Analysis for Strategic Marketing

Vithala R. Rao

Johnson School of Management
Cornell University

Joel H. Steckel

Stern School of Business
New York University

 **ADDISON-WESLEY**

An imprint of Addison Wesley Longman, Inc.

Reading, Massachusetts • Menlo Park, California • New York • Harlow, England
Don Mills, Ontario • Sydney • Mexico City • Madrid • Amsterdam

To Our Parents

four of the greatest people the world ever knew

V. Kameswaramma and V. Sitaramamurty

Hazel and Phillip Steckel

Publishing Partner	Michael Roche
Editorial Assistant	Ruth Berry
Managing Editor	Jim Rigney
Production Supervisor	Billie Porter
Senior Manufacturing Supervisor	Hugh Crawford
Cover Supervisor	Gina Hagen
Cover Design/Illustration	Linda Manly Wade
Composition, Design, and Project Coordination	Elm Street Publishing Services, Inc.

Library of Congress Cataloging-in-Publication Data
Rao, Vithala R.
    Analysis for strategic marketing / Vithala R. Rao, Joel H. Steckel.
        p.   cm.
    Includes bibliographical references and index.
    ISBN 0-321-00198-2
    1. Marketing.   I. Steckel, Joel H.   II. Title.
  HF5415.R3242   1998
  658.8'02—dc21
                                                  97-3230
                                                      CIP

1 2 3 4 5 6 7 8 9 10—MA—00 99 98 97

PREFACE

Marketing touches every person in one way or another. Marketing and innovation are perhaps the only two significant engines for the growth of any economy. Successful growth of a company, an organization, or an industry (and an economy) depends heavily on insightful, systematic, and scientific application of marketing principles and methods. But the word *marketing* to a layperson is likely to elicit thoughts of commercials with special effects, catchy slogans, and celebrity endorsers touting new and improved products and services. This visible output of the marketing process is a creative and artistic activity and implies a sole purpose of persuading the customer to buy things. Fortunately, marketing professionals know better. Behind those enticing commercials are often hours of quantitative analysis that attempt to uncover what customers want, how alike people or organizations are who want the same things, how to design a new product or improve an existing one, and how successful a new or improved product is likely to be. These analyses are necessary to make a commercial successful. What the layperson sees as art is often the result of hours of scientific work.

The distinction between art and science in marketing is reflected in the evolution of marketing practice. In the first half of the twentieth century, the task of marketing began with the product as given. The main job was to think of "artistic," creative, and often clever ways to persuade customers to buy a product or service. With technological and industrial progress, new industries have evolved, leading to ever-changing ways to satisfy customer needs and wants. The structure of competition among firms has also changed due to the emergence of new competitors and the eventual exit of some old ones. Existing boundaries between industries and product markets have blurred. Firms have to seek new ways to satisfy the needs and wants of customers better than their dynamic competitors. Accordingly, focus has shifted to the importance of gaining deeper understanding of both customer and competitor behavior in discovering new product opportunities to satisfy unmet customer needs. Both the academic community and consulting firms, often in cooperation, have developed sets of analytical and scientific methods directed toward assisting firms in tackling the newer challenges.

Marketing executives make decisions for their products and services at both tactical and strategic levels. The tactical decisions are often the day-to-day tasks for managing an existing business with more attention paid to current problems. These include designing price promotions, formulating advertising slogans, and identifying and targeting market segments. These managerial tasks fall under the rubric of brand or product management and planning. Strategic decisions consider issues such as how the market and industry will change in the future, what competitive advantages are sustainable, which newer product markets to enter, and how the firm can compete in those markets. Strategic marketing is more concerned with the long-term viability of a business and even the corporation as a whole.

Needless to say, effective planning is required to implement decisions at both the tactical and strategic levels. In order to survive, the modern corporation must continually search for new product opportunities. Once a firm enters a new market with either a new or an existing/modified product, the markets must be managed effectively. Both levels of planning also require relevant and intelligently performed analyses to be successful. To be useful, analyses must provide information that impacts corporate decisions. This book was written in response to a perceived void in the literature related to effective analyses for the strategic marketing function.

Two areas of marketing are related to the specific topics covered in *Analysis for Strategic Marketing:* they are strategic marketing and marketing research. Books on strategic marketing tend to describe frameworks and paradigms that emphasize the questions management ought to consider when formulating a strategic decision. However, such books generally do not provide sufficient detail about the specific research approaches needed to answer these questions. In contrast, most marketing research books are oriented toward techniques of data collection and analysis. They concentrate on the formulation of research designs and the technology of conducting research projects.

Features

No book exists until now that takes the questions relevant to strategic market planning and describes precisely how to conduct the research and analyses needed to answer them. This book starts with issues faced and decisions to be made by a strategic marketer and describes various methods of analyses that can be used to assist management in this endeavor. *Analysis for Strategic Marketing*

1. Provides a deeper understanding of the issues that encompass marketing strategy (investigating product-market opportunities, discovering unmet consumer needs, analyzing competitors, determining competitive advantage, predicting environmental changes so as to be proactive in the marketplace, forecasting results of strategies, and allocating resources)
2. Describes with applications a set of well-tested methods that address each of the issues and
3. Shows how to implement or guide the implementation of research with these methods.

It is an exciting time to be writing this book. Several developments have occurred or are on the horizon that will facilitate the kinds of analyses described in this book. Generally speaking, the seeds for a marketing information revolution are sown in a fertile environment amply supplied by technology, communication, and brain power. Using supermarket scanners to collect data on customer behavior is now commonplace; new interactive computer-aided interview methodologies have emerged; and who knows what new opportunities the information superhighway and digital television-cum-computers will bring for collection of data that can help one address strategic questions related to customers and competitors? Further, decision-support systems are being designed to implement the results of various analyses in a more or less routine manner.

One of the attractive aspects of the material in this book is that it is quite robust in its treatment of all these changes. The tools and techniques described here will be as applicable in the future as they are today. The thing to look forward to is that the future will bring richer data collected by better methods for applying the strategic marketing methods discussed in this book.

Acknowledgments

Our thinking on this subject has of course been shaped by each other as well as by generations of our students at Cornell University (Johnson School) and New York University (Stern School), consulting clients, teachers, and colleagues. First, we thank Barry Bayus (Kenan-Flagler School at the University of North Carolina) for permitting us to include his cases on the compact disc market in the book. We want to acknowledge the valuable research assistance of Jayaram Chigurupati, Rahul Bhalla, Tetsuo Yamada, and Maurice Doyon (all MBA and Ph.D. students at Cornell University). Special thanks to Tetsuo Yamada for permitting us to use the cases on the athletic industry. We also wish to thank Kimberly Banks, Gina Plaia, Tracy Pollastri, and Joseph Weglein (all MBA students at NYU) for their work on the Victoria Moore project in Chapter 9. Citibank and Directions for Decisions also graciously allowed us to use materials in Chapter 9.

We also want to thank the reviewers of portions of the manuscript who were kind enough to take time from their hectic schedules to assist us. Our thanks and appreciation go to Edward McLaughlin (Cornell University), Edward Fern (Virginia Tech University), Dipak Jain (Kellogg School at Northwestern University), Alan Shocker (University of Minnesota), and Russ Winer (Hass School at University of California at Berkeley). We owe a particularly large debt to Joe Alba (University of Florida), who provided invaluable direction in organizing the material in several of the chapters. Barb Drake at the Johnson School assisted immensely by creating well-formatted manuscript from our handwritten scrawl. Chris Moore and Shaaron Gomes of the Stern School helped with much of the artwork. We also thank Saroj Rao for her help and patience throughout this project.

It is our privilege to particularly acknowledge the inspiration of Professor Paul E. Green of the Wharton School of the University of Pennsylvania. Paul served on both of our doctoral dissertation committees as Chair and member, respectively. His example in thought and deed has been felt by every marketing academic, practicing researcher, consultant, and manager in the United States and indeed the whole world. He has provided us with a model to emulate. People who have read his extensive contributions to the marketing literature will undoubtedly see his influence in various parts of this book.

Finally, we are pleased to be associated with Addison Wesley Longman, an excellent organization, and with two of their superb editors—Mike Roche and Anne Smith, who, along with their assistants, Ruth Berry and Jay O'Callaghan, guided us throughout this project. Billie Porter supervised the production of this book. Phyllis Crittenden of Elm Street Publishing Services, Inc. served as the project editor for this book. We are grateful to Gary Lilien and Arvind Rangaswamy (both of Penn State University) for allowing us to piggyback on their *Marketing Engineering* project for the supplementary software available with this book.

Vithala R. Rao
Ithaca , New York

Joel H. Steckel
New York City

July 1997

Contents

Chapter 3

Identifying Unmet Needs: What Do the Customers Want?   76

Chapter 4

Identifying Competitors: Whom Will We Compete Against?   119

Chapter 5

Understanding and Forecasting the External Environment: Demographic, Social, Economic, and Political Factors   156

Chapter 6
Understanding and Forecasting the Market Environment: Technological Factors and Forecasting   221

Chapter 7

Analyzing Competitive Advantage: How to Compete? 269

Chapter 8
Resource Allocation Methods   324

Chapter 9

Actual Case Examples: Analyses in Action   383

The Role of Analysis in Strategy Formulation

INTRODUCTION

Formulating marketing strategy is a difficult task. Managers rarely have all the information that they would like to have at their disposal to make the required decisions. Furthermore, the information that they do have may be difficult to interpret, especially if it relates to future business environments. Consider the following illustrations.

The Victoria Moore Company designs and manufactures women's dress and casual clothing, shoes, jeans, accessories, men's wear, and children's wear.* The vast majority of their business is in women's clothing, the area in which the company began. As the company desires to continue to grow, it needs to investigate whether new products or new markets will best fuel that growth. If new products are the answer, the company then needs to determine what new products will best serve its purposes. Victoria herself wondered whether activewear was a future growth opportunity. In order to determine the appropriate course of action, she needed to answer these questions:

1. How could she identify her target activewear customers? What potential do they represent?
2. Who would her competitors most likely be—other designers of casual wear or sports apparel manufacturers?
3. What benefits do potential customers look for in leisure sports apparel—Fit, fashion, comfort?
4. Is the Victoria Moore brand name an advantage in this category? And if so, what is its value?

In the early 1990s Citibank attempted to differentiate its classic Visa and MasterCard by placing a photograph of the customer on them.† The credit card market had become extremely competitive and competitors like Citibank had to find reasons for potential customers to choose their card. The intent behind the photo was to appeal to security-conscious consumers who might fear that fraudulent charges could be made with a lost card. The bank felt that the new card would reinforce its

---

*Victoria Moore is a fictitious name for a real company. The company has provided data used later in the book and has asked that its name be withheld.

†Photocards were available in the early 1980s from some regional banks (such as Baybank in Boston). These cards were abandoned because of excessive production costs. By the early 1990s technology had advanced to a point where cost was no longer an issue.

Bankcard Division's positioning statement, "No other credit card gives you the security and confidence of Citibank MasterCard and Visa because no one is as responsive to your needs." Before the photocard was introduced on a wide scale, Citibank was interested in customers' reactions to various aspects of obtaining and using its cards. In particular, the bank wanted insight into the relative importance of the photo in customers' decision to acquire and use the card.

In the early 1990s, the athletic footwear industry entered its mature stage. Growth in sales flattened as the number of people participating in exercise peaked and the domestic economy began to falter. After a decade of double-digit retail growth, 1993 saw essentially no growth at all. Sales to women actually declined. Seeing clouds on the horizon, Reebok, the number two company in this industry (behind Nike), recognized the need to identify growing market segments in the industry. This involved two subtasks: segmenting the market and forecasting each segment's growth.

During the 1970s, Xerox customers had become disappointed with Xerox quality and service. The company's early competitive advantage was gone. Consequently, the company lost its leadership in the copier industry it created with the introduction of its model 914 in 1959. In 1983 Xerox began to regain lost share by initiating a "Leadership through Quality" program that emphasized product quality, customer satisfaction, and new products. To monitor the success of the program, Xerox felt it had to develop a set of tools to continuously measure customer satisfaction. In its view, customer satisfaction was a leading indicator of financial performance.[1]

In the first half of the 1990s, many electronics companies were investigating high-definition television (HDTV), a new technology that produced higher picture resolution in addition to superior digital stereo sound. Zenith, the only American-owned television producer, was particularly interested in this development. To best decide whether and how to proceed, it had to forecast demand for the new technology and study consumer preferences for the new format.[2]

Coffee is the largest product category in the General Foods portfolio. Unfortunately for the company, health concerns have led to a decline in national coffee consumption. This trend has not affected all aspects of the coffee business equally, however. In particular, decaffeinated gourmet brands, such as the General Foods International Coffees, have been less affected than regular and mass-market ones. General Foods—and the Maxwell House division in particular—must decide how to allocate its resources among its brands so as to maximize its performance.[3]

These situations differ in a wide variety of ways. They involve distinct strategic decisions. Some (Zenith's) involve market entry; others (Citibank's) involve product differentiation, and others (General Foods') involve resource allocation. The role the company plays in its industry differs. Some of the situations involve market leaders (Citibank); others involve market challengers (Reebok). The situations also represent industries in different stages of growth. Some involve mature industries (General Foods'); others involve embryonic industries (Zenith's). The situations also differ with respect to issues as fundamental as whether the company of interest is a participant in the industry in question. Some involve companies contemplating entry into a new industry (Victoria Moore); others involve companies already there (Xerox). Despite these many differences, they have one thing in common: They all require the collection and/or analysis of information (data) in order to make the appropriate decision. That is what this book is about—the analysis of information necessary to make strategic marketing decisions.

In this chapter, we begin by outlining what a strategic marketing decision is. We continue by classifying strategic situations and demonstrating that specific needs for analysis vary systematically across these situations. Then we show what role analysis plays in the process of strategic decision making. The chapter concludes by discussing the link between these issues and the remainder of the book.

BOUNDARIES OF STRATEGIC MARKETING

If you ask most managers what a strategy is, you will invariably elicit a response akin to "the way you go about accomplishing your objectives." This is rather vague, and for good reason. The word *strategy* is ubiquitous in common language. It is used not only in conjunction with business in general and marketing in particular; it is associated with politics, military action, and sports as well. For example, consider the longtime rivalry between tennis players Martina Navratilova and Chris Evert. Each match they played would follow the same pattern. Martina would try to attack the net and hit a winning shot; she tried to shorten the points as much as possible. In contrast, Chris would try to hit the ball deep and keep Martina away from the net until Martina made a mistake; she tried to lengthen the points as much as possible. Each player tried to establish the pattern of points in which she had the best chance of winning. Martina wanted short points because she was such a dynamic, attacking player and could hit winning shots with the greatest of skill; if the game were determined by who could hit the first winning shot, her skill at attacking would be the determining factor and she would most likely win. Chris wanted long points because she was steady and if the points were determined by who made the first mistake, her steadiness made it unlikely that this would be her. In this context, strategy reduces to pattern of points (short, long) and method of winning points (attacking, being steady).

In marketing, the pattern of points corresponds to the selection of markets companies will compete in, the products they design, and the companies they acquire. Method of winning points becomes the way companies get sales from customers— what marketing skills they employ. These ideas are reflected in the strategic gameboard designed by Roberto Buaron, the well-known McKinsey consultant. As shown in Fig. 1.1, strategic choice can be boiled down to two questions, where to compete and how to compete.[4]

The question of where to compete can manifest itself in a variety of forms. It can involve deciding whether to enter a new industry, as is the case with Victoria Moore. It can focus on the pursuit of certain segments within a given industry, which is Reebok's task. Finally, given that a firm may compete in several industries and/or segments, it must decide the relative emphasis and resources it will place on each. Such is the dilemma confronting the Maxwell House division of General Foods.

Although determining how to compete seems to encompass an almost infinite number of alternatives, Michael Porter argues that there are really only two general classes of options.[5] One is to be the low-cost producer. If a firm is the low-cost

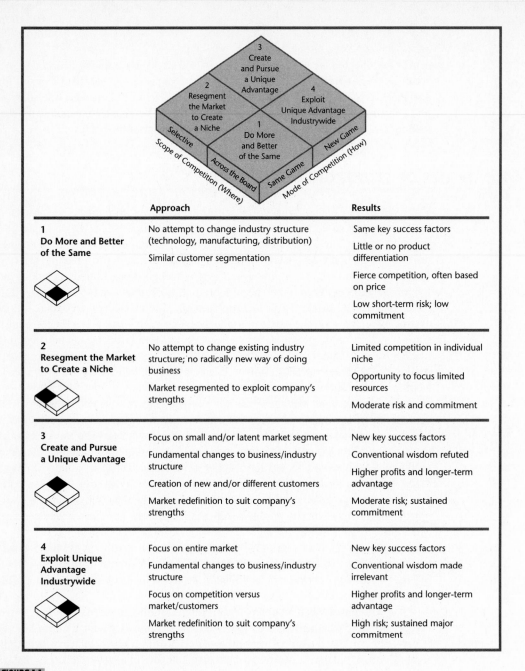

	Approach	Results
1 **Do More and Better of the Same**	No attempt to change industry structure (technology, manufacturing, distribution) Similar customer segmentation	Same key success factors Little or no product differentiation Fierce competition, often based on price Low short-term risk; low commitment
2 **Resegment the Market to Create a Niche**	No attempt to change existing industry structure; no radically new way of doing business Market resegmented to exploit company's strengths	Limited competition in individual niche Opportunity to focus limited resources Moderate risk and commitment
3 **Create and Pursue a Unique Advantage**	Focus on small and/or latent market segment Fundamental changes to business/industry structure Creation of new and/or different customers Market redefinition to suit company's strengths	New key success factors Conventional wisdom refuted Higher profits and longer-term advantage Moderate risk; sustained commitment
4 **Exploit Unique Advantage Industrywide**	Focus on entire market Fundamental changes to business/industry structure Focus on competition versus market/customers Market redefinition to suit company's strengths	New key success factors Conventional wisdom made irrelevant Higher profits and longer-term advantage High risk; sustained major commitment

FIGURE 1.1   **The Strategic Gameboard**

Source: Buaron, Roberto (1981), "How to Win the Market-Share Game? Try Changing the Rules," *Management Review* 70 (January), 10.

producer, it will perform at or above the industry average if it can sustain prices at or near the industry average. The second way for a firm to compete is by differentiating its product/service from its competition. Some companies differentiate via product features. Citibank is putting pictures on credit cards; Victoria Moore makes clothes of softer fabric; Reebok makes athletic shoes with a built-in air pump. Others focus on what Ted Levitt calls "intangibles."[6] These include both things that customers expect, such as service from Xerox, and things that they do not, such as the newsletters with helpful hints that software providers SPSS and WordPerfect regularly mail to their users. The choice between low cost and differentiation (as well as the exact basis of differentiation) should be dictated by the skills and resources a firm possesses.

Formally, then, we define the boundaries of strategic marketing as those issues which guide decisions that impact either directly or tangentially on either or both of the following components:

1. *Market Scope*—those industries or market segments that a firm wishes to target. Market scope can be defined with respect to segments of customers, customer needs, products produced, or technologies employed by the firm.
2. *Competitive Advantage*—the assets, skills, and resources a firm possesses and the positional advantages (differentiation, low cost) they lead to that enable a firm to achieve superior performance.

Porter cross-classifies the two forms of positional advantage with two degrees of scope (broad target, narrow target) to produce four generic strategies.[7] See Fig. 1.2. The figure is essentially a more formal representation of the strategic gameboard in Fig. 1.1.

CLASSIFICATION OF STRATEGIC SITUATIONS

The specific strategic issues a firm faces in its choice of market scope and competitive advantage will differ as its circumstances differ. Charles Hofer has surveyed the business strategy literature and uncovered 54 variables that marketing, policy, and economic theorists have determined to be of major importance to a firm's choice of strategy. These include broad-based environmental (economic, demographic, socio-cultural, political, and legal) variables, supplier variables (such as degree of supplier integration), industry structure variables (degree of product differentiation, price/cost structure), competitor variables (number of competitors, aggressiveness of competition), consumer variables (buyer needs, market size), and firm characteristics (market share, quality of product).[8] Some of these variables are faced by *all* firms in an industry; others are *unique to each firm* in an industry.

Fortunately, as Hofer points out, these factors are not completely independent. Many factors faced by all firms in an industry are systematically related to the stage of an industry's development. Furthermore, industry progressions are not completely random. Much commonality exists across them. For example, early in its development, *any* industry will tend to have few competitors and low degrees of product differentiation. The relationship of stage of industry development to other

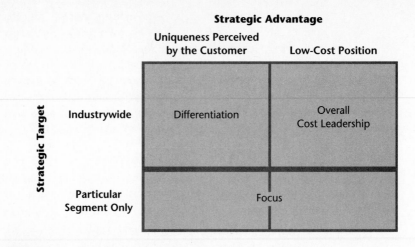

Strategic Advantage

	Uniqueness Perceived by the Customer	Low-Cost Position
Industrywide	Differentiation	Overall Cost Leadership
Particular Segment Only	Focus	

Strategic Target

FIGURE 1.2 **Porter's Generic Strategies**

Source: Porter, Michael E. (1980), *Competitive Strategy,* New York: Free Press, 39. Reprinted with the permission of The Free Press, a Division of Simon & Schuster, from COMPETITIVE STRATEGY: Techniques for Analyzing Industries and Competitors by Michael E. Porter. Copyright (c) 1980 by The Free Press.

important strategy-determining factors makes it a useful variable for characterizing strategic environments.

There are many ways to categorize industry development.[9] These schemes differ according to the number of discrete stages, their names, and what determines the transition from one to another. We use the approach suggested by Kotler. His framework suggests that an industry evolves through emergence, growth, maturity, and decline.[10]

Before a market emerges, it exists in a latent condition; that is, a group of people has an unmet need or want that no existing product currently satisfies. The people who have this need may not even recognize it themselves. Yet some entrepreneur does recognize this need and derives a solution to the problem. The need exists in a general form and general satisfaction of it will usually suffice. The Bowmar Brain (the first handheld calculator) was developed in response to a latent need for people to perform calculations more rapidly than could be done with paper and pencil, an abacus, or a slide rule. The precise form of a product in the emergence stage is not usually a major issue. Buyers' preferences will in some sense be formed to fit the alternatives that the market provides.[11] A firm's ability to gain competitive advantage in the emergence stage is largely keyed to its ability to satisfy a generic need. Satisfying it better than others is not that great a problem at this point, since there are few if any others. However, it must make sure that the technology it adopts is not likely to become obsolete in the near future. One of the major risks the entrepreneur faces here is a lack of knowledge of how extensive the generic need is. This determines the potential size of the market.

If sales in an emergent market are good, other firms will enter the market and help it grow. Often this will occur because customers recognize that there is something the product could do better. For example, the original Bowmar Brain handheld calculators could be made smaller. Many firms entered the market, making smaller and smaller calculators. As a market gains experience with a product, it learns how to use it and begins to understand its requirements. A key to the market's development is to recognize that not all consumers will have the same requirements. Different segments will have different needs unmet by existing offerings. These unmet needs represent opportunities for potential entrants. A potential entrant's ability to gain competitive advantage in this growth stage is therefore keyed to its ability to recognize and satisfy diverse consumer preferences. The Bowmar Brain was not only too large, it did not perform enough functions. Calculators with more scientific functions than addition, subtraction, multiplication, and division began to emerge.

Normally, the number of competitors increases rapidly during the growth stage. Industry sales generally increase as well, since the latent need capitalized on in the emergence stage is becoming more obvious to the population as a whole. For example, the Victoria Moore Company is trying to enter a market where more and more customers are recognizing the need to integrate fashion with athletic activity.

Since the growth market is still evolving in a somewhat turbulent manner, its ultimate potential and the depth of the underlying need are still uncertain. Increased competitive activity begins to worry industry participants. They look for ways to erect barriers to entry. High barriers to entry exist when there are large economies of scale; customers have high degrees of brand identification; there are large capital requirements or setup costs; entrenched companies have cost advantages; access to distribution channels is scarce; and the government has placed regulations on the industry.[12] Victoria Moore's ability to circumvent such barriers and erect some of its own make the activewear market attractive. The company can take advantage of economies of scale in fabric purchases; it has strong brand identification; and manufacturing equipment is already in place.

When most of the population has recognized the need the product satisfies and consequently has entered the market, sales increases will necessarily slow or perhaps even disappear. Industry sales levels become predictably stable and the industry enters the maturity stage. To increase revenues, firms have to either take sales from existing competitors in existing markets or discover new markets.

Customer requirements in existing markets will become more and more precise, largely because firms comply. They will be willing to tailor their offerings to more refined segments because it is the only way they can continue to succeed. Unfortunately for them, the degree of potential success decreases. As market segments' requirements become increasingly refined, the segments will necessarily fragment and shrink. Furthermore, satisfying these requirements will usually entail the research costs of modifying existing products and developing new ones. In the wake of these dynamics, profits may also shrink. But because the industry is still profitable, firms will still enter it.

Consider the credit card industry. Profits have traditionally come from retailer discounts, annual fees, and interest on balances. A visit to one's own mailbox should demonstrate that more and more companies are offering cards every day. These offerings waive annual fees, charge lower interest rates, and decrease retailer discounts. This forces traditional competitors to either match these terms or provide customers some other incentive to use their card. In the face of sharply declining profits, Citibank is trying to satisfy the precise needs of a security-conscious segment with the photocard.

New markets can be found in the guise of either new *users* (new customers) or new *uses*. Ted Levitt discusses how each might work by looking at the history of the nylon industry.[13] Early uses for nylon were primarily military. Nylon was the substance from which parachutes, thread, and rope were made. Later on it became the dominant material for women's hosiery. New users could conceivably have come from merchandising to teenagers. Advertising using youthful social and style leaders would have been appropriate. Most of nylon's successes, however, came from new uses. After military and hosiery uses, nylon became incorporated into warp knits, tire cord, textured yarns, and carpet yarns.

Eventually markets enter a stage of decline. New technologies emerge that make previous products obsolete. New competitors no longer enter the market; in fact, existing competitors may leave it. A firm can remain in the market only if it either looks for an enduring pocket of demand in the declining market, such as General Foods has done with its decaffeinated brands of coffee, or becomes the dominant competitor in the declining industry. The choice of which, if either, a firm should do is contingent on its forecast of how fast the decline will be and how strong it is relative to its competitors.[14]

In sum, a firm's decisions related to market scope and competitive advantage vary as the stage of development of its industry evolves. Firms in an emergent industry face different circumstances than those in a mature industry. Consequently, a firm's specific needs for information and analyses related to customers and competitors and its ability to forecast the market will also vary as the industry evolves. Table 1.1 summarizes the major variations in these situations that in turn affect a firm's needs for analysis.

The type of research and analysis that a firm needs depends not only on its stage of development but on the role it plays in its industry as well. A firm can be an industry leader, challenger, follower, or nicher.[15] In addition, there are potential entrants to any industry.

The *market leader* is the firm with the largest market share. It is a beacon for competitors to consciously challenge, imitate, or avoid. In general, the strategies available to a leader include increasing market share, defending market share, and expanding the market by attracting new users, developing new usage situations, or increasing the usage of current users. Citibank is the market leader in the credit card industry. The photocard is Citibank's attempt to increase market share by differentiating its product in a meaningful way.

A *market challenger* usually holds the second, third, or sometimes lower rank in market share. Its strategic objectives are usually framed in terms of increasing market share with the underlying assumption being that increased market share will lead to increased profits.[16] The tasks that a market challenger must face include identifying which competitor or class of competitors to try to take share from and whether the challenger's attack would pit its strengths against the competitor's strengths, pit its strengths against the competitor's weaknesses, or apply its strengths to areas the

TABLE 1.1 Strategic Environments at Different Stages of Development

| Stage of Industry Development | Market Scope–Related | | | Ability to Gain Competitive Advantage | Forecasting Difficulty | Important Strategic Questions |
	Segments	Buyers' Needs and Wants	Product Variety			
Emerging	None	Undefined, but to be developed	None	Easy once need is identified	Extremely high	a. Is there a market for this product? b. To what extent is there a latent generic need for this product's benefits? c. What will be the dominant technology?
Growing	Beginning to form	Defined but need to be differentiated; buyers beginning to gain technical aspects of product	Limited but growing	Keyed to differences in customer preferences	Uncertain—errors still likely	d. What segments of (more precise) consumer needs will emerge? e. What competitors can we expect and with what strategies? f. How can we erect barriers to entry?
Mature	Many and diverse	Differentiated; buyers are well versed technically	High (may be in terms of cosmetic features such as size, flavor, or technical features)	Difficult	Straightforward	g. What segments of precise consumer needs have emerged? h. Do we have the skills and resources to be able to satisfy these needs? i. Is the market segment large enough to be profitable? j. Are there new uses for this product or a new set of users that have not been mined?
Declining	Many (perhaps fewer) and diverse	Changing in dramatic style	High at first, but eventually small as brands begin to evaporate	Very difficult	Straightforward	k. What segments of consumer needs persist? l. What strengths do we have that will allow us to succeed in these segments? m. How fast will the decline be?

9

competitor has not yet taken advantage of. Reebok has consistently been a challenger to Nike's position in athletic footwear. In attempting to identify growth segments, Reebok is choosing the last of these options.

Market followers tend to follow rather than challenge the market leader. Their philosophy is that a market leader will react strongly to any threats. If a firm does not have the ability to seriously threaten a market leader with a product innovation or distribution breakthrough, it may be better off recognizing that any attempt at challenging the market leader's position will at best be a Pyrrhic victory. Market followers usually clone, imitate, or adapt the leader's products.

For the smaller firm, an alternative to being a market follower is to be a *market nicher*. Firms can avoid major competitors in two ways. They can deliberately not be a threat in the overall market or they can target small segments (niches) of the market that have little or no appeal for the leader. They become specialists in some end use, customer group, quality level, or channel. In producing the General Foods International Coffees line, the Maxwell House division of GF is acting like a market nicher by going after the gourmet segments and other consumers who entertain often. These segments are much smaller than the mainstream daily beverage market.

Finally, any industry is subject to potential entrants. As suggested by Michael Porter's five forces of competition (see Fig. 1.3), potential entrants are one of the basic forces that determine the long-run profitability of an industry.[17] The seriousness of the threat of new entrants depends on the barriers to entry present and the degree to which potential entrants can expect harsh retaliation from firms already in the industry. We have already discussed barriers to entry. Harsh reactions from incumbents can be expected when the incumbents possess substantial resources, have excess capacity, or industry growth is slow.[18]

Potential entrants can come from almost anywhere. However, the firms that are most likely to enter a given market are those that operate adjacent to the market. Two of these classes of firms can also be found among Porter's five forces, the suppliers and customers of those firms that operate in the industry. These firms would enter if the benefits of buying a buyer or seller (operating economies, access to supply or demand, control over the product system) justified the increased costs (operating costs, inexperience in a new business, reduced flexibility). Other potential entrants operating adjacent to a given industry include firms that sell different products to the same market and firms that make and sell similar products to different markets. Victoria Moore makes products similar to activewear in form (apparel) and sells them to the same market (the upscale consumer). Thus, Victoria Moore is a potential entrant.

Industries at different stages of development will have different concentrations of firms with given roles. Emergent industries usually have one or maybe two firms competing. Even after new technology and design have been established, an emergent industry may have no competitors until a product has been commercialized. Such is the case with the HDTV market described in the Zenith vignette. As an industry grows, other firms enter to challenge and imitate the leader. Once an industry matures, niche players emerge. Finally, as an industry declines there is rarely room for more than one or two competitors. These roles are summarized in Table 1.2.

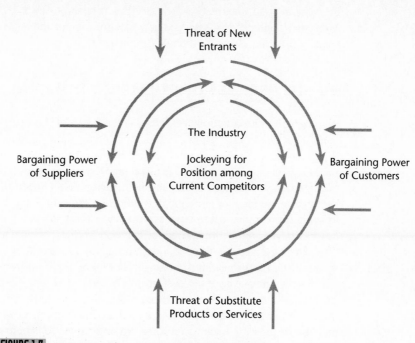

FIGURE 1.3 **Porter's Five Forces of Competition**

Source: Porter, Michael E. (1979), "How Competitive Forces Shape Strategy," *Harvard Business Review* 57 (March-April), 141.

TABLE 1.2 **Strategic Relevance of Competitive Roles at Different Development Stages**

Stage of Industry Development	Market Leader	Market Challenger	Market Follower	Market Nicher	Potential Entrant
Emerging	?	?	0	0	X
Growing	X	X	X	0	X
Mature	X	X	X	X	X
Declining	X	?	?	?	0

X = Strategically most relevant

0 = Strategically least relevant

? = May or may not be strategically relevant

The important point to remember here is that the analysis needs of a firm depend not only on the stage of development of its industry, but on the role the firm plays in that industry as well. For example, Citibank and Reebok both compete in mature industries. Citibank is a market leader; Reebok is a market challenger. As a market leader, Citibank needed to reinforce its positioning statement. In particular, it wanted to affirm its "security and confidence" aspects. That is why Citibank was interested in promoting photocard usage. In contrast, as a market challenger, Reebok had to try to do something substantively different. Thus it began to look for growth segments. More specifically, Reebok needed new ways of segmenting the market and selecting some of these segments for intensive pursuit.

ANALYSIS AND THE PROCESS OF STRATEGIC THINKING

As implied by the situations described at the outset of this chapter, good judgment is not enough to make good strategic decisions—thorough analyses are required. When a strategist views a situation primed for a strategic decision with respect to market scope and/or competitive advantage, he or she generally encounters areas of uncertainty that directly impact the decision. This uncertainty can usually be captured in the form of strategic questions like those in Table 1.3. Chris Evert and Martina Navratilova had an easier time when they played tennis than most businesses do when they plot strategy. Chris and Martina knew where the lines were. They knew the net was three feet high in the middle and three and a half feet high at the posts. In contrast, businesses do not know their environs as well. They do not always know who their customers are, who their competitors are, and what government, the economy, and technology hold in store for them. Tennis is a matter of execution. Strategy is a matter of figuring out what the arena is; only then does execution become an issue. Strategic questions help managers envision their "tennis court."

TABLE 1.3   Examples of Strategic Questions

Customer Related

Who are the potential customers?

(a,c,g,j)

Are there any customers not being served adequately?

(b)

Competitor Related

Who are the potential competitors?

(e)

What are the bases of the firm's advantage over its competitors?

(h,l)

Environment Related

What factors in the external environment influence how the firm will perform?

(c)

How will these factors change?

(m)

Company Decision Related

How much emphasis should the firm place on each market it participates in?

(f)

What are the expected results of any given strategy?

(i)

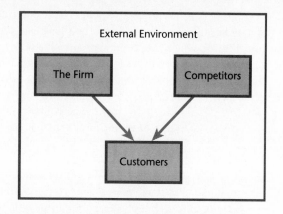

External Environment

The Firm   Competitors

Customers

FIGURE 1.4   **Framework for Analyzing Market Scope and Competitive Advantage**

The questions in Table 1.3 are generalizations of those found in the right-hand column of Table 1.1. The related Table 1.1 questions are listed in parentheses below each question in Table 1.3. Formal analyses are often necessary to answer these strategic questions. The manager then uses the answers to these questions when making decisions. For strategic questions to be meaningful, they must relate to a firm's ability to attain a competitive advantage within a given market scope. The general entities that primarily influence competitive advantage are customers, competitors, the firm itself, and the external environment. See Fig. 1.4.

Strategic questions relating to customers tend to focus on defining market segments and understanding their motivations. Market segments can be defined in terms of customers, product technologies, or uses. Segments are important because they provide a framework for defining market scope (determining what segments will be served). Customer motivations are important to understand because the skills and assets needed to address these motivations (which may currently be unmet by existing competitors) present the key to a firm striving for competitive advantage in a given segment.

Strategic questions relating to competitors generally come in two forms, "Who are they?" and "What are their strengths and weaknesses?" The notion of competitive advantage usually involves exploiting a competitor's weakness or neutralizing a competitor's strength. Firms often define their competition too narrowly. For example, the myopia of the railroad industry in the middle of the twentieth century in not recognizing the competitive threat of the airline industry is well documented.[19] Similarly, activewear manufacturers would be remiss if they ignored companies like Victoria Moore.

Strategic questions about the firm itself usually mirror the strengths and weaknesses aspect of competitor questions. These again provide the basis for assessing competitive advantage. The major difference between assessing one's own and competitors' strengths and weaknesses lies in the level of information available.

Finally, each firm faces important forces outside it that shape its strategic options and choices. These forces include political, economic, social, and technological factors. Strategic questions about these involve how they will change and what impacts they will have on particular markets. Do they present any new opportunities or threats? For example, the last 20 years have seen an increase in the fitness consciousness of many Americans. This as much as anything has produced the opportunity for Victoria Moore to enter the activewear market.

We should keep in mind, however, that firms usually participate in multiple markets. Therefore, the framework presented in Fig. 1.4 has to be replicated for each market the firm is considering. From an analytic perspective, each replication has its own set of strategic questions. From a decision-making perspective, this leads, of course, to the question of how much effort the firm should allocate to each market.

This book presents a set of formal analytic methods and concepts useful for answering strategic questions like these. Some of these involve quantitative methods; others simply structure managerial judgment. Whenever possible, we have focused on methods and concepts that have been found to work satisfactorily in practice and are easy to use. Whenever these criteria are violated, we do our best to point it out.

A skeptic might look at the questions in Table 1.3 and argue that any competent manager experienced in a given industry could answer them with a modicum of introspection and without much trouble. Maybe, maybe not. The next subsection suggests why.

Judgmental Biases

Research in the behavioral sciences suggests that managers (and humans in general) are not nearly as smart as they think they are. This view can be traced back to the Nobel Prize–winning economist Herbert Simon.[20] He argues that managers face a very complex world. Even when they have complete information about this world, they cannot draw the appropriate conclusions because their mental ability to process this information is limited. Managers often blame their inappropriate or inaccurate decisions or unwillingness to arrive at conclusions on a lack of relevant information. They tend to complain that they simply do not have enough.

Russell Ackoff suggests that not only do managers have enough information, they often have *too much* information at their disposals. Their difficulty is in determining which precise pieces of information are most relevant to their current decisions. Consequently, they may base their decisions on the wrong information.[21] Managers are often reluctant to admit their limitations in this regard. This is ironic in light of the fact that we all accept the deficiencies and limitations of our memory. We all use some kind of aids (address books, daily calendars) to help us avoid the penalties of faulty memory.

In order to deal with the abundance of information about a complex world, managers simplify the world they are trying to learn about to make it more manageable. After all, humans are not computers. More complex worlds (those with changing technology, dynamic competition, uncertain consumer requirements) require greater simplification. Simplification allows managers to draw correct, if simplified, conclusions from their evidence. However, there is no guarantee that these conclusions are correct for their original, complex world. Simon calls this *bounded rationality* (that is, the manager is rational within the bounds of the way he or she views the world).[22]

Simplifying information about the world for judgment and decision making often results in the use of simple rules, or *heuristics.* These simple rules introduce bias into decision making. For example, suppose that a Reebok executive is on a flight to Miami Beach. On that flight, he notices a number of senior citizens wearing athletic shoes. He makes the simplification that the proportion of senior citizens on that flight is typical of the proportion in the population as a whole. He therefore assumes that senior citizens are a growth market for athletic shoes. What he has done is use a rule that specific instances that are easily observed or recalled can serve as a basis for future-oriented decisions. This is an example of the well-known *availability heuristic* and *availability bias.*[23] The Reebok executive is focusing on the mental availability of the number of senior citizens on the flight wearing athletic shoes and ignoring the possibility that a flight to Miami Beach might have a higher proportion of senior citizens than does the population as a whole. Similar results would occur if the executive conducted a consumer survey with a sample that did not reflect the population at large.

Formal analysis helps resolve the difficulties imposed by judgmental biases in at least two ways. First, approaches based on quantitative methods, unlike humans, use all the information at hand, derive appropriate weights for it, and process it in an unbiased manner. Second, formal analytic approaches are based on relationships between variables (for example, customer motivation and purchase behavior). This is true for both quantitative and nonquantitative approaches. At the very least, these relationships provide a logical structure for managerial judgments. If the Miami-bound Reebok executive had conducted a study of footwear usage, he might have found that all segments believed comfortable shoes are essential for travel. This would redirect his attention from senior citizens to air travelers and allow him to avoid the availability bias. He was concentrating on senior citizens only because they had a significant presence on the Miami flight. If the flight were going to Juneau, he might have come to the same conclusion about Eskimos. Even by just conceptualizing the study, he would have been forced to consider customer motivation and probably avoided the erroneous conclusion.

Thorough Analysis Does Not Always Lead to Good Outcomes

Unfortunately, even after obtaining the best answers to the appropriate strategic questions, a manager may still make a decision that has a bad outcome. This can occur because managers do not interpret the results correctly, the analyses cannot completely eliminate uncertainty, or the analyses lack relevance.

The key to why thorough analyses do not guarantee success is found in the last subsection, judgmental biases. The process of interpreting how the answers to strategic questions point to appropriate managerial decisions can also exhibit bounded rationality. Decisions are often arrived at with the use of heuristics and consequently can be biased. Biased decisions are less likely to lead to good outcomes.

Second, formal analyses do not eliminate uncertainty. Consider Zenith and the HDTV. It would be surprising indeed if any forecast were perfectly accurate. There are so many unknowns, so many strategic questions. How will the technology develop? What competitive technologies (if any) will emerge? How will consumers react to the technology? How will it be priced? Each of these will affect the number of HDTVs sold. Not knowing the answers to these questions necessarily imparts some uncertainty to the forecast. Whether a manager likes it or not, decision making usually takes place in the face of uncertainty. In fact, if there were no uncertainty in a situation, a manager would not likely be needed. All decisions could be made by a robot or a computer that could unambiguously interpret the appropriate information.

If it cannot eliminate uncertainty, what then does analysis do? Analysis provides information in a form that *reduces* the uncertainty implicit in strategic questions. The manager's job is to then take the information and exercise his or her judgment in making decisions. The good decision maker acknowledges (and doesn't fret) that uncertainty is unavoidable and that each decision is a risk. Therefore, we distinguish between bad decisions and bad outcomes. Good decisions can have bad outcomes if the uncertainty gets resolved in a manner that was both unlikely before the decision was made and unfriendly to the chosen strategy. Suppose that before the decision, we could have said that it was likely that the uncertainty would be resolved in a manner friendly to the chosen strategy. In this case, the decision would still be correct; it would just have turned out wrong. More likely than not, this decision would have produced a good outcome. For example, suppose that Zenith used consumer surveys to forecast HDTV demand and that these revealed a lucrative market. Suppose further that Zenith interviewed television network representatives and determined that they believed that they had a 90 percent likelihood of being able to develop transmission procedures that would take advantage of the high-resolution properties of HDTV. This hypothetical example twists on a final supposition, that the network executives were wrong. If this were to happen, HDTV would provide no benefit to the consumer and sales would fall far short of the forecast. The decision was the right one because it was likely the uncertainty in transmission would be resolved in a manner friendly to HDTV. Unfortunately, it was not. The decision would have been bad if the unfriendly manner in which the transmission uncertainty was resolved could have been viewed as likely before the fact.

A third reason that thorough analyses frequently do not lead to success is that they are often conducted without a direct link to the decision involved. For example, suppose Citibank was reluctant to initiate the photocard line. Feeling nervous, bank management requested a study of how other banks solicit new cardholders. The connection between this and the go–no go decision for the photocard is tangential at best. This story demonstrates an all too common function of research and analysis. It serves to postpone the decision for managers who have cold feet. Furthermore, the lack of a direct relationship to the decision renders the analysis relatively useless. A relevant, useful analysis should have a direct impact on the decision. For example, Citibank's attempt to determine whether the photocard generates feelings of security and confidence is more directly related to the card's introduction. If it does, the appropriate decision is to introduce; if it doesn't, the appropriate decision is to pull back. This last statement indicates one way to ensure that analyses are relevant to a decision at hand. If a manager can make a statement of the form, "If the results of the analysis say *X,* then I should do *A;* if the results of the analysis say *Y,* then I should do *B,"* he or she knows that the forthcoming information is relevant to the decision.

The Remedy: Planning Processes

As indicated earlier, uncertainty is something we can never eliminate. There is a way, however, to ensure relevance and minimize a decision maker's susceptibility to bounded rationality: use of a formalized, structured, comprehensive planning process. Just as structure helps answer strategic questions, it also ensures that many of the "right" strategic questions get asked. This in turn ensures that any analysis is relevant. Of course, the answers to the strategic questions and the conduct of anlyses often requires a fair amount of creativity. The proposed Citibank study of competitors' solicitation procedures would never be allowed. Comprehensiveness ensures that enough pieces of information are seen so that the decision maker can best approximate the complex world he/she operates in and avoid biases such as availability. It is important that enough gets seen and no more! If too much information gets seen, then the decision maker may be susceptible to other bounded rationality considerations.

Planning processes are usually conducted according to strict guidelines and follow a strict schedule. Companies have formal planning manuals that dictate how the process is to be conducted.[24] The product of the process is usually a formal written document that reflects and justifies the firm's strategic intentions. Unfortunately, too often in corporate America the product (the plan) is emphasized at the expense of the process (the planning). After all, planners are hired to prepare plans. When the plan itself takes on paramount importance, the planning process usually turns into one of essentially completing a checklist of separate tasks prescribed by the manual without paying attention to whether the thinking behind it is coherent. As General Eisenhower said during World War II, "Planning is everything, plans are nothing." Although this is somewhat of an exaggeration, it emphasizes the point that the decision-making activity is more important than the written document. In fact, one could argue that if the planning process was conducted properly, the decisions that emerged from it would be logically based as well as understood and accepted by everyone involved. The written document would almost be superfluous except as a historical record. The purpose of planning is not to create a plan. The purpose of planning is to ask the right strategic questions, answer them to the extent possible, and use those answers in making decisions.

FRAMEWORK OF THE BOOK

This book is structured around formal analytic methods that can be used to answer the strategic questions described in Table 1.3. As noted, these questions all relate to customers, competitors, the company itself, and the external environment. They are linked in the decision-making framework in Fig. 1.5. The process begins with an analysis of the current marketplace. One way of summarizing the results of this analysis is to develop a set of plausible future demand, competitive, and environmental scenarios. The firm must forecast which of these are most likely to occur.

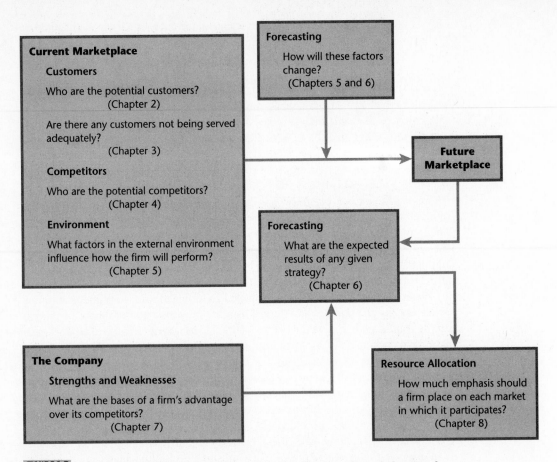

FIGURE 1.5   **Decision-making Framework for the Remainder of the Book**

It then generates a set of strategies that capitalize on its strengths and avoid its weaknesses. Choosing among them is dictated by how well each strategy is expected to perform in the most likely scenarios. The result is an allocation of the firm's resources.

Fig. 1.5 demonstrates the relationship between the questions of Table 1.3 and the chapters that answer them. We now discuss each question in more depth to set the stage for the remainder of the book.

Who are the potential customers? Analyzing the marketplace begins with a thorough understanding of the behavior of a firm's customers and their needs. Part of determining market scope is deciding which customers will comprise the firm's future. To do this effectively, the marketing strategist must first determine what segments currently exist in the marketplace. This is the task facing Reebok at the beginning of the chapter. Only then can intelligent choices be made with respect to whose needs the firm will meet. The identification of these segments is the subject of Chapter 2.

Are there any customers not being served adequately? In order to grow, a firm must expand its portfolio of offerings by modifying existing products and services as well as adding new ones. A change in its market scope must constantly be under consideration. In either case, the firm must understand the current and future needs of various customer segments, such as the security-conscious segment Citibank is interested in. The firm's objectives must then include both the satisfaction of needs currently met by other firms, perhaps inadequately, and the satisfaction of needs not currently being met in the marketplace. Chapter 3 is devoted to methods of identifying both classes of needs.

Who are the potential competitors? In order to attain growth objectives, firms must strive to enter new markets as well as strengthen their positions in existing ones. Marketing strategists searching for new markets to enter must identify the existing and potential competitors in them. For example, Victoria Moore wanted to know who her competitors would be. Similarly, firms defending their positions in existing markets must be able to anticipate potential entrants. Thus maintaining viable market positions requires careful analysis of present and potential competition. The identification of both types of competitors forms the subject matter of Chapter 4.

What factors in the external environment influence how the firm will perform? Any given industry's fortunes naturally depend on the behavior of its customers, competitors, and suppliers. At a macro level, these behaviors are influenced by a variety of demographic, economic, social, political, and technological factors. Such environmental factors can be instrumental in providing opportunities for and imposing threats on the firm. General Foods was faced with a health-conscious population decreasing its consumption of coffee. Determining the critical environmental factors represents a major component of so-called SWOT (strengths, weaknesses, opportunities, and threats) analysis. Chapter 5 describes analytic methods for understanding those factors most important to the firm.

How will these factors change? Effective marketing strategy requires more than just an understanding of the current environment. Only a vision of the future can enable management to assess any market's attractiveness appropriately. When forecasting for established products and markets, standard techniques that rely on historical data, such as regression, can be used. When dealing with new products and new markets as is Zenith with HDTV, forecasting can be particularly difficult because little data will generally be available. Here creative thinking is required. Issues related to these tasks are introduced in Chapter 5 and form the basis for Chapter 6.

What are the bases of a firm's advantage over its competitors? Analyzing the environment will generally reveal the opportunities and threats facing a firm. Its ability to capitalize on those opportunities and avoid those threats hinges on its strengths and weaknesses relative to competitors. Chapter 7 is devoted to the measurement of these strengths and weaknesses and completes the SWOT analyses that form the basis of strategic market planning. Such an analysis enabled Xerox to become aware of its problems.

How much emphasis should a firm place on each market it participates in? Strategic decisions based on previous analyses require an allocation of resources among competing activities. These allocations are performed at various levels within the organization. In general, resources at the corporate level are allocated among divisions and among the different strategic business units (SBUs) within each division. Allocation decisions are also made among existing products and new opportunities. Furthermore, new opportunities may reside within existing SBUs or lead to the creation of new SBUs. Methods of allocating resources have to account for possible interdependencies and synergies among the SBUs, existing brands, and new opportunities. Of course, the resources allocated to a brand or opportunity depend in part on the return expected from it. The expected return is in turn a function of the specific marketing activities on which the resources are spent. This leads us to the question, *What are the expected results of any given strategy?* For established brands, this question translates to modeling marketing mix response. (Forecasting this return is part of the subject matter of Chapter 6.) For development projects and new brands, this translation is not as precise. Therefore, we may need different approaches to allocate resources at the separate levels. These approaches provide the subject matter for Chapter 8.

The concluding chapter of the book, Chapter 9, presents a series of studies the authors have encountered that use methodologies discussed in Chapters 2 through 8 to address the questions posed in this section. All these studies were performed in the real world to increase the informational input managers had to make the required decisions. Our intent here is that the reader will better learn having seen full-fledged, real-world examples.

Review Questions

1. The strategic gameboard (Fig. 1.1) is one paradigm for thinking about competitive strategies. Evaluate how the following firms in the watch industry have effectively used this paradigm in their strategies.

    a. Swiss firms (as a group)

    b. Timex

    c. Bulova

    d. Seiko.

2. The rental car industry has approximately 2 percent of the almost $200 billion domestic travel market in the United States. The market approaches 600,000 car rentals per day. Hertz is the market leader with a 45 percent share. Avis is the challenger with a 30 percent share. The remainder of the market is divided among companies like Budget and Dollar. In the past decade growth has slowed and profits have declined. Primary demand may have reached saturation levels. Hertz and Avis have begun gift giveaways. Use Porter's five forces to analyze the car rental industry. Discuss whether the current situation could have been predicted.

3. Compare and contrast the market scope and competitive advantage strategies of the following firms in the ice cream industry: Haagen-Dazs, Breyers, Baskin-Robbins, and your local private label.

4. One of the ways in which a firm can grow is product line expansion. Two contrasting strategies that serve this purpose are "class to mass" and "mass to class." Discuss the pros and cons of each. Illustrate your answer with examples from common experience.

5. Table 1.1 demonstrates how the critical strategic questions a firm faces may vary according to its stage in the industry life cycle. How do you think these questions may vary with respect to the competitive roles described in Table 1.2?

Notes

1. This example is fully discussed in "Xerox Corporation: The Customer Satisfaction Program" (1991), Harvard Business School Case #9-591-055, Boston, MA.

2. This case is discussed in "Zenith: Marketing Research for High Definition Television (HDTV)" (1990), Harvard Business School Case #9-591-025, Boston, MA.

3. This example is based on "U.S. Retail Coffee Market (A)" (1982), Harvard Business School Case #9-582-087, Boston, MA; "U.S. Retail Coffee Market (B)" (1982), Harvard Business School Case #9-582-088, Boston, MA; and "Brim (A)" (1982), Harvard Business School Case #9-582-089, Boston, MA.

4. Buaron, Roberto (1981), "How to Win the Market-Share Game? Try Changing the Rules," *Management Review* 70 (January), 8–19.

5. See Porter, Michael E. (1980), *Competitive Strategy,* New York: Free Press.

6. See Levitt, Theodore (1980), "Marketing Success through Differentiation—of Anything," *Harvard Business Review* 58 (January-February), 83–91.

7. Porter, *Competitive Strategy,* 39.

8. See Hofer, Charles W. (1975), "Toward a Contingency Theory of Business Strategy," *Academy of Management Journal* 18 (December), 784–810.

9. *Ibid.* Several alternatives are mentioned.

10. See Kotler, Philip (1994), *Marketing Management: Analysis, Planning, and Control,* Englewood Cliffs, NJ: Prentice-Hall, 374–377.

11. For example, Carpenter, Gregory S., and Kent Nakamoto (1989), "Consumer Preference Formation and Pioneering Advantage," *Journal of Marketing Research* 26 (August), 285–298, suggest that consumer preferences in an emerging market are labile and influenced by the specific design of the pioneering product. Uneducated consumers are not really capable of understanding the variety of potential benefits a product can offer and therefore need the manufacturers to tell them what is really important.

12. These conditions are outlined in more detail in Porter, *Competitive Strategy,* 139–140.

13. He tells the story in Levitt, Theodore (1965), "Exploit the Product Life Cycle," *Harvard Business Review* 43 (November-December), 81–94.

14. See Harrigan, Kathryn R., and Michael E. Porter (1983), "End Game Strategies for Declining Industries," *Harvard Business Review* 61 (July-August), 111–120.

15. This classification is proposed in Kotler, *Marketing Management: Analysis, Planning, and Control,* 382.

16. For a discussion of the market share–profitability relationship, see Buzzell, Robert D., Bradley T. Gale, and Ralph G. M. Sultan (1975), "Market Share—A Key to Profitability," *Harvard Business Review* 53 (January-February), 97–106.

17. Porter, Michael E. (1979), "How Competitive Forces Shape Strategy," *Harvard Business Review* 57 (March-April), 141.

18. *Ibid.* These conditions are outlined in more detail on page 140.

19. See Levitt, Theodore (1960), "Marketing Myopia," *Harvard Business Review* 38 (July-August), 45–56.

20. See Simon, Herbert A. (1997), *Administrative Behavior,* 4th ed., New York: Free Press for a complete presentation of Simon's viewpoint.

21. Simon, Herbert A. (1997), *Administrative Behavior,* 4th ed., New York: Free Press, Chapter 5.

22. See Ackoff, Russell L. (1967), "Management Misinformation Systems," *Management Science* 14, B147–B156 (C), for a complete discussion.

23. See Tversky, Amos, and Daniel Kahneman (1973), "Availability: A Heuristic for Judging Frequency and Probability," *Cognitive Psychology* 5, 207–232, for a more complete discussion.

24. Hopkins, David S. (1981), *The Marketing Plan,* New York: The Conference Board presents excerpts from some of these manuals.

Bibliography

Ackoff, Russell L. (1967), "Management Misinformation Systems," *Management Science* 14, B147-B156 (C).

"Brim (A)" (1982), Harvard Business School Case #9-582-089, Boston, MA.

Buaron, Roberto (1981), "How to Win the Market-Share Game? Try Changing the Rules," *Management Review* 70 (January), 8–19.

Buzzell, Robert D., Bradley T. Gale, and Ralph G. M. Sultan (1975), "Market Share—A Key to Profitability," *Harvard Business Review* 53 (January-February), 97–106.

Carpenter, Gregory S., and Kent Nakamoto (1989), "Consumer Preference Formation and Pioneering Advantage," *Journal of Marketing Research* 26 (August), 285–298.

Harrigan, Kathryn R., and Michael E. Porter (1983), "End Game Strategies for Declining Industries," *Harvard Business Review* 61 (July-August), 111–120.

Hofer, Charles W. (1975), "Toward a Contingency Theory of Business Strategy," *Academy of Management Journal* 18 (December), 784–810.

Hopkins, David S. (1981), *The Marketing Plan,* New York: The Conference Board.

Kotler, Philip (1994), *Marketing Management: Analysis, Planning, and Control,* Englewood Cliffs, NJ: Prentice-Hall.

Levitt, Theodore (1960), "Marketing Myopia," *Harvard Business Review* 38 (July-August), 45–56.

Levitt, Theodore (1965), "Exploit the Product Life Cycle," *Harvard Business Review* 43 (November-December), 81–94.

Levitt, Theodore (1980), "Marketing Success through Differentiation—of Anything," *Harvard Business Review* 58 (January-February), 83–91.

Porter, Michael E. (1979), "How Competitive Forces Shape Strategy," *Harvard Business Review* 57 (March-April), 137–145.

Porter, Michael E. (1980), *Competitive Strategy,* New York: Free Press.

Simon, Herbert A. (1976), *Administrative Behavior,* 3rd ed., New York: Free Press.

Tversky, Amos, and Daniel Kahneman (1973), "Availability: A Heuristic for Judging Frequency and Probability," *Cognitive Psychology* 5, 207–232.

"U.S. Retail Coffee Market (A)" (1982), Harvard Business School Case #9-582-087, Boston, MA.

"U.S. Retail Coffee Market (B)" (1982), Harvard Business School Case #9-582-088, Boston, MA.

"Zenith: Marketing Research for High Definition Television (HDTV)" (1990), Harvard Business School Case #9-591-025, Boston, MA.

Segmenting Markets

Who Are the Potential Buyers?

INTRODUCTION

Market segmentation involves identifying groups of consumers who behave differently in response to a given marketing strategy. Their behavior is conceptualized as homogeneous within a segment and heterogeneous across segments. Recall from the first chapter that much of strategic decision making is devoted to determining market scope; that is, deciding which product markets to invest in. Segmentation then structures these decisions by defining the alternative product markets, or at least the customers in them.

The operational decisions underlying the determination of market scope include what products will be offered, how they will be positioned, and what customers will be pursued. These decisions and the precise knowledge of consumer behavior required for making them differ slightly for new and existing products (see Table 2.1). In both product design and modification decisions the most important behavioral concept is benefits required (including low price). Managers working on product design issues should then look for groups (market segments) that have homogeneous benefit requirements. Similarly, managers searching for effective product positions (for both new and existing products) need to find segments that have homogeneous product perceptions.

Socioeconomic and technological trends have made market segmentation more pervasive in recent years.[1] Expanding disposable incomes and higher education levels have produced consumers with sophisticated (and varied) tastes and lifestyles. Consequently, they have diverse benefit requirements for the goods and services they purchase. Furthermore, new, more focused advertising media (magazines, cable TV, radio, direct marketing) have emerged, facilitating the implementation of well-defined marketing programs targeted to groups with special interests. Finally, new technologies such as computer-aided design and modular assemblies have enabled manufacturers to customize a wide variety of products to meet the requirements of these special interest groups. These trends can only accelerate as marketers and consumers alike learn to make efficient use of the Internet and World Wide Web. To date, the role of the web in marketing has been as an information source for consumers and, to a lesser extent, a vehicle for order taking. Its potential is much greater.

TABLE 2.1 **A Framework for Market Scope Determination**

	Decision	Questions about Customer Behavior
New Products	Product design	What benefits do customers want in a new product?
	Positioning	How are existing brands perceived in the marketplace?
	Price points	How price sensitive are customers?
	Customer selection	What classes of customers want certain benefits and have certain perceptions?
Existing Products	Product modification	What benefits do customers want in a specific product?
	Positioning	How are existing brands (including ours) perceived in the marketplace?
	Promotions	How price sensitive are customers?
	Customer selection	What customers would be most receptive to our offering?

These trends not only make market segmentation viable, they make it possible to reach smaller distinct segments. With the population not growing as fast as it has been (the U.S. Census Bureau projects just 7.2 percent growth during the 1990s) and many standard product markets maturing, competition is necessarily becoming more and more intense. To survive, firms must pay more specific attention to their customers' precise requirements. It follows then that the market segments facing companies are shrinking. Indeed, many companies are addressing segments of size one! Advances in database marketing (to be discussed later) enable some firms (such as catalog houses and financial institutions) to design and address their offerings to each particular customer.

Most manufacturing and service organizations, however, find segments of size one either infeasible to target because of limited information on individual customers or unprofitable because they are too small. Therefore, they resort to a partial aggregation strategy. For example, business schools cannot tailor a curriculum for each student even if each one has different interests. Therefore, they group students interested in a specific functional area (say, marketing or finance) and do not typically attempt to segment the market any further (say, by developing a program for students interested in pharmaceutical marketing, another for students planning a finance career in the hotel industry, etc.).

The bulk of this chapter will revolve around this type of partial aggregation approach. We take the viewpoint that firms will try to find groups of customers with similar (if not perfectly identical) *perceptions* or *benefit requirements,* the variables implied by Table 2.1 to be most important for setting marketing strategy. Table 2.1 also includes price sensitivity; however, this is really just a (very important) specific benefit requirement. Therefore this chapter focuses on the measurement of perceptions and benefit requirements and aggregation of customers. We return then to a discussion of segments of size one by introducing some basics of database marketing and conclude with a brief discussion on the selection of strategically relevant market segments.

Before embarking on this path, though, we do note that although we emphasize differences in consumer perceptions and benefit requirements in strategy choice, many other variables have been used in both academic theory and practice. Any discussion of market segmentation that did not address them would be incomplete. For that reason, we begin by discussing these variables.

BASES OF SEGMENTATION

Consumers differ on literally thousands of dimensions (age, sex, religion, etc.). Each can potentially serve as a basis for segmenting markets. Not all dimensions will be equally useful in all situations. Nevertheless, Table 2.2 presents some of the more popular ones.

The table divides the variables in several ways. First, it separates those more useful for consumer markets from those more useful for industrial markets. Some variables (such as geographic location and benefits sought) are useful for both. Others (race and SIC codes) are more specific for one. Second, the table separates out those variables that describe the consumer in general from those that specifically relate to various aspects of the consumer's choice and behavior. This distinction will become very important shortly.

Consumer Markets

Demographics are among the most popular variables used in segmenting consumer markets for several reasons. First, they are easy to measure. Furthermore, segments defined by demographics are often very large and accessible by various communications media and distribution channels. In addition, demographic data can be very inexpensive. Relevant publications, such as the *U.S. Statistical Abstract, Rand McNally's Commercial Atlas and Marketing Guide, Sales and Marketing Management's Survey of Buying Power,* and the *U.S. Census of Population and Housing,* are available at almost every library in the United States. Finally, demographics are often projectable. Consider, for example, that today's male teenager will be a young adult male in 10 years.

The term *psychographics* has emerged to describe psychological elements such as personality, values, and lifestyle that can be used to describe consumers. There is no universally accepted definition of psychographics.[2] Despite this, the area has thrived over the last two decades. Psychographics are intended to supplement (not replace) demographics.

Psychographic variables are not nearly as easy to identify as demographic ones. The usual approach is to ask a sample of consumers a large battery of attitude, interest, and opinion (AIO) questions, some custom made and others taken from standard attitude or personality tests used in psychology, and use factor analysis to uncover the

TABLE 2.2 Bases of Segmentation

(A) Consumer Markets

General Descriptive Customer Characteristics	Characteristics Related to Consumer Behavior
Demographics	Benefits sought
Sex	
Age	Desired application
Marital status	
Number and age of children	Purchase and loyalty patterns
Stage in life cycle	Usage characteristics
Subcultures	Heavy versus light
Race	User versus nonuser
Ethnic group	Store loyalty
Geographic location	
	Participation in the adoption and diffusion process
Socioeconomic characteristics	Information and influence patterns
Income	Innovativeness
Education	
Occupation	Brand behavior
Social class	Loyalty
	Attitudes
Psychographics (personality and lifestyle characteristics)	Intentions
Personality	Perceptions
Attitudes	Preferences
Interests	
Opinions	Sensitivity to marketing mix elements
Lifestyle	Price
	Advertising
Occasion for use/consumption	Promotion

(B) Industrial Markets

General Descriptive Customer Characteristics	Characteristics Related to Consumer Behavior
General organizational characteristics	Benefits sought
SIC Code	
Size	Product usage
Geographic location	
Structure	Source loyalty
Power relationships	
Reward system	Buying process
Technology	
	Attitudes
Psychographics	
Direction	Perceptions
Achievement motivation	
General degree of conflict	Preferences
Organizational climate	

Source: Updated and adapted from Frank, Ronald E., William F. Massy, and Yoram Wind (1972), *Market Segmentation,* Englewood Cliffs, NJ: Prentice-Hall.

TABLE 2.3 Examples of AIO Questions

Following is a series of statements. The subjects are asked how much they agree or disagree with each one.

c. I'd say I'm rebelling against the way I was brought up.

g. In general, it's more important to understand my inner self than to be famous, powerful, or wealthy.

h. My greatest achievements are ahead of me.

i. I believe a woman can work outside the home even if she has small children and still be a good mother.

m. It's very important to me to feel I am part of a group.

o. Overall, I'd say I'm very happy.

s. I would rather spend a quiet evening at home than go out to a party.

w. A woman's life is fulfilled only if she can provide a happy home for her family.

cc. Air pollution is a major, worldwide danger.

dd. I often feel left out of things going on around me.

ff. It is wrong for an unmarried man or an unmarried woman to have sexual relations.

gg. Women should take care of running their homes and leave running the country to men.

hh. It would be best for the future of this country if the United States continues to take an active part in world affairs.

jj. The purchase and use of marijuana should be legalized.

nn. I think we are spending too much money on military armaments.

Sources: These questions are taken from Mitchell, Arnold (1983), *The Nine American Lifestyles*, New York: MacMillan. The particular ones presented here were chosen by William O. Bearden, Richard G. Netemeyer, and Mary F. Mobley (1983), *Handbook of Marketing Scales: Multi-Item Measures for Marketing and Consumer Behavior Research*, Newbury Park, CA: Sage Publications, 90–91. Copyright © 1993. Reprinted by permission of Sage Publications, Inc.

psychographic dimensions underlying the responses. This is done by grouping together those items to which consumers respond similarly. Table 2.3 presents an excerpt from one such survey. The chapter appendix presents more details on factor analysis.

Table 2.4 presents the results of a factor analysis designed to consolidate psychographic dimensions to be used in segmenting the market for department stores in a large southwestern community. The table summarizes a psychographic analysis of 29 statements given to 754 residents of that community. Such an analysis could impact strategy in several ways. For example, a new department store might choose to carry high-quality, old-fashioned merchandise if there is a large enough segment in its region that scores high on the statements comprising the traditionalist dimension.

As is apparent from our description, psychographic studies can be very complex and costly. Syndicated or standardized research services can often provide lower- (but still high-) cost substitutes. Instead of hiring someone to take a survey, firms can subscribe to a survey already taken. Suppliers such as Yankelovich Partners and Donnelly Marketing Services have derived general lifestyle segments that can be used as possible segmentation bases. Probably the best known of these is Stanford SRI

TABLE 2.4 Psychographic Analysis for Southwestern Department Stores

Dimension or Factor	Sample Statement*
Traditionalist	I have some old-fashioned tastes and habits.
Outgoing/Individualist	I would rather fix something myself than take it to an expert.
Quality/Service	I will go out of my way to find a bank with good service.
Socially conscious	If my clothes are not in fashion, it really bothers me.
Other directed	I usually ask for help from other people in making decisions.

*All AIO statements were operationalized as five-point scales ranging from strongly disagree to strongly agree. Samples are statements that are very important to (load highly on) that factor.

Source: Bearden, William O., Jesse E. Teel, Jr., and Richard M. Durand (1978), "Media Usage, Psychographic, and Demographic Dimensions of Retail Shoppers," *Journal of Retailing* 54 (Spring), 65–74. Reprinted by permission of the publisher.

International's VALS (Values and Lifestyles) program.[3] The latest version, VALS2, proposes the eight lifestyle segments illustrated in Figure 2.1a and 2.1b. Services such as VALS2 are still growing in popularity. However, in the end, their effectiveness may still be somewhat limited since the lifestyle research is general in nature and not really directed to purchasing behavior in any particular product or market category.

Another syndicated service that attempts to describe consumers at a much more micro level is Claritas Corporation's PRIZM (Potential Rating Index for Zip Markets) clusters. In 1974, Jonathan Robbin, a computer scientist, devised a system that matches zip codes with census data and consumer surveys (which measure VALS2 typologies, among many other things). He sorted the 36,000 zip codes into 40 lifestyle clusters. Each zip code belongs to one of the clusters. The idea is, as Robbin says, "Tell me someone's zip code, and I can predict what they eat, drink, drive—even think."[4] For example, one of the authors of this book lives in Greenwich Village in New York City, zip code 10012. His neighborhood belongs to the Bohemian Mix PRIZM cluster. Figure 2.2 tells a lot about his neighbors and where else people like them live. The 40 PRIZM clusters are fully described in a popular press book by Michael J. Weiss.[5] Clients of Claritas, though, can access its database in much more detail. They can find out what people in a single zip code buy, what zip codes tend to buy their products, what people in a zip code read, and so on. These clusters are updated with each census. The most recent version has 62 clusters.

The second major group of segmenting variables in Table 2.2 consists of those directly related to consumer behavior. These are important in that they are related to the focus of the marketer's activity: buying the firm's products and services. Measuring segmentation variables based on consumer behavior is the focus of much of the remainder of this chapter.

Industrial Markets

The state of knowledge regarding industrial market segmentation is not nearly as well developed as that of consumer market segmentation. That is one reason why the industrial segmentation bases are not structured as well. There are some clear parallels between the two, however, in particular as they relate to general customer descriptive characteristics. Industrial markets have their corresponding demographics. One study on hospitals used size, number of beds, budget, percent occupancy, teaching versus nonteaching status, and community size as demographic variables (and explicitly called them so).[6]

Perhaps the most often used industrial demographic is the SIC (Standard Industrial Classification) code. The SIC code is a hierarchical numerical classification system controlled by the Statistical Policy Division of the Office of Management and Budget. It divides all economic activity into major categories (such as agriculture, manufacturing, construction, mining, wholesale trade, and retail trade). It further subdivides each activity into major groups, each identified with a two-digit code. For example, the two-digit number 35 represents General Industrial Machinery and Equipment under the major category of manufacturing. The major groups are divided into subgroups, and a third digit is added. Subgroup 357 represents the Office, Computing, and Accounting Machines subgroup of group 35. A more and more detailed industry classification emerges when more digits are added to the code. Category 3572 denotes typewriter manufacturers; 3573 denotes manufacturers of electronic computing equipment, and so on. The level of detail can extend to the seventh digit. In any event, industrial marketers have been using SIC codes as tools for segmenting their markets for many years.

Beyond demographics, organizations, like consumers, can be described on non-demographic, psychological descriptor dimensions (openness of communication, clarity of organizational objectives, achievement motivation, resistance to change, and maybe even strategy). Thus, we have an organizational analogy to psychographics.[7]

The parallels between industrial and consumer segmentation bases begin to lessen, though, when we turn our attention to characteristics related to buying behavior. As complex as consumer buying processes may appear, they pale in comparison to industrial buying processes. There are usually many more people involved in industrial buying; a wider variety of technological and economic factors must be considered; large sums of money are frequently involved; and the duration of some buying processes can exceed a year.

Often, the most difficult task for a marketer is to discover who in an organization influences the buying decision and who is responsible for eventually making it. Imagine the difficulty of a salesperson trying to interest a prospect in a product as he or she gets to the front door of the company's building, looks at the directory, and cannot figure out who to see. One of the keys to the early success of Federal Express in the 1970s was its understanding that the decisions to use some of its products (Standard Air Services and Priority One mail) were made by traffic managers, and the decisions to use others (Courier Pak) were made by executives and secretaries.[8]

Fortunately, it is often possible to segment potential customers by the identities of the decision makers. For example, one study on industrial air conditioners, described in Table 2.5, found four segments. The raw data for the analysis that produced this table were collected via a survey in which respondents from the potential market were asked who (in terms of job title) would influence the purchase decision. A cluster analysis (see the chapter appendix) was then performed to group the respondents into segments.

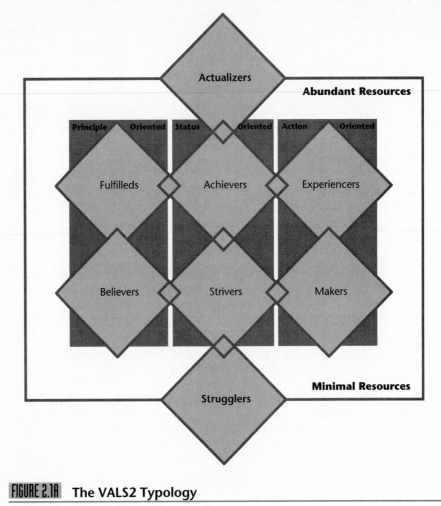

FIGURE 2.1A   **The VALS2 Typology**

Source: SRI International.

Descriptor or Behavioral Variables: Which Are Better?

Selecting a variable or set of variables to use as bases of segmentation for a specific product category can be problematic. Where to start? Which are more likely to be useful, descriptor variables or behavioral variables? The answer is that both are necessary.

Segmentation is an expensive proposition. It not only requires the financial costs of creating multiple programs, it also requires time and effort, which result in opportunity costs. For the costs of segmentation to be balanced by its benefits, the company has to be able to create an offering more tailored to the way a consumer behaves. That behavior might be reflected in benefits sought or the way a consumer responds to other marketing variables. That is why behavioral variables are impor-

Actualizers: 8% of population. Median age is 43. Highest income; median is $58,000. Successful, take-charge individuals interested in personal growth and exploration. Image is more of an expression of cultivated tastes than a status symbol. Wide interests. Enjoy finer things in life.

Fulfilleds: 11% of population. Many are retired. Median age near 50. Mature, comfortable, reflective people. Median income $38,000. Interested in broadening knowledge. Have strongly held principles and appear self-assured. Demand value and durability in products.

Believers: 15% of population. Median income $21,000. Conservative, conventional people with concrete beliefs. Few have any college. Follow established routines surrounding family, religion, and social groups. Favor known brands.

Achievers: 13% of population. Mostly in 30s. Median income is $50,000. Self-definition comes through career success. Like to feel in control. Image is important as a status symbol.

Strivers: 13% of population. Mostly in 30s. Few have college experience. Median income $25,000. Money is measure of success. Most feel cheated by their limited resources. Concerned about opinions of others. Like style and emulate those with higher means.

Experiencers: 12% of population. Mostly in 20s. Median income is $19,000 but disposable income is high since they share living quarters. Vital, enthusiastic, rebellious. Savor what is new, offbeat, and risky. Sports and outdoors provide outlets for abundant energy.

Makers: 13% of population. Median age is 30. Median income is $23,000. Craftspeople and do-it-yourselfers. Practical, self-sufficient people. Like to build. Conservative and suspicious of new ideas. Few have college background.

Strugglers: 12% of population. Have hard time making ends meet. Chronically poor, low skilled, poorly educated. Two-thirds are women. Median age over 60. Median income below poverty level. Focused on meeting urgent needs of moment. Concerns are for security and safety. Cautious consumers who are limited but brand loyal.

FIGURE 2.1B The VALS2 Typology

Source: Descriptions are based on Piirto, Rebecca (1991), *Beyond Mind Games: The Marketing Power of Psychographics,* Ithaca, NY: American Demographics Books, 80–83.

tant. They reflect the behavior the company has tailored its offering to. Now the company has to find those consumers who respond to the new, tailored offering in the way that the company has predicted. That is why descriptor variables are important. They allow the company to pinpoint those consumers who will have the desired response.

Consider chewing gum. One brand, Cry Baby, made by the Philadelphia Chewing Gum Corp., has an extremely sour taste.[9] It makes your eyes water and your body sweat. Why would anybody buy it? The company (behaviorally) segments on two benefits sought: the desire to prove that you can "take it" and the opportunity to play practical jokes. Who seeks these benefits? Twelve- to thirteen-year-old junior high school students, of course. They want to prove they're adults. That is why the

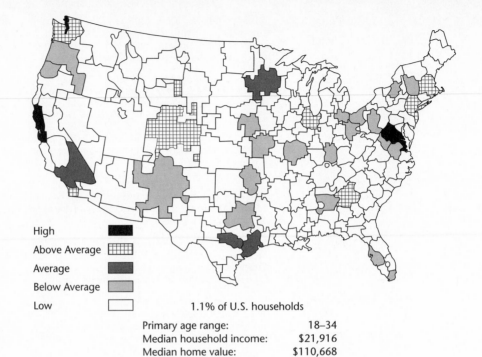

High

Above Average

Average

Below Average

Low

1.1% of U.S. households

Primary age range:	18–34
Median household income:	$21,916
Median home value:	$110,668

Thumbnail Demographics

bohemian inner-city neighborhoods
multi-unit housing
racially-mixed singles
white-collar jobs

Politics

Predominant ideology:	liberal
1984 presidential vote	Mondale (65%)
Key issues:	nuclear arms, federal budget

Sample Neighborhoods

Greenwich Village, New York, New York (10012)
Dupont Circle, Washington, D.C. (20036)
Cambridge, Boston, Massachusetts (02139)
Lincoln Park, Chicago, Illinois (60614)
Shadyside, Pittsburgh, Pennsylvania (15232)
Haight-Ashbury, San Francisco, California (94117)

FIGURE 2.2A   **The Bohemian Mix PRIZM Cluster**

Source: Michael J. Weiss (1988), *The Clustering of America,* New York: Harper & Row, 301–302.

Lifestyle

High Usage	Low Usage
Environmentalist organizations	Cigars
Travel by railroad	Hunting
Downhill skiing	Wall paneling
Drink Irish whiskey	Standard-size cars
Country clubs	Christmas/Chanukah clubs
Classical records/tapes	CB radios
Wine by the case	Chewing tobacco
Common stock	Watch roller derby

Magazine/Newspapers

High Usage	Low Usage
Atlantic Monthly	*Seventeen*
Harper's	*Saturday Evening Post*
Gentlemen's Quarterly	*Working Woman*
The New Yorker	*1001 Home Ideas*

Cars

High Usage	Low Usage
Alfa Romeos	Buick LeSabres
Saabs	Ford Crown Victorias
Peugeots	Mercury Grand Marquises
BMW 3 Series	Dodge Diplomats
Mitsubishi Mirages	Pontiac Bonnevilles

Food

High Usage	Low Usage
Whole-wheat bread	White bread
Frozen waffles	Pretzels
Fruit juices and drinks	Frozen pizzas
TV dinners	Meat tenderizers

Television

High Usage	Low Usage
"Late Night with David Letterman"	"Who's the Boss?"
"At the Movies"	"Highway to Heaven"
"Nightline"	"CBS Sports Saturday"
"Good Morning America"	"Santa Barbara"

FIGURE 2.2B **The Bohemian Mix PRIZM Cluster**

Source: Michael J. Weiss (1988), *The Clustering of America*, New York: Harper & Row, 301–302.

TABLE 2.5 Major Segments of Organizations in the Industrial Air-Conditioning Study

	Segment 1	Segment 2	Segment 3	Segment 4
Segment Size (% of Potential Market)	12%	31%	32%	25%
Major decision participant categories in equipment selection decision (Frequencies of involvement)	Plant managers (1.00) HVAC consultants (.38)	Production engineers (.94) Plant managers (.70)	Production engineers (.97) HVAC consultants (.60)	Top management (.85) HVAC consultants (.67)

Source: Reprinted from "A New Approach to Industrial Market Segmentation," by Jean-Marie Choffray and Gary L. Lilien. *Sloan Management Review,* Issue 19, 1978, pp. 17–30, by Sloan Management Review Association. All rights reserved.

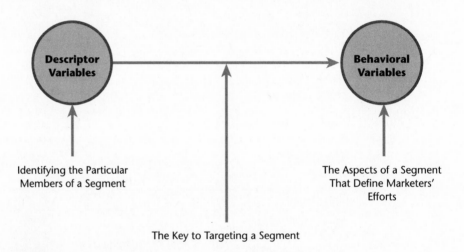

FIGURE 2.3 Relationships for Segment Targeting

gum does not sell well to younger children (who have no illusions of adulthood) or older children (who do not need to resort to these symbols).

   This interesting (if unconventional) example illustrates a further point. Not only are both descriptor and behavioral variables important, but the link between them is essential. What good would it do the company to just know the benefits without knowing who sought them? It would not know how to promote or distribute the product. Fig. 2.3 summarizes these ideas.

Descriptor or Behavioral Variables: Which Come First?

Given the importance of descriptor-behavior pairings and links, managers must make a decision as to how to proceed. They essentially have two choices. They can form prototype segments with descriptor variables and search for commonalities in behav-

TABLE 2.6 Annual Household Beer Consumption by Income and Education

Annual Family Income	Years of Education (Head of Household)				
	6	10	12	14	16
Less than $9,000	$30.03	$19.59	$18.54	$36.81	$46.53
$9,000–$14,999	$83.22	$60.81	$35.10	$52.20	$5.37
$15,000–$23,999	$75.69	$78.09	$67.89	$72.81	$50.40
$24,000–$29,999	$83.16	$72.63	$96.42	$63.84	$69.69
$30,000–$44,999	$102.72	$72.15	$64.62	$61.89	$72.54
$45,000+	$109.74	$37.50	$70.47	$117.51	$53.58

Source: Updated and adapted from Bass, Frank M., Douglas J. Tigert, and Robert T. Lonsdale (1968), "Market Segmentation: Group versus Individual Behavior," *Journal of Marketing Research* 5 (August), 270.

ior among consumers with common descriptors, or they can start with behavioral variables and search for descriptors that correspond to the relevant behavior. We call the two approaches *descriptor-first* and *behavior-first*. The behavior-first approach involves a sequence of four steps:

1. Identify the behavior of interest.
2. Measure it for a sample of consumers.
3. Cluster the sample into segments.
4. Find descriptors that are appropriate for each segment.

In the descriptor-first approach, steps 3 and 4 are specified in advance.

Since omitting the last two steps simplifies the process, the descriptor-first approach has the advantage of more easily formed prototype segments. It is usually developed with the use of a classification table containing one or more descriptor variables in its rows and/or columns. The entries in the table are some behavioral variables. Table 2.6 presents an example. Household beer consumption is cross-classified by income and education of the head of the household. The table shows the mean annual dollar purchases for each cell. As implied by the table, consumption varies widely according to socioeconomic characteristics.

In addition, descriptor-first segmentation is appropriate when a company has a strong position with a segment of customers defined by a set of descriptor variables. For example, Johnson & Johnson may have a stronger reputation among mothers than among the population as a whole. It makes sense, then, for it to examine the needs (behavior) of mothers (descriptor) in a descriptor-first way in search of possible line extensions.

Finally, certain behaviors and measurement devices do not lend themselves to individual consumer measurement and clustering (for example, perceptual maps to be discussed later). They are more meaningful when measured at some aggregate level. In these cases a descriptor-first approach is mandated.

Unfortunately, though, many descriptor-first attempts to segment buyer behavior do not prove fruitful. In an industrial marketing study of the nonintelligent data-terminal market published over a decade ago, 300 recent buyers of this product category were surveyed about the major benefits they sought in their terminals.[10] While the customer company's size was somewhat related to benefits sought, its industry, as reflected by SIC code, was not very helpful. Retail establishments, financial institutions, and manufacturers all reported similar relative importances for several characteristics (speed, service, reliability, delivery). The company that sponsored the study segmented the market by SIC code. The results of the study implied that the company was designing product and promotional programs for very specific segments of the market that do not behave differently than the market as a whole!

With the behavior-first approach, however, we are guaranteed divergent behaviors among segments. So which should come first? It depends. If strategic or methodological considerations call for decriptors first, then so be it. If not, perhaps the risk of nonmeaningful results is enough to overcome the simplicity of descriptor-first approaches, especially since a primary data collection effort is often required anyway. Therefore, when one has a choice, we recommend behavior-first approaches. We now turn to a discussion of the two behaviors previously singled out, perceptions and benefits required.

PERCEPTION MEASUREMENT AND SEGMENTATION

Consumers are guided in their choices by their perceptions of the product and service alternatives they face. These perceptions are the result of mental selection, interpretation, and integration of a tremendous amount of product information (such as features) and marketing information (advertising, word of mouth) into a coherent picture. As such, perceptions are subjectively determined. Two products that are physically distinct may be perceived as substitutes if their dissimilarities are not perceived as being important. On the other hand, products that are essentially identical may be perceived as different. Take beer, for example. Go to the supermarket and you can buy "relaxing" Michelob ("Weekends were made for Michelob"), "light" Amstel, and "refreshing" Miller ("It's Miller time"). Yet, in blind taste tests, most consumers cannot generally identify the brand they usually drink. So what consumers perceive is more important than what really is. This philosophy is based on a theory drawn from psychology called Brunswik's Lens model, in which perceptions are a lens through which the consumer views product and marketing information to form preferences.[11] Thus, to effectively affect choice, marketers must understand consumer perceptions.

Perceptions are formally integrated into marketing strategy through the concept of *positioning*. A product's position can be defined as how it is perceived relative to its competitors by a relevant group of customers (the target segment). Segmentation and positioning are too often treated as independent concepts in practice and in the literature. However, positioning has no value unless it is appropriate for a target segment. For example, will an airline's economy positioning make business travelers who care more about schedules and on-time performance buy tickets?

How consumers process marketing information, form perceptions, and establish product positions in their minds will be a function of their prior beliefs, knowledge, and experiences. Not all consumers come to the product category with the same beliefs, knowledge, and experiences, however. Therefore, different consumers bombarded with the same information may form different perceptions and view product positions differently. Hence marketers should not consider overall product positioning, but focus on positionings of the product perceived by various market segments. One group (singles) may view the Ford Explorer as a fun car, while others (young marrieds) may view it as a family vehicle.

In choosing target segments, managers must look at positioning-segment pairs. They can begin by selecting a positioning they find attractive and continue by searching for descriptors of segments that view their product that way. Alternatively, they can select a target segment with descriptors and come up with a suitable positioning. Of course, there is no guarantee that a preselected segment will have similar perceptions. In either case, the best recipe is probably to proceed iteratively in analyzing positioning and segment selections.

To accomplish these tasks, we need to measure consumer perceptions. We describe two ways: direct questioning and perceptual maps.

Direct Questioning

The easiest way to get insight into people's perceptions is to ask them directly. Consumers can be asked in person, on the phone, or through the mail to rate a product, or more likely several products within a category, on a selected set of attributes. Questions like the following are common.[12]

Please rate Crest on the following attributes:

	Very Poor			Very Good
Decay prevention	____	____ ____ ____	____
Price	____	____ ____ ____	____
Tooth whitening	____	____ ____ ____	____

Questions asked in this format are unfortunately vulnerable to a *"halo" effect;* that is, if someone has an overall liking for Crest, he or she is likely to rate it highly on all attributes. The information gained from this process is not likely to be useful. To minimize the halo effect, multibrand studies should be conducted attribute by attribute rather than brand by brand as follows:

Please rate the following brands in terms of decay prevention:

	Very Poor			Very Good
Aim	____	____ ____ ____	____
Crest	____	____ ____ ____	____
Colgate	____	____ ____ ____	____

Of course, nothing can be done to totally eliminate halo, but the attribute-by-attribute format forces explicit comparisons along specific criteria.

As an example of studying perceptions, a credit union was interested in determining how it had positioned itself in the minds of its members relative to other county financial institutions.[13] In particular, it was interested in what elements of its services customers were least happy with. It initiated a mail survey of 700 of its members. The sample was asked to rate the credit union, along with two other institutions, on 12 dimensions. The results are presented graphically in Fig. 2.4. The credit union's major shortcoming appears to be an inconvenient location, although this was obviously not the case for people who worked near the credit union (a potentially useful descriptor variable). Location was not something the credit union could do anything about. However, it was something the credit union could deemphasize relative to other characteristics in its communications to customers who didn't work nearby. This insight also gave it a place to look for new customers—right in its own backyard. Note how critical the link between behavior (perception) and descriptors (location) is to decision making in this example.

Responses to direct questioning can be either used directly or further reduced by factor analysis to see if there is any underlying structure to the perceptions. One study of 14 nonalcoholic beverages found that 65 consumers' ratings for nine attributes could be parsimoniously summarized by three major underlying characteristics or factors:[14]

Underlying Characteristic	Rated Attributes
Maturity	Served hot, adult orientation, relaxing
Nutrition	Healthful, consumed with food (versus best alone), sweet
Refreshing	Filling, energy giving, thirst quenching

Collectively, these factors explain 77 percent of the variation in the original data set. As will be discussed in the next section, factor analysis results can be used in constructing perceptual maps.

Perceptual Mapping

A *perceptual map* is a visual representation of consumers' perceptions of and preferences for a given set of products or brands. Products are plotted as points on a set of axes. The distance between two products can be interpreted as the psychological similarity between them.

Fig. 2.5 shows a perceptual map based on the nonalcoholic beverage study briefly described in the previous section. Since the study showed that there were three underlying characteristics in the nine attributes, the resulting map is three-dimensional. Unfortunately, we cannot present a three-dimensional structure on a two-dimensional page. Some companies actually have a set of Tinkertoys on hand to create three-dimensional maps! The best we can do in Fig. 2.5 is to present two two-dimensional structures (maturity versus nutrition and maturity versus refreshing).

Many mathematical techniques have emerged for constructing perceptual maps. These include *multidimensional scaling, factor analysis,* and *multiple discriminant analysis.*[15] These are complex computer-intensive techniques that we unfortunately

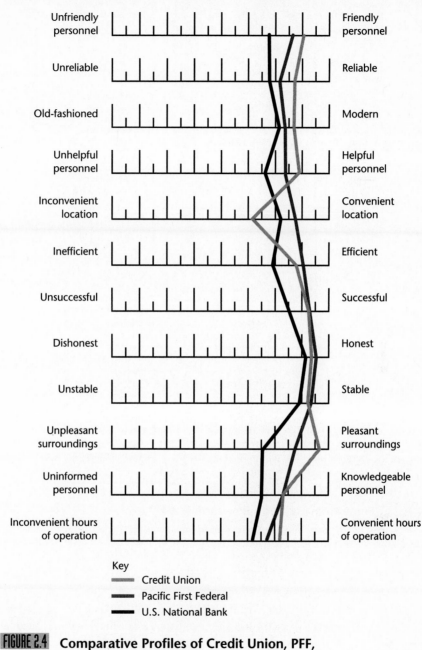

FIGURE 2.4 **Comparative Profiles of Credit Union, PFF, and U.S. National Bank**

Source: Green, Paul E., Donald S. Tull, and Gerald R. Albaurn (1988), *Research for Marketing Decisions*, 5th ed. Englewood Cliffs, NJ: Prentice Hall, 685.

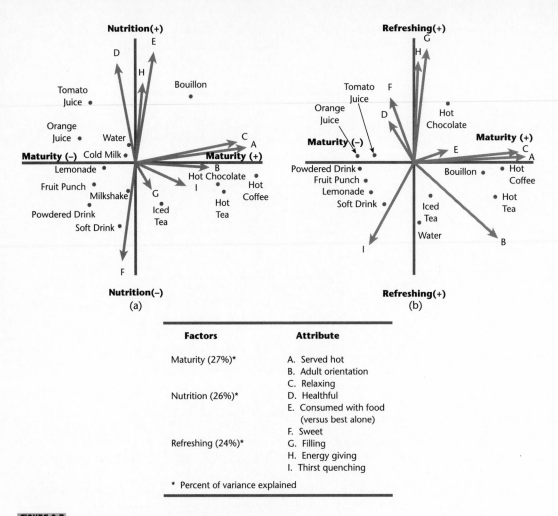

Factors	Attribute
Maturity (27%)*	A. Served hot
	B. Adult orientation
	C. Relaxing
Nutrition (26%)*	D. Healthful
	E. Consumed with food
	(versus best alone)
	F. Sweet
Refreshing (24%)*	G. Filling
	H. Energy giving
	I. Thirst quenching
* Percent of variance explained	

FIGURE 2.5 **Perceptual Map of a Beverage Market**

Sources: Adapted from Hustad, Thomas P., Charles S. Mayer, and Thomas W. Whipple (1975), "Consideration of Context Differences in Product Evaluation and Market Segmentation," *Journal of Academy of Marketing Science,* Vol. 3 (Winter), p. 39–41; Aaker, David A. (1981), "Multidimensional Scaling" in *Multivariate Analysis in Marketing,* D. A. Aaker (ed.), Palo Alto, CA: Scientific Press, 185–191.

can only convey limited insight into here. Fortunately, though, specialized computer packages including MARKPACK and PC-MDS have emerged that can produce perceptual maps from a variety of data. In one study, though, factor analysis procedures seemed to work as well or better than the other two with respect to predictability, interpretability, and ease of use.[16]

Fig. 2.5 was produced by factor analysis. Since the respondents rated 14 beverages, they will each have 14 scores for each of the three factors, as described in the chapter appendix. Given that, we can (in principle) create a perceptual map for each individual by plotting the factor scores for that individual. However, this is not practical. One of the benefits of perceptual maps is their parsimonious visual nature, which is compromised at the individual level. The more practical approach is to position each beverage in the three-dimensional space according to the average factor score for that beverage across individuals in a predefined (descriptor-first) segment. Given the mathematical relationship between the original attributes and the derived factor scores, it is possible to draw the original attributes on the derived factor map as directed lines or vectors. The direction of each vector indicates the factor with which the attribute is most closely associated; the length indicates the strength of the association. Consider the attribute, G, "filling," for instance. Its position in panel (a) indicates that it is not strongly associated with either "maturity" or "nutrition." On the other hand, its position in panel (b) indicates that it is strongly associated with "refreshing."

BENEFIT MEASUREMENT AND SEGMENTATION

Of the myriad bases of segmentation, benefits sought is often viewed as the most relevant for marketing strategy. The benefits a company decides to provide can determine its entire marketing strategy. For example, toothpaste users can be divided into those who want whitening power, those who want decay prevention, those who want good taste and nice appearance, and so on. When the company decides to provide one of these benefits, other decisions such as target segment (in terms of descriptors), product design, and product positioning follow immediately.

Tables 2.7 and 2.8, and Figure 2.6 contain the results of benefit segmentation studies of toothpaste, financial aid management services for educational institutions, and electrical components.

TABLE 2.7 Toothpaste Market Benefit Segments

	Sensory Segment	Sociable Segment	Worrier Segment	Independent Segment
Principal Benefit Sought	Flavor and product appearance	Brightness of teeth	Decay prevention	Price
Demographic Strengths	Children	Teens, young people	Large families	Men
Special Behavioral Characteristics	Users of spearmint-flavored toothpaste	Smokers	Heavy users	Heavy users
Brands Disproportionately Favored	Colgate	MacLeans, Ultra Brite	Crest	Cheapest brand
Lifestyle Characteristics	Hedonistic	Active	Conservative	Value oriented

Source: Haley, Russell I. (1968), "Benefit Segmentation: A Decision Oriented Tool," *Journal of Marketing* 32 (July), 30–35.

TABLE 2.8 Financial Aid Management Benefit Segments

	Segment I	Segment II	Segment III	Segment IV
Potential Benefits Sought	Accuracy	Accuracy	Accuracy	Accuracy
	More time to counsel students	Consistency in award making	Consistency in award making	Consistency in award making
	Stored data	More time to counsel students	Better control of funds	More time to counsel students
	Speed and time savings	Speed and time savings	Cost savings	Better control of funds
Institution Type (Predominantly)	Public (54%)	Public (64%)	Public (56%)	Public (68%)
	Private (46%)	Private (36%)	Private (44%)	Private (32%)
	Four-year and two-year colleges	Four-year and two-year colleges	Vocational/technical schools	Universities and two-year colleges
Undergraduate Enrollment	Under 1,500	Under 1,500	Under 1,500	Over 1,500
Number of Financial Aid Applications Processed/Year	Under 500	Over 500	Under 500	Over 500
Purchase Intentions*	Concepts 6 and 7	Concepts 3, 5, 6, 7	Concepts 3 and 6	Concept 6

*Intentions were measured for eight service concepts: (1) data storage and retrieval; (2) applicant ranking; (3) needs matching; (4) financial aid correspondence; (5) aid disbursement; (6) aid profile; (7) special request report; (8) custom survey.

Source: From Mark Moriarty and M. Venkatesan, "Concept Evaluation and Market Segmentation," *Journal of Marketing*, Vol. 42, July 1978, pp. 82–86. Reprinted by permission of the American Marketing Association.

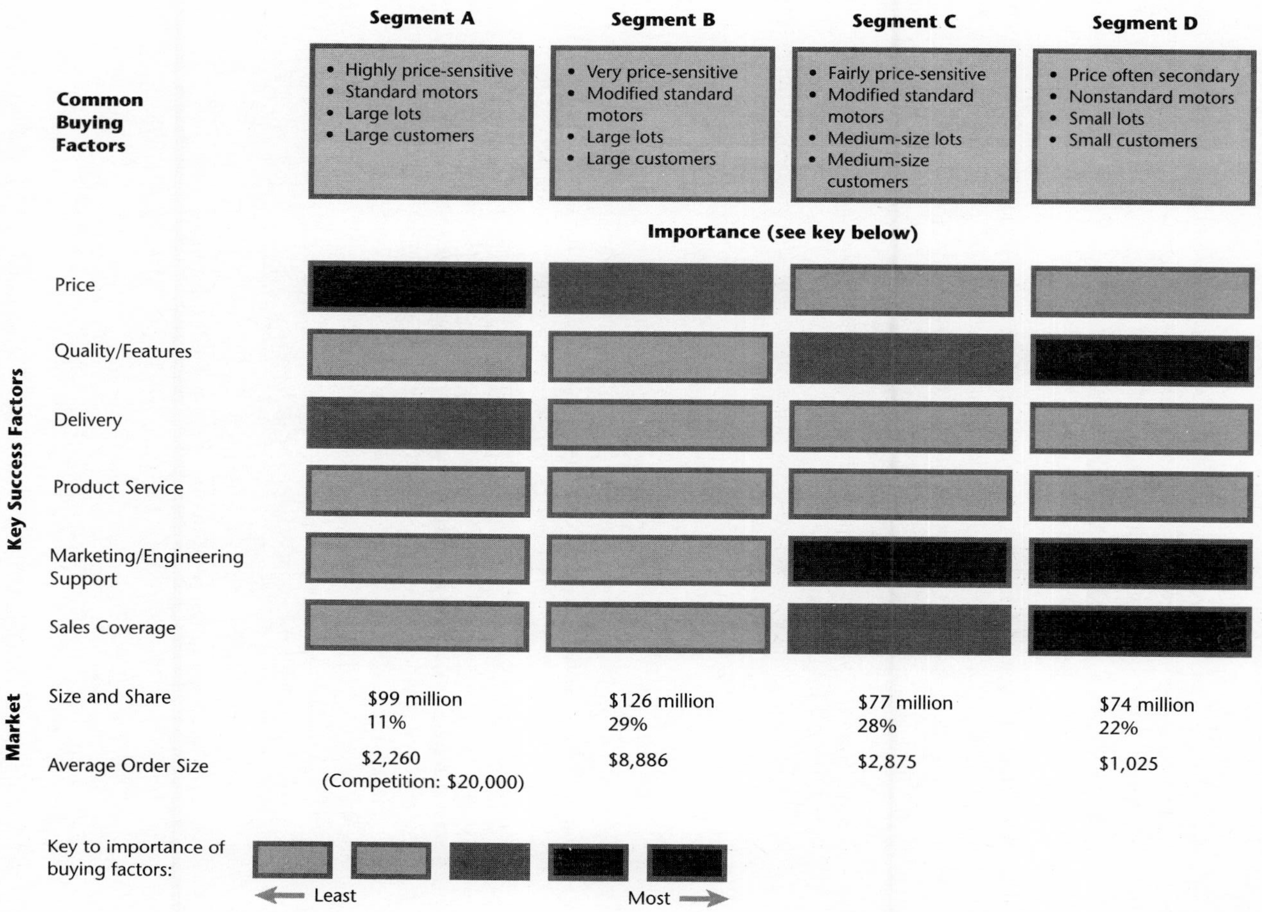

Common Buying Factors

	Segment A	Segment B	Segment C	Segment D
	• Highly price-sensitive • Standard motors • Large lots • Large customers	• Very price-sensitive • Modified standard motors • Large lots • Large customers	• Fairly price-sensitive • Modified standard motors • Medium-size lots • Medium-size customers	• Price often secondary • Nonstandard motors • Small lots • Small customers

Importance (see key below)

Key Success Factors

Price

Quality/Features

Delivery

Product Service

Marketing/Engineering Support

Sales Coverage

Market

	Segment A	Segment B	Segment C	Segment D
Size and Share	$99 million 11%	$126 million 29%	$77 million 28%	$74 million 22%
Average Order Size	$2,260 (Competition: $20,000)	$8,886	$2,875	$1,025

Key to importance of buying factors:

← Least   Most →

FIGURE 2.6 Segmentation by Key Buying Factors—Electrical Components

Source: Garda, Robert A. (1981), "Strategic Segmentation: How to Carve Niches for Growth in Industrial Markets," *Management Review* (August), 21.

43

The segments in the first two examples are very useful in that the benefits are tied to specific descriptor variables, which help to uncover potential market opportunities or identify target segments. In the toothpaste example, there is probably an opportunity for a brand to better provide the benefits sought by the sensory segment than does Colgate, its favorite brand. In the financial aid example, a package stressing aid disbursement (concept 5) would best be targeted to small schools with a high percentage of students applying for financial aid.

The electrical components study proved to be a major boon to its sponsor, a company with a 24 percent market share and a 10 percent price premium that covered special features and services provided to makers of high-quality specialty products. The company found it had only an 11 percent share in the price-sensitive segment A. Furthermore, its average order from segment A was only $2,260, while its competitors were getting $20,000 per order. Recognizing that the company could not compete in segment A because of its antiquated facilities, top management decided to price itself out of segment A by raising prices 25 percent. As expected, none of the major competitors followed. The company retained essentially all of its specialty business at a significantly higher margin.

We describe three ways to measure benefits sought: direct questioning, perceptual mapping, and conjoint analysis.

Direct Questioning

As with perceptions, the easiest way to learn about the benefits people seek is to ask them directly. Survey respondents may be asked to rate a list of potential benefits in a specific product category on a five-point (or any other) scale according to how important they are in making a choice between products.

These responses can then be either used directly or reduced by factor analysis to see if there is any underlying structure to the benefits. For example, suppose we are interested in segmenting the snack market. We might come up with the following list of potential benefits: tastes good, filling, nonfattening, contains vitamins, easy to serve, provides energy, clean, inexpensive, good for teeth, can be eaten out of hand, juicy, and easily available. After factor analyzing the survey responses, we might find that there are really three underlying major benefits:

Taste: tastes good, provides energy, juicy

Nutrition: nonfattening, contains vitamins, good for teeth

Convenience: filling, easy to serve, clean, inexpensive, can be eaten out of hand, easily available.

Each respondent's factor scores reflect the relative importance of the underlying benefit for him or her.

Direct questioning suffers from two major limitations in the benefits sought context. First, people are sometimes unwilling to say what is really important to them. Their answers may have what is called a *social desirability bias*. Indeed, researchers have shown that fewer mothers serve their children nutritious snacks than would be indicated by their direct importance ratings.[17] Second, they may not really *know* what is important to them. People sometimes make product choices without reflecting on the benefits of the products. When asked why they made a specific choice, they may not have a good answer, or they may state why they think they made a choice without it being the real reason.[18] This has stimulated the use of a number of indirect approaches, perceptual mapping and conjoint analysis in particular.

Perceptual Mapping

Benefits sought are captured in a perceptual map by a construct called an ideal point. A consumer's *ideal point* is the location on the map that his or her ideal product would occupy. Products located closer to the ideal point are preferred to those farther away.

As an example, consider the perceptual map of 8 small cars and two respondents in Fig. 2.7. The ideal points for respondents I and J indicate that their favorite cars are the Toyota Corolla and Nissan Sentra, respectively.

Notice that each consumer has his own ideal point on the map; yet, the brands have fixed locations for all consumers. Essentially, this means that everyone perceives the market in the same way. This is consistent with the descriptor-first approach discussed in the perceptual segmentation section. In benefit segmentation with perceptual maps, we often make the assumption that the *entire market* perceives the set of offerings similarly. Whatever differences exist in the ways consumers psychologically evaluate them lie in their preferences or benefits sought (as reflected by the variation in ideal points). This assumption is often referred to as the *homogeneous perceptions–heterogeneous preferences assumption*. Nevertheless, with each individual having a unique ideal point and representation of benefits required, we have the potential for behavior-first segmentation within this context.

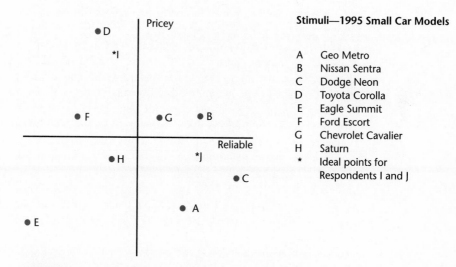

Stimuli—1995 Small Car Models

A   Geo Metro
B   Nissan Sentra
C   Dodge Neon
D   Toyota Corolla
E   Eagle Summit
F   Ford Escort
G   Chevrolet Cavalier
H   Saturn
*   Ideal points for
     Respondents I and J

FIGURE 2.7 **Perceptual Map of Automobiles**

Ideal points can be fit to a preexisting perceptual map by a variety of procedures. The general logic behind many of them is implicit in the following scenario. Suppose a respondent supplies a preference order. A computer algorithm then searches for a point on the map that satisfies the condition that the point is closer to the most preferred item than to any other item. It is closer to the second most preferred item than it is to any other item farther down the list, etc. For example, point I is consistent with a preference order of Toyota Corolla, Ford Escort, Chevrolet Cavalier, Saturn, Nissan Sentra, etc.; point J could have been derived from a preference order of Nissan Sentra, Dodge Neon, Chevrolet Cavalier, Geo Metro, Saturn, etc.

Perceptual maps are useful graphical tools for positioning products for segments. Questions of specific design and analysis of price-attribute trade-offs are better examined by conjoint analysis.

Conjoint Analysis

Conjoint analysis is a technique useful for sorting out the relative importances of a product's attributes (benefits). Its popularity has increased exponentially. A survey of commercial applications estimates that upwards of 2,000 applications are performed annually.[19]

Conjoint analysis starts with a consumer's overall preference judgments (desirability ratings, purchase intention, preference rankings) about a set of complex products with common attributes. It then decomposes these evaluations into separate and comparable utility scales, which can be used to either reconstruct the original preference judgments or predict preferences for a new set of alternatives with the same attributes. The engine driving conjoint analysis is the analysis of trade-offs. Simply put, if a consumer states in an interview or a survey that the most preferred option is low-price, high quality (LH) and that a high-price, high-quality option (HH) is preferred to a low-price, low-quality one (LL), we can conclude that the difference in quality is more important to him or her than the monetary difference. Likewise, if LL is preferred, we infer that the respondent would not be willing to pay that difference for the increase in quality. Conjoint analysis is an extension of these ideas.

Suppose a company wants to decide what benefits to include in a new credit card.[20] Management believes that consumer preference is dictated by five factors: annual fee, the size of cash rebate (if any) given at year's end, establishments accepting the card, whether the card carries retail purchase insurance, and whether the card carries rental car insurance. For simplicity, assume there are three potential annual fees ($0, $20, $50), three potential cash rebates (none, 0.5 percent, 1 percent), three categories of card acceptance (AHC—air, hotel, rental cars; AHCR—AHC plus most restaurants; AHCRG—AHCR plus most general retailers). In addition, the only option for retail purchase or rental car insurance involves a 90-day expiration date, and the only option for rental car insurance has a $30,000 maximum.

Management is concerned with how consumers value the various benefits. Relevant questions might include:

TABLE 2.9 Conjoint Analysis of Credit Cards

	Annual Fee	Cash Rebate	Card Acceptance	Retail Purchase Insurance	Car Rental Insurance	Respondent Evaluation (rank number)
1	$50	0.5%	AHCRG	No	No	13
2	$50	None	AHCR	No	Yes	11
3	$50	1.0%	AHC	Yes	No	17
4	$20	0.5%	AHCR	Yes	Yes	2
5	$20	None	AHC	No	No	14
6	$20	1.0%	AHCRG	No	No	3
7	$ 0	0.5%	AHC	Yes	Yes	12
8	$ 0	None	AHCRG	No	No	7
9	$ 0	1.0%	AHCR	No	No	9
10	$50	0.5%	AHC	No	No	18
11	$50	None	AHCRG	Yes	Yes	8
12	$50	1.0%	AHCR	No	No	15
13	$20	0.5%	AHCRG	No	No	4
14	$20	None	AHCR	No	No	6
15	$20	1.0%	AHC	Yes	Yes	5
16	$ 0	0.5%	AHCR	No	No	10
17	$ 0	None	AHC	No	No	16
18	$ 0	1.0%	AHCRG	Yes	Yes	1*

*Highest rank.

Is retail purchase insurance worth more than rental car insurance?

Would a consumer pay a $50 annual fee to get cash rebates?

What is more important, annual fee or card acceptances?

Conjoint analysis can answer all of these questions.

The basic conjoint model is called the *part-worth model*:

$$U_i = \sum u_{ij}$$

where U_i is the utility for the ith brand (credit card) and u_{ij} is the utility of the jth attribute possessed by card i. The u_{ij} are usually called part-worths. They reflect the part of the total worth of the brand contributed by the jth attribute.

In a typical conjoint study, a respondent would be presented (usually in a personal interview) with some well-constructed fraction of the $3 \times 3 \times 3 \times 2 \times 2 = 108$ total possible credit cards.[21] See Table 2.9. This fraction is carefully designed so as to maximize the information provided in the subject's responses in a statistical sense. The respondent would then either rank or rate them according to his or her preference. Early in the development of conjoint analysis, most respondent tasks involved ranking alternatives; however, rating scales seem to dominate more recent applications because of both technical reasons (statistical validity) and ease of implementation (it's easier to get a respondent to rate a large number of items than to rank them). The preference rankings or ratings play the role of the left-hand side of the part-worth equation (utility). Conjoint analysis then derives the part-worths that would make the model as consistent with the respondent's preference data as possible. Many mathematical procedures are available, but multiple regression is the easiest, most commonly used,[22] and works as well as any. The chapter appendix provides more detail on how to set up a conjoint problem as a regression.

The data in Table 2.9 were analyzed to reproduce the following part-worths:

Annual Fee	Cash Rebate	Acceptance	Retail Insurance	Rental Car Insurance
$50 = 0.0	None = 0.0	AHCRG = 0.9	No = 0.0	No = 0.0
$20 = 0.5	0.5% = 0.1	AHCR = 0.6	Yes = 0.1	Yes = 0.5
$ 0 = 0.9	1.0% = 0.3	AHC = 0.0		

These in conjunction with the part-worth equation can be used to answer the earlier questions. Indeed, rental car insurance is worth more than retail purchase insurance (it adds more to overall utility); annual fee is more important than cash rebate (the range of part-worths for annual fee is 0.9 and for cash rebate is 0.3; thus fee has a larger effect on utility than rebate); and a consumer would be indifferent between a $50 fee with AHCRG acceptance and AHC acceptance with no annual fee but with other identical features (they have the same part-worth sums).[23]

Before leaving benefits, we should assert that benefits sought are constantly changing. For example, one survey shows that in 1992 "a reasonable price" had become a more important determinant of brand choice in general than "manufacturer's reputation for quality." In 1985, the opposite was true.[24] The message here is that companies need to constantly reevaluate their segments lest they change and leave the company behind.

SEGMENTING WITH OTHER BEHAVIORAL BASES

Of course, the particular variables included in a segmentation study depend on the purposes of the study and the strategic alternatives faced by the company. If, for example, a company were interested in growing essentially by selling more of its current products to current customers, it would be most interested in identifying its current markets, and customers' usage characteristics (distinguishing heavy from light users) would be most relevant. If, on the other hand, it were interested in selling current products to new customers, purchasing behavior (buyers versus nonbuyers) would be noteworthy. From a more tactical perspective, a company interested in evaluating a pricing schedule, promotion, or media plan would be interested in responsiveness to specific marketing mix elements.

To grow with current products or services in a given geographic market, companies can proceed in two ways. They can pursue either people who do not use the product or light users. Pursuing people who do not use the product does not imply targeting the nonuser segment and creating a communications program to reach them—quite the opposite. Better logic dictates that future customers are likely to be similar to current customers. Reaffirming a marketing program directed to current customers appears to be the way to go. Indeed, Yamaha uses this approach for choosing sites for new dealerships.[25] It identifies the demographic characteristics (descriptors) of previous buyers (behavior). It then uses Census Bureau data to search for geographic areas with similar demographic profiles.

Finally, marketers can better fine-tune their tactics if they know the characteristics of those consumers who are more sensitive to specific marketing mix elements. Consumers can be segmented by responsiveness to any one of a large number of marketing stimuli: price, coupon, advertising, even package size and variety.

Consider a study conducted by AT&T after a rate increase.[26] The company contacted a sample of those customers who maintained (or even increased) their usage (behavior) after the rate increase and a sample of those who decreased their usage. They found that members of the price-insensitive segment had a higher income and were either single, newly married, or had teenagers living in the house (descriptors). One of the implications of this study was to inform lower-income customers about lower rates for off-peak and weekend calls.

Response segmentation of this type is likely to increase greatly in the coming years with the growing availability of scanner data. These are essentially sales data obtained from optical scanners at the cashier or the consumer's home. Two research companies, A.C. Nielsen Inc. and Information Resources Inc. (IRI), have set up some markets in which consumers present a magnetically coded identification card when they buy their groceries.* The research company can then determine exactly what a consumer buys, at what price, and under what competitive conditions in the store that day, all of which are known to the research company. These consumers can then be characterized by descriptor variables also known to the research company. Subscribing companies can then identify segments that switch brands in response to a promotion, price change, end-of-aisle display, and so on.[27] The representativeness of such analyses is increasing as Nielsen and IRI continue to add more and more markets to their operations. Although this activity centers around finding "deal-prone" (price-sensitive) consumers, it really is just another form of benefit (economy or value) segmentation.

GROUPING CONSUMERS INTO SEGMENTS

The importance of this step depends on the nature of the approach to the segmentation problem. In particular, grouping becomes superfluous in the descriptor-first approach discussed earlier. Grouping was implicitly done at the time the descriptor variables were selected. On the other hand, if behavior measurement comes first, there needs to be some way to identify groups that exhibit that behavior. With respect to the two primary behavioral variables examined in this chapter, the grouping step tends to be more critical to segmentation by benefits sought. The omnipresence of maps in the study of perception, along with the impracticality of producing one for

---

*Nielsen's SCANTRACK markets include Sioux Falls, S. Dak., and Springfield, Mo. IRI's INFOSCAN markets include Cedar Rapids, Iowa, Eau Claire, Wis., Grand Junction, Colo., Marion, Ind., Midland, Tex., and Pittsfield, Mass.

each individual, has led to the common practice of maps being produced for segments predefined on the basis of specific descriptor variables. On the other hand, benefits sought can usually be recorded in numerical forms that lend themselves to further summary by grouping procedures.

Cluster analysis is the standard multivariate method used for grouping consumers into segments. Any (or all) of the measures described to this point in the chapter (whether elicited through direct questioning, perceptual maps, or conjoint analysis) for each consumer can be input into a standard computer program that will group them according to similarity and derive discrete clusters (or segments) of consumers.

Two examples of clustering ideal points in perceptual maps are shown in Figs. 2.8 and 2.9. In the food product perceptual map, ideal points tended to group them-

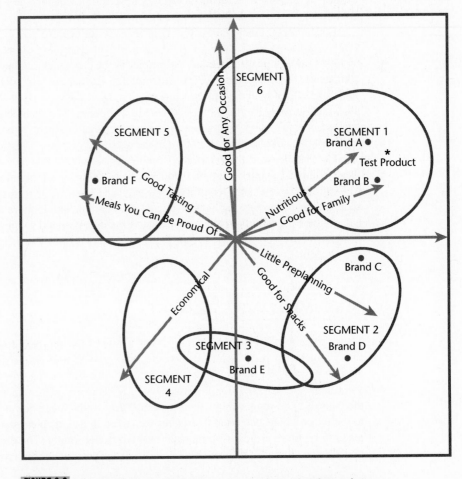

FIGURE 2.8 **Segments and Positions for a New Food Product**

Source: Adapted from Assael, Henry (1975), "Evaluating New Product Concepts and Developing Early Predictions of Trial," *Marketing Review* (May), 13.

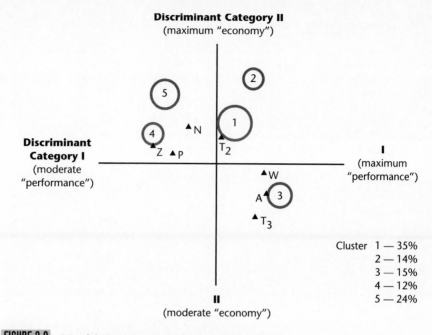

Discriminant Category II
(maximum "economy")

Discriminant Category I
(moderate "performance")

I
(maximum "performance")

II
(moderate "economy")

Cluster 1 — 35%
2 — 14%
3 — 15%
4 — 12%
5 — 24%

FIGURE 2.9   **Machining Center Market Structure***

*The suppliers are coded as follows: A=Adaptive, N=NC, P=Punchole, T1=Terrific 100 product, T2=Terrific 200 product, T3=Terrific 300 product, W=Warlock, and Z=Zit.

Source: Adapted from J. Curtis Jones, "Market Segmentation Strategy Decisions," *Combined Proceedings of the American Marketing Association,* Thomas V. Greer (ed.), pp. 114–117. Reprinted by permission of the American Marketing Association.

selves into clusters (circles or ovals). Certainly, many ideal points are found outside the circles, but the picture provides an excellent approximation. The picture implies that any opportunity for the test product lies with segment one. However, two brands are already well positioned for that segment.

The machining center picture demonstrates there is a perceived economy/performance relationship. Those suppliers highest on the economy dimension tend to be lower on the performance dimension and vice versa. Segment 2, prospects desiring high-performance and high-economy machining centers, is left unsatisfied. Warlock, Adaptive, and Terrific 300, all competing for segment 3, are perceived to have approximately the same levels of (high) performance. Terrific, though, is thought to have the least economic product. It has a job to do in altering the market's perceptions of its product. The wisdom of these three suppliers, though, can be severely questioned when one recognizes that segment 3 represents only 15 percent of the market.

Table 2.10 presents a segmentation analysis for scientific and technical information (STI) services.[28] Conjoint analyses were performed on 274 scientists, information specialists, and managers who represented 163 Pennsylvania companies randomly selected from industries involved in R&D work. A part-worth utility

TABLE 2.10   **Relative Importance of the 12 STI Factors by the Five Utility Segments**

STI Factor	Segment 1	Segment 2	Segment 3	Segment 4	Segment 5
Speed of information	12.8%	8.8%	7.4%	13.5%	30.8%
Purchase arrangement	1.9	1.9	1.3	1.7	0.9
Nature of output	13.6	13.9	10.7	17.9	4.7
Output format	15.9	23.9	21.6	10.4	16.3
Mode of search	1.3	4.3	3.4	1.1	2.5
Distribution	8.3	5.8	8.3	4.1	2.3
Mode of payment	2.9	3.2	1.6	1.9	3.0
Type of supplies	10.1	6.5	4.8	4.9	2.4
Language used	7.2	0.0	1.0	0.5	5.2
Topical coverage	6.3	3.9	0.7	2.0	4.3
Period coverage	10.9	7.1	4.6	1.8	0.9
Price	8.9	20.7	34.8	40.2	26.6

Source: Wind, Yoram, John F. Grashof, Joel D. Goldhar (1978), "Market-based Guidelines for Design of Industrial Products," *Journal of Marketing* 42 (July), 33.

function was estimated for each respondent. The part-worths were then grouped into five clusters. The values in Table 2.10 are the relative importances of the 12 attributes examined in the study for each of the five segments. (Relative importance is defined in the cluster analysis section of the chapter appendix.)

Examining the table and the original part-worths suggests the following profiles for the five segments:

Segment 1 (48 percent)—the least price-sensitive segment. Members are concerned with system characteristics. They are the only ones who want an English language system and for whom complete coverage is important. They are primarily concerned with the nature and format of the output.

Segment 2 (8 percent)—predominantly concerned with output format and nature. Members are not very price-sensitive and would pay for a system that offers desired characteristics.

Segment 3 (20 percent)—one of the two most price-sensitive segments. Members have a concern for output format and secondary concerns for nature of output and mode of distribution.

Segment 4 (11 percent)—the most price-sensitive segment. Members are also concerned with nature of output, speed of information, and output format. Nothing else carries any real weight.

Segment 5 (13 percent)—a speed-of-information segment. This is the most important factor for members of this segment, followed by price and output format.

These are all nice examples in the sense that the clusters come out very neatly. This need not be the case. For example, Figure 2.10 presents the distribution of importances of nutrition and convenience stated by mothers choosing snack foods for their children. This figure shows much more of an amorphous mass of benefits sought than the others.

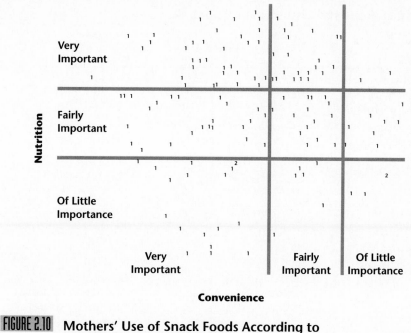

FIGURE 2.10 **Mothers' Use of Snack Foods According to Nutrition and Convenience**

Source: From W. Thomas Anderson, Jr., Eli P. Cox III, and David G. Fulcher, "Bank Selection Decisions and Market Segmentation," *Journal of Marketing,* Vol. 40, January 1976, 40–45. Reprinted by permission of the American Marketing Association.

DESCRIBING SEGMENTS

As in the last section on grouping, this step is superfluous in descriptor-first segmentation. On the other hand, once segments have been formed on the basis of behavior, the analyst or manager has the task of describing them. He/she must decide which of the descriptor variables discussed earlier in this chapter differ among (at least some of) the segments. This can be done either by visually inspecting the descriptors for the consumers in each segment or, more formally, with the use of the statistical technique of the analysis of variance. The *analysis of variance* is a multivariate generalization of the familiar two-sample t-test. It can test the hypothesis that the mean descriptor (or set of descriptors) is equal across segments.

Table 2.11 presents a set of descriptions of two statistically distinct benefit (convenience or service) segments for banks. Convenience-oriented bank customers are more likely to have fewer children, lower incomes, and unemployed spouses than service-oriented bank customers.

Consider the industrial air conditioner example presented in Table 2.5. Table 2.12 provides descriptor variables that distinguish between the segments defined in Table 2.5. For example, companies in segment 4 tend to be smaller, more satisfied with their current air conditioning system, and more concerned with the economic

TABLE 2.11   Profiles of Distinct Bank Benefit Segments

Variable	Segment 1: Convenience-oriented Bank Consumers	Segment 2: Service-oriented Bank Consumers	Significance Level
Deal with one of the five principal downtown banks	51% yes 49% no	21% yes 79% no	.0000
Frequency of downtown shopping	56% twice/week or more often 18% 2–3 times/month 13% once a month 8% 2–6 times/year 5% almost never	5% twice/week or more often 15% 2–3 times/month 14% once a month 16% 2–6 times/year 50% almost never	.0000
Marital status	76% married 14% single 10% other	86% married 9% single 5% other	.0162
Stage in the family life cycle	13% single 30% childless 23% preteenage children 17% teenage children 7% postteenage children 10% other	9% single 28% childless 32% preteenage children 18% teenage children 9% postteenage children 4% other	.0435
Family member selecting principal bank	67% husband 9% wife 22% both 2% other	69% husband 14% wife 15% both 2% other	.0000
Annual family income	20% above $20,000 53% above $10,000 and below $20,000 27% below $10,000	31% above $20,000 46% above $10,000 and below $20,000 23% below $10,000	.0279
Employment status of the spouse	27% full time 20% part time 53% not employed	42% full time 14% part time 44% not employed	.0044
Source of information concerning bank selection	10% television 1% radio 8% newspapers 78% conversations 3% billboards	5% television 0% radio 3% newspapers 90% conversations 2% billboards	.0067

Source: From W. Thomas Anderson, Jr., Eli P. Cox III, and David G. Fulcher, "Bank Selection Decisions and Market Segmentation," *Journal of Marketing,* Vol. 40, January 1976, 40–45. Reprinted by permission of the American Marketing Association.

consequences of their decisions. Accordingly, the managerial function is more involved in the purchase, with expertise being provided by external consultants. On the other hand, in larger companies (segments 2 and 3) the decision is essentially made by engineering people who are less concerned with economy. Therefore,

TABLE 2.12   **Characteristics of Each Industrial Air Conditioner Segment**

	Segment 1	Segment 2	Segment 3	Segment 4
Satisfaction with Current A/C System	Medium-High	Low	Low-Medium	High
Consequence if A/C System Is Less Economical than Projected	Medium-High	Low	Low-Medium	High
Consequence if A/C System Is Less Reliable than Projected	Medium-High	Low	High	Low-Medium
Company Size	Medium	Large	Large	Small
Percentage of Plant Area Requiring A/C	Medium-Large	Small	Large	Medium
Number of Separate Plants	Medium-Large	Small	Large	Small-Medium

Source: Reprinted from "A New Approach to Industrial Market Segmentation," by Jean-Marie Choffray and Gary L. Lilien. *Sloan Management Review,* Issue 19, 1978, pp. 17–30, by Sloan Management Review Association. All rights reserved.

knowledge of the size of a company tells the marketer a great deal about how to market air conditioners to that company.

Finally, Table 2.13 shows the major descriptor variables that discriminate among the five segments in the STI conjoint study described in the last section. The two major PC software conjoint analysis packages, those produced by Sawtooth Software in Idaho and Bretton-Clark in New Jersey, both have the facility to cluster respondent part-worths and explicitly relate them to descriptor variables.

Multiple regression sometimes affords the opportunity to describe segments without the clustering step. Consider a regression model of the form

$$Benefit\ sought = a_0 + a_1X_1 + \cdots + a_kX_k,$$

where the Xs are descriptor variables and the as are regression coefficients. The statistical significance of the as should provide insight into which descriptor variables are related to the particular benefit sought (be it a stated importance, ideal point coordinate, or conjoint part-worth). This would be sufficient to create a table that would provide insights similar to those of Table 2.11. Unlike in the analyses leading to Table 2.11, we would not know which consumers belonged to which segments, but we might not have to. This approach may also prove useful when distinct segments (clusters) cannot be found.[29]

In a study performed by one of the authors, segments based on conjoint analysis–derived part-worth importances for the inclusion of certain camera features (such as built-in exposure meter, automatic focus adjustment, shutter speed adjustment, and built-in automatic flash) were related to camera ownership, film usage, photography as a hobby or profession, and magazine readership.[30] One of the more interesting findings of this study is that the only segment responsive to the inclusion of an automatic flash

TABLE 2.13 Key Discriminating Characteristics among the Five Utility Segments in the STI Segmentation Study

	Segment 1 (131)	Segment 2 (23)	Segment 3 (55)	Segment 4 (30)	Segment 5 (35)
Organizational Characteristics:					
Average organization size	Large	Small	Medium	Medium	Small
Ratio of scientists to total employees	12.9%	7.3%	9.7%	11.5%	17.4%
Ratio of information support people to scientists	7.6%	4.5%	8.3%	2.1%	4.2%
Research Activities:					
Percent of firms doing no research	11%	26%	9%	13%	14%
Percent engaged primarily in chemistry research	19%	13%	24%	33%	20%
Percent engaged primarily in engineering research	49%	48%	36%	33%	51%
Respondent Characteristics: Education:					
Percent with doctoral degrees	5%	4%	16%	10%	11%
Percent with master's degrees	25%	17%	20%	10%	26%
Percent with college degrees	50%	57%	55%	60%	49%
Job Responsibility:					
R&D manager	25%	40%	27%	13%	20%
R&D scientist	10%	13%	16%	17%	6%
General management (president, controller, plant manager, etc.)	26%	8%	26%	37%	24%
Research librarian & information specialist	21%	4%	6%	13%	20%

Source: Wind, Yoram, John F. Grashof, and Joel D. Goldhar (1978), "Market Guidelines for Design of Industrial Products," *Journal of Marketing* 42 (July), 34.

was heavy readers of *Popular Photography* and *New Yorker* magazines. This has direct implications for where cameras with built-in flashes should be advertised (as well as for where cameras without them should not be advertised).

Before we end this section, we would be remiss if we did not point out that attempts to relate behavioral measures to descriptor variables have met with mixed success. In one perceptual mapping study of computer buyers, for example, it was found that all classes of consumers essentially sought hardware reliability as the most important benefit.[31] Different types of consumers had different second most important benefits; buyers who were employed as data processors were more concerned with technical backup features, while buyers who were employed in other capacities were more concerned with a performance/cost ratio. Regression studies demonstrate that the amount of variation that descriptor variables explain is small—statistically significant, but small nevertheless.[32] Similar comments can be made about cluster analyses of conjoint part-worths.[33] The major conclusion seems to be that descriptor variables can be useful in discriminating among benefit segments but often not nearly as useful as we would like.

DATABASE MARKETING: SEGMENTS OF SIZE ONE

Today's customer information systems enable many firms to assemble, coordinate, and integrate data about their current and potential customers. These data come from a variety of sources: ongoing business (orders, inquiries, refusals), external sources (rented or purchased lists, joint ventures with other companies, database compilation services), or customized sources (primary marketing research, warranty cards, satisfaction surveys). These databases enable companies to communicate information (usually either by direct mail or telephone) about products to potential customers that either directly or indirectly increases sales and/or profits. Each customer is treated as a "segment of size one" and that (very small) segment is evaluated for economic viability. In that sense, database marketing is essentially a mechanism for customer selection.

Customer selection through database marketing is performed by relating the information in the database to likely response. This tends to be conducted in two general (but related) ways, tagging and formal response modeling. *Tagging* involves the identification of very specific items, usually some aspect of consumer behavior, in the database that raise the customer's likelihood of response to an offering. This is the thrust of American Express's Personalized Rewards campaign.[34] The major component of American Express's customer database is the set of transactions each customer has made. By inspecting these, American Express can pinpoint customers for whom specific offers are more relevant. CEO Harvey Golub explains the general idea this way, "A Northern Italian restaurant opens in midtown Manhattan. . . . We know from the spending of card members which of them have eaten in Northern Italian restaurants in New York, whether they live in New York or Los Angeles. We make the offer of a free or discounted meal available only to those card members." In this way, members who have eaten in such restaurants are "tagged" to receive the offer. This not only reduces printing and mailing costs for American Express, it makes the customer's Personalized Rewards statement more personal by only including those offers most relevant. Similarly, Citibank uses tags to sell its variety of financial services. For example, large credit card balances and purchases at select upscale stores (such as Tiffany's) will get a customer a mail solicitation for premium banking services. In sum, the marginal cost for obtaining a customer goes way down, allowing the firm to obtain more customers.

Formal response modeling involves a more comprehensive analysis of data and presupposes a more complex relationship between database items than can be captured by simple tagging. Suppose there are many items in a customer's data file (demographics, purchase history) that might relate to his/her likelihood of responding to a particular offer. Suppose further that some of these relationships are stronger than others. The appropriate tool to use in predicting response from a set of predictor variables is regression analysis. *Regression analysis* creates a set of coefficients or weights that are then applied to the respective variables and totaled to produce a single "score" for each customer. This score varies with the likelihood of response and becomes the natural basis for selecting customer prospects from the database.

As an illustrative example, consider the analysis of a credit card solicitation one company conducted in the Netherlands in the early 1990s.[35] The database used contained information on demographic (age, family structure), socioeconomic, and psychographic (leisure interests, reading behavior) characteristics as well as product ownership of one million of the just over six million Dutch households. Credit card ownership was also included. A logistic regression to predict credit card ownership was run on a sample of 2,000 randomly selected households using the remaining database elements as potential predictor variables.* The specific predictor variables described in Table 2.14, along with the notation that was used, emerged from the analysis. These variables effectively discriminated between owners and nonowners of credit cards among the sample of 2,000 households. The results of the logistic model are also summarized in Table 2.14. For the model to be used successfully it would have to predict current or impending ownership for the remaining households. Such predictions can be made by inserting the data for each household into the logistic regression formula in order to create an index such that if the index value were above a certain cutoff, the prediction would be that the household *would* own. If the index value were below a certain cutoff, the prediction would be that the household *would not* own. The model created for this example predicted correctly for 94.3 percent of the individuals in another randomly selected collection of 34,225 households.

How such an analysis generalizes to database marketing is straightforward. Imagine the firm mailing a credit card solicitation to 2,000 households randomly selected from its database of 1,000,000 households. It would then estimate a model intended to predict response to the solicitation based on those households. It could then use that model to predict response for the remaining 998,000 households in the database and use those predictions to efficiently select its target customers.

---

*A logistic regression is a type of regression that instead of using a linear model as a basis, uses a nonlinear model of the form $y = 1/[1 + \exp(b_0 + b_1X_1 + \cdots + b_kX_k)]$. This model has some nice properties for this example. These are explained in the regression section of the chapter appendix.

TABLE 2.14 Database Marketing Illustration (Logistic Regression)

Variables:

CAR	The monetary value of the car owned by the household
	0 = No car
	1 = 0–15,000 (NLG)*
	2 = 15,000–20,000
	3 = 20,000–25,000
	4 = 25,000–30,000
	5 = 30,000–35,000
	6 = 35,000–40,000
	7 = 40,000–45,000
	8 = 45,000–50,000
	9 = 50,000 and more.
NRC	Daily newspaper
	1 = If the household reads the newspaper
	2 = Otherwise
NHS	National Health Service
	0 = If the household is compulsorily covered by the National Health Service
	1 = Otherwise
MW	Microwave
	1 = If the household owns a microwave
	0 = Otherwise
SKI	Ski
	1 = If a member of the household is interested in skiing
	0 = Otherwise
RES	Restaurant
	1 = If the household frequently visits a restaurant
	0 = Otherwise
IF	Investment Funds
	1 = If the household has invested money in an investment
	0 = Otherwise

*NLG stands for Dutch guilders.

		Logistic Model		
Variable	Description	Parameter	Standard Error	t-Score
Intercept		–0.906	0.053	—
CAR	Value of car owned	0.040	0.009	4.44
NRC	Newspaper readership	0.195	0.053	3.68
NHS	Coverage by national health service	0.230	0.051	4.51
NW	Ownership of microwave	0.173	0.042	4.11
SKI	Interest in skiing	0.153	0.042	3.64
RES	Restaurant patron	0.065	0.039	1.67
IF	Investor in funds	0.171	0.04	3.48

Source: Bult, Jan Roelf (1993), "Semiparametric versus Parametric Classification Models: An Application to Direct Marketing," *Journal of Marketing Research*, 30 (August), p. 385, 386.

Alternatively, a model can be estimated on the complete data set and used to predict response for a future offering deemed similar to this one in fundamental ways.

A final word on database marketing is that the database is the primary asset that makes the engine go. Like other assets (brand name, quality design) it must be nourished as time goes on. Each contact with the customer produces a new piece of information that should be added to the database so that it can become a more powerful asset in the same way that product designs must be improved for the company to remain competitive in the face of escalating competition.

SELECTING TARGET SEGMENTS

After segments have been defined, the next step in the strategic process is the selection of those segments in which the company wishes to compete. That selection should be based on the answers to three questions for each segment:

1. Is the segment attractive?
2. Does the firm have a competitive advantage in the segment?
3. Is that competitive advantage sustainable?

If the answer to any one of these questions is no, the segment in question is probably not one in which the company should compete.

Although as George Day says, "attractiveness will ultimately be in the eye of the beholder,"[36] all firms look for segments that exhibit growth prospects and that they believe have above-average profitability. Such segments may be large, such as the price-sensitive retail segment pursued by Wal-Mart. They may also be small segments in which the firm can command a large price premium. Witness Ford's entry into the luxury car segment via the purchase of Jaguar. A firm might also find a segment attractive if it does not have any dominant competitors. Such was the case with the authors' decision to write this book. There was no dominant book in the strategy market that treated the subject from an analytic viewpoint.

In order for a company to be successful in a given segment in the long run, it must have some competitive advantage in that segment. This can only be determined after a thorough analysis of the company's (and its competitors') strengths and weaknesses. The central question is, What assets or skills does the company possess that allow it to provide the benefits desired by the consumers in that segment? Analyzing strengths and weaknesses is the topic of Chapter 7.

The final question in the assessment of a segment is whether the advantage a firm has in it is sustainable. Wal-Mart's early strategy made its advantage sustainable by not leaving any room for competitors. It deliberately located early stores in small towns with populations that were not large enough to support a second large-scale mass merchandiser. Thus, Wal-Mart avoided competition by selecting segments it knew would not be attractive to potential competitors.[37]

These questions have to be modified only slightly for dealing with segments of size one. This is the problem of database marketing. The resulting questions follow:

    A. What is the probability of converting a given prospect into a customer?

    B. Given conversion, what is the lifetime value of the customer?

Question A is analogous to our earlier question 2, while question B is essentially a consolidation of questions 1 and 3.

    Question A can be answered with the tagging and formal modeling approaches discussed in the last section and illustrated by the credit card example of Table 2.14. With respect to question B, the word *lifetime* is an exaggeration for some reasonable long-term planning horizon. Indeed, Citibank uses the word to denote the next five years! Tagging and analytical modeling can both be used here as well to compute the lifetime value of a (potentially) converted prospect. After more than five years in business, a company could compute the mean amount spent in their first five years by a set of customers who began their relationship with the company over five years ago and match the prospect on a specific set of descriptors. This is essentially a tagging approach. Alternatively, the company could construct a lifetime value prediction equation by regressing the amount spent against the same set of descriptors. The multiplicative product of the answers to A and B then becomes the expected lifetime value of the prospect and the basis for a segment (of size one) selection decision.

SUMMARY

Market segmentation is critical to the construction of marketing strategies in that it provides a structure for product-market selection. Markets can be segmented in as many different ways as consumers differ. The vast array of variables used to segment markets tend to fall into one of two categories: *behavioral variables,* which reflect differences in consumer behavior in the product category, and *descriptor variables,* which physically and psychologically describe differences in consumers on dimensions independent of the product category. Both are essential for a coherent segmentation. A marketer must pinpoint what behavior he/she wishes to affect (through behavioral variables) and determine who exhibits or is prone to this behavior (through descriptor variables). Perceptions and benefits required are the most useful behavioral variables for marketing strategy in that they determine consumer needs to be satisfied and how products are positioned to satisfy those needs. *Direct questioning, perceptual mapping,* and *conjoint analysis* are useful measurement tools.

    The segmentation task involves grouping consumers in ways that produce segments that exhibit homogeneous behavior within segments and heterogeneous behavior across segments. This can be done either a priori according to certain descriptors (*descriptor-first segmentation*) or ex post facto with the aid of cluster analysis (*behavior-first segmentation*).

    Increased competition in many industries makes it more critical that customers' needs be completely satisfied. This has necessarily led to smaller and smaller market segments. In the extreme, companies mine large databases to investigate individual consumers—segments of size one. No matter how large or small the segments a company faces, the decision of where to compete is a function of how attractive the segment is and whether the company has a competitive, sustainable advantage within that segment.

Review Questions

1. What are the advantages and disadvantages of using demographics in guiding marketing strategy?

2. What are the roles of descriptor and behavioral variables in market segmentation?

3. What are the similarities and differences between perceptual mapping and conjoint analysis? Given that they are both useful for measuring benefit requirements, how should you choose between them?

4. What is the target segment for your business school? How does it differ from the target segments of other business schools? Do you think your school has made an appropriate choice? Why or why not?

5. Why is it necessary for companies to change their view of market segments over time?

Notes

1. The following arguments are adapted from Orville C. Walker, Harper W. Boyd, and Jean-Claude Larreche, *Marketing Strategy: Planning and Implementation,* copyright (c) 1992. Reprinted with permission of The McGraw-Hill Companies.

2. See Wells, William D. (1975), "Psychographics: A Critical Review," *Journal of Marketing Research* 12 (May), 196–213, for a discussion of this issue and some interesting case studies.

3. Piirto, Rebecca (1991), *Beyond Mind Games: The Marketing Power of Psychographics,* Ithaca, N.Y.: American Demographics Books provides a superb discussion of the history of the VALS program along with its criticisms and modifications. She also outlines several examples.

4. Quoted in Weiss, Michael J. (1988), *The Clustering of America,* New York: Harper & Row, 1.

5. *Ibid.*

6. See Robertson, Thomas S., and Yoram Wind (1980), "Organizational Psychographics and Innovativeness," *Journal of Consumer Research* 7 (June), 24–31.

7. *Ibid.*

8. See "Federal Express" (1977), Harvard Business School Case #9-577-042, Boston, MA.

9. See *Business Week,* "Tastes Yucky, Sells Like Hotcakes!," May 18, 1993, 56.

10. This study is fully described in Moriarty, Rowland T. (1983), *Industrial Buying Behavior: Concepts, Issues, and Applications,* Lexington, MA: Lexington Books.

11. The lens model was originated by Brunswik, Egon (1952), *The Conceptual Framework of Psychology,* Chicago: University of Chicago Press.

12. The toothpaste example and the discussion of halo are adapted from Lehmann, Donald R. (1989), *Market Research and Analysis,* Homewood, IL: Irwin, 149–150.

13. This example is adapted from Green, Paul E., Donald S. Tull, and Gerald R. Albaum (1988), *Research for Marketing Decisions,* 5th ed., Englewood Cliffs, NJ: Prentice-Hall, 685.

14. This study is reported in Hustad, Thomas P., Charles S. Mayer, and Thomas W. Whipple (1975), "Consideration of Context Differences in Product Evaluation and Market Segmentation," *Journal of the Academy of Marketing Science* 3 (Winter), 34–47, and presented in this format by Aaker, David A. (1981), "Multidimensional Scaling" in *Multivariate Analysis in Marketing,* D. A. Aaker (ed.), Palo Alto, CA: Scientific Press, 185–191.

15. For a complete exposition of these techniques, see the classic book by Green, Paul E., and Vithala R. Rao (1972), *Applied Multidimensional Scaling: A Comparison of Approaches and Algorithms,* New York: Holt, Rinehart, and Winston.

16. See Hauser, John R., and Frank S. Koppelman (1979), "Alternative Perceptual Mapping Techniques: Relative Accuracy and Usefulness," *Journal of Marketing Research* 16 (November), 495–506.

17. Myers, James H. and Edward W. Forgy, "Getting More Information from Customer Surveys," *California Management Review* 18 (Winter), 66–72.

18. Nisbett, R. E., and T. D. Wilson (1977), "Telling More Than We Can Know: Verbal Reports on Mental Processes," *Psychological Review* 84, 231–259, provide evidence of this point.

19. See Wittink, Dick R., and Phillipe Cattin (1989), "Commercial Use of Conjoint Analysis: An Update," *Journal of Marketing* 53 (July), 91–96.

20. This example is adapted from Green, Paul E., and Yoram Wind (1975), "New Way to Measure Consumer Judgments," *Harvard Business Review* 53 (July-August), 107–117; and Green, Paul E., and Abba M. Krieger (1991), "Product

Design Strategies for Target-Market Positioning," *Journal for Product and Innovation Management* 8, 189–202. Reprinted (Adapted) with permission from *Journal of Product Innovation,* Vol. 8, Paul E. Green and Abba M. Krieger, Product Design Strategies for Target-Market Positioning, pp. 189–202, 1991, Elsevier Science Inc.

21. To see how to construct these fractions, see Green, Paul E. (1974), "On the Design of Choice Experiments Involving Multifactor Alternatives," *Journal of Consumer Research* 1 (June), 61–68.

22. Regression was used in 54% of the applications reported in Wittink and Cattin, "Commercial Use of Conjoint Analysis."

23. For more information about conjoint analysis, see Green, Paul E., and V. Srinivasan (1978), "Conjoint Analysis in Consumer Research: Issues and Outlook," *Journal of Consumer Research* 5 (September), 103–123; and Green, Paul E., and V. Srinivasan (1990), "Conjoint Analysis in Marketing Research: New Developments and Directions," *Journal of Marketing* 54 (October), 3–20. Cattin, Phillipe, and Dick R. Wittink (1982), "Commercial Use of Conjoint Analysis: A Survey," *Journal of Marketing* 46 (Summer), 44–53; and Wittink and Cattin (1989), "Commercial Use of Conjoint Analysis," study the state of industry practice.

24. This study is described in Heline, Holly (1993), "Brand Loyalty Isn't Dead," *Brandweek,* June 3, 14–15.

25. See *Marketing News* (1981), "Computer Mapping of Demographic Lifestyle Data Locates 'Pockets' of Potential Customers at Microgeographic Levels," November 27, 16.

26. See Assael, Henry, and A. Marvin Roscoe, Jr. (1976), "Approaches to Market Segmentation Analysis," *Journal of Marketing* 40 (October), 67–76, for a detailed description of this study.

27. Curry, David J. (1993), *The New Marketing Research Systems,* New York: Wiley discusses these research suppliers and their capabilities in great detail.

28. This study is described in detail by Wind, Yoram, John F. Grashof, and Joel D. Goldhar (1978), "Market-based Guidelines for Design of Industrial Products," *Journal of Marketing* 42 (July), 27–37.

29. Some relatively recent developments in marketing science have modeled benefits sought directly as a function of descriptor variables rather than trying to relate derived benefit measures to descriptor variables after the fact. In these cases the parameters of interest are those that relate the descriptors to (say) conjoint part-worths as in Green, Paul E., and Wayne S. DeSarbo (1979), "Componential Segmentation in the Analysis of Consumer Trade-offs," *Journal of Marketing* 43 (Fall), 83–91; and Green, Paul E. (1984), "Hybrid Models in Conjoint Analysis: An Expository Review," *Journal of Marketing Research* 21 (May), 155–169; or ideal points as in DeSarbo, Wayne S., and Vithala R. Rao (1986), "A Constrained Unfolding Methodology for Product Positioning," *Marketing Science* 5 (Winter), 1–19.

30. See Rao, Vithala R., and Frederick W. Winter (1978), "An Application of the Multivariate Probit Model to Market Segmentation and Product Design," *Journal of Marketing Research* 15 (August), 361–368, for full details on this study.

31. This study is fully described in Green, Paul E., Donald S. Tull, and Gerald R. Albaum (1988), *Research for Marketing Decisions,* 5th ed., Englewood Cliffs, NJ: Prentice-Hall, 682–684.

32. For examples see Massy, William F., Ronald E. Frank, and Thomas M. Lodahl (1968), *Purchasing Behavior and Personal Attributes,* Philadelphia: University of Pennsylvania Press.

33. See Moore, William L. (1980), "Levels of Aggregation in Conjoint Analysis: An Empirical Comparison," *Journal of Marketing Research* 17 (November), 516–523.

34. See Solomon, Stephen D. (1995), "American Express Applies for a New Line of Credit," *New York Times Magazine,* July 30, 35–47, for additional discussion.

35. This example is drawn from Bult, Jan Roelf (1993), "Semiparametric versus Parametric Classification Models: An Application to Direct Marketing," *Journal of Marketing Research* 30 (August), 380–390.

36. Day, George (1990), *Market Driven Strategy: Processes for Creating Value,* New York: Free Press, 201.

37. See "Wal-Mart Discount Store Operations" (1987), Harvard Business School Case #9-387-018, Boston, MA, for a full discussion.

Bibliography

Aaker, David A. (1981), "Multidimensional Scaling" in *Multivariate Analysis in Marketing,* D. A. Aaker (ed.), Palo Alto, CA: Scientific Press, 185–191.

Anderson, W. Thomas, Jr., Eli P. Cox III, and David G. Fulcher (1976), "Bank Selection Decisions and Market Segmentation," *Journal of Marketing* 40 (January), 40–45.

Assael, Henry (1975), "Evaluating New Product Concepts and Developing Early Predictions of Trial," *Marketing Review* (May), 13.

Assael, Henry, and A. Marvin Roscoe, Jr. (1976), "Approaches to Market Segmentation Analysis," *Journal of Marketing* 40 (October), 67–76.

Bass, Frank M., Douglas J. Tigert, and Robert T. Lonsdale (1968), "Market Segmentation: Group versus Individual Behavior," *Journal of Marketing Research* 5 (August), 264–270.

Bearden, William O., Richard G. Netemeyer, and Mary F. Mobley (1993), *Handbook of Marketing Scales: Multi-Item Measures for Marketing and Consumer*

Behavior Research, Newbury Park, CA: Sage Publications.

Bearden, William O., Jesse E. Teel, Jr., and Richard M. Durand (1978), "Media Usage, Psychographic, and Demographic Dimensions of Retail Shoppers," *Journal of Retailing* 54 (Spring), 65–74.

Brunswik, Egon (1952), *The Conceptual Framework of Psychology,* Chicago: University of Chicago Press.

Bult, Jan Roelf (1993), "Semiparametric versus Parametric Classification Models: An Application to Direct Marketing," *Journal of Marketing Research* 30 (August), 380–390.

Business Week (1992), "Tastes Yucky, Sells Like Hotcakes!," May 18, 56.

Cattin, Phillipe, and Dick R. Wittink (1982), "Commercial Use of Conjoint Analysis: A Survey," *Journal of Marketing* 46 (Summer), 44–53.

Choffray, Jean-Marie, and Gary L. Lilien (1978), "A New Approach to Industrial Market Segmentation," *Sloan Management Review* 19 (Spring), 17–30.

Curry, David J. (1993), *The New Marketing Research Systems,* New York: Wiley.

Day, George (1990), *Market Driven Strategy: Processes for Creating Value,* New York: Free Press.

DeSarbo, Wayne S., and Vithala R. Rao (1986), "A Constrained Unfolding Methodology for Product Positioning," *Marketing Science* 5 (Winter), 1–19.

"Federal Express" (1977), Harvard Business School Case 9-577-042, Boston, MA.

Frank, Ronald E., William F. Massy, and Yoram Wind (1972), *Market Segmentation,* Englewood Cliffs, NJ: Prentice-Hall.

Garda, Robert A. (1981), "Strategic Segmentation: How to Carve Niches for Growth in Industrial Markets," *Management Review* (August), 15–22.

Green, Paul E. (1974), "On the Design of Choice Experiments Involving Multifactor Alternatives," *Journal of Consumer Research* 1 (September), 61–68.

Green, Paul E. (1984), "Hybrid Models in Conjoint Analysis: An Expository Review," *Journal of Marketing Research* 21 (May), 155–169.

Green, Paul E., and Wayne S. DeSarbo (1979), "Componential Segmentation in the Analysis of Consumer Trade-offs," *Journal of Marketing* 43 (Fall), 83–91.

Green, Paul E., and Abba M. Krieger (1991), "Product Design Strategies for Target-Market Positioning," *Journal for Product and Innovation Management* 8, 189–202.

Green, Paul E., and Vithala R. Rao (1972), *Applied Multidimensional Scaling: A Comparison of Approaches and Algorithms,* New York: Holt, Rinehart, and Winston.

Green, Paul E., Donald S. Tull, and Gerald R. Albaum (1988), *Research for Marketing Decisions,* 5th ed., Englewood Cliffs, NJ: Prentice-Hall.

Green, Paul E., and V. Srinivasan (1978), "Conjoint Analysis in Consumer Research: Issues and Outlook," *Journal of Consumer Research* 5 (September), 103–123.

Green, Paul E., and V. Srinivasan (1990), "Conjoint Analysis in Marketing Research: New Developments and Directions," *Journal of Marketing* 54 (October), 3–20.

Green, Paul E., and Yoram Wind (1975), "New Way to Measure Consumer Judgments," *Harvard Business Review* 53 (July-August), 107–117.

Haley, Russell I. (1968), "Benefit Segmentation: A Decision Oriented Research Tool," *Journal of Marketing* 32 (July), 30–35.

Harman, Harry H. (1967), *Modern Factor Analysis,* Chicago: University of Chicago Press.

Hauser, John R., and Frank S. Koppelman (1979), "Alternative Perceptual Mapping Techniques: Relative Accuracy and Usefulness," *Journal of Marketing Research* 16 (November), 495–506.

Heline, Holly (1993), "Brand Loyalty Isn't Dead," *Brandweek,* June 3, 14–15.

Horowitz, A. D. and J. N. Sheth (1977), "Segmenting the Ridesharing Market," A. Woodside and J. N. Sheth (eds.), *Consumer and Industrial Buying Behavior,* New York: North-Holland, 152–185.

Hustad, Thomas P., Charles S. Mayer, and Thomas W. Whipple (1975), "Consideration of Context Differences in Product Evaluation and Market Segmentation," *Journal of the Academy of Marketing Science* 3 (Winter), 34–47.

Jones, J. Curtis (1973), "Market Segmentation Strategy Decisions," in *Combined Proceedings of the American Marketing Association* 35 Thomas V. Greer (ed.), Chicago: American Marketing Association, 114–117.

Kaufman, Leonard, and Peter J. Rousseeuw (1990), *Finding Groups in Data: An Introduction to Cluster Analysis,* New York: Wiley.

Lehmann, Donald R. (1989), Market Research and Analysis, Homewood, IL: Irwin, 149–150.

Marketing News (1981), "Computer Mapping of Demographic Lifestyle Data Locates 'Pockets' of Potential Customers at Microgeographic Levels," November 27, 16.

Massy, William F., Ronald E. Frank, and Thomas M. Lodahl (1968), *Purchasing Behavior and Personal Attributes,* Philadelphia: University of Pennsylvania Press.

Mitchell, Arnold (1983), *The Nine American Lifestyles,* New York: MacMillan.

Moore, William L. (1980), "Levels of Aggregation in Conjoint Analysis: An Empirical Comparison," *Journal of Marketing Research* 17 (November), 516–523.

Moriarty, Mark, and M. Venkatesan (1978), "Concept Evaluation and Market Segmentation," *Journal of Marketing* 42 (July), 82–86.

Moriarty, Rowland T. (1983), *Industrial Buying Behavior: Concepts, Issues, and Applications,* Lexington, MA: Lexington Books.

Myers, James H., and Edward W. Forgy, "Getting More Information from Customer Surveys," *California Management Review* 18 (Winter), 66–72.

Nisbett, Richard E., and T. D. Wilson (1977), "Telling More Than We Can Know: Verbal Reports on Mental Processes," *Psychological Review* 84, 231–259.

Piirto, Rebecca (1991), *Beyond Mind Games: The Marketing Power of Psychographics,* Ithaca, NY: American Demographics Books.

Rao, Vithala R., and Frederick W. Winter (1978), "An Application of the Multivariate Probit Model to Market Segmentation and Product Design," *Journal of Marketing Research* 15 (August), 361–368.

Robertson, Thomas S., and Yoram Wind (1980), "Organizational Psychographics and Innovativeness," *Journal of Consumer Research* 7 (June), 24–31.

Solomon, Stephen D. (1995), "American Express Applies for a New Line of Credit," *New York Times Magazine,* July 30, 35–47.

Walker, Orville C., Harper W. Boyd, and Jean-Claude Larreche (1992), *Marketing Strategy: Planning and Implementation,* Homewood, IL: Irwin, 176.

"Wal-Mart Discount Store Operations" (1987), Harvard Business School Case #9-387-018, Boston, MA.

Weiss, Michael J. (1988), *The Clustering of America,* New York: Harper & Row.

Wells, William D. (1975), "Psychographics: A Critical Review," *Journal of Marketing Research* 12 (May), 196–213.

Wind, Yoram, John F. Grashof, and Joel D. Goldhar (1978), "Market-Based Guidelines for Design of Industrial Products," *Journal of Marketing* 42 (July), 27–37.

Wittink, Dick R., and Phillipe Cattin (1989), "Commercial Use of Conjoint Analysis: An Update," *Journal of Marketing* 53 (July), 91–96.

Appendix

Analysis Techniques

Regression Analysis

Most readers of this book will have been exposed to regression analysis in prior work. Therefore, we present only a cursory review at this point. Regression analysis has the objective of producing a linear equation that can be used for predicting a single criterion or dependent variable from a set of several predictor or independent variables. The basic model is

$$Y = B_0 + B_1 X_1 + B_2 X_2 + \cdots + B_k X_k + \text{error}.$$

In this model Y is the dependent variable; the X's are the independent variables; and the B's are regression coefficients or weights. Y and the X's are known; the B's are not. The B's are estimated by finding those values (b's) that will make the predicted values of $Y = (b_0 + b_1 X_1 + b_2 X_2 + \cdots + b_k X_k)$ as close to the real values as possible. This is done (with standard computer software, of course) by minimizing the sum of squared differences between Y and its predicted values.

Regression has two major uses. First, given a new set of values of predictor variables, it enables us to predict the criterion. For example, marketers have long used regression to help them forecast sales, given marketing decisions such as price and advertising. Second, regression allows us to test whether a specific variable (or set of variables) is useful in predicting a criterion. This is done by testing the statistical significance of coefficients.

Often in marketing, it is necessary to predict a variable that must fall between 0 and 1 (e.g., market share, choice probability). In those cases, the multiple regression model just presented will not be adequate since there is nothing to prevent the predicted value of the dependent variable (Y) from being negative or greater than one. This problem can be solved by letting the model's dependent variable Y be $\text{Ln}(p/1 - p)$ where p is the quantity between 0 and 1 that we really want to predict. The logistic regression model then becomes $\text{Ln}(p/1 - p) = B_0 + B_1 X_1 + B_2 X_2 + \cdots + B_k X_k + \text{error}$. Ln is the natural logarithm. If we solve for p and substitute the notation for estimates, b's, for the B's, we obtain

$$p = 1/[1 + \exp(b_0 + b_1 X_1 + \cdots + b_k X_k)],$$

where $\exp(z)$ is the exponential function e^z. It is easy to see that this model yields a prediction between 0 and 1. If the linear combination in parentheses is very large, $\exp(z)$ becomes very large, and $1/(1 + \text{very large})$ approaches zero. On the other hand, if the same combination is very negative, $\exp(z)$ becomes very small, and $1/(1 + \text{very small})$ approaches one.

Factor Analysis

Factor analysis is used for the general purpose of reducing a set of variables to a more manageable, yet informative, set. It has the general goal of identifying a set of underlying dimensions in a data set that capture most of the information in the data set and yet retain interpretability and ease of use. Some of the contexts in this chapter where factor analysis can be used include:

Psychographic Segmentation: Often in attempting to define psychographic descriptor variables that might prove useful for segmenting a given market, companies conduct studies in which consumers are asked a large battery of attitude, interest, opinion, lifestyle, and personality questions. Attempting to be comprehensive, they may (and hopefully will) create a battery of items that are closely correlated. For example, the degree to which a consumer agrees or disagrees with the two statements "I go to many sports events" and "I exercise whenever I can" is likely to be somewhat positively correlated. So when we ask about each, we might not really be asking about two distinct underlying lifestyle or psychographic dimensions. Rather, we may be asking about only one: interest in sports. Identifying such latent driving dimensions (factors) can make further analysis more manageable.

Perceptual Structures: To effectively position its products and identify customers for whom an intended positioning would be fruitful, a firm must understand how the market perceives its and its competitors' products. To find this out, the firm asks a sample of consumers to rate each product on a number of attributes. Survey designers are faced with the need to invest a small number of attributes to keep further analysis manageable. In so doing, however, they run the risk of not being comprehensive enough. A more common approach is to err on the side of being overly comprehensive and potentially redundant. Just as in the previous example, analysts can search the data for latent perceptual dimensions that underlie the larger set of original ones.

Benefit Structures: In attempting to find out what benefits consumers seek in a product category, we might ask them to tell us how important several specific benefits are. Again, to be comprehensive, we create a large battery of potential benefits, some of which may be closely correlated. For example, calories and nutrition are negatively correlated in snack foods. So when we ask about each, we might not really be asking about two distinct underlying benefits.

These three problems all have a common structure. In attempting to comprehensively describe the market (customers or products), consumers are asked to rate one or more entities on a (much too) large battery of items. The resulting data set looks like this:

Respondent	_____	Item 1	Item 2	—	Item N
1	Entity 1	—	—	—	—
	Entity 2	—	—	—	—
	—	—	—	—	—
	Entity M	—	—	—	—
2	Entity 1	—	—	—	—
	Entity 2	—	—	—	—
	—	—	—	—	—
	Entity M	—	—	—	—
—	—	—	—	—	—
—	—	—	—	—	—
K	Entity 1	—	—	—	—
	Entity 2	—	—	—	—
	—	—	—	—	—
	Entity M	—	—	—	—

In psychographic segmentation, there is only one entity, the respondent; the items are the AIO and personality questions. In perceptual structures, the entities are the products or brands involved and the items are the complete set of attributes posited at the outset of the study. Benefit analyses again have one entity, the product category in question; the items are the variety of potential benefits suggested in the survey. In all cases, the dimensions are the immediate object of concern.

The factor analysis model assumes that the N specific items we ask about (Is) are a weighted combination of a set of q underlying general factors (fs), (such as psychographic dimensions, perceptual dimension, product benefit). It is formally stated as

$$I_1 = L_{11}f_1 + L_{12}f_2 + \cdots + L_{1p}f_q + e_1$$
$$I_2 = L_{21}f_1 + L_{22}f_2 + \cdots + L_{2p}f_q + e_2$$
$$I_N = L_{N1}f_1 + L_{N2}f_2 + \cdots + L_{Np}f_q + e_N$$

where N is the number of items in the battery we give consumers and the es are random error terms. Factor analysis finds the Ls, usually called loadings, that relate the (unobservable) factors to the (observable) items measured. Procedures to do this are widely available in most computer statistics packages (for example, BMDP, SAS, SPSS, and SYSTAT). Each has a variety of estimation algorithms useful for obtaining Ls.

The Ls can be shown to represent the correlation between each specific item and a factor. When several items have high Ls on the same factor, or as is commonly stated, "load" highly on the same factor, they are assumed to be somewhat redundant.

TABLE A2.1   Factor Analysis of Ridesharing Benefits

Specific Benefit	Factor 1	Factor 2
Convenient	0.85	0.03
Reliable	0.83	0.03
Pleasant	0.84	0.04
Comfortable	0.80	0.00
Saves time	0.76	0.16
Expensive	0.00	0.58
Energy consuming	0.03	0.70
Traffic problems	0.03	0.83
Pollution	0.03	0.84
% of Variance	37.2	24.8
Apparent Underlying Dimension	Time-convenience	Private and public cost

Source: Adapted from Horowitz, A.D., and J.N. Sheth (1977), "Ridesharing to Work: An Attitudinal Analysis" in *Predicting Carpool Demand*, Transportation Research Board, National Research Council, Washington, D.C.

	Very Low						Very High
	1	2	3	4	5	6	7
Expensive	☐	☐	☐	☐	☐	☐	☐
Comfortable	☐	☐	☐	☐	☐	☐	☐
Pleasant	☐	☐	☐	☐	☐	☐	☐
Reliable	☐	☐	☐	☐	☐	☐	☐
Saves time	☐	☐	☐	☐	☐	☐	☐
Convenient	☐	☐	☐	☐	☐	☐	☐
Safe from crime	☐	☐	☐	☐	☐	☐	☐
Energy consuming	☐	☐	☐	☐	☐	☐	☐
Traffic problems	☐	☐	☐	☐	☐	☐	☐
Pollution	☐	☐	☐	☐	☐	☐	☐

FIGURE A2.1   Measurement Scales for Automobile Ridesharing Benefits

The number of items that load highly on some specific factor reflect how much more parsimonious the battery of dimensions could perhaps be made.[1]

As an example, consider the ridesharing benefit analysis summarized in Table A2.1.[2] We see here that data on nine specific benefits collected from a questionnaire such as that in Fig. A2.1 can be reduced to two more general benefits. The two underlying factors identified, "time-convenience" and "private and public cost," are inferred from those specific items that load highly on the two factors.

The degree to which these factors capture the totality of information in the original data-set is reflected in an item included on all factor analysis outputs, *percent of variance explained.* Each factor has its own percent of variance explained. It is a summary measure that reflects how much of the variance of the original *N* dimensions is accounted for by that factor. One of the decisions required in factor analysis is how

TABLE A2.2 **Factor Analysis of Bank Service Benefits**

	Factor 1	Factor 2	Factor 3	Factor 4
Large	−0.004	−0.069	0.215	0.541
Wide variety of services	0.330	0.318	−0.046	0.371
Does lot of advertising	0.041	0.219	0.161	0.641
Convenient branches	0.692	0.140	0.005	0.149
Good reputation	0.552	0.252	0.129	0.261
High savings interest	0.685	0.187	0.103	−0.044
Modern	0.011	0.002	0.548	0.353
Pleasant offices	0.199	0.156	0.661	0.149
Encourages financial responsibility	0.305	0.399	0.432	0.165
Convenient hours	0.813	0.166	0 .085	0.043
Community concern	0.406	0.324	0.396	0.070
Parking	0.493	0.030	0.280	0.084
Friendly	0.545	0.379	0.295	−0.014
Loans available	0.126	0.790	0.119	0.083
Quick service	0.694	0.320	0.181	−0.106
Low loan interest	0.395	0.685	0.018	0.010
Bank for all	0.229	0.414	0.241	0.170
% of Variance	66.4	16.6	10.2	6.8
Apparent Underlying Dimension	Convenience and value	Loans	Facilities	Size and advertising

many factors should be studied. The percent of variance statistic is useful in this regard. Analysts strive for few factors with high percent of variance explained. There is a trade-off. More factors means more variance explained but less parsimony. The two factors in the ridesharing example collectively explain 62 percent of the variance in the original data set.

Table A2.2 presents another example, one that is not as clean as the ridesharing one. What makes it less clean is that not all items have loadings that are very high or very low on the factors. In such cases, the factors may be difficult to name. This is only one case where quantitative analyses require creative input.

Although the factors themselves are not directly observable, they are related to the observed items or dimensions by the system of equations presented earlier. Indeed, the factor loadings are the centerpiece of any factor analysis output, and with good reason. They are the primary tool used in identifying the factors. Fortunately, factor values for each row of the previous data structure can be derived from the factor analysis procedure. Most computer programs can provide these "factor scores." As described in the body of the chapter, these scores are used to plot the positions products occupy in perceptual mapping. These factor scores also tell how important each respondent rates each underlying attribute and how each respondent values each psychographic dimension.

Multiple Regression for Conjoint Analysis

The part-worth model can be estimated by multiple regression if the attributes are coded as *dummy variables* (dummy variables only take on the values 0 or 1). For example, suppose in the credit card illustration that annual fee was coded with dummy variables Z_1 and Z_2, with Z_1 taking on the value 1 for annual fee $20 and 0 otherwise, and Z_2 taking on the value 1 for annual fee $0 and 0 otherwise. Annual fee $0 then can be coded with Z_1 and Z_2, both taking on the value 0. In sum, then, the three annual fees can be coded as follows:

	Z_1	Z_2
$50	0	0
$20	1	0
$0	0	1

Similarly, we can code cash rebate and card acceptance with two dummy variables each and retail purchase and rental car insurance with one dummy variable each as follows:

Cash Rebate				Card Acceptance		
	Z_3	Z_4			Z_5	Z_6
None	0	0	AHC		0	0
0.5%	1	0	AHCR		1	0
1.0%	0	1	AHCRG		0	1

Retail Purchase Insurance		Car Rental Insurance	
	Z_7		Z_8
No	0	No	0
Yes	1	Yes	1

Suppose now that we arbitrarily set the following part-worths to 0: $50 annual fee, no cash rebate, AHC card acceptance, no retail purchase insurance, and no car rental insurance. We can do this without loss of generality because adding or subtracting a constant to the utility for all levels of an attribute does not affect how they differ from one another. So we can add or subtract whatever it takes to make these chosen levels 0. This enables us to rewrite the part-worth model for this example as a regression model:

$$Preference = b_0 + b_1Z_1 + b_2Z_2 + b_3Z_3 + b_4Z_4 + b_5Z_5 + b_6Z_6 + b_7Z_7 + b_8Z_8,$$

where "Preference" is supplied by the respondent. It can be a rating on a liking or purchase intention scale or a rank in a preference order. If the respondent ranks the eighteen stimuli in Table 2.10 from 1 to 18 according to his or her preference, (19 minus the preference rank) becomes an increasing measure of preference.

In the above equation, b_0 is an additive constant and does not matter because of the reason mentioned earlier; b_1 and b_2 are the part-worths for annual fees \$20 and \$0; b_3 and b_4 are the part-worths for cash rebates 0.5 percent and 1.0 percent; b_5 and b_6 are the part-worths for AHCR and AHCRG card acceptances; b_7 is the part-worth for retail purchase insurance; and b_8 is the part-worth for car rental insurance. The utility for a combination that has no annual fee, a 1 percent cash rebate, AHCR acceptance, and rental car insurance but no retail purchase insurance is $b_0 + b_2 + b_4 + b_5 + b_8$, which is consistent with the part-worth model except for b_0, which will appear in all utilities and therefore cannot determine differences between them. All one would need to do to estimate the part-worths is to code the data in Table 2.10 and run the regression model. The results are the estimates provided in the body of the chapter.

Cluster Analysis

As its name implies, the purpose of cluster analysis is to aggregate individual observations into groups in which the observations are more similar to each other than to those in other groups. Similarity is defined with respect to a set of variables. Traditionally, the most common use of cluster analysis in marketing is the one described in this chapter, grouping consumers into segments. Recent applications have focused on grouping products or brands into competitive sets. These will be described in Chapter 4. Whatever the nature of the application, there are two major components to cluster analysis: defining a measure of similarity between observations and deciding how to group them.

Measures of Similarity   Some measures of similarity are readily apparent from the variables that form the basis of the clustering. For example, if the intent of an application is to group consumers with respect to similar ideal points on a perceptual map, the (Euclidean) distance between ideal points is an obvious (dis)similarity measure. With other data, measuring similarity may be somewhat more problematic. Consider relative importances of benefits as measured by direct questioning or conjoint part-worths. There may be scale biases in how people respond to certain questions that do not really impact how different respondents evaluate product offerings. In particular, respondents to direct questioning might have a scale bias that leads them to favor either higher or lower values. A respondent that rates three benefits as a 5, a 4, and a 3 in importance has a very similar evaluation mechanism to one that rates them as a 3, a 2, and a 1. Computing the absolute differences in importance ratings indicates that these are dissimilar. In fact, they would be less similar than the 5, 4, and 3 ratings would be to 3, 4, and 5. Since correlations do not depend on such scale biases, a more appropriate measure of similarity between these respondents might be the correlation between importance ratings.

Depending on how a conjoint analysis is performed, it too may be vulnerable to scale biases. These can be mitigated by computing the relative importance of attributes. The range (maximum value – minimum value) of the part-worths for a given attribute reflect how much each could potentially impact the dependent variable in the part-worth model. If the data collected are ratings and not rankings, which must be comparable in scale across respondents, the part-worths and their ranges can be vulnerable to scale biases. These can be eliminated by transforming the importance of attribute m (range of part-worths for that attribute), IMP_m, into

$$\frac{IMP_m}{\sum_n IMP_n},$$

where n indexes all the attributes. Then the distance between two consumers' stated importances can be computed as the sum of the absolute value of the differences of the revised importances or the Euclidean distance between them.

A final example of a similarity measure is apparent from the industrial air conditioning study in Table 2.5. Two organizations are more similar if they have similar patterns of involvement in the purchasing process. One can list a variety of job titles and assign each a one or zero for each organization depending on whether or not that individual has influence in the purchase. The similarity between two organizations can then be taken as the number of 0-1 elements that match in the two lists.

Grouping Observations   After a similarity measure is developed, a grouping algorithm must be chosen. More often than not, this is dictated by what computer program is available. A wide variety of algorithms exist. These differ on (among other things) whether clusters are built up from individual observations or broken off from the aggregate and the definition of similarity between an observation and a cluster.[3]

The most common procedures fall into a class called *hierarchical* agglomorative *methods.* These involve the sequential building up of clusters into a hierarchy. As an example, consider a collection of n = 10 items (brands) as in Figure A2.2(a). The most direct way to begin a cluster analysis is to group together the two most similar items. Suppose these two are items 1 and 5. Once this is done, 9 objects remain, 8 single items and one cluster. See Figure A2.2(b). The items in the cluster should obviously be represented next to each other in the hierarchy. The next step is to take the next two most similar items and group them. To determine whether the next grouping should be between two single items or a single item and the already formed cluster, we need a way to define the distance between a single item and a cluster. Alternatives include the minimum, maximum, and mean distance between the single item and each item in the cluster.

If the next grouping is between two single items, say items 7 and 9, we have eight objects remaining, $N - 4$ single items and two clusters each containing two elements. See Figure A2.2(c). On the other hand, if the second similarity search yields the most similar item pair as the first cluster and a third single item, say 9, we have eight items remaining—seven single items and one three-item cluster. This can be graphically represented as in Figure A2.2(d). Repeated application of this logic with successive pairings depicted as higher couplings in the hierarchy will produce diagrams such as that in Figure A2.3.

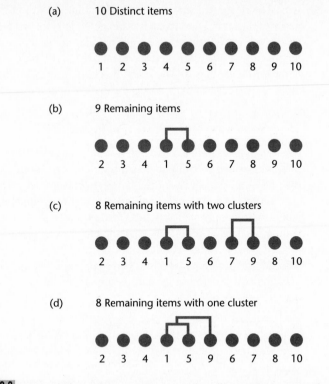

(a)   10 Distinct items

(b)   9 Remaining items

(c)   8 Remaining items with two clusters

(d)   8 Remaining items with one cluster

FIGURE A2.2   **How Hierarchies or Trees Arise from Cluster Analyses**

There are two critical components to hierarchical agglomerative clustering computer outputs. The first is a tree diagram, often called a *dendrogram,* such as that shown in Figure A2.3. This demonstrates how objects link together at various levels of similarity. If sliced at the appropriate level, dendrograms can also be used to assign items to clusters for all possible numbers of clusters. For example, the two-cluster solution, {1,3,16,2,4,5,7,14,9,6,8,10,11,15,12} {13}, has item 13 in one cluster and all other items in the other; the three-cluster solution, {1,3,16,2,4,5,7,14,9,6,8,10,11,15} {12} {13}, has item 13 in one, item 12 in a second, and all others in a third. The four-cluster solution can be described as {1,3,16,2,4,5,7,14,9} {6,8,10,11,15} {12} {13}. The five-cluster solution is {1,3,16,2,4,5} {7,14,9} {6,8,10,11,15} {12} {13}. We could go on.

Often a user finds it desirable to work with a single solution with a specific number of clusters. This selection is usually made on the basis of cluster interpretability and goodness of fit among statistics.[4] This leads to the second important component of cluster analysis output, a table of means of the clusters on the variables used to define the clusters. For example, a clustering of ideal points would include each cluster's mean ideal point for all individuals in that cluster.

Other clustering approaches commonly used include *hierarchical divisive* and *K-means clustering*. Hierarchical divisive clustering also produces a tree diagram. It dif-

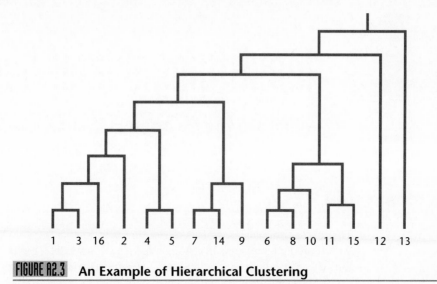

FIGURE A2.3 An Example of Hierarchical Clustering

fers from the previous approach in that all items begin in one cluster and it sequentially removes dissimilar objects instead of sequentially adding items. K-means clustering takes a fixed number of clusters and assigns items to them by maximizing the ratio of the variance between cluster means to the variance within clusters about their means.

Notes

1. Harman, Harry H. (1967), *Modern Factor Analysis,* Chicago: University of Chicago Press, discusses factor analysis in much more detail.
2. This example is based on Horowitz, A. D., and J. N. Sheth (1977), "Segmenting the Ridesharing Market," A. Woodside and J. N. Sheth (eds.), *Consumer and Industrial Buying Behavior,* New York: North-Holland, 152–185.

3. See Kaufman, Leonard, and Peter J. Rousseeuw (1990), *Finding Groups in Data: An Introduction to Cluster Analysis,* New York: Wiley for more detailed information on clustering algorithms.
4. For example, Kaufman and Rousseeuw (*Ibid.*, Chapter 5) discuss a statistic they call the *agglomerative coefficient.*

Identifying Unmet Needs

What Do the Customers Want?

INTRODUCTION

To grow, a firm must design a strategy for expanding its portfolio of offerings. The Ansoff product-market matrix,[1] shown in Fig. 3.1, provides a useful way for a firm to identify growth options for a business. Ansoff classifies a firm's current products as "existing" and calls all future products (including those yet to be developed) "new." He uses similar terminology for the markets currently served by the firm and for those yet to be developed. The resulting 2×2 combinations form the product-market matrix. The strategies corresponding to the four cells are *market penetration* for expanding existing products in existing markets; *product development* for developing new products for existing markets; *market development* for marketing existing products in new markets; and *diversification* for marketing new products in new markets.

The product development growth direction involves modifying existing products and/or developing new products and services for current markets. However, in the process of developing new products, the firm may seek entirely new markets (not served by the firm so far) or investigate segments in markets it currently serves. Internal development of products is a viable option if the firm has the technological capabilities. If not, it may need strategic alliances, licensing, or acquisition. When a firm engages in acquisition, it may also be diversifying its product portfolio.

To achieve success with product development (product modification or creation of new products), the firm must understand the current and future needs of various customer segments. Its objectives must include both the satisfaction of needs currently met by other firms, perhaps inadequately, and the satisfaction of needs not currently being met in the marketplace. Many companies in a wide variety of industries have used the satisfaction of unmet needs as a major vehicle to growth. The following are some examples.

Self-Moving Industry: Ryder Truck Rental, Inc., recognized an unmet need of customers for an easy and convenient moving experience and repositioned its truck-renting operation accordingly.[2]

Health Care Industry: Doctors and nurses always want to be sure about a diagnosis. The use of artificial intelligence (that is, computer-assisted diagnosis) can prevent not only misdiagnosis, but misadministration of drugs. The Discern program of the Kansas City-based Cerner Corporation is an example; it uses Boolean algebra to

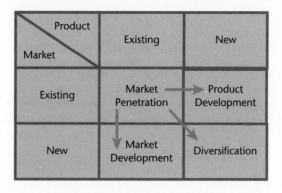

FIGURE 3.1 **Vector of Growth Directions for a Given Product-Market Combination**

Source: Adapted from Figures 6.1 and 7.1 in Ansoff, Igor (1965), *Corporate Strategy,* New York: McGraw-Hill.

take advantage of what computers can do best and leaves to human doctors what they can do best.[3]

Van Design: The remote-controlled side passenger door in GM's new minivans meets van drivers' previously unmet need to be able to open and close the side door with ease.[4]

Energy for Electric Vehicles: Energy Partners, Inc., and other companies are pursuing the development of a fuel cell as a lighter weight, higher power, long-lasting alternative to batteries in an electric vehicle; progress in the use of electric vehicles has been slow, owing to the significant unmet need for a suitable energy source.[5]

Battery Discharge in an Automobile: Many motorists have experienced their car battery remaining charged after they have left the car headlights on by mistake. A new product, Battery Buddy, developed by Masco Industries, offers a neat solution to this problem. It switches off the flow of electricity before it is drained too far. The Battery Buddy consists of a microprocessor that monitors the electrical flow and outside temperature. It is strapped to the battery and connected to the terminal.[6]

Computerized Auto Service Systems: The development of a computer-chip nerve center for an automobile will save a lot of time and energy in diagnosing problems. Rather than replacing a faulty computer chip to correct how a car runs, the new technology will allow mechanics to diagnose the problem and reprogram the chip by downloading a new program onto it. The process takes only a few minutes.[7]

Genetic Engineering of Foods: The food industry is likely to be revolutionized by developments in gene-splicing technology. The gene-spliced tomato, called Flavr Savr—the product of eight years and $20 million in research by Cialgene, Inc., in Davis, California—is one example; Flavr Savr has been genetically engineered to retard rotting.[8] Other potential opportunities include:

Light Beer Industry: Although the light beer market is sizable and growing in the United States, the most significant unmet need is for a low-calorie beer (with fewer than the present 90 or so calories per 12 oz) with the robust flavor of a full-calorie beer. At the same time, no light beer is sold in countries such as Trinidad, and the need for a light beer may not even be perceived in these countries.

Ice Cream Industry: The U.S. ice cream industry is somewhat stable, but segments served with appropriate products may offer growth potential. These include vegetarian and vegan populations.

Personal Computer Industry: In the PC market, the unmet needs include total software compatibility between the Macintosh and DOS systems, standardized open architectures, standardized networking solutions between DOS and Mac, and standardized ISDN and multimedia solutions with adequate communication bandwidths.

Notebook Computers: In this industry, there is an unmet need for low-priced machines as well as longer lasting batteries.

Cellular Phones: Two unmet needs with regard to the use of cellular phones are automatic number identification (ADN) and security.

Ready-to-Drink Tea: In the growing ready-to-drink tea industry, a significant unmet need is a 100 percent natural product as well as good-tasting diet alternatives.

Pay Phones in Remote Places: Hikers, boaters, and other travelers sometimes need to call friends and families. Currently, phone lines do not exist in remote places.[9]

Classifying Unmet Needs

One way to organize customers' unmet needs is from the perspective of a firm marketing a product for a specific consumption situation. Fig. 3.2 shows a convenient way to categorize customer needs. In general, customers recognize a majority of the (potential) needs existing in a situation.* Further, because existing products in the marketplace meet most of the needs recognized by customers, the opportunity for developing new products based on meeting such needs is rather minimal. However, firms can either modify/reposition their existing products or develop new products to meet those needs recognized by firms but not served by current products. In a similar vein, some of the needs yet to be recognized by customers are, in fact, recognized and understood by firms due to their research and development efforts, which produce new technologies. Finally, a group of unmet needs remains unknown to both customers and firms.

For example, consider the development of the cordless telephone and its various features during the last 10 years or so. Assume that the current product with the ability to store numbers in memory is produced by several firms and meets customers' need for flexibility in using the telephone. Nevertheless, the product can be modified to include an answering machine (an unmet need recognized by customers). Similarly, the cordless telephone can be redesigned to have the capability of sending/receiving a facsimile, but it may require designing an entirely new product. Among the developments that would possibly meet needs not yet recognized by customers are a cordless telephone with the previous enhancements *and* the capability for use in home banking and a phone unit that performs as a palmtop computer with

---

*We use the term *needs* very broadly; it is not restricted to essentials for survival.

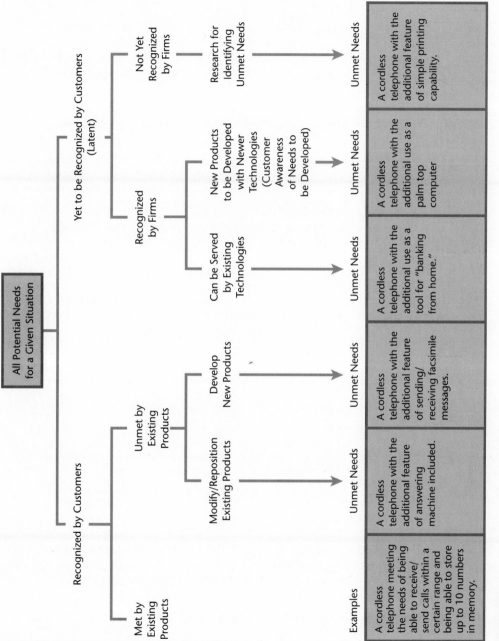

FIGURE 3.2 A Classification of Customer Needs

TABLE 3.1   **Classifying Unmet Needs for the Computer Industry**

Case	Category	Case Example
1	Recognized by customers, unmet by existing products; modify/reposition existing products	While popular with scientific users, Novell Inc.'s Unix operating system software has not been used greatly in business because of incompatibilities in different versions. Thus, the need to standardize exits. Novell is planning to modify the software to a standard, ready-to-ship product.
2	Recognized by customers, unmet by existing products; develop new products	Recognizing the need of travelers to send faxes to the hotel front desk and to get printouts, Canon introduced a powerful 7.7-lb laptop with a built-in inkjet printer.
3	Yet to be recognized by customers, recognized by firms; existing technologies	Understanding the potential demands placed on computer terminals not in use yet turned on, Berkeley Systems developed screen savers such as its tropical fish After Dark product.
4	Yet to be recognized by customers, recognized by firms; new products to be developed along with customer awareness	In response to its perception of the ways people naturally share and swap information on a network, Lotus developed Notes, a product that enables large groups of users to collaborate on projects. Documents can be created, revised, and organized with a minimum of meetings and management interventions. Lotus's intent was to minimize the need for bureaucracies.
5	Yet to be recognized by customers, yet to be recognized by firms	Recognizing the coming need for increased user-friendliness of the point and click features of the Windows operating system, Microsoft developed the Word for Windows word-processing package. This pulled the rug out from under WordPerfect's DOS market leadership position.

Sources: Fisher, Lawrence M. (1993), "Novell to Try to Make Unix More Acceptable," *New York Times*, September 22; Lewis, Peter H. (1993), "Canon's New Laptop Packs a Nice Printer Inside," *New York Times*, April 18; Lefton, Terry (1993), "Microsoft into Saving Screens," *Brandweek*, July 26; Luscombe, Belinda (1993), "Products that Make Markets," *Fortune*, June 14; *Business Week* (1993), "The Glitch at WordPerfect," May 17.

printing capabilities. The first modification utilizes existing technology, while the second might require technological development.

Developments in the computer industry offer another illustration of our categorization of unmet needs (see Table 3.1). Examples range from product repositioning (modification of Novell software) to the potential development of a product that would cater to needs yet to be recognized by customers or firms (Word for Windows).

Characteristics of Markets with Unmet Needs

Is it possible to identify a set of general characteristics of market situations that point to unmet needs? Continuing our previous discussion, a firm may first wish to explore strategies for market expansion in current markets with current products before considering product development. Beyond that, the following may represent opportune situations for studying unmet needs:

- Current markets are reaching a high level of saturation.
- Customers are highly dissatisfied with current products (of the firm as well as of its competition).
- New technologies are emerging that may significantly alter the production processes of current products.
- New societal trends are emerging that alter the lifestyle of current customers.
- New international markets are opening up for a firm's domestic products, but cultural differences exist between these markets and the current markets; the same holds for geographic submarkets.

We proceed from the premise that studying customers and other groups in a creative manner will enable the strategic market planner to uncover these opportunities. The remainder of this chapter will be devoted to methods for identifying unmet customer needs.

METHODS FOR IDENTIFYING UNMET NEEDS

There are two broad sources of unmet needs: (1) manifest or latent problems with the currently available offerings designed to solve a set of customer needs and (2) general changes in the environment that lead to changes in consumption habits. Several research methods exist for identifying the unmet needs that may arise from these two sources. Table 3.2 categorizes selected research methods for identifying unmet needs.

The first group of research methods shown in Table 3.2 involves insightful analyses of various aspects of the consumption of the available products and the degree to which they satisfy customer needs. We identify four specific aspects of the consumption process: how customers evaluate products offered in the marketplace; the problems customers experience during the actual buying transaction; the difficulties customers experience while using or disposing of the products; and how well satisfied customers are with the products.

A range of research methods exists for studying these aspects of consumption with an eye to identifying problems (and, implicitly, unmet needs). Focus groups,* perceptual mapping, and benefit structure analysis are generally suitable to study how customers evaluate existing offerings. Mystery shopper surveys are an interesting way to understand any problems during the actual transaction process. The techniques of so-called "problem" research, which involve detecting and inventorying problems, are perhaps ideal for studying customers' difficulties using or disposing of products. The methods of customer satisfaction research—surveys and complaint

---

*The focus group is only one of the methods available to the strategic analyst for exploring unmet customer needs. In practice, it is a variation of the brainstorming method.

TABLE 3.2 Selected Methods for Identifying Unmet Needs

Source of Unmet Needs	Associated Aspects of Buying/Consumption Process	Research Methods	Examples of Unmet Needs Uncovered
A. Problems with existing offerings (own and competitors')	Evaluation of existing alternatives	• Focus groups	Identification of the need for a warranty program for items bought on a credit card
		• Perceptual mapping methods	Identification of locations in the perceptual map not well served by existing products
		• Benefit structure analysis	Identification of gaps between benefits wanted and benefits offered by existing products
	Transactional aspects of buying (mechanics of buying)	• Mystery shopper surveys	Unmet need for a totally courteous service while shopping for goods
	Aspects of using and disposing of a product	• Problem research (detection analysis and inventory analysis)	Unmet need for an environmentally safe product (such as paper towels or baby diapers)
	Satisfaction with the use of a product	• Customer satisfaction surveys • Customer complaints analysis	Unmet need for a defect-free automobile at a "reasonable" price
B. Changes in the environment	Some fundamental changes in various aspects of consumption process	• Environmental scanning • Analysis of trends in population changes, society, and technology*	Unmet needs for nutritious and convenient products (arising due to both adults working outside home)

*These methods are covered in Chapters 5 and 6.

analysis—are relevant for studying the degree of satisfaction with products. Table 3.2 gives examples of the unmet needs that could be uncovered with these methods. The methods are described more fully in the following sections.

The second set of methods involves tracking and analyzing changes in the environment and evaluating them to identify any unmet needs. This research requires studying environmental factors relevant to the business under review. In addition to studying demographic trends of the market, the strategic analyst should identify and evaluate the effects of other environmental trends. These include economic, social, technological, and legal factors. Environmental scanning can help forecast potential changes in consumption habits, which may lead to identifying unmet needs. While our discussion in this chapter is confined only to this technique, we cover the variety of methods for studying and forecasting environmental factors in Chapters 5 and 6.

METHODS FOR UNCOVERING PROBLEMS WITH EXISTING OFFERINGS

We will describe in this section the various methods for identifying problems with existing offerings in the marketplace listed in Table 3.2. These methods are focus groups, perceptual mapping, benefit structure analysis, mystery shopper surveys, problem research, customer satisfaction surveys, and customer complaint analysis.

Focus Groups

Developed as a basic qualitative research technique in marketing research, *focus groups* are an effective way for a firm to gain insights and to generate hypotheses about customer behavior toward its products. When skillfully administered, this technique can help identify unmet consumer needs. Focus groups are quite widely employed in marketing; because they are based on small samples, we must caution that they are not to be used as a substitute for large-scale quantitative studies.

American Express used insights gathered from focus groups as an important input when developing the program that extended warranties.[10] The marketing department at American Express first developed a set of 10 ideas potentially valuable to its customers. Using focus groups, it reduced this list to a handful to ensure that the firm was pursuing ideas of some interest to customers. The reduced list of ideas was subsequently tested using quantitative research techniques. The result of this research process, in which focus groups played a significant part, was the design of a buyer's assistance program that extended warranties on products bought with an American Express card. The program was successful; it increased both card usage and card sales.

Focus group methodology was also instrumental for Johnson Wax in understanding consumers' problems in using shampoo.[11] Having identified that oiliness was a major problem for teenage users of shampoo, the company developed a successful formulation for its Agree creme rinse, a brand that took a significant lead over its competitors in the market.

Recently, one of the authors conducted a focus group among executives of biotechnology companies to ascertain how Cornell's Center for Advanced Technology (CAT) can serve their unmet needs in research and technological support. This exercise identified a significant unmet need for networking among companies and CAT to exchange information more effectively.

The emphasis in this technique is on group interaction, *focused* on a series of topics introduced by an experienced moderator. The discussion is open ended and takes place among the members of the group, with minimal input from the moderator. The group size is about 8 to 12 people, and each group is relatively homogeneous in terms of background characteristics (age, social status, and so on). Homogeneity of a group enables easy exchange of views among the members. To ensure that focus groups generate a wide spectrum of insights, it is necessary to conduct several focus group sessions. At least four group discussions are held for a given project and groups vary in their composition; for example, only users of the firm's products, only users of competitive products, and mixed groups.

Screening interviews are conducted, usually by telephone, to determine which individuals will participate in a particular focus group. It is important to avoid individuals who have participated in prior focus groups, because some of them may second-guess the purposes of the focus group study and express opinions simply to be consistent with such purposes. A focus group of members who behave like "experts" will not provide useful information.

The moderator directing the focus group attempts to follow a rough outline of issues while simultaneously directing that each member's comments be considered by the group. Each participant in the focus group is thereby exposed to the ideas of others in the group and offers his or her own ideas to the group for consideration. A typical focus group lasts from $1^{1}/_{2}$ to 2 hours. The participants are typically compensated for their time, the amount depending on the subject matter of the focus group and, therefore, the occupation of participants (for example, secretary versus physician).

The moderator of a focus group should be cognizant of the meanings behind group members' nonverbal communications and direct the group to enable open exchange of ideas.[12] Two significant aspects of nonverbal communications are the signs/signals used and posture of the members of the group. Various nonverbal communications that arise in a group discussion context can be illustrated in a 2×2 chart such as Fig. 3.3. If a group member uses closed signs (legs crossed, arms folded across body, and so on) with a tense posture (symmetrical body position, tense hands, etc.), he or she may be seeking confirmation of his or her views. On the other hand, he or she may be controlling the group by using closed signs with a relaxed posture (indicated by asymmetric body posture, leaning, or tilting one's head backwards). Open signals (maintaining eye contact, arms at sides) and relaxed posture will enable an open exchange of views among the group. The goal of the group moderator is to create an atmosphere of open signals and relaxed posture; the moderator should recognize the signals conveyed by the participants at any given moment in the group discussion and take appropriate steps to move the interview along. He or she should also use body language to keep the discussion going by either mirroring others' postures or contradicting them. Further, pacing may be a useful technique to help group members verbalize their thoughts.

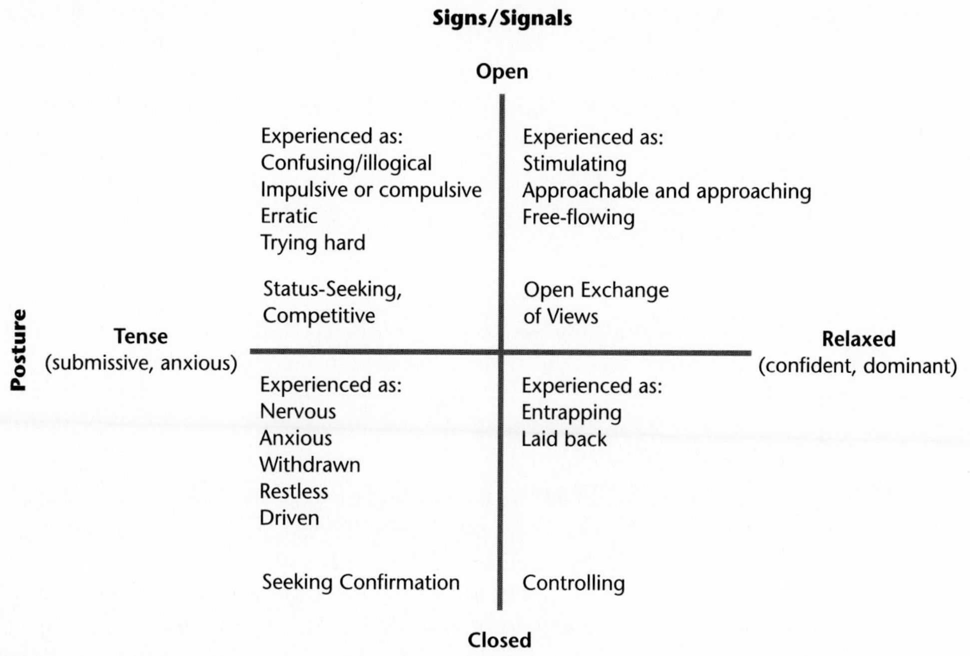
Signs/Signals
Open
Experienced as:
Confusing/illogical
Impulsive or compulsive
Erratic
Trying hard
Status-Seeking,
Competitive
Experienced as:
Stimulating
Approachable and approaching
Free-flowing
Open Exchange
of Views
Posture
Tense
(submissive, anxious)
Relaxed
(confident, dominant)
Experienced as:
Nervous
Anxious
Withdrawn
Restless
Driven
Seeking Confirmation
Experienced as:
Entrapping
Laid back
Controlling
Closed

FIGURE 3.3 Meaning of Nonverbal Communications

Source: Gordon, Wendy, and Roy Langmaid (1988), *Qualitative Market Research,* Brookfield, VT: Gower Publishing Company, 88.

An Illustration of the Use of Focus Groups* The following is an illustration of how focus groups were used to determine the unmet needs of commercial vehicle operators: truckers, product delivery salespeople, and parcel delivery salespeople employed by firms such as UPS and Federal Express. Assume that an electronics firm has several technological capabilities and can develop various tracking and monitoring systems that could be installed in both existing and future commercial vehicles. The company is interested in knowing more about the unmet needs of these commercial vehicle operators. How will it go about this task? A suitable technique is focus groups of commercial operators. In fact, the firm conducted several such focus groups.

In this case, these focus groups revealed a number of unmet needs of the commercial vehicle operators, including the following:

Communication with the Base: An operator needs to let the base personnel know how much of the work has been completed and to receive any new or revised directions (for example, to change the route to perform an urgent task).

*This illustration is patterned after a real application conducted for a large automobile corporation. Owing to confidentiality, only cursory information is provided.

Routing: The firm managing the commercial vehicles needs to identify the optimal route for each operator in the local area; using the information on the particular deliveries that need to be made in the area, one may develop a route that minimizes either total driving time (considering traffic patterns) or number of deliveries made later than the expected or promised time.

Safety and Security: The operator needs to contact the base quickly and perhaps unobtrusively when there is a danger on the road. This need may be critical for a vehicle that carries valuable goods or cash.

Locating: The home base also needs to locate each vehicle in a local area.

With this information, the electronics firm can design and test suitable tracking and monitoring systems that could be installed in commercial vehicles.

Perceptual Mapping

Perceptual mapping methods are used to develop maps that show various competitive products as points in order to describe their relationships; for example, the degree of similarity between them. The axes of these maps are the salient attributes of the products. Consumers are positioned as points in the perceptual maps to describe their most desired combination of the attributes. A mapping study of a product category will reveal gaps in the current attribute combinations offered in the marketplace and therefore can suggest potential new products.

We will illustrate the perceptual mapping method with two applications. The first, given in Fig. 2.8, shows the derived perceptual positions of six brands of a food product labeled A through F (shown as dots in the figure) and a test product, located by an asterisk.[13] The analysis was based on data on attribute ratings by a sample of consumers and data on their preferences toward the existing brands (A–F). The perceptual map was derived using factor analysis. The arrows show the attributes in the space; for example, brand F, positioned in the direction of "good tasting," is rated highest on that attribute. Brand E does not have a distinct position in the market.

The ideal points of the consumers are clustered into six segments of consumers and these segments are positioned in the perceptual map. The segments, labeled 1 through 6, are shown as circles or ellipses in the figure, the size of which represents the relative size of the corresponding segment. For example, Segment 1, which encompasses brands A and B, prefers these two brands as well as the test concept. Segment 2 prefers brands C and D, and so on. Further, this map suggests that the test product may need to compete head on with brands A and B to achieve any realistic market share. On the other hand, positioning the test product as "good for any occasion" may establish it as a viable choice alternative for Segment 6, which is not essentially well served by the current brands (that is, Segment 6 has an unmet need). Similarly, Segment 4 has an unmet need as well.

Fig. 3.4 shows an illustration of mapping of preferences of existing cars (Brazilia, Beetle, Datsun, and Renault) in relation to three new car concepts (S-car, T-car, and V-car) under consideration by an automobile manufacturer in a foreign market.[14] The perceptual map, developed from responses of 1,000 automobile

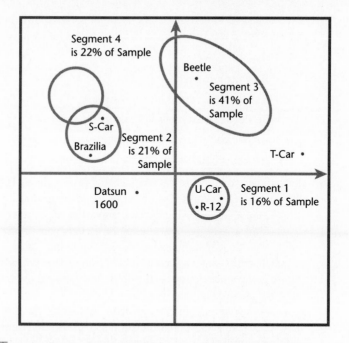

FIGURE 3.4 **Position of Seven Popular Car Concepts Based on Customer Preferences**

Source: From *Consumer Behavior and Marketing Action,* by Henry Assael, Copyright (c) 1981, page 464. By permission of South-Western College Publishing, a division of International Thomson Publishing, Inc., Cincinnati, Ohio 45227.

owners, shows four distinct segments of car owners. It clearly points out that the T-car concept is not meeting the needs of any group of consumers, while there is a clear unmet need for Segment 4 (about 22 percent of the sample), which may be served by a repositioned S-car concept.

Benefit Structure Analysis

Benefit structure analysis is a survey-based approach developed especially to find new product opportunities (presumably based on unmet needs) in broadly defined product/service categories, such as household cleaning products, banking services, or tools for home repair or redecoration.[15] The method involves two phases. In the first phase, some 50 in-depth interviews (or six or so focus groups) elicit information on all possible occasions for the product category, products used, benefits sought, and product attributes. (This phase may be omitted entirely if a company already has extensive information about the product/service area from previous research.) A comprehensive questionnaire on various benefits wanted versus benefits received for a number of alternative products for several consumption occasions is developed with the information from the first phase. Using this questionnaire, a large-scale survey of 500 or so prime users of the category is conducted in the second phase.

Data collected in this phase are the major source of benefit structure analysis. The data collected can be analyzed in terms of the following dimensions:

- Benefits wanted.
- Benefits received.
- Ratings of product characteristics.
- Product(s) used by use occasion.
- Brands chosen by use occasion.
- Various background data on respondents.

Each dimension in these data may have 5 to as many as 100 categories, depending on the context. Data combined on all of these dimensions, called the *complete benefit matrix,* are analyzed using various univariate and multivariate methods. The objectives of these analyses are to explore various gaps in the products available in the market, to identify deficiencies in existing brands with regard to benefits delivered versus benefits wanted, and to identify any use occasions that can be exploited for future product development. In addition to simple cross-tabulation, factor and cluster analyses are used to identify gaps.

One analysis of interest is cross-tabulating the degree to which a benefit is wanted versus received in the products in use and summarizing the table into a deficiency index for each benefit. Simply stated, a *benefit deficiency index* is the average of the score "benefit wanted minus benefit received" for a benefit; the benefit wanted and benefit received are usually rated on a four-point scale: (1) not at all, (2) somewhat, (3) pretty much, and (4) a whole lot. The difference score will have seven values ranging from −3 to +3. The number of respondents with each difference score is computed from the cross-tabulation. This cross-table is called a *benefit deficiency matrix.*

Next, various plots show the average benefit wanted scores versus average deficiency scores for each benefit, the average positive deficiency score versus proportion of sample with some deficiency, and the average benefit wanted score versus proportion wanting the benefit "pretty much" or "a whole lot" who felt some deficiency. Similar plots can also be made for product characteristics. These plots enable a market planner to identify "opportunity points": benefits that are wanted but not received or product characteristics that are received but not wanted or wanted but not received. The analyses for product characteristics may help direct the research and development labs to modify existing products by either adding or removing certain product characteristics.

Third, various benefits can be clustered into benefit groups using the information on benefit wanted, and the resulting benefit groups can be analyzed to show which is more sizable. Finally, a combined analysis of use occasions and benefits wanted can reveal at a glance which general use occasions require which general benefits.

As an illustration, consider the category of household cleaning products. The qualitative phase would identify various use occasions such as cleaning windows, cleaning appliances and broiler pans, cleaning floors, and cleaning bathrooms. Further, it would identify various benefits and product characteristics for this product category. In a study reported by Myers, over 25 benefits and product characteristics were reported; a subset of these is shown in Part A of Table 3.3.

Part B of Table 3.3 shows the benefit deficiency matrix for the benefit "removes grease," using data from 493 respondents. While a large majority of these people are satisfied with the amount of benefit received versus wanted, a subgroup finds deficiencies in the benefit.

For the benefit, "removes grease," the average benefit wanted score is 2.70 versus the average benefit received score of 2.36, yielding a deficiency of –0.34. From this table, the average positive deficiency computed by ignoring negative deficiencies (setting them equal to zero) accurately reflects the extent to which respondents wanted a particular benefit and did not get it; its value for the "removes grease" benefit is 0.57. For this benefit, 15 percent of the sample have a negative deficiency score. Also, the number of respondents with deficiency in this benefit is 162 (= 34 + 26 + 27 + 23 + 30 + 22), about 33 percent of the sample.

In this study, the primary benefits that people want in cleaning products are grouped into seven categories, A through G, shown in Part C of Table 3.3. Here, not only are the percentages of the sample wanting a benefit "pretty much or more" shown, but the importance of making an improvement in the benefit is gauged by the percentages of the sample having a deficiency (wanting more than received). While 75 percent of the sample wants the benefit group, "removes dust/dirt/film" pretty much or more, only 32 percent of the sample finds a deficiency in this benefit in the existing products. On the other hand, although only 35 percent of the sample want more of the benefit "gentle on hands/skin," 56 percent find a deficiency in this benefit as received from various products. Thus, a marketer may need to evaluate which of these two product improvements offers greater economic potential.

Mystery Shopper Surveys

This method is useful in determining whether there are any deficiencies in the services delivered in a retail environment. The *mystery shopper survey* involves sending a few individuals trained to pose as shoppers to describe various special needs and gather information on the way the firm's products are described relative to those of the competition. The data gathered here can reveal areas where existing products can be improved. If these studies are done by a retail organization, they may indicate areas where service improvements are necessary.

This approach can profitably be employed by a firm such as IBM in exploring how its ThinkPad laptop computers are being described by salespeople in such retail stores as CompUSA. The firm can dispatch interviewers to shop for a laptop computer at the stores identified. These "mystery shoppers" will keep track of their interaction with salespeople, particularly with respect to the way the IBM laptops are described and compared with other laptops in the store. The resulting information can be valuable for IBM in its communication with the stores and also in providing appropriate information to the stores in training sales personnel. It is also worth pointing out that company executives can gain some firsthand knowledge of their products by visiting stores as mystery shoppers.

TABLE 3.3   Illustration of Benefit Structure Analysis: Household Cleaning Products

A. Benefits and Product Characteristics

Benefits	Product Characteristics
Bleaches	Strong smell
Removes stains	Abrasive/scratchy
Removes grease	Can wipe on
Cleans tub ring	Self-polishing
Doesn't leave residue	Biodegradable
Doesn't streak	Can spray on
Doesn't hurt hands	Economical
Seals porous floors	Stains
Strips wax	Contains deodorant

B. Benefit Deficiency Matrix

Benefit #49: "Removes grease"

					Marginal Sums	
Benefit Wanted	"Not at all" (1)	"Somewhat" (2)	"Pretty Much" (3)	"A Whole Lot" (4)	Wanted	Got
Not at all (1)	108	13	10	12	143	187
Somewhat (2)	22	15	13	6	56	84
Pretty much (3)	23	30	25	20	98	75
A whole lot (4)	34	26	27	109	196	147
Total	187	84	75	147		

Wanted minus received = (deficiency)		−3	−2	−1	0	1	2	3
Number of respondents*		12	16	46	257	79	49	34
Averages: Wanted: 2.70	Received: 2.36							

*These numbers are obtained from different combinations of the table data; for example, 49 is obtained as the sum of 26 (wanted "a whole lot" and received "somewhat") and 23 (wanted "pretty much" and received "not at all").

C. Comparative Size of Major Benefit Wanted Segments and Benefit Deficiencies

Benefit Grouping		% Sample Wanting Benefit Pretty Much or More	% Sample Having Deficiency
A.	Removes dust/dirt/film	76%	32%
B.	Removes porcelain stains	63	28
C.	Leaves no film/residue/scratches	61	26
D.	Removes grease/wax/stains	59	41
E.	Convenient to use/store	58	34
F.	No unpleasant odor during/after use	54	62
G.	Gentle on hands/skin	35	56

Source: Myers, James H. (1976), "Benefit Structure Analysis: A New Tool for Product Planning," *Journal of Marketing* (October): 23–32. Reprinted by permission of the American Marketing Association.

Another natural application of mystery shopper surveys is in evaluating how franchisees are implementing the policies of the franchiser, such as the McDonald's Corporation. In this case, a sample of franchise locations can be visited by a number of interviewers who "shop" and gather information on the relevant policies being evaluated (say, prices, displays, and premium offers).

Problem Research

There are essentially two methods for problem research. The first method is to ask consumers what problems they encountered with each of the existing products they use and to have them rate the severity of each problem identified. Each solution may lead to a new product idea or opportunity. We call this the *product problem detection system.* The other method is to present consumers with a long inventory of problems and ask them to identify what product comes to mind as having each problem; this approach is called *problem inventory analysis.*

Problem Detection System   Developed in the late 1970s by BBDO Advertising Agency, the problem detection system involves two major steps: (1) problem generation and (2) problem evaluation. (The method was formerly called problem detection analysis.) The first step is to develop a long and thorough list of possible problems for a particular product or service (or those with a broadly defined end use such as cooking or housecleaning). This is done by such methods as focus group interviews among prime prospects for the product or service, analysis of secondary sources such as past consumer surveys, expert judgment, and researcher insight.

The second step of problem evaluation involves reducing the list developed in the first step to yield a list of "big" or "major" problems. For this purpose, personal interviews among 150 to 200 prime prospects are conducted. Each problem generated is put on a separate card, and three questions are asked for each problem. The data collected include a rating of the perceived importance of the problem, frequency of occurrence, and preemptibility (whether the solution to the problem was preempted by some other product or service). Using these data, two scores—the problem score (PS) and the opportunity score (OS)—are computed for each problem. The problem score is a weighted score of frequency of occurrence by importance, while the opportunity score is a weighted score of all three items of data including preemptibility.

The formulae for computing these scores for a sample of n respondents as a whole are as follows:

$$PS_j = \frac{1}{n}\sum_{i=1}^{n} IMP_{ij} \times FREQ_{ij} \text{ and}$$

$$OS_j = \frac{1}{n}\sum_{i=1}^{n} IMP_{ij} \times FREQ_{ij} \times PREEMPT_{ij}$$

where

IMP_{ij} = importance rating given by the ith respondent for the jth problem (on a 10-point scale, 10 being high);

$FREQ_{ij}$ = frequency of occurrence of the jth problem as experienced by the ith respondent (measured in terms of number of times per month); and

$PREEMPT_{ij}$ = 1 if no product or service has preempted solving the jth problem and 0 otherwise according to the ith respondent.

The larger the PS score for a problem, the more severe the problem is from the consumers' perspective. Various problems can first be ranked by problem scores. Those with high opportunity scores can be chosen for possible product enhancements or for the development of a new product. Usually, the top two or three problems are identified for this purpose.

These computations are illustrated in Table 3.4 for five respondents, using hypothetical data for a banking service. These five respondents are assumed to have equal sales potential. The problem "Lines are too long" receives the highest score on both problem score and opportunity score compared to the other two problems, "Service is too slow" and "Banking is too complicated." The bank under consideration may benefit by taking steps to correct the problem of long lines.

TABLE 3.4   Computations of Scores in Problem Detection Analysis for a Banking Service

Respondent	Measure	Service Is Too Slow	Banking Is Too Complicated	Lines Are Too Long
			Problem	
1	Importance	8	6	10
	Frequency	3	2	4
	Preempt	1	1	0
2	Importance	7	8	9
	Frequency	2	1	4
	Preempt	1	0	0
3	Importance	7	8	7
	Frequency	3	3	5
	Preempt	0	1	1
4	Importance	4	4	6
	Frequency	1	2	2
	Preempt	0	0	0
5	Importance	8	7	5
	Frequency	3	3	6
	Preempt	0	1	1
	Problem Score	17.4*	14.6	30.6
	Opportunity Score	7.6†	11.4	13.0

*17.4 is computed as $\frac{1}{5}[(8 \times 3) + (7 \times 2) + (7 \times 3) + (4 \times 1) + (8 \times 3)]$.

†7.6 is computed as $\frac{1}{5}[(8 \times 3 \times 1) + (7 \times 2 \times 1) + (7 \times 3 \times 0) + (4 \times 1 \times 0) + (8 \times 3 \times 0)]$.

TABLE 3.5   Product Detection System Application

Product/Service Category	Problem Detection System: "Biggest" Problems	Benefit Identification Approach: Most "Desired" Benefits
Dog food	1. Is expensive	1. Balanced diet
	2. Does not smell good	2. Nutrition
	3 Does not come in different sizes for different dogs	3. Contains vitamins
	4. Does not keep teeth clean	4. Tastes good to the dog
	5. Does not chew like a bone	5. Easy to prepare
Banking	1. Service is too slow	1. Modern
	2. Banking is too complicated	2. Innovative
	3. Lines are too long	3. Friendly
	4. Can't get a loan	4. Low interest rates

Source: Extracted from "BBDO's Problem Detection System," a presentation by BBDO, June 1993 (with permission).

It is worth noting that the problem detection system can also be implemented for industrial products. For such products, the sample of respondents will typically be small, and the relative weights of the respondents in terms of their sales potential will need to be incorporated in the computation of the scores.

BBDO has used this technique for several of its clients. It claims that the problem detection approach is superior to the approach of asking customers the benefits desired in a product or service because customers simply play back benefits previously heard in advertising. These distinctions are quite apparent for the two cases—dog food and banking—shown in Table 3.5. While the benefit approach uncovered "good" aspects of a product or service, the problem detection system identified those areas where a firm can improve a product or develop a new product to solve the problems.

Although we have developed aggregate measures for various problems, the analysis can be done at an individual respondent level in order to identify those customers with the most severe problems. Such an analysis can identify segments of customers who may be good prospects for improved products.

The problem detection approach was applied on a small scale for the product category of laundry detergents. The results (both consumer problems and potential product enhancements to solve these problems) are shown in Table 3.6. Also shown are descriptions of selected brands that seem to address some or all of the consumer problems.

Undoubtedly, the success of the problem detection approach depends on the customers' ability to tell their needs and problems in the first stage of the method. Once a list has been identified, the second-step analysis of the data collected seems quite straightforward.

Problem Inventory Analysis   This approach is aimed at rectifying any difficulties in developing a list of consumer problems when the problem detection method is

TABLE 3.6   **Problem Research for Laundry Detergents**

A. Problems and Product Enhancements

Selected Consumer Problems	Potential Product Enhancements
Brighter clothes, whiter whites	Include bleach in detergent, add optical brighteners
Cleaner clothes	Add phosphates
Use any water temperature	Add cleaning agents geared for any water temperature
Allergic reactions	Eliminate dyes and perfumes, eliminate enzymes
Softer clothes	Add fabric softener
Convenience: all in one	Add softener, bleach, and phosphates
Smaller package	Superconcentrated formulas

B. Description of Selected Brands

Selected Brands	Powder/Liquid	Bleach	All Temp	Non-allergenic	Softener	Super Concentrate
Tide Ultra	P	Y/N	X			X
Cheer Free	P/L		X	X		
Solo	L		X		X	
Yes	L	X	X		X	
Dash	P		X			X
Bold Ultra	P		X		X	X
All	L		X	X		

employed. Rather than asking consumers to indicate problems with a specific product or service, this method presents a list of problems and asks a consumer to indicate what products come to mind as having that problem. The method is implemented in a self-administered survey using the sentence completion technique.

The method was implemented by Tauber for food products in a survey among 200 women using the mall-intercept method.[16] Tabulated results for 10 statements are reproduced in Table 3.7. These results indicate possibilities for product enhancement. But caution must be exercised in making changes to existing products from these results without further analysis. Certain "stock" or "expected" results may not represent true opportunities because they may not be important problems to consumers. For example, as Tauber reports, General Foods introduced a compact cereal box, which was a failure.

Customer Satisfaction Studies

Perhaps a more fruitful way for a firm to uncover the unmet needs of customers is to study the degree to which current customers are satisfied or dissatisfied with its

| TABLE 3.7 | **Results of a Problem Inventory Study about Food** |

Questions Asked and Percent of Respondents Answering

1. The package of _____ doesn't fit well on the shelf.

   | cereal | 49% |
   | flour | 6% |

2. My husband/children refuse to eat _____.

liver	18%
vegetables	5%
spinach	4%

3. _____ doesn't quench my thirst.

Soft drinks	58%
Milk	9%
Coffee	6%

4. Packaged _____ doesn't dissolve fast enough.

jello/gelatin	32%
bouillon cubes	8%
pudding	5%

5. Everyone always wants different _____.

vegetables	23%
cereal	11%
meat	10%
desserts	9%

6. _____ makes a mess in the oven.

Broiling steaks	19%
Pie	17%
Roast/pork/ribs	8%

7. Packaged _____ tastes artificial.

   | instant potatoes | 12% |
   | macaroni and cheese | 4% |

8. It's difficult to get _____ to pour easily.

catsup	16%
syrup	13%
gallon of milk	11%

9. Packaged _____ looks unappetizing.

hamburger helper	6%
lunch meat	3%
liver	3%

10. I wish my husband/children could take _____ in a carried lunch.

    | a hot meal | 11% |
    | soup | 9% |
    | ice cream | 4% |

Source: Tauber, Edward M. (1975), "Discovering New Product Opportunities with Problem Inventory Analysis," *Journal of Marketing* 39 (July): 67–70. Reprinted by permission of the American Marketing Association.

products. The topic of consumer satisfaction/dissatisfaction (under the acronym CS/D) has received more prominence in the last 10 years or so. Simply stated, if a product performs higher than expected by a consumer (or buyer), the consumer is satisfied; otherwise the consumer is dissatisfied. Of course, the expectation of performance and the observation of performance do not necessarily occur in the same time frame. While an analysis of sources of dissatisfaction can identify problems with the firm's products and areas of improvement, it can also identify customers' unmet needs.

Sources of Data   Firms can use one or more of the following sources of data to identify problems with existing products and sources of consumer dissatisfaction:

- Consumer panels and consumer surveys to track market shares.
- Consumer surveys of customer satisfaction.

TABLE 3.8   **Some Measures and Analysis Methods of Customer Satisfaction**

Measure of Customer S/D	Satisfaction (S) or Dissatisfaction (D)	Type of Measure	Source of Data	Analysis Method
Market share	S	Objective	Share data obtained through surveys or panels	Computation of market share using a relevant competitive set of items
Repeat purchase	S	Objective	Data on consecutive purchases of items obtained through surveys or panels	Analysis of a brand-switching matrix and transition probabilities
Switching out rate	D	Objective	Data on consecutive purchases of items obtained through surveys or panels	Analysis of movements relative to a random-switching model
Frequency of unsolved "objective" problems or complaints	D	Objective	Consumer letters, consumer surveys	Content analysis of letters received and open-ended data in surveys
Stated satisfaction or dissatisfaction	S/D	Subjective	Consumer surveys	Means and distribution of overall satisfaction ratings
Frequency of consumer problems	D	Subjective	Consumer surveys, consumer letters	Frequency analysis over time
Frequency of warranty claims	D	Objective	Data on warranty claims settled	Frequency analysis over time

Source: Adapted from Andreasen, Alan R. (1977), "A Taxonomy of Consumer Satisfaction/Dissatisfaction Measures," *Journal of Consumer Affairs* 11 (Winter): 11–24. Reprinted by permission of The University of Wisconsin Press.

- Consumer complaint letters.
- Warranty claims.

Analyses of these data using simple statistical methods can identify consumers' potential unmet needs. The firm should develop an information system to maintain these databases and enhance their accuracy over time. Care must be taken to assure comparability over time by using the same questions in repeated surveys.

Measures of Customer Satisfaction   As shown in Table 3.8, measures of customer satisfaction can be either objective or subjective and focus on satisfaction or dissatisfaction. Various measures are self-explanatory. The statistical techniques called for in building these measures are generally quite straightforward; they include developing profiles of the standing of the firm's products against competing products, developing frequency counts of various problems experienced by consumers, analyzing the content of letters received from customers, and so on. Also, some comparisons of actual consumer switches from the firm's brand to a competing brand can be made relative to a model of random switching. For example, one may compute a flow measure (F) such as

$$F_{ij} = \frac{N_{ij}N_{..}}{N_{i.}N_{.j}}$$

where N_{ij} is the number of consumers switching from brand i (the firm's) to another brand j (a competitor's) over two purchase occasions. $N_{i.}$ and $N_{.j}$ are the number of consumers who purchased brand i in the first occasion and brand j in the next occasion, and $N_{..}$ is the total number of consumers. If this measure exceeds 1.0, then the firm marketing brand i should examine its product carefully to understand the reasons for this high switching from i to j. This measure may indicate potential problems with brand i and perhaps some unmet needs among its buyers.

It is important to develop the F-measure using brand-switching data of a longer duration (for example, panel data for a year) to reflect "stable" market conditions. Measures based on shorter intervals are subject to the effects of sales promotions and other tactical marketing variables and will not be useful for identifying potential problems with a brand.

Consumer Satisfaction Surveys   Studies of customer satisfaction are becoming very popular in almost every area of marketing. The methodology of conducting such studies is quite similar to that of any marketing research survey. For details, see Hayes (1992).

We will illustrate this research with a study by the Bank Marketing Association.[17] The Bank Marketing Association's 1992 National Consumer Study on Service Quality in Banking surveyed by mail over 20,000 consumers across the United States. Questionnaires were mailed to a nationally representative sample of consumers throughout the nine census regions of the United States. Survey respondents included customers of commercial banks, thrifts, and credit unions.

Consumers' views were elicited on eight service areas: accessibility, appearance, clarity, competence, courtesy, features, reliability, and responsiveness. Each service area was measured using 6 to 11 questions: accessibility (10 questions), clarity (6 questions), competence (7 questions), courtesy (8 questions), features (10 questions), reliability (9 questions), and responsiveness (11 questions). Questions included the importance of various attributes and satisfaction ratings of the consumer's financial institution. The survey data were weighted to reflect the true distribution of the U.S. population. A number of statistical analyses were performed to search for differences by region, type of financial institution, and/or customer demography.

The analyses relevant to customer satisfaction included computation of five measures for each of the eight service areas: 1. service magnitude (importance weighted by the degree of satisfaction); 2. service gap (the distance between maximum satisfaction and expressed satisfaction weighted by importance); 3. maximum attainable satisfaction

TABLE 3.9   **Results of Customer Satisfaction Study for Two Banks***

	Customers of Bank A			Customers of Bank B		
Service Area	Service Magnitude	Service Gap	Maximum Attainable Satisfaction	Service Magnitude	Service Gap	Maximum Attainable Satisfaction
Accessibility	5.7	4.3	9.0	6.7	3.3	8.0
Appearance	8.2	1.8	9.0	7.5	2.5	9.5
Clarity	3.7	6.3	8.0	6.3	3.7	7.6
Competence	5.0	5.0	9.0	6.0	4.0	7.5
Courtesy	4.0	6.0	10.0	4.5	5.5	9.2
Features	7.2	2.8	7.0	6.0	4.0	8.5
Reliability	7.5	2.5	8.0	8.5	1.5	8.5
Responsiveness	4.5	5.5	7.0	5.5	4.5	9.0

* Data shown are average ratings.

(customer satisfaction standards); 4. improvement potential (room for improvement); and 5. satisfaction impact (effect on overall satisfaction).

These five measures can be computed for each financial institution and its particular competitors (or, more generally, national and regional institutions as a whole). Table 3.9 presents illustrative results for customers of Bank A and customers of its competitor, Bank B, for three measures on all eight service areas. It is clear from these data that customers of Bank B, are more satisfied than those of Bank A. These data reveal areas where Bank A can improve so as to satisfy its customers' unmet needs. Bank A is considered by its customers to be deficient in clarity (providing clear statements and the like), courtesy (friendly tellers), and responsiveness (reacting to suggestions). Bank A can meet its customers' unmet needs by designing programs such as training its personnel, redesigning its statements, and inviting suggestions on a routine basis.

Consumer Complaint Analysis   There has been extensive research on consumer complaint behavior. Andreasen and Best's 1977 study (sponsored by the Call for Action and the Center for Study of Responsive Law), based on a telephone survey of 2,419 households in the continental United States, contains interesting information on the incidence of nonprice problems and the actions consumers undertake to solve them. Nonprice problems are problems mentioned by consumers regarding the quality of product or service but not price; an example of a nonprice problem is "The product did not last long." In this study, consumers were asked to indicate their degree of satisfaction, any problems they experienced (by simple questioning and by

TABLE 3.10   **Satisfaction, Nonprice Problems, and Voiced Complaints**

Product Category	Number of Purchases	Percent Purchases Unsatisfactory	Percent Nonprice Problems	Percent Complaints Voiced
Infrequently Purchased Products				
Eyeglasses	834	12.9%	20.8%	63.7%
Television sets	495	9.9	20.8	72.9
Tires	1,041	6.3	12.0	46.3
Floor coverings	522	7.8	18.5	52.5
Lamps	340	2.6	8.5	55.6
Frequently Purchased Products				
Mail-order goods	537	19.6	31.1	74.5
Books, records	1,566	5.9	12.7	61.1
Clothing	2,135	13.8	28.1	40.4
Toys	1,049	16.0	30.7	31.6
Cosmetics, toiletries	1,939	3.9	9.2	19.7
Services				
Car repair	1,277	22.9	35.0	63.0
Film developing	1,250	9.8	18.5	43.4
Medical or dental care	1,910	8.1	14.9	38.3
Credit	1,191	8.0	10.6	58.0
Averages				
Infrequently purchased products	7,241	9.8	19.9	62.5
Frequently purchased products	13,550	11.2	20.1	44.6
Services	7,783	13.9	20.9	54.6
All Items	28,574	11.6	20.2	52.0

Source: Adapted from Andreasen, Alan R., and Arthur Best (1977), "Consumers Complain—Does Business Respond?," *Harvard Business Review* (July-August): 93–101.

probing), and whether they took any action to solve the problem. Table 3.10 presents an abstract of results for a set of selected products and services. While dissatisfaction with purchases ranged from under 3 percent (lamps) to 23 percent (car repair service), consumers experienced problems of a nonprice nature at a much higher level. For example, only 8.5 percent of lamp purchases resulted in nonprice problems, while consumers experienced nonprice problems in over a third of the car repair purchases. Furthermore, consumers tend to voice only about half of their complaints. This study reveals two important facts for a manufacturer to keep in mind: (1) Even when consumers are satisfied with their purchase, they can still experience problems with the products; and (2) frequency of complaints is not a full measure of the problems with a manufacturer's products. With respect to immediate handling of consumer complaints, a firm is well advised to set up a system to achieve maximum synchronization between the type of complaint and the type of response.[18]

Thus, while studies on consumer complaints can be a valuable source for uncovering consumer problems with a firm's products, they may not fully represent all of the dissatisfaction among customers. Nevertheless, such information can potentially lead to identification of consumers' unmet needs.

Warranty Claims   In 1993, based on five cases of warranty claims reports, the Chevrolet division of General Motors took preventive action by advising its dealers of a potential problem involving automatic transmissions offered on the full-size Caprice sedan and on its C, K, S, and T series of trucks. The company said that it was not recalling the vehicles, but only advising dealers what to look for in making transmission repairs to prevent future problems. This example is illustrative of the use of even limited data on warranty claims in the prevention of consumer problems.

Studies focusing on purchase encounters, rather than global assessments of consumer satisfaction, can be a valuable method of uncovering problems with products and services. Further, there could be trade-offs between achieving consumer satisfaction and meeting market share goals.[19]

CHANGES IN THE ENVIRONMENT

Consumer needs change as changes occur in the environment. These changes provide opportunities for new products. We will discuss various methods for understanding and forecasting environmental forces in Chapters 5 and 6. Here, however, we will describe a simple method known as environmental scanning to complete our discussion of various methods for identifying unmet needs.

Environmental Scanning

Environmental scanning involves the strategic marketer's keeping abreast of various environmental trends and identifying any consequent unmet consumer needs related to the firm's product line. For this purpose, the firm should have a system for compiling data on various demographic, social, political, technological, and other trends in the United States and around the world and should analyze their implications for its several businesses. Sources of information include newspapers such as *The Wall Street Journal* and *New York Times,* weeklies such as *Business Week* and *Newsweek,* television reports, analyses of congressional proceedings, and the like. It is worth pointing out that some organizations make it their business to analyze and report on major trends in the society at large; one of these is Megatrends, Inc., which published the book *Megatrends 2000: Ten New Directions for the 1990s.* There are also newsletters such as *John Naisbitt's Trend Letter* and *Kipplinger's Letter,* which report on trends on a regular basis.

METHODS FOR IDENTIFYING SOLUTIONS TO UNMET NEEDS

To be successful, a firm needs to adopt a systematic process for translating identified needs into solutions. The various steps of the new product development process are well suited for this translation—see Urban and Hauser (1993) for a comprehensive discussion on new product development. Usually, the steps involve internal research and development. In some cases, however, a firm may be able to license products or processes or join alliances with other firms for developing new products and processes. (A successful example of alliance is the development of the Power PC by a consortium of microcomputer firms including Apple and IBM.)

Customers play a significant role in finding a solution to their unmet needs. In fact, studying customers is one of the early phases of a new product development process. Table 3.11 illustrates five methods in which customers play a significant role in finding solutions to unmet needs. The methods are studies among lead users, brainstorming techniques, synectics, morphological connections, and kansei analysis. While brainstorming and synectics methods are in general extensions of focus group techniques, lead-user research is a composite of several research techniques. It not only includes focus groups, but involves conducting surveys among current users of the firm's and competitors' products to identify a group of users who are much more sophisticated than others. The solutions developed by this group of users (called the lead users) to solve problems encountered with the current products are then used to develop and test new products.

TABLE 3.11 **Selected Methods for Identifying Solutions to Unmet Needs**

Methods	Examples
Lead-user analysis	Seeking a solution to problems experienced by users of scientific instruments by studying lead users
Brainstorming techniques	Seeking solutions to the general problem of making a household's life easier and better (by redesigning existing appliances or by adding new appliances)
Synectics	Seeking a solution to the problem of car leaks with a group discussion method
Morphological forced connections	Identifying several combinations of existing attributes as a way to identify new solutions
Kansei analysis	Identifying product features to enhance a new product's appeal

The last two research methods, morphological connections and kansei analysis, are also useful in the identification of potential products that could meet certain unmet needs. Morphological connections is a technique of systematically enumerating all possible products that could be developed from various product attributes and locating potential new products. Kansei analysis method utilizes behavioral concepts to identify product features that could enhance a new product's appeal to potential customers.

Lead-User Analysis

Lead users, a term coined by Eric von Hippel, are current product users whose present strong needs will become general in the marketplace months or years in the future.[20] Since lead users are more knowledgeable about future conditions of product use than most others, they can serve as a laboratory for testing future (and currently unmet) needs.

Lead-user analysis consists of three essential steps: (1) identifying an important trend that affects the firm's current markets; (2) identifying lead users; and (3) conducting extensive surveys and focus groups to determine how the lead users are solving problems (or needs) not yet clear-cut in the marketplace. The lead-user data on usage in step 3 are also employed for projecting future market demand for the solutions developed by lead users, should they be commercialized by the firm. Further, lead users can become a sounding board for evaluating the viability of new product concepts under development. Open-ended data collected in lead-user surveys on need statements also contain information about possible solutions to the need under consideration.

Lead-user research employs focus groups among other marketing research techniques. Studies on lead users are more advantageous than conventional focus groups on customers in general because members of conventional focus groups are generally constrained in their discussions by current uses and current products. It requires a creative moderator to bring out future use situations in focus groups similar to those experienced by present lead users. Further, lead users' experience is needed for conducting marketing research in fast-moving product categories such as semiconductors.

Two examples reflect successful applications of lead-user research. The first was the development and marketing of an automated optical pattern generator by GCA/David Mann and Company in 1967 for the manufacture of semiconductor masks, which involved projecting on a photographic plate mounted on an X–Y table; such a design can be adjusted to obtain any desired mask pattern. Initial development of this product occurred at IBM (a lead user) in the mid-1960s and perhaps elsewhere. The second was Monsanto's introduction of butyl benzyl phthalate (BBP) in 1946 as a plasticizer for several rubber and polyvinyl chloride (PVC) products, which enabled processing of PVC at lower temperatures (110° to 130°C rather than 150° to 160°C) on standard rubber-processing machines. BBP was developed initially by Bayer in the 1930s as a plasticizer for cellulose nitrate.

TABLE 3.12 **Identification of Lead Users: An Illustration for the PC-CAD**

	Group 1	Group 2 (Lead Users)
Number of respondents	98	38
Characteristics		
Percent building own PC-CAD	1%	87%
Innovativeness (four-point scale; 1 = Low; 4 = High)	2.4	3.3
Satisfaction with commercial products (seven-point scale; 1 = Low; 7 = High)	5.3	4.1
First use of a CAD (year)	1980	1973

Source: Extracted from Table 1 in Urban, G. L., and E. von Hippel (1988), "Lead User Analysis for the Development of New Industrial Products," *Management Science* 34 (May).

The lead-user analysis is well illustrated by the study reported by Urban and von Hippel (1988) for the development of computer-aided design (CAD) systems used to design printed circuit boards (PC-CAD).[21] The methodology involved conducting a survey among current users of a product to identify a group of lead users and designing and testing new product concepts based on the solutions of lead users. The sample was clustered into two groups of 98 and 38 users of a PC-CAD system on the basis of characteristics measured in the survey. The characteristics included building own PC-CAD, innovativeness, satisfaction with commercial products, and year of first use of a CAD. Table 3.12 shows descriptions of these two clusters. Cluster 2 was labeled "lead users" because it tended to be set apart from the first cluster on a number of characteristics; this cluster is also highly consistent with prior assumptions/conjectures about lead users. For example, 87 percent of the lead-user group built its own PC-CAD system, compared with 1 percent of the first cluster. The lead-user group is more innovative and is less satisfied with commercially available systems. Also, it used a PC-CAD many years earlier than the other group. Using various techniques of group interactions and group discussions among a sample of the identified lead users, Urban and von Hippel developed a concept for a new PC-CAD system. The "lead-user" concept was tested against other product concepts in a questionnaire survey in order to test the validity of this method for identifying new product possibilities (or, stated differently, users' unmet needs). The lead-user concept received 78.6 percent first choices as against 9.8 percent for respondents' current PC-CAD; only 4.9 percent preferred the best system commercially available, and 6.5 percent preferred a specialized user system. This illustration shows that a firm (particularly one marketing technological products) can not only identify unmet customer needs, but can design products to satisfy such needs using the methodology of lead users.

Brainstorming

Brainstorming is a group discussion method specifically developed to generate creative solutions to problems. Developed by Osborn, the brainstorming technique[22] has become quite popular in various segments of society, including business. Under the general direction of an experienced moderator, groups in a brainstorming session devote their energies solely to creative thinking, each building upon the ideas expressed by the other members. We will describe how brainstorming may be used to identify unmet needs among consumers.

First, a few important rules for a successful brainstorming session: criticism is ruled out; freewheeling is welcomed; quantity of solutions is explicitly sought; and combination and improvement of previously expressed ideas is sought. A brainstorming session may be held among 10 people or so at a time and may last about 90 minutes. The moderator of a brainstorming session should explain the rules at the beginning of the session and should try to maintain an informal atmosphere during the session. Participants should be encouraged to express any and all ideas that occur to them because one can never really tell how one idea (good or bad) may lead to another that may be worthwhile. The subsequent idea may not occur to another without the stimulus of a prior idea. Osborn presents considerable evidence that application of these rules generates a large number of ideas for solving problems.

Assume that a brainstorming session is planned for identifying unmet needs in a household to make its daily life a little better. First, the moderator may write a background memo prior to the session to each recruited participant, laying out the purpose of the session and asking him or her to think about any ways in which his or her daily life can be improved by either new products or new services. The moderator may also suggest some examples of individual new products for various rooms in the house (electronic faucets that are turned on and off automatically; an electronic fence for the yard, etc.). The moderator should also come up with a set of ideas; some of these may be suggested during the session when the flow of new ideas has slowed. Once the session is over, the whole set of ideas may be grouped under various categories that may become the starting points for determining unmet needs in a household. This list may be refined with the information gathered in subsequent groups.

Synectics

Synectics, a word of Greek origin, means the joining together of different and apparently irrelevant elements. The group discussion theory of synectics applies to the integration of opinions and judgments of diverse individuals into a problem-stating or problem-solving context. The application to the problem-stating context is relevant to finding unmet needs for a firm. The method is systematic and consists of establishing a synectics group in three distinct phases:[23] (1) selecting firm personnel such as salespeople, managers, and so on, or a sample drawn from customers at large; (2) training the group of selected people in the theory and methods of synectics; and (3) reintegrating the group into the firm's environment.

The technique of synectics was developed using two basic and interrelated approaches to encourage creativity: (1) procedures, such as the use of analogy and other indirect means, that lead to imaginative speculation and (2) disciplined ways of behaving in the group so that speculation is not cut down, but is valued and encouraged. In this endeavor, an experienced group leader is critical.

Three stages are critical in a synectics session: (1) choice of a goal as understood by the group members, (2) generation of ways to view the unfamiliar (strange) problem in familiar ways and to view familiar solutions in a strange manner so as to come up with several "solutions," and (3) close examination of one solution to force development of a worthwhile group viewpoint. Fig. 3.5 shows the steps in a synectics session as a flowchart. The group leader asks several types of questions to make the strange familiar and the familiar strange. These questions fall into three categories: asking for specific examples, asking for personal analogies, and asking for a book title (a two-word phrase) to capture the idea. As an illustration, when the group is trying to find a solution for a thermos-bottle closure, a specific example for a closure could be a door or a mental block. While a door may be a familiar concept, the stranger example of a mental block may lead the group into a new line of speculation that may result in a novel solution. Personal analogies can aid in developing material to help look at the problem in a strange, new context. In response to a personal analogy question, group members may simply describe facts, may describe emotions in the first person, or may identify empathetically with the subject matter. For example, for the leader's question, "You are a tuning fork. How do you feel?," these three responses could result:

Description of facts: I am made of metal and have very precise dimensions. When struck, I vibrate with a fixed frequency.

First-person description of emotions: I feel sensitive, but only to very special things. You can hit me with a hammer and I do not care at all, but if you whistle just the right note, I feel I am going all to pieces.

Empathetic identification with the subject matter: My nerves are shot. Here I am, a high-grade piece of steel, and when the right tone sounds, I have a breakdown! But, I am intensely responsible and narrow-minded. Dead to anything until my frequency comes around and then WOW![24]

The third option, of empathetic identification, generally produces more useful material.

A complete transcript of a synectics session is given in the appendix to this chapter.

Various principles and cautions should be followed while conducting a synectics session. These include such obvious things as avoiding impatience, acknowledging the contribution of others to the session, and listening attentively, as well as more subtle things such as temporarily suspending all feelings of disbelief, avoiding negative evaluation of one's own thoughts and of others' suggestions, and not insisting on precision.[25]

A company with the same name as the technique, Synectics®, was founded in 1960 by George M. Prince and three of his colleagues (all members of Arthur D. Little). This company sought to explore innovative thinking and how it could be applied reliably to organizations. The firm focuses on research and new product development.

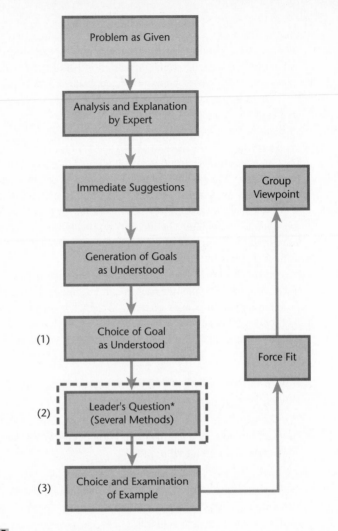

FIGURE 3.5 **A Synectics Flowchart**

*There are three types of leader's questions leading to three types of analogy: example, personal analogy, and book title. Source: Adapted from Prince, G. (1970), *The Practice of Creativity,* New York: Harper & Row. Copyright (c) 1970 by George M. Prince. Reprinted by permission of HarperCollins Publishers, Inc.

Synectics® employs three major ways to involve consumers and experts in creative thinking for new product development efforts: (1) consumer exploratory sessions; (2) customers and experts as creative resources; and (3) consumer development labs. As stated in its brochures, details for these three methods are as follows:[26]

Consumer Exploratory Sessions

Before undertaking any concept generation process, Synectics® works with groups of targeted consumers to uncover needs, tap insights, and catalyze their creative thinking in direct and indirect ways. The Synectics team applies many of the techniques the company is best known for, such as utilizing metaphors and analogies to uncover frustrations and wishes that direct questions do not surface effectively. We then discuss, learn from, and translate this information to maximize the usefulness of consumer and client team insights in subsequent idea generation and development work.

Customers and Experts as Creative Resources

Since the early seventies, Synectics has incorporated outside experts, customers, and other resources to think with clients in the invention and development phases of new product development projects. These "outsiders" provide depth and unexpected creativity to the client team. Synectics continues to utilize this very successful approach in Innovation and Development Sessions using our ability to draw on over 200 diverse "expert thinkers," based on project need or client request.

In addition, we frequently work with clients and relevant outside experts to creatively explore new directions, strategies, trends, or hypotheses our clients believe represent fertile opportunities. These short sessions usually precede new product idea generation, allowing us to prepare a synthesis of the discussion and learnings as stimulus for generating ideas.

Consumer Development Labs

For the last 10 years, Synectics has expanded its new product development services to involve consumers in the development and refinement of concepts created by our clients. Typical groups include internal and external customers or consumers, the trade, distributors, and other important constituents of the concepts generated. Using its proprietary approach, Synectics works with these groups to creatively transform beginning ideas into workable concepts by incorporating the consumer's needs and wishes. Typical projects have included refining new product or service concepts for quantitative or qualitative testing and creating innovative promotions, positionings, and names.

This firm has successfully implemented the synectics approach for the design of such products as Silkience by Gillette, which became one of the 10 top-selling brands of shampoo.[27] Synectics® Inc. has worked in most major industries and has served such organizations as NYNEX, AT&T, Black & Decker, Gillette, Kodak, and DuPont.

Morphological Forced Connections

Morphological forced connections[28] enables a strategic marketer to identify new product possibilities. This method involves identifying a list of salient attributes in the current alternatives used to solve a consumer need (or problem). For each attribute, a number of alternative possibilities are also identified. Given the premise that all new inventions are merely new ways of combining old bits and pieces, the method looks for new combinations not yet available as possible solutions.

An example, drawn from Koberg and Bagnell, shows how a new ballpoint pen can be developed[29] (see Fig. 3.6). First, one lists all of the attributes of a ballpoint pen. Below each attribute, one then lists all possible alternatives one can think of. Once these lists have been completed, many random runs are made through the alternatives, one from each column, in order to assemble the combinations into entirely new forms of the original ballpoint pen. The attributes and levels, along with a potential invention, are shown in Fig. 3.6.

Attributes and Alternatives

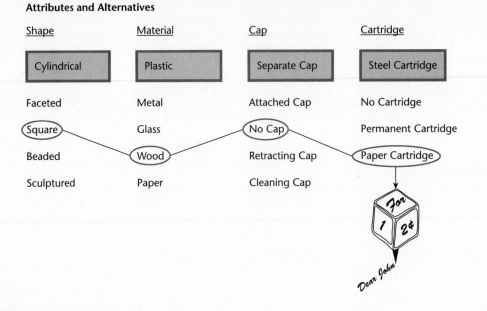

FIGURE 3.6   **Morphological Connection Method**

Source: Koberg, Don, and Jim Bagnell (1980), *The Universal Traveler*, Los Altos, CA: William Kaufmann.

The first row in Fig. 3.6, marked with rectangles, shows the combination of an existing ballpoint pen, whereas the combination resulting from those alternates marked with ovals is a potential ballpoint pen. This combination led to the invention of a square-shaped ballpoint pen made of wood, with a paper cartridge, and no cap. When this product was designed, it led to a cube-shaped pen, one corner of which writes, leaving six faces for ads, calendars, photos, and so on, as shown in the figure.

The recent introduction of AT&T international fax service is an example of a service design intended to solve business users' unmet need to send facsimile documents when either the receiver's international fax number or the telephone line is busy or not operational. In this situation, the sender of the fax can transmit his or her facsimile document to the number 1-800-THRUFAX, which transmits the fax to the receiver later, when the lines are free. Morphological connections can be used to identify the features of such service innovations.

Kansei Analysis

Given the concern that verbal reports are not always accurate predictors of purchase behavior, methods have been developed that probe into people's feelings. One such method is *kansei analysis*—a technique developed in Japan. *Kansei* ("sensitivity" in Japanese) is a successor to a popular phrase, *human engineering*. Mazda Chairman Kenichi Yamamoto gave speeches in 1986 on the need to understand the rapport between the driver and the car and the need to appeal to his or her senses, or kansei. Two main branches of this method are in vogue—methods for evaluating abstract feelings about a product and methods for analyzing facial muscle movements when people look at or discuss various products.

In the first branch of kansei analysis, the researcher develops a list of abstract constructs of feelings (elegance, sportiness, comfort, feel, noise, shape, color, etc.) and identifies one or two of relevance to the product category under study. For ascertaining feelings, a sample of customers is presented a variety of alternatives in the product category (physical items or pictures or models of, for example, coffee cups or sports cars) and asked to compare them with respect to an abstract construct (say, elegance for coffee cups, sportiness for cars). The responses (recorded on 10-point scales) are analyzed to determine the features of the product that most contribute to the construct. (In this sense, the method is quite similar to a regression analysis of judgment data as in conjoint analysis.)

In the second branch, sensors are put on customers' faces to record movements of facial muscles as they test prototypes of products. The data are collected through a telemeter system. Customers speak into a microphone to give their spontaneous reactions while using the product. In this approach, the manufacturer can determine which aspects of the product are causing difficulty for the customer. Mazda used this approach to identify which features of gear shifts were cumbersome for drivers. The premise is that facial muscle data give more accurate readings on subtle nuances than do verbal reports.

Mazda recently adopted these approaches to determine physical and emotional responses to noise, shape, and color in its automobiles, according to Shuji Mata, senior research engineer at its Yokohama Research Center.[30] The procedures consisted of testing its image creative system and vehicle sound synthesizer. For the image creative system, 20 people were shown slides of places, objects, colors, and shapes and asked to provide written responses to each image. Cameras were also used to follow eye movements stimulated by each image. The vehicle sound synthesizer, on the other hand, was used to determine the "ideal blend" of engine noise and miscellaneous sounds for different car models; a sample of mixes of engine noises and other sounds was tested.

In a similar vein, Nissan Motor Company employs the "kansei factor" in developing new technologies. It uses kansei methods to determine the look and feel of the exterior or interior of a car. Its approach uses more personal judgment than Mazda's.

Kansei approaches are also useful in developing strategies for customer satisfaction, according to Jack Matson.[31] In this context, kansei means being "in congruence with nature and natural harmony." Given that hassles at the time of a sales transaction can be a serious turnoff for a customer, firms can satisfy customers by understanding their feelings using the nonverbal methods.

For example, the policy of Radio Shack to collect personal data such as the name and address of a customer purchasing even a small item such as a phone jack can be a turnoff and decrease repeat business. Understanding such reactions can be valuable in developing appropriate customer-satisfaction strategies.

ROLE OF CREATIVITY

While certain streamlined research methods exist for uncovering consumers' unmet needs, the foregoing discussion makes it clear that the process for identifying unmet needs is undoubtedly a creative one. It is, therefore, essential for a firm to foster an environment that encourages creativity among employees. Several volumes have been written on different aspects of creativity of the human mind. We will offer a brief account of a few.

Using their experience in a graduate course at Stanford, Ray and Myers (1986) suggest the following ideas to encourage creativity in business: (1) Have faith in your creativity by letting things follow their own course and surrendering to your own creativity even after initial failure; (2) make an all-out attack on barriers to your creativity by destroying judgment of things or people; (3) pay attention by using all sensory skills—seeing, looking, and listening, and (4) ask questions even if they seem dumb. They further identify several ways of developing inspiration and implementing creative ideas. These include methods for reducing stress and methods for being in the world at large but not belonging to it and developing a sense of balance and purpose in life.[32]

In a similar vein, Ackoff presents a number of illustrations and a potentially rational approach to problem solving in management. His approach is derived from a paradigm: Given a set of objectives the decision maker identifies and determines the relationship between outcomes and controllable and uncontrollable variables. But he suggests some useful ways of developing insights from any given situation. The following are some of the principles or morals he offers: Irrationality is usually in the mind of the observer, not in the mind of the actor; that which is lost may not be found where the loss is found; it is often harder to solve a problem created by others than it is for them to solve the problem created by the solution; and the way variables act may not be nearly as important as how they interact.[33] These ideas are generally useful in guiding one's own thinking about things in general and in spotting needs unmet by existing products. They are useful while employing group discussion techniques described earlier in the chapter.

The business press contains several articles describing ways in which firms devote time and money to coming up with breakthrough ideas.[34] These methods are the brainstorming techniques described earlier or some variations of them. A recent technique is the use of metaphors, called the ZMET.[35] This technique offers a systematic way to elicit nonverbal communication from customers and to understand their opinions. It uses personal interviews among a sample of product customers to elicit the metaphors, constructs, and mental models that drive customers' thinking and actions. Customers are asked to bring pictures of a topic of the study, which then form the basis of the interview. The customer is asked to sort the pictures in order to develop connections between them to tell a story. To facilitate this process, the customer is asked to compare three pictures at a time and is asked to indicate which two are similar to each other but different from the third and why. The metaphors used by customers are elicited during a series of interviews, as is a mental map. Digital imaging techniques are also used in the process of summarizing images of consumers' thinking.

For example, in a study of assessing financial success, a participant whose assignment was to take/collect pictures of "financial success" brought 23 pictures; she further sorted them into eight groups including social things or situations (2 pictures), living spaces (6 pictures), personal grooming and health (6 pictures), family (1 picture), and others before developing connections among them. The mental map for financial success for this participant included such constructs as achievement, confidence, responsibility, excitement, and indulgence. Further, the composite picture developed using digital techniques was that of a decadent dinner with friends in a fancy dining room, with music and lots of attention from a waiter. A consensus map developed from mental maps of a sample of participants will reveal the ingredients of financial success expressed by the participants. Proprietary data indicated that ZMET generates more ideas than focus groups and that the consensus map includes constructs generated by focus groups. Thus, ZMET enables a firm to gain more insights. The technique, although in its early phases of development, has been used by a few companies in helping make a variety of marketing decisions. It can potentially be employed for identifying unmet customer needs.

SUMMARY

Because growth of a firm's revenues will naturally involve new products, identifying unmet consumer needs is an essential step in the market research process. In this chapter, we have classified the sources of unmet needs into two groups: problems with existing offerings in the marketplace and changes in the environment. We have described a wide range of methods for identifying problems with existing products; these included focus groups and mystery shopper surveys as well as more formal methods such as perceptual mapping, benefit structure analysis, and problem research. Further, analysis of objective and subjective data on customer satisfaction can offer clues to the sources of customer dissatisfaction, which can also lead to an identification of unmet needs. Problems arising out of changes in the environment can be ascertained by the general method of environmental scanning. Methods for understanding various environmental factors and forecasting trends in the environment are extensively covered in Chapters 5 and 6.

We have also discussed methods for identifying solutions to unmet needs. These included lead-user research, brainstorming techniques, and synectics. The group discussion techniques, brainstorming and synectics (which may be thought of as extensive modifications of focus groups), are also productive ways to generate ideas; they can therefore be used to identify potential unmet needs. We have also described two miscellaneous methods, morphological connections and kansei analysis, useful in identifying new product possibilities.

We concluded this chapter with a brief discussion of methods for increasing creativity among consumers or managers. We now turn to a discussion of methods for identifying business competition.

Review Questions

1. Consider the following new products introduced over the last 30 years in the marketplace. For each product, identify the "unmet consumer need" that may have led to its development. Briefly discuss your answer.

Portable tape/CD player

Laptop computer

Videocassette recorder

Air bag for an automobile

Handheld calculator

Post-It Brand note pad

2. Discuss the role of determining unmet customer needs in a product category as a first step in developing new products and new markets for a company. (Consider such product categories as soft drinks, luxury automobiles, and athletic shoes.)

3. Recently, a new product—caffeinated and clear bottled water—was introduced in the marketplace. Speculate what unmet customer needs this product is intended to solve.

4. Discuss two different marketing situations in which the mystery shopper technique is suitable for identifying unmet needs.

5. Compare and contrast the techniques of focus groups, brainstorming, and synectics. Identify the most appropriate uses of these techniques as ways of developing new products for growth.

6. Assume that you are in charge of designing new word-processing software. Show how the method of morphological connections can be used for this purpose.

7. Conduct five in-depth interviews among users of shampoo to uncover any problems experienced. Based on this information, develop three product development ideas for a shampoo maker.

8. What is kansei analysis? Discuss its role in the design of a keyboard for a personal computer.

9. Assume that you are in charge of a project aimed at assessing the future prospects for laser printers. As you know, laser printers are currently connected to personal computers, and documents created on a personal computer are printed onto paper using the printers. The printed documents are delivered/transmitted to other people via mail or fax or similar means. But several trends in the environment point to the emergence of a paperless office in the near future. These trends include the emergence of the Internet, interactive TV, and e-mail as major communication options. Thus there may be a shift in the major usage of personal computers from document creation to communication. Against this background, discuss how you might design a research program to uncover the emerging "printing" needs of the future.

10. Discuss how a customer satisfaction study can help uncover unmet needs of customers. Illustrate your answer with the example of designing services offered by a luxury hotel.

Notes

1. See Ansoff, Igor (1965), *Corporate Strategy,* New York: McGraw-Hill.

2. Schwartz, Judith D. (1993), "Ryder Redraws the Self-Move Map with Service, Convenience," *Brandweek* (January), 34–35.

3. Oliver, Suzanne (1994), "Take Two Aspirin; The Computer Will Call in the Morning," *Forbes,* March 14, 110–111.

4. *New York Times* (1993), "Opening a Van Door the Hands-Free Way," March 24, D2.

5. Wald, Matthew L. (1993), "Going Beyond Batteries to Power Electric Cars," *New York Times,* March 3, D2.

6. Cuff, Daniel F. (1993), "For the Forgetful Motorists," *New York Times,* February 14.

7. Halpert, Julie Edelson (1993), "Who Will Fix Tomorrow's Cars?" *New York Times,* November 7, F4.

8. Hamilton, Joan and James E. Ellis (1992), "A Storm is Breaking Down the Farm," *Business Week,* December 14, 98–101.

9. *The Wall Street Journal* (1993), Western edition, "Hikers, Phone Home," July 1, 1.

10. Trachtenberg, Jeffrey A. (1987), "Listening, the Old-fashioned Way," *Forbes,* October 5, 202.

11. See *Marketing News* (1979), "Key Role of Research in Agree's Success is Told," January 12, 14.

12. See Gordon, Wendy, and Roy Langmaid (1988), *Qualitative Market Research: A Practitioner's and Buyer's Guide,* Aldershot, UK or Brookfield, VT: Gower Publishing Company, Chapter 7.

13. This illustration is drawn from Assael, Henry (1975), "Evaluating New Product Concepts and Developing Early Predictions of Trial" (May): 13–18. See also Lautman, Martin R. (1993), "The ABCs of Positioning," *Marketing Research* 5, No. 1 (Winter): 12–18 for a method for screening potential positionings of a brand in the perceptual space.

14. See Assael, Henry (1981), *Consumer Behavior and Marketing Action,* 1st ed., Belmont, CA: Wadsworth, 464.

15. See Myers, James H. (1970), "Benefit Structure Analysis: A New Tool for Product Planning," *Journal of Marketing* (October), 23–32.

16. Tauber, Edward M. (1975), "Discovering New Product Opportunities with Problem Inventory Analysis," *Journal of Marketing* 39 (July): 67–70.

17. *Bank Marketing* (1992), "BMA National Service Quality Study Zeroes in on News Bankers Can Use" (March), 37–38.

18. See Resnik, Alan J., and Robert R. Harmon (1993), "Consumer Complaints and Managerial Response: A Holistic Approach," *Journal of Marketing* 47 (Winter): 86–97 for an exploratory study that examined the perceptions of managers and consumers regarding complaint letters. Also see Wilkie, William L. (1986), *Consumer Behavior,* New York: John Wiley and Sons, 558–583, for a comprehensive discussion of consumer satisfaction/dissatisfaction research.

19. See Anderson, Eugene W., Claes Fornell, and Donald R. Lehmann (1993), "Economic Consequences of Providing Quality and Customer Satisfaction," Working Paper, Cambridge, MA: Marketing Science Institute, Report Number 93–112, August.

20. See von Hippel, Eric (1986), "Lead Users: A Source of Novel Product Concepts," *Management Science* 32 (July): 791–805. See also von Hippel, Eric (1988), *The Sources of Innovation,* New York and Oxford: Oxford University Press.

21. See Urban, G. L., and E. von Hippel (1988), "Lead-User Analysis for the Development of New Industrial Products," *Management Science* 34 (May): 569–582.

22. Osborn, Alex F. (1957), *Applied Imagination: Principles, Procedures of Creative Thinking,* rev. ed., New York: Charles Scribner's Sons.

23. Gordon, William J. R. (1961), *Synectics: The Development of Creative Capacity,* New York: Harper & Brothers.

24. See Prince, G. (1970), *The Practice of Creativity,* Harper and Row.

25. For more discussion, see Ibid.; and Procter, R. A. (1989), "The Use of Metaphors to Aid the Process of Creative Problem Solving," *Personnel Review* 18 (4), 33–42.

26. The following information is from several brochures from Synectics® Inc., Cambridge, MA 02138. We thank Ms. Pamela W. Moore of Synectics® for sharing these materials.

27. Olivero, Magalay (1990), "Get Crazy! How to Get a Breakthrough Idea," *Working Woman* 15 (September): 144–147, 222.

28. See Adams, James L. (1986), *Conceptual Blockbusting: A Guide to Better Ideas,* Reading, MA: Addison-Wesley, 109–110.

29. Koberg, Don, and Jim Bagnell (1980), *The Universal Traveler,* Los Altos, CA: William Kaufmann.

30. Maskery, Mary Ann (1994), "Mazda Looks for Numbers to Explain Kansei Concept," *Automotive News* (January). Reprinted with permission from *Automotive News,* 5/5/97, Copyright Crain Comm, Inc. All rights reserved.

31. Brown, Thomas L. (1993), "A Job for Management: Eliminate the Hassles," *Industry Week,* September 20, 23. Reprinted with permission from *Industry Week,* (September 20, 1993). Copyright Penton Publishing, Inc., Cleveland, Ohio.

32. See Ray, Michael, and Rochelle Myers (1986), *Creativity in Business,* New York: Doubleday & Company.

33. See Ackoff, Russell L. (1978), *The Art of Problem Solving,* New York: John Wiley & Sons.

34. See, for example, Olivero, "Get Crazy! How to Have a Breakthrough Idea"; Nellozuech (1992), "Identifying and Ranking Opportunities for Machine Vision in a Facility," *Industrial Engineering* (October); McLaughlin, Mark (1987), "It Is OK to Say Oops: Consultants Encourage Creativity by Easing Fear of Making

Mistakes," *New England Business,* February 2: 50, 53.

35. Zaltman, Gerald, and Robin A. Higie (1993), "Seeing the Voice of the Customer: The Zaltman Metaphor Elicitation Technique," Working Paper, Report Number 93-114, Cambridge, MA: Marketing Science Institute.

Bibliography

Ackoff, Russell L. (1978), *The Art of Problem Solving Accompanied by Ackoff's Fables,* New York: John Wiley & Sons.

Adams, James L. (1986), *Conceptual Blockbusting: A Guide to Better Ideas,* 3rd ed., Reading, MA: Addison-Wesley.

Andreasen, Alan R. (1977), "A Taxonomy of Consumer Satisfaction/Dissatisfaction Measures," *Journal of Consumer Affairs* 11: 11–24.

Andreasen, Alan R., and Arthur Best (1977), "Consumers Complain—Does Business Respond?," *Harvard Business Review* (July-August): 93–101.

Andriole, Stephen J. (1983), *Handbook of Problem Solving: An Analytical Methodology,* New York: Petrocelli Books.

Bearden, William O., and Jesse E. Teel (1983), "Selected Determinants of Consumer Satisfaction and Complaint Reports," *Journal of Marketing Research* 20: 21–28.

Elizur, D. (1970), *Adapting to Innovation: A Facet Analysis of the Case of the Computer,* Jerusalem: Jerusalem Academic Press.

Folkes, Valerie S. (1984), "Consumer Reactions to Product Failure: An Attributional Analysis," *Journal of Consumer Research* 10: 398–409.

Gordon, William J. (1961), *Synectics: The Development of Creative Capacity,* New York: Harper & Row.

Hayes, Bob E. (1992), *Measuring Customer Satisfaction,* Milwaukee: ASQC Quality Press.

Levenstein, Aaron (1965), *Use Your Head: The New Science of Personal Problem-Solving,* New York: Macmillan.

Makridakis, Spyros G. (1990), *Forecasting, Planning, and Strategy for the 21st Century,* New York: Free Press.

Martino, Joseph P. (1993), *Technological Forecasting for Decision Making,* 3rd ed., New York: McGraw-Hill.

Mason, Joseph G. (1960), *How to Be a More Creative Executive,* New York: McGraw-Hill.

Morgan, Gareth (1988), *Riding the Waves of Change: Developing Managerial Competencies in a Turbulent World,* San Francisco: Jossey-Bass.

— (1993), *Imagination: The Art of Creative Management,* Newberry Park, CA: Sage Publications.

Myers, James H. (1976), "Benefit Structure Analysis: A New Tool for Product Planning," *Journal of Marketing* 40 (October): 23–32.

Norris, E. E. (1975), "Seeking Out the Consumers' Problems," *Advertising Age,* March 17, 43–44.

Oliver, Richard L. (1980), "A Cognitive Model of the Antecedents and Consequences of Satisfaction Decisions," *Journal of Marketing Research* 17: 460–469.

Osborne, Alex F. (1952), *Your Creative Power: How to Use Imagination,* New York: Scribners.

— (1957), *Applied Imagination: Principles and Procedures of Creative Thinking,* New York: Scribners.

— (1963), *Applied Imagination,* 3rd ed. New York: Scribners.

Parasuraman, A., Valerie A. Zeithaml, and Leonard L. Berry (1986), "SERVQUAL: A Multiple Item Scale for Measuring Customer Perceptions of Service Quality," *Journal of Retailing* 64: 12–40.

Prince, George M. (1970), *The Practice of Creativity: A Manual for Dynamic Group Problem Solving,* New York: Harper & Row.

Ray, Michael, and Rochelle Myers (1986), *Creativity in Business,* New York: Doubleday.

Resnick, Allan J., and Robert R. Harmon (1983), "Consumer Complaints and Managerial Response: A Holistic Approach," *Journal of Marketing* 47: 86–97.

Russ, Sandra W. (1993), *Affect and Creativity: The Role of Affect and Play in the Creative Process,* Hillsdale, NJ: Lawrence Erlbaum Associates.

Stein, Morris I. (1974), *Stimulating Creativity, Volume 1: Individual Procedures,* New York: Academic Press.

— (1975), *Stimulating Creativity, Volume 2: Group Procedures,* New York: Academic Press.

Tauber, Edward M. (1972), "HIT: Heuristic Ideation Technique—A Systematic Procedure for New Product Search," *Journal of Marketing* 36: 58–73.

— (1975), "Discovering New Product Opportunities with Problem Inventory," *Journal of Marketing* 39: 67–70.

Taylor, Irving A., and J. W. Getzels (eds.) (1975), *Perspectives in Creativity,* Chicago: Aldine Publishing Company.

Urban, Glen L., and John R. Hauser (1993), *Design and Marketing of New Products,* 2nd ed., Englewood Cliffs, NJ: Prentice-Hall.

Urban, Glen L., and Eric von Hippel (1988), "Lead User Analyses for the Development of New Industrial Products," *Management Science* 34: 569–582.

von Hippel, Eric (1978a), "Successful Industrial Products from Customer Ideas," *Journal of Marketing* 42: 39–49.

— (1978b), "Users as Innovators," *Technology Review* (January): 31–39.

— (1982), "Get New Products from Customers," *Harvard Business Review* 60 (March-April): 117–122.

— (1986), "Lead Users: A Source of Novel Product Concepts," *Management Science* 32: 791–805.

— (1988), *The Sources of Innovation,* New York: Oxford University Press.

Wheelwright, Steven C., and W. Earl Sasser, Jr. (1989), "The New Product Development Map," *Harvard Business Review* (May-June): 112–125.

Zangwill, Willard I. (1993), *Lightning Strategies for Innovation: How the World's Best Firms Create New Products,* New York: Lexington Books.

Appendix

Synectics Session Tackling the Problem of Car Leaks

Problem as Given: To quickly and inexpensively detect minute leaks in car wheels during final stages of production.

Analysis: A manufacturer of the steel car wheel upon which tubeless tires fit had trouble with undetected "leakers." Some were shipped with minute, undetected holes and used by new car manufacturers. Finished cars parked in a holding area are only inches apart. When a "leaker" let the tire go flat, the tilting car damaged the finish on itself and the car next to it. The wheel manufacturer started 100 percent inspection, but it was further necessary to power-spray the weld area of the wheels with dye and inspect with black light. The "leakers" were detected, but several cents' cost was added.

Goals as Understood:

1. How can we make leakers identify themselves?
2. How can we prevent leakers in the first place?
3. How can we make leakers cure themselves?

Preventing leakers is clearly the most desirable solution of all and was not neglected, but the group leader was influenced by the need for immediate action.

LEADER Let's take number 3 but put it aside for now and don't think of the problem. In the world of psychology, think of an example of healing itself.

RON Forgetting.

LEADER Yes . . . would you say a little more?

RON I think forgetting a painful experience may be a healing of yourself.

LEADER If I understand, rather than continually being upset over something you forget it?

RON That's it.

HORACE *(the expert)* A prejudice.

LEADER A prejudice, yes. . . .

HORACE I think a prejudice is most often formed to allow a person to tolerate . . . or perhaps cope with a feeling, anxiety, or insecurity. I am not sure of that.

LEADER That doesn't matter. Are you saying that I have a feeling of discomfort with a black person—so to heal that unease I form a prejudice?

HORACE That's close to my meaning but you may have the anxiety and the prejudice without ever really being with a black person.

LEADER I see. Good. Let's take this prejudice idea. Take twenty seconds and I want you to turn yourself into a prejudice. Then tell me how it feels to be a prejudice. *(Pause.)* Yes, Dick? *(Dick has given a signal he is ready.)*

DICK I feel invincible and a little contempt for the person I am in. He never questioned my credentials, and in his hierarchy of prejudices I am just as important as his don't-jump-out-of-the-window prejudice. I've got it made.

LEADER Anyone have other feelings?

AL I feel very grateful to my host because if he didn't nourish me and keep me, where would I be? I try to serve him and come to his mind often to keep that anxiety away.

RON I am ambitious, and once I am established I keep trying to grow. No matter what my owner does that bothers him I try to take credit. He squashes his finger in the car door and I say, "See, that black man on the way home put a hex on you."

HORACE I feel maligned by the way you guys talk—a person might think there were no good prejudices like me. I am for fair play and I have a constant fight for attention. I am put on red alert every time a hasty impulse comes along.

LEADER OK, let's take this material on prejudice and make some book titles—capture the essence but include a paradox.

HORACE *Impulsive Care.*

RON *Anxious Contempt.*

HORACE *Insecure Invincibility.*

AL *Malignant Gratefulness.*

LEADER Good. Let's go to the world of modern tribal customs—can you give me an example of anxious contempt?

DICK Speeding—we customarily break the speed laws and so we are showing contempt but there is nearly always, at least in me, a little anxiety about it.

LEADER Yes, I don't think anything of going 45 in a 25-mile-per-hour zone, but if I see a cop—even if he is looking the other way—I feel it strongly, so I am anxious all the time I am being contemptuous. Is that what you mean?

DICK Yes.

AL Cigarette smoking.

LEADER Yes, go ahead.

AL I know it is bad, but I keep right on.

LEADER Do you mean that your actions show contempt, but in your mind you're anxious?

AL Yes. It is stupid. We smoke because we are anxious, and it makes us anxious in another way when we smoke.

LEADER OK, let's examine speeding. What does this speeding idea bring to mind?

RON There is an exhilaration about speeding that is very sensual. It is, in a way, almost as exciting as sex.

DICK Yes, even when you are not in control of it, like at take-off when they open up those engines.

HORACE I wonder if that is a male thing or do girls feel the same way?

LEADER What do you think, Horace?

HORACE It's probably in different degrees. I'm thinking of the difference in recklessness of girl drivers and boy drivers.

AL I find that difference simply astonishing. Even young kids—say ten years old—girls have a different perception of consequences. . . . They are more in the real world.

HORACE Right. But I think they turn suddenly unrealistic and into romantics at twenty-five.

DICK I don't know about that. I believe women tend to be realistic most of the time.

LEADER Probably both can be true, but let's use this: Let's go back to our problem: How can we make leakers cure themselves? How can we use this speeding idea—any of them—to help us?

AL I think of a cop speeding to the scene of . . . of a leak?

LEADER Yes, and then how can we—

RON He pulls his gun and fills the hole with lead.

DICK The picture that came to my mind was he plugs it with his thumb like the little Dutch boy and the dike.

LEADER We would fill his gun with thumbs . . . but what is this saying?

HORACE I like the cop idea because we can do that—our dye speeds to the scene of the crime, but then it just lies there.

RON You know, on the side where you look for leaks with black light?

HORACE Yes.

RON Could you shoot lead or something wherever you see dye coming through?

HORACE You know, we have never thought of making a repair at that point. We were so obsessed with detecting we haven't thought of that. That is a good thought, but lead bothers me.

LEADER What concerns you, Horace?

HORACE These holes are really small—like pores, really. Black light shows you a stain, but that only tells the general area. We would have to have a very thin dye-like lead that would stay molten until we knew it had filled the pore.

AL Horace, could you use two different dyes—boy-girl type dyes? That turn thick?

HORACE Yes, I like two components . . . like an epoxy. A slow-curing one. . . . But we have to make it really penetrate somehow.

DICK I thought Al meant boy on one side, girl on the other.

HORACE That is it! A two-component epoxy, both thin as dye. Spray one on the outside, the other on the inside . . . they meet and react in the hole.

Source: Prince, G. (1970), *The Practice of Creativity,* New York: Harper & Row Publishers, 147–150. Copyright (c) 1970 by George M. Prince. Reprinted by permission of HarperCollins Publishers, Inc.

Identifying Competitors

Whom Will We Compete Against?

INTRODUCTION

Competitive analysis has become more than just a planning activity these days. It's a job description as well. Many firms have employees whose formal responsibility is to analyze competitors. These include Citicorp, Mitsubishi, Adolph Coors Co., Motorola, McDonnell Douglas, and Marriott. Employees in these firms have such job titles as "manager for competitive intelligence."

Suppose now that you are a consultant at Great Spring Waters of America, Inc. You have been charged with the apparently simple exercise of profiling the competition for its Poland Spring brand. Your first decision relates to which brands and firms you should collect information on. You likely begin with Great Spring Waters's other brands, Deer Park and Great Bear. Not only are these marketed by the same company as Poland Spring, they come from springs in the same state: Maine. You might also want to profile Vermont Pure Spring Water. It comes from a nearby state. Other American brands such as Spa are probably relevant too. It might be the case, though, that stores will not carry *all* these brands. A casual trip to the local grocery store would reveal that while in some categories, the store will carry virtually all the major brands, in others, it will carry only a few selected brands. If brands are not carried by the same stores, then, should one consider them all competitors? Perhaps not.

Suppose further that non-American brands like Naya from Canada and Evian from France were available in the same outlets as Poland Spring. Are these competitors? Probably. After all, these products are also brands of bottled water. People who prefer one are probably not likely to turn down another if offered it at a party. What about Perrier? It is essentially water; it is clear; but it is carbonated. Furthermore, it comes flavored—fruit flavored no less! How can a carbonated, fruit-flavored beverage compete with bottled waters? Nevertheless, a bottled water drinker who is really thirsty is not likely to refuse a lemon-flavored Perrier when offered. He or she might even buy it at a restaurant if that is the closest thing to bottled water that is available.

What about Seven-Up or Sprite? They are also clear, carbonated, and fruit flavored. If Perrier is a competitor of Poland Spring, why not Seven-Up or Sprite? Some might argue that you should not include them because they are sold on different shelves than is Poland Spring. Consumers are not likely to be holding Poland

Spring and Sprite in their hands, trying to decide between them. To others, a more compelling reason not to include Seven-Up and Sprite may be that they have calories. If calories are so important, there's Diet Seven-Up and Diet Sprite. If these are included, then why not Diet Coke and Diet Pepsi or Coke and Pepsi? If thirsty enough, most people would be likely to drink any one of them. Not to mention beer. Where do you stop? The seemingly simple exercise can become a nightmare. Fig. 4.1 represents the dilemma. At what branch of the tree do you make the cut?

IMPLICATIONS OF THE POLAND SPRING DILEMMA

Three principles emerge from the previous discussion. First, *competition is a matter of degree.* It is not realistic to say that products either are or aren't competitors. A more accurate picture emerges if you allow Evian to be a more serious competitor to Poland Spring than Perrier than if you are forced to make a yes or no decision on each. With this in mind, we still characterize a *competitive set* as those brands or products that are the most serious competitors of a given brand or product. We must never lose sight, though, that this concept, while often useful to managers because of its simplicity, is an approximation of what is really a continuum.

Second, *competition is governed by consumer behavior.* If a consumer views Poland Spring, Perrier, and Caffeine-Free Diet Pepsi all as capable of quenching her thirst without providing calories or caffeine and that is all she cares about, these brands all compete with each other *for that customer!* One implication of the dependence of competition on consumer behavior is that competitors can often be found outside the primary product category. This is extremely important for marketing strategy. Consider the story of the demise of the railroad industry as chronicled by Ted Levitt.[1] Thirty-five years ago the major railroads fell upon hard times because they "assumed themselves to be in the railroad business rather than in the transportation business."[2] They never considered the airlines as potential competitors and consequently never saw the coming threat. People did not need to take the train to get from New York to Washington or Paris to London. They could fly.

Third, *marketing intermediaries can influence the determinants of competitive sets.* This point is a direct consequence of the dependence of competitive sets on consumer behavior. Marketing intermediaries (stores, salespeople, distributors) act as gatekeepers. Without their cooperation, consumers will never have a particular brand available to them. Without availability, there can be no consumer behavior. The most direct competitors a brand has today will be those that can be found by customers in the same place. Thus, a manufacturer's direct customers (the retailers) partially determine which brands will be competitors of the manufacturer. Similarly, a retailer's suppliers (manufacturers) partially determine which stores will be competitors. Stores that comprise a retailer's competitive set will be those that carry the most similar product assortments (that is, purchase from the same manufacturers).

Michael Porter proposed a model that generalizes this notion of the impact of suppliers and customers on competitive sets. He argued that the nature and degree of competition in an industry depends on five forces: the threat of new entrants, the bar-

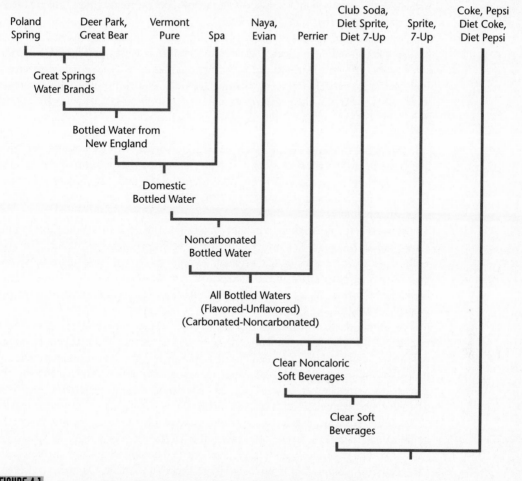

FIGURE 4.1 **Competitive Structure for Poland Springs Example**

gaining power of customers, the bargaining power of suppliers, the threat of substitute products, and the competition among current participants.[3] These are diagrammed in Fig. 1.3. Each of these forces is a source of potential conflict with the firm of interest. Porter's view is that the stronger these forces are relative to the firm of interest, the lower the firm's potential economic returns will be. Thus, each force is a competitor in a very real sense.

For example, Procter & Gamble has had a long history of conflict with its immediate customers (retailers) that has negatively impacted its economic performance. In 1919, in the early days of the firm, William Cooper Procter decided to eliminate wholesalers and distribute directly to retailers to cut the number of steps between factory and kitchen cabinets so that he could hold costs down. P&G also dictated that the smallest shipment it would issue was five cases. Small retailers who used to be able to buy single cases of P&G products from wholesalers were no longer able to. They were so angry that they canceled orders.

More recently, Wal-Mart, P&G's largest customer at $1.5 billion retail per year, has become dissatisfied because Procter & Gamble is trying to shift its emphasis away from efficient distribution to using its marketing and advertising expertise. Wal-Mart's success depends on continual product availability and high inventory turnover. Wal-Mart is interested in shortening the path from factory to shelf. It wants to be sure that the customer can always find P&G products in its stores. Procter & Gamble is more concerned with building its own brand names. Wal-Mart could not care less about the power of P&G's brand names. In fact, Wal-Mart would probably like these brands to be weaker so that Wal-Mart could maintain the upper hand in negotiations between the two firms. Wal-Mart's size implicitly pressures P&G to accede to its demands. Interests conflict. P&G's economic welfare declines. Competition emerges.[4]

However, the most direct competition a product faces comes from others in the same product category. The most likely firm to be competing against Coca-Cola ten years from now is PepsiCo. The products may not be as we know them today and there might be other firms in the market, but few would deny that the most likely brand Coke will be trying to stare down in its battle for soft-drink supremacy ten years from now will be Pepsi.

Nevertheless, firms are often faced with competition from products outside their category. Understanding competition in a broader sense allows managers to be not only more keenly aware of potential threats, but more likely to spot opportunities as well. The National Basketball Association recognized that if fans were not watching its games, they were likely to be watching other television, going to the movies, and so on. The NBA was competing with entertainment vehicles more than other sports events. Recognition of the entertainment nature of the competition led to a repositioning of the game as entertainment. In the late 1980s, the league actually moved its weeknight cable TV "Game of the Week" from Thursday to Tuesday to avoid competing with "The Bill Cosby Show." Similar issues with respect to the Atlanta Olympics concerned Hollywood in the summer of 1996. Were people going to watch the games on TV rather than go to the movies? As another example, cable television and telephone companies are scrambling nowadays to set up signposts on the information superhighway. They are ignoring the electric companies, which already have wires running to almost every home in the developed world. What role these companies play in the highway's eventual route can impact the more visible interested parties.[5]

While the narrower within-category view of competition is relevant to both marketing strategy and day-to-day planning, the broader view is more germane to marketing strategists. They must be concerned not only with current and direct competition from similar brands and offerings but the potential, less direct competition from other diverse product categories that might be substantial threats in the future by satisfying the same need and rendering the original product obsolete.

The second and third Poland Spring implications highlighted earlier correspond to the distinction proposed by Day, Shocker, and Srivastava between demand- and supply-oriented approaches to the identification of competitors.[6] Demand-oriented

TABLE 4.1 **Foci of Various Competitive Orientations**

	Supply Oriented	Demand Oriented
Strategic Decisions	Product categories	Consumer needs and wants
Tactical Decisions	Brands within category	Preferences

approaches define competitive sets with respect to customer needs, requirements, and behavior. Supply-oriented approaches focus on physical product, manufacturing process, or perhaps distribution considerations.

Competitor identification approaches thus differ as to whether they supply inputs more appropriate to strategic (broader) or tactical (within product category) decision making as well as whether they are supply or demand oriented. Table 4.1 reflects the focus of each of the four combinations of these competitive orientations. For example, from a supply-oriented perspective, Federal Express at one level of management (perhaps that of a marketing manager) is concerned with other overnight courier services. At another level (that of a corporate strategist), it must follow the progress in plain-paper fax machines to determine the types of documents that only it and its direct competitors could deliver successfully. A more demand-oriented perspective would have Federal Express examining specific product preferences at the tactical (or marketing manager) level—What benefits should it promote?—and basic needs and wants at the strategic (corporate) level—What are the basic needs the company has to satisfy?—to guide new product/service development.

The primary objective of this chapter is to describe those methodologies and frameworks useful for identifying competition. These methods are listed in Table 4.2. We discuss both demand- and supply-oriented approaches as well as methods that can be used to identify competition outside the traditional category. Since demand-oriented approaches correspond to aspects of consumer behavior, it makes sense to use a prototypical consumer decision process as a framework. The concept of a supply-oriented definition of competitive sets invites the use of the strategic group concept as discussed in the industrial organization and strategy literature. Indeed, strategic groups are often defined as firms that follow similar strategies.

The methods use data from a wide variety of sources: managerial judgment, consumer judgment, secondary data, financial data, and scanner panel data. There are important trade-offs among these data sources. Consumer judgments may provide the most explicit information as to how products compete. They can also provide insight into the potential acceptability of products with new attributes (such as caffeine-free colas). On the other hand, they are time consuming and expensive to collect. Furthermore, if elicited from people not interested in the product category, the judgments then may not be of use. Secondary data are relatively inexpensive, available almost immediately, and highly reliable. Unfortunately, these data cannot be tailored to answer managers' questions. Managerial judgment is the easiest, quickest, and least expensive data source around. However, it can be the least reliable.

TABLE 4.2   **Methods for Identifying Competitors**

Method	Demand or Supply Oriented	Appropriate for Identifying Competition Outside of Category	Usual Data Sources
Substitution in use analysis	Demand	Yes	Consumer judgment
Perceptual mapping	Demand	Yes	Consumer judgment
Brand-switching analyses	Demand	No	Scanner panel data, surveys
Forced choice and product deletion	Demand	Yes	Consumer judgment
Analysis of interpurchase times	Demand	No	Scanner panel data
Strategic groups analysis	Supply	No	Secondary data, product lists, price lists, managerial judgment
Porter's five forces	Usually supply, but could be either	Yes	Company sales records, purchasing requisitions, product lists, price lists, managerial judgment
Ansoff's product market matrix	Usually supply, but could be either	Yes	Product lists, price lists, managerial judgment

As discussed in Chapter 1, human judgment in general and managerial judgment in particular suffers from systematic flaws and biases induced by bounded rationality.[7] Managers often focus on only a small amount of the available information—an amount they can process—and make judgments on the basis of that. These judgments would not necessarily be correct even if *all* the information were correctly used. This simplification of complex problems to simpler ones is what leads to flawed, biased judgments.

Perhaps the bias most relevant to competitor identification results from what Tversky and Kahneman call the "representativeness" heuristic. According to this, judgments are often made on the basis of how similar one event or object is to another class of objects.[8] This would lead to managers forming competitive sets on the basis of physical feature similarity. If elements in the marketing environment dictate that factors other than physical similarity govern the set of brands consumers make choices from, their conclusions can be erroneous. Returning to the Poland Spring example, suppose retail outlets that sold both Poland Spring and Spa were few in number. As suggested earlier, classification of these brands in the same competitive set might be inappropriate despite their physical similarity.

IDENTIFYING COMPETITORS BY ANALYZING CONSUMER DECISION PROCESSES

Many authors of consumer behavior textbooks conceptualize consumer decision making as a multistage process.[9] The names of the specific stages may differ from book to book, but all essentially conform to the following story. A consumer encounters a need that requires a purchase to satisfy. He/she then seeks out and evaluates alternative products or brands that would satisfy the need. Eventually the consumer makes a choice, which is followed by some postpurchase reflection.

If two products are competitors for the same consumer, he/she must either see them as satisfying the same need or evaluate them as being similar enough that he/she could choose either on a single occasion. Consistent with this paradigm, we classify demand-oriented methods for identifying competitive sets as to whether they correspond to *need recognition, alternative evaluation,* or *choice.* As implied by Table 4.1, these stages correspond to levels of analysis and decision making. Need recognition approaches are useful for higher levels of management with broad concern about potential competition from alternative categories that could satisfy the same essential needs their products do. Choice approaches are more useful for the marketing manager who is competing for share within a category in the short term and needs to know what brands he or she might lose share to or take share from.

Need Recognition

Needs get recognized when consumers have a problem that no immediately available brand or product addresses adequately. Chapter 3 discussed ways of uncovering unmet needs. When a new product is designed that meets these needs, an old product is necessarily displaced. When designing this new product (or brand), the firm would therefore like to know which old products (categories or brands) it will substitute for (compete with). The key element in identifying those products is knowing what people currently use for the new product's intended use. This idea can be easily adapted to determining competitive sets among an existing group of products. Products in different categories or brands within the same category are said to compete if they can substitute for each other in the same usage situations. A technique that capitalizes on this logic is substitution-in-use analysis.

Substitution-in-Use Analysis   *Substitution-in-use analysis* presumes that interproduct competitiveness is largely based on usage situations. Products in the same and different categories can be viewed as competitors if they are used in the same situations. For example, bottled water and soft drinks may both be consumed when a consumer is thirsty. The more similar the usage situations, the more competitive two products are. Bottled water, soft drinks, and wine may all be used as beverages accompanying a meal; however, wine is not likely to be used to quench thirst. Beer can be used to quench thirst, as a beverage with meals, and as a beverage at parties. Wine is appropriate for parties. Soft drinks and bottled water may be less so.

The typical substitution-by-use analysis, as described by its developer, Volney Stefflre (1972), involves three stages.[10] In the first, or *idea generation* stage, a sample of 20 to 30 consumers is given a target set of products, asked to list to which uses these products are put, and asked to list other products that could be used for the same purposes. These data can be used to formulate a comprehensive list of products and uses. A firm interested in a specific product class can assemble lists of

1. the major products that comprise the bulk of the product class;
2. a few peripheral products that represent characteristics that might be of interest (might substitute for some uses);
3. the major uses of the products;
4. and a few particular and/or idiosyncratic uses to aid in interpretation (Stefflre, 1977, pp. 442–444).

One of the major advantages of substitution-in-use analysis lies in the second consumer-generated list. By including peripheral products, the manager can identify potential competition outside the product category. For example, a soft drink manager can identify which other beverages (not only which brands of the same beverage) compete with his or her product.

In the second, or *data collection* stage, an independent sample of consumers is asked whether they see each product on the list as suitable for each use on the list. This enables the analyst to create a matrix of products by uses in which the entry in the ith row and jth column is a 1 if the respondent would consider the product in the ith row for the use in the jth column and a 0 otherwise. Products are then determined to be more similar if they have more uses in common; in other words, a similarity measure for two products (matrix rows) is the number of uses (columns) for which the products both have 1s. The overall similarity of a pair of products is then deemed to be the average of the similarity measures for that pair over all consumers in the sample.

The final, or *data analysis* stage submits these similarity measures to either a hierarchical cluster analysis or perceptual mapping program.[11] As discussed in Chapter 2, cluster analysis is a multivariate statistical technique that groups together items according to how similar they are. Cluster analysis software often produces output that is visually represented as a hierarchy or tree diagram such as that in Fig. 4.2. Brands or products grouped together farther down the tree are those among which there is more substitutability. Thus, we infer that these are seen by consumers as more similar and, consequently, should be viewed by managers as more competitive with each other than with others.*

Fig. 4.2 presents the output of the third stage of a substitution-in-use analysis where the target product was bank credit cards. It depicts the broad structure of financial services and what competes with what. This analysis produced a couple of insights for the managers of the sponsoring bank. They were exposed to the notion that convenient credit services (credit card account checks, overdraft protection, cash

---

*Further understanding of the similar usage nature of the competitive structure can be gained by examining what uses are appropriate for the products close to each other at the base of the hierarchy.

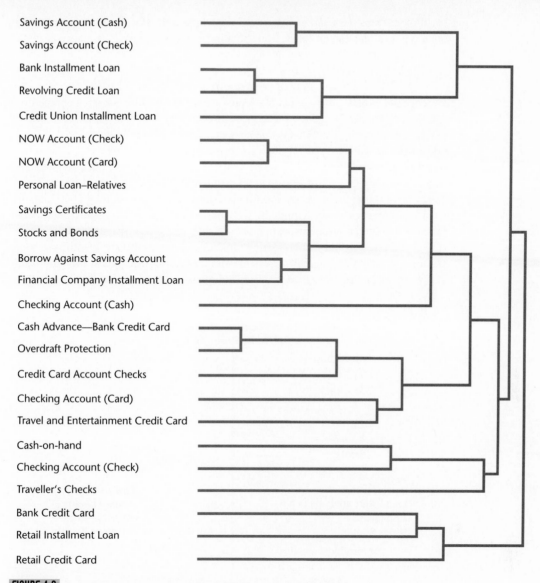

FIGURE 4.2 **Structuring Competition in Financial Services**

Source: From Srivastava, Rajendra K., Robert P. Leone, and Allan D. Shocker (1981), "Market Structure Analysis: Hierarchical Clustering of Products Based on Substitution-In-Use," *Journal of Marketing* 45 (Summer), 45. Reprinted by permission of the American Marketing Association.

advances on bank cards) were more competitive with checking accounts (a debit instrument) than with other credit instruments such as installment loans. The usual (apparently incorrect) practice was to categorize services into debit or credit instruments. The analysis found that functional usage was more important to categorizing a service than whether the service was a credit or debit instrument. In addition, the managers found it noteworthy (although quite reasonable in retrospect) that retail installment loans were more competitive with bank and retail credit cards than with other types of installment loans. The shopping use was the key.

Perception of Alternatives

Perceptual Maps   Perceptual maps provide another way of assessing competitive sets. Recall that two brands are positioned close together on the map if they are seen as psychologically "similar." This is true no matter whether the map was created via multidimensional scaling or factor analysis. It follows then that if two brands are close together on a perceptual map, they are seen as substitutes by potential customers and should therefore be part of the same competitive set. For example, in Fig. 4.3, one competitive set might be {Chrysler, Buick, Oldsmobile}; another might be {Lincoln, Cadillac, Mercedes}; a third might be {Datsun, Toyota}. These competitive sets could be formed either by visual inspection or by cluster analysis of the map coordinates.

One interesting way of collecting similarities data useful for identifying competitors through a perceptual map is the similarity of consideration sets approach. Respondents are asked to pick a subset of brands or products that they would con-

FIGURE 4.3   A Perceptual Map of Automobiles

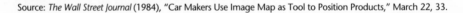

Source: *The Wall Street Journal* (1984), "Car Makers Use Image Map as Tool to Position Products," March 22, 33.

sider buying out of a larger set. The similarity measure is then taken to be the number of times that two products were both included in this "consideration set." The appeal of this approach is twofold. First, the similarity of consideration question is akin to asking a respondent which products have a chance to compete for his or her purchase. Second, since the researcher defines the set of products, the researcher can include anything he or she feels appropriate—both Poland Spring Water and Diet Pepsi, for example.

A slight variant of this approach begins with a set of cards, each with the name of a different product on it.[12] The respondent is then instructed to sort the cards into as many groups as he or she wishes. The groups should contain similar products. Once the respondent has done this, he or she is asked to describe or label each group. A similarity measure is then formed for each respondent by assigning a 1 to a pair of products if the respondent put the two products in the same group. Otherwise a 0 is assigned. The overall similarity measure is defined by adding the similarity measures for all individuals in the sample.

Choice

If competition is rooted in consumer behavior, then consumers who choose more than one product or brand on successive occasions should provide insight into the structure of competition. After all, the set of products or brands a consumer uses competes with other sets from purchase occasion to purchase occasion. In this section, we describe three approaches to analyzing competition based on consumer choices: brand-switching analyses, forced choice and product deletion methods, and analysis of interpurchase times.

Brand-switching Analyses   Marketers of packaged consumer goods have long known that consumers tend to purchase (and consume) many brands within a product category. In one study on soft drinks, consumers bought the same brand as on the previous usage occasion only 45 percent of the time.[13] The academic literature contains many explanations for this "brand-switching" phenomenon. In particular, if consumers are price sensitive, they may gravitate to whichever brand (if any) is on promotion at any given time.[14] Brand-switching behavior is usually summarized in what is called a *brand-switching matrix*. In such a matrix, the rows and columns represent the brands in the product category of interest. The element in the ith row and jth column reflects the conditional probability that a consumer will buy the brand in the jth column on the purchase occasion following one on which the brand in the ith row was bought. For example, in Table 4.3, 12 percent of the people who bought Tide on a given purchase occasion bought Wisk on the next one. The diagonal elements of Table 4.3 are the repeat purchase probabilities for each brand. Note that these are the largest elements in each row. It makes sense that a purchaser of a given brand would be more likely to purchase that brand than any other on the next purchase occasion.

Most brand-switching matrices for American products are compiled from the scanner panel data collected by Nielsen and Information Resources, Inc. These data

TABLE 4.3   **Matrix of Switching Probabilities—Liquid Laundry Detergent Market**

	Tide	Wisk	Era	Surf	Solo	Cheer	All	Bold-3	Fab
Tide	0.558	0.120	0.055	0.135	0.021	0.043	0.020	0.023	0.023
Wisk	0.156	0.481	0.071	0.119	0.022	0.041	0.046	0.026	0.039
Era	0.094	0.102	0.590	0.101	0.027	0.032	0.016	0.024	0.014
Surf	0.140	0.170	0.074	0.424	0.033	0.051	0.038	0.030	0.038
Solo	0.086	0.076	0.057	0.130	0.515	0.017	0.017	0.071	0.030
Cheer	0.221	0.127	0.085	0.161	0.009	0.303	0.030	0.048	0.015
All	0.130	0.189	0.059	0.144	0.059	0.048	0.333	0.018	0.067
Bold-3	0.128	0.138	0.066	0.179	0.072	0.041	0.034	0.307	0.034
Fab	0.195	0.132	0.070	0.151	0.026	0.048	0.022	0.066	0.290

Note: Based on brand switches of 1924 panelists.

Source: Bucklin, R. E., G. J. Russell, and V. Srinivasan (1994), "A Relationship Between Price Elasticities and Brand Switching Probabilities in Heterogeneous Markets," mimeo.

reflect products bought in supermarkets (both Nielsen and IRI collect data on these) or drugstores (only IRI collects these data). Data suppliers usually provide customers with data for all brands within the customer's product category, *as seen by the supplier.* Any analysis of competition that is based on these data is constrained by the scanner supplier's definition of that category. For example, one cannot easily form switching matrices that contain both Poland Spring Water and Diet Pepsi because Nielsen and IRI do not compile their data in ways that would allow it. They would more likely separate soft drinks and bottled water.

One property of brand-switching matrices illustrated by this table is that they are asymmetric. The probability of switching from Tide to Cheer does not equal the probability of switching from Cheer to Tide. This asymmetry is well known with respect to different price tiers of packaged goods. The probability of switching from a moderate- or low-priced brand to a premium brand is much lower than the reverse. The reason for this is that typical moderate- or low-price buyers (those who typically buys Bold-3 or Fab) will buy a premium brand (such as Tide) when it's on promotion because they can get what they believe to be superior quality for the same price as the nonpremium brand. On the other hand, typical premium buyers will not buy lower priced brands when they are on promotion because they are unwilling to sacrifice quality.[15]

In any event, it stands to reason that brands to which buyers tend to switch from a given brand are likely to be competitive with the given brand. The underlying logic is that if consumers tend to use two brands in a given product category, these brands are likely to be seen as substitutes. Table 4.3 suggests that Tide's most serious competitor is Surf, although Wisk is a close second. Wisk's most serious competitor is Tide; Era's is Wisk; Wisk's is Tide, and so on.

As another example, consider the switching matrix for Japanese brands of soy sauce found in Table 4.4. This matrix contains data from two national brands (Yamasa and Kikkoman), two store brands, and a fictional agglomeration of all other brands.

TABLE 4.4   Japanese Soy Sauce—Switching Matrix

Previous Brand	New Brand					
	Yamasa	Kikkoman	Store Brand A	Store Brand B	Store Brand C	All Others
Yamasa	0.680	0.247	0.011	0.018	0.020	0.024
Kikkoman	0.251	0.680	0.019	0.023	0.004	0.023
Store Brand A	0.149	0.439	0.368	0	0	0.044
Store Brand B	0.394	0.276	0	0.300	0	0.029
Store Brand C	0.297	0.063	0	0	0.617	0.023
All Others	0.318	0.409	0.040	0.055	0.007	0.172

Note: Based on data from 4,594 panelists.

Source: *1990 Category Facts Book*, Tokyo: Distribution Economics Institute of Japan.

According to this matrix, Yamasa is the biggest competitor of store brands B and C while Kikkoman is the largest competitor of store brand A. While this is probably due to distribution effects,* it demonstrates how these data can be used. This type of analysis is straightforward to perform. However, it is very ad hoc and so does not really provide a formal basis for partitioning the market into distinct competitive sets.

One way to accomplish this is to convert the switching data into similarity measures and use cluster analysis to form clusters or competitive sets. As in any cluster analysis, the first step is to define an appropriate similarity measure. In order to make such a definition, we need to establish some notation. Let

n_{ij} = number of consumers who switched from brand i on one choice occasion to brand j on the next,

$n_{i.}$ = number of consumers who purchased brand i on the first choice occasion,

$n_{.j}$ = number of consumers who purchased brand j on the second choice occasion, and

$n_{..}$ = number of consumers in the sample.

Then an appropriate similarity measure is the flow measure discussed in Chapter 3.

$$F_{ij} = \frac{n_{ij} n_{..}}{n_{i.} n_{.j}}.$$

This measure can be interpreted as the ratio of the *actual* number of consumers switching from i to j to the *expected* number switching from i to j under the assumptions that

---

*Store A carries Kikkoman while store C carries Yamasa. The data in the matrix suggest that store B carries both but may devote more shelf space to Yamasa.

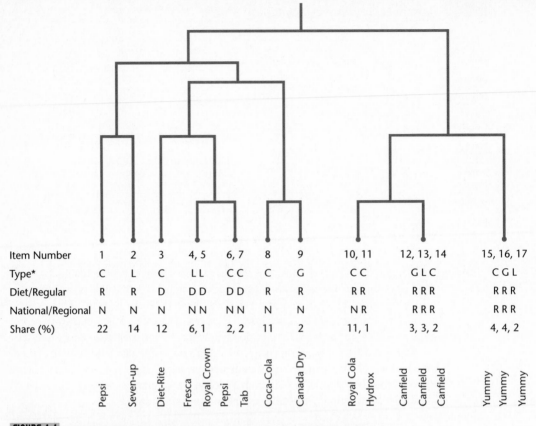

Item Number	1	2	3	4, 5	6, 7	8	9	10, 11	12, 13, 14	15, 16, 17
Type*	C	L	C	L L	C C	C	G	C C	G L C	C G L
Diet/Regular	R	R	D	D D	D D	R	R	R R	R R R	R R R
National/Regional	N	N	N	N N	N N	N	N	N R	R R R	R R R
Share (%)	22	14	12	6, 1	2, 2	11	2	11, 1	3, 3, 2	4, 4, 2

Pepsi · Seven-up · Diet-Rite · Fresca · Royal Crown · Pepsi · Tab · Coca-Cola · Canada Dry · Royal Cola · Hydrox · Canfield · Canfield · Canfield · Yummy · Yummy · Yummy

FIGURE 4.4 **Hierarchical Competitive Structure for Soft Drinks**

*C = Cola, L = Lemon/Lime, and G = Ginger ale

From Vithala R. Rao and Darius J. Sabavala, "Inference of Hierarchical Choice Processes from Panel Data," *Journal of Consumer Research,* Vol. 8, June 1981, pp. 85–96. Reprinted with permission of The University of Chicago Press.

the two choice occasions are independent and that the choice probabilities of *i* and *j* are given by the two choice shares, respectively.

One problem with inputting these measures into most clustering programs is that the programs usually require that similarities be symmetric; that is, that $S_{ij} = S_{ji}$. That is not the case with this measure. One can modify it, though, to make it symmetric by replacing the n_{ij} term with the weighted average $.5n_{ij} + .5n_{ji}$.

Fig. 4.4 depicts the hierarchical structure of a cluster analysis one of the authors performed using a soft drink-switching matrix.[16] The diagram contains paths that link each brand with every other brand. The way to interpret this diagram is that more switching occurs between pairs of brands linked with a path towards the bottom of the diagram than towards the top. For example, in Fig. 4.4, there is more switching between Diet Pepsi and Tab than between Tab and Diet-Rite; there is also more switching between Tab and Diet-Rite than between Tab and Coca-Cola.

As with the earlier substitution-in-use analyses, products closer together at the base of the hierarchy or connected at a lower node in the hierarchy are more compet-

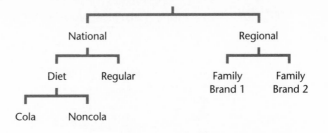

FIGURE 4.5 Summary Interpretation of Soft Drink Hierarchy

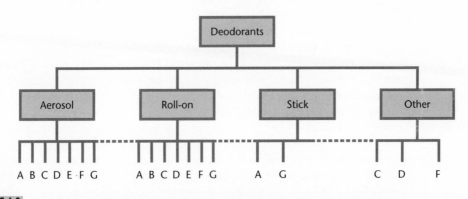

FIGURE 4.6 Hypothetical Hierarchical Competitive Structure for Deodorant

Source: Rao, Vithala R. (1981), "New Product Sales Forecasting Using the Hendry System," in *New Product Forecasting*, Y. Wind, V. Mahajan, and R. W. Cardozo (eds.), Lexington, MA: Lexington Books, 505.

itive with each other. In particular, national brands (left-hand side of the tree) have a greater degree of competitiveness (exhibit more intragroup switching) with each other than they do with regional brands (right-hand side), regardless of flavor. Additionally, within regional brands, brand name forms a strong basis of competition (that is, there is more intrabrand switching than intraflavor switching among regional brands).

The hierarchical or tree nature of this output enables the analyst or manager to ascribe a choice process to the brand-switching matrix. Fig. 4.5 provides a summary interpretation of Fig. 4.4.[17] National/regional distribution (or perhaps price) is the most important attribute—the one consumers use first. The subtree for the national brands has diet/regular as the next important feature, followed by flavor.

While hierarchical cluster analysis certainly makes best use of commonly available statistical software, an approach developed by the Hendry Corporation about 25 years ago produces essentially the same output: a hierarchical representation of the consumer choice process. However, the Hendry Model requires some prior hypotheses concerning what that representation might be. One hypothesized hierarchy for the deodorant market is shown in Fig. 4.6.

The Hendry System proceeds from an assumption similar to that implicit in hierarchical clustering: that brand switching occurs to a greater extent within branches

TABLE 4.5   **Automobile-Switching Matrix (1960)**

Previous Car	New Car			
	General Motors	Ford	Other	Chrysler
General Motors	0.68	0.14	0.12	0.06
Ford	0.21	0.60	0.12	0.07
Other	0.15	0.18	0.62	0.05
Chrysler	0.20	0.17	0.16	0.46

Source: Colombo, Richard A., and Donald G. Morrison (1989), "A Brand Switching Model with Implications for Marketing Strategies," *Marketing Science* 8 (Winter), 89–99.

originating farther down the hierarchy than within branches farther up. For example, switching between brand A aerosol and brand B aerosol in Fig. 4.6 is greater than switching between aerosol and roll-on. Its driving force is the ratio between actual switching probabilities and those derived from the presumption that switching between products is the result of independence between choice occasions and constant brand choice probabilities. A large ratio implies that there is a great deal of interproduct switching and, consequently, joint membership in a hierarchy branch originating nearer the bottom.[18] Unfortunately, the Hendry System is proprietary and the published descriptions are necessarily incomplete. The Hendry Corporation remains the lone conclusive authority. Much academic debate has occurred over the years amid several published testimonials from satisfied users. Nevertheless, the logic behind the system can be a great help in thinking about how brands compete against each other.

One final comment on brand-switching analyses is in order. The vast majority of brand-switching analyses and switching matrices are created for frequently purchased packaged goods, for two reasons. First, the interpurchase times must be short enough so that repeat purchases and switches in particular can be observed. Second, the major source of data tracking a consumer's brand choices over time is scanner panel data, which are primarily available only for frequently purchased packaged goods. However, one should not take this to mean that switching matrices cannot be constructed for infrequently purchased consumer durables. Ford Motor Company used to conduct a survey each year of 20,000 new car buyers. Among the questions asked was what car was traded in for the car just bought. Table 4.5 presents a switching matrix constructed from the data collected in 1960.

Each year Rogers National Research collects trade-in data for a large sample of U.S. new car buyers. Table 4.6 presents a switching (car-traded-in to buy-a-new-car) matrix created from the 1979 data. Table 4.6 is constructed on the segment level. Here one can view competition not between brands but between product subcategories. One fact apparent from this matrix is that owners of midsize specialty cars are most likely to switch to small specialty or medium-price standard cars, given that they do not remain in the subcategory. Consequently, these subcategories provide the biggest threat to the midsize specialties. A manager in Ford's Thunderbird division must keep an eye on what is happening with the Chevrolet Camaro, for example. A

TABLE 4.6A Segment Composition of 1979 Model Cars

1. Subcompact/Domestic (SUBD)
   Bobcat
   Chevette
   Horizon
   Monza
   Omni
   Pinto
   Spirit
   Sunbird

2. Subcompact/Captive Imports (SUBC)
   Arrow
   Champ
   Colt
   Colt Hatchback
   Fiesta
   Opel

3. Subcompact/Imports (SUBI)
   Datsun 210
   Datsun 310
   Fiat 128
   Honda Civic
   Honda CVCC
   Honda Accord
   Renault LeCar
   Toyota Corolla
   Volkswagen Rabbit
   —Gas
   —Diesel

4. Small Specialty/Domestic (SMAD)
   Camaro
   Capri
   Corvette
   Firebird
   Horizon TC-3
   Mustang
   Omni O24
   Pacer
   Skyhawk
   Starfire

5. Small Specialty/Captive (SMAC)
   Challenger
   Sapporo

6. Small Specialty/Imports (SMAI)
   Datsun 280ZX
   Fiat Spider 2000
   Fiat X1/9
   Toyota Celica
   Volkswagen Scirocco

7. Low-Price Compact (COML)
   Concord
   Fairmont
   Nova
   Volare

8. Medium-Price Compact (COMM)
   Aspen
   Omega
   Phoenix
   Skylark
   Zephyr

9. Import Compact (COMI)
   Audi Fox
   Datsun 510
   Fiat Brava
   Toyota Corona
   Volkswagen Dasher

10. Midsize Domestic (MIDD)
    Century
    Cougar
    Cutlass Supreme
    Diplomat
    Granada
    LeBaron
    LeMans
    LTD II
    Malibu
    Monarch

11. Midsize Imports (MIDI)
    Audi 5000
    BMW 320I
    Datsun 810
    Toyota Cressida
    Volvo 242/244
    Volvo 245/265
    Volvo 264

12. Midsize Specialty (MIDS)
    Cordoba
    Cougar XR-7
    Cutlass Supreme
    Grand Prix
    Magnum XE
    Monte Carlo
    Regal
    Thunderbird

13. Low-Price Standard (STDL)
    Chevrolet
    Ford

14. Medium-Price Standard (STDM)
    Buick
    Chrysler
    Dodge
    Mercury
    Oldsmobile
    Pontiac

15. Luxury Domestic (LUXD)
    Cadillac
    El Dorado
    Lincoln Continental
    Mark V
    Riviera
    Seville
    Toronado
    Versailles

16. Luxury Import (LUXI)
    BMW 528I
    BMW 733I
    BMW 633CSI
    Mercedes-Benz 240D
    Mercedes-Benz 300D
    Mercedes-Benz 300SD
    Mercedes-Benz 280E/SE
    Mercedes-Benz 450SEL
    Mercedes-Benz 450SL/SLC
    Porsche 911
    Porsche 924

Source: Rogers National Research, Toledo, Ohio. Matrix adapted from Harshman, Richard A., Paul E. Green, Yoram J. Wind, and Margaret E. Lundy (1982), "A Model for the Analysis of Asymmetric Data in Marketing Research," *Marketing Science* 1 (Spring), 205–242.

TABLE 4.6B Car Subcategory—Switching Matrix 1979

	SUBD	SUBC	SUBI	SMAD	SMAC	SMAI	COML	COMM	COMI	MIDD	MIDI	MIDS	STDL	STDM	LUXD	LUXI
SUBD	0.2102	0.0134	0.0949	0.1716	0.0004	0.0209	0.1115	0.0367	0.0049	0.114	0.0043	0.1475	0.0384	0.0214	0.0086	0.0011
SUBC	0.1774	0.0607	0.1643	0.1448	0.0013	0.03	0.0523	0.0487	0.0122	0.0911	0.0122	0.1097	0.0505	0.0294	0.0134	0.002
SUBI	0.1404	0.015	0.3216	0.1213	0.0006	0.0668	0.0404	0.0167	0.0279	0.0643	0.0162	0.1033	0.0286	0.0199	0.0133	0.0036
SMAD	0.0958	0.0097	0.091	0.3136	0.0006	0.0398	0.0493	0.0191	0.0076	0.0694	0.0096	0.195	0.0264	0.0361	0.0336	0.0033
SMAC	0.137	0.0175	0	0.3411	0.0117	0	0	0.1429	0	0.3207	0	0.0292	0	0	0	0
SMAI	0.0653	0.008	0.1335	0.1272	0.0006	0.1934	0.041	0.0115	0.0272	0.0601	0.0394	0.1819	0.0125	0.0332	0.0483	0.0169
COML	0.1368	0.0138	0.0902	0.1131	0.0005	0.0121	0.2013	0.0459	0.0062	0.1551	0.0042	0.1138	0.0722	0.0268	0.0068	0.0013
COMM	0.1526	0.0102	0.086	0.0938	0.0006	0.009	0.0916	0.11	0.0083	0.1417	0.0064	0.1433	0.053	0.081	0.0113	0.0013
COMI	0.1122	0.0207	0.2998	0.0796	0.0004	0.0439	0.0561	0.0271	0.066	0.1176	0.0432	0.0425	0.0195	0.0426	0.0233	0.0055
MIDD	0.1045	0.0074	0.0697	0.0938	0.0003	0.0133	0.0665	0.0385	0.008	0.1678	0.0068	0.1942	0.0887	0.1074	0.031	0.0022
MIDI	0.0612	0.0054	0.1346	0.0588	0.0002	0.0365	0.0713	0.0214	0.0267	0.1807	0.1447	0.1115	0.0279	0.0498	0.0412	0.0281
MIDS	0.0798	0.006	0.0508	0.1162	0.0006	0.0212	0.0227	0.0107	0.0057	0.071	0.0081	0.3443	0.0674	0.1149	0.0771	0.0036
STDL	0.1085	0.0074	0.0506	0.0624	0.0001	0.0052	0.0738	0.0228	0.0046	0.1105	0.0037	0.1458	0.2651	0.1127	0.0257	0.0012
STDM	0.0751	0.0056	0.0488	0.0498	0.0002	0.0081	0.0336	0.0268	0.0056	0.091	0.0046	0.1311	0.0665	0.3554	0.0955	0.0024
LUXD	0.0345	0.004	0.0429	0.0546	0.0001	0.0057	0.0153	0.0096	0.0044	0.0283	0.0077	0.0792	0.0274	0.0849	0.5868	0.0146
LUXI	0.0115	0.0044	0.1088	0.0658	0	0.0372	0.0082	0.006	0.0192	0.0165	0.0643	0.0827	0.0172	0.0825	0.1347	0.341

Source: Rogers National Research, Toledo, Ohio. Matrix adapted from Harshman, Richard A., Paul E. Green, Yoram J. Wind, and Margaret E. Lundy (1982), "A Model for the Analysis of Asymmetric Data in Marketing Research," *Marketing Science* 1 (Spring), 205–242.

subcategory manager must pay attention to what trends exist in the small specialty (Are they getting larger?) and medium-price standard (Are they getting sportier?) subcategories to anticipate future competition.

Forced Choice and Product Deletion   In sports, there is a saying that no place is worse than second place. The runner-up in any competition often takes little solace from the fact that he or she was the second-best player or supplied the most competition for the eventual winner. In a consumer's brand choice, the runner-up is never known. If it were, the manager of the runner-up brand would know that his or her brand was the most competitive with the chosen brand for the consumer in question. This could provide valuable input into the definition of competitive sets, particularly for durable goods where switching data are more difficult to obtain.

Consider the following marketing research interview question. Suppose a consumer were asked to make a choice from a prespecified set of brands. Once this is done, the researcher informs the consumer that his or her preferred brand is no longer available. Which one does the consumer choose then? Another way of phrasing this question is, "What brand benefits most if the preferred brand drops out of the picture?" This question captures the essence of what we intuit as competition. The logic behind this research approach very much parallels that of brand-switching analyses. Both ask "who affects who"–type questions. The major differences lie in the nature of the switch and the data source from which it is measured.

A hypothetical data set emerging from this analysis is shown in Table 4.7. The second column of the table lists the distribution of the forced choices of 100 respondents given the choice set in the first column. The remaining columns present the distribution of forced choices that emerges when the product listed in that row is deleted for those who preferred it. For example, six of the ten respondents that preferred a Peugeot diesel now prefer a Cutlass diesel, eight prefer some type of diesel, and only one stayed with the Peugeot brand and switched to a gasoline engine. Similar statements could be made for those who preferred Cutlass and Jetta diesels. Two possible competitive structures are "diesel versus gasoline" and "brand name specific." The data in Table 4.7 seem to suggest that "diesel versus gasoline" is a more appropriate structure.

Following the logic behind this approach, Urban, Johnson, and Hauser have formally defined a submarket as a group of products whose choice probabilities are more likely to be affected when one of them is deleted from the overall product category or market. The size of this (positive) effect for a remaining brand is proportional to its market share. Urban and his colleagues developed a formal statistical methodology, using forced choice and product deletion data, to test whether a hypothesized partitioning of products into submarkets satisfies this property.[19]

Interpurchase Times   Today's scanner panel data contain much more information than simply the sequence of purchases needed to compute a brand-switching matrix. The actual dates and amounts of purchase are available too. This enables one to compute interpurchase times and the quantities associated with them, providing more fuel to identify competitive sets.

Consider a market containing two brands, A and B. Also consider a consumer who consumes these two brands at the same rate and makes a purchase immediately

TABLE 4.7   **Automobile Forced Choice Matrix**

	Number of Choices	Diesel			Gasoline			
		Peugeot	**Cutlass**	**Jetta**	**Cavalier**	**Peugeot**	**Cutlass**	**Jetta**
Diesel								
Peugeot	10	—	6	2	1	1	0	0
Cutlass	20	10	—	4	0	2	4	0
Jetta	15	7	2	—	1	1	1	3
Gasoline								
Cavalier	20	0	2	4	—	0	4	10
Peugeot	15	3	1	1	0	—	5	5
Cutlass	10	0	1	0	3	3	—	3
Jetta	10	0	0	2	1	5	2	—

Source: Urban, G. L., P. L. Johnson, and J. R. Hauser (1984), "Testing Competitive Market Structures," *Marketing Science* 3, No. 2 (Spring), 96.

upon running out of the brand previously purchased. Consider the time interval (in days) between two successive purchases of brand A. Brand B may or may not have been bought in the interpurchase interval. In either case, if A and B are being used as substitutes, the interpurchase time should depend on the amount of A and the amount of B bought during this interval. We can write this in algebraic form as

$$Y_A = a_A(Q_A + Q_{BA}),$$

where Y_A is the interpurchase interval, a_A is a parameter that measures the time it takes to consume one unit of A, Q_A is the quantity of brand A purchased on the first purchase occasion, and Q_{BA} is the amount of B purchased in the interpurchase interval.*

If, on the other hand, A and B are not substitutes, the interpurchase time should be related to the amount of A bought at the beginning of the time period only. This would be written as

$$Y_A = a_A Q_A.$$

The question of whether A and B are substitutes (can be classified into the same competitive set) then becomes the question of which of the two above relationships is correct. The analyst can perform a linear regression with the two independent variables, Q_A and Q_{BA}

$$Y_A = \beta_A Q_A + \beta_{BA} Q_{BA}$$

---

*This relationship can be extended in a straightforward manner if there is a third brand, say C, in the market. The extension becomes $Y_A = a_A (Q_A + Q_{BA} + Q_{CA})$, where Q_{CA} is the quantity of C bought in the interpurchase interval. Extensions to larger markets are obvious.

where the regression constant is constrained to be equal to zero. The test of whether A and B are competitors is the test of the hypothesis that the coefficient of Q_{BA} is zero. If this hypothesis cannot be rejected, it would imply that the interpurchase time between A's is independent of the amount of B purchased in the same interval. Therefore, it makes sense to conclude that B has no impact on the usage of A and is consequently not a competitor of A. Standard computer packages (such as SAS) allow this test to be constructed and the constant to be constrained with a couple of simple program instructions.

These ideas can be extended to several brands. The analyst can include a variety of brands in the extended brand regression:

$$Y_A = \beta_A Q_A + \Sigma_i \beta_{iA} Q_{iA}$$

where i is taken over all other potential brands in the competitive set of A, and Q_{iA} is the amount of the ith brand purchased in the interpurchase interval. The corresponding tests for whether each brand is a competitor of A then become tests that each of the coefficients of the Q_{iA} is zero.[20]

The foregoing discussion implicitly assumed that A and B were either perfect substitutes or not related at all. This is obviously not always the case. While Perrier and Poland Spring Water may not be perfect substitutes (one is carbonated and may be used somewhat differently), it would be inappropriate to assert that they are not related at all. The variable β_{BA} can be not equal to zero, yet not very large. The truth is that these brands, if not most brands in most categories, are *imperfect substitutes* for each other. For example, if the b coefficients of brands A, B, and C in the extended model

$$Y_A = \beta_A Q_A + \beta_{BA} Q_{BA} + \beta_{CA} Q_{CA}$$

are 1, 0.8, and 0.2, respectively, the most accurate statement might be that B is fairly competitive with A, and C is not very much so. Recall that competition is a matter of degree.

In principle, these analyses are intended to be performed at the individual level, meaning a separate analysis is needed for each household. However, if usage rates and the times taken to consume each member of the product category do not vary much across households, data from several households can be pooled and the analysis performed at the aggregate level. If the manager believes this is appropriate, the resulting inferences relate to the market as a whole rather than to a particular household. If, on the other hand, usage rates and the times taken to consume each member of the product category do vary significantly across households, the previous regressions need to be modified to account for this variation. We turn to this now.

We begin with the case where two households have potentially different usage rates for each of two brands. An aggregate model that accounts for this heterogeneity is

$$Y_A = (\beta_{A1} D_1 + \beta_{A2} D_2) Q_A + (\beta_{BA1} D_1 + \beta_{BA2} D_2) Q_{BA},$$

where D_1 (D_2) is a dummy variable that takes on the value 1 if the interpurchase time in question is from household 1 (household 2) and 0 otherwise. With this formulation it is easy to show that the interpurchase time model is

$$Y_A = \beta_{A1} Q_A + \beta_{BA1} Q_{BA}$$

for household 1 and

$$Y_A = \beta_{A2}Q_A + \beta_{BA2}Q_{BA}$$

for household 2. So by estimating the full aggregate model, we can get household differences. It should be straightforward for the reader to extend this approach to any number of households and brands by increasing the number of dummy variables and using the extended brand equation in the body of the chapter.

A Final Comment on Competitors outside the Category

Many of the research and analysis techniques described to this point in the chapter can be used to identify competitors outside the product category of interest simply by substituting product categories for brands in the data collection process. The financial services example used to illustrate substitution-in-use analysis already reflects this. As another example, consider the perceptual map of breakfast foods in Fig. 4.7. This map was based on judged similarities of the different items. Sweet items such as jelly donut, cinnamon bun, and glazed donut all appear on the left side of the map. Nonsweets such as buttered toast, toast and margarine, and hard roll with butter appear on the right side. There are also many natural groupings of items such as toast pop-up and cinnamon toast, toast with margarine and buttered toast, and so on. These groupings contain items that obviously compete with each other.

The set of techniques based on scanner panel data (analyses of switching matrices and interpurchase times) do not lend themselves to identifying competitors outside the product category, since the data are usually assembled within a specific category.

STRATEGIC GROUPS ANALYSIS: COMPETITOR IDENTIFICATION FROM A SUPPLY-SIDE PERSPECTIVE

The Poland Spring example discussed at the outset of the chapter suggests that while consumer behavior is at the core of competitor identification, it would be naive to suppose that supplier behavior had no effect. The decisions suppliers make influence the ways consumers make choices. One may get a chance to buy Poland Spring only if it is distributed through her favorite grocery store. The dependence of competition on supplier behavior is reflected in the notion of *strategic groups* popularized in the strategic management literature.

Industrial organization economists have long held the view that firms within a given industry are homogeneous, except for differences in market share.[21] This is of course an abstraction that theoreticians have found useful but is not reflected in reality. We would not be writing this book if companies within the same industry did not employ different strategies. For example, in the handheld calculator industry, Texas Instruments seeks competitive advantage in large, standard markets based on a long-run low-cost position; Hewlett-Packard seeks competitive advantage in small markets based on unique, high-value products.[22] This has implications for differences in marketing, manufacturing, and development. TI must aim for rapid growth, must fully

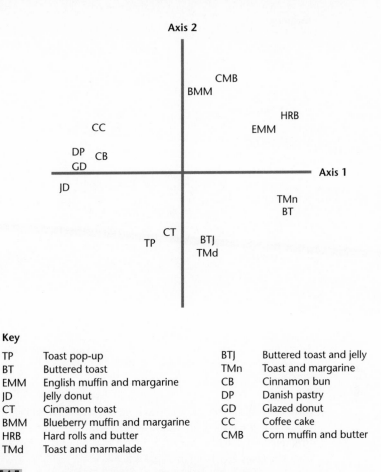

Key

TP	Toast pop-up	BTJ	Buttered toast and jelly
BT	Buttered toast	TMn	Toast and margarine
EMM	English muffin and margarine	CB	Cinnamon bun
JD	Jelly donut	DP	Danish pastry
CT	Cinnamon toast	GD	Glazed donut
BMM	Blueberry muffin and margarine	CC	Coffee cake
HRB	Hard rolls and butter	CMB	Corn muffin and butter
TMd	Toast and marmalade		

FIGURE 4.7   **A Perceptual Map of Breakfast Foods**

Source: Green, Paul E., and Vithala R. Rao (1972), *Applied Multidimensional Scaling,* New York: Holt, Rinehart and Winston, 29.

utilize its assets, and must design products to cost specifications. On the other hand, H-P must try for controlled growth, must provide quality, and must design products to performance specifications.

Recognizing the intra-industry variability of firm strategies, Michael Porter proposed that the strategic group should be the relevant unit of analysis for corporate strategy. *Strategic groups* are firms that follow "similar strategies."[23] The traditional application to strategic group analysis involves identifying strategy-defining variables, then applying cluster analysis to a data set that contains these variables for a set of firms to be divided.

Strategic management authors and economists, however, have had a problem identifying what "similar strategies" really means. Thus, they have not reached agreement on what specific variables to use in defining strategic groups. They have generally settled on the logic that a strategic group should be defined in such a way that

TABLE 4.8   **Sources of Mobility Barriers**

Market-Related Strategies	Industry Supply Characteristics	Characteristics of Firms
Product line	Economies of scale: Production	Ownership
User technologies	Marketing Administration	Organization structure
Market segmentation		Control systems
Distribution channels	Manufacturing processes	Management skills
Brand names	R&D capability	Boundaries of: Firms

Geographic coverage	Marketing and
	  distribution systems
		Diversification
		  Vertical integration

Selling systems		Firm size

		Relationships with
		  influence
		  groups

Source: McGee, J., and H. Thomas (1986), "Strategic Groups: Theory, Research, and Taxonomy," *Strategic Management Journal* 7 (March–April), 141–160.

firms outside a strategic group should not be able to make decisions similar to those within it without incurring significant costs. It is then natural to conceptualize the key strategic variables as those that affect the heights of these mobility barriers. Many such variables are listed in Table 4.8.[24]

As an example, consider business schools. Private schools charge high tuition's as opposed to state schools, which are subsidized by the state. Graduates of private schools thus graduate with greater loan indebtedness. Schools differ in their selectiveness as well. More selective schools take a lower percentage of applicants with higher salaries in their pre-M.B.A. jobs. Schools also invest heavily in placement activities. Those that invest more get more job offers for their graduates, help generate more offers per graduate, and consequently generate higher satisfaction among graduates. Funding, selectivity, and placement investment are not things schools could change without incurring significant costs. Thus, the following variables could be considered as defining mobility barriers: tuition, percent applicants accepted, pre-M.B.A. salary, post-M.B.A. salary, percent graduating with no job, average number of offers, outstanding M.B.A. loan, and graduates' grade for placement. Table 4.9 presents the results of a cluster analysis of the top 20 business schools in the 1992 *Business Week* rankings on these variables. The results of this analysis indicate that one competitive set consists of UCLA, UC Berkeley, and North Carolina. It is hard to imagine that there are many students these three schools compete for. California residents who get rejected from UCLA and Berkeley would not likely consider North

TABLE 4.9 **Strategic Groups of *Business Week's* Top 20 Business Schools (1992)**

Variable	Strategic Group 1	Strategic Group 2	Strategic Group 3	Strategic Group 4	Strategic Group 5
Tuition	$17,730*	$19,028	$9,234	$17,730	$12,302
Percent applicants accepted	36.48%	21.00%	21.72%	37.92%	35.04%
Pre-M.B.A. salary	$37,358	$46,568	$41,341	$33,874	$33,376
Post-M.B.A. salary	$58,926	$75,150	$61,945	$52,512	$49,117
Percent graduating with no job	14.4%	7.2%	15.3%	27.0%	21.9%
Average number of offers	2.08	2.68	2.10	1.66	1.90
Outstanding M.B.A. loan	$25,967	$34,518	$17,417	$24,350	$16,030
Graduates' grade for placement[†]	1.58	1.58	2.66	3.00	1.00
Members of the strategic group or cluster[‡]	Michigan (5) Columbia (9) Virginia (11) Duke (12) Cornell (14) NYU (15) Vanderbilt (19)	Northwestern (1) Chicago (2) Harvard (3) Wharton (4) Dartmouth (6) Stanford (7) MIT (13)	North Carolina (10) UCLA (16) UC Berkeley (18)	Carnegie Mellon (17) Washington-St. Louis (20)	Indiana (8)

*All cell entries are means for that strategic group.

[†]Scale: 1 = Best, 3 = Worst.

[‡]Numbers in parentheses represent *Business Week* ranks in 1992.

Carolina (assuming they could get accepted). Coming from out of state, such applicants would not have the benefit of low in-state tuition available to them. Such is the limitation of a supplier-oriented mobility barrier–based definition of strategic groups and competitive sets that do not account for the customer at all.

Unlike economists and strategic management authors, marketers have clear notions of what they mean when they describe strategy. As identified in Chapter 1, the relevant strategic variables relate to market scope and choice of competitive advantage. Using these variables as the basis for strategic group formation introduces a demand-side perspective into the conceptualization of competitive sets. Firms in the same strategic group will be competing for the same customers in the same ways. The importance of this stems from the fact that competitive set determination is the result of both supplier *and* customer behaviors. Both must be accounted for in a complete determination of who a firm's competitors really are. Using marketing-oriented strategy variables accomplishes this.

In this vein, Abell proposed three dimensions for the classification of a business that might be useful in defining strategic groups: customer groups served, customer needs served, and technologies employed (ways to satisfy these needs).[25] The first two are essentially product-market selection variables. "Customer groups served" implies target segments. Firms that compete for customers in the same segment are part of the same strategic group (or competitive set). In a given industry, the manager of one firm can estimate the proportion of each competitor's sales that comes from each target segment. These data, along with hard data on a firm's own segment breakdown, provide a complete profile of segment activity for the industry. If a trade association or another disinterested third party were conducting the study, it could get this hard data from each firm. One such independent academic study of the medical supply industry, using Abell's dimensions, found that most firms can be classified as serving hospitals, serving physicians, or serving both.[26]

Customer needs served can be reflected either by the products a firm offers or the specific benefits those products offer. Firms that offer similar products or products with similar benefits are clearly in the same competitive set (strategic group). In the medical supply industry, firms sell supplies, equipment, or both supplies and equipment. This trichotomy forms three broad categories of needs that a firm can serve. Firms that sell just equipment are rare. Furthermore, even if two firms sold similar equipment, they might still provide different benefits. For example, some CT scanners might emphasize scan time. Others might emphasize picture resolution. Lists of the products and/or benefits they offer (possibly obtained from a manager's judgment) form a profile of the customer needs served by the firms in the industry.

Firms attain competitive advantage through either having lower costs or meaningfully differentiating their products or services. (See the discussion of Porter's generic strategies in Chapter 1.) Measures of costs and differentiation may be difficult to obtain. Nevertheless, useful surrogates are available. Experience curve theory (see Chapter 7) tells us that costs are related to cumulative experience, which is related to market share. Furthermore, low costs tend to lead to low prices. Therefore, price and market share are two variables that potentially lend insight into costs. Differentiation is also difficult to measure. However, highly differentiated products usually must be advertised heavily in order to communicate the relevant differentiation. Thus, the ratio of advertising to sales can reflect differentiation.

In sum, the following variables can reflect a firm's marketing strategy: percentage of sales from each segment, specific products offered, specific benefits offered, price, market share, advertising-to-sales ratio. Each firm can be described on these variables, which reflect both supplier decisions and consumer reactions to them. A cluster analysis can then be performed on these variables, which yields the industry's strategic groups and consequently tells us which companies compete with which others. The medical supply industry study further revealed six judgmentally formed strategic groups: Hospital Supply, Hospital Supply and Equipment, Physician Supply, Physician Supply and Equipment, Hospital and Physician Supply, Hospital and Physician Supply and Equipment.

FORECASTING COMPETITORS' ACTIONS

There are two major components to competitor analyses in marketing plans at any level: identification and prediction of action. Once competitors have been identified, firms need to forecast their actions. After all, what competitors do shapes the opportunities (unmet needs) and threats (alternative brands and emerging substitutes) that a firm faces.

Consider American Airlines' innovation of frequent flyer programs. American's major competitors—United, Delta, and, at the time, Eastern and Pan Am (all facing potential passenger losses)—were able to match this plan almost immediately with ones of their own. This not only canceled American's advantage, but led it to give away free trips. Passengers who did not have to pay and increased administrative costs led everyone in the industry, including American, to make less money. Given a chance to take its decision back, American would in all likelihood do so. The airline's attempt to take advantage of an opportunity became a threat to its own position. American's error was in not forecasting the reactions of competitors correctly. This error was compounded later when American, recognizing that 92 percent of domestic fares were sold at a discount, tried to raise its prices, expecting competitors to follow. Not only did they not follow, some actually lowered prices in attempts to steal American's customers. Here American did indeed forecast competitor action; but its forecasts were 180 degrees off![27]

That competitors shape opportunities and threats applies not only to the actions of firms currently in the category, but to firms that may enter the category as well. If EMI, the British music company that pioneered the CT scanner market, had foreseen the entry of General Electric into the product category, it would have made very different choices. EMI had a monopoly and became complacent about its technological superiority. General Electric developed a superior machine and, with its greater marketing expertise in medical electronics, buried EMI. Without the superior technology, EMI had nothing to offer. If EMI had predicted the entry of GE or some such giant, it would have either licensed the product it had developed or tried to advance the technology faster to maintain an advantage.[28]

The American Airlines and EMI stories suggest that forecasting competitive activity consists of two components: predicting the activity of existing competitors and predicting the entry of future competitors. In the next sections we discuss both.

FORECASTING THE ACTIONS OF EXISTING COMPETITORS

To systematically forecast how a competitor will behave requires at least a model of that behavior. Such a model must evaluate the factors that determine behavior and transform them into a predicted action. Fig. 4.8 presents one such model for a firm puzzling over how a competitor will react to a potential price cut. In deciding whether to cut price, the firm needs to forecast the competitor's long- and short-term reactions to such a cut. Following Michael Porter, the model includes as determinants of the competitor's behavior its likely payoffs assessed against its

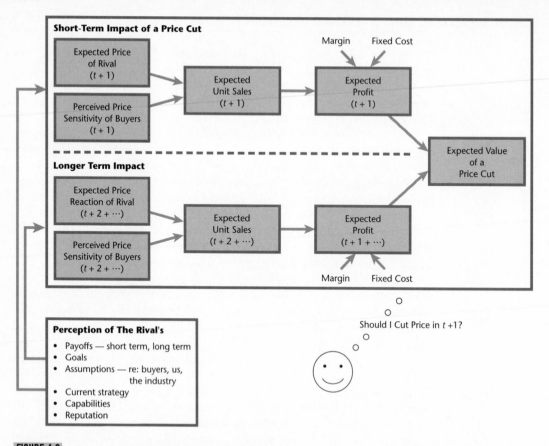

FIGURE 4.8 **Forecasting the Reaction to a Price Cut**

Source: Adapted from Moore, Marian Chapman, and Joe E. Urbany (1994), "Blinders, Fuzzy Lenses, and the Wrong Shoes: Pitfalls in Competitive Conjecture," *Marketing Letters* 5 (July), 249.

goals; the competitor's assumptions about itself, its buyers, and its industry; and its strategy, capabilities, and reputation.[29] In forecasting competitor behavior, the firm must be more interested in how the competitor sees itself than in how it sees the competitor. This figure pinpoints two sources of potential errors in competitor forecasts: the firm could incorrectly perceive how the competitor perceives itself or incorrectly transform its correct perceptions into forecasts of action.

If a firm's forecasts of how a competitor will react to a given set of factors is devoid of both incorrect perceptions of how a competitor perceives itself and errors in transformation, they are said to conform to the rational expectations hypothesis. The rational expectations hypothesis states that a firm forecasting a competitor's decisions uses essentially the same model that the competitor does in making the decisions. If competitor forecasts of all firms in the industry conform to the rational expectations hypothesis and each firm rationally pursues its own self-interest (maximizes its own utility function) without concern for how well or poorly competitors do, then the literature on game theory can provide useful predictions of competitor behavior.

Game Theory

All game theory models have a common structure. Assumptions about firm payoffs are mathematically expressed; these payoffs are interdependent (each firm's payoff depends on the competitor's decisions); all firms share these assumptions; and each competitor myopically pursues its own payoff. These circumstances mathematically lead to what game theorists call an *equilibrium solution*. The first three components of the structure reflect rational expectations. Everyone knows what each firm feels is in its own interest and how each firm believes it can achieve it. This is the essence of the rational expectations hypothesis.

As an illustration of game theory, consider the well-known game theoretic *principle of maximal differentiation,* as reflected in the following story.[30] Two ice cream stands sell identical ice creams. Each has to decide where to locate along a boardwalk running along a beach in an east-west direction. People are equally likely to sit anywhere on the beach. Since the ice creams are identical, people go to the closest stand. The solution to this problem is that one stand should locate at the easternmost point on the boardwalk; the other stand should locate at the westernmost point. This way they each will get half the market. If the easternmost stand were to move closer to the center, it could get more than half the market* but that gives an incentive to the western stand to also move closer to the center to retain its half of the market. Taking this logic to the extreme, both stands would end up at the same place, in the center. This is why the stands are located at opposite extremes.† The only basis for competition left is price. Prices will then have to fall, with profits following.

This logic can form the basis for forecasting competition in certain circumstances. If a manager believes that the competitive situation in which he or she is embroiled can be approximated by the assumptions of game theory, then the behavior prescribed by game theory becomes a very compelling forecast. In particular, if

a. both ice cream stand owners understand that the payoff to each is a function of how many people they are the closest to;

b. both ice cream stand owners understand that people are uniformly distributed along the beach; and

c. each stand owner correctly maximizes his or her own profits without regard to the profitability of the competitor,

then each stand owner can predict that the competitor will locate at the opposite end of the beach from him or her.

---

*It would be closer to all those people along the beach east of center as well as some of those people just to the west of center who used to be closer to the other stand.

†The general principle captured by the ice cream stand story is as follows. Two firms, each trying to position a product on a single attribute, over which the distribution of consumer preferences is uniform, and to price it accordingly should differentiate the product as much as possible. That is, the firms should position their products at opposite extremes of the attribute.

Why Rational Expectations and Game Theory May Not Work

The dual presumptions of correct perceptions of how the competitor perceives itself and correct transformation of these perceptions to competitor action have as much potential to be biased and incorrect as any aspect of human judgment.

Two cognitive biases may be particularly powerful in establishing incorrect perceptions of how the competitor sees itself: the fundamental attribution error and the illusion of superiority.[31] The *fundamental attribution error* refers to the tendency to attribute an observed behavior to the individual or group exhibiting that behavior rather than to the situation the individual or group finds itself in. With respect to the price cut example in Fig. 4.8, a competitor may not have matched a previous price cut because of low inventory. The firm, not knowing the competitor's inventory levels, may mistakenly make the attribution that the competitor has a differentiation-through-quality strategy that does not allow it to match price cuts. The *illusion of superiority* reflects the tendency for individuals to see themselves as better than others. In contemplating a price cut reaction, a firm may expect one, thinking that its product has comparable quality to the competitor's. The competitor, however, may view its product as being of superior quality and consequently believe that it does not need to react.

Errors in transformation of competitor perceptions to action can be induced by what is called the *false consensus effect.*[32] False consensus refers to the tendency of humans to view other people the way they view themselves. In the case of forecasting competitive action, a firm may use its perceptions to predict that the competitor will act as it would. For example, in the price cut situation, a firm run by very competitive individuals may forecast a reaction to a price cut simply by transferring its own managers' values to the competitor. The firm may do this even if it knows about a competitor's low inventory.

The presence of these biases will inhibit the applicability of rational expectations and game theory. Fortunately, there are other ways to forecast competitor action.

WHAT TO DO WHEN RATIONAL EXPECTATIONS THEORY DOES NOT APPLY

In the absence of the rigorous predictions made by game theory, managers can resort to three ways to predict competitors' actions: let them tell you, infer from past behavior, or role-play by putting yourself in their position.

Firms will often make public announcements about intended actions. For example, they often preannounce new products. They do this for several reasons.[33] Perhaps they are trying to position a product in the most profitable segment. Perhaps they are trying to develop initial levels of support or word of mouth to accelerate the acceptance of the product. It could be that they are simply trying to discourage competitors. Maybe they just want to signal to the investment community that they have exciting new products to elevate their stock price. Or perhaps they are trying to associate their company's name with the product in question. Digital Equipment (DEC) recently announced that it is working on a little pipe organ that sits on a PC chip and absorbs excess heat.[34] It produces vapors that rise to the top of the machine and are cooled by the PC's fan. With this announcement, DEC has become identified with the device. Any customer worried about excess heat will think of DEC as a potential choice, even if others later duplicate the device. Of course, DEC has made it more likely that others will duplicate the product (and do it more quickly) by making the preannouncement. In telling potential customers, firms also tell competitors. Benefits usually come with costs. In any event, a competitor of DEC didn't need to look any farther than *Business Week* to forecast DEC's new product feature.

Patterns in a company's behavior will often appear. Around the chemical industry, you may hear the phrase "DuPont personality." This refers to DuPont's established pattern of trying to differentiate its products in terms of value. DuPont does this in spite of the fact that much of what it produces can be classified almost as a commodity. The implication of the "DuPont personality" is that DuPont is less likely than other firms in the chemical industry to respond to a price cut with a matching price cut.[35] As another example, Phillip Morris tends to enter businesses in which heavy advertising is a custom. Consequently, it purchased General Foods. It would not be likely to purchase a company that makes commodities such as sponges.

Finally, companies can put themselves in their competitors' positions and try to role-play their behavior. This requires a thorough understanding of the competitors' strengths, weaknesses, assets, and liabilities (see Chapter 7). A manager can ask the rhetorical question, "Given this knowledge of my competitors, what would I do?" A vehicle for formalizing the answer is to have one's staff write a marketing plan for the competitor. One apocryphal story involves two competitors in the manufacture of jet engines. An executive from one company was giving a courtesy plant tour to his peer at the other company. During his visit, the guest saw a loose-leaf binder labeled "Competitor's Marketing Plan" on a table. He inquired what it was. The host informed him that his people did competitive analyses by creating hypothetical competitor marketing plans. The guest replied, "Wow! That sounds like a very interesting document. Could I get a copy?"

In a competitive, nonbusiness scenario, high-ranking American military officers during the Vietnam War split into two groups, one representing the United States and the other North Vietnam.[36] Various strategic interactions were simulated. U.S. officers proposed actions; North Vietnamese representatives role-played reactions. Limited bombing by the United States was a failure in this role-play. Unlimited bombing was a bit more favorable, but no more so than no bombing. Ultimately, the results of the role-play were ignored and the American forces chose the limited bombing strategy, which was ineffective and extremely costly.

Scott Armstrong suggests that the following rules would enhance the realism and consequently the effectiveness of role-plays:[37]

1. Use props to make the situation realistic. Special clothing sometimes helps. In some situations, it helps to rearrange the furniture.
2. The actors should not step out of their roles; that is, once the actors meet, they should "be" that person at all times. A good idea here is to ask the role players to separate, and then return to the meeting place a few minutes later, after they have mentally prepared themselves and are ready to stay with their new identities.

3. The actors should improvise as needed and should throw themselves into the role-playing session.

IDENTIFYING FUTURE COMPETITORS

In making long-run-oriented strategic decisions, management needs to be concerned not only with today's competitors, but with potential competition from firms that do not compete in the same product-market today but may threaten to in the future, either as new entrants or by repositioning their products as substitutes for those of the firm. In packaged goods, Procter & Gamble has such strong relationships with supermarkets, drug, and discount stores and so much experience and marketing know-how that it is a potential entrant in virtually any packaged category that can be sold in these stores. Arm & Hammer baking soda provides an example of a product that can be positioned as a substitute in other product categories. It has provided competition for toothpastes, household deodorizers, and kitty litters, among others.

Identifying future competitors is a difficult task indeed. By definition, these firms are not yet in the market, so they are firms that the company has less knowledge about. Fortunately other frameworks and techniques could prove useful in identifying competitors outside the product category. In this section we discuss two conceptual models of corporate strategy, Porter's model of five competitive forces and Ansoff's product-market matrix, which offer insight into where to look for future competitors from outside the market.

Porter's Five Forces

Early in this chapter, we discussed Porter's five forces of competition. Porter's view is that competition comes in a variety of forms. In some sense, buyers, suppliers, potential entrants, and substitutes are as much competitors as other firms competing in the market at the current time. See Fig. 1.3.

Our viewpoint here is somewhat different from Porter's. Instead of the five agents being competitors in an existing environment, we think of the four peripheral forces as potential direct competitors in a future environment. These should each be scrutinized. For example, suppliers and/or customers can become competitors by vertically integrating. Vertical integration occurs whenever a firm internalizes multiple transactions in the chain that extends from raw materials to final consumer. Suppliers of a given firm can become its competitors by *forward* integrating (entering the market in which their products are used as ingredients or components); customers can become competitors by *backward* integrating. Whether to backward integrate is often called a "make-or-buy" decision.

The polystyrene industry is one in which firms vary widely with respect to vertical integration.[38] Polystyrene is a plastic widely used in packaging. It is made from styrene, which is manufactured from ethane, which is derived from natural gas. Major producers include Arco Chemical, Dow Chemical, Huntsman, Fina Chemicals, and Polysar. Dow is highly integrated. It produces nearly all of the styrene needed in its basic chemicals division. It also manufactures the (styrene) cartons in which fast-food hamburgers are often sold. Thus Dow has integrated both forward and backward. On the other hand, Huntsman, the industry leader in terms of capacity, has no end-use markets and buys much of its styrene from outside vendors.

There are many benefits and costs to vertical integration. The benefits include guaranteed access to supply or demand, considerable reduction of transaction costs, and control of supply and/or end-product quality. The costs include increased operating costs, reduced flexibility as a result of increased investment, and possibility of complacency without the threat of direct competition. Obviously, each firm makes its vertical integration decisions by weighing these benefits against the costs. A firm can assess whether a customer or supplier might be a future competitor by role-reversal simulations; that is, by subjectively placing itself in the customer's or supplier's shoes and evaluating these considerations.

Ansoff's Product-Market Matrix

Ansoff's product-market matrix, described in Fig. 3.1 on page 77, provides another framework for identifying future entrants.[39] As previously discussed, the rows represent different products the firm produces. The columns represent markets, or "missions," as Ansoff calls them. A market or *mission* is a description of the job the product is intended to perform and for whom. A product can have multiple missions. For example, Ansoff describes the missions of the Lockheed Aircraft Corporation. One of them is to provide commercial air transportation for passengers; another is to provide the Air Defense Command with airborne early warning; yet a third is to provide the ability to perform hand-to-hand combat.[40]

The original purpose of Ansoff's matrix was to structure and identify possible growth paths. A firm can continue with the same products in the same markets (market penetration), sell the same products in different markets (market development), sell different products in the same markets (product development), or sell different products in different markets (diversification).

With respect to new entrants, we note that if the matrix structures the strategic growth decision for a firm, it must do the same for its competitors. The manager can then put himself or herself in the place of other firms looking for growth and examine the directions suggested by the matrix. In particular, firms that either sell the same product or sell to the same markets (but not both*) are potential future competitors. If one of these firms extends its scope to the manager's markets or products, it becomes a direct competitor. Indeed, it stands to reason that the most likely future competitors will be firms with some expertise in the same arenas. The most obvious candidates are those that know how to make the same product or that sell to the same markets.

Procter & Gamble mass-produces, markets, and sells packaged goods through supermarkets for general consumer use. Virtually any packaged good that can be marketed this way is a potential extension for P&G. Any company that makes a packaged good must consider P&G a potential competitor. Scott Paper Company

---

*If the firm does both, it already is a competitor.

makes, among other things, paper towels for consumer use. The Fort Howard Paper Company makes paper towels for institutional and industrial customers. These two companies sell essentially the same product in different markets. Each must be wary of the other as a potential competitor.

SUMMARY

Identifying competitors is not always a straightforward task. Some may even come from outside the industry a firm operates in. Two principles about competition help to identify it: (1) competition is a matter of degree; and (2) competition is rooted in consumer behavior. Two products are competitors if and only if a consumer only needs one of them on any given occasion. For example, railroads and airlines are competitors. This is not universally true, though, since while both are reasonable ways to travel from New York to Boston, they are not equally reasonable ways to travel from New York to Oslo, Norway. Thus competition exists only to a degree.

This chapter presented a series of methodologies and frameworks useful in identifying competitors. Some, such as those based on brand-switching matrices, are more useful within the product category of interest. Others, such as substitution-in-use analysis, are more useful for identifying potential competitors outside the category. In either case, once competitors have been identified, a manager has to try to predict their actions. Indeed, it is these actions that shape the opportunities and threats a firm faces. Consequently, forecasting competitor action is a prerequisite for long-run success.

Review Questions

1. Can you characterize the types of companies that have most of their competitors outside their industry? Consider product, customer, need, and technology.

2. Sketch a tree diagram to outline the competition for your school or organization.

3. What are the trade-offs between using brand-switching approaches and forced choice and product deletion methods for illuminating market structure?

4. True or false: Rational expectations is a good approximation to the way much competitive analysis is conducted. Why or why not?

5. Using Porter's five forces and/or Ansoff's product-market matrix, outline potential future competition for the world's leading business schools.

Notes

1. See Levitt, Theodore (1960), "Marketing Myopia," *Harvard Business Review* 38 (July-August), 45–56.
2. *Ibid.,* 45.
3. This model was proposed in Porter, Michael E. (1979), "How Competitive Forces Shape Strategy," *Harvard Business Review* 57 (March-April), 137–145.
4. The Procter & Gamble stories are told by Swasy, Alecia (1993), *Soap Opera: The Inside Story of Procter & Gamble,* New York: Times Books.

5. Potential roles are outlined in *New York Times* (1994), "Big Hopes Put on Electric Wires," July 6, D1.
6. See Day, George S., Allan D. Shocker, and Rajendra K. Srivastava (1979), "Customer-Oriented Approaches to Identifying Product-Markets," *Journal of Marketing* 43 (Fall), 8–19, for more complete discussion.
7. One of the landmark discussions of these biases can be found in Tversky, Amos, and Daniel Kahneman (1974),

"Judgment Under Uncertainty: Heuristics and Biases," *Science* 185, 1124–1131.

8. For more detail see Kahneman, Daniel, and Amos Tversky (1972), "Subjective Probability: A Judgment of Representativeness," *Cognitive Psychology* 3 (3), 430–454; and Kahneman, Daniel, and Amos Tversky (1973), "On the Psychology of Prediction," *Psychological Review* 80 (4), 237–251.

9. See for example Engel, James F., Roger D. Blackwell, and Paul W. Miniard (1995), *Consumer Behavior,* 8th ed., Fort Worth, TX: Dryden Press, and Wilkie, William L. (1994), *Consumer Behavior,* 3rd ed., New York: Wiley.

10. The original discussion by Stefflre (1972) is a generalization of the methods proposed here. Stefflre was interested in grouping both products and uses. We are concerned just with products. That enables us to invoke a somewhat simplified set of procedures.

11. Srivastava et al. (1981) suggest hierarchical cluster analysis and Stefflre (1972) suggests perceptual mapping. Both sets of techniques use similarity measures as input. Both are equally interpretable. In situations like this, the choice is often made on the basis of software availability.

12. This approach is described in Bourgeois, Jacques C., George H. Haines, Jr., and Montrose S. Sommers (1979), "Defining an Industry," *Market Measurement and Analysis,* Proceedings of the First Market Measurement and Analysis Conference, D. Montgomery and D. Wittink (eds.), Cambridge, MA: Marketing Science Institute, 120–133.

13. See Bass, Frank M., Edgar A. Pessemier, and Donald R. Lehmann (1972), "An Experimental Study of Relationships between Attitudes, Brand Preference, and Choice," *Behavioral Science* 17 (November), 532–541.

14. Neslin, Scott A., and Robert W. Shoemaker (1989), "An Alternative Explanation for Lower Repeat Rates after Promotion Purchases," *Journal of Marketing Research* 26 (May), 205–213, develop an intriguing model of how promotions impact repeat purchase probabilities.

15. Blattberg, Robert C., and Kenneth J. Wisniewski (1989), "Price Induced Patterns of Competition," *Marketing Science,* 8 (Fall), 291–309 develop a very compelling model that explains this.

16. See Rao, Vithala R., and Darius J. Sabavala (1981), "Inference of Hierarchical Choice Processes from Panel Data," *Journal of Consumer Research* 8 (June), 85–96, for complete details.

17. *Ibid.*

18. For more complete descriptions of the Hendry System, see Kalwani, Manohar U., and Donald G. Morrison (1977), "A Parsimonious Description of the Hendry System," *Management Science* 23 (January), 467–477; and Rao, Vithala R. (1981), "New Product Sales Forecasting Using the Hendry System," in *New Product Forecasting,* Y. Wind, V. Mahajan, and R. W. Cardozo (eds.), Lexington, MA: Lexington Books, 499–527.

19. See Urban, Glen L., Philip L. Johnson, and John R. Hauser (1984), "Testing Competitive Market Structures," *Marketing Science* 3 (Spring), 83–113, for complete details.

20. Grover, Rajiv, and Vithala R. Rao (1988), "Inferring Competitive Market Structure Based on a Model of Interpurchase Intervals," *International Journal of Research in Marketing* 5, 55–72, present a more sophisticated approach which estimates elasticities of substitution from interpurchase times allowing for preference heterogeneity and multiple usage occasions. In their framework brands are perfect substitutes if their elasticity of substitution is equal to 1.

21. See Hall, M., and L. Weiss (1967), "Firm Size and Profitability," *Review of Economics and Statistics* 49 (August), 319–331, for an explication of this view.

22. This example is discussed more fully in Kotler, Phillip (1991), *Marketing Management: Analysis, Planning, and Control,* 7th ed., Englewood Cliffs, NJ: Prentice-Hall, 227.

23. See Porter, Michael (1976), *Interbrand Choice, Strategy, and Bilateral Market Power,* Cambridge: Harvard University Press.

24. The spectrum of variables is described in the review by McGee, John, and Howard Thomas (1986), "Strategic Groups: Theory, Research, and Taxonomy," *Strategic Management Journal* 7, 141–160.

25. See Abell, Derek (1980), *Defining the Business,* Englewood Cliffs, NJ: Prentice-Hall.

26. This study is described by Frazier, Gary L., and Roy D. Howell (1980), "Business Definition and Performance," *Journal of Marketing* 47 (Spring), 59–67.

27. The story of American Airlines and airline pricing is told in Smith, Timothy K. (1995), "Why Air Travel Doesn't Work," *Fortune,* April 3, 42–56.

28. The demise of EMI is reported in Barron, Cheryll (1979), "What Scarred EMI's Scanner," *Management Today* (February), 67ff.

29. For a more complete discussion, see Porter, Michael E. (1980), *Competitive Strategy,* New York: Free Press, Chapter 3.

30. This principle was formulated by D'Aspremont, Claude, Jean Jaskold-Gabszewicz, and Jacques-Francois Thisse (1979), "On Hotelling's 'Stability in Competition'," *Econometrica* 47, 1145–1150.

31. Both of these are discussed in great detail by Fiske, Susan T., and Shelley E. Taylor (1991), *Social Cognition,* 2nd ed., New York: McGraw-Hill.

32. False consensus is reviewed by Marks, G., and N. Miller (1987), "Ten Years of Research on the False-Consensus Effect: An Empirical and Theoretical Review," *Psychological Bulletin* 102, 72–90.

33. Robertson, Thomas S., and Jehoshua Eliashberg (1988), "New Product Preannouncing Behavior: A Market Signalling Study," *Journal of Marketing Research* 25 (August), 282–292, discuss many of these in depth.

34. See *Business Week* (1994), "Little Fridges for those Hot PC's," July 25, 82.

35. For more information on how firms react to price cuts, see Rao, Vithala R., and Joel H. Steckel (1995), "A Cross-Cultural Analysis of Price Responses to Environmental Changes," *Marketing Letters* 7 (January), 5–12.

36. This exercise is fully described in Halberstam, David (1973), *The Best and the Brightest,* London: Barrie and Jenkins, 558–560.

37. These clues are taken from Armstrong, J. Scott (1985), *Long-Range Forecasting: From Crystal Ball to Computer,* 2nd ed., New York: Wiley, 125.

38. The polystyrene industry is discussed by Oster, Sharon M. (1994), *Modern Competitive Analysis,* 2nd ed., New York: Oxford, 196–197.

39. The matrix is fully described in Ansoff, H. Igor (1988), *The New Corporate Strategy,* New York: Wiley.

40. A complete description of the Lockheed example can be found in Ansoff, H. Igor (1957), "Strategies for Diversification," *Harvard Business Review* 35 (September/October), 113–124.

Bibliography

Abell, Derek (1980), *Defining the Business,* Englewood Cliffs, NJ: Prentice-Hall.

Ansoff, H. Igor (1957), "Strategies for Diversification," *Harvard Business Review* 35 (September/October), 113–124.

— (1988), *The New Corporate Strategy,* New York: Wiley.

Armstrong, J. Scott (1985), *Long-Range Forecasting: From Crystal Ball to Computer,* 2nd ed., New York: Wiley.

Barron, Cheryll (1979), "What Scarred EMI's Scanner," *Management Today* (February), 67ff.

Bass, Frank M., Edgar A. Pessemier, and Donald R. Lehmann (1972), "An Experimental Study of Relationships between Attitudes, Brand Preference, and Choice," *Behavioral Science* 17 (November), 532–541.

Blattberg, Robert C., and Kenneth J. Wisniewski (1989), "Price Induced Patterns of Competition," *Marketing Science* 8 (Fall), 291–309.

Bourgeois, Jacques C., George H. Haines, Jr., and Montrose S. Sommers (1979), "Defining an Industry," *Market Measurement and Analysis,* Procedings of the First Market Measurement and Analysis Conference, D. Montgomery and D. Wittink (eds.), Cambridge, MA: Marketing Science Institute, 120–133.

Bucklin, Randolph E., Gary J. Russell, and V. Srinivasan (1994), "A Relationship Between Price Elasticities and Brand Switching Probabilities in Heterogeneous Markets," *Mimeo* (June).

Business Week (1994), "Little Fridges for those Hot PC's," July 25, 82.

Colombo, Richard A., and Donald G. Morrison (1989), "A Brand Switching Model with Implications for Marketing Strategies," *Marketing Science* 8 (Winter), 89–99.

D'Aspremont, Claude, Jean Jaskold-Gabszewicz, and Jacques-Francois Thisse (1979), "On Hotelling's 'Stability in Competition'," *Econometrica* 47, 1145–1150.

Day, George S., Allan D. Shocker, and Rajendra K. Srivastava (1979), "Customer-Oriented Approaches to Identifying Product-Markets," *Journal of Marketing* 43 (Fall), 8–19.

Engel, James F., Roger D. Blackwell, and Paul W. Miniard (1995), *Consumer Behavior,* 8th ed., Fort Worth, TX: Dryden Press.

Fiske, Susan T., and Shelley E. Taylor (1991), *Social Cognition,* 2nd ed., New York: McGraw-Hill.

Frazier, Gary L., and Roy D. Howell (1980), "Business Definition and Performance," *Journal of Marketing* 47 (Spring), 59–67.

Green, Paul E., and Vithala R. Rao (1972), *Applied Multidimensional Scaling,* New York: Holt, Rinehart, and Winston.

Grover, Rajiv, and Vithala R. Rao (1988), "Inferring Competitive Market Structure Based on a Model of Interpurchase Intervals," *International Journal of Research in Marketing* 5, 55–72.

Halberstam, David (1973), *The Best and the Brightest,* London: Barrie and Jenkins.

Hall, M., and L. Weiss (1967), "Firm Size and Profitability," *Review of Economics and Statistics* 49 (August), 319–331.

Harshman, Richard A., Paul E. Green, Yoram J. Wind, and Margaret E. Lundy (1982), "A Model for the Analysis of Asymmetric Data in Marketing Research," *Marketing Science* 1 (Spring), 205–242.

Kahneman, Daniel, and Amos Tversky (1972), "Subjective Probability: A Judgment of Representativeness," *Cognitive Psychology* 3 (3), 430–454.

— (1973), "On the Psychology of Prediction," *Psychological Review* 80 (4), 237–251.

Kalwani, Manohar U., and Donald G. Morrison (1977), "A Parsimonious Description of the Hendry System," *Management Science* 23 (January), 467–477.

Kotler, Phillip (1991), *Marketing Management: Analysis, Planning, and Control,* 7th ed., Englewood Cliffs, NJ: Prentice-Hall, 227.

Levitt, Theodore (1960), "Marketing Myopia," *Harvard Business Review* 38 (July-August), 45–56.

March, James G., and Herbert A. Simon (1958), *Organizations,* New York: Wiley.

Marks, G., and N. Miller (1987), "Ten Years of Research on the False-Consensus Effect: An Empirical and Theoretical Review," *Psychological Bulletin* 102, 72–90.

McGee, John, and Howard Thomas (1986), "Strategic Groups: Theory, Research, and Taxonomy," *Strategic Management Journal* 7, 141–160.

Moore, Marian Chapman, and Joe E. Urbany (1994), "Blinders, Fuzzy Lenses, and the Wrong Shoes: Pitfalls in Competitive Conjecture," *Marketing Letters* 5 (July), 249.

Neslin, Scott A., and Robert W. Shoemaker (1989), "An Alternative Explanation for Lower Repeat Rates after Promotion Purchases," *Journal of Marketing Research* 26 (May), 205–213.

New York Times, (1994), "Big Hopes Put on Electric Wires" July 6, D1.

1990 Category Facts Book, Tokyo: Distribution Economics Institute of Japan.

Oster, Sharon M. (1994), *Modern Competitive Analysis,* 2nd ed., New York: Oxford.

Porter, Michael E. (1976), *Interbrand Choice, Strategy, and Bilateral Market Power,* Cambridge: Harvard University Press.

— (1979), "How Competitive Forces Shape Strategy," *Harvard Business Review* 57 (March-April), 137–145.

Rao, Vithala R. (1981), "New Product Sales Forecasting Using the Hendry System," in *New Product Forecasting,* Y. Wind, V. Mahajan, and R. W. Cardozo (eds.), Lexington, MA: Lexington Books, 499–527.

Rao, Vithala R., and Darius J. Sabavala (1981), "Inference of Hierarchical Choice Processes from Panel Data," *Journal of Consumer Research* 8 (June), 85–96.

Rao, Vithala R., and Joel H. Steckel (1995), "A Cross-Cultural Analysis of Price Responses to Environmental Changes," *Marketing Letters* 6 (January), 5–14.

Robertson, Thomas S., and Jehoshua Eliashberg (1988), "New Product Preannouncing Behavior: A Market Signalling Study," *Journal of Marketing Research* 25 (August), 282–292.

Simon, Herbert A. (1957), *Models of Man,* New York: Wiley.

Smith, Timothy K. (1995), "Why Air Travel Doesn't Work," *Fortune,* April 3, 42–56.

Srivastava, Rajendra K., Robert P. Leone, and Allan D. Shocker (1981), "Market Structure Analysis: Hierarchical Clustering of Products Based on Substitution-In-Use," *Journal of Marketing* 45 (Summer), 38–48.

Stefflre, Volney J. (1972), "Some Applications of Multidimensional Scaling to Social Science Problems," in R. Shepard, A. K. Romney, and S. Nerlove (eds.), *Multidimensional Scaling: Theory and Applications in the Behavioral Sciences,* New York: Academic Press, 211–243.

— (1977), "New Products: Organizational and Technical Problems and Opportunities," in *Analytic Approaches to Product and Marketing Planning,* A. D. Shocker (ed.), Cambridge, MA: Marketing Science Institute, 415–480.

Swasy, Alecia (1993), *Soap Opera: The Inside Story of Procter & Gamble,* New York: Times Books.

The Wall Street Journal, "Car Makers Use Image Map as Tool to Position Products," (1984), March 22, 33.

Tversky, Amos, and Daniel Kahneman (1974), "Judgment Under Uncertainty: Heuristics and Biases," *Science* 185, 1124–1131.

Urban, Glen L., Philip L. Johnson, and John R. Hauser (1984), "Testing Competitive Market Structures," *Marketing Science* 3 (Spring), 83–113.

Wilkie, William L. (1994), *Consumer Behavior,* 3rd ed., New York: Wiley.

Understanding and Forecasting the External Environment

Demographic, Social, Economic, and Political Factors

INTRODUCTION

Having identified the trends in customer behavior, unmet customer needs, and competitive forces, the analyst has to turn to the other environmental forces affecting the strategies of a business. In general, this analysis will need to be conducted at the level of the industry in which the specific business unit competes. Any given industry's fortunes will naturally depend on the behavior of its customers, competitors, and suppliers. At a macro level, these behaviors are influenced by a variety of environmental factors, which can be categorized into four groups: political, economic, social (demographic, cultural, and sociological), and technological factors. The acronym PEST will help you remember these categories. The PEST factors can be instrumental in providing opportunities for and imposing threats on the firm.

The technological trends in the computer industry offer an interesting illustration. The technological developments in the semiconductor industry leading to the development of the personal computer offered significant business opportunities for several firms (Apple, IBM, Dell, and Compaq) and at the same time contributed significantly to the precipitous decline in sales of mainframe computers. A firm like IBM faced both an opportunity and a threat due to the technological innovation of the personal computer in the 1980s. A few years later, the personal computer industry was threatened by the technology of miniaturization that led to the introduction of laptop computers. Interestingly, although this industry is in first bloom, it may face difficulties due to the advent of even smaller computers, called *PDAs* (or *personal digital assistants*).[1]

Analysis of environmental (PEST) factors is a major component of SWOT (Strengths, Weaknesses, Opportunities, and Threats) analysis for any particular business. The results can be summarized as a number of potential future scenarios and a set of strategic questions. The strategic questions are "What if?"-type questions intended to ascertain the likely impact of a specific environmental trend or a set of related trends. They can be answered when the strategy analyst has developed a forecasting system, including "scenario analysis" methods.

The second part of the SWOT analysis relates to the determination of strengths and weaknesses of the business relative to its present or potential competition. This analysis also involves an assessment of the firm's resources and other capabilities to compete in the environment of the future.

This and the next two chapters will cover relevant methods for comprehensive SWOT analysis. In this chapter, we will describe analytic methods for identifying various factors in the external environment that are most important to the growth of a firm's business. We discuss some ways of determining the likely future environmental trends. In Chapter 6, we continue this discussion and will cover various analytical methods for forecasting market dynamics. In Chapter 7, we cover methods for analyzing strengths and weaknesses of a business relative to its competitors.

In the next section of this chapter, we enumerate various factors in the environment to be considered in an opportunities-threats analysis. We also identify characteristics of strategic situations where environmental understanding is paramount. In the third section, we classify various available techniques for looking at specific aspects of the environment and the various sources of data. In the fourth section, we describe a subset of these techniques in some depth and provide examples. Finally, we conclude with ways of assessing the impact of one or more environmental trends.

SITUATIONS WHERE ENVIRONMENTAL UNDERSTANDING IS CRITICAL

In general, it is necessary for a manager to keep up with changes in the external environment and to adapt business strategies to it. It is also essential for a manager to be proactive and to anticipate the kinds of changes likely to occur in the future so that he or she is well armed with contingent strategies to meet the opportunities and threats posed. Table 5.1 categorizes various environmental trends as political, economic, social/cultural/demographic, and technological factors; it also shows potential consequences of these trends as opportunities and threats for selected businesses. For example, the creation of NAFTA will offer opportunities for certain high-technology industries while at the same time reducing demand for certain U.S. supplier industries due to possible relocation of their customer companies to Mexico.

The effects of environmental changes may be very small in certain mature industries such as detergent and toothpaste, where demand trends are essentially governed by changes in the population size (or customer base). Even here, a firm seeking to focus on a specific market segment may need to understand how changes in the

TABLE 5.1   Environmental Trends, Opportunities, and Threats

Environmental Factors	Opportunities	Threats
Political Factors		
NAFTA	Export possibilities for certain high-technology industries such as computers and software	Potential loss of demand for certain supplier industries in the U.S. due to relocation of their customers
Passage of legislation taxing alcohol and cigarettes	Demand for products such as nonalcoholic beer	Potential lowering of demand for alcohol industry products such as wine or whiskey
Economic Factors		
Economic development in South Asian countries	Potential for certain U.S. companies to form strategic alliances with local firms	Potential for increases in costs of production in those industries that have enjoyed low-cost sources in these countries
Lowering of capital gains taxes	Potential availability of capital for emerging industries	
Social/Cultural/Demographic Factors		
Increasing participation of women in the workforce	Increasing demand for convenience goods Increasing demand for direct-mail shopping	Potential decline in the demand for certain leisure-oriented industries
Aging of the U.S. population	Increasing demand for various health care services	Likely reduction in the school-going population and demand for educational services Potential reduction in the demand for durable goods due to a decrease in the number of households
Increasing diversity of the U.S. population	Several emerging niche markets Increasing opportunities for special media vehicles to appeal to minorities	Potential decrease in the demand for certain well-established industries
Technological Factors		
Developments in genetic engineering	Increasing demand for certain pharmaceutical products	Potential decline in certain well-established pharmaceutical products
Miniaturization of microprocessors	Increasing demand for notebook or palmtop computers and software for such computers	Potential decline in desktop computer and workstations

environment affect the size of that segment; for example, a toothpaste marketer focusing on selling a brand of toothpaste aimed at cleaning dentures may need to understand the demographic trends in the population that determine the potential market size for such a product.

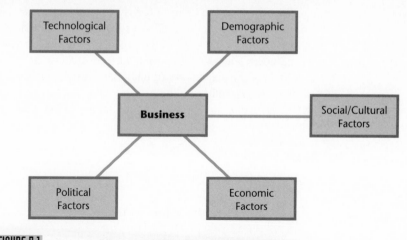

FIGURE 5.1 **External Forces Affecting Any Business**

Understanding and forecasting the effects of environmental changes is essential in nascent industries such as multimedia. Assume you are in charge of a business in such an industry and wish to direct your staff to monitor various aspects of the external environment that might affect your business. As a manager of this business, you may be called upon to provide direction on the specific environmental trends and facts you will need to monitor to make such decisions. The PEST framework described earlier will enable you to reflect upon various factors to be considered in providing direction on data collection. Based on the environmental information gathered and your own knowledge of the business, you might consider changing your product positioning or price, adding new products, or even deleting some existing products.

Fig. 5.1 shows the external forces that impinge on any business and that therefore should be systematically monitored.

The task is to obtain relevant data on these various forces on a periodic basis and to interpret them. In addition to collecting current and past information on these factors, it is necessary to gain some insight into the future. This task involves forecasting trends. Careful interpretation of the results will enable a manager to not only understand the present but make specific assumptions about the future environment in which the business is expected to be operating and make the appropriate strategic adaptations. It is worth pointing out that these adaptations need to be made continuously. In strategy development, it is almost impossible to stand still.

Demand Analysis Framework

Various environmental factors affecting a business can be integrated in terms of the total demand or sales for the product or service (or at the industry level). First, we assume that the analyst has identified market segments relevant to the product or service. We will describe them in terms of demographic, social, and cultural factors. Next, we decompose the total sales of a product or service in any time period as simply the sum of the sales of the product or service arising from the different market segments. The sales from each market segment can be further decomposed as the product of the (1) number of potential customers in the segment; (2) proportion of these units purchasing the product; and (3) average rate of purchase of the product or service by the members of the segment. Using this logic, we can write the demand D_t as:

$$D_t = \sum_{s=1}^{S_t} N_{st} \pi_{st} R_{st} \tag{1}$$

where

S_t = number of market segments at time t;

N_{st} = number of potential customers in the s-th segment at time t;

π_{st} = proportion of the s-th segment units purchasing the product or service; and

R_{st} = average purchase quality of the product or service by the members of the s-th segment at time t.

Equation (1) describes the decomposition of demand in terms of market segments at a given point in time. The same equation can also be used for forecasting the future demand for the product, using forecasts of the components of demand.

Fig. 5.2 shows the following relationships between various environmental factors and demand components:

1. The demographic, social/cultural, and economic factors are the essential factors in the determination of number of market segments and their sizes for a product or service. The figure also recognizes the possibility that the number of segments used in the demand decomposition can vary over time. This feature is important, as it incorporates new ways of segmenting the market as the business environment changes.

   As in Chapter 2, variables such as product benefits are used in determining segments. Even in that case segments will ultimately need to be defined in terms of demographic, social, and economic factors before appropriate strategies can be decided upon.

2. The proportion of units in any market segment purchasing the product or service will be influenced by economic factors as well as social/cultural and political/legal factors. In addition, technological factors that determine new product introductions will also influence the proportion of units buying the product.

3. While purchase rates are naturally influenced by economic factors, they are also affected by social/cultural and political/legal factors. In particular political/legal factors may restrict the availability of products to certain segments of the market; such restrictions will naturally influence purchase rates. For exam-

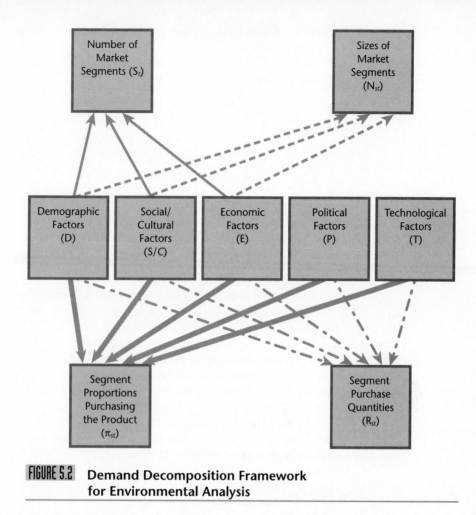

FIGURE 5.2 **Demand Decomposition Framework for Environmental Analysis**

ple, people under 21 are not allowed to purchase beer from supermarkets in some states.

It is important for a strategic analyst to understand the particular environmental forces that affect his/her business and identify appropriate strategies in anticipation of significant changes in the market environment. For example, an athletic footwear marketer will benefit significantly from understanding emerging health and fitness trends. Several firms have made fortunes by designing and marketing walking shoes as more middle-aged people have taken to walking to keep fit.

Against this background, we will now discuss ways of analyzing various environmental factors.

METHODS FOR UNDERSTANDING AND PREDICTING ENVIRONMENTAL FACTORS

Factors to Consider

The particular factors to be considered will depend on the characteristics of the industry in which the business competes. For a multiproduct corporation, different factors may affect individual businesses; for example, the factors that affect the mainframe computer business of IBM are not the same as those that affect its laptop computer business. Whereas the need for organizations to maintain and process large volumes of data could boost the mainframe business, the technological trends toward miniaturization and larger computing power in portable computers may reduce the prospects for mainframes. The same trends, when combined with customer desires for convenience of portability, will enhance the demand for laptop computers.

Overview of Methods

Table 5.2 lists several questions specific to each environmental dimension of interest to managers. Selected methods of analysis specific to each environmental dimension are also indicated. For example, the social and cultural dimensions of the environment affect not only the size of the market in the future but also the demand for specific products. Similarly, regulation will affect the ability of a firm to market certain products (such as environmentally unsafe products). Various methods—from those used in demographic analysis to sophisticated methods for forecasting technology—are needed to perform a full-fledged analysis of environmental factors. It should be clear from this table that because of the importance of a variety of environmental dimensions, a combination of methods is always called for in this phase of strategic analysis.

Sources of Data

The strategic analyst has to consult several public and private sources of data to be confident that he or she has analyzed the trends in a comprehensive manner. In addition to public sources such as the publications of the U.S. Government's Department of Commerce (census publications and reports of economic surveys), the analyst may consult reports of surveys conducted by private organizations such as Roper, Gallup, and Yankelovich. It is particularly important to include private sources in any information search because they tend to focus on a limited array of topics and are often timely. On the other hand, governmental surveys and censuses cover a broad range of topics and generally take much longer to become available; nevertheless, they are quite useful in determining general trends.

Appendix 5A contains a comprehensive description of strategies for conducting a secondary search for environmental analysis of interest in marketing strategy. It also contains an illustration of search as applied to the pharmaceutical industry. The reader is urged to go through this material to fully appreciate the wealth of information available in public sources.

TABLE 5.2 **Dimensions and Methods of Environmental Analysis**

Environmental Dimension	Managerial Questions	Suitable Methods of Analysis
Political/ Governmental	(a) What changes in the regulation are possible? How will they affect the business demand?	Analysis of regulations Environmental monitoring Public opinion polls
	(b) What political risks exist in countries the firm wishes to expand to?	
Social/Cultural/ Demographic	(a) What trends are emerging in the sociological, cultural, and lifestyle areas in the markets (countries) where the firm is operating?	Content analysis of popular press Lifestyle analysis
	(b) How would these trends affect the demand for existing products or help create new products?	General-purpose consumer surveys
	(c) What trends of population growth and population movement are emerging in the next few years?	
	(d) What are some opportunities and threats due to these trends?	
Economic	(a) What are the economic prospects in the markets (countries) where the firm currently operates or plans to operate in the future?	Macroeconomic forecasting models
	(b) How would they affect the business?	
Technological	(a) What are some emerging technologies that will affect the current products or their production processes?	Technological forecasting methods
	(b) What are the life-cycle trends of the current technologies?	Life-cycle analysis
All aspects	(a) Given various trends, what future environmental scenarios are likely to emerge?	Scenario analysis Cross-impact analysis
	(b) How should the firm adapt to these changes?	

In Appendix 5B, we list various sources of interest to a marketing strategist. These sources include corporate annual reports, publications by such organizations as Standard & Poor's and Dow Jones, and publications based on media and consumption surveys of Simmons Market Research Bureau, SRDS, Mediamark, and the like. In addition, many companies compile data from several sources and make them accessible to marketing strategists; these include Gale Research, Claritas, and Equifax. *American Demographics,* a monthly magazine, also synthesizes various census, private, and public survey data and publishes articles on trends and population projections.

Assessing the Quality of Published Data

It is crucial for an analyst to ensure that the data compiled from secondary sources are of the highest possible quality. We urge the analyst to keep in mind the following factors that may affect the quality of published data:

1. *Consider the caliber and reputation of the organization collecting the secondary data.* Look for possible biases of the organization collecting the data. If the organization has been in business for a long time, it may have been scrutinized by others and rectified any problems.
2. *Consider the organization sponsoring the study from which the data are taken.* The sponsoring organization may have a specific objective in collecting the data, such as "proving" a particular point of view. In such cases, the published data may be biased.
3. *Consider the objectives of the study, which formed the basis for secondary data.* The objectives in the secondary study may be reflected in the sample used, questions asked, and so on. Thus, while the data reported may be accurate, they may be relevant only for a particular segment of the population.
4. *Look at the particular statistical methods employed in the secondary data.* One should carefully examine the weighting methods used for projecting the results to the whole population before using the total numbers.
5. *Look at the classifications and definitions used in the tabulations employed in the published data.* The classifications (or groupings) used for such variables as age, income, and occupation may not correspond to those in which the marketing strategic analyst is interested. In such a case, the analyst may need to adjust the published data. For example, one may be looking for data by sales territories that span parts of several states and data may be available only by state; in such a case, the analyst may need to adjust the published data.

    Finally, the definitions of some variables in published data may change over time. The analyst has to be cognizant of such changes before utilizing such data.
6. *Consider the timeliness of the published data.* Some data, such as census data, may not be timely enough for the project at hand. The researcher has to consider ways of updating such data to ensure that they are reasonably current.
7. Avoid significant problems with published data by adopting the following simple tips:

    a. *If possible, go to the original source.* This procedure avoids errors in transcription from one source to another.

    b. *Cross-check the data with other sources.* Cross-checking data is particularly useful if the different sources used distinct methods for producing the data reported. Also, one should cross-check against past data on the same subject; if the change between past and current data is not dramatic and is in line with other trends in the economy, one may be confident of the accuracy of the data. If not, one must look deeply to determine the reasons for large changes before using the data.

c. *Determine whether there exists any legal authority for the organization collecting the data.* For example, the Internal Revenue Service has legal data-collecting authority in connection with tax returns, which increases compliance or coverage. One may therefore be reasonably confident that such data are quite accurate. But trade associations do not necessarily have such authority to ensure compliance from members. Thus, it becomes important to look at the procedures used by such organizations for increasing response.

d. *It is important to look at the footnotes and endnotes to various tables reported in secondary sources.* These notes contain information that will enable the analyst to evaluate the scope and accuracy of such data. For example, some data reported may be only estimates while others are actual data.

e. *Stay alert to any changes in research designs by the organization reporting the data over time.*

f. *Consult the most current original source.* It is likely to contain adjustments made to time series data, particularly if changes are made to definitions and research designs over time.

Role of Experts

While published data generally refer to past trends and give some direction for the future, strategy analysts may consult experts in particular fields to ascertain the import of specific trends and how the technologies of certain industries are likely to develop. Such consultation is particularly necessary in fast-moving, technology-intensive industries such as biotechnology, genetic engineering, multimedia, and microprocessors.

METHODS FOR ANALYZING DEMOGRAPHIC FACTORS

Owing to the considerable importance of demographic data in strategic analysis, we will discuss methods for demographic analysis separately.

Understanding Census Data

The 1990 census contains a rich set of data on population and housing characteristics highly valuable for marketing analysis. In addition to reports on the decennial census, the U.S. Census Bureau publishes periodic reports that provide projections and estimates on the size and characteristics of the population. Some items in the census are collected for the whole population, while others are collected on a sample basis. Among the items collected on complete count are number of persons in household, relationship among household members, sex, race, age, year of birth, marital status, and Hispanic origin of each person in the household; and such housing characteristics as number of units in the structure, number of rooms in the unit, tenure (owned or rented), and value of home or monthly rent. Information on social characteristics (education, place of birth, citizenship, language), economic characteristics (labor force status, occupation, work experience), and some housing

TABLE 5.3 1990 U.S. Census: Complete Enumeration and Sample Component Questionnaires

Complete Enumeration	
Population	**Housing**
Number of persons in household	Number of units in structure
Relationships of household members	Number of rooms in unit
Sex of each person in the household	Tenure (owned or rented)
Race of each person in the household	Value of home or monthly rent paid
Age and year of birth of each person in the household	Lot size of the house (more than 10 acres or not)
Marital status of each person in the household	Congregate housing (meals included in rent)
Hispanic origin of each person in the household	Vacancy characteristics of the housing unit

Sample Component	
Population	**Housing**
Social Characteristics of Each Person in Household	Condominium status
	Number of bedrooms
Education (enrollment and attainment)	Year structure built
Place of birth, citizenship, and year of immigration	Lot size of the house (less than one acre or not)
Ancestry	Year moved into residence
Language spoken at home	Farm residence
Migration (residence in 1985)	Shelter costs, including utilities*
Disability	Plumbing and kitchen facilities
Fertility (number of children born)	Telephone in unit
Veteran status	House heating fuel
Economic Characteristics of Each Person in Household	Source/method of water and sewer
	Number of vehicles available
Labor force status	
Occupation and industry of worker	
Place of work and journey to work	
Work experience in 1989	
Year last worked	
Income in 1989	

*Detailed questions added in this category.

Source: Adapted with permission from Dowell Myers, *Analysis with Local Census Data.* (Boston: Academic Press, 1991).

characteristics (number of bedrooms, telephone, house heating fuel, and number of vehicles available) are collected on a sample basis. The contents of the 1990 census are shown in Table 5.3.

Census data are also available at the level of smaller geographic areas (such as census block) and at higher levels of aggregation (county, city, state). Several cross-tabulations of the population characteristics can be made. For marketing purposes, housing characteristics such as number of bedrooms and possession of a telephone are often as useful as demographic characteristics.

Forecasts of Population Trends Based on the census data and other information, demographers develop periodic forecasts of the entire population or subgroups. A marketing analyst should keep abreast of such forecasts. A good source is the U.S. Bureau of the Census. Occasionally, *American Demographics* magazine publishes forecasts of facets of the population trends that are either direct compilations or based on additional analyses.

Methods of Population Analysis

Population Forecasting Methods All methods for forecasting the population of any geographic area use the fundamental equation:

Population at time $t + 1$ = Population at time t + Number of births during the period $(t, t+1)$ − Number of deaths during the period $(t, t+1)$ + Immigration during $(t, t+1)$ − Emigration during $(t, t+1)$.

Population forecasters forecast each component on the right-hand side of this equation and combine them. They use the age distribution of the population and age-specific rates of births and deaths to predict the numbers of births and deaths. (The distribution of the female population and age-specific fertility rates are used to forecast the number of births. Also, prediction of sex ratio at birth is used to obtain separate estimates of babies born of each sex.) The immigration forecasts are made by examining any legal limits set by the geographic area or by forecasting past trends. A similar procedure is used for emigration. In either case, forecasts are made by age group.

The Census Bureau estimates birth and death rates for subgroups defined on a larger number of characteristics (age, sex, occupation, education, and so on), forecasts the numbers of births and deaths for each subgroup defined, and aggregates the forecasts for the population as a whole. This procedure will yield not only a forecast of the total population, but forecasts by age and perhaps sex. The forecasts of population by age and sex can subsequently be used in developing forecasts for the next and subsequent years using a similar procedure. Usually, such projections are made for five-year intervals because much of the population data are grouped into five-year age intervals. This procedure uses knowledge of age-specific birth and death rates, which in turn are dependent on developments in medicine and social and cultural norms, among others.

While this procedure is suitable for predicting the population of a country, it is much more difficult to use for predicting the future population of smaller geographic areas such as states, cities, and towns. The problem is due to the difficulty in forecasting the component of migration; typically data on internal movements are hard to come by.

We show two forecasts in Tables 5.4 and 5.5, respectively, for number of households for the years 1990–2000 and number of African-Americans during the period 1990–2010.

Two implications of the forecasts in Tables 5.4 and 5.5 are the following:

1. The number of households in the United States should exceed 100 million by the end of the century. Household population growth is slowing; the trend is toward smaller households. These trends have significant consequences for various

TABLE 5.4 **Household Projections: 1990–2000 (Number of family and nonfamily households by age of head of household, with percent distributions; households in thousands)**

Age	1990	Percent	1995	Percent	2000	Percent	Percent Change, 1990–2000
Total households	91,951	100%	98,265	100%	103,828	100%	13%
Under 35	25,138	27	24,274	25	23,072	22	–8
35 to 54	35,059	38	40,921	41	45,441	44	30
55 and older	31,754	35	33,070	34	35,315	34	11
Family households	65,336	100%	70,073	100%	74,174	100%	14%
Under 35	17,370	27	16,807	24	15,905	21	–8
35 to 54	28,399	43	33,147	47	36,810	50	30
55 and older	19,567	30	20,119	29	21,459	29	10
Nonfamily households	26,615	100%	28,192	100%	29,654	100%	11%
Under 35	7,768	29	7,467	26	7,167	24	–8
35 to 54	6,660	25	7,774	28	8,631	29	30
55 and older	12,187	46	12,951	46	13,856	47	14

Source: Dexter, Thomas E. (1992), "Middle-Aging Households," *American Demographics*, July. Reprinted with permission. (c) 1992 *American Demographics,* Ithaca, New York.

TABLE 5.5 **African-Americans: 1990–2010**

	1990		2010		Percent Change, 1990–2010	
	Men	Women	Men	Women	Men	Women
All Ages	14,204	15,782	17,841	19,558	26%	24%
Under age 5	1,297	1,272	1,366	1,312	5%	3%
5 to 14	2,499	2,497	2,931	2,822	17	13
15 to 24	2,581	2,658	2,888	2,826	12	6
25 to 34	2,840	2,984	2,617	2,666	–8	–11
35 to 44	1,978	2,290	2,595	2,778	31	21
45 to 54	1,162	1,484	2,620	2,933	125	98
55 to 64	895	1,181	1,628	2,084	82	76
65 to 74	636	884	741	1,171	17	33
75 and older	316	532	454	964	44	81

Source: Dexter, Thomas E. (1992), "Blacks to 2010," *American Demographics*, December. Reprinted with permission. (c) 1992 *American Demographics,* Ithaca, New York.

consumer packaged goods marketers, such as the need to develop smaller package sizes, for example.

2. African-Americans are the largest ethnic market, with over 30 million people. The number of African-Americans between 25 and 34 will actually decline, while those between 45 and 64 will increase at a rate faster than the national average. Thus, middle-aged people will dominate the population of African-Americans by the year 2010.

Other forecasts of population show that Hispanics and Asian-Americans are quickly increasing their numbers in the United States. In the year 1990 there were 22.4 million Hispanics and 7.3 million Asian-Americans. The rate of growth for Hispanics during the decade from 1980 to 1990 was 53 percent, and over 100 percent for Asians. These trends offer exciting opportunities for developing niche markets in various industries.

The Standardization Technique—A Method for Comparing Two Areas

In marketing, one often needs to make comparisons between the sales performance of two geographic areas, such as states, countries, or market areas. It is particularly important to understand why two areas are performing differently. This understanding can assist in forecasting the future sales performance of one area if it attains the same age-specific consumption rates as the other.

For example, one might wish to understand why sales of a particular product per 1,000 persons in one area differ from the corresponding measure for another area. The *standardization technique,* used in demographic analysis, is useful for this purpose. We illustrate it with hypothetical data, shown in Table 5.6, for sales of a consumer product (shampoo) in two areas, A and B, that differ in population size. Further, we assume we have sales data broken down by the age of the head of household. The relevant data then will be sales in A and B broken down by age and number of households with corresponding ages. These data can be collected through a consumer survey or through scanner panels.

The respective populations in areas A and B are 1,400,000 and 551,000. The respective sales volumes are 5040 thousand and 1613 thousand units. Because they differ, one way to compare sales in A and B is by using per capita sales, shown at the bottom of the Sales Rate columns in Table 5.6. The rate of sales per thousand people in A is 3.60 versus 2.92 in B. On the face of it, this difference is 0.68. The observed difference could be due to various factors. In particular, it could be due to age differences in population or to age-specific sales rates. The age-specific sales rates are shown in the Sales Rate columns. Standardization enables one to determine whether the difference is due mainly to population structure or to rate differences. There are

TABLE 5.6   **Illustration of Standardization**

| Age Group | Area A | | | | Area B | | | |
| | Population | | | | Population | | | |
	Number (000s)	Percent Population (w_{ia})	Sales (000s)	Sales Rate (R_{ia})	Number (000s)	Percent Population (w_{ia})	Sales (000s)	Sales Rate (R_{ib})
Under 25 years	462	33%	340	0.74	209	38%	100	0.48
25–34 years	280	20	2520	9.00	105	19	756	7.20
35–44 years	210	15	1750	8.33	72	13	570	7.92
45–54 years	168	12	315	1.875	44	8	110	2.50
55 years and older	280	20	115	0.41	121	22	77	0.64
Total	1400	100%	5040	3.60	551	100%	1613	2.92

two ways of standardizing for comparing A with B: by using the population structure of A with B's age-specific sales rates or by using the population structure of B with A's age-specific sales rates. These standardized rates follow, along with observed sales rates.

| | Use of Age-Specific Sales Rates of | |
Population Structure of	A	B
A	3.60*	3.31
B	3.21	2.92*

*Observed sales rates

The standardized rate of A, computed using the age-specific rates of B is 3.31. When compared with the unstandardized rate for A of 3.60, this indicates that the age-specific rates of A and B are quite different but, not as different as per capita sales rates would suggest. A direct comparison of 3.60 with 2.92 masks this difference in the age-specific rates. Further, when B's population structure is used with A's age-specific rates, we get a standardized rate of 3.21. Again, a comparison with 2.92 (sales rate of B) points to the fact that the difference between the sales rates of A and B is due both to population structure factors and to age-specific rates.

The formulas used in standardization can be generalized as follows:

Let R_a and R_b be the sales rates of the areas A and B, and w_{ia} and w_{ib} be the percentages of the populations in the age group i for A and B. Further, let the age-specific sales rates for A and B be R_{ia} and R_{ib}, respectively. Then the sales rate of A $= R_a$ $= \Sigma w_{ia} \times R_{ia}$. Similarly, $R_b = \Sigma w_{ib} \times R_{ib}$.

The standardized sales rate of A using the age-specific sales rates of B is $\Sigma(w_{ia} \times R_{ib})$, while the standardized sales rate of A using the population structure of B is $\Sigma(w_{ib} \times R_{ia})$. These can be used in identifying the sources of the differences and in interpreting them.

To determine the separate contributions of population structures and age-specific rates in the difference between R_a and R_b, the following formula is often used:

$$R_a - R_b = \Sigma(w_{ia} + w_{ib}) \times (R_{ia} - R_{ib}) / 2 + \Sigma(R_{ia} + R_{ib}) \times (w_{ia} - w_{ib}) / 2.$$

The first component is a measure of the contribution due to the age-specific rate differences, and the second term is the contribution of the population structure differences. Now, returning to our example in Table 5.6, these two components are 0.39 and 0.29, respectively, making up the total difference of 0.68. This decomposition indicates that the contribution due to the age-specific rate differences is larger than that due to the difference in the population structures.

Although we have shown the method of standardization with one variable—age—it can be applied to classifications using multiple variables—age, sex, occupation, length of residence.[2] It will help pinpoint the sources of the difference in sales behavior of any two entities. The technique can be particularly helpful in making international comparisons.

Cohort Analysis

Description *Cohort analysis* is a technique that helps in understanding whether existing patterns of consumption will persist in the future. A *cohort* is a generation of people born in the same period of time (say, five years). Because they are born in the same period, one can expect that they are subjected to the same set of environmental trends and societal events. These common experiences can manifest themselves as a common set of values. In particular, we may expect that they may adopt the same patterns of consumption behavior. For example, people in their twenties (born around 1970) were raised on television and intense but brief stimulation is required to catch their attention. As time passes, this generation will tend to hold on to this set of values. Thus, understanding the value systems of people belonging to various cohorts makes it possible to extrapolate trends that may emerge in the future.

An industry view of cohorts is shown in Table 5.7. Perkins, a vice-president/account manager for an advertising agency, has identified four possible cohorts based on more than two years of research using such methods as focus groups (with emphasis on younger generations), expert testimony culled from published articles, and field research.

TABLE 5.7 **One View of Cohorts in Current Society**

Cohort	Born During	Core Values	Implications for Marketer
Traditionalists	1920s or earlier	Patriotic, seek financial security, strong religious ethics, respect authority, etc.	Quality and value oriented. Use wisdom and experience in making decisions
Transitioners	1930s and 1940s	Protective and sentimental, desire choices, mistrust other nations	Brand loyal, value oriented, not impulsive in decision making; influenced by celebrity endorsements
Challengers	1950s and 1960s	Individualism and self-fulfillment concerns, "me"-focused, idealistic, moralistic, short-term thinkers, still believe in having it all, self-indulgent lifestyle	Seek information before purchase. Constantly fight the aging process. No longer trendsetters
Space-agers	1970s or later	Skeptical, concerned about the future, economically liberal, politically conservative, show the "just do it" attitude	Street-smart consumers, value products developed for them, look for lasting values, intangible benefits and instant gratification

Source: Adapted from Perkins, Natalie (1993), "Zeroing in on Consumer Values: Cohort Analysis Reveals Some Key Differences Among the Generations," *Advertising Age*, March 22.

Use in Analysis of Consumption   The data on consumption of a product at a point in time can be divided by age group to understand how consumption differs by age. Consider the following data on consumption of soft drinks per person for 1979 adapted from Rentz, Reynolds, and Stoudt.[3] (For this illustration we use some hypothetical data also.)

Age Group (years)	Per Capita Consumption (gallons)	Population Percent
10–19	48.6	16.6%
20–29	48.3	18.3
30–39	42.1	21.5
40–49	34.8	17.9
50+	23.5	25.7

Based on these data, the per capita consumption of soft drinks is 38.23 gallons. It is also clear from these data that per capita consumption varies dramatically by age: younger people drink soft drinks much more than older people. If we were interested in projecting (forecasting) the rate of consumption for a future year, we could obtain population forecasts for the year and use the per capita rates shown above to calculate the average rate of consumption for the future. (Note that population forecasts are available from the Census Bureau.) Such a procedure assumes that the rate of consumption for the age groups will be the same in the future as it is today. Given that the future population will have fewer young people, this forecasting method will yield a lower forecast for the consumption of soft drinks. This method uses cross-sectional data on rates of consumption without invoking any trends. However, this cross-sectional analysis can be wrong because it does not consider the fact that consumption habits, once established at an early age, tend to persist over a lifetime.

Cohort analysis is distinct from analysis of segments defined by age in two ways. Cohort analysis requires data on rates of consumption for at least two periods; segmentation by age requires data for one point in time. Cohort analysis considers not just trends in consumption data across time periods but persistence in behavior of a cohort of people through time. Naturally, this feature is not available in age segmentation analysis.

Cohort analysis explicitly considers the possibility of such persistence. In this method, the 1989 rate of consumption for the 30–39 age group is taken to be that of the 20–29 age group in 1979; that is to say, cohort analysis assumes the consumption habits of the 20–29 age group will persist through their life stages as they age. In fact, these rates are forecasted using historical data on the rates of consumption by age for several time periods. Usually, such data are compiled from longitudinal panel or cross-sectional surveys conducted at periodic intervals. Such cohort tables are illustrated below:

Age	1960	1970	1980	
10–19	31.4	40.0	48.6	
20–29	30.2	42.1	48.3	C7
30–39	21.1	34.7	42.1	C6
40–49	17.3	28.4	34.8	C5
50+	11.8	22.5	23.5	C4
		C1	C2	C3

This cohort table contains information on seven cohorts, C1 through C7. C1 is the cohort of people born prior to 1910 (who were 50 years old or older in 1960), C2 is the cohort of people born between 1911 and 1920 (who were in the 40–49 age group in 1960 and in the 50+ age group in 1970). Similarly, the cohort C4 consists of people aged 20–29 in 1960, 30–39 in 1970, and 40–49 in 1980. Their rates of consumption of soft drinks are 30.2 in 1960, 34.7 in 1970, and 34.8 in 1980. The trend in these three data points can be used to project their consumption in 1990. In a like manner, we can look at the cohort C5, aged 40–49 in 1980, whose rates of consumption were 31.4 in 1960, 42.1 in 1970, and 42.1 in 1980, and project its future rate of consumption in 1990 and later years.

The next table shows the forecasted rate of consumption in 1990 by age group, assuming no specific trends in the rates for the purposes of illustration. Of course, one will have to make a guess for the first age group in 1990. For completeness, we assume that the rate in 1990 for age group 10–19 is the same as that in 1980.

	Projected Rate in 1990	
Age	Cohort Analysis	Cross-sectional Analysis
10–19	48.6	48.6
20–29	48.6	48.3
30–39	48.3	42.1
40–49	42.1	34.8
50+	34.8	23.5

Based on these rates and the expected population distribution of 1990, we can estimate the rate of consumption of soft drinks for the year 1990 to be 37.63 gallons when data on cross-sectional rates are used and 43.59 when estimates from cohort analysis are used. Details are presented in Table 5.8. The actual consumption rate for 1990 was 42.5 gallons. It appears that the estimate from cohort analysis is much closer to the actual rate.

Compared to age-segmentation analysis, cohort analysis has yielded forecasts closer to actual rates for coffee consumption as well.[4] The method was applied to predict three variables: penetration (proportion of persons over ten years old drinking coffee), cups per drinker of coffee, and cups per person (both coffee drinkers and nondrinkers). The first two multiplied together produce the third. Thus, forecasts of the first two are sufficient for a forecast of the third. The results follow.

	Penetration	Cups per Drinker	Cups per Person
1980 actual	.566	3.57	2.02
Cross-sectional forecast	.595	3.35	2.14
Cohort forecast	.519	3.39	2.07
1989 Actual	.525	3.34	1.75

Cross-sectional forecasts predicted an increase in penetration as a result of an aging population despite a decreasing penetration rate for younger cohorts (people born during the period since 1950). While the cross-sectional forecast was closer for the cups per drinker indicator, the cohort forecast was closer for cups per person. This is probably due to the higher accuracy of the cohort forecast for the penetration variables.

TABLE 5.8   **Use of Cohort Analysis to Estimate Consumption of Soft Drinks**

Age Group	Population Percent		Age-specific Rate of Consumption According to	
	1980	1990	Cohort Analysis	Age-Segmentation Analysis
10–19 years	17.3%	13.8%	48.6	48.6
20–29 years	18.1	16.2	48.6	48.3
30–39 years	14.0	16.0	48.3	42.1
40–49 years	10.0	12.6	42.1	34.7
50+ years	26.0	25.4	34.8	23.5
Total (10 years +)	85.4%	84%		
Per capita consumption (Gallons)	35.0	42.5	43.59	37.63
	(Actual)		(Estimated)	

In practice, cohort analysis uses regression to forecast the age-specific rates into the future. For this purpose, data on age-specific consumption rates for a number of years are regressed against three predictors: year for which data are applicable (trend variable), age group, and cohort membership. These regressions capture not only the trends over time, but also the effects of age and cohort membership. They can then be used to predict the future consumption rates of different age groups. It is worth pointing out that ad hoc methods will be necessary to estimate the consumption rate for the new cohort—members born recently and for whom there is no historical information.

METHODS FOR ANALYZING SOCIAL/CULTURAL FACTORS

One might argue that the 1992 decision by the Ralph Lauren company to use a 12-year-old girl in its ads for Polo for Boys, a product line that has always sold well with girls, was an adaptation to changes in the country's cultural attitudes.[5] It appears the firm has embarked on a 25-year project to broaden its image by deemphasizing the icon of the Wasp male in its advertisements. Such changes in strategy require a careful analysis of social and cultural trends.

Understanding of changes in social values and cultural norms can be gained by a thorough content analysis of various human interest and other stories reported in the media (newspapers, magazines, and television shows). Given the importance of this kind of analysis, some firms have chosen to analyze these reports and speculate on evolving trends. We will describe two such content analysis efforts—*The Popcorn Report* and *Megatrends 2000*. In addition, we will review three other ways to assess the impact of social/cultural trends: future shock, lifestyle analysis, and general-purpose consumer surveys. The last two approaches are based on information gathered through survey research, while the first two are based on content analysis and creative assessment and speculation.

Content Analysis of the Popular Press

Content analysis of the popular press has become an accepted way to understand social and cultural trends and to predict trends in a broad sense. These predictions are at a highly aggregated level and are not generally useful for the design of a marketing strategy for a specific product, but they do provide a social context in which to interpret the sales patterns of existing products and to glean new product opportunities. To gain maximum advantage from such predictions, one may have to be creative and forgo insisting on a quantitative basis for predictions. It must be underscored that knowledge of broad trends will provide a context in which a specific marketing strategy can be crafted and evaluated. The particulars of any strategy will naturally depend on the specific demand and competitive situation encountered by the business in question.

The task of collecting the necessary information and interpreting social and cultural trends in society is quite involved and requires constant vigilance. In light of the importance of this activity and its ensuing difficulties, several consulting firms have emerged to help industrial clients follow various trends. This information helps a firm in the process of designing and changing marketing strategies. We now describe *The Popcorn Report* and *Megatrends 2000.*

The Popcorn Report   *The Popcorn Report,* published periodically by Faith Popcorn, describes nine so-called BrainReserve Trends:[6]

1. *Cashing Out:* Working women and men, questioning personal/career satisfaction and goals, opt for simple living;
2. *Cocooning:* People feel the need to protect themselves from the harsh, unpredictable realities of the outside world;
3. *Down-Aging:* Nostalgic for their carefree childhood, baby boomers find comfort in familiar pursuits and products of their youth;
4. *Egonomics:* The sterile computer era breeds the desire to make a personal statement;
5. *Fantasy Adventure:* The modern age whets our desire for roads untaken;
6. *99 Lives:* Too fast a pace, too little time causes societal schizophrenia and forces us to assume multiple roles and adapt easily;
7. *Small Indulgences:* Stressed-out consumers want to indulge in affordable luxuries and seek ways to reward themselves;
8. *Staying Alive:* Awareness that good health extends longevity leads to a new way of life;
9. *The Vigilante Consumer:* The consumer manipulates marketers and the marketplace through pressure, protest, and politics.

While these assessments are essentially the judgments of members of the Popcorn group, they may contain an element of truth. They are based on an extensive analysis of many sources of information. The BrainReserve Reading List consists of some 130 magazines, newspapers, newsletters, and trade publications covering the various subjects shown in Table 5.9. Trends reported in these sources are culled out and then incorporated into the company's TrendBank. The group also interviews various executives and other thinkers for additional information on emerging trends.

TABLE 5.9   **Sources Consulted by the BrainReserve Group**

Topic	Number of Publications	Examples
General interest/Information	21	*Newsweek, Working Mother*
Men	5	*Men's Health, Esquire*
News	7	*The Wall Street Journal, The New York Times*
Science	5	*Science Digest, Omni*
Health	7	*American Health, Self*
Food/Liquor	5	*Gourmet, Vegetarian Times*
Home	3	*Architectural Digest, HG*
Travel/International	9	*Travel & Leisure, Tokyo Journal*
Entertainment/Gossip	10	*National Enquirer, Entertainment Weekly*
Literary/Art	9	*The New Yorker, The Atlantic*
Business	6	*Business Week, Business Ethics*
Economics	2	*The Economist, Japan Economic Journal*
Politics	8	*New Republic, The Washington Spectator*
Environment	8	*Greenpeace, Ecosource*
Newsletters and trade publications	22	*Research Alert, Advertising Age, John Naisbitt's Trend Letter*
New Age	6	*Whole Earth Review, Yoga Journal*
Offbeat	5	*Utne Reader, Paper*

Source: From THE POPCORN REPORT by Faith Popcorn. Copyright 1991 by Faith Popcorn. Used by permission of Doubleday, a division of Bantam Doubleday Dell Publishing Group, Inc.

The BrainReserve group analyzes the impact of various trends on a particular industry or firm consists of project definition, gathering of input, idea development, refinement/presentation, and implementation or action plan. It uses a technique called *discontinuity trend analysis,* which simply involves measuring the specific target industry, business, service, or product against the more universal trends assessed by the firm. As an example, let us look at the implications of nine trends uncovered by the BrainReserve Group for the supermarket industry. Popcorn asserts that the supermarket industry is not keeping up with any of the trends, except perhaps down-aging. She argues that the supermarket industry is heading for calamity. Her recommendation for correcting the trend in the supermarket industry is extensive use of electronic media (virtual reality), which can result in maximum shopping satisfaction because consumers can get detailed nutrition and other information on products.

TABLE 5.10 Megatrends Identified by Naisbitt and Aburdene

1982 List	1990 List
1. Industrial Society ➤ to Information Society	1. The Booming Global Economy of the 1990s
2. Forced Technology ➤ to High Tech/High Touch	2. A Renaissance in the Arts
3. National Economy ➤ to World Economy	3. The Emergence of Free-Market Socialism
4. Short Term ➤ to Long Term	4. Global Lifestyles and Cultural Nationalism
5. Centralization ➤ to Decentralization	5. The Privatization of the Welfare State
6. Institutional Help ➤ to Self-Help	6. The Rise of the Pacific Rim
7. Representative Democracy ➤ to Participatory Democracy	7. The Decade of Women in Leadership
8. Hierarchies ➤ to Networking	8. The Age of Biology
9. North ➤ to South	9. The Religious Revival of the New Millennium
10. Either/Or ➤ to Multiple Option	10. The Triumph of the Individual

Source: Naisbitt, John, and Patricia Aburdene, (1990), *Megatrends 2000*, New York: Avon Books.

Megatrends John Naisbitt and Patricia Aburdene updated their 1982 analysis of social trends and published *Megatrends 2000,* which identifies 10 major societal trends that they deem to be gateways to the twenty-first century. They content-analyze newspapers, magazines, and the like. Table 5.10 compares these new trends with those identified earlier.

One important aspect of their recent analysis is the effect of the Cold War ending and the consequent reduction in the arms race. Undoubtedly, this has some interesting consequences for emerging businesses in the countries of the former Soviet Union. Further, they identify the privatization of the welfare state as a megatrend. This trend has already occurred in countries such as India, which have opened their economies for private foreign investment even in such important sectors as power generation. It opens up great opportunities for various U.S. firms to do business abroad.

A further trend indicated is that of the "age of biology," which involves the development of biotechnologies including genetic engineering. These technological developments will create opportunities for new products and processes in the future. A success story in this regard is that of Calgene Inc., marketer of Flavr Savr tomato seeds, which were genetically engineered to retard rotting.[7] The ultimate success of this new tomato will naturally depend on consumer and channel acceptance.

This brief discussion is intended to alert the marketing strategist about the necessity to keep up with various trends in society and to evaluate their potential impact on current and potential products. Further, *John Naisbitt's Trend Letter,* a biweekly newsletter published by the Global Network, is helpful in keeping people up to date on emerging trends.

Consumer Trends for the Twenty-first Century

Based on an analysis of a variety of survey and other information, Judith Waldrop, research editor of *American Demographics* magazine, compiled a list of 21 trends for the twenty-first century.[8] While several relate to the workplace, some have implications for marketing strategies of U.S. businesses. We next present a sample of these trends and briefly comment on their strategy analysis implications.

Trend a: Everyone belongs to a minority group. Current trends indicate that by 2020, immigration will play an important role in the growth of the U.S. population and, consequently, the population will be highly diversified. This diversity will offer great opportunities and challenges for businesses to cater to a diversity of consumer needs and wants. Niche marketing may become even more important to a range of consumer product marketers.

Trend b: Family must be redefined. The current trends in marriage and divorce imply that more than half of all children will spend part of their lives in single parent families by 2000. Further, one in three married couples with children will have a stepchild or an adopted child by 2010. More children will never know a time when their mothers did not work outside home. These trends will need to be carefully integrated by advertisers in the design and execution of advertising strategies.

Trend c: The retirement population explodes. By July 2009, there will be 37 percent more people aged 62 or older than in the previous year and 63 percent more than in 1990. Combined with economic incentives for early retirement, this boom will continue for several decades to come. The growth in this population will offer a significant increase in the demand for travel and related products and services.

Trend d: Life becomes leisurely. There is a distinct trend toward Americans feeling that leisure time is more important than the time they spend at work. Further, the population seeking activities to fill this leisure time will be affluent. Thus, they will be willing to spend more on relaxation products and services.

Trend e: Cooking from scratch means pushing the right buttons. Even when the population gets older, people will not turn into better cooks. Fast foods and ready-to-serve foods will be in great demand. The microwave will become an important cooking appliance in America.

Future Shock

As far back as 1970, Toffler speculated on several societal changes that will affect our products, communities, and organizations.[9] He labeled the change phenomenon "future shock" and may have essentially shocked various business executives with his predictions. Some—such as the death of technocracy (implicitly, the decline of planned economies like the former Soviet Union); acceleration of scientific discovery; and transience in such crucial societal matters as marriage, diversity of lifestyles, multiple choices in product varieties, and the like—have in fact come true. He forcefully argued that any corporation that has not adapted to changes will not survive. The case in point was his assessment of the situation at American Telephone and Telegraph Company (AT&T) in 1972. In his report to the AT&T board, he identified several environmental problems it faced including competitive pressures from companies like MCI, Caterfone, and CATV; the emergence of IBM and other major communications-minded companies; mounting consumerist pressures; the concern that the AT&T system hire more African-Americans and hard-core unemployed;

pressure to prevent pollution and recycle waste; and rising community resistance to new service installations. He argued that the firm faced the enormous task of defining and becoming a superindustrial enterprise based on more advanced technology and radically different organizational styles, among other features. The controversial strategy he recommended for the firm to adapt to changes in technology and other environmental trends was to divest several of its operations, creating "Baby Bell" companies, and concentrate on providing long-distance services. His 1972 report, published in 1985, shows the need for a firm to be flexible, resilient, and responsive to changes in the environment.[10]

As an example, consider the technological changes likely to affect one aspect of a corporation, the sales function. Changes in communication and data storage and retrieval can affect how salespeople carry out their day-to-day activities. Scofield and Shaw predict that the following trends may alter current sales methods and caution managers not to commit to any technology too rigidly:[11]

Computing tools that enable easy transfer of data and software between various computers will become standardized. Such standardization will help easy transfer of sales reports by electronic mail and electronic data interchange.

Artificial intelligence software technologies will help the sales force identify prospects more effectively than ever before.

Pad and tablet computers that recognize handwriting will appear on the market and will enable easy data entry. These are likely to become a major hardware platform for automating some functions of a sales force, such as placing orders.

The continuing reduction of the price of cellular telephones will facilitate effective communication among the field sales force, customers, and home office personnel.

The development of object-oriented software systems, which are easier to understand, learn, and modify, is likely to have a tremendous impact on the way the sales process can be automated. The effects will be felt in the way sales records are maintained and retrieved.

Emerging multimedia trends blending several technologies, including voice, sound, video, still pictures, monochrome, and color graphics, will have applications in sales training, visual product demonstrations, order entry systems, and the like.

The essential message to a marketing strategy analyst is to compile and analyze any trends that are even remotely applicable to one's business and to evaluate their potential impact.

Lifestyle Analysis

Clearly, many social and cultural trends manifest themselves in lifestyles. Thus, one of the methods of understanding and even forecasting the impact of social and cultural trends is through lifestyle or psychographic analysis. We have described these methods in Chapter 2.

To implement any marketing strategy at a local geographic level, it may be useful to combine lifestyle data with demographic data on the population at the level of smaller geographic areas. SRDS is one firm that publishes such data. Its most recent publication is *The Lifestyle Market Analyst 1995*. SRDS divides the United States into 211 designated market areas (DMAs), each consisting of a few counties. The Lifestyle Market Analyst is a joint venture of SRDS and NDL (National Demographics & Lifestyles, Inc., a part of R. L. Polk & Co.). The demographic and lifestyle profiles of various DMAs are updated annually by SRDS. These data can be used to identify geographic areas where lifestyle activity rates differ from the nation's average.

Lifestyle data are collected from households by inserting consumer information questionnaires into packaged consumer goods, including electronic equipment, appliances, apparel, sporting and camping goods, and other products. These questionnaires solicit demographic and lifestyle information, which NDL analyzes for its client companies. The information is based on some 30 million questionnaires. The county-level profiles are based on a sample of 19.3 million households, representing questionnaires received over a one-year period, from November 1993 to November 1994. NDL adjusts its raw data to extrapolate results from those sampled to the population at large and to compensate for possible flaws in the data collection process. NDL follows standard statistical procedures in making these adjustments, and these results are checked against updated figures computed from U.S. census counts. Therefore, the demographic statistics reported by NDL can be deemed reliable and reflect the entire U.S. adult population.

To convey the flavor of these data, we present information from *The Lifestyle Market Analyst 1995* for the Binghamton DMA, covering the counties of Broome, Chenango, Delaware, and Tioga in New York State. NDL divides the lifestyle activities into seven major groups: home life activities such as book reading, good-life activities such as attending cultural/arts events, investing and money activities such as casino gambling, great outdoor activities such as camping/hiking, hobbies and interests such as automotive work or sewing, sports/leisure activities such as bicycling or running/jogging, and high-tech activities such as using electronics or photography. Table 5.11 shows these data for the Binghamton area relative to the U.S. population. The table also shows the projected number of households who participate in each of these activities. We find that the average number of activities per U.S. household is 14.1. (A household is considered to participate in an activity if one or more adult members participates in it.) The number of households participating in the range of activities varies considerably. From a marketing perspective, participation in any activity translates immediately to demand for the products that will be used or needed for that activity. (As an example, the development and marketing of walking shoes by Reebok can be attributed to the trend toward walking for health; over 33 million U.S. households participate in this activity according to NDL.)

A ratio index is computed to compare the participation rates for the Binghamton area to those of the United States as a whole. Further, the rank of the Binghamton area index relative to other DMAs is shown for each activity. These are shown in the last two columns of Table 5.11. These data show that household participation in the Binghamton area are lower than the U.S. average in some activities and higher in others. For example, the rates are generally lower for the so-called good-life activities but higher for the great outdoor activities. Further, Binghamton's rank relative to

TABLE 5.11 Lifestyle Activities of Binghamton DMA Compared to the United States

Lifestyle Group and Activity	United States		Binghamton DMA			
	Households (000s)	Participation Rate (%)	Households	Participation Rate (%)	Index	Rank
Home Life						
Avid Book Reading	36,802	38.1%	55,818	40.0%	105	46
Bible/Devotional Reading	18,063	18.7	20,653	14.8	79	186
Flower Gardening	31,489	32.6	50,934	36.5	112	61
Grandchildren	22,023	22.8	35,724	25.6	112	95
Home Furnishing/Decorating	19,415	20.1	25,816	18.5	92	167
Houseplants	31,779	32.9	50,097	35.9	109	67
Own a Cat	25,307	26.2	44,654	32.0	122	32
Own a Dog	32,649	33.8	50,376	36.1	107	145
Subscribe to Cable TV	61,724	63.9	99,914	71.6	112	27
Vegetable Gardening	21,734	22.5	38,375	27.5	122	82
Good Life						
Attend Cultural/Arts Events	13,137	13.6%	15,489	11.1%	82	103
Fashion Clothing	12,944	13.4	15,210	10.9	81	158
Fine Art/Antiques	9,852	10.2	13,396	9.6	94	105
Foreign Travel	13,716	14.2	13,815	9.9	70	107
Frequent Flyer	20,188	20.9	24,141	17.3	83	78
Gourmet Cooking/Fine Foods	16,421	17.0	21,211	15.2	89	77
Own a Vacation Home/Property	10,625	11.0	16,048	11.5	105	62
Travel for Business	18,739	19.4	25,397	18.2	94	79
Travel for Pleasure/Vacation	36,223	37.5	49,957	35.8	95	95
Travel in USA	33,711	34.9	47,027	33.7	97	86
Wines	11,398	11.8	16,885	12.1	103	42
Investing and Money						
Casino Gambling	10,915	11.3%	12,140	8.7%	77	121
Entering Sweepstakes	13,620	14.1	18,280	13.1	93	174
Moneymaking Opportunities	11,398	11.8	13,396	9.6	81	199
Real Estate Investments	6,085	6.3	6,977	5.0	79	143
Stock/Bond Investments	15,262	15.8	19,676	14.1	89	112
Great Outdoors						
Boating/Sailing	10,336	10.7%	14,234	10.2%	95	89
Camping/Hiking	21,830	22.6	34,886	25.0	111	81
Fishing Frequently	22,989	23.8	32,654	23.4	98	172
Hunting/Shooting	14,875	15.4	30,421	21.8	142	89
Motorcycles	7,245	7.5	11,582	8.3	111	94
Recreational Vehicles	7,824	8.1	12,838	9.2	114	89
Wildlife/Environmental	15,841	16.4	26,374	18.9	115	26
Sports, Fitness, and Health						
Bicycling Frequently	16,518	17.1%	18,280	13.1%	77	147
Dieting/Weight Control	19,801	20.5	26,514	19.0	93	182
Golf	19,126	19.8	32,514	23.3	118	36
Health/Natural Foods	14,489	15.0	18,839	13.5	90	113
Improving Your Health	22,796	23.6	30,979	22.2	94	146

(Continued on next page)

TABLE 5.11   **Continued**

Lifestyle Group and Activity	United States		Binghamton DMA			
	Households (000s)	Participation Rate (%)	Households	Participation Rate (%)	Index	Rank
Sports, Fitness, and Health (continued)						
Physical Fitness/Exercise	32,842	34.0%	42,143	30.2%	89	132
Running/Jogging	11,011	11.4	11,443	8.2	72	169
Snow Skiing Frequently	7,148	7.4	12,559	9.0	122	55
Tennis Frequently	5,602	5.8	6,977	5.0	86	85
Walking for Health	33,132	34.3	49,120	35.2	103	78
Watching Sports on TV	37,479	38.8	53,306	38.2	98	125
Hobbies and Interests						
Automotive Work	14,779	15.3%	23,164	16.6%	108	110
Buy Prerecorded Videos	15,455	16.0	22,188	15.9	99	105
Career-Oriented Activities	8,887	9.2	11,024	7.9	86	128
Coin/Stamp Collecting	6,762	7.0	10,466	7.5	107	50
Collectibles/Collections	10,818	11.2	17,443	12.5	112	39
Crafts	26,756	27.7	45,771	32.8	118	38
Current Affairs/Politics	15,455	16.0	19,955	14.3	89	141
Home Workshop	21,149	25.0	38,794	27.8	111	36
Military Veteran in Household	24,149	25.0	35,305	25.3	101	131
Needlework/Knitting	16,807	17.4	30,142	21.6	124	34
Our Nation's Heritage	4,733	4.9	7,396	5.3	108	57
Self-Improvement	17,966	18.6	23,025	16.5	89	174
Sewing	18,353	19.0	27,769	19.9	105	138
Supports Health Charities	15,551	16.1	24,839	17.8	111	23
High-Tech Activities						
Electronics	10,432	10.8%	14,234	10.2%	94	99
Home Video Games	11,398	11.8	16,606	11.9	101	116
Listen to Records/Tapes/CDs	47,814	49.5	67,261	48.2	97	92
Own a CD Player	48,683	50.4	64,051	45.9	91	106
Photography	18,063	18.7	27,211	19.5	104	43
Science Fiction	8,500	8.8	12,280	8.8	100	73
Science/New Technology	8,404	8.7	11,582	8.3	95	75
Use a Personal Computer	35,257	36.5	48,003	34.4	94	76
Use an Apple/Compatible	8,597	8.9	7,675	5.5	62	160
Use an IBM/Compatible	29,364	30.4	42,422	30.4	100	58
Mean Number of Interests	14.1					
Total Number of Households	96,594,092		139,545			

The Top Ten Lifestyles Ranked by Index for Binghamton DMA

Hunting/Shooting	142	Golf	118
Needlework/Knitting	124	Crafts	118
Own a Cat	122	Wildlife/Environmental	115
Vegetable Gardening	122	Recreational Vehicles	114
Snow Skiing Frequently	122	Flower Gardening	112

Source: SRDS, 1995, *The Lifestyle Market Analyst 1995,* Des Plaines, IL: SRDS. Extracted from pages 81 and A-35.

other DMAs also varies across activities. The top ten lifestyles in Binghamton relative to the entire United States are shown in the bottom part of the table; these include hunting/shooting, needlework/knitting, and so on.

Consider the photography and home workshop, for which the Binghamton DMA indexes are 104 and 111 relative to 100 for the United States as a whole. If a marketer that produces products for these activities wishes to get a higher share for its business, it may design strategies such as intensifying its distribution among existing Binghamton outlets, locating its own retail outlets, and even creating a direct marketing campaign. For a direct marketing campaign, the marketer may look for a suitable mailing list.

General-Purpose Consumer Surveys

Organizations such as the Roper Organization and Yankelovich Partners conduct periodic surveys to keep track of consumer confidence and sentiment as well as attitudes toward social and cultural trends. These provide a further understanding of how social and cultural factors influence the opportunities and threats for a given business. For example, societal attitudes toward smoking in public will naturally affect the demand for cigarettes. Similarly, attitudes toward lobbying by such groups as MADD (Mothers Against Drunk Driving) will influence the general demand for alcoholic beverages consumed outside the home.

METHODS FOR ANALYZING ECONOMIC FACTORS

We now turn to a discussion of how economic factors affect a business. The general economic environment is measured by various indicators such as the total gross national product, degree of unemployment, industrial production, and the rate of inflation. The U.S. Bureau of the Census and the Bureau of Labor Statistics routinely compile various statistics and report them to various congressional bodies and to the president. These are published in many forms. The most accessible is the *Statistical Abstract of the United States.* (Similar abstracts exist for other countries as well.) This abstract contains a wealth of statistical information on economic factors relevant to any business.

Economic Statistics

Analysis of economic statistics enables a marketing strategy analyst to understand the broader economic climate in which the business operates. Some firms specialize in publishing historical data on various economic indicators.[12] The analyst should correct historical series of economic data for inflation before interpreting inherent trends. In general, overall economic trends may not be uniform across all sectors of the economy. For example, the slow growth of the U.S. economy in 1990 was largely due to low consumer expenditures for durable goods although there was steady growth in the service sector.

Table 5.12 presents selected economic indicators for the United States for the years 1986 through 1992. These data are extracted from various sources by a firm that specializes in publishing data on economic indicators. It is interesting to note the 5 to 8 percent per year growth trend in the gross national product in nominal terms. Corrected for inflation, U.S. economic growth was relatively slow during these years. Further, the steady growth in the consumer expenditures devoted to services as opposed to durable goods is perhaps indicative of the shift in the economy toward the service sector. It is also worth noting that the slow growth of the economy is naturally reflected in low consumer expenditures for durable goods.

Future economic trends can be gleaned from the composite index of leading economic indicators; the bottom part of Table 5.12 shows the movement of this index. It is a composite of 11 indicators: average weekly hours in manufacturing, average weekly initial claims for unemployment insurance, manufacturers' new orders, the Standard & Poor's index of stock prices of 500 common stocks, contracts and orders for plant and equipment, index of new private housing units, vendor performance (slow deliveries), consumer expectations, change in manufacturers' unfilled orders, change in sensitive material prices, and M2 money supply (which includes all currency, checking accounts, and other checkable deposits as well as other liquid assets such as money market funds, money market deposit accounts, savings accounts, and small time deposits). This composite index tends to signal the onset of a recession or recovery some months before the economy actually registers the change. It is generally held that a change in the direction of the indicator must be sustained for at least three months before the indicator is an accurate predictor of a change in the economy. As shown in the table, the movements in this index seem to correspond to the trend in total GNP.

Understanding the potential of each geographic area requires compilation of economic and demographic data at various disaggregated geographic levels in the country. Economic and demographic data at the county and city level are routinely compiled from a variety of sources and published for use by marketing analysts. As an illustration, Table 5.13 presents such data for Ithaca, a small city in New York State. It is instructive to reflect on the potential uses of these data for a number of business firms. For example, a firm selling building materials will be interested in changes in the level and value of construction authorized by building permits in the city. Similarly, a firm marketing scanning equipment for retail operations will be interested in any changes in the number of establishments engaged in retail trade.

Economic Surveys

To evaluate how well a business is faring in the marketplace, it is necessary to compare its sales volume with the size of the total market or the corresponding industry by computing a measure of market share. The data published by the Bureau of the Census (described in Appendix 5B) are useful in estimating the denominator. In addition, the data collected by the U.S. Bureau of Economic Analysis's *Survey of Current Business* are useful in determining the total expenditure on broader categories (such as clothing, shoes, and telephone and telegraph) by all consumers in

TABLE 5.12   Selected Economic Indicators for the United States (Actual Dollars)

Year	Gross Domestic Product (Billions$)	Personal Consumption Expenditures			
		Total (Billions$)	Durable Goods (Billions$)	Nondurable Goods (Billions$)	Services (Billions$)
1986	$4,268.6	$2,850.6	$389.6	$ 952.2	$1,508.8
	(5.7%)	(6.9%)	(10.4%)	(3.6%)	(8.1%)
1987	4,539.9	3,052.2	403.7	1,011.1	1,637.4
	(6.4%)	(7.1%)	(3.6%)	(6.2%)	(8.5%)
1988	4,900.4	3,296.1	437.1	1,073.8	1,785.2
	(7.9%)	(8.0%)	(8.3%)	(6.2%)	(9.0%)
1989	5,250.8	3,523.1	459.4	1,149.5	1,914.2
	(7.2%)	(6.9%)	(5.1%)	(7.0%)	(7.2%)
1990	5,546.1	3,761.2	468.2	1,229.2	2,063.8
	(5.6%)	(6.8%)	(1.9%)	(6.9%)	(7.8%)
1991	5,722.9	3,906.4	457.8	1,257.9	2,190.7
	(3.2%)	(3.9%)	(−2.2%)	(2.3%)	(6.7%)
1992	6,038.5	4,139.9	497.3	1,300.9	2,341.6
	(5.5%)	(6.0%)	(8.6%)	(3.4%)	(6.9%)

Note: Percent changes over previous year shown in parentheses.

(Continued on next page)

TABLE 5.12 Continued

Implicit Price Deflator for Gross Domestic Product (1987 = 100)

Year	Quarter			
	1	2	3	4
1986	96.0	96.5	97.2	98.0
1987	98.8	99.5	100.3	101.2
1988	102.1	103.2	104.5	105.5
1989	106.9	108.1	109.1	110.1
1990	111.5	112.7	113.8	115.0
1991	116.4	117.3	118.2	118.9
1992	120.4	120.9	121.2	118.9
1993	123.3	124.0	121.2	122.2

Composite Index of 11 Leading Indicators (1987 = 100)

Month	1989	1990	1991	1992	1993
January	100.9	99.4	96.0	97.5	98.9
February	100.7	98.9	96.4	97.8	99.1
March	100.1	99.4	96.8	98.1	98.4
April	100.4	99.2	96.8	98.1	98.4
May	99.6	99.4	97.0	98.3	98.1
June	99.4	99.3	97.0	98.2	98.1
July	99.2	99.1	97.9	98.1	97.9
August	99.1	98.4	97.7	97.9	98.4
September	99.2	97.8	97.7	97.8	98.6
October	98.9	97.2	97.6	98.0	98.6
November	99.0	96.5	97.4	98.2	—
December	99.4	96.5	97.2	99.2	—

— = Not available.

Source: Darnay, Arsen J. (ed.) (1994), *Economic Indicators Handbook*, 2nd ed., Detroit: Gale Research. Compiled from several sources of the U.S. government: Time Series, Conversions, Documentation, pp. 14, 18, 20, 22, 24, 73, 168.

TABLE 5.13   Compilation of Data from Several Sources: Profile of Ithaca, New York

Land area (1990)	14.1 sq km	

Population

Population in 1990	
Total persons	29,541
Density (per sq km)	2,095
Population in 1980	28,732
% change in population 1980–1990	2.8

Population Characteristics

a. Race	Percent
White	81.8
Black	6.5
Am. Indian, Eskimo, Aleut.	0.3
Asian and Pacific Islander	10.0
Other races	1.4
Hispanic	3.6
Foreign born	11.5

b. Age	Percent
Under 5 years	3.0
6 to 14 years	5.4
15 to 24 years	52.7
25 to 34 years	14.8
35 to 44 years	8.6
45 to 54 years	4.1
55 to 64 years	3.7
65 to 74 years	3.7
75 years and older	4.0

c. Sex	
Percent female	48.3

Households

Number in 1990	9,617
Percent change 1980–1990	4.9
Persons per household in 1990	2.26
Percent female family householder	8.3
Percent families with one person	36.5
Persons in group quarters	7,649

Persons in institutions	235
Persons identified as homeless	13

Crimes

Serious crimes known to police, 1991	2,178
Violent crimes	82
Rate per 100,000 inhabitants	7,345

Education, 1990

School Enrollment

Public	5,648
Private	12,862

Educational Attainment

Percent completing 12 years or more	86.7
Percent completing 16 years or more	50.2

Money Income, 1989

Per capita ($)	9,213
Median household income ($)	17,738
Percent change in household income 1979–1989 (constant $)	2.8
Percent households with $100,000 or more	2.5
Percent below poverty, 1989	
Persons	39.4
Households	15.0

Housing Units, 1990

Total	10,075
Percent change, 1980–1990	5.8
Vacant units for sale or rent	322
Occupied units	
Number	9,617
Percent owner occupied	28.9
Median value ($)	95,300

Labor Force

Civilian Labor Force,1991 (Persons 16 years and older)

Total	17,584
Percent change, 1990–1991	–1.4

Unemployment

Total	665
Percent	3.8

Civilian Employment, 1990 (Persons 16 years and older)

Total	13,066

Rate per 1,000 employees

Professional, managerial and technical	47.6
Precision, production, craft, and repair	3.4

Disability, 1990

Work disabled persons (percent)	3.7

Value of Construction, Authorized by Building Permits

Total ($1,000)	7,698
Nonresidential	
Total ($1,000)	244
Residential	
New construction ($1,000)	1,960
Number of units	18
Percent single family	5.6
Alterations and additions	1,085

Manufacturers, 1987 Establishments

Total	74
Percent with 20 or more employees	24.3

All Employees

Number ($1,000)	2.0
Percent change, 1982–1987	–23.1

(Continued on next page)

TABLE 5.13   Continued

Annual payroll (millions of dollars)	45.5

Production Workers

Number (1,000)	1.2
Work hours (millions)	2.4
Wages	
Total (millions of dollars)	20.4
Average per production worker (dollars)	17,000
Value added by manufacture (millions of dollars)	97.3
Value of shipments (millions of dollars)	180.0
New capital expenditures (millions of dollars)	5.3

Wholesale Trade, 1987

Establishments	53
Sales (millions of dollars)	100.2
Paid employees	488
Annual payroll (millions of dollars)	10.1

Retail Trade

All Establishments, 1987

Number	596
Sales (millions of dollars):	
Total	388.7
General merchandise group	D*
Food stores	74.4
Apparel and accessory stores	22.6
Eating and drinking places	38.6

Establishments with Payroll, 1987

Number of paid employees	5,007
Percent change, 1982–1987	18.5
Annual payroll (millions of dollars)	46.4

Taxable Service Industries Establishments with Payroll

Number	366

Receipts (millions of dollars)

Total	111.7
Selected business types:	
Hotels, motels and other lodging types	D*
Health services	32.3
Legal services	8.3
Paid employees	2,564
Annual payroll (millions of dollars)	38.0

Selected Federal Funds, Fiscal 1991 ($1,000)

Procurement Contracts

Defense	35,513
Other	5,398

Grant Awards

Total	137,645
Health and family welfare	28,290
Energy and environment	6,244
Education	4,127
Housing and community development	753

Direct Payments for Individuals

Educational assistance	11,828
Housing assistance	2,006
Form of gov't.	Mayor-council

City Government Finances, 1990

General Revenue

Total (millions of dollars)	23.4
Intergovernmental total (millions of dollars)	5.8
Percent from state government	67.0

Taxes

Total (millions of dollars)	11.6
Per capita (dollars)	
Total	393
Property	195
Sales and gross receipts	182

General Expenditure

Total (millions of dollars)	24.9
Per capita (dollars)	
Total	843
Capital outlays	152

Percent of Total for:

Public welfare	0.0
Highways	12.8
Parking facilities	1.1
Transit subsidies	0.0
Education	0.0
Health and hospitals	0.0
Police protection	12.2
Sewer and sanitation	7.7
Parks and recreation	9.5
Housing and community development	3.8
Interest on debt	5.4

Debt Outstanding

Total (millions of dollars)	26.2
Per capita (dollars)	882
Percent utility	4.0

Climate

Average Daily Temperature (degrees Fahrenheit)

Mean:	
January	22.2
July	68.8
Average daily minimum for January	13.8
Average daily maximum for July	80.3
Annual precipitation (in inches)	35.27
Heating degree days	7,177
Cooling degree days	328

*Figure has been withheld to avoid disclosure of information pertaining to specific organization or individual, or because it does not meet statistical standards for publication.

Source: Slater, Courtney M., and George E. Hall, eds. (1993), *1993 County and City Extra: Annual Metro, City and County Data Book*, 2nd ed., Lanham, MD: Bernam Press.

the market. Other sources for obtaining data on consumer expenditures include the *Survey of Consumer Finances* conducted annually by the Survey Research Center of the University of Michigan and the surveys done by the Conference Board. The *Survey of Consumer Finances* also measures consumers' confidence in their future well-being. Thus, it offers insight into the tendencies of consumers to purchase various high-ticket items.

Economic Forecasts

It is not a surprise that forecasts of economic trends are in great demand by both business and government. This demand is met by several firms whose main activity is to develop and publish such forecasts of various economic indicators. The methods they use range from formal macroeconomic demand systems to informal, back-of-the-envelope judgmental forecasts. (We will describe several forecasting techniques in the next chapter.)

Given the difficulty of forecasting turning points in an economy, forecasters often miss declines in output; details for 1990 and 1991 are shown in Table 5.14, which shows the forecasts of the Congressional Budget Office (CBO) and Blue Chip (a consensus of private forecasters).

METHODS FOR ANALYZING POLITICAL FACTORS

Analysis of Regulatory Data

One of the ways in which political factors manifest themselves as business influences is through regulation. Another is through movements such as the green movement or through action groups for protecting the environment and so on. A list of the laws affecting marketing is found in Table 5.15. A strategy analyst should keep abreast of existing laws and pending legislation as they affect the businesses of interest.

The events occurring in the cigarette industry illustrate the importance of a marketing strategist keeping up with legal developments affecting business. In March 1994, Philip Morris Cos., the largest tobacco company in the nation, sued ABC TV for $10 billion, accusing the network of libel for reporting that cigarette makers artificially spike their products with nicotine.[13] Congressional hearings were being held to determine whether the government should regulate tobacco products as drugs. The heart of the story is the Food and Drug Administration's consideration of designating nicotine a drug, a move that the FDA commissioner told Congress would probably take most tobacco products off the market. There would be immediate consequences for the sales of cigarettes and the fortunes of various tobacco firms like Philip Morris.

Green Marketing Trends

One political trend of note concerns protecting the environment—mainly, reducing pollution and ensuring the appropriate disposal of both industrial and domestic waste. Businesses are becoming more responsible in dealing with these problems. Their

TABLE 5.14   **How Accurate Are Macroeconomic Forecasts?**
(GNP growth, 4th quarter over 4th quarter)

Forecast Date	1989	1990	1991
February 1989			
CBO	2.9	2.2	
Blue Chip	2.3	1.9	
January 1990			
CBO		1.8	2.5
Blue Chip		1.8	2.4
March 1991			
CBO			1.3
Blue Chip			0.9
Actual	1.8	−0.3	−0.3

Source: From Rudiger Dornbush and Stanley Fischer, *Macroeconomics,* Sixth Edition, copyright (c) 1994. Reprinted with permission of The McGraw-Hill Companies.

approaches have been labeled "green marketing." These strategies include the development and production of products with biodegradable packages, use of recycled materials, and the design and marketing of products that are environmentally safe to produce and use and reduce air pollution. Frankel notes that 1993 was a year of steady progress in the worlds of corporate environmentalism and green business. He notes that environmental responsibility is being institutionalized in product development and R&D.[14] For example, the Mobil Corporation spends over $1.3 billion and employs over 700 people simply to deal with environmental issues that relate to the firm all over the world.[15] In a different vein, the Sun Company of Philadelphia, the twelfth-largest oil company in the United States, became the first Fortune 500 company to endorse the Valdez Principles, a code of environmental conduct devised after the 1989 Alaskan oil spill.[16]

It is fair to assume that business will in general face stricter environmental laws. It is therefore essential for a marketing strategist to develop internal procedures to monitor these laws and to institute and implement appropriate policies. Several "green marketing" legal actions have been taken against companies, for example. Claims at issue in these actions include the following[17]

- *Compostability and Recyclability:* Mr. Coffee, White Castle Systems
- *Degradability:* Archer Daniels Midland, North American Plastics Corp.
- *Energy Savings:* Osram Sylvania
- *Environmentally Friendly/Safe:* BPI Environmental, de Mert & Dougherty, Mr. Coffee, Nationwide Industries, Orkin Exterminating
- *Ozone Friendly:* G. C. Thorsen, Perfect Data, Redmond Products, Texwipe Company

Two companies that are finding strategic environmental management a powerful competitive tool are Bristol-Myers Squibb (New York, N.Y.) and IBM

TABLE 5.15   Milestone U.S. Legislation Affecting Marketing

Sherman Antitrust Act (1890)	Prohibits (a) "monopolies or attempts to monopolize" and (b) "contracts, combinations, or conspiracies in restraint of trade" in interstate and foreign commerce.
Federal Food and Drug Act (1906)	Forbids the manufacture, sale, or transport of adulterated or fraudulently labeled foods and drugs in interstate commerce. Supplanted by the Food, Drug, and Cosmetic Act, 1938; amended by Food Additives Amendment, 1958, and the Kefauver-Harris Amendment, 1962. The 1962 amendments deal with pretesting of drugs for safety and effectiveness and labeling of drugs by generic name.
Meat Inspection Act (1906)	Provides for the enforcement of sanitary regulations in meat-packing establishments and for federal inspection of all companies selling meats in interstate commerce.
Federal Trade Commission Act (1914)	Establishes the commission, a body of specialists with broad powers to investigate and to issue cease-and-desist orders to enforce Section 5, which declares that "unfair methods of competition in commerce are unlawful."
Clayton Act (1914)	Supplements the Sherman Act by prohibiting certain specific practices (certain types of price discrimination, tying clauses and exclusive dealing, intercorporate stockholdings, and interlocking directorates) "where the effect . . . may be to substantially lessen competition or tend to create a monopoly in any line of commerce." Provides that violating corporate officials could be held individually responsible; exempts labor and agricultural organizations from its provisions.
Robinson-Patman Act (1936)	Amends the Clayton Act. Adds the phrase "to injure, destroy, or prevent competition." Defines price discrimination as unlawful (subject to certain defenses) and provides the FTC with the right to establish limits on quantity discounts, to forbid brokerage allowances except to independent brokers, and to prohibit promotional allowances or the furnishing of services or facilities except where made available to all "on proportionately equal terms."
Miller-Tydings Act (1937)	Amends the Sherman Act to exempt fair-trade (price-fixing) agreements from antitrust prosecution. (The McGuire Act, 1952, reinstates the legality of the non-signer clause.)
Wheeler-Lea Act (1938)	Prohibits unfair and deceptive acts and practices regardless of whether competition is injured; places advertising of foods and drugs under FTC jurisdiction.
Antimerger Act (1950)	Amends Section 7 of the Clayton Act by broadening the power to prevent inter-corporate acquisitions where the acquisition may have a substantially adverse effect on competition.
Automobile Information Disclosure Act (1958)	Prohibits car dealers from inflating the factory price of new cars.
National Traffic and Safety Act (1958)	Provides for the creation of compulsory safety standards for automobiles and tires.
Fair Packaging and Labeling Act (1966)	Provides for the regulation of the packaging and labeling of consumer goods. Requires manufacturers to state what the package contains, who made it, and how much it contains. Permits industries' voluntary adoption of uniform packaging standards.

(Continued on next page)

TABLE 5.15   Continued

Child Protection Act (1966)	Bans sale of hazardous toys and articles. Amended in 1969 to include articles that pose electrical, mechanical, or thermal hazards.
Federal Cigarette Labeling and Advertising Act (1967)	Requires that cigarette packages contain the statement: "Warning: The Surgeon General Has Determined that Cigarette Smoking is Dangerous to Your Health."
Truth-in-Lending Act (1968)	Requires lenders to state the true costs of a credit transaction, outlaws the use of actual or threatened violence in collecting loans and restricts the amount of garnishments. Establishes a National Commission on Consumer Finance.
National Environmental Policy Act (1969)	Establishes a national policy on the environment and provides for the establishment of the Council on Environmental Quality. The Environmental Protection Agency was established by "Reorganization Plan No. 3 of 1970."
Fair Credit Reporting Act (1970)	Ensures that a consumer's credit report will contain only accurate, relevant, and recent information and will be confidential unless requested for an appropriate reason by a proper party.
Consumer Product Safety Act (1972)	Establishes the Consumer Product Safety Commission and authorizes it to set safety standards for consumer products as well as exact penalties for failure to uphold the standards.
Consumer Goods Pricing Act (1975)	Prohibits the use of price maintenance agreements among manufacturers and resellers in interstate commerce.
Magnuson-Moss Warranty/FTC Improvement Act (1975)	Authorizes the FTC to determine rules concerning consumer warranties and provides for consumer access to means of redress, such as the class-action suit. Also expands FTC regulatory powers over unfair or deceptive acts or practices.
Equal Credit Opportunity Act (1975)	Prohibits discrimination in a credit transaction because of sex, marital status, race, national origin, religion, age, or receipt of public assistance.
Fair Dept Collection Practice Act (1978)	Makes it illegal to harass or abuse any person and make false statements or use unfair methods when collecting a debt.
Toy Safety Act (1984)	Gives the government the power to recall dangerous toys quickly when they are found.

Source: Kotler, Philip (1994), *Marketing Management: Analysis, Planning, Implementation, and Control*, 8th Ed., Prentice-Hall.

Corporation (Armonk, N.Y.). Among the strategies implemented by these firms are the following:

Bristol-Myers Squibb: Analyzed the environmental performance of all existing and new products of the firm. This analysis led to the replacement of methylene chloride, a regular toxic chemical, with water in the company's Bio/Chemical Division by a major product reformulation, development of the first alcohol-free hair spray by Clairol in response to pressure from California residents calling for reduced volatile organic compounds in consumer products, and a product life-cycle assessment for the company's Ban roll-on deodorant leading to reduction of chemical usage and manufacturing cycle time. All this results in lower costs.

IBM Corporation: Created an engineering Center for Environmentally Conscious Products. The center contributed extensively to the development of the IBM PS/2E personal computer with superb environmental performance. The environmental features of the PS/2E include design for disassembly by reducing number of parts and fasteners, some reusable parts, increased content of recycled materials, potential for recycling the case, energy efficiency, and the use of PCMIA technology, which increases transferability from PC machine to a laptop computer. These environmental features bode well for the long term.

Companies can be proactive in the general area of the environment by first recognizing the importance of various environmental laws that affect their business and by implementing appropriate policies. Such actions will enable them to deal with any potential threats likely in this area of growing importance. According to the Roper Organization surveys, Americans are becoming more concerned about the environment and are willing to pay 5 to 20 percent more for environmentally safe products; also, the share of Americans who take actions that benefit the environment almost doubled, rising from 11 to 20 percent.[18] A productive way to deal with environmental issues is to undertake an "environmental audit."

Public Opinion Polls

Tens of thousands of public opinion polls or surveys are undertaken in the United States and elsewhere every year. A variety of topics of interest to a marketing strategist are explored in these surveys. The topics include attitude toward big business, attitude toward product safety, consumer confidence and sentiment, general intentions to purchase products, concern for the environment, attitude toward privacy, and information technology. It is essential that a marketing strategy analyst understand which organization is conducting the survey, the time period of the survey, how the questions are worded, consistency in the results of the various survey organizations, and in which medium the results are reported to the public. Results from public opinion polls and surveys provide a good sense of the general public's tone and of the broader environment in which a business has to operate.

A partial list of survey organizations that conduct public opinion polls and surveys includes Gordon S. Black Corporation, Louis Harris and Associates, National Opinion and Research Center, Opinion Research Corporation, Princeton Survey

Research Associates, Survey Research Center of the University of Michigan, The Cambridge Reports, Inc., The Gallup Poll Organization, The Roper Organization for Surveys, and Yankelovich Partners. In addition, various news media organizations (such as *The Washington Post, New York Times,* National Broadcasting Corporation, American Broadcasting Corporation, Columbia Broadcasting Corporation, and Cable News Network) conduct or sponsor public opinion polls on current issues and report the results. It is advisable for a marketing strategy analyst to find out through an appropriate bibliographic search whether there is a recent survey on an environmental trend or potential environmental threat.

As an example, we describe in Table 5.16 public opinion trends on the issue of privacy and information technology as collected in different public opinion surveys. This table shows the results on a few questions on this issue as reported by six survey organizations: Cambridge Reports, The Gallup Organization, Harris Survey Organization, Maritz Marketing Research Inc., National Opinion Research Center, and Roper Center for Public Opinion Research. They indicate, for example, that Americans believe that privacy loss will be a larger concern in the future than it is today and that governmental actions to protect privacy have decreased. These results are quite significant for companies in such industries as credit cards, telecommunications, direct marketing, and electronic communication networks like the Internet, as well as the U.S. government. Both business and government have to keep up with trends of this nature to be able to design defensive or proactive strategies to contend with public concerns.

SUMMARY

In this chapter, we have identified analysis methods for understanding and forecasting the influence on a business of various factors in the external environment. Five sets of factors—demographic, social/cultural, economic, political, and technological—were identified, along with methods for analyzing their impact on demand. In addition, we have looked at various sources of data that a marketing strategist should keep up with in order to monitor trends.

We will continue with this discussion in the next chapter, which focuses on the technological factors. We will discuss various methods for forecasting technological trends and sales of existing and new products. We will also consider methods for evaluating the joint influence of several factors via scenario analysis and cross-impact analysis.

Review Questions

1. The Dow Jones Industrial Index recently celebrated 100 years of existence. Among the original companies that composed the index, only GE remains. Other initial companies included coal and railroad companies. How would you explain this change?

TABLE 5.16 **Extracts from Public Opinion Surveys on Privacy and Technology**

1. How concerned are you about threats to your personal privacy in America today? Would you say you are very concerned, somewhat concerned, only a little concerned or not concerned at all?

	Harris Survey			Cambridge Reports	
	11/78	7/82	9/83	Q1/88	Q1/89
Very concerned	31%	45%	47%	38%	44%
Somewhat concerned	33	29	30	37	32
Only a little concerned	17	14	15	18	17
Not concerned at all	19	11	8	7	6
Don't know	1	1	0	1	1
	101%	100%	100%	101%	100%
Number of respondents	1,256	1,513	1,506	1,471	1,448

2. Here is a list of some different kinds of problems people might or might not be facing 25 to 30 years from now. Would you go down that list, and for each one tell me whether you think it will or will not be a serious problem your children or grandchildren will be facing 25 to 50 years from now . . . Lack of privacy (government surveillance, data files, etc.)?

	1/75	1/77	1/79	2/81	2/83	2/85
Will be serious problem	55%	56%	59%	55%	63%	61%
Will not be serious problem	30	30	30	35	27	32
Don't know	15	14	11	11	10	7
	100%	100%	100%	101%	100%	100%
	2,005	2,000	1,997	2,000	2,000	1,977

3. Even though some of those things are likely to happen, you may feel they will have different effects on our society. Would you read down that list again and tell me which ones you see as serious threats to our society and life as we know it in the United States?

	5/74	5/76	5/78	4/80	5/84
Increasing invasion of privacy	25%	30%	30%	22%	27%
N	1,984	2,002	2,003	2,002	2,000

Source: Roper Surveys

4. What about in future years—how concerned are you about the invasion of your personal privacy in the future: are you very concerned, somewhat concerned, not too concerned, or not concerned at all?

	1st Quarter 88
Very concerned	45%
Somewhat concerned	35
Only a little concerned	13
Not concerned at all	6
Don't know	1
	100%
Number of respondents	1,513

Source: Cambridge Reports

(Continued on next page)

TABLE 5.16 **Continued**

5. Some people say that Americans begin surrendering their privacy the day they open their first charge account, take out a loan, put something on the installment plan, or apply for a credit card. All in all, do you tend to agree or disagree with this statement?

	3/74	1/76	3/77	6/78	11/78	9/83
Agree	48%	47%	67%	71%	76%	69%
Disagree	43	47	25	24	21	30
Not sure	9	6	8	5	3	1
	100%	100%	100%	100%	100%	100%
N	1,495	1,532	1,522	1,259	1,513	1,256

Source: Harris Surveys

6a. Have you ever decided not to apply for something like a job, credit, or insurance, because you did not want to provide certain kinds of information about yourself?

	Harris 11/78	Maritz 1–2/89*
Yes, did not apply	14%	11%
No	85	89
Can't remember, not sure, DK	1	0
	100%	100%
N	1,513	981

*Actual question used in this survey was: Have you ever refused to apply for something like a job, credit, or insurance because you did not want to provide all the information you thought they would ask?

6b. Have you ever refused to provide information on an application that you felt they had no right to ask?

	1–2/89
Yes	35%
No	67
Don't Know	0
	100%
N	981

Source: Maritz Surveys

7. Do you believe that personal information about yourself is being kept in some files somewhere for purposes not known to you, or don't you believe this is so?

	Harris				Cambridge Reports	
	3/74	1/76	3/77	9/83	Q1/88†	Q1/89†
Believe	44%	47%	54%	68%	69%	68%
Do not believe	44	43	32	30	17	20
Not sure	12	9	14	2	13	12
	100%	99%	100%	100%	99%	100%
N	1,495	1,532	1,522	1,256	1,471	1,448

†The wording used in the Cambridge Reports in place of "not known to you, or do not believe this is so" is "not known to you or not."

8. Do you think we need new laws to protect personal privacy, or are existing laws adequate?

	Q1/88	Q1/89
Need new laws	48%	50%
Existing laws adequate	37	37
Don't know	15	13
	100%	100%
N	1,471	1,448

Source: Cambridge Reports

(Continued on next page)

TABLE 5.16   Continued

9. In your opinion, do you feel that the present uses of computers are an actual threat to personal privacy in this country, or not?

	1974	1976	1977	1978	1983
Are a threat	38%	37	41%	54%	52%
Not a threat	42	51	44	32	43
Not sure	20	12	15	14	5
	100%	100%	100%	100%	100%
N	1,495	1,532	1,522	1,513	1,256

Source: Harris Surveys

10. As computer usage increases in business and the general society, more and more information on individual consumers is being acquired and stored in various computers. How serious a threat to your personal privacy is this development? Is it a very serious threat, somewhat serious, only slightly serious, or not a serious threat to your privacy at all?

	1983	1984	1985	1986	1988	1989
Very serious	19%	26%	26%	28%	23%	22%
Somewhat serious	27	29	28	31	38	33
Slightly serious	24	18	16	18	19	23
Not at all	24	21	22	18	14	17
Don't know	5	5	8	5	6	5
	99%	99%	100%	100%	100%	100%
N	1,466	1,429	1,430	1,455	1,471	1,448

11. To the extent that the increased use of computers does pose a threat to personal privacy, do you think the greater threat comes from the improper use of computers by businesses or by government?

	1985	1986	Q1/88	Q1/89
Business	22%	22%	21%	20%
Government	26	26	24	22
Both (voluntary)	35	40	42	44
Neither (voluntary)	7	6	5	6
Other (voluntary)	2	—	1	1
Don't know (voluntary)	9	6	8	7
	101%	100%	101%	100%
N	1,430	1,455	1,471	1,448

Source: Cambridge Reports

12. Everything considered, would you say that in general you approve or disapprove of wiretapping?

	1974	1975	1977	1978	1982	1983	1985	1986	1988	1989
Approve	17%	16%	18%	19%	19%	19%	23%	22%	22%	26%
Disapprove	80	80	78	78	77	78	74	74	78	69
Don't know	4	4	3	3	4	4	3	4	1	5
	101%	100%	99%	100%	100%	101%	100%	100%	101%	100%
N	1,484	1,490	1,530	1,532	1,506	1,599	1,534	1,470	927	1,000

Source: NORC Surveys

Source: Extracted from Katz, James E., and Annette R. Tassone (1990), "The Polls Report: Public Opinion Trends: Privacy and Information Technology," *Public Opinion Quarterly* 54 (Spring): 125–143. Copyright (c) 1990. Reprinted by permission of The University of Chicago Press.

2. A young firm that sells widgets asks you to compare the sales in units of its northeast and southern markets. You are given the following data.

	Northeast				Southern			
	Population				**Population**			
Age Group	Number (000s)	%	Sales (000s Units)	Sales Rate	Number (000s)	%	Sales (000s Units)	Sales Rate
< 25 years	700		1400		220		422	
25–34 years	500		1250		330		792	
35–44 years	300		900		220		660	
45–54 years	240		960		550		2310	
> 55 years	260		1196		880		3960	
Total	2000		5706		2200		8144	

a. Compare these two markets using the standardization technique. What are your conclusions?

b. Considering the age distribution of the population, what can you say about long-term sales for the Northeast market?

3. What is the principal problem of *The Popcorn Report* and *Megatrends 2000?* What would be a proper use of these reports?

4. What is the problem with using cross-sectional data to forecast consumption? How can that problem be solved?

5. **a.** Many analysts believe that the future of the tobacco industry in North America is dark. Using Table 5.1 as a guide, conduct a PEST analysis of that industry.

b. Recently a new cigarette, Eclipse, was introduced in the U.S. market. This cigarette is expected to deliver smoking pleasure with much less nicotine and is expected to have no secondhand smoke problem. Given your PEST analysis in part a, discuss the prospects for this new brand (and type) of cigarette.

6. Using the framework of this chapter, conduct a demand analysis for the personal computer industry. Discuss how various environmental factors are likely to affect the future of this industry.

Notes

1. For details on the PDA industry, see Barbara Kantrowitz (1993), "This is Your Life. Maybe," *Newsweek,* November 15, 45–46.

2. For details, see Das Gupta, Prithwa (1978), "A General Method of Decomposing a Difference Between Two Rates into Several Components," *Demography* 15 (February): 99–112.

3. Rentz, Joseph O., Fred O. Reynolds, and Roy G. Stoudt (1983), "Analyzing Changing Consumption Patterns with Cohort Analysis," *Journal of Marketing Research* 20: 12–20.

4. Rentz, Joseph O., and Fred D. Reynolds (1991), "Forecasting the Effects of an Aging Population on Product Consumption: An Age-Period Cohort Framework," *Journal of Marketing Research* 28 (August): 355–60.

5. See Grimes, William (1992), "Ralph Lauren's Revised Guest," *New York Times,* September 13, C1.

6. From THE POPCORN REPORT by Faith Popcorn. Copyright 1991 by Faith Popcorn. Used by permission of Doubleday, a division of Bantam Doubleday Publishing Group, Inc.

7. Hamilton, Joan O. (1992), "A Storm Is Breaking Down on the Farm," *Business Week,* December 14, 98–101.

8. Waldrop, Judith (1990), "You Will Know It's the 21st Century When...," *American Demographics* December:

22–27. Reprinted with permission. (c) 1990 *American Demographics,* Ithaca, New York.

9. Toffler, Alvin (1970), *Future Shock,* New York: Bantam Books.

10. See Toffler, Alvin (1985), *The Adaptive Corporation,* New York: McGraw-Hill.

11. Scofield, Todd, and Donald R. Shaw (1993), "Avoiding the Future Shock," *Sales & Marketing Management* (January): 16.

12. See, for example, Darnay, Arsen J. (ed.) (1992), *Economic Indicators Handbook,* Detroit: Gale Research Inc.; and Russell, Cheryl, and Margaret Ambry (1993), *The Official Guide to American Incomes,* Ithaca, NY: New Strategist Publications & Consulting.

13. See the news story, "Cigarette Firm Sues ABC," *Ithaca Journal,* March 25, 1994.

14. Frankel, Carl (1993), "1993 in Review: Steady as She Goes," *Green Marketing Alert* 4 (December): 1–2.

15. Based on a speech given by Lucio A. Noto, chairman and CEO of Mobil Corporation, at Cornell University, April 4, 1994.

16. *New York Times* (1993), "Sun Oil Takes Environmental Pledge," February 11.

17. *Green Marketing Alert* (1993) 4, 12, Bethlehem, CT (December): 4–5. Reprinted with permission from GREEN MARKET ALERT.

18. *American Demographics* (1993), January, 9–10.

Bibliography

Aaker, David A. (1992), *Strategic Market Management,* New York: John Wiley & Sons.

Aaker, David A., and George S. Day (1990), *Marketing Research,* 4th ed., New York: Wiley.

Ansoff, Igor, and Edward McDonnell (1990), *Implanting Strategic Management,* Englewood Cliffs, NJ: Prentice-Hall.

Clancy, Kevin J., and Robert S. Shulman (1991), *The Marketing Revolution: A Radical Manifesto for Dominating the Marketplace,* New York: Harper Business.

Larreche, Jean-Claude, and Reza Moinpour (1983), "Management Judgment in Marketing: The Concept of Expertise," *Journal of Marketing Research* 20 (May): 110–121.

Little, John D. C., and Leonard M. Lodish (1981), "Commentary on 'Judgment-Based Marketing Decision Models,'" *Journal of Marketing,* 45 (Fall): 24–29.

Naisbitt, John (1982), *Megatrends,* New York: Warner Books.

Naisbitt, John, and Patricia Aburdene (1990), *Megatrends 2000: Ten New Directions for the 1990s,* New York: Avon.

Newson-Smith, Nigel (1986), "Desk Research," in *Consumer Market Research Handbook,* Robert Worcester and John Downham (ed.), Amsterdam: North-Holland, 7–28.

Neubaven, F. Friedrich, and Norman B. Solomon (1977), "A Managerial Approach to Environmental Assessment," *Long Range Planning* 10 (April): 13–26.

Popcorn, Faith (1992), *The Popcorn Report,* New York: Harper.

Porter, Michael E. (1980), *Competitive Strategy,* New York: Free Press.

Rentz, Joseph O., Fred O. Reynolds, and Roy G. Stoudt (1983), "Analyzing Changing Consumption Patterns with Cohort Analysis," *Journal of Marketing Research* 20: 12–20.

Reynolds, Fred D., and Joseph O. Rentz (1981), "Cohort Analysis: An Aid to Strategic Planning," *Journal of Marketing* 45: 62–70.

Sigford, J. V., and R. H. Parvin (1965), "Project PATTERN: A Methodology for Determining Relevance in Complex Decision Making," *IEEE Transactions on Engineering Management* 12, 1 (March): 9–13.

Wheelwright, Steven C., and Spyros G. Makridakis (1981), "Technological Forecasting," in *Corporate Strategy and Product Innovation,* 2nd ed., Robert R. Rothberg (ed.), New York: Free Press, 290–299.

Wheelwright, Steven C., and Spyros G. Makridakis (1980), Forecasting *Methods for Management,* 3rd ed., New York: John Wiley, 267–288.

Appendix 5A

Strategies for Conducting Secondary Research for Environmental Analysis*

While most of us realize the need for scanning the environment to stay ahead of the competition, few of us know what this process actually entails. Understanding and assessing the external environment as an undifferentiated entity is far too overwhelming a task. For purposes of exploration, we will divide the external environment into four distinct areas: political/regulatory, economic, social/demographic, and technological. We investigate each of these separately and identify the relevant information resources, readily available in most business libraries. At the end of this section, we will walk through the process a second time to illustrate exactly how these secondary research strategies are applied to a single industry, the pharmaceutical industry.

The Regulations: Political/Regulatory Environs

Each industry has some regulatory body overseeing its activities. Some industries are more heavily regulated than others. The *Federal Register* is the daily compilation of decisions, rules, and notices from the federal regulatory agencies. At the end of the year, this information is codified and is released as the *Code of Federal Regulations (CFR)*. The code is organized into a series of 50 titles representing broad areas that come under federal regulatory authority. For example, Title 7 covers agriculture, Title 12 covers banks and banking, and Title 15 covers commerce and foreign trade. Appendix D of the *United States Government Manual* has an alphabetical listing of all federal regulatory agencies and their corresponding title numbers in the *Code of Federal Regulations.*

Introductory texts on government and business should be available in most business library collections. Two books that provide overviews of the connection between business and government are H. Craig Petersen's *Business and Government,* Harper Collins College Publishers, fourth edition, 1993, and Martin C. Schnitzer's *Contemporary Government and Business Relations,* Houghton Mifflin Co., fourth edition, 1990.

Monitoring regulatory activity is much easier if you have access to electronic full-text search services such as Lexis/Nexis, Dow-Jones News/Retrieval, or Dialog Information Services. Commercial subscriptions are expensive, but one can gain access to a variety of business, industry, and government databases through these commercial database vendors. Electronic access also enables one to see the reaction of the press and various industry specialists to changes reported in the regulatory

---

*Prepared by Lynn Brown, Librarian, Johnson Graduate School of Management Library, Cornell University, Ithaca, NY, 1995. Reprinted by permission of the author.

environment. This broader access provides greater insight as to the impact of these new directives. Currency of the information may also be a critical factor in your analysis and future strategic decision making. If currency is important, you need to weigh the cost/benefit of electronic alternatives versus a paper format.

Trade literature, including publications of specialized industry and trade associations, will generally highlight activities in the regulatory environment. Perhaps this information will not be hot off the wire, but it might provide a more in-depth assessment of the situation. Professional and trade associations can be identified in the *Encyclopedia of Associations.*

Standard & Poor's Industry Surveys analyzes trends and future prospects for several major industries. Current as well as anticipated regulatory activities are often discussed at length in this quarterly publication.

Economic Environs

Business cycles, economic trends, and forecasting are generally the purview of economists. At first glance, these gross measures seem too general to warrant close monitoring. When analyzed in light of our other external environmental factors, however, economic measurements may provide valuable information for market forecasting. Standard economic indicators, most of which are statistical releases of the federal government, are often republished in a variety of major periodicals, including the popular press. Several general business magazines such as *Business Week, Fortune,* and the *Economist* include brief economic scoreboards in each edition. Frederick M. O'Hara and Robert Sicignano's *Handbook of United States Economic and Financial Indicators,* Greenwood Press, 1985, does a thorough job of describing the major economic indicators. Each description includes the indicator's publisher/compiler, frequency of publication, and place of publication.

Although there are numerous indicators, many businesses pay close attention to two composite indexes that are published by the U.S. Department of Commerce in *Business Conditions Digest:* the Leading Indicators Composite Index and the Lagging Indicators Composite Index. The Leading Indicators Composite Index is comprised of 12 economic indicators. These indicators tend to change in advance of a business cycle's peak or trough, hence the term *leading.* The six lagging indicators experience a similar pattern except they tend to lag behind other indicators that define a particular cycle. There is actually a third composite called the Coincident Index. The four indicators in this index have peaks and troughs that actually correspond with the business cycle chronology.

The U.S. Bureau of Labor Statistics produces two indicators that are usually viewed as barometers of inflation: the Consumer Price Index (CPI) and the Producer Price Index (PPI). These indexes are published monthly. The PPI is particularly valuable in that it is a measurement of the prices received by producers throughout the manufacturing process. This index focuses on three stages of processing: finished goods (manufacturing process is completed), crude materials (materials that have not yet entered the manufacturing process), and intermediate goods (those that have been incorporated into the manufacturing process).

Financial markets should also be tracked with respect to the industry being analyzed. The financial press publishes a variety of market indices such as the Dow Jones Industrial Index and the Standard & Poor's Composite Index. Standard & Poor's publishes many industry-specific indexes that serve as industry benchmarks. Electronic investment tools such as Bloomberg Financial Markets and Dow Jones News/Retrieval provide up-to-the-minute assessment of financial market performance.

When People Count: Social/Demographic Environs

The decennial Census of Population and Housing is conducted to meet the constitutional mandate for legislative apportionment. The census is a comprehensive statistical snapshot of America's population. Michael Lavin, in *Business Information: How to Find It, How to Use It,* Oryx Press, second edition, 1992, refers to the census as the "mother lode of demographic data in the United States." In his book, Lavin does an excellent job of describing the various available census reports. He also defines census geography. The Census Bureau uses three main categories of geography: administrative, governmental, and statistical. Administrative units are defined only for the purpose of collecting data; governmental units are defined by political boundaries, such as states, counties, cities, towns, and so forth; and statistical units are areas defined by the Census Bureau for the purpose of statistical reporting. These units include blocks, block groups, tracts, and metropolitan areas. Since census geography is also used in many commercial demographic sources, being familiar with these defined reporting levels will facilitate data analysis.

Most large public libraries and academic institutions will receive census publications through the U.S. government's depository program. Much of this material is now available on easy-to-use CD-ROMs and on the World Wide Web.

As is true for most government data, the census is in the public domain. This means that it is not copyrighted and may be duplicated and distributed. Commercially available population data products are almost always based on the data originally gathered via the decennial census and the intermittent reports known as the *Current Population Reports* and the *Current Housing Reports.* In many instances, the commercially produced products are easier to use and often incorporate population projections vital to your research. A good example of this type of product is *The Sourcebook of County Demographics,* published by CACI Marketing Systems. CACI also publishes a comparable resource at the zip code level.

Similar information can be gotten electronically from D&B-Donnelley Demographics (Donnelley Marketing Information Services), a computer database that is accessible via Dialog Information Services. Electronic file access, like the Donnelley database, usually means steep costs, and most of this data is available in print resources such as the ones from CACI. The Census Bureau itself has a database called Cendata, which is available through Dialog and CompuServe. Cendata contains selected statistical releases from the Census Bureau, including the most recent decennial census, and Summary Tape Files 1 and 3. The Summary Tape Files provide data that were gathered from the short census form (STF 1) and the long form (STF 3). A common mistake is to assume that information delivered electronically is always more current than that available in print form. It is important to remember that a total enumeration of the population is done only every 10 years. *Current Population Reports,* which are conducted between censuses, are surveys, not total enumerations of the population. Therefore, regardless of format, the information will generally reflect the most recent decennial period or survey release from the Census Bureau. Population projections, especially those done at the county level or smaller geographic areas, are usually products of commercial services.

The demographic component of your market research should be one of the easiest to complete. Demographic data is readily accessible in a variety of formats and using demographic information to analyze your potential market is extremely cost effective.

In addition to the numbers derived from the demographic profiles, businesspeople need to know about customer behavior. Effective strategic planning is based on the successful merger of demographic projections with statistics on purchasing behavior. Ultimately, your demographic data need to be analyzed in light of your customer base. An excellent reference to guide you through this type of analysis is Penelope Wickham's *Insider's Guide to Demographic Know How: Everything Marketers Need to Know About How to Find, Analyze and Use Information About Their Customers,* American Demographics Press, 1988.

Sales transaction data can be an excellent source of statistics on customer purchasing behavior. This data not only tracks inventory and popularity of a product, but it often provides insight into the characteristics of the consumer. Purchasing behavior data can also come from other sources, such as credit card data; test market information; store scanners; and surveys such as the *Consumer Expenditure Survey,* an ongoing survey published by the U.S. Bureau of Labor Statistics. A complete consumer information system will incorporate two other components, psychographics and media use. *The Lifestyle Market Analyst,* from SRDS (Standard Rate and Data Service), is a good example of a resource that focuses on psychographics. This resource links data generated by the most recent decennial census and other data sources with consumer information obtained from questionnaires enclosed in the packaging of a variety of consumer goods. The end result is segment market profiles that identify lifestyle preferences for people in certain geographic areas and socio-economic groups.

Media use is tracked through monitoring devices and surveys. Survey researchers want to know what people watch on television and listen to on the radio, and what magazines they read. Nielsen and Arbitron are well-known groups that track TV viewing. Simmons Market Research Bureau publishes *Study of Media and Markets,* which surveys about 20,000 adults each year about their media use. This information is then published as a series of cross-tabulations against standard demographic data elements.

Much of this demographic and consumer analysis can be done with tools readily available in most business library collections and without a formal background in demographic research. This work can also be contracted out—for a price! Numerous marketing research organizations offer this type of service. Each January, a *Directory of Marketing Information Companies* is published as a supplement to *American Demographics* magazine. The directory identifies the top 100 marketing information services and products. Many of the companies identified in the directory now offer cluster analysis products. Cluster analysis manipulates data from the decennial census, syndicated surveys, and other sources to classify U.S. neighborhoods by their residents' demographics, attitudes, purchase behavior, and media habits.[1] These cluster analysis tools sort demographic data on a variety of dimensions such as median household income, educational attainment, and occupation of residents. Neighborhoods across the United States that share similar characteristics are assigned to a cluster. Most marketing research firms recognize about 40–60 different clusters to describe all U.S. neighborhoods. New ventures in cluster analysis and the application of geographic information systems in business yield exciting possibilities for future marketing research techniques.

A word of caution: no system, technique, or research company is foolproof. Generally, the smaller the geographic area being analyzed, the greater the potential level of inaccuracy when attributes that are linked to larger areas are allocated to smaller ones. It is important to determine the level of accuracy necessary for your research project. Whether you attempt to do the demographic analysis on your own or go with a commercial vendor, the power of the information will contribute significantly to your market research analysis.

What's on the Horizon? Technological Environs

Technological changes and product innovations can be tracked by methodically culling the trade literature and searching patent databases. Most companies consider their research and development activities to be extremely proprietary in nature, and so it is not until patent applications are filed that we generally have an opportunity to see what directions companies are taking. Perhaps this is not quite cloak and dagger, but competitive intelligence is tough work, and it is not uncommon to come up empty-handed. My suggestion, as an information specialist, is to try to take advantage of those resources that usually do most of the legwork for you. Many of the nation's leading companies are publicly traded firms. The major brokerage houses produce investment research reports on industries and the public companies that make up the industry. Although the purpose of these reports is to make investment recommendations, the information contained in them often highlights new product initiatives and technological innovations. The reports themselves are often very expensive, but they are also available from some of the online information services mentioned earlier. A commercial subscription to Lexis/Nexis, for example, provides you with access to both the Investext database and several databases providing patent information.

The Predicasts, Inc., family of services includes very specialized indexes covering the business and trade press. Many of these indexes organize the information by Predicasts codes. This is a numeric classification system based on the Standard Industrial Classification (SIC) system. This unique classification scheme enables researchers to identify specific product line information. *Predicasts F&S Index* covers both industry issues and company-specific information. The service focuses on new product announcements, new capacities, sales, market, and management. The index is available in three different sets: the United States, Europe, and International. Predicasts

PROMT (Predicasts Overview of Markets and Technology) database is available in both print and electronic formats. PROMT provides abstracts and some full-text articles covering such topics as new technologies, new product lines, market share, financial trends, contracts, and new joint ventures. The Predicasts databases can be accessed through a variety of commercial database vendors.

Secondary Research in the Pharmaceutical Industry: An Illustrative Example

We will now revisit the four external environments with respect to marketing research strategies in the pharmaceutical industry. As a starting point, we will assume that the market researcher is familiar with his or her company's internal environment and product lines, and is ready to focus on external factors and their potential impact.

If you need a quick refresher in order to review the basic issues facing the industry, consider starting your research by reading the pharmaceutical section in *Standard & Poor's Industry Surveys*. This illustrative example was prepared in May 1994, and the issues raised throughout the exercise reflect that time period.

Political/Regulatory Environment
Issues:

Current administration's political agenda—impact of proposed national health plan

- Health plan calls for greater price controls and increased use of generic drugs.
- Managed health care providers insist on generic substitutes in their health plans.
- Proposal in health care plan would empower Secretary of Health and Human Services to identify certain high-priced products and eliminate them from Medicare reimbursement.

Self-regulated price controls versus government price controls

- Several leading drug manufacturers agree to hold prices to the annual rate of inflation (CPI). Previous attempts at self-regulation have been criticized by various congressional leaders as ineffective. For past data on price indexes, see Table 5A.1.

Food and Drug Administration regulatory activity

- Industry would like the approval process to be shortened. See Table 5A.2 for data on new drug filings with FDA.
- Development of computer-assisted new drug application systems could speed up approval process.

International political ramifications

- Political restructuring of Europe into a single economic community will result in increased international competition. Europe hopes to adopt a single system approval process, tighter patent protection, and free-market pricing.

TABLE 5A.1 Producer Price Indexes for Selected Drug Products (1982 = 100)

Product	1988	1989	1990	1991	1992
Ethical Preparations	169.0	184.4	200.8	217.5	231.7
Systemic anti-infectives	134.2	138.7	146.3	155.0	162.4
Anti-arthritics	125.3	130.4	136.5	148.2	159.2
Cardiovascular therapy	185.8	201.8	220.8	240.5	256.8
Hormones	126.6	143.4	161.5	175.6	187.9
Diuretics	161.0	176.7	192.4	206.5	221.5
Analgesics, internal	181.1	203.0	218.5	230.8	252.2

Source: *Standard & Poor's Industry Surveys* (1994), April, H–21. Reprinted by permission of Standard & Poor's and the McGraw-Hill Cos.

TABLE 5A.2 New Drug Filings with Food & Drug Administration*

Year	Original INDs Submitted	Original NDAs Submitted	NDAs Approved	New Molecular Entities
1992	2576	100	91	26
1991	2116	112	63	30
1990	1530	98	64	23
1989	1345	118	87	23
1988	1337	126	67	20
1987	1346	142	69	21
1986	1623	120	98	20
1985	1904	148	100	30
1984	2112	217	142	22
1983	1798	269	94	14

*IND—Investigational new drug. NDA—New drug application

Source: *Standard & Poor's Industry Surveys* (1994), April, H–25. Reprinted by permission of Standard & Poor's and the McGraw-Hill Cos.

Applicable Sources

ABI/INFORM (ProQuest database)

OneSource U.S. Public (OneSource database)

Encyclopedia of Business Information Sources, ninth edition

Federal Register

PMA Statistical Fact Book (Pharmaceutical Manufacturers Association)

Standard & Poor's Industry Surveys

James Taggart, *The World Pharmaceutical Industry,* 1993

U.S. Industrial Outlook (U.S. Department of Commerce, publication ceased in 1995)

Economic Environment

Issues:

Cost of doing business

- R&D-intensive business, several years of testing, and millions of dollars before FDA approved (see Table 5A.3 for data on R&D expenditures in the pharmaceutical industry).
- Tax shelters being reduced on manufacturing operations in Puerto Rico (see Table 5A.4 for the impact of Puerto Rican tax credits).
- Annual increases in producer price indexes (see Fig. 5A.1 for trend in price indexes for drugs).

Increased popularity of formularies

- Formularies, a method of limiting the range of drugs physicians may prescribe, used primarily by HMOs, have strong impact on holding down drug prices.

Projected industry growth and earnings

- Annual value of total shipments of pharmaceutical preparations rises at a slower rate than previous trend (see Tables 5A.5 and 5A.6 for trends in value of shipments of drugs).
- Industry is typically recession resistant. Aging population will continue to account for large segment of sales.

TABLE 5A.3   Research & Development Expenditures

Company	1990 Millions of Dollars	1990 Percent of Sales	1991 Millions of Dollars	1991 Percent of Sales	1992 Millions of Dollars	1992 Percent of Sales
Abbott	$567	9%	$666	10%	$772	10%
American Home Products	369	5	431	6	552	7
Bristol-Meyers/Squibb	873	9	983	9	1,083	10
Johnson & Johnson	834	7	980	8	1,127	8
Eli Lilly	703	14	767	13	925	15
Glaxo	748	13	841	14	1,047	15
Marion Merrel Dow	358	15	393	14	465	14
Merck	854	11	988	11	1,112	12
Pfizer	640	10	757	11	863	12
Schering-Plough	380	11	426	12	522	13
SmithKline Beecham	700	9	765	9	841	9
*Syntex	271	18	316	17	374	18
Upjohn	427	14	491	14	549	15
Warner-Lambert	397	8	423	8	473	8
Wellcome	343	16	385	15	455	15

*Fiscal year ending July 31

Source: *Standard & Poor's Industry Surveys* (1994), April, H–21. Reprinted by permission of Standard & Poor's, and the McGraw-Hill Cos.

TABLE 5A.4   **Impact of Puerto Rican Tax Credit**

Company	Effective Tax Rate (Percent)*	Tax Savings from Puerto Rican Manufacturing
American Home Products	33.3%	−6.1%
Bristol-Myers/Squibb	22.6	−8.7
Johnson & Johnson	26.4	−7.2
Eli Lilly	30.0	_7.5
Merck	31.3	−5.1
Pfizer	28.6	−8.2
Schering-Plough	24.5	−6.8
Upjohn	22.0	−11.0
Warner-Lambert	25.0	−6.8

*Note: The U.S. statutory tax rate is 34.0%

Source: *Standard & Poor's Industry Surveys* (1994), April, H–20. Reprinted by permission of Standard & Poor's, and the McGraw-Hill Cos.

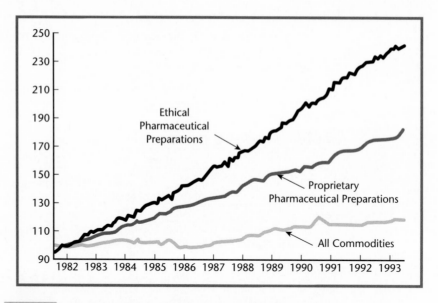

FIGURE 5A.1   **Producer Price Indexes—Drugs (1982 = 100)**

Source: *Standard & Poor's Industry Surveys* (1994), April, H–18. Reprinted by permission of Standard & Poor's, and the McGraw-Hill Cos.

- U.S. market is single largest market (see Fig. 5A.2 for the trend in U.S. health care expenditures).

Corporate restructuring/downsizing

- Downsizing and restructuring efforts have resulted in substantial tax savings.
- Merger/acquisition activity and strategic alliances will continue in order for firms to better position themselves in a more highly regulated market.

TABLE 5A.5 Trends and Forecasts: Drugs (SIC 283) (in millions of dollars except as noted)

Item	1987	1988	1989	1990	1991	1992[1]	1993[2]	1994[3]	Percent Change: (1989–1994)					
									88-89	89-90	90-91	91-92	92-93	93-94
Industry Data														
Value of shipments[4]	39,263	43,987	49,114	53,720	60,835	65,317	68,973	70,452	11.7	9.4	13.2	7.4	5.6	2.1
2833 Medicinals & botanicals	3,350	4,150	4,753	4,919	6,308	6,548	7,044	7,178	14.5	3.5	28.2	3.8	7.6	1.9
2834 Pharmaceutical preps	32,094	35,825	40,028	44,182	47,376	51,295	54,101	55,183	11.7	10.4	7.2	8.3	5.5	2.0
2835 Diagnostic substances	220	2,261	2,325	2,462	4,746	4,940	5,188	5,340	2.8	5.9	92.8	4.1	5.0	2.9
2836 Bio prod ex diagnostic	1,614	1,750	2,008	2,156	2,406	2,534	2,640	2,751	14.7	7.4	11.6	5.3	4.2	4.2
Value of shipments (1987$)	39,263	40,942	41,998	42,773	45,470	46,277	47,153	48,089	2.6	1.8	6.3	1.8	1.9	2.0
2833 Medicinals & botanicals	3,350	3,960	4,213	4,274	5,141	5,234	5,328	5,429	6.4	1.4	20.3	1.8	1.8	1.9
2834 Pharmaceutical preps	32,094	32,988	33,581	34,144	33,767	34,357	35,010	35,710	1.8	1.7	-1.1	1.7	1.9	2.0
2835 Diagnostic substances	2,205	2,237	2,275	2,282	4,280	4,366	4,453	4,542	1.7	0.3	87.6	2.0	2.0	2.0
2836 Bio prod ex diagnostic	1,614	1,757	1,929	2,073	2,282	2,320	2,362	2,408	9.8	7.5	10.1	1.7	1.8	1.9
Total employment (000)	172	175	184	183	184	—	—	—	5.1	-0.5	0.5	—	—	—
2833 Medicinal & botanicals	1.6	11.3	11.4	10.9	12.5	—	—	—	0.9	-4.4	14.7	—	—	—
2834 Pharmaceutical preps	132	133	142	144	129	133	136	—	6.8	1.4	-10.4	3.1	2.3	—
2835 Diagnostic substances	15.4	16.2	16.1	14.9	30.5	—	—	—	-0.6	-7.5	104.7	—	—	—
2836 Bio prod ex diagnostic	13.3	13.7	14.5	13.3	12.1	—	—	—	5.8	-8.3	-9.0	—	—	—
Production workers (000)	79.6	81.0	82.8	81.4	82.7	—	—	—	2.2	-1.7	1.6	—	—	—
2833 Medicinals & botanicals	6.1	6.2	6.6	6.5	7.2	—	—	—	6.5	-1.5	10.8	—	—	—
2834 Pharmaceutical preps	59.9	60.8	62.4	61.5	59.2	60.4	61.6	—	2.6	-1.4	-3.7	2.0	2.0	—
2835 Diagnostic substances	6.8	7.5	6.8	6.6	9.9	—	—	—	-9.3	-2.9	50.0	—	—	—
2836 Bio prod ex diagnostic	6.8	6.5	7.0	6.8	6.4	—	—	—	7.7	-2.9	-5.9	—	—	—
Average hourly earnings ($)	12.22	12.67	13.48	14.22	15.36	—	—	—	6.4	5.5	8.0	—	—	—
2833 Medicinals & botanicals	15.32	16.09	16.29	17.35	20.06	—	—	—	1.2	6.5	15.6	—	—	—
2834 Pharmaceutical preps	12.42	12.93	13.83	14.71	14.77	—	—	—	7.0	6.4	0.4	—	—	—
2835 Diagnostic substances	10.74	10.93	11.54	11.80	18.17	—	—	—	5.6	2.3	54.0	—	—	—
2836 Bio prod ex diagnostic	8.87	9.13	9.30	9.15	11.00	—	—	—	1.9	-1.6	20.2	—	—	—
Capital expenditures	1,749	2,058	2,392	2,280	2,669	—	—	—	16.2	-4.7	17.1	—	—	—
2833 Medicinals & botanicals	115	151	219	195	487	—	—	—	45.0	-11.0	149.7	—	—	—
2834 Pharmaceutical preps	1,471	1,725	1,933	1,809	1,772	—	—	—	12.1	-6.4	-2.0	—	—	—
2835 Diagnostic substances	93.5	93.3	117	147	302	—	—	—	25.4	25.6	105.4	—	—	—
2836 Bio prod ex diagnostic	69.9	89.1	124	130	108	—	—	—	39.2	4.8	-16.9	—	—	—

(Continued on next page)

TABLE 5A.5 Continued

Item	1987	1988	1989	1990	1991	1992[1]	1993[2]	1994[3]	Percent Change: (1989–1994)					
									88–89	89–90	90–91	91–92	92–93	93–94
Product Data														
Value of shipments[5]	35,283	39,532	43,796	47,832	51,880	55,607	58,428	—	10.8	9.2	8.5	7.2	5.1	—
2833 Medicinals & botanicals	4,224	4,948	5,393	5,789	6,647	6,898	7,116	—	9.0	7.3	14.8	3.8	3.2	—
2834 Pharmaceutical preps	26,610	29,555	32,713	35,280	37,416	40,532	42,750	—	10.7	7.8	6.1	8.3	5.5	—
2835 Diagnostic substances	2,683	3,063	3,471	4,234	4,973	5,176	5,435	—	13.3	22.0	17.5	4.1	5.0	—
2836 Bio prod ex diagnostic	1,765	1,966	2,220	2,529	2,844	3,001	3,127	—	12.9	13.9	12.5	5.5	4.2	—
Value of shipments (1987$)	35,283	36,939	37,753	38,649	39,269	39,984	40,737	—	2.2	2.4	1.6	1.8	1.9	—
2833 Medicinals & botanicals	4,224	4,721	4,781	5,030	5,417	5,514	5,611	—	1.3	5.2	7.7	1.8	1.8	—
2834 Pharmaceutical preps	26,610	27,214	27,443	27,264	26,668	27,148	27,664	—	0.8	-0.7	-2.2	1.8	1.9	—
2835 Diagnostic substances	2,683	3,030	3,396	3,924	4,484	4,574	4,665	—	12.1	15.5	14.3	2.0	2.0	—
2836 Bio prod ex diagnostic	1,765	1,974	2,132	2,431	2,699	2,748	2,797	—	8.0	14.0	11.0	1.8	1.8	—
Trade Data														
Value of imports	—	—	3,531	3,884	4,812	5,958	6,743	—	—	10.0	23.9	23.8	13.2	—
2833 Medicinal & botanicals	—	—	2,354	2,303	2,854	3,277	3,604	—	—	-2.2	23.9	14.8	10.0	—
2834 Pharmaceutical preps	—	—	868	1,103	1,442	1,859	2,105	—	—	27.1	30.7	28.9	13.2	—
2835 Diagnostic substances	—	—	118	207	191	336	371	—	—	75.4	-7.7	75.9	10.4	—
2836 Bio prod ex diagnostic	—	—	191	271	325	486	662	—	—	41.9	19.9	49.5	36.2	—
Value of exports	—	—	4,345	5,050	5,731	6,774	7,207	—	—	16.2	13.5	18.2	6.4	—
2833 Medicinals & botanicals	—	—	1,794	1,908	2,064	2,444	2,442	—	—	6.4	8.2	18.4	-0.1	—
2834 Pharmaceutical preps	—	—	974	1,258	1,478	1,818	2,055	—	—	29.2	17.5	23.0	13.0	—
2835 Diagnostic substances	—	—	739	909	1,160	1,370	1,494	—	—	23.0	27.6	18.1	9.1	—
2836 Bio prod ex diagnostic	—	—	839	974	1,028	1,142	1,216	—	—	16.1	5.5	11.1	6.5	—

[1]Estimate, except exports and imports.

[2]Estimate.

[3]Forecast.

[4]Value of all products and services sold by establishments in the drugs industry.

[5]Value of products classified in the drugs industry produced by all industries.

Note: Changes in the mix of products produced by drug making establishments caused them to be reclassified among the SICs shown between 1990 and 1991 distorting the magnitude of the changes for the four-digit SICs.

Source: U.S. Department of Commerce: Bureau of the Census; International Trade Administration (ITA). Estimates and forecasts by ITA.

TABLE 5A.6 Value of Product Class Shipments of Pharmaceutical Preparations, Except Biologicals: 1982 to 1991

Product Code	Product Description	1991	1990	1989	1988	1987	1986	1985	1984	1983	1982
	Pharmaceutical preparations:										
28341	Pharmaceutical preparations affecting neoplasms, endocrine system, and metabolic diseases, for human use	3340.8	2743.2	2507.4	2071.2	1994.9	2140.6	2110.2	1946.8	1885.7	1705.3
28342	Pharmaceutical preparations acting on the central nervous system and the sense organs, for human use	7820.3	7218.5	6441.3	6172.7	5740.5	5946.0	5737.6	5029.7	4439.0	3841.4
28343	Pharmaceutical preparations acting on the cardiovascular system, for human use	5009.3	4814.6	4874.9	4449.9	3795.9	3570.3	3170.9	2708.1	2264.2	1842.5
28344	Pharmaceutical preparations acting on the respiratory system, for human use	3757.8	3724.1	3286.2	3224.0	2811.4	2492.2	2202.4	1816.4	1750.4	1590.1
28345	Pharmaceutical preparations acting on the digestive or the genito-urinary systems, for human use	5605.8	4840.2	4363.0	3860.8	2954.8	1864.5	1875.9	1765.4	1611.7	1419.5
28346	Pharmaceutical preparations acting on the skin, for human use	1621.4	1558.0	1451.7	1388.5	1288.3	1327.3	1213.3	1132.9	1037.7	819.1
28347	Vitamin, nutrient, and hematinic preparations for human use	2596.8	2587.9	2672.4	2538.5	2570.7	2665.9	2291.2	2286.9	2454.8	2170.8
28348	Pharmaceutical preparations affecting parasitic and infective diseases, for human use	5731.0	5411.0	4936.2	4593.6	4024.9	3821.0	3386.2	3046.6	2820.2	2438.0
28349	Pharmaceutical preparations for veterinary use	1163.1	1056.8	1071.1	1051.5	997.1	853.7	817.7	843.1	847.2	789.0

Source: U.S. Department of Commerce, Bureau of the Census, Industry Division, Washington, D.C. 20233.

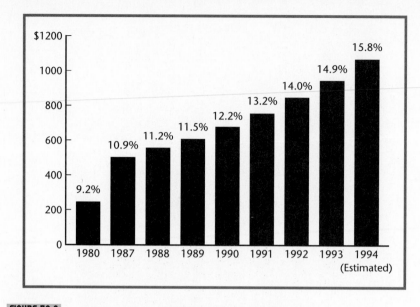

FIGURE 5A.2   **Health Care Expenditures (in billions of dollars and as a Percentage of GDP)**

Source: *Standard & Poor's Industry Surveys* (1994), April, H–1.

Patent expirations and generic drug increase

- Generic drug firms will become more competitive as patents for several drugs are due to expire. Expiration of patents enables the generics to produce and market the same preparation at a much lower price.

International competitiveness

- Exchange rates: As the dollar increases in strength abroad, prices rise for many U.S. preparations, making the domestic product more competitive.

- Foreign currency sales are negatively impacted by the stronger dollar.

- Foreign government health care systems set pricing norms that have negatively impacted foreign sales.

- Unified common market (EC), when established, will pose serious competitive threats.

Applicable Sources

ABI/INFORM (ProQuest database)

Annual Survey of Manufacturers (Bureau of the Census)

OneSource U.S. Public (OneSource database)

Current Industrial Reports (Bureau of the Census)

Drug Topics

Predicasts F&S Index

PPI Detailed Report (Producer Price Index, Bureau of Labor)

Medline (National Library of Medicine database)

Standard & Poor's Industry Surveys

Standard & Poor's Statistical Service

Social/Demographic Environment

Issues:

Aging of population

- The elderly, 65+, consume three times more pharmaceutical preparations than those younger (see Table 5A.7 for personal health care expenditures by age in 1987 versus 1977).
- The baby boomer generation is aging (see Fig. 5A.3 for population projections for 2030 and 2050).

Consumer activism

- Public demand for price controls. Active lobbies among elderly for increased Medicare benefits covering prescription drugs.

TABLE 5A.7 Personal Health Care Expenditures, by Age: 1977 and 1987

Age and Type of Expenditure	Aggregate Amount (billions)			Per Capita Amount		
	1987	**1977**	**1977***	**1987**	**1977**	**1977***
Total Expenditures						
All ages	$447.0	$150.3	$281.9	$1776.0	$658.0	$1234.1
Under 19 years	$51.9	$19.5	$36.6	$745.0	$269.0	$504.5
19 to 64 years	$233.1	$85.6	$160.5	$1535.0	$651.0	$1220.9
65 years and over	$162.0	$45.2	$84.8	$5360.0	$1856.0	$3480.9
Private Expenditures						
All ages	$271.8	$92.6	$173.7	$1079.0	$405.0	$759.6
Under 19 years	$38.1	$14.4	$27.0	$547.0	$198.0	$371.3
19 to 64 years	$173.0	$62.3	$116.8	$1139.0	$474.0	$889.0
65 years and over	$60.6	$15.9	$29.8	$2004.0	$653.0	$1224.7
Public Expenditures						
All ages	$175.3	$57.8	$108.4	$696.0	$253.0	$474.5
Under 19 years	$13.8	$5.2	$9.8	$198.0	$711.0	$133.2
19 to 64 years	$60.0	$23.2	$43.5	$395.0	$177.0	$332.0
65 years and over	$101.5	$29.3	$55.0	$3356.0	$1204.0	$2258.1

*1977 in 1987 constant dollars; source of data: Health Care Financing Administration, Office of the Actuary, data from the Office of National Cost Estimates.

Source: "Sixty-Plus in America," *Population Reports—Special Studies*, P23-178 RV, 3–19.

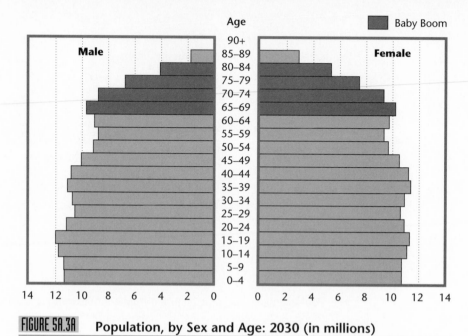

FIGURE 5A.3A   Population, by Sex and Age: 2030 (in millions)

Source: "Sixty-Plus in America," *Population Reports-Special Studies,* P23-178 RV, 2–8. Reprinted by permission of Standard & Poor's, and the McGraw-Hill Cos.

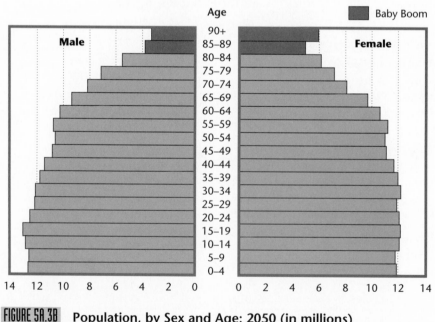

FIGURE 5A.3B   Population, by Sex and Age: 2050 (in millions)

Source: "Sixty-Plus in America," *Population Reports-Special Studies,* P23-178 RV, 2–8. Reprinted by permission of Standard & Poor's, and the McGraw-Hill Cos.

- Increased popularity of mail-order prescriptions.
- Consumer complaints about cross-border price differentials; willingness to buy drugs in Canada and Mexico.
- Consumer support for national health care plan and more controls over pricing.
- Greater political activism, especially among groups representing the elderly.

Social issues

- Lobbying groups organized around religious/moral concerns have brought pressure to bear on R&D efforts in areas such as the abortion pill.
- Animal rights activists' opposition to testing procedures.

Applicable Sources

ABI/INFORM (ProQuest database)

American Demographics

Current Population Reports, Special Studies P23-178RV, "Sixty-Five Plus in America"

Drug Topics

Social Science Index

Standard & Poor's Industry Surveys

Technological Environment

Issues:

Research and development-intensive industry

- Costly R&D, lengthy process for drug approval, and small number of drugs that get approval, all affect pricing. Price controls discourage innovation by limiting the profit motive.

Organizational structure and technology

- Companies need to foster innovation by incorporating technological environmental scanning into the overall strategic planning of the firm.
- Strong linkages between technology and marketing are necessary to ensure commercial success.

Applicable Sources

ABI/INFORM (ProQuest database)

Annual Survey Report (Pharmaceutical Manufacturers Association)

Applied Science and Technology Index

Medline (National Library of Medicine database)

PTS PROMT (Predicasts database)

James Taggart, *The World Pharmaceutical Industry,* 1993

Note

1. Francese, Peter (1994), "What Is Cluster Analysis For?"
Marketing Tools (April/May): 50.

Appendix 5B

A Guide to Information Sources for Marketing Strategy Analysis*

I. Company Information

Bloomberg Financial Markets. Online system providing financial analysis of firms, company news, and analysis of national and international financial markets.

Company Annual Reports and 10K's. Annual reports can be requested directly from firms. Also available electronically from a variety of vendors. Edgar Database of Corporate Information is on the World Wide Web (http://www.sec.gov/edgarhp.htm).

Moody's Manuals. Bound annual volumes with current updates. Includes corporate histories and basic financials.

Bank and Finance	OTC Industrial
Industrial	OTC Unlisted
International	Public Utility
Municipal and Government	Transportation

Standard and Poor's Stock Reports. Brief overviews of stock performance, updated quarterly.

Value Line Investment Survey. Investment recommendation service tracking current performance of firms and industries.

OneSource: U.S. Public. CD/ROM product by OneSource. Includes historical financial data; full-text investment reports for companies and industries; annual stock trade data and weekly data; and article abstracts for companies and industries.

OneSource U.S. Private+. Information on privately held companies. Includes article abstracts.

Dow Jones News/Retrieval. Online service providing access to a variety of business databases. Full-text articles from *The Wall Street Journal, Barrons,* and business press general companies, industries, and financial markets.

Compustat PC Plus and Compustat Daily Prices. Twenty years of financial data on public companies. Includes segment-level data for firms, comparative company and industry data and market share information. Compustat Daily Prices contain price histories on equities and market indexes.

II. Industry Information

Predicasts Forecasts. Quarterly analysis of industries by SIC code. Annual growth data, sales, production data, and consumption data are routinely reported. Short and long-term forecasts are included.

---

*Compiled by Lynn Brown, Librarian of the Management Library, Cornell University, Ithaca, NY, 1995. Reprinted by permission of the author.

Standard & Poor's Industry Surveys. Detailed reports on industries, products, and major competitors. Industry trends and the regulatory environment are often discussed.

Standard Industrial Classification Manual. Detailed description of SIC codes and the industries, products, and services represented by this numerical classification system.

III. Economic and Demographic Statistical Data Sources

Census of Population and Housing (U.S. Bureau of the Census). Decennial census is a total enumeration of the U.S. population and household units.

Current Population Reports (U.S. Bureau of the Census). Detailed statistical series on the population of the United States. Provides information on specific population characteristics and projected population trends.

Consumer Income (Series P-60)
Household Economic Studies (Series P-70)
Local Population Estimates (Series P-26)
Population Characteristics (Series P-20)
Population Estimates and Projections (Series P-25)

Economic Census Reports (U.S. Bureau of the Census). Economic censuses are run every five years. Annual surveys are also conducted to update the data. Data elements include value of shipments, capital expenditures, number of employees, payroll data, and number of establishments. Data is arranged by SIC code and by geographic area.

Census of Construction Industries
Census of Finance, Insurance & Real Estate
Census of Manufactures
Census of Mineral Industries
Census of Retail Trade
Census of Service Industries
Census of Transportation
Census of Wholesale Trade

Sourcebook of County Demographics (CACI Marketing Systems). Statistics on income and purchasing power available at the county level. Measures potential demand for products and services at the county level.

Sourcebook of Zip Code Demographics (CACI Marketing Systems). Statistics on income and purchasing power at the zip code level.

Survey of Current Business (U.S. Bureau of Economic Analysis). Monthly periodical tracking economic indicators, industry data, and import/export data. Special issue in July, "National Income and Product Accounts," includes "Personal Consumption Expenditures by Type of Product."

IV. Consumer Markets:

Almanac of Consumer Markets (American Demographic Press). Provides demographic statistics, arranged by age cohorts, to help marketers identify potential consumer markets.

Consumer Expenditure Survey (U.S. Bureau of Labor Statistics). Nationwide, ongoing study of household spending.

Consumer Power: How Americans Spend Their Money. Ambry, Margaret K., Ithaca, NY: New Strategist, 1996. Consumer market survey tracking household expenditures. Original data source for this work is the Consumer Expenditure Survey.

Handbook of Demographics for Marketing and Advertising: New Trends in the American Marketplace. Lazer, William, New York: Lexington Books, 1994. Discusses the impact of changing demographics on markets, the importance of market segmentation, and the need to understand lifestyle differences and their marketing implications.

Insider's Guide to Demographic Know-How: Everything Marketers Need to Know About How to Find, Analyze and Use Information about Their Customers. Wickham, Penelope, Ithaca, NY: American Demographics Press, 1988.

Lifestyle Market Analyst (SRDS). Provides profiles of consumers by bringing together demographic, geographic, and lifestyle information for each ADI market.

The Official Guide to Household Spending: The Number One Guide to Who Spends How Much On What. Ambry, Margaret K., Ithaca, NY: New Strategist, 1993.

Study of Media and Markets (Simmons Market Research Bureau). Profiles consumers by identifying their socioeconomic characteristics and their purchasing behavior.

Survey of Buying Power (Special issue of *S&MM*). Tracks retail sales, population trends, and provides an "effective buying income" index for all metros, counties, and major U.S. cities. Ranks metros by their sales and by specific socioeconomic characteristics.

V. Advertising and Brand Data

Ad $ Summary. Identifies brands and their respective media expenditures across ten media dimensions. Ranks industries and companies by total media expenditures.

Standard Rate and Data Service. Multivolume set tracks circulation statistics and advertising costs for consumer and business magazines, advertising costs for television and radio spots, and newspaper advertising cost information. Provides basic household demographic data.

Superbrands. Includes detailed analysis of the top 2000 U.S. brands.

Marketing and Media Decisions. Publishes a special "brand report" in several of its issues. Typical reports cover the airlines, apparel, pet food, wine, etc.

VI. Indexing and Abstracting Services and Full-Text Services

ABI/INFORM. Provides abstracts of articles from both the general business press and scholarly business journals.

American Statistics Index. (Congressional Information Service). Comprehensive guide to government statistical publications.

Business Periodicals Index. Provides citations to the general business press and the scholarly press.

Dialog's Business Connection. Includes full-text articles covering company and industry information. An especially good source for market data/information.

Lexis/Nexis. Online service providing access to full-text articles from the national and regional press, and business periodicals. The "Market" library of files contains full-text articles from the marketing and advertising literature.

Market Research Abstracts. Indexes and abstracts articles appearing in scholarly journals.

Predicasts F&S Index. Indexes articles by company name and by industry classification (SIC code). Excellent source for tracking articles from the trade literature and for obtaining market information.

VII. General Information Sources

Business and Government. Petersen, H. Craig. New York: Harper Collins College Publishers, 4th ed., 1993.

Business Information: How to Find It, How to Use It. Lavin, Michael R., Phoenix, AZ: Oryx Press, 1992.

Business Information Sources. Daniells, Lorna M., Berkeley, CA: University of California Press, 3rd ed., 1993.

Contemporary Government and Business Relations. Schnitzer, Martin., Boston, MA: Houghton Mifflin, 2nd ed., 1983.

Encyclopedia of Business Information Sources. Detroit, MI: Gale Research Co., 10th ed., 1995/1996.

Handbook of United States Economic and Financial Indicators. O'Hara, Frederick M., Westport, CT: Greenwood Press, 1985.

International Business Information: How to Find It, How to Use It. Pagell, Ruth A., Phoenix, AZ: Oryx Press, 1994.

Statistical Abstract of the United States. Washington, DC: U.S. Department of Commerce, Social and Economic Statistics Administration, Bureau of the Census, 115th ed., 1995.

Understanding the Census: A Guide for Marketers, Planners, Grant Writers, and Other Data Users. Lavin, Michael R., Kenmore, NY: Epoch Books, 1996.

6 Understanding and Forecasting the External Environment

Technological Factors and Forecasting

INTRODUCTION

We saw in the previous chapter how changes in the demographic, social, cultural, political, and economic factors in the environment influence the choice of a strategy for a business. Choice of a specific business strategy involves assessing the impact of environmental factors on the future of the business and on competitors so that the firm can ready an appropriate response to likely competitor reactions. In this chapter we continue this discussion by focusing on the need to understand and forecast changes in technological aspects of the environment.

Managers utilize their experience and judgment to conjecture the relevant changes in the environment. As we have seen earlier, such conjectures are subject to various biases. In situations with limited historical data, firms will not be able to avoid using judgmental forecasts. However, in other cases it can use analytical methods such as regression to forecast competitor responses; in the same vein, it can use regression to identify what strategic decisions can lead to a prespecified objective. However, use of regression assumes that the future environment is not likely to change dramatically from the conditions that prevailed when the data were gathered.

The business press reports technological developments on a regular basis. For example, consider the following two developments that might revolutionize the health sector and the entertainment industry:

1. A gene therapy treatment that unclogs cholesterol damage was implemented by Dr. James Wilson of the University of Pennsylvania's Institute for Gene Therapy (*USA Today,* April 1, 1994). Gene therapy experiments are also reported to be under way for a variety of diseases, including cystic fibrosis and certain cancers. Such developments can have a significant effect on the demand for various drugs and health services in the future.

2. Developments in multimedia technology will give people an opportunity to control interactively various household electronics. There is a clear need to develop products that will enable such interactive control in a household from the same device.

UNCERTAINTY AND ROLE OF JUDGMENT

Typically, historical data can be employed in forecasting the future using statistical methods. But when historical data are not available, gauging the future becomes essentially a judgmental activity. Even when forecasts are developed from historical data, it becomes necessary to revise them using various qualitative information not easily incorporated in the forecasting model. Such revisions also involve managerial judgment.

Managerial judgment is also called for in dealing with other uncertainties in strategic decision making—assessing future actions of competitors, future trends in technology, and changes in the political environment. Managers will need to identify these uncertainties and the risks involved. Such judgments are an important input to the design of appropriate strategies.

Behavioral decision researchers have documented biases that affect people's judgments. We show in Table 6.1 various biases of human judgment relevant to future-oriented decisions in general. The biases particularly relevant to forecasting are conservatism, recency, illusory correlations, and optimism or wishful thinking about the future. Strategic decision makers must recognize these human limitations and biases and take steps to minimize their impact on forecasts and the decisions based on them.

FORECASTING TECHNOLOGY

Technology plays an essential part in the success of any firm. We therefore focus on the ways in which a strategy analyst can forecast technological trends as an input into the formulation of a business strategy. The techniques described in this chapter, however, are also generally applicable to forecasting other aspects of a business such as sales or costs; therefore, the reader should not exclusively identify the techniques with the task of forecasting technology.

Alternatives to Formal Forecasting   Alternatives to a formal process for forecasting technological developments include no forecast, anything can happen, the glorious past, window-blind forecasting, crisis action, and genius forecasting.[1] Some pros and cons of these approaches follow.

1. *No forecast:* This means that a firm is facing the future blindfolded. In most cases, the firm thinks that the future is constant or will change to only a negligible extent.
2. *Anything can happen:* This option implicitly assumes that the future is a gamble. This attitude can create serious trouble and the business can be short lived.

TABLE 6.1 **Common Biases in Future-oriented Decisions and Ways to Avoid or Reduce Their Negative Impact**

Type of Bias	Description of Bias	Ways to Avoid or Reduce Negative Impact of Bias
Conservatism	Failure to change (or changing slowly) one's own mind in light of new information/evidence.	• Monitor for changes in the environment and build procedures to take actions when such changes are identified.
Recency	The most recent events dominate those in the less recent past, which are downgraded or ignored.	• Realize that cycles exist and that not all ups or downs are permanent. • Consider the fundamental factors that affect the event of interest.
Anchoring	Predictions are unduly influenced by initial information, which is given more weight in the forecasting process.	• Start with objective information (e.g., forecasts). • Ask people to discuss the types of changes that are possible; also ask the reasons when changes are being proposed.
Illusory correlations	Belief that patterns are evident and/or two variables are causally related when they are not.	• Verify statistical significance of patterns. • Model relationships, if possible, in terms of changes.
Optimism, wishful thinking	People's preferences for future outcomes affect their forecasts of such outcomes.	• Have the forecasts made by a disinterested third party. • Have more than one person independently make the forecasts.
Underestimating uncertainty	Excessive optimism, illusory correlation, and the need to reduce anxiety result in underestimating future uncertainty.	• Estimate uncertainty objectively. Consider many possible future events by asking different people to come up with unpredictable situations/events.

Source: Reprinted with the permission of The Free Press, a Division of Simon & Schuster, from FORECASTING, PLANNING, AND STRATEGY FOR THE 21ST CENTURY by Spyros G. Makridakis. Copyright (c) 1990 by Spyros G. Makridakis.

3. *The glorious past:* This attitude implies that the future will be as glorious as the past because the firm has prospered with the decisions of the past. This approach to dealing with future uncertainties can lead to disaster.

4. *Window-blind forecasting:* This approach to forecasting assumes that existing technology can only get better, faster, higher, or bigger. This view can lead an organization into unpleasant surprises owing to unanticipated future changes.

5. *Crisis action:* This approach involves waiting until a significant change has occurred. An organization following this method of managing technology will probably not make any progress toward its goals. A firm can avoid crisis action by anticipating the future in a systematic manner.

6. *Genius forecasting:* This method consists of asking a genius (or an expert) to find out what future technological developments will be. In a sense, it is a forecasting

method. But there is no rational way to examine the assumptions behind and seek corroboration for such a forecast.

It should be clear from the foregoing discussion that there are several disadvantages to not using a formal method for forecasting future possibilities. These disadvantages are particularly relevant for forecasting technological developments owing to the opportunities (and fortunes) that could be lost when a firm selects a specific path of technology. Even large firms like Sony have lost out in the VCR market by banking on Betamax technology and not focusing on VHS technology. In the same manner, Zenith lost out in the video storage and transmission market by focusing on videodiscs when success clearly lay in videocassettes. Our view is that a firm will have a significant advantage if it develops forecasts in a systematic manner and makes technological choices based on as much information on the future as possible. The gains of developing such forecasts far outweigh the costs. We must, however, point out that mere availability of technological forecasts does not guarantee right choices. But we do believe that a firm is better off employing a formal forecasting technique and supplementing it with managerial judgment wherever necessary. Even with the availability of forecasts, a firm has to make choices regarding the specific technologies to be employed. The remainder of this section will briefly review a few formal techniques for forecasting technological trends. The reader may note that these are but a subset of techniques generally used for forecasting. We will elaborate on how these techniques are applied to sales forecasting in the next section.

Measuring Technology

To forecast technological trends, a first step is to define and measure technology using one or two critical parameters. Two measures available for measuring technology are functional and technical parameters. *Functional parameters* measure the utility to the user of the technology or a product developed from that technology, while *technical parameters* are those that the technology developer can manipulate to yield the desired utility to the user. For example, a functional parameter for an incandescent bulb would be light output measured in lumens, while a technical parameter would be filament temperature, which a product designer may vary to yield the desired lumens. In the case of a personal computer, a functional parameter would be the speed with which the computer can execute a command, while a corresponding technical parameter would be the speed of the microprocessor chip.

The measure selected for forecasting a technology should satisfy some criteria. First, the measure itself must actually be measurable. Next, the measure should represent the state of the art of technology and should be applicable to all different technologies that may be considered in forecasting. (For example, when one considers aircraft speed as a technical measure for aircraft technology, it enables comparison of propeller-driven and jet-propelled aircraft. Aircraft weight would not allow such a comparison.) Of course, appropriate data should be available for the measure selected and the measure should be consistent with the stage of innovation represented in the data. It would be inappropriate to compare technologies in their early stages of development with technologies in much later stages of development. For example, it would be inappropriate to compare the physical size of a computer of an earlier generation with that of a current-generation laptop computer.

Once the data for the selected measures have been collected, the analyst may adopt any one of several techniques for forecasting.* These include trend extrapolation methods and fitting growth curves. (Trend extrapolation methods are a subset of various time-series techniques.) Further, the analogy method may also be appropriate to forecast the impact of a new technology. The analogy method involves identifying a trend exhibited in one or more existing technologies quite similar to the one under consideration and applying the observed trend to the technology being forecasted.

An Illustration of Forecasting Technology   To make the technological forecasting problem concrete, assume that one is interested in assessing when the next Intel microprocessor chip will be introduced and what its speed will be. Undoubtedly, this is a complicated forecasting task. We suggest how some methods can be utilized to complete it.

First, we will be interested in finding out the historical data on the introduction of microprocessor chips by Intel. Fortunately, some details on Intel's introductions in the recent past were reported in *The Wall Street Journal.* The following data can be extracted from this article.

Date of Introduction	Intel Corporation's Chip	Chip Speed (MIPS)	Number of Months Elapsed since June 1979	Number of Months from Previous Chip
June 1979	8088	0.5	0	0
February 1982	80286	1.1	23	23
October 1985	80386	1.5	67	44
April 1989	80486	20.0	109	42
March 1993	Pentium-60MHZ	100.0	156	47
March 1994	Pentium-100MHZ	200.0	168	12

Data drawn from *The Wall Street Journal,* December 7, 1994.

Methods for Forecasting Technology   Various methods described in this chapter are relevant to develop forecasts of *when* and *what* in connection with Intel's chip introductions. First, we will be able to forecast by fitting a mathematical function

---

*Techniques for forecasting technology are often described as exploratory or normative. The essential distinction is whether the forecast depends on some knowledge currently available to the forecaster. Thus, techniques such as trend extrapolation, regression, and the like will be called exploratory. Normative techniques include methods of relevance trees and morphological analysis. The reader will recall our description of the method of morphological connections for finding solutions in Chapter 3. We will not delve into the normative techniques in this book.

to go through various data points of time of introduction (when) and million instruction per second (MIPS) (what) and use the curve to forecast when the next processing chip will be introduced and with what speed. Various functions such as linear or exponential trend lines and growth curves (a broad class of *curve-fitting methods*) can be used. In particular, the *S*-shaped curve, when fitted to the data on MIPS, can reveal how large a speed is feasible for a microprocessor chip. These techniques do not call for any more information than shown here. Hence, they suffer from the disadvantage of not being able to incorporate any knowledge of technological developments in the microprocessor chip industry.

One method that utilizes such knowledge is the *Delphi technique* and involves eliciting opinions of experts in one or more rounds. A third method, the *method of analogy,* involves applying the developments in an analogous industry to the chip industry.

Accuracy of Technology Forecasts   Wise analyzed the accuracy of predictions of future technological changes and their effects made by Americans between 1890 and 1940 and found that less than half (40 percent) either were or are in the process of being fulfilled.[2] His analysis was based on 1556 predictions in 18 specified areas of technology such as energy sources, communications, new materials, heating and cooling, computers, and weapons. He also found that the batting average of experts (44.4 percent) was significantly better than that for nonexperts (33.6 percent). Further, the study showed that effects of technology were harder to predict than the technological changes themselves. This finding suggests that social and economic changes evolve in response to an array of technological changes rather than to a single technological innovation.

These findings are quite consistent with those of Schnaars and Berenson, who looked at market growth forecasts published in the business press from 1960 to 1979.[3] Out of the 90 market growth forecasts they examined, 48 (53 percent) failed to materialize. The reasons attributed to these failures and successes, summarized below, indicate the need for careful analysis of a multitude of factors while making forecasts of marketplace innovations.

Reasons for Failure	Reasons for Success
Overevaluation of technological wonders	Demographic forecasts
No relative advantage for the consumer	A focus on fundamental market factors
Shift in the relative advantage demanded by the consumer	Consistent advances in product and market
Changes in social and demographic trends	
Technical problems	
Undue pessimism	
Politics	

These reasons show that for a successful forecast requires that a strategy analyst conduct appropriate analyses of customer and competitive behavior as well as the external environment. The various methods described in earlier chapters and in this chapter will undoubtedly be helpful.

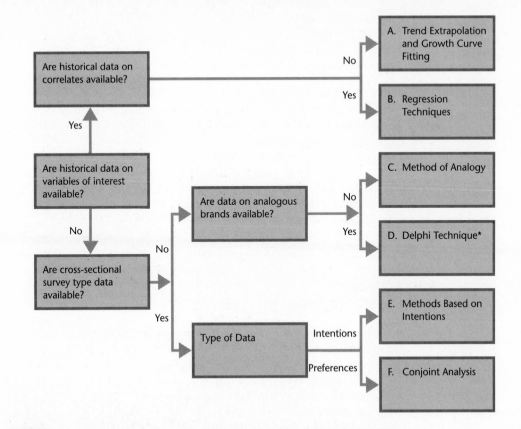

FIGURE 6.1   **A Data-Based Taxonomy of Major Forecasting Methods**

*Not exhaustive.

Source: Adapted from Vithala R. Rao and James E. Cox, *Sales Forecasting: A Review of Recent Developments.* Copyright (c) 1978. Reprinted by permission of Marketing Science Institute. (Please note that this report is out of print.)

SELECTED FORMAL FORECASTING METHODS*

Various forecasting methods[4] can be organized in several ways. One classification is shown in Fig. 6.1. It is based on the four variables: (i) whether historical data on the variable of interest are available; (ii) whether historical data on the variables of interest correlate; (iii) whether data on analogous situations are available; and (iv) type of cross-sectional survey data available. As the flowchart indicates, various combinations of these variables will lead to six categories of forecasting techniques:

A: trend extrapolation and growth curves;

B: regression;

*We thank Rahul Bhalla, Cornell MBA, 1995, for his assistance in developing various analyses used in this section.

C: method of analogy;

D: Delphi technique;

E: methods based on intentions and

F: conjoint analysis.

Although our focus up to this point has been on technology, the first four methods have widespread use including sales forecasting. The last two methods are more specifically geared to sales forecasts. Consistent with this, we draw examples from both technology and sales forecasting.

Trend extrapolation and fitting growth curves do not utilize any data other than the variables of interest (e.g., sales), while regression requires the analyst to obtain data on some correlates of the variable being forecasted. Multiple regression is the most versatile for developing forecasts. In the analogy method, historical data on a number of analogous situations are analyzed to forecast the variable under question (usually sales). The Delphi technique involves a series of surveys of a panel of experts, with feedback of their opinions after each round. The last two categories of methods (E and F) involve data obtained in surveys on purchase intentions and evaluations of hypothetical products.*

Advantages and disadvantages of these techniques are described in Appendix 6A.

Industry Use of Forecasting Methods   In a survey among executives of 500 U.S. corporations, Sanders and Manrodt[5] (1994) found that respondents are more familiar with quantitative forecasting methods than in the past, but the level of usage has not increased. The data are based on usable responses from 96 executives with such job titles as vice-president of sales and marketing, director of marketing, and director of corporate planning. Although over 90 percent of the executives are familiar with regression, they continue to rely largely on judgmental forecasting methods. The major obstacles to the use of formal quantitative forecasting methods such as multiple regression are lack of relevant data and low level of organizational support.

Executives also adjust data judgmentally while using quantitative techniques to reflect their knowledge of special conditions of the data.

Extrapolation and Curve Fitting

When the analyst has access to a series of data over time, a forecast can be developed using any one of several trend extrapolation methods or by fitting a growth curve. While trends can be extrapolated with any type of function, we will consider only linear and exponential trends. Growth curves are based on a loose analogy between

---

*We limit our discussion to methods A through D. The techniques based on surveys of purchase intentions are beyond the scope of this book because they deal mainly with short-term forecasting. The technique of conjoint analysis described in Chapter 2 can also be employed for forecasting sales of a new product.

growth in sales and growth of a living organism. Typically, there will be slow growth in the early period, followed by rapid growth. Later on, the growth tapers off, reaching a plateau. The general shape is that of an *S*-curve. We consider two particular growth curves, called the Pearl curve and Gompertz curve. The mathematical equations for trend and growth curves and ways of estimating them are shown in Appendix 6B.

Trend Extrapolation   Essentially, extrapolating a trend involves visually identifying a pattern in the growth of sales over time and fitting an appropriate mathematical function to the observed pattern. While any mathematical function can be used to describe a time trend, linear and exponential trend functions are usually appropriate and sufficient for consideration; these two patterns are shown in Fig. 6.2.

Once a trend pattern has been selected, the analyst fits the trend to the observed data using the method of least squares. Usually, one or two data points at the end are not used in the fitting of the trend. The fitted trend is then used to forecast the data for the points withheld. The prediction is then compared with the observed data to check how well the trend line fits the data. If the fit is good enough, the trend line may then be reestimated using all data points. The updated trend line is used to forecast future patterns. Given the ease with which linear functions can be fitted using the method of least squares, the exponential trend function is linearized by taking logarithms on both sides.

Growth Curves   Among the several curves that can be employed to forecast growth, the Pearl curve and the Gompertz curve are the most suitable. The procedure for fitting them is the same as that for trend extrapolation. The growth curve is transformed to yield a linear function while fitting the curve.

We show the patterns for the two growth curves along with their equations in Fig. 6.3.

Illustration of Trend and Growth Curves: Cellular Telephone Sales   We illustrate this process of extrapolating trends and fitting growth curves using the sales data for cellular telephones during the period 1983 to 1992. The data are shown in Table 6.2. A visual examination of these data shows a phenomenal growth of sales during this period.

We fitted both the linear and exponential trends to these sales data for the years 1983–1990 and used the estimated trends to forecast sales for 1991 and 1992. We then compared the forecasts with actual sales. The results are shown in the top part of Table 6.3. As can be seen, the errors are very large.

The bottom part of Table 6.3 shows the results of the fit of growth curves—Pearl and Gompertz—to the same data. In this estimation, one needs to assume a value for the upper limit (L) of the growth curve equation; we estimated these curves with a value of 5,000 for L. We tested the sensitivity of the results for different values of the upper limit, L. The estimates of parameters vary, of course, with the value of L. In general, the forecasts increase as L increases. This should be expected because the

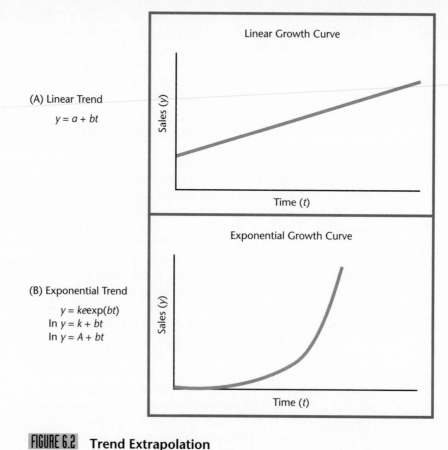

(A) Linear Trend

$$y = a + bt$$

(B) Exponential Trend

$$y = keexp(bt)$$
$$\ln y = k + bt$$
$$\ln y = A + bt$$

FIGURE 6.2   **Trend Extrapolation**

whole growth curve is pushed upwards as L increases. Once L is known, the growth curve equation can be linearized and estimated by the method of least squares.

The fit measures (R = squares) are all very high for each of these curves. Nevertheless, the forecasts show varying amounts of error. The forecasts from all of these methods are summarized below by the absolute error in the forecast as a percentage of the actual value.

	1991	1992
Linear trend	48.4%	40.6%
Exponential trend	42.0	202.1
Pearl curve	1.4	25.9
Gompertz curve	45.4	33.2

The results indicate the Pearl growth curve yielded not only a better fit but also forecasts for 1991 and 1992 much closer to actual figures. But, it was subject to a large error

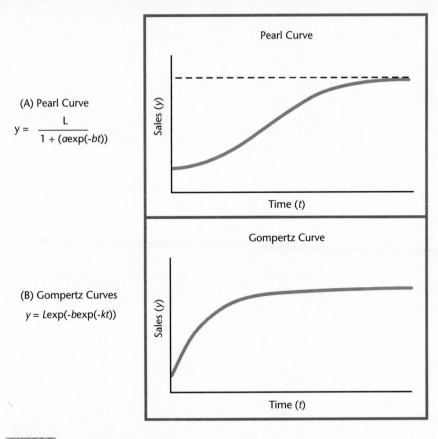

(A) Pearl Curve

$$y = \frac{L}{1 + (a\exp(-bt))}$$

(B) Gompertz Curves

$$y = L\exp(-b\exp(-kt))$$

 **Growth Curves**

TABLE 6.2 U.S. Sales of Cellular Phones: 1983–1992

Year	t	Sales (thousands of units)
1983	0	5*
1984	1	25
1985	2	75
1986	3	280
1987	4	300
1988	5	500
1989	6	870
1990	7	2100
1991	8	3100
1992	9	3750

*This number is actually shown as not available (N/A). We use 5 as an approximation.

Source: *1993 Electronic Market Data Book*, p. 33. Marketing Services Dept., Electronics Industries Association, Washington D.C.

TABLE 6.3 Fit and Predictions from Different Trend and Growth Curves for Cellular Phone Sales Data (1983–1990)

Trend or Growth Curve	Mathematical Equation	Parameter Estimates and Standard Errors (S.E.)			Degree of Fit (R-Square)	Actual and Forecasted Values for			
						1991		1992	
		Parameter	Estimate	S.E.		Actual	Predicted	Actual	Predicted
Trend									
Linear trend	$y = a + bt$	a	−1,761.62		0.71	3,100	1,600	3,750	1,840
		b	240.13	63.30					
Exponential trend	$y = ae^{bt}$ or	ln a	1.314		0.95	3,100	5,324	3,750	11,329
	$\ln y = a + bt$	b	0.755	0.071					
Growth Curves									
Pearl curve	$y = \dfrac{L}{1+ae^{-bt}}$	a			0.96	3,100	3,057	3,750	3,902
	(L is set at 5,000)	b	0.8148	0.067					
Gompertz curve	$y = Le^{-be^{-Kt}}$	b	15.002		0.94	3,100	2,047	3,750	2,505
	(L is set at 5,000)	K	0.2565	0.0259					

for the year 1992. The Pearl growth curve is drawn along with the actual data and predictions in Fig. 6.4. The Gompertz growth curve gave poor predictions for both years.

The exponential trend perhaps is not appropriate for these data; it showed greater errors than the linear trend for the year 1992, although the error from it is less than that for the linear trend for 1991.

This illustration shows the potential mistakes an analyst can make in forecasting with linear and exponential trend curves. In general, it is more appropriate to rely on growth curves because sales growth is generally constrained.

Regression Techniques

Regression is highly suitable for forecasting the sales of established products (or brands). In developing a regression model for sales of an established product, the analyst needs first to develop a conceptually defensible framework to describe the process of sales formation (a similar framework is necessary for using regression to forecast the development of a technology). This framework should enable the analyst to determine which predictors to include in the regression model for forecasting sales. For example, consider forecasting the sales of new cars in a country; the conceptual framework relevant for this problem may be derived from the economic theory of consumption; variables such as disposable income, credit conditions,

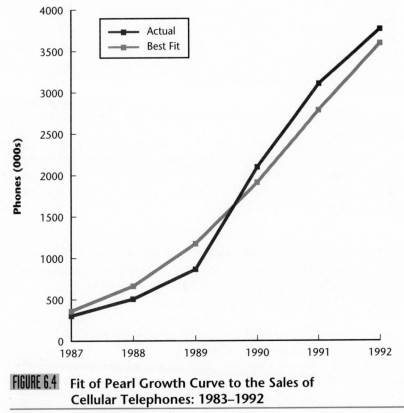

FIGURE 6.4   **Fit of Pearl Growth Curve to the Sales of Cellular Telephones: 1983–1992**

Note: 1992 point is extrapolated.

prices, and stock of automobiles of different ages may be important predictors for forecasting the demand for new automobiles. In a like manner, population size, age distribution, and disposable income may be relevant predictors for sales of pharmaceutical products.

Regression Procedure   The procedure for building a regression model for sales forecasting involves the following steps:

Step 1: Identify an appropriate conceptual model for sales.

Step 2: Identify predictor variables that affect sales; let Y be the sales variable and $X_1, X_2, \ldots, X_n$ be the n predictors affecting sales.

Step 3: Collect historical data on sales (Y) and predictor variables (Xs).

Step 4: Make the series comparable in units used over time; for example, ensure that any dollar measures are in constant terms over time.

Step 5: Use dummy variables to account for any sudden changes in the conditions over the period of series of data.

Step 6: Estimate the postulated regression equation between sales and the X-variables (including any additional dummy variables); test the goodness of fit and interpret the equation.

Step 7: Develop estimates for the future values of the X-variables in the equation using external information. It may be useful at this stage to consider multiple sets of future values for the X-variables. (Each set of future values defines a scenario that could occur in the future.)

Step 8: Assuming that the regression model is acceptable, use it to forecast Y for each scenario.

Step 9: Test for the sensitivity of assumptions made either in the model or in the future values of predictors used in forecasting future sales.

We illustrate this approach with two examples. In the first example, we estimate a forecasting equation for cable television subscriptions in the United States using the time-series data for the period 1963–1990 and make a forecast for the year 1991. In the second example, we develop a forecasting equation to predict the penetration of telephones in a country using cross-sectional data across various countries.

Example 1: Forecasting CATV Penetration   Because the number of cable television subscribers will be highly related to the population size, we use the number of CATV subscribers per 100,000 households as the dependent variable in the regression equation. We can multiply this forecast by the projected number of households to obtain a forecast of the total number of CATV subscribers. This procedure will enable us to forecast an underlying behavior (rate of CATV subscription) rather than forecast a total, which would naturally be affected by population size. (Note that it is important to separate out those reasons for an increase in sales due to a change in underlying behavior from those simply due to population growth with no change in the underlying consumption behavior.) We conjecture that two variables—monthly rate for the cable television service and disposable income per household—would be useful in predicting the penetration of CATV for this illustration.

We collected relevant data for the period 1975–1989 and estimated a regression equation. The predictor variables were monthly subscription rate for CATV, adjusted for inflation, and disposable income per household measured in 1987 constant dollars. The variable monthly subscription rate reflects the managerial decisions of the CATV systems, while disposable income reflects households' economic status. This forecasting model does not account for differences among households because data are at the aggregate level.

The results are shown in panels A, B, and C of Table 6.4. Panel A shows data compiled and identifies the manipulation of data before running the regression. Panel B shows the results of regression analysis: R-square measuring the degree of fit of the regression, the intercept of the regression, the two regression coefficients, their standard errors, and t-values. Panel C shows the forecasts made for the years 1991–1993 using the regression model, along with actual values and forecasting errors.

The R-square for this regression is 0.94, indicating an extremely good fit of this model to predict CATV penetration. The two regression coefficients are statistically significant. They are negative for monthly subscription rate and positive for disposable income, as one would expect. According to this regression, a 1-unit decrease in the adjusted monthly subscription rate will increase the penetration rate of CATV by 2.10 units, while a $100 increase in disposable income would increase the rate of penetration by 0.99 units.

We now use the model to see how well it predicts for the years 1991–1993. The forecasts for the three-year period are very close to the actual values. The forecast errors are 6.9 percent for 1991, 3.2 percent for 1992, and 0.9 percent for 1993. The regression model underpredicts the actual penetration rate of cable TV for all of these years. The actual versus predicted rates of penetration are shown in Fig. 6.5.

Example 2: Forecasting Telephone Penetration in Countries   This example involves developing a regression model to predict the penetration of telephones across 29 countries spanning all continents of the world for the year 1988. Given that these countries are at various stages of development, the data can be thought of as a time-series even though the data correspond to one year.

We compiled data on number of telephones per 100 people, percent urban population, and railway passenger-kilometers per 100 people in each country. While the first variable obviously contributes to greater telephone usage, the second variable is a measure of the infrastructure of a country. These two variables combined measure the extent of industrialization of a country, and are thereby important determinants of telephone penetration. We developed a regression model for predicting telephone penetration using these two predictors. Considering that some countries are highly industrialized, we estimated a multiple exponential

TABLE 6.4   Illustration of Forecasting with Regression: CATV Data

Panel A: Data Used

Year	Number of Subscribers (000s)	Subscription Rate per Month (current $)	Price Index (value of a 1982–1984 dollar)	Adjusted Monthly Subscription Rate (constant $)	Disposable Income (1987 $)	Number of Households (000s)	Penetration Rate (per 100 households)	Predicted Rate of Penetration
1975	9,800	$ 7.85	1.859	$14.593	$10,906	71,120	13.78	6.56%
1976	11,000	7.87	1.757	13.828	11,912	72,867	15.10	18.13
1977	12,200	7.92	1.649	13.060	11,406	74,142	16.45	14.73
1978	13,400	8.09	1.532	12.394	11,851	76,030	17.62	20.54
1979	15,000	8.44	1.380	11.647	12,039	88,330	16.98	23.97
1980	17,500	8.80	1.215	10.692	12,005	80,776	21.66	25.64
1981	21,500	9.02	1.098	9.904	12,156	82,368	26.10	28.79
1982	25,400	9.57	1.035	9.905	12,146	83,527	30.41	28.69
1983	29,450	9.84	1.003	9.870	12,349	83,198	35.40	30.77
1984	32,850	10.08	0.961	9.687	13,029	85,407	38.46	37.88
1985	35,430	10.42	0.928	9.670	13,258	86,789	40.82	40.18
1986	38,740	10.31	0.913	9.413	13,552	88,458	43.79	43.63
1987	41,200	10.15	0.880	8.932	13,545	89,479	46.04	44.58
1988	44,200	10.18	0.846	8.612	13,890	91,124	48.51	48.66
1989	47,390	10.21	0.807	8.240	14,030	92,830	51.05	50.83
1990	50,455	10.38	0.766	7.951	14,154	93,347	54.05	52.67

Panel B: Regression Results

R-Square = 0.94; Adjusted R-Square = 0.93

ANOVA

	df	Sum of Squares	Mean Square	F-Ratio	P-Value
Regression	2	2,849.90	1,424.95	106.59	< .00001
Residual	13	173.79	13.37		
Total	15	3,023.68			

	Coefficients	Standard Error	t-Value	P-Value
Intercept	−70.69	36.23	−1.95	0.073
Monthly rate	−2.10	1.03	−2.04	0.0625
Disposable income	0.0099	0.0021	4.77	0.0004

Panel C: Forecasts

Year	Actual Number of Subscribers (000s)	Monthly Rate (current $)	Price Index	Adjusted Monthly Rate (constant $)	Disposable Income (1987 $)	Number of Households (000s)	Actual Penetration Rate*	Predicted Penetration Rate*	% Error = (Actual − Predicted) x 100 / Actual
1991	52,600	$10.27	0.734	$7.538	$13,990	94,312	55.77	51.91	6.9%
1992	54,300	10.06	0.713	7.173	14,219	95,669	56.76	54.94	3.2
1993	56,300	9.11	0.692	6.304	14,330	96,391	58.41	57.87	0.9

*Per 100 households.

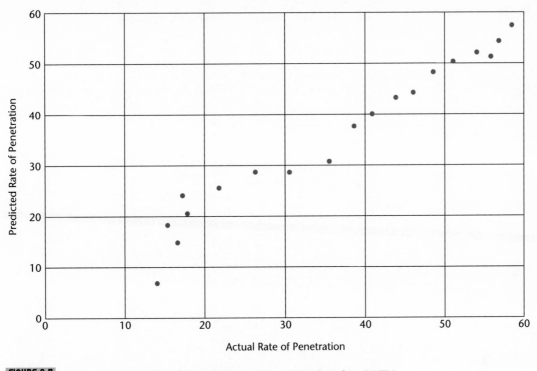

FIGURE 6.5 **Actual versus Predicted Rates of Penetration for CATV**

model to describe a growth pattern across the countries. We linearized the model by transforming these variables into logarithms. This procedure is described in Appendix 6C.

The results of this analysis are shown in Table 6.5. The data used in the regression are shown in the top panel and the results are shown in the middle panel. The forecasts are shown in the bottom panel. We made the data comparable across all countries by estimating any data missing in the original source.

The regression coefficients for the two variables—percent urbanization and infrastructure—are highly significant. The respective coefficients are both positive (as could be expected); the regression coefficient in the multiple exponential model (which is shown in Appendix 6C to be the elasticity) for the urbanization variable is 2.38, indicating a 2.38 percent change in telephones per 100 people for each percent change in the degree of urbanization. Similarly, the elasticity for the infrastructure measure is 0.44. The R-square of the model is 0.77, indicating a good fit.

We used the model to predict telephone penetration for five countries—Argentina, Japan, Sri Lanka, Norway, and South Africa—not included in the estimation: the results were mixed. The forecasting errors are very large for the less-developed countries and quite low for developed countries. In particular, the model forecasts telephone penetration for Norway and South Africa very well.

TABLE 6.5   **Forecasting of Telephone Penetration in Various Countries**

Panel A: Data Used

Country	1988 Population (in thousands)	Telephones per 100 People in 1988 (Y)	Adjusted* % Urban (1988) (X_1)	1988 Railway Passenger-Km (in millions)	Passenger-Km per 100 people (X_2)
Austria	7,651	54.30	57.6	7,994	104,488
Belgium	9,845	49.90	95.7	6,348	64,479
Bolivia	7,002	2.80	50.0	369	5,270
Brazil	144,246	9.60	73.7	13,891	9,630
Canada	25,999	51.30	76.6	2,989	11,496
Chile	12,736	6.80	84.1	1,013	7,954
Cuba	10,400	5.20	72.6	2,627	25,260
Czechoslovakia	15,600	25.50	75.3	19,408	124,414
Denmark	5,130	88.20	84.6	4,850	94,547
Finland	4,956	49.90	59.7	3,147	63,496
France	55,880	45.20	72.8	63,290	113,261
Germany	62,356	68.20	85.0	41,760	66,970
Greece	10,008	43.10	61.3	1,963	19,614
India	796,502	0.60	25.0	263,731	33,111
Indonesia	173,356	0.50	27.3	7,863	4,536
Ireland	3,517	23.80	54.7	1,180	33,551
Kenya	23,290	1.50	22.0	2,608	11,198
Malaysia	16,967	9.70	41.3	1,518	8,947
Netherlands	14,765	65.90	88.4	9,664	65,451
Peru	21,132	2.30	69.8	596	2,820
Spain	38,726	28.00	77.5	15,716	40,582
Sweden	8,474	66.20	83.8	6,081	71,760
Switzerland	6,619	88.20	60.5	12,391	187,203
Tanzania	24,023	0.60	19.5	855	3,559
Thailand	54,975	1.80	21.4	10,301	18,738
Turkey	55,211	11.70	58.6	6,708	12,150
United Kingdom	57,009	45.50	88.9	34,412	60,363
United States	245,535	49.60	74.9	9,156	3,729
Venezuela	18,747	9.30	89.6	29	155

*These are estimated using 1990 data and growth rates during 1985–1990.

Source: *UN Statistical Yearbook*, 1992.

Panel B: Regression Results for the Exponential Model
       (Regression of Ln Y on Ln X_1 and Ln X_2)

R-Square = 0.77; Adjusted R-Square = 0.75

ANOVA

	df	Sum of Squares	Mean Square	F-Value	Significance of F
Regression	2	58.14	29.07	43.37	< .0005
Residual	26	17.43	0.67		
Total	28	75.57			

(Continued on next page)

TABLE 6.5   Continued

Panel B: Regression Results for the Exponential Model (Regression of Ln Y on Ln X_1 and Ln X_2)

ANOVA

	Coefficients	Standard Error	t-Statistic	P-Value
Intercept	−11.40	1.51	−7.52	< .0001
Ln X_1	2.39	0.33	7.21	< .0001
Ln X_2	0.44	0.10	4.22	0.0002

Panel C: Forecasts

Country	X_1	X_2	Y	Ln X_1	Ln X_2	Predicted Ln Y	Actual Ln Y	% Error
Argentina	85.6	32,609	11.50	4.45	10.39	3.745	2.442	53.34%
Japan	76.9	290,865	40.20	4.34	12.58	4.441	3.694	20.23
Sri Lanka	21.3	11,248	1.10	3.06	9.32	−0.0359	0.0953	−137.6
Norway	74.1	62,187	47.80	4.31	11.03	3.682	3.867	−4.78
South Africa	48.6	63,391	14.60	3.88	11.05	2.685	2.681	0.14

However, these results indicate that the model has not captured all of the essential aspects of the process of telephone penetration in a country. Perhaps, additional variables are needed to develop a better forecasting model.

Precautions in Using Regression   Some precautions in using multiple regression for forecasting should be pointed out. First, it is important to have a theoretically sound basis to identify the predictor variables to be included in the regression model and to develop suitable measures for them. This problem is quite evident in the second example; although we believe that infrastructure is an important construct in predicting telephone penetration in any country, we probably did not capture it well by the measure of railway passenger-kilometers. This was due to lack of suitable data. A related issue is that the analyst should include those variables for which forecasts are available so that the fitted regression model can be used to forecast the dependent variable. Next, it is important to choose a functional form for the regression equation that describes the structure of the data and the underlying demand formation process. We used two different functional forms—linear and exponential. Choice of a functional form is a complicated subject; discussion of this topic is beyond the scope of this book.[6] Further, the analyst has to ensure that the fitted model has face validity so that the regression coefficients can be suitably interpreted. The two examples given do satisfy this consideration. It is also important that the model fits the data well; this is seen by the large value of R-square.

   Another concern in using the regression model for forecasting is to ensure that the model predicts for the data points withheld from the estimation stage of the analysis well. While the first example did better on this criterion, there is room for improvement in the second. Another way to judge the forecasting ability of the model is by examining whether it predicts any turning points in the data. (We did not encounter this problem in our examples.) A final problem is high correlation between the included predictors in the model. This problem is called *multicollinearity*. While high multicollinearity is not detrimental to using the model for forecasting, it causes the estimated coefficients to be unstable and hard to interpret. Further discussion of this issue is beyond the scope of this book.

Analogy Method

In cases when the new product has no sales history, the task of forecasting its growth is quite monumental. Researchers have developed some creative ways to arrive at a reasonable forecast in such situations. They tend to look for similar past situations for which historical data now exist or seek the advice of experts. The corresponding methods are called the analogy method and the Delphi technique. We discuss these in some detail.

When a new product appears, it is possible to compare it to an existing product and try to forecast its growth from the experience accumulated with the existing product. This approach is essentially qualitative in that only general trends can be forecasted. However, when one can utilize the experience of several existing products, it is possible to relate the growth rate of each to a set of characteristics that describe them. When a relationship between the growth rate of a product (using a measure such as rate of penetration in the ten years since its introduction) and its characteristics (such as speed and cost) is developed, it can be used to forecast the future growth of the new product using information on its characteristics. Generally, the method of multiple regression can be employed for this purpose.

Forecasting HDTV Diffusion   As an illustration, consider the potential diffusion among U.S. households of the high-definition television (HDTV), based on a new technology under development. The manner in which HDTV will be diffused can be forecasted using the experience with television and related innovations. Fig. 6.6 shows how color television, multiple TV sets, cable TV, and VCR have diffused in the United States over the period between 1950 and 1990.

These growth curves can be used to compute the penetration of color TV and the VCR, whose technology may be "analogous" to that of HDTV. Further, because the price of HDTV is likely to be substantially higher than that of either of these two innovations, one may forecast that the diffusion of HDTV would be slower (perhaps much slower). In fact, the projections made by the FCC's working group (shown in Fig. 6.7) seem to be consistent with this view.

Bayus has assessed viability of existing forecasts for the HDTV using the method of analogy.[7] He first identified some 27 new products (or different technologies) that were introduced at various times during the last 70 years or so; these products included black and white television, color television, room air conditioner, lawn mower, turntable, and VCR. Utilizing data on the growth patterns of these products and the path of their prices over time, he estimated three parameters to describe the technology for each product. These are coefficient of innovation, coefficient of imitation, and a learning coefficient that depicts the decrease in costs due to experience.

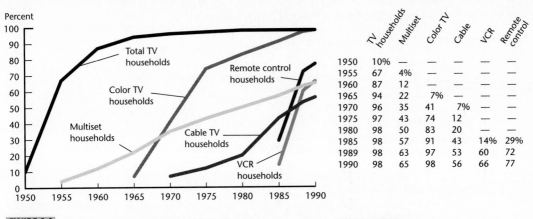

	TV households	Multiset	Color TV	Cable	VCR	Remote control
1950	10%	—	—	—	—	—
1955	67	4%	—	—	—	—
1960	87	12	—	—	—	—
1965	94	22	7%	—	—	—
1970	96	35	41	7%	—	—
1975	97	43	74	12	—	—
1980	98	50	83	20	—	—
1985	98	57	91	43	14%	29%
1989	98	63	97	53	60	72
1990	98	65	98	56	66	77

FIGURE 6.6 **U.S. Growth of TV and Related Innovations, 1950–1990**

Source: Extracted from the Harvard Business School Case, "Zenith: Marketing Research for High Definition Television (HDTV)" Case #9-591-025, Exhibit 2.

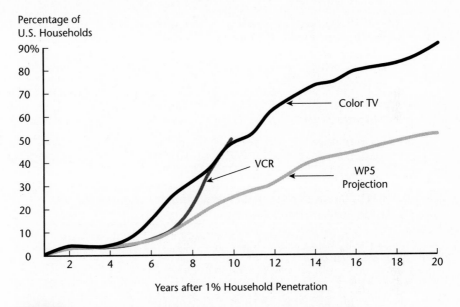

FIGURE 6.7 **FCC WP5 Estimate of U.S. HDTV Penetration Rates**

Source: Extracted from the Harvard Business School Case, "Zenith: Marketing Research for High Definition Television (HDTV)" (1990), Case #9-591-025, Exhibit 10.

(The innovation and imitation parameters describe the way a new product gets diffused in the market; we will describe them in a later section of this chapter.) The 27 products were then clustered into five appliance segments. Table 6.6 shows the characteristics of these segments.

Bayus then analyzed the estimates of demand for HDTV for 1996–2007 published by the American Electronics Association (AEA), Electronics Industries

TABLE 6.6   Use of Analogy for Forecasting HDTV Demand

Panel A: Segment Mean Characteristics

Segment	Products	Coefficient of Innovation (x 10^{-2})	Coefficient of Imitation	Market Potential (x 10^3)	Price	Price Trend	Learning Coefficient
1	Electric toothbrush, fire extinguisher, hair setter, slow cooker, styling dryer, trash compactor, turntable	8.30 (0.91)	0.22 (0.03)	38,903.8 (8,379.5)	108 (53.5)	0.051 (0.01)	0.216 (0.04)
2	Can opener, cassette tape deck, curling iron, electric blanket, heating pad, knife sharpener, lawn mower, waffle iron	2.32 (0.74)	0.32 (0.04)	36,323.6 (12,781.0)	151 (53.7)	0.086 (0.01)	0.279 (0.02)
3	B&W TV, blender, deep fryer, electric dryer, food processor, microwave oven, room A/C	1.41 (0.46)	0.48 (0.05)	38,231.7 (14,328.1)	623 (208.0)	0.054 (0.01)	0.119 (0.02)
4	Color TV, refrigerator, VCR	0.20 (0.14)	0.54 (0.07)	42,646.1 (23,566.5)	2109 (338.7)	0.090 (0.03)	0.158 (0.05)
5	Calculator, digital watch	2.49 (0.45)	0.27 (0.15)	382,722.7 (194,664.2)	140 (33.0)	0.182 (0.05)	0.472 (0.11)

Note: Standard error in parentheses.

Panel B: HDTV Parameter Estimates and Market Potential for the Three Forecasting Schemes

	AEA	EIA	NTIA
Coefficient of innovation (x 10^{-2})	0.20	0.20	1.85
Coefficient of imitation	0.54	0.54	0.46
Market potential (x 10^3)	42,646	42,630	38,261

Source: Bayus, B. L. (1993), "High-Definition Television: Demand Forecasts for Next Generation Consumer Durable," *Management Science* 39 (November), 1319–1333.

Association (EIA), and National Telecommunications Information Administration (NTIA). He used their sales estimates to infer the coefficients of innovation and imitation for HDTV. He also analyzed the assumed price paths to determine the coefficient of the learning curve for price for each set of sales estimates. (The procedure for computing these is described in the experience curve section of Chapter 7.) The parameter estimates obtained from this analysis of published demand estimates for HDTV were then combined with the grouping information of the 27 products to obtain a revised estimate of U.S. diffusion of HDTV. Bayus then used these revised parameters to judge the reasonableness of each of the published demand estimates for HDTV. These revised estimates are also shown in Table 6.6. Given the high initial price for HDTV, he concluded that a market potential of 50 million households was more reasonable for HDTV in the United States. He further concluded that the estimate published by the AEA for the period 1996–2007 is consistent with the sales histories of the 27 products he analyzed.

To use the method of analogy for forecasting, the analyst has to be able to identify appropriate analogous situations. Analogies may be identified on several dimensions. In addition to technological criteria, these dimensions include economic, managerial, political, and social criteria. For example, when forecasting the diffusion of VCR, the fact that its function is complementary to color television can be used in forecasting its diffusion; such an analogy will be based on technological dimensions. One may also use economic criteria such as price and use the diffusion paths of products with comparable prices (say, medium-priced cameras or medium-priced stereo systems). Because product diffusions just do not happen without appropriate managerial actions, one may look at the diffusion paths of products marketed by the same firm (or similar firms) as the one under consideration and use that experience in developing a forecast. Similar arguments can be made for other criteria. The basic idea is to identify products that have similar characteristics and use their experience in analogy forecasting.

Delphi Technique

The Delphi technique is a method to combine the expertise of several individuals knowledgeable about the variable of interest. The technique has been successfully used by the RAND Corporation for forecasting various technologies. In a survey of applications among individuals who either conducted or participated in Delphi studies, Brockhaus and Mickleson found that about one-fourth of the studies tackled business and economics forecasting problems.[8] The respondents felt that topics such as material shortages, energy crisis, pollution control, and long-range forecasting for various industries and product types were well handled by the Delphi technique. The respondents also noted that the Delphi technique was chosen mainly due to its low cost.

We will discuss this technique in terms of forecasting technological trends. The analyst selects a panel of experts in the technology of interest, such as research scientists, engineers, or university professors. The panel will consider various developments in the technology of interest and speculate on the specific developments likely to occur in the future (say, during the next five years). Panel members will also provide their best estimate of the probability of occurrence of each development identified. Usually, but not always, they will also guess the date when they believe the development is likely to occur. (In cases of complicated technologies, the experts may be asked to indicate the specific reasons why they believe the developments will occur; such information may be valuable in ascertaining trends that contribute to the growth of a particular technology.) The anonymous responses are collected by an independent moderator, who collates the suggested developments and summarizes the data using the median and interquartile range of the probabilities assigned by the experts. In some cases, the median and the interquartile range of the date may also be fed back to the panel so members can modify their previous predictions. This process is iterated a few times until the experts reach consensus. Various studies found that three or four iterations are sufficient for reaching consensus. In sum, this technique is characterized by anonymity and iteration with controlled feedback and statistical inference.

Advantages   The Delphi technique eliminates the disadvantages of using a committee to develop a composite forecast. These include the social pressure a group places on its members, the tendency for the group to be swayed by misinformation from any single member, and the undue influence of dominant members of the group. It also retains the advantages of a group approach such as the ability to consider a diversity of views and preserve the total amount of information presented by members.

Disadvantages   Nevertheless, the Delphi technique has been criticized for its nonscientific nature in that survey research procedures are not rigorously followed. Accordingly, a few variations are adopted in practice to ensure the rigor of the Delphi exercise. These include providing a better description of the context for developing the forecast, providing initial descriptions of potential future events, eliciting confidence bands for the predictions made by the panelists, and conducting the Delphi study for a large number of rounds until a consensus is achieved.

Studies assessing the validity of the Delphi technique of forecasting point to the significant role expertise of the panel members plays in the accuracy of the forecast obtained. Thus it is essential to ensure that a high degree of expertise is represented on the panel.

Applications of Delphi   We now describe two applications of the Delphi technique. The first application dealt with a 10-year forecast of the electronics industry developed for Corning Glass Works, and the second, a 40-year forecast developed for the Alaskan economy for the year 2000 and beyond.

Application 1: The Corning Electronics Delphi Study   The standard Delphi process was modified by researchers at Corning Glass Works in their attempt to forecast component sales in the electronics industry for a 10-year period. While actual results are not available, Johnson[9] described the various steps Corning followed in adapting the Delphi technique to business forecasting purposes.

In a standard Delphi study, experts are asked to predict the date by which a specific event will occur. Corning researchers modified this procedure by first selecting a date and then asking experts to predict the extent to which a specific change will have taken place by that time. This variation was found to be much more useful for business forecasting because the business environment changes rather gradually. In fact, predictions were sought for two specific points in time, making it possible to look at trends.

Given that outside experts were needed in this study and that the electronics industry is very diversified, Corning researchers found it difficult to find individuals with enough detailed knowledge to qualify as experts. The problem was compounded by the need for confidentiality. These considerations led the researchers to develop three different panels—one for consumer-oriented businesses, one for industrial businesses, and one for government businesses; their respective sizes were 15, 19, and 12 members. By the end of the third round, the number of responses had dropped to 14 for consumer-oriented businesses, 17 for industrial businesses, and 9 for government businesses; thus, there was a high degree of commitment on the part of panel members. The researchers found there was also a high degree of consensus in these diverse panels concerning over 80 percent of the questions either at the beginning or by the end of the third round. The biggest problem experienced was the amount of time taken for this study at Corning—nine months, as compared to the original estimate of six months.

Application 2: Forecasting the Economy of Alaska   An interesting application of the Delphi technique is that of forecasting the Alaskan economy for the year 2000 and beyond.[10] This forecast was developed by a 91-member panel drawn from several categories of decision makers, technical experts, and advocates. The panel was large in part to ensure balance of the group in expertise, advocacy orientation, responsibility areas represented, and geographic affiliation. By deliberately including opposing viewpoints, the research group attempted to achieve objectivity. The panel developed forecasts of policies, trends, and events suitable for forecasting the dynamics of the changing Alaskan economy.

In addition to the use of a large panel, the basic Delphi technique was modified in two other ways: first by conducting parallel interviews to obtain input from Alaskan natives and also by designing several scenarios and using cross-impact analysis (to be discussed later) to ascertain the likelihood of future events. The research design attempted to resolve some of the problems with the Delphi method described earlier.

The innovations in this research design proved valuable in practice. The study yielded the probabilities and timing of key events in the growth of the Alaskan economy. For example, the Delphi study predicted that the population of Alaska will reach 633,000 by the year 2000. It seemed very consistent with an independent projection by the U.S. Census Bureau of 630,000. Given the insights obtained from this study, two other Delphi projects were undertaken by state agencies. Further, the report of this Delphi study continued to be in demand even $1\frac{1}{2}$ years after its completion; consequently, it had to go into a fourth printing.

SCENARIO ANALYSIS METHODS

More traditional quantitative forecasting methods try to extrapolate from the knowledge and experience of the past to make predictions about the future. They assume that the patterns of the past are also applicable to the future. Such an assumption is not tenable when the future world is likely to change dramatically from the past.

One way to make the forecasts more realistic is to incorporate the qualitative knowledge of current trends held by people who are directly involved with the marketplace, such as local managers. Even then, extrapolation can overlook new trends, risks, and opportunities that face a business, particularly when conditions change rapidly. Under these situations, the strategy analyst needs a method that supplements traditional techniques. Scenario analysis serves this purpose well.

There is no single accepted procedure for implementing scenario analysis. The term scenario has become somewhat of a management buzzword with several meanings. In general, a *scenario* is not a forecast of the future but a description of a possible future environment. Several factors that may influence the outcome of a particular strategy are identified, and combinations of the identified factors become a scenario. The analyst will select a few of the many possible scenarios for analysis and will attempt to predict the future potential for a given strategy. In this sense, scenario analysis is a qualitative forecasting technique.

Depending on the forecasting task, scenarios can be quite general or very specific. For example, if the strategic task is to forecast the demand for energy in a country and the particular strategy the country may need to pursue, the scenarios will be defined in terms of the world political situation and technological developments regarding the development of energy sources such as solar energy. Such scenarios need not describe specific corporate technological investments. On the other hand, when the task is to develop forecasts for the potential sales of a product of significance to a company and to choose an appropriate strategy, scenarios will need to be defined not only in terms of general economic and political conditions, but also in terms of competitive situations.

Methodology of Scenario Analysis   Scenario analysis consists of three phases: *phase one*—identifying the problem and relevant external influences; *phase two (development path analysis)*—identifying paths of development for various relevant external influences, and *phase three*—synthesizing of various influences. The methods used in phase one include brainstorming and its variations. The objective in this phase is to develop a list of external factors relevant to the specific forecasting problem at hand. The second and third phases involve determining the relative impact of the various factors on each other and synthesizing their influences; different quantitative techniques are used in these two phases. The general objective is to identify a few plausible scenarios using the data collected in phase two and synthesized in phase three. While cross-impact analysis is used in the second and third phases of scenario analysis, it can also form the core of a scenario analysis by itself.

Alternate Methods for Scenario Analysis   In application, the various scenario analysis methods can be divided into three classes: cross-impact analysis, the Battelle method, and the method developed by Brauers and Weber.[11] These methods differ in the specific techniques used in the three phases of scenario analysis, particularly in synthesizing interdependencies between factors. We show the details in Table 6.7. A sce-

TABLE 6.7 A Comparison of Three Scenario Analysis Methods

Method Details	Cross-Impact Analysis	Battelle Method	Brauers and Weber Method
Identification of relevant factors	Brainstorming and similar techniques to generate a set of events of the future	Same; but each factor is defined in terms of a set of possible future outcomes	Same as the Battelle method
Definition of a scenario	A combination of presence or absence of the identified events	A combination of possible future outcomes of the identified factors	Same as the Battelle method
Data input for analysis	Marginal and conditional probabilities for the pairs of events	Compatibility estimates for all pairs of factor outcomes	Compatibility estimates for all pairs of factor outcomes and estimated probabilities for each outcome by factor
Selection of scenarios	Based on the highly probable scenarios, using the estimated probabilities according to a model	Scenarios are selected for which compatibility scores are very high based on the matrix of compatibility values for all pairs of factor outcomes.	A bounded enumeration of all possible factor outcomes is examined to check for compatibility of the scenario.
Computation of scenario probabilities	Computed according to a formal linear programming model Kluyver-Moskowitz's models)	No probabilities are computed for the scenarios	Procedure is similar to cross-impact analysis
Determination of some main scenarios	Selected on the basis of ranking of the scenario probabilities, defined as combinations of events	A few disparate and compatible scenarios are chosen	Done through cluster analysis based on the characteristics of the scenarios in terms of the factor outcomes

nario is defined differently in each of these three methods. While cross-impact analysis defines a scenario as a combination of the presence or absence of identified events (each defined by only two outcomes), the other two methods allow for several outcomes for each factor. (See Table 6.7.)

Cross-impact analysis requires marginal and conditional probabilities for the pairs of events as input. The data collection task for eliciting these probabilities is very demanding on the decision maker. Also, the estimates may not satisfy probability theory axioms; consistency tests and corrections are often required. The output from this analysis is a ranking of the scenarios in terms of their likelihood of occurring in the future. Because the likelihoods for several scenarios are extremely small, individual scenarios are often grouped to represent composite scenarios.

The Battelle method, on the other hand, requires much simpler input: the compatibility estimates for every possible pair of factor outcomes. The interdependence between the individual outcomes is evaluated by experts using some scale of compatibility. For example, in a 1 to 5 scale of compatibility, if two outcomes are incompatible, they are assigned a value of 1. A compatibility rating of 5 indicates that they are very compatible. The intermediate values of 2, 3, and 4 represent increasing degrees of compatibility between factor outcomes. The resulting matrix of compatibility ratings (k_{ij}) is symmetric. The matrix is used to generate a number of compatible scenarios with the help of advanced mathematical procedures. In this process, only a few scenarios are used for further investigation. Because the Battelle method does not use probabilities, the selected scenarios may in fact have very small probabilities of occurrence and may not be a reliable basis for a meaningful planning effort.

The method proposed by Brauers and Weber is generally similar to the Battelle method but differs in the way the scenarios are selected. While the Battelle method determines a few disparate and compatible scenarios as the main ones to consider for strategic purposes, Brauers and Weber identify main scenarios using cluster analysis.

Industry Utilization   Table 6.8 presents some data on the degree to which scenario analysis is used among large corporations in the United States. The typical long-range planning horizon for a majority of the Fortune 100 companies was five years, according to this survey. About one-half of the companies have used scenario analysis in their strategic planning process (e.g., for evaluating major investments, such as building a new facility, making an acquisition, and entering a new business area). Among 25 percent of the companies, multiple scenarios are fully integrated into the formal planning process and are used regularly, while over a third of the companies use multiple scenarios but not on a regular basis.

Three major uses of multiple scenarios are identification of potential new business opportunities; evaluation of flexibility, adaptability, or robustness of strategies; and evaluation of major investments. About one-fifth of the firms intend to use multiple scenarios on an experimental basis, while a similar number intend to use the technique often or less regularly.

A Case History of the Use of Scenario Analysis   Battelle's method of scenario analysis was applied to the Goodyear Aerospace Corporation in forecasting the international environment and U.S. defense expenditures to 1995.[12] The procedure involved identifying 16 key factors and trends, which Battelle calls "descriptors." These descriptors included Soviet-American strategic balance, arms control, international conflict, defense technologies, and U.S. defense expenditures in their international context. As we described earlier, Battelle researchers prepared a five-page essay on each descriptor that explained why it was important, gave data on past trends, and projected alternative states for the descriptor for 1995 with assigned prior probabilities of occurrence based on trend analysis and expert opinion. The alternative states are mutually exclusive and exhaustive of all reasonable possible outcomes.

TABLE 6.8 **Selected Results from a Survey of Environmental Scenario Use**

	Fortune 1000 Industrials (*n* = 215)	Fortune 500 Nonindustrials (*n* = 85)	Fortune Foreign 500 Industrials (*n* = 105)
ALL RESPONDENTS' LONG-RANGE PLANNING HORIZON			
3–4 years	14%	20%	5%
5 years	63%	53%	61%
6–9 years	2%	3%	3%
10 years	15%	12%	21%
Over 10 years	6%	12%	10%
Have a formal environmental unit (or department)	20%*	24%	44%
USERS OF SCENARIOS			
Firms that use multiple scenarios in the strategic planning process and/or for evaluating major investments, such as new facilities, acquisitions, or new businesses.	50%†	58%	53%
Length of time that firms have been using scenarios			
1 to 2 years	36%	33%	21%
3 to 4 years	26%	22%	52%
5 years or more	38%	45%	27%
The extent of use of multiple scenarios in arriving at strategic decisions			
Multiple scenarios are used on an experimental basis	6%	7%	14%
Multiple scenarios are used, but not regularly	35%	37%	23%
Multiple scenarios are used often, but are not fully integrated into the formal planning process	34%	37%	42%
Multiple scenarios are fully integrated into the formal planning process and are used regularly	25%	17%	20%
Other	—	2%	1%
How multiple scenarios are used in arriving at strategic decisions			
Scenarios are used to indicate new potential areas of business/product/market activity	67%	66%	68%
Scenarios are used to design and/or to evaluate the flexibility/adaptability/robustness of strategies	76%	75%	79%
Scenarios are used to evaluate the feasibility of major investments (such as building a new plant)	85%	70%	76%
ALL RESPONDENTS			
Planned extent of future use of multiple scenarios in the strategic planning process			
Multiple scenarios will not be used	11%	8%	8%
Multiple scenarios will be attempted on an experimental basis	20%	9%	23%
Multiple scenarios will be used, but not regularly	24%	30%	24%
Multiple scenarios will be used often, but will not be fully integrated into the formal planning process	21%	22%	20%
Multiple scenarios will be fully integrated into the formal planning process and will be used regularly	24%	28%	25%
Other	—	3%	—

*Adjusted for nonrespondent bias: 10%.

†Adjusted for nonrespondent bias: 35%.

Source: Linneman, Robert E., and Harold E. Klein (1985), "Using Scenarios in Strategic Decision Making." Reprinted from *Business Horizons,* January–February 1985. Copyright 1985 by the Foundation for the School of Business at Indiana University. Used with permission.

TABLE 6.9   **A Cross-Impact Matrix**

		U.S. Defense Expenditures		
		9%–13% of GNP	6%–9% of GNP	3%–6% of GNP
U.S. Strategic Nuclear Delivery Vehicles	2400+ (0.10)	2	−1	−2
	2000–2400 (0.30)	1	0	−1
	1700–2000 (0.40)	−1	0	1
	< 1700 (0.20)	−2	−1	2

Note: This 3 × 4 matrix is a block of a larger 49 × 49 matrix; to be read columnwise.

Source: Millett, S. M., and F. Randles (1986), "Scenarios for Strategic Business Planning: A Case History for Aerospace and Defense Companies," *Interfaces* 16:6 (November–December): 64–72.

The prior probabilities add to 1.0 for each descriptor. In all there were 49 possible alternative states across all 16 descriptors.

Battelle researchers then applied cross-impact analysis to determine the relative impact (increase or decrease) of each alternate state of any descriptor on the probabilities of occurrence of all other descriptor states. The 49 × 49 matrix of cross-impacts was filled in with numbers ranging from −3 (greatly decreases) to +3 (greatly increases); each entry describes the impact of the column state on the row state of the descriptors. A section of the large cross-impact matrix is shown in Table 6.9 for the two descriptors U.S. Strategic Nuclear Delivery Vehicles and U.S. Defense expenditures.

The researchers used the BASICS program to calculate all possible cross-impact index values and to adjust the prior probabilities of the alternate states of the 16 descriptors. These adjustments were made so that prior probabilities of alternate states of descriptors were driven to 1.0 (will occur) or 0 (will not occur). The program ran several simulations (or scenario sequences of descriptor state occurrences and nonoccurrences based on the BASICS algorithm) and organized them into scenarios (combinations of the alternate states of the descriptors). The more likely combinations are the more likely future scenarios, which can be employed in the design of future plans for the defense contractor firm.

The most likely future uncovered by this analysis was a combination of the following: the size of the U.S. and Soviet strategic arsenals would remain stable, the Strategic Arms Limitation Talks (SALT) regime would continue, and strategic doctrine (deterrence with a triad of strategic forces) would endure. The mainline forecast prepared in 1984 proved to be entirely correct during the first year of its ten-year period, much to the delight of the forecasters. Further, U.S. defense expenditures were forecasted to be between 3 and 6 percent of GNP by 1995. The Goodyear managers were able to incorporate the results from the scenario analysis in their yearly strategic planning. This involved their identifying the implications of the mainline forecast for market conditions and for each of their products in a systematic manner. This "what needs to be done" approach followed directly from an interpretation of the scenarios to answer the question, "What are the future prospects for our products?"

This detailed description illustrates the mechanics and use of scenario planning. The reader may note that cross-impact analysis is just one part of the whole process of scenario analysis.

Illustration of Brauers and Weber Method   Brauers and Weber applied their method to a forecasting problem by considering three environmental subsystems: Society, Technology, and Economy, defined respectively by 4, 1, and 2 factors. Their definitions and levels for each are as follows:

Subsystem	Factor	Levels
Society	S1: Dominant political opinion	Socialist, liberal, or conservative
	S2: Government influence on the economy and society	Strong or weak
	S3: Consumer spending	Strong or weak
	S4: Environmental protection	Strong or weak
Technology	T1: Rate of technological innovation	High or low
Economy	E1: Economic growth	Rising or stagnating
	E2: Unemployment	Rising, no change, or falling

When combined, these factors yield a total of 16 (= 3 + 2 + 2 + 2 + 2 + 2 + 3) outcomes, labeled e1-e16. The analysis then consists of obtaining compatibility ratings for all pairs of the 16 factor outcomes, along with probabilities for the outcomes of each factor. Illustrative data are shown in Table 6.10.

Given these compatibility rating data, Brauers and Weber determined the main scenarios and their probabilities using a three-step procedure: (1) determine compatible scenarios; (2) determine scenario probabilities through linear programming for the compatible scenarios; and (3) identify some main scenarios using cluster analysis. First, a scenario is deemed incompatible if the compatibility rating for an outcome pair is 1 and compatible if the rating is 5 on a 1 to 5 scale. In the example, there are 288 (= $3 \times 2 \times 2 \times 2 \times 2 \times 2 \times 3$) possible future scenarios defined on the seven factors. The first step reduced this number to 32 compatible scenarios. Note that each scenario is a combination of the outcomes of the factors and therefore a compatibility matrix for the factor outcomes of that scenario is part of the larger matrix of compatibilities.

The second step is more complicated mathematically. It involved setting up a large-scale linear programming model. This procedure is too complicated to describe in detail here, but we will convey some of its flavor. For this purpose,

TABLE 6.10   **Brauers and Weber Method**

p(i)	Factor	Outcomes (e₁–e₁₆)	S1 1	S1 2	S1 3	S2 1	S2 2	S3 1	S3 2	S4 1	S4 2	T1 1	T1 2	E1 1	E1 2	E2 1	E2 2	E2 3
0.3	S1: Dominant	S11: Socialist	x															
0.4	political opinion	S12: Liberal	1*	x														
0.5		S13: Conservative	1	1	x													
0.6	S2: Goverment	S21: Strong	5	1	3	x												
0.4	influence on the economy and society	S22: Weak	1	5	3	1	x											
0.6	S3: Consumer	S31: Strong	2	3	4	3	3	x										
0.4	spending	S32: Weak	4		2	3	3	1	x									
0.7	S4: Environmental	S41: Strong	5	3	2	3	3	1	4	x								
0.3	protection	S42: Weak	1	3	5	3	3	4	2	1	x							
0.8	T1: Rate of technical	T11: High	2	5	3	3	3	5	2	4	3	x						
0.2	innovation	T12: Low	4	2	3	3	3	2	5	2	3	1	x					
0.2	E1: Economic	E11: Rising	2	4	3	2	4	5	1	2	4	5	1	x				
0.8	growth	E12: Stagnating	4	2	3	3	3	2	4	3	3	3	3	1	x			
0.3	E2: Unemployment	E21: Rising	2	3	2	2	4	2	4	2	3	2	4	1	5	x		
0.5		E22: No change	3	3	4	3	3	3	3	4	3	3	3	3	3	1	x	
0.2		E23: Falling	4	3	3	4	2	4	2	3	3	4	2	5	1	1	1	x

*Compatibility/ratings of the row factor outcome on the column factor outcome.

equations are developed to express joint probabilities of occurrence of all pairs of the outcomes of the factors associated with a scenario in terms of observed compatibility ratings. The linear program is solved so as to minimize the difference between preliminary probabilities and final joint probabilities. The preliminary probabilities are obtained so that they conform to the theory of probability (that is, probabilities for the outcomes of any factor should each be nonnegative and should sum to 1.0). This step will generate probabilities of outcomes for each factor and probabilities for each scenario.

In the third step, scenarios are profiled in terms of the outcomes of the factors. They are then clustered to determine the typical scenarios of the total set. In this example the 32 scenarios are clustered to yield three clusters of sizes 10, 15, and 7 scenarios. The center of the first cluster represented by the factor outcomes is shown in Table 6.11. This cluster represents the future defined by conservative public opinion, relatively weak influence of government on the economy, strong consumer spending, weak protection for the environment, high rate of technological innovation, relatively neutral economic growth, and essentially no change in unemployment. The other two clusters will yield different scenarios. The strategy analysts can then utilize these three scenarios to prepare plans for a business.

TABLE 6.11	**Description of the Center of a Scenario Cluster (Brauers and Weber Method)**			
Factor	**Description**	**Minimum**	**Center**	**Maximum**
S1	Political opinion	2 (liberal)	2.6	3 (conservative)
S2	Influence of government	1 (strong)	2.4	3 (weak)
S3	Consumer spending	1 (strong)	1.0	1 (strong)
S4	Environmental protection	3 (weak)	3.0	3 (weak)
T1	Rate of technological innovation	1 (high)	1.0	1 (high)
E1	Economic growth	1 (rising)	1.8	3 (stagnating)
E2	Unemployment	1 (rising)	2.2	3 (falling)

Source: Brauers, Jutta, and Martin Weber (1988), "A New Method of Scenario Analysis for Strategic Planning," *Journal of Forecasting* 7 (January–March): 31–47.

Illustration of Battelle Scenario Analysis   The Battelle Consulting firm has been performing scenario analysis since 1980 with an approach called BASICS (Battelle Scenario Inputs to Corporate Strategy). The method is an adaptation of the cross-impact techniques developed at the RAND Corporation and the University of Southern California. It was coupled with Battelle's computer-based algorithm, developed in Geneva, Switzerland. An expert judgment methodology is also an element of the Battelle system.

This procedure was applied in 1988–1989 to the problem of evaluating the changes in the European market for an information technology company with a disguised name, REM Inc.[13] Battelle employed three essential BASICS steps to tackle this problem. These were (1) identifying the issues, (2) trend analysis, and (3) cross-impact analysis.

For the first step, Battelle researchers interviewed the REM managers most familiar with the marketplace and conducted three group dynamics sessions using the *nominal group technique* (a procedure that solicits the professional judgment of experts and is similar to a focus group method). These group sessions were conducted both in Europe and the United States. The participants were drawn from REM's managers and technologists, plus economists and market analysts employed at Battelle. The first step produced a list of the most important factors that would determine the extent of EC single-market cohesion by the end of 1992.

The second step involved writing an essay on each of the 20 factors identified in the first step. These essays showing the alternative outcomes possible for each of the factors were composed by Battelle researchers and other knowledgeable individuals. The outcome possibilities—equivalent to the attribute levels in conjoint analysis—were reviewed by peers in the consulting firm. A total of two to four possible outcomes were developed for each factor. Prior probabilities of occurrence of the possible outcomes by 1992 were assigned for each factor by the researchers.

The third step in the procedure was to elicit cross-impacts of change in the occurrence of a possible outcome of a factor on the occurrence of other factor outcomes. These data were elicited with the help of the BASICS computer program system. These judgments were made by a few individuals and any differences were discussed and reconciled. The BASICS algorithm used these cross-impact indexes to evaluate the likely conditions for a variety of initial probabilities of factor outcomes. It also organized outcomes with high probabilities into sets that were internally consistent. Having examined the patterns, the analysts prepared a report outlining four possible principal scenarios for use in the REM company's strategic planning. The four scenarios were as follows.

Scenario 1: EC Works. In this scenario, a single market will emerge in Europe, but it will possibly lack monetary unification. Also, the information technology market in Europe will experience medium to high growth.

Scenario 2: EC Disappoints. This scenario identified a much slower emergence of a single market than did Scenario 1. The information technology market was expected to grow moderately despite the slower unification.

Scenario 3: The EC Fails. This scenario painted a gloomier picture for a common market. The information technology market was expected to grow very slowly.

Scenario 4: The U.S. of Europe. This scenario showed the emergence of a common market that exceeded the expectations of Scenario 1. In addition to a common currency, it predicted a more unified governmental structure. Information technology market growth was expected to be high under this scenario.

This scenario analysis led REM management to undertake several strategic actions, including increasing local presence in every EC country by expanding marketing and service networks, committing to expansion of its Brussels office to monitor changes in EC commission policies, making plans to expand capacity within one particular EC country, and the like.

Practical Issues in Scenario Analysis   Some practical questions that arise when conducting scenario analysis and their possible resolutions:

1. *How many scenarios should be used in the final analysis?* The general consensus is that three final scenarios are best; identifying more than three final scenarios is too cumbersome.
2. *How should the scenarios be arrayed?* The final scenarios should be arrayed according to some criterion. Some commonly used criteria are favorability of the scenario to the project sponsor, likelihood of occurrence of the scenarios, plausible outcomes for a single dominant factor (such as the potential for government regulation), and composite themes of the environment (for example, environmental concern, economic expansion, or technological domination).

   When using the criterion of favorability to the sponsor, it is good to use one surprise-free or baseline scenario. Other scenarios to include could be optimistic and pessimistic. Various techniques are used to estimate the probability of outcome of a scenario as described earlier. The themes for arraying the scenarios could include economic expansion, technological domination, economic contraction, and the like.
3. *How should scenarios be selected?* In the early development of scenario analysis, highly qualitative or intuitive methods were employed in selecting three or four scenarios to consider. But quantitative methods such as cross-impact analysis and

TABLE 6.12   Comparison of Selected Scenario-generating Procedures

	Becker (1983)	deKluyver (1980)	Linnman and Klein (1977)	MacNulty (1977)	Vanston et al. (1977)	Wilson (1978)	Zenter (1975)
Number of scenarios	3	3	3 or 4	3 or 4	3 to 6	3 or 4	3
Length of scenarios	—	—	1 or 2 paragraphs	—	7–10 pages	—	< 50 pages in all
Base scenario	Most likely	Most likely	None	Surprise free	Most likely	Surprise free	None
Alternative scenarios	Optimistic/ pessimistic	Optimistic/ pessimistic	Themed	Themed	Themed	Optimistic/ pessimistic	Themed
Are probabilities assigned?	No	Yes	No	—	No	No	No
Does it use cross-impact analysis?	No	No	No	Yes	No	Yes	No
How is the number of factors reduced?	Considers only key factors	Considers only key factors	Considers only key factors	It is not done	Considers many factors	Scoring by probability and importance	—
How are the scenarios selected?	Selects plausible combinations of key factors	Judgmental translation into optimistic/ pessimistic and most likely	Selects plausible combinations of key factors	Judgmental integration of trends and intuition	To conform to the themes	Scenario writing and cross-impact analysis	—

Sources: Reprinted from *Long Range Planning,* Vol. 20 No. 1, Steven P. Schnaar, "How to Develop and Use Scenarios," pp. 105–114, Copyright 1987, with kind permission from Elsevier Science Ltd, The Boulevard, Langford Lane, Kidlington 0X5 1GB, UK.

models for stimulating probabilities are now available. In general, an eclectic approach that combines both methods is highly recommended. Table 6.12 shows a comparison of selected scenario-generating procedures.

METHODS FOR FORECASTING SALES OF DURABLE PRODUCTS

The demand for durable products in any year comes from three sources: initial purchases, replacements, and additions. The third part is usually small. In the early stages of life cycle (introduction and growth), initial (or first-time) purchases will be a major component. In the later stages of the life cycle (maturity and decline), replacement purchases will become significant.

Forecasting Initial Purchases

An approach that has proven valuable in estimating initial purchases is the diffusion model of new product acceptance developed by Bass.[14] We describe it as a major method for forecasting first-time purchases of durable goods. We describe a procedure to estimate replacement demand using additional survey data on failure rates.

The Bass model of diffusion is essentially a model of timing of initial purchases of *new* consumer durable goods. New generic classes of products (not new brands) are covered by this model. The model is useful in making long-range planning decisions (such as whether to expand plant capacity). A typical pattern of first-time sales of a new durable product over time is shown in Fig. 6.8. Sales grow to a peak and then level off at some magnitude lower than the peak. Stability occurs owing to relative growth in replacement purchases and decline of initial purchases. The model applies to initial purchases.

In this model, first-time sales of a new product are the result of two consumer forces—innovation and imitation. Thus, an individual's probability of buying the new product for the first time is a sum of two components: an inherent ability to innovate and an inherent ability to imitate others who bought it.

Assuming that there will be a maximum of *m* initial purchases of the new product over the life of the product, the Bass model derives as an equation for first purchasers at any time:

$$S(T) = pm + (q - p)Y_{T-1} - \left(\frac{q}{m}\right)Y_{T-1}^2$$

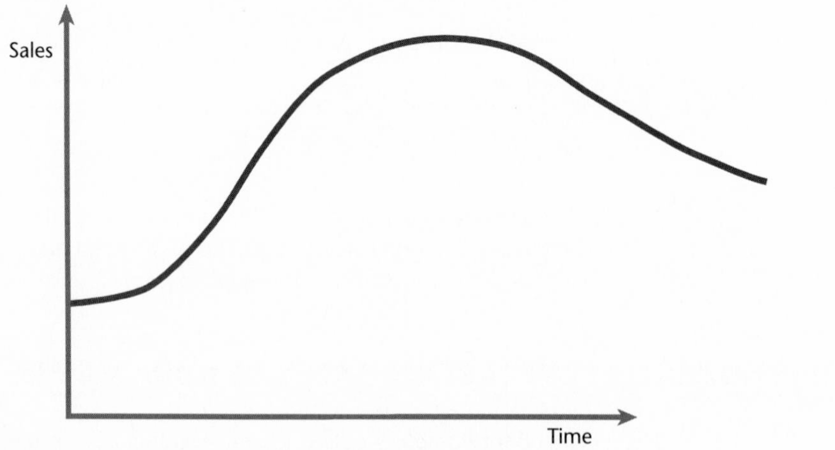

FIGURE 6.8   **Typical Pattern for First-Time Sales of a New Durable Product**

where:

p = coefficient of innovation for the population of consumers

q = coefficient of imitation for the population of consumers

Y_{T-1} = cumulative number of initial purchases up to T and

$S(T)$ = sales during the period T.

The sales curve $S(T)$ will reach a peak and then decline when the imitation coefficient (q) is larger than the innovation coefficient (p); it will decrease continuously from the beginning when the imitation coefficient is smaller than the innovation coefficient. These cases are shown in Fig. 6.9.

The model can be estimated by a regression of S_T on Y_{T-1} and Y_{T-1}^2:

$$S(T) = a + bY_{T-1} + cY_{T-1}^2; \quad T = 2, 3, \ldots$$

The estimated values of a, b, and c in this regression are used to solve the parameters p, q, and m. The equations used are

$$a = pm \quad b = q - p \quad c = -\frac{q}{m}$$

$$b = q - p = -cm - \frac{a}{m}$$

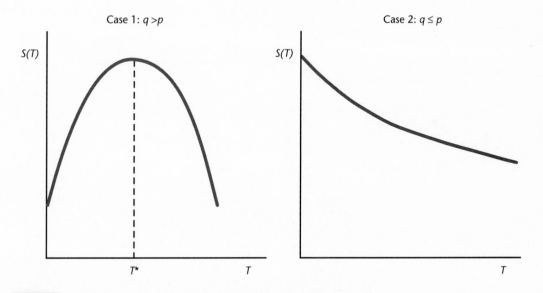

Case 1: $q > p$ Case 2: $q \le p$

$S(T)$ T^* T $S(T)$ T

FIGURE 6.9 **Two Cases of the First-Time Sales of a New Durable Product according to the Bass Model**

$$m = \frac{-b \pm \sqrt{b^2 - 4ca}}{2c}$$

There will be two solutions to the equation for m and the positive value of m will be selected for the potential number of adopters of the product. The values of parameters a, b, and c can be employed in making sequential predictions of sales.

We show in Table 6.13 the results of estimation of this model for several durable goods.

The model can be used to predict when sales are likely to reach a maximum. This information is useful in building up adequate capacity in the industry. For $q \le p$, sales will decline over time; maximum sales occur in the initial period. For $q > p$, the maximum occurs when cumulative sales reach the level of $m\left(\dfrac{q-p}{2q}\right)$ (approximately $\dfrac{m}{2}$ for most products since $q \gg p$). The peak value of $S(T)$ occurs when $T = T^* = \dfrac{1}{q}\ln\left(\dfrac{q+p}{p}\right)$ and the sales level at the peak is $S(T^*) = \dfrac{m(q+p)^2}{4q}$. Fig. 6.10 shows the way one can graphically estimate the peak time.

The model was applied to data for various products and services. Bayer's forecasts of HDTV sales utilize this model.

Some examples of predictions made from this model versus actual peak sales are shown in the following table. We illustrate the computations for color television sets using the estimates of m, p, and q

Product	Predicted Peak Time (years)	Actual Peak Time	Peak Sales (x 10⁶) Predicted	Actual
Black-and-white televisions	7.9	7	7.5	7.8
Steam irons	6.8	7	5.4	5.9
Electric bed coverings	14.9	14	4.9	4.9
Color TVs (retail)	6.0	8	5.7	5.5

shown in Table 6.13. The predicted value of peak time is

$$T^* = \frac{1}{q}\ln\left(\frac{q}{p}\right) = \frac{1}{0.836874}\ln\left(\frac{0.8368744}{0.0054447}\right)$$

$$= \frac{1}{0.83687}\ln(150.93) = 5.995, \text{ or } 6 \text{ years.}$$

Also, the predicted level of peak sales for color televisions is

TABLE 6.13   **Estimation of New Product Diffusion Model for Several Durable Goods**

Product	Time Period	m(x 10^3)	p	q	R^2
Black-and-white televisions	1946–1961	96,702	0.02784	0.25101	0.576
Steam irons	1949–1960	55,696	0.028632	0.32791	0.828
Electric bed coverings	1949–1961	76,590	0.005881	0.24388	0.975
Color TV sets, retail	1959–1969	27,050	0.0054447	0.83687	0.663

Sources: Computed from data shown in Bass, Frank M. (1969), "A New Product Growth Model for Consumer Durables," *Management Science* 15 (January): 215–227; and reprinted from "Extensions of a New Product Model," by John V. Nevers. *Sloan Management Review,* Issue 13, Winter 1972, pp. 77–91, by permission of the publisher. Copyright 1972 by Sloan Management Review Association. All rights reserved.

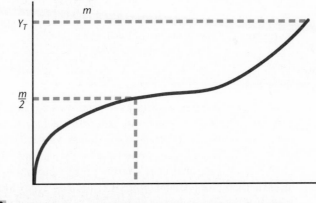

FIGURE 6.10   **Cumulative First-Time Sales of a New Durable Product (Bass Model for $q > p$)**

$$S(T^*) = \frac{m(q+p)^2}{4q} = \frac{27{,}050{,}000(0.83687 + 0.0054467)^2}{4(0.83687)}$$

$$= 5{,}733{,}453, \text{ or approximately 5.7 million units}$$

These predictions compare very well with the actual values shown.

Estimating Replacements

Using a survey of ownership of durable goods one can estimate the age distribution of existing durable goods. These data can be used to estimate the failure rate of the durable good at each age. If necessary, technical sources can be utilized in addition to estimate failure rates.

The data would look as follows for a durable good in year 4.

Age (years)	Failure Rate	Number That Age in Year *t*
1	0.1	100
2	0.2	90
3	0.4	72
4	1.0	43
Total Population		305

Estimate of number of units replaced next year (year 5) $(t + 1) = (100 \times 0.1) + (90 \times .2) + (72 \times .4) + (43 \times 1.0) = 90.8$.

Final Forecast

The final forecast for any given year is obtained by adding the estimates of first-time purchases and replacements of the durable product.

SUMMARY

This chapter covered a variety of techniques for developing forecasts useful for strategic planning. The methods described include formal quantitative techniques such as trend extrapolation and regression as well as the Delphi and analogy methods. These methods are equally applicable for forecasting sales of a product and techno-logical trends. We developed a taxonomy of various forecasting techniques that span the criteria of the availability of historical data, type of data available, and the avail-ability of data on analogous situations.

We then described a set of methods known as scenario analysis that combine expectations of the impact of several factors. These judgmental methods involve identifying various factors relevant to any complex forecasting situation and deter-mining their impacts on each other. The data on their relative impact are synthesized to develop a small number of plausible future scenarios. These scenarios then become the basis for developing any contingent strategies for a business.

The problem of forecasting the sales of durable products requires special atten-tion due to the diffusion processes inherent in the adoption of a new durable good. We described methods useful for forecasting the diffusion of a new durable good as well as for forecasting the sales due to replacement.

The discussion in this and the previous chapter covers an array of methods avail-able to a strategy analyst for understanding and forecasting the various environmen-tal forces that affect any business. We now turn to methods for determining the strengths and weaknesses of business competitors.

Review Questions

1. Define the following terms and identify the forecasting technique with which they are associated. Give an example of how the corresponding technique might be used.

Gompertz curve

Multicollinearity

Pearl curve

R-square

Coefficient of imitation versus coefficient of innovation

Controlled feedback

2. Describe a possible application of the following scenario analysis techniques. Briefly describe their differences.

Brauers and Weber method

Battelle method

Cross-impact analysis

3. Compare and contrast the techniques of window-blind forecasting and genius forecasting used in technological forecasting. Give potential examples of their use.

4. Consider the product category of subcompact cars. For this category, identify three functional and three technical parameters. Discuss how they can be forecasted for the future.

5. What is the difference between a strategy and a tactic? Is formal forecasting more appropriate for strategic or tactical decisions? Why?

6. According to the survey reported in the chapter, a large proportion of U.S. firms do not use formal forecasting methods. What can you infer from this finding?

7. In the second regression technique example, "Forecasting Telephone Penetration in Countries," a railway-passenger kilometers variable was used to measure the infrastructure of a country. What is the problem with using this variable to measure infrastructure in North America? What would be a better set of variables (assuming their availability)?

8. Do you think that scenario analysis could be an advantage for a firm that evolves in a sector characterized by frequent structural change? Why? Give an example.

Notes

1. From Joseph P. Martino, *Technological Forecasting for Decision Making,* Third Edition, copyright (c) 1993. Reprinted with permission of The McGraw-Hill Companies.

2. See Wise, George (1976), "The Accuracy of Technological Forecasts, 1890–1940," *Futures* (October): 411–419.

3. See Schnaars, Steven P., and Conrad Berenson (1986), "Growth Market Forecasting Revisited: A Look Back at a Look Forward," *California Management Review* 28 (Summer): 71–88.

4. See Armstrong, J. Scott (1985), *Long-Range Forecasting,* New York: Wiley for a comprehensive treatment of forecasting techniques.

5. See Sanders, Nada R., and Karl B. Manrodt (1994), "Forecasting Practices in U.S. Corporations: Survey Results," *Interfaces* 24 (March-April): 92–100.

6. See any text on econometrics such as Gujarati, Damodar (1992), *Essentials of Econometrics,* McGraw-Hill; Wittink, Dick R. (1988), *The Application of Regression Analysis,* Allyn and Bacon; Johnston, J. (1984), *Econometric Methods,* 3rd ed., McGraw-Hill.

7. See Bayus, Barry L. (1993), High Definition Television: Demand Forecasts for Next Generation Consumer Durable, *Management Science* 39 (November): 1319–1333.

8. See Brockhaus, William L., and John F. Mickelsen (1977), "An Analysis of Prior Delphi Applications and Some Observations on its Future Applicability," *Technological and Social Change* 10: 103–110.

9. See Johnson, Jeffrey L. (1976), "A Ten Year Delphi Forecast in the Electronics Industry," *Industrial-Marketing Management* 5 (February): 45–52.

10. See Eschienbach, Ted G., and George A. Geistatus (1985), "A Delphi Forecast for Alaska," *Interfaces* 15: 6 (November-December), 100–109.

11. See Brauers, Jutta, and Martin Weber (1988), "A New Method of Scenario Analysis for Strategic Planning," *Journal of Forecasting* 7 (January-March): 31–47.

12. See Millett , Stephen M., and Fred Randles (1986), "Scenarios for Strategic Business Planning: A Case of

History for Aerospace and Defense Companies," *Interfaces* 16: 6 (November-December) 64–72.

13. See Millett, Stephen M. (1992), "Battelle's Scenario Analysis for a European High-Tech Market," *Planning Review* (March-April): 20–24.

14. See Bass, Frank M. (1969), "A New Product Growth Model for Consumer Durables," *Management Science* 15 (January): 215–227.

Bibliography

Armstrong, J. Scott (1985), *Long-Range Forecasting From Crystal Ball to Computer,* 2nd ed., New York: Wiley.

Bayus, Barry L. (1993), "High-Definition Television: Demand Forecasts for Next Generation Consumer Durable," *Management Science* 39 (November): 1319–1333.

Becker, Harold S. (1983), "A Tool of Growing Importance to Policy Analysis," *Technological Forecasting and Social Change* 23, 95–120.

Brauers, Jutta, and Martin Weber (1988), "A New Method of Scenario Analysis for Strategic Planning," *Journal of Forecasting* 7 (January–March): 31–47.

Cazes, Bernard (1976), "The Future of Work: An Outline of a Method for Scenario Construction," *Futures,* (October): 405–410.

Dalkey, Norman (1972), "An Elementary Cross-Impact Model," *Technological Forecasting and Social Change* 3, 341–351.

deKluyver, Cornelis A. (1980), "Bottom-up Sales Forecasting through Scenario Analysis," *Industrial Marketing Management* 9, 167–170.

Duperin, J. C., and M. Godet (1975), "SMIC 74—A Method for Constructing and Ranking Scenarios," *Futures,* (August): 302–312.

Gershuny, J. (1976), "The Choice of Scenarios," *Futures,* (December): 496–508.

Gordon, T. J., and H. Hayward (1968), "Initial Experiments with the Cross Impact Matrix Method of Forecasting," *Futures* 1, 100–116.

Helmer, Olaf (1981), "Reassessment of Cross-Impact Analysis," *Futures* 13, 389–400.

Jackson, J. Edward, and William H. Lawton (1976), "Some Probability Problems Associated with Cross-Impact Analysis," *Technological Forecasting and Social Change* 8, 263–273.

Johnson, Jeffrey L. (1976), "A Ten-Year Delphi Forecast in the Electronics Industry," *Journal of Industrial Marketing Management* 5, 45–52.

Linneman, Robert E., and Harold E. Klein (1983), "The Use of Multiple Scenarios by U.S. Industrial Companies: A Comparison Study, 1977-1981," *Long Range Planning* 16 (6): 94–101.

Linneman, Robert E., and Harold E. Klein (1985), "Using Scenarios in Strategic Decisions Making," *Business Horizons* (January-February): 64–74.

Lootsma, F. A. , P. G. M. Boonekamp, R. M. Cooke, and F. Van Oostvoorn (1990), "Choice of a Long-term Strategy for the National Electricity Supply via Scenario Analysis and Multi-criteria Analysis," *European Journal of Operational Research* 48, 189–203.

MacNulty, Christine A. R. (1977), "Scenario Development for Corporate Development," *Futures* 9 (April), 128–138.

Mahajan, Vijay, Eitan Mueller, and Frank M. Bass (1990), "New Product Diffusion Models in Marketing: A Review and Directions for Research," *Journal of Marketing* 54 (January): 1–26.

Martino, Joseph P., and Kuei-Lin Chen (1978), "Cluster Analysis of Cross Impact Model Scenarios," *Technological Forecasting and Social Change* 12, 61–71.

Millett, Stephen M. (1992), "Battelle's Scenario Analysis of a European High-Tech Market," *Planning Review* (March/April): 20–24.

Millett, Steven M., and Fred Randles (1986), "Scenarios for Strategic Business Planning: A Case History for Aerospace and Defense Companies," *Interfaces* 16 (November-December): 64–72.

Mitchell, R. B., and J. Tydeman (1978), "Subjective Conditional Probability Modeling," *Technological Forecasting and Social Change* 11, 133–152.

Mitchell, Robert B., John Tydeman, and John Georgiades (1979), "Structuring the Future—Application of a Scenario-Generation Procedure," *Technological Forecasting and Social Change* 14, 409–428.

Rao, T. R. (1984), "Scenarios for the Indian Iron and Steel Industry," *Long Range Planning* 17 (4): 91–101.

Russ, William R. (1988), "A Move Toward Scenario Analysis," *International Journal of Forecasting* 4, 377–388.

Sanders, Nada R., and Karl B. Mandrot (1994), "Forecasting Practices in U.S. Corporations: Survey Results," *Interfaces* 24 (March-April): 92–100.

Sarin, Rakesh K.(1978), "A Sequential Approach to Cross-impact Analysis," *Futures* 10, 53–62.

Schnaars, Steven P. (1987), "How to Develop and Use Scenarios," *Long Range Planning* 20 (1): 105–114.

Schnaars, Steven P., and Conrad Berenson (1986), "Growth Market Forecasting Revisited: A Look Back at a Look Forward," *California Management Review* 27 (Summer): 71–88.

Turoff, Murray (1972), "An Alternative Approach to Cross Impact Analysis," *Technological Forecasting and Social Change* 3, 309–339.

Vanhonacker, Wilfried R., and Lydia J. Price (1975), "Estimating the Response Effect of Future Events Based on Historical Analogy: A Methodology and Illustration on Generic Substitution of Brand-Name Drug Sales Following Patent Expiration," *Marketing Letters* 6: 1, 73–85.

Vanston, John H., Jr., W. P. Frisbie, S. C. Lopreato, and D. L. Poston (1977), "Alternative Scenarios Planning," *Technological Forecasting and Social Change* 10, 159–180.

Wilson, Ian H., W. P. George, and P. J. Solomon (1978), "Strategic Planning for Marketers," *Business Horizons* 21, 65–73.

Wise, George (1976), "The Accuracy of Technological Forecasts, 1890–1940," *Futures* (October): 411–419.

Zenter, Rene D. (1975), "Scenarios in Forecasting," *Chemical and Engineering News* 6 (October), 22–34.

Appendix 6A

Descriptions, Advantages, and Disadvantages of Selected Methods of Forecasting

Technique	Description	Main Advantages	Main Disadvantages
A. Trend Extrapolation			
Linear trend fitting	A line is fitted to the data by minimizing the squared error between the estimated curve and actual observations.	Logically reproducible; can apply to most series	Poor turning point indication
Exponential trend fitting	An exponential curve is fitted to the data.	The curve has known properties.	Projections may be much higher than actual amounts given the exponential growth.
B. Regression			
Simple regression	Functionally relates sales to one (economic, competitive, etc.) explanatory variable	Statistical estimates of confidence can be developed. True causal relationships should be more stable and lead to more accurate forecasts.	May not be possible to forecast explanatory variables with adequate accuracy High degree of statistical competence needed
Multiple regression	Functionally relates sales to more than one explanatory variable and takes into account the explanatory variables' intercorrelations	Allows more than one explanatory variable Same as simple regression	May not be possible to forecast explanatory variables High degree of statistical expertise required

Technique	Description	Main Advantages	Main Disadvantages
C. Analogy			
Method of analogy	Attempts to find relationships in past known situations and uses them in forecasting for a new product or technology	Uses past information even when the product/ technology is new Offers some basis for developing forecast	Difficult to find analogous situations Conditions relevant to past products may not apply to the current situation
D. Delphi			
Conventional Delphi	Attempts to elicit expert opinion in a systematic manner by use of questionnaire; feeds back iteratively until convergence of opinion or a point of diminishing returns	Eliminates relationship interactions May take into account factors difficult to quantify	Forecasts cannot be made rapidly It may be difficult to obtain cooperation
Panel consensus	Group forecast by experts who have defended their thinking before each other	Check and balance of several opinions May take into account factors difficult to quantify	Relationship interactions may give poor forecast Rapid forecast may not be possible

Appendix 6B

Estimating Equations for Trend and Growth Curves

This chapter has utilized four functional forms of trend and growth curves. These are

$$\text{Linear trend: } y_t = a + bt \tag{1}$$

$$\text{Exponential trend: } y_t = Ke^{bt} \tag{2}$$

$$\text{Pearl curve: } y_t = \frac{L}{1 + ae^{-bt}} \tag{3}$$

$$\text{Gompertz curve: } y_t = Le^{-be^{-kt}} \tag{4}$$

where y_t is sales at time t and a, b, and L are unknown parameters. All of these curves (or parameters) can be estimated using a time-series of sales data (y_t for various values of t).

Estimating Equation (1) for linear trend is straightforward; it requires regressing the y_t-values on time (t). The method will yield estimates of a and b. Once a and b are known, the function can be used for forecasting values of y for future values of t.

Equation (2) can be transformed into a linear equation by taking logarithms on both sides. This step will yield:

$$\ln y_t = \ln K + bt$$

This equation is linear in $Y_t = \ln y_t$. We can write it as:

$$Y_t = A + bt \tag{5}$$

where $A = \ln K$. Equation (5) can now be estimated using regression to obtain estimates of A and b. Then, the estimate of $K = e^A$. Once K and b are known, Equation (2) can be used in forecasting values of y for future time periods.

The Pearl curve of Equation (3) is a bit more difficult to estimate. The function can be linearized by using algebra. The steps are as follows:

$$\frac{L}{y_t} = 1 + ae^{-bt}$$

$$\frac{L}{y_t} - 1 = ae^{-bt}$$

$$\frac{L - y_t}{y_t} = ae^{-bt}$$

$$\ln\left(\frac{L - y_t}{y_t}\right) = \ln a - b$$

We may write this as:

$$Z_t = C - bt \qquad (6)$$

where $Z_t = \ln\left(\dfrac{L - y_t}{y_t}\right)$ and $C = \ln a$.

Equation (6) is now linear in Z_t, but we do not know the value of L. This equation is estimated by assuming a value of L and checking how well the function fits the data. If the fit is not satisfactory, the procedure is repeated with a different value for L until a satisfactory fit is obtained. This procedure yields estimates of L, C, and b. The parameter b is directly obtained from regression and a is estimated as e^C.

The Gompertz curve of Equation (4) can be linearized using the following algebraic steps:

$$\frac{y_t}{L} = e^{-be^{-kt}}$$

$$\ln\left(\frac{y_t}{L}\right) = -be^{-kt}$$

$$-\ln\left(\frac{y_t}{L}\right) = be^{-kt}$$

$$\ln\left[-\ln\left(\frac{y_t}{L}\right)\right] = \ln b - kt$$

This equation can be written as:

$$V_t = D - kt \qquad (7)$$

where $V_t = \ln\left[-\ln\left(\frac{y_t}{L}\right)\right]$ and $D = \ln b$.

V_t is linear in t as per Equation (7). But V_t depends upon the unknown parameter L. As before, we assume a value for L and check how well the function is fitted. If the fit is not satisfactory, the procedure is repeated with a different value of L until a satisfactory fit is obtained. This procedure yields estimates of L, D, and b. While L and b can be used directly in the function, a is estimated as e^D.

Appendix 6C

Estimating the Multiple Exponential Model

The multiple exponential model in 2 X-variables is

$y = a x_1^{b_1} x_2^{b_2}$ where y is sales, x_1 and x_2 are sales correlates, and a, b_1, and b_2 (1)
are unknown parameters. By taking logarithms on both sides, we get:

$\ln y = \ln a + b_1 \ln x_1 + b_2 \ln x_2$ or   (2)

$Y = A + b_1 X_1 + b_2 X_2$ (3)

where $Y = \ln y$; $X_1 = \ln x_1$, $X_2 = \ln x_2$ and $A = \ln a$.

In this model, b_1 measures the change in Y for one unit change in X_1, keeping X_2 constant; it is also the percent change in y for one percent change in x_1, keeping x_2 constant. Thus, b_1 is the (partial) elasticity of y with respect to x_1. Similarly b_2 is the (partial) elasticity of y with respect to x_2.

Equation (3) is estimated by multiple regression of Y on X_1 and X_2. This procedure yields estimates of A, b_1, and b_2. While b_1 and b_2 are directly estimated, a is estimated as e^A.

Analyzing Competitive Advantage

How to Compete?

INTRODUCTION

Marketing strategy is largely concerned with the development and implementation of means by which firms can achieve superior long-run financial performance. Firms achieve such returns either by making themselves more attractive to customers or by producing at a lower cost while not making themselves less attractive to customers. We can describe this process as a search for *competitive advantage*. While most authors agree that firms need some form of competitive advantage to succeed, they do not necessarily agree on exactly what the phrase "competitive advantage" means.

As Day and Wensley point out, authors usually imply one of two things when they use the term.[1] Some use the term as a synonym for "distinctive competence." In this context, it refers to specific skills or resources (such as money, superior technology, patents, personnel) that a firm possesses. Others use it to signify "positional superiority." Here it refers to a firm's providing its customers with superior value or attaining lower costs.

A complete view of competitive advantage, however, requires both perspectives as well as an understanding of how superior performance is measured. See the framework in Fig. 7.1. In pursuit of competitive advantage businesses are charged with developing certain skills and resources that enable them to better accomplish their chosen goals and objectives. Firms must then apply these skills and resources either to deliver their products and services at lower cost or to provide superior customer value by differentiating their offerings in a meaningful way. These positional advantages (in terms of superior value or lower cost) then produce marketplace results. The profits derived from marketplace results are then used to sustain or improve the business's skills and resources in a cyclical manner as in Fig. 7.1. If a particular source of advantage, positional advantage, or performance outcome is superior to a competitor's, we term it a relative *strength*; if it is inferior, we term it a relative *weakness*. The long-term welfare of a firm obviously depends on its balance of strengths and weaknesses.

This logic is consistent with a framework called the *resource based view of the firm (RBV)* that has recently gained prominence in the strategy literature.[2] The RBV

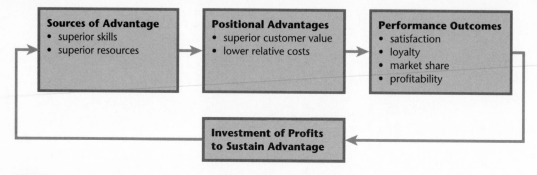

FIGURE 7.1   **The Elements of Competitive Advantage**

Source: From "Assessing Advantage: A Framework for Diagnosing Competitive Strategy," *Journal of Marketing,* Vol. 92, April, pp. 1–20. Reprinted by permission of the American Marketing Association.

sees companies as unique collections of assets and capabilities (or skills and resources in our language) that allow them to outperform their competitors over a sustained period of time. Each company is different because each has had a different set of experiences, acquired different skills and resources, and built different organizational cultures. It follows from the RBV that a company will be positioned to succeed if it has the best and most appropriate inventory of skills and resources for its chosen strategy. Fig. 7.1 goes a bit further than the RBV in that it links the use of skills and resources to performance through competitive position.

The skills and resources that form the sources of competitive advantage can range from the tangible and concrete, such as money and superior technology, to the procedural and attitudinal, such as how a company serves and relates to its customers and employees. For example, if a company involves its customers in its design process it has a better chance of producing winning products. Gillette's Sensor razor, Reebok's Pump sneaker, Motorola's MicroTac cellular phone, and IBM's ThinkPad computer were all developed with the use of ethnographic techniques, such as videotaping human behavior and observing the work environment.[3] Furthermore, the early success of the Saturn automobile was attributed to the degree of control employees had in running the company. They were involved in selecting suppliers, future products, and advertising campaigns. Employee enthusiasm enabled Saturn to become one of the highest quality U.S.–made cars, despite three early product recalls.[4]

The feedback loop at the bottom of Fig. 7.1 is required by the fact that competition is always striving to erode a firm's competitive advantage. Therefore, profits derived from the application of skills and resources and the attainment of superior positions must be reinvested to reaffirm the skills and resources that led to the profits in the first place (or perhaps develop new ones). Consider the contrasting experiences of Honda and EMI, a Japanese and a British company, in the American motorcycle and medical electronics markets.[5] In the face of a stagnant market dominated by American and British producers of large motorcycles used mostly for primary transportation, Honda produced smaller bikes that appealed to the middle class for use as a secondary recreational vehicle. It mass-produced, lowered costs, employed heavy advertising and extensive distribution, and consequently produced superior customer value. The profits generated from initial success were reinvested to cut costs further and develop new models for specialized use (such as dirt bikes). Honda was always a step ahead of its competitors on the differentiation track. EMI, on the other hand, developed the CT scanner to a welcoming and waiting market. Being the technology pioneer, they concentrated on building a reputation, sales, and production. Before long, companies like General Electric leapfrogged EMI in technology, and EMI's competitive advantage was gone. There was no reason for anyone to buy an EMI CT scanner. General Electric offered a better product at no higher a price. EMI's mistake was not to reinvest profits in the further development of the skills and technology that led to its success in the first place. We will return to the EMI story later in the chapter. For now, the moral of the Honda and EMI stories is that if a strength is to become a sustainable advantage, it must be nurtured, not neglected.

According to Stevenson, skills and resources can relate to any of three forms, all of which begin with *e*: *existence, efficiency,* or *effectiveness* of an attribute. Consider a personal computer manufacturer. An example of an existence-type resource is whether that company offers 24-hour technical support. How many support calls that same technical staff can handle in an hour is an example of an efficiency skill. Finally, the overall quality of support service (perhaps defined as the proportion of problems solved) is an example of an effectiveness skill or resource.

Once a firm has analyzed the components of competitive advantage of both itself and its competitors relative to each market segment, it can select those segments for which its strengths provide an advantage and its weaknesses do not impose a significant handicap. It can then create programs that capitalize on that advantage. A key question for management to study then is, "What are our strengths and weaknesses relative to those of our competitors?" Thus the focus of this chapter is on assessing the strengths and weaknesses of the firm and its competitors. Strengths and weaknesses can be assessed from a variety of perspectives corresponding to each of the components of Fig. 7.1. We can assess strengths and weaknesses in the sources of advantage (skills and resources), positional advantages (value and cost), or performance outcomes.

The assessment is essentially a two-stage process. In the first stage, we ask for what dimensions does a firm need to assess strengths and weaknesses? Clearly those dimensions appropriate for one type of business may not be appropriate for others, as the following analysis of college book publishing and machine tools illustrates:[6]

Market	Source of Advantage	Positional Advantage
College book publishing	• Relationships with quality authors • Strong editorial capabilities • Publisher strength in discipline • Backlist depth	• Quality of published books • Publisher reputation • Fit with other published works
Machine tools	• Design and manufacturing quality • Simplification of parts variability • Instant response from central depots • Raw material stock	• Tool quality • Parts availability

The second stage involves the application of specific measurement approaches to those dimensions identified as "critical" in the first stage. The bulk of this chapter will discuss the two stages. Within each stage, we discuss each of the three components (sources, position, and outcomes) of competitive advantage in turn.

ON WHAT DIMENSIONS SHOULD STRENGTHS AND WEAKNESSES BE ASSESSED?

The number of dimensions on which relative strengths and weaknesses could potentially be assessed is as large as the number of ways on which firms can differ. Myriad checklists, such as the one in Table 7.1, can be found in the literature.

Does a firm need to be superior to its competitors on all (or even most) of these dimensions to gain competitive advantage? Clearly the answer is no. Firms with different competitive advantages coexist in a variety of industries. Consider the note-

TABLE 7.1 **Checklist of Assets and Skills**

Research and Development (Innovation)	Production (Manufacturing)	Finance	Organization (Management)	Marketing Skills	Relations with External Entities
Technical Resources Technological ability Patents	*Cost Structure* Experience process efficiency Scale economies Access to raw material	*Access to Capital* From operations From parent From net short-term assets	*Organizational Synergies* *Key People* Loyalty Knowledge of business	*Customer Orientation* *New Product Development* *Marketing Research*	*Customers Loyalty* *Retailers* *Distributors*
Key People					
Financial Resources Internally generated Government supplied	*Product Quality* *Flexibility* *Workforce Attitudes and Motivation* *Capacity*	*Ability to Use Both Debt and Equity*	*Quality of Planning Process* *Speed of Response* *Culture* Entrepreneurial thrust	*Reputation* Brand-name quality *Advertising* *Sales Force* Size *Customer Service* *Product Line Breadth*	*Banks* *Political Figures*

Source: Adapted from Lehmann, Donald R., and Russell S. Winer (1991), *Analysis for Marketing Planning*, 2nd ed., Homewood, IL: Irwin, 74–75.

book computer industry. Here the Japanese and American firms divide the market almost in half. The Japanese firms have much greater expertise in design and manufacturing than the American firms. Producing small computers would be next to impossible without the miniaturization techniques that the Japanese electronic firms have mastered in calculators, camcorders, and watches. Furthermore, the Japanese possess the ability to produce better LCD screens. On the other hand, the American firms possess superior technology in producing miniature disk drives. In addition, spearheaded by Apple and IBM, the American firms are light-years ahead of the Japanese in marketing. Finally, Intel remains the world's major source of microprocessor chips. The coexistence of all these firms would not be possible if one firm had to dominate on all dimensions to succeed.[7]

In contrast, a single dimension of superiority may not be quite enough. One study found that firms tend to exercise between four and five dimensions of competitive advantage.[8] IBM has several strengths that enable it to continue, even in times of trouble. These include a huge software business (over $11 billion in revenue), semiconductor technology (IBM is still the world's largest chip maker), research labs (employing three Nobel Prize winners), the brand name (none carries more weight in the computer industry), and unmatched global marketing and service.[9]

So we are left with the question of which dimensions are most relevant in creating competitive advantage in any given industry.

Critical or key success factors have been described elsewhere as

> . . . the limited number of areas in which results, if they are satisfactory, will ensure successful competitive performance for the organization. They are the few key areas where "things must go right" for the business to flourish. If results in these areas are not adequate, the organization's efforts will be less than desired.[10]
>
> . . . the handful of skills and resources that will exert the most leverage on positional advantage and performance outcomes. These . . . must be managed obsessively to ensure success. Poor performance on these factors will almost certainly mean failure.[11]

The second description directly alludes to the sources of advantage depicted in Fig. 7.1. The first, however, is a bit more ambiguous. It can be interpreted in light of any sources of advantage, positional advantages, or performance outcomes. To be consistent with our framing of competitive advantage, the next three sections concentrate on determining the critical dimensions of sources of advantage, positional advantage, and performance outcome. Since managers are less interested in skills, resources, and positions for their own sake than in how they produce performance outcomes, it is pedagogically useful to begin with performance outcomes and go backward to see how they are generated.

IDENTIFYING CRITICAL PERFORMANCE OUTCOMES

The objective of most corporations is to maximize long-run profitability. Unfortunately, long-run profitability is extremely difficult to measure. For one thing, we would have to wait for the long run to do it. Given this inherent difficulty, managers often work towards optimizing short-run variables believed to lead to long-run profitability. The question remains, though, which variables should be maximized?

We begin by examining some general answers from pooled business experience and move towards a method for analyzing data to come up with a more industry- or company-specific answer.

PIMS Analyses

While critical or key success outcome measures certainly vary from industry to industry or even firm to firm, it stands to reason that some things are necessary (or perhaps sufficient) for any business to succeed. The PIMS (Profit Impact of Market Strategy) project database allows one to investigate these. Researchers affiliated with the Strategic Planning Institute have built regression models that analyze data from over 3,000 strategic business units (in approximately 500 companies covering a wide variety of industries) in an attempt to determine those factors that explain differences in profitability among various kinds of businesses. Buzzell and Gale[12] and Kerin, Mahajan, and Vadarajadan[13] review the spectrum of factors that seem to govern profitability. It seems that profitability is positively related to market share, degree of vertical integration (in mature markets only), market growth rate, R&D (in mature markets), and breadth of product line (in growing markets). Profitability is negatively related to costs, vertical integration (in growing markets), and investment intensity (net assets per dollar value added). This suggests that managers would be well advised to consider market share, new product activity, degree of vertical integration, and investment intensity as key performance outcomes.

The PIMS project can provide only a starting point for any analysis of success factors. Its results are very general. Any specific firm or industry will face some requirements implied by PIMS and others that are not. Furthermore, PIMS suffers from a number of limitations;[14] it uses the Strategic Business Unit* (SBU) as a level of analysis and ignores any synergies that SBUs within a firm may have; it treats a set of extremely diverse firms as being of the same population without the appropriate statistical tests; the data are based on single time periods; and there are statistical problems (such as multicollinearity) in the regressions.

Do these limitations render the PIMS results useless? Absolutely not! They merely highlight the proper role of PIMS in assessing critical success factors. It provides a starting point—no more, no less. We will return to PIMS for resource allocation in Chapter 8.

Elasticity Analysis

Elasticity analysis depends on the existence of sufficient historical data on performance measures and the factors that might influence them. It requires a regression model of the form

---

*In many organizations SBUs are identified with product categories.

$$(\% \text{ change in long-run profitability}) = e_0 + e_1 \, (\% \text{ change in potential success measure 1})$$

$$+ \, e_2 \, (\% \text{ change in potential success measure 2})$$

$$+ \cdots$$

$$+ \, e_k \, (\% \text{ change in potential success measure } k).$$

The coefficients, the es, reflect the percent change in the performance measure resulting from a 1 percent change in each of the potential success factors. This conforms to the economic definition of elasticity, hence the name of the technique. Of course the most critical success measures are those for which the es are highest in absolute value.

For example, if one were to perform an elasticity analysis of the notebook computer market, one might regress percent change in long-run profitability against percent change in production costs, percent change in R&D expenditures, percent change in number of products, percent change in market share, and so on. The variables with the highest coefficients would warrant special attention.

There is one major problem, though. We are still missing a good way to operationalize long-run profitability. Net profit in the current period (short run) is still unsatisfactory. One possibility is to use net profit a certain number of years after the measures on the right-hand side of the previous equation. While indeed we do have (long-run) profits that are more likely to be the result of the other (short-run) measures, this requires much more data than may be available. Furthermore, it presumes that the requirements of success are constant over that time period.

An interesting alternative is to use shareholder value in the current period. Shareholder value reflects the stock market's valuation of the long-run prospects of the firm. The market will look at the firm with less bias and prejudice than a manager might. We know of no firm that does this.

IDENTIFYING CRITICAL POSITIONAL ADVANTAGES

Once succcess measures are identified, the question turns to what positional advantages drive the success measure.

Porter's generic strategies, discussed in Chapter 1 (see Fig. 1.2), suggest that most positional advantages fall into two major categories: low cost and differentiation. However, these categories can be manifested in several different ways. Low cost can be the result of no-frills services, streamlined operations and designs, or scale economies. Differentiation may be in terms of physical features that promise and/or deliver superior performance; it may also be in terms of delivery time and place, terms of sale, or different types of service support such as consulting or repair.[15] In any particular industry, all roads may not provide equal access to the promised land. So the question remains: Which ones provide a higher likelihood of success?

A preliminary answer can be found in the PIMS studies introduced in the last section. They suggest that companies high in relative perceived quality are more profitable.[16] A study more directed towards identifying key positional advantages (albeit only for industrial products firms) is Project NewProd. Project NewProd, conducted by Cooper, is offered in the same spirit as the PIMS project. Like PIMS, NewProd is essentially an empirical multifirm, multi-industry investigation into what separates successful and unsuccessful firms and products.[17] Also like PIMS, it can provide a useful starting point. Unlike PIMS, it focuses on new rather than existing products.

Project NewProd

The original version of the project, published in 1979, was based on analyses of 195 industrial products (102 successes and 93 failures) introduced by 177 firms.[18] In addition, many new data have been added to the database.[19] These include European data and data from consumer goods and financial services firms. The most recent results of the project are summarized in Table 7.2. It appears that the single most critical success position is product superiority and quality, thereby confirming the PIMS result. Cooper

TABLE 7.2 Project NewProd Summary

Factors not discriminating between success and failure include Technical Complexity and Magnitude, Product Customness, Product Determinateness, Existence of a Dominant Competitor, Proficiency of Production Startup, Proficiency of Precommercialization Activities, and Product Uniqueness/First to Market.

Factor Name and Description	Relative Value of the Factor
Product Superiority/Quality: the competitive advantage the product has by virtue of features, benefits, quality, uniqueness, etc.	1.48
Economic Advantage to the User: the product's value for the money for the customer	0.86
Overall Company/Project Fit: the product's synergy with the company—marketing, managerial, business fit	1.19
Technological Compatibility: the technological synergy with the company—R&D, engineering, production fit	0.23
Familiarity to the Company: how familiar or "close to home" the project is to the company (as opposed to new or "step out")	0.49
Market Need, Growth, and Size: the magnitude of the market opportunity	0.70
Competitive Situation: how easy the market is to penetrate from a competitive standpoint (as opposed to a tough and competitive market)	0.25
Defined Opportunity: whether the product has a well-defined category and established market (as opposed to a true innovation and new category of products)	0.30
Project Definition: how well defined the product and project are	0.23

Sources: Adapted from Robert G. Cooper, "The Dimensions of Industrial New Product Success and Failure," *Journal of Marketing,* Vol. 93, Summer 1979, pp. 93–103. Reprinted by permission of the American Marketing Association; Cooper, Robert G. (1992), "The NewProd System: The Industry Experience," *Journal of Product Innovation Management* 9 (June): 113–127.

suggests that this is often so obvious that it tends to be overlooked. Project/company fit also plays a critical role as does the economic advantage the product affords the customer. The original 1979 study also highlighted three barriers to success: high price, being in a market with many new product introductions, and being in a market where customers are already well satisfied.

As stated earlier, the general nature of the PIMS and NewProd analyses raises the likelihood that, while they may represent the population as a whole or an identifiable part thereof, they may not represent any particular industry or firm within it. Indeed, a study by Vasconcellos found that while critical positional advantages can indeed be identified, they tend to differ across industries.[20] For example, high quality is more important for high-capital-goods businesses such as major equipment than it is for operating supplies. In contrast, low cost is more critical for operating supplies. Finally, timely delivery (outbound logistics) is more essential for components and raw materials than it is for either major equipment or operating supplies.

This variation along with the limited set of factors identified by PIMS and NewProd dictate that other approaches to identifying critical positional advantages be invoked. Aaker suggests that a way to frame the analysis is simply to judgmentally compare the successful firms in an industry with the unsuccessful ones and see how they differ.[21] These differences can suggest critical or key positional advantages. While this is a very powerful idea, additional structured approaches and frameworks can help implement it more successfully. This is where the PIMS and NewProd results can prove most valuable—by providing suggestions as to where to look first for these differences. In the remainder of this section we discuss consumer preference models and a new theoretical framework (the value chain) that have the potential to prove useful in isolating critical positional advantages.

Consumer Preference Models

Consumer input can be essential in determining the positions that a business needs to achieve to be successful in the long run. This input usually comes in the form of a "market-back" approach, where the analyst begins with analyses of customer motivations or preferences within given market segments and works backward to the company to identify those benefits the company needs to deliver better than the competition. For example, suppose the part-worths in the credit card conjoint analysis described on pages 46–48 in Chapter 2 were representative of a specific market segment. The part-worths in that example indicated that annual fee and range of establishments accepting the card were the two most important attributes in consumers' evaluations. That would indicate that a critical positional advantage would be having the widest variety of participating establishments. Similarly, the perceptual map of the machining center market (Fig. 2.9) suggests that maximizing "economy" would be a critical positional objective with respect to segment 5.

Another model useful in the analysis of consumer preference is the multinomial logit model. Its development begins with the presumption that the consumer makes choices in order to maximize utility. Furthermore, this utility, say u_k for brand k, is the sum of two components

$$u_k = v_k + \varepsilon_k$$

where v_k is a component of the consumer's utility that can be calculated from observable variables and ε_k is a random component of the consumer's utility. The observable variables could include product attributes, prices, whether a brand is on promotion, whether it is displayed at the end of an aisle, and so on. The random component varies from choice occasion to choice occasion, possibly due to variables that the analyst cannot observe.

McFadden has shown that if some very specific (but empirically useful) assumptions are made about the random component, the consumer's probability of choosing brand k, p_k, has a remarkably simple form

$$p_k = \frac{\exp(v_k)}{\sum_{i-1}^{T} \exp(v_i)},$$

where $\exp(z)$ is the exponential function. This expression is the multinomial logit model.[22]

Suppose further that the observable variables are denoted by $x_{1k}, x_{2k}, \ldots, x_{Tk}$ for brand k. We model v_k in a linear fashion

$$v_k = b_{0k} + \sum_{j-1}^{T} b_j x_{jk},$$

where b_j is the utility weight of variable j and b_{0k} is the brand-specific constant for brand k. The brand-specific constant is often interpreted as a measure of brand equity. It reflects the nonvarying component of utility (brand image) that can be attributed to aspects of a brand unique to that brand and that cannot be captured by observable variables. It is easy to see that the higher the value of b_{0k} is, the more likely brand k is to be chosen.

This model is usually estimated by the statistical method of maximum likelihood. The independent variables are the observable x's and the dependent variable is the brand chosen. All standard statistical packages contain programs that can be easily modified to estimate the parameters of the multinomial logit. Some even contain specific programs for it (for example, SYSTAT, MINITAB, SPSS, and SAS). Obviously, a certain amount of quantitative expertise is required to implement the multinomial logit.

Although McFadden's development is for an individual, the most successful marketing applications (and there have been many in the packaged goods arena) have been at the market or segment level. At these levels choice probability becomes market share. The presence of IRI and Nielsen scanner data has made it simple to create data sets on which this model can be estimated. In these contexts, the observable variables usually reflect a firm's marketing activity (such as price and promotion). The output usually reflects those marketing variables most critical for success. The coffee market study by Guadagni and Little was the first such application of this model to market-level response with scanner data to be published.[23] Their analysis indicated that a brand got a bigger boost from a price promotion than it did from a price cut of equal magnitude, thereby suggesting that having more effective promotions than the competition is a critical success position in this industry.

An Important Limitation   The methods for isolating critical success positions described thus far suffer from an important limitation. They all focus on the way business *has been* done. In particular, PIMS, and consumer preference models either focus on historical data or consumer reactions to products in a familiar category. None of these methods lends itself to answering the question, "What positions or factors are critical in the acceptance of a really innovative offering?"

For example, Savin went from a minor plain-paper copier company with $63 million in annual sales to a major force with $200 million in annual sales within two years in the late 1970s.[24] Its leading products used a liquid toner technology that the industry had avoided until that time because of uneven copy quality. This technology change, coupled with appropriate manufacturing, distribution, and service approaches, enabled Savin to offer its machines at a much lower price. By 1978, Xerox's market share in the low end shrank to 10 percent.

If Savin had focused on historical business or current customer needs, it would not have been able to isolate the critical success position (low price) for success of its new strategy. One tool that will now be discussed, the value chain, would have given Savin more hope. With this they could have asked the questions, "How can we provide value to our customers?" and "What do we need to be able to do to provide this value?"

The Value Chain

Porter describes a firm as "a collection of activities that are performed to design, produce, market, deliver, and support its product."[25] The value chain, depicted in Fig. 7.2, represents the interrelationships among these activities. Porter argues that, if a firm is to gain competitive advantage, it must perform one or more of these activities either better or at a lower cost than its competitors.

As Fig. 7.2 suggests, the activities of the value chain can be divided into two major categories: primary and support activities. The primary activities, detailed in Table 7.3, are performed in the physical creation of the product as well as its sale and/or transfer to the buyer along with any after-sale service that the firm may provide. The support activities allow the primary ones to take place by providing purchased inputs, technology, and human resources, among other ingredients.

Porter isolates five primary value activities: inbound logistics, operations, outbound logistics, marketing and sales, and service. The objectives and content of these activities are detailed in Table 7.3. These value chain activities can be analyzed as to whether they provide opportunities for differentiation or cost reduction.

For example, American Express's Personalized Rewards program provides (differentiation) value to its customers via marketing and sales.[26] This program uses the vast amounts of information it collects on what its customers purchase to provide offers and tailor rewards to individual cardholders. A monthly statement could bill a London cardmember for a flight on British Airways at the same time that it offers a 20 percent discount on all British Airways flights booked in the next month with the American Express card. The offer would be printed adjacent to the charge on the statement. These offers create additional transactions for American Express.

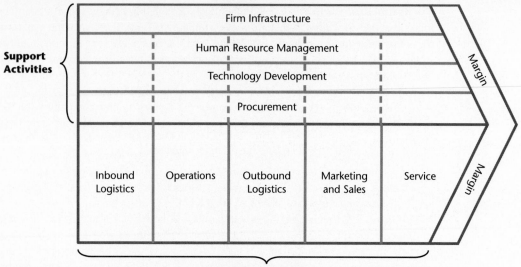

FIGURE 7.2   **The Value Chain**

Source: Reprinted/Adapted with the permission of The Free Press, a Division of Simon & Schuster, from COMPETITIVE ADVANTAGE: Creating and Sustaining Superior Performance by Michael E. Porter. Copyright (c) 1985 by Michael E. Porter.

TABLE 7.3   **Generic Categories of Primary Value Activities**

Generic Category of Primary Activities	Inbound Logistics	Operations	Outbound Logistics	Marketing and Sales	Service
Objective of the value activity	To receive, store, and disseminate inputs to products	To transform inputs into the final form	To collect, store, and physically distribute the product	To provide means by which buyers can buy the product and to induce them to buy it	To provide service to enhance or maintain the value of the product
Value activities performed	Material handling, warehousing, inventory control, vehicle scheduling, returns to suppliers	Machining, packaging assembly, equipment maintenance, testing, printing, facility operations	Finished goods, warehousing, material handling, delivery operation, order processing, scheduling	Advertising, promotion, sales force, pricing, channel selection, channel relations	Installation, repair, training, parts supply, product adjustment

Sources: Reprinted/Adapted with the permission of The Free Press, a Division of Simon & Schuster, from COMPETITIVE ADVANTAGE: Creating and Sustaining Superior Performance by Michael E. Porter. Copyright (c) 1985 by Michael E. Porter; Kerin, Roger A., Vijay Mahajan, and P. Rajan Varadarajan (1990), *Contemporary Perspectives on Strategic Market Planning*, Boston: Allyn and Bacon, 315.

Texas Instruments (TI) has differentiated itself in the dynamic random-access memory (DRAM) market through outbound logistics.[27] It was able to gain this position by distributing orders to the least busy factories physically closest to customers. By decreasing factory and shipping delays, TI improved on-time delivery from 77 percent in 1990 to 96 percent in 1995.

Successful implementation of differentiation requires a link between identified value activities and firm performance. Will personal rewards actually produce more transactions for American Express? Often, focus groups can be helpful in answering questions like these. Sometimes, especially for activities in the pre-marketing and sales parts of the value chain, managers will have to resort to their inferential abilities.

One of the recurring themes of this book has been that managers, like humans in general, have limited abilities to make judgments and decisions. Errors and biases arising from these limitations appear in assessing relative strengths and weaknesses as well as other aspects of the strategic planning process. These biases can be overcome by making people aware of them, training them to be more systematic in their judgments, and providing structure for the particular judgment at hand. The value chain is one framework for providing such structure, as it relates to identifying critical success factors (positions) in particular.

IDENTIFYING CRITICAL SOURCES OF ADVANTAGE

The final step in identifying critical success factors is to determine the critical sources of advantage. The sources of advantage are the most difficult of the three competitive advantage components to identify. This is because they are invisible to everyone except those inside the firm. Internal company sources may allow a manager to examine the sources of advantage of his or her own firm. However, those of the competition are difficult to assess. Even if Airbus knows that Boeing is the low-cost producer of airplanes, it may not know how Boeing achieved that position.[28] Boeing will know, presumably because it is part of its strategic plan.

Prahalad and Hamel use the metaphor of a fruit tree.[29] While the fruit is often easy to see, the roots of the tree are not. Examining positional advantages and performance outcomes is analogous to examining the fruit, leaves, branches, and trunk. However, to understand the growth patterns of a tree (or a firm), a firm must examine the roots of itself, its competitors, and identifiable potential competitors.

For example, Canon's expertise in optics and imaging technology (its "roots") allowed it to diversify from a camera company into image, information, and communication products in the 1960s.[30] It changed its name from Canon Camera Inc. to Canon Inc. in 1969. The portion of Canon's business that came from business machines rose from 0 percent in 1960 to 81.3 percent in 1992. Only 12.2% came from cameras. Without understanding its roots, Canon would not have been able to exploit its sources of advantage into such tremendous growth. Furthermore, if Xerox viewed Canon simply as a camera maker and not the possessor of its technology, it may have been surprised to see Canon enter the photocopier market. In fact, Canon's superior design was able to eliminate the need for the very service requirement at which Xerox excelled. This, along with the emergence of low-cost competitors like Savin, sent Xerox into a tailspin. It took Xerox's "Leadership through Quality" program to pull the company out of it.

Two consequences of the invisibility of roots is that customers are less useful in supplying information and that direct observation is often not possible (unless the competitor tips its hand or a financial report or magazine story proves illuminating). Managerial inferences must be made by examining positional advantages and diagnosing what could have led to them. Behavioral scientists have called this type of process "thinking backward."[31] Thinking backward "involves looking for patterns, making links between seemingly unconnected events, testing possible chains of causation to explain an event, and finding a metaphor or theory to help in looking forward."[32]

As in most judgmental processes, thinking backward has the potential to be contaminated by biases and errors. Thus, we begin this section by demonstrating how value chain analysis can be extended to aid the manager in structuring the critical sources of advantage judgment. We continue with a structured interviewing technique (the Critical Success Factor method) that has a similar objective, but also benefits from the influence of an unbiased observer. Finally, we close this section with a discussion of one concept, order of entry, which it has been suggested relates to both low cost and superior differentiated value positions. It is often thought that early entry is a critical source of advantage. We present this view, challenge it, and highlight the trade-offs, leaving the question as to whether early entry, and market pioneering in particular, is a key source of advantage in a specific industry to a student of that industry.

The Value Chain

The objectives and content of the support activities of the value chain are shown in Table 7.4: procurement, technology development, human resource management, and firm infrastructure. As illustrated in Fig. 7.2, these activities can support any or all of the primary value activities. If the primary activities form the basis of positional advantage, then, since support activities allow the primary ones to happen, these must provide the sources of advantage.

Consider again American Express's Personalized Rewards. The source for Amex's marketing and sales competitive advantage can be found in the support activities of technology development and procurement. Unlike Mastercard and Visa, American Express operates a "closed-loop network"; it handles every step of cardholder and merchant transactions, including actual charge and final billing. Mastercard and Visa do not have data collection systems with comparable capabilities. Furthermore, the success of the program depends largely on the company's ability to procure partners to participate in the program.

Texas Instruments provides another example of the relationship between primary and support activities. Texas Instrument's advantage in outbound logistics originated in both firm infrastructure and technology development. By forming strategic alliances with worldwide companies, such as Hitachi, TI was able to produce a

company that became a minor player very quickly. The first notebook, however, appeared in October 1988 under the NEC UltraLite brand name. Compaq followed a year later. Experts report that the Compaq and NEC product lines are still two of the most successfully differentiated lines available today.

In a recent study, Tellis and Golder identified another category of firms called "early leaders," firms that are the market leaders during the growth stage of the product life cycle.[39] They conclude that these firms have average market shares in maturity of about three times those of pioneers. While early leaders may or may not be pioneers, their performance is driven by five factors: "a vision of the mass market, managerial persistence, financial commitment, relentless innovation, and asset leverage."[40] What this implies to us is that there is no enduring advantage intrinsic to pioneering. Rather, it appears that a firm's skills and resources lead to competitive advantage. The case for pioneering may seem more advantageous because it is these same skills and resources that often lead to pioneering opportunities. For example, Intel's position in the microprocessor market has been sustained because of its overlapping development cycles. The next generation chip is under development even before the current generation has been mass-marketed. The technological ability and foresight that led Intel to pioneer one generation of chip allow it to sustain dominance and pioneer the next. This traces back to the feedback loop of Fig. 7.1 and the lesson EMI never learned.

What is clear, though, despite the confusion about pioneer and order of entry advantage, are the trade-offs of early versus late entry. Furthermore, order of entry is an unambiguous piece of information. Any firm can put the potential pros and cons of early entry on opposite sides of the ledger as strengths and weaknesses and make decisions accordingly.

The next few sections make the transition to the second stage of the competitive advantage assessment process, application of specific measurement approaches to the critical dimensions identified in the first stage. Much of the discussion will be presented as if the measurements are to be made with respect to a single company. However, the word *advantage* has an implicit comparative connotation—advantage over who or what? Therefore, the reader should keep in mind that all measures need to be made either relative to a competitor or for each competitor so that they can be compared.

MEASURING PERFORMANCE OUTCOMES

All strategic and marketing plans contain a page or two of goals and objectives. Usually a set of performance outcomes the firm is striving to achieve are included among these. The ultimate evaluation of such plans is contingent on whether these objectives in general, and the strived-for performance in particular, have been achieved. To evaluate this, performance must be measured. Recognizing the difficulties inherent in measuring the most desirable performance outcome, long-run profitability, we must address other performance variables. In this section we discuss the measurement of market share, customer satisfaction, and a concept General Electric has found useful—something it calls *customer franchise*.

Market Share

It would seem that measuring market share would be one of the most straightforward analyses that a manager could perform. However, there are decisions that must be made. Day and Wensley argue that "a single market share obscures as much as it reveals." There are two reasons for this, competition and level of definition. First, market share must be evaluated relative to competition. Consider a 10 percent market share. That 10 percent market share can look quite different depending on whether the largest competitor has a 50 percent share or a 2 percent share.

Second, the level of definition matters. Ten percent of the market may be quite good; 10 percent of the target end-user segment may be unsatisfactory. Ten percent of the entire market can translate into 50 percent or more of the target segment. Indeed, many low-share companies are quite successful by concentrating their efforts in segments where they have a competitive advantage. Crown, Cork, and Seal, the metal can manufacturer, maintained higher profit margins and return on equity than high-share competitors Continental Can and American Can by focusing on cans for hard-to-hold products, such as beer and soft drinks, and aerosols. This allowed it to attain a cost advantage by building plants close to a few large customers.[41]

Market share is unique with respect to the different elements of competitive advantage because it is both a measure of performance and a measure of competitive strength.[42] As a source of strength or competitive advantage, market share carries a lot of perks. Market share makes it easier to get shelf space. It makes it easier to get a consumer new to the product category to pay attention to the brand. The power market share exerts on the consumer's mind is illustrated in the battery market. Eveready's Energizer battery and the pink bunny that dominated its television commercials have been responsible for one of America's favorite advertising campaigns in recent years; yet Duracell, the market leader, watched its share continue to grow while Eveready's declined!

The solution to this paradox lies in the results of Video Storyboard Tests Inc.'s survey of television viewers. Energizer was America's second favorite ad campaign in the first quarter of 1990. Duracell broke into the top ten, too, at number seven. The interesting aspect of Duracell's ranking was that no new major campaign was instituted in the first quarter of 1990. Forty percent of the people who cited the bunny commercial as being the most outstanding said that it was a Duracell commercial! They associated the bunny with a battery, did not remember the brand, and just assumed it was the one they and their friends used the most often—market leader Duracell.[43]

In the early nineties, Toshiba has been the share leader in the laptop (notebook) computer market. Because of the advantages it accrues as a consequence, Toshiba can command a price premium over most of its competitors for a comparably equipped machine. Indeed, a casual visit to a local computer store will show that Toshiba is one of the higher priced machines on the shelf.

Customer Satisfaction Surveys

As discussed in Chapter 3, customer satisfaction surveys can help identify unmet needs by pinpointing customer motivations not met by any existing offering in the marketplace. These represent opportunities for firms not competing in the industry and threats for those that are. The Apple Macintosh was developed in response to a need for a user-friendly system. The underlying technology has proved to be an important strength for Apple.[44]

More relevant to the present chapter, many companies periodically sample their customers to evaluate the quality of their products, the efficiency of their delivery, the friendliness of their service, and so on. Notebook computers evolved as a response to the unwieldy early laptops. Users found it very difficult to open, close, and comfortably handle 10- to 14-lb machines on an airplane.

Usually customer satisfaction surveys elicit responses to questions on a five- to ten-point bipolar (very dissatisfied–very satisfied) scale. For example, Fig. 7.3a presents a questionnaire that McDonald's asks its customers to take when they leave the restaurant, fill out at home, and return. Fig. 7.3b shows how McDonald's gets customers to actually return the questionnaire. It is printed on the back of a $1.00 check. All the customer has to do is deposit the check in his/her account, and McDonald's gets the consumer's responses when the check is returned.

Xerox collects extensive amounts of customer satisfaction data as part of its "Leadership through Quality" program. Each month it mails surveys to 40,000 randomly selected customers. It solicits information about satisfaction on a variety of levels: overall satisfaction with Xerox, likelihood of buying additional products from Xerox, likelihood of recommending Xerox, and satisfaction with several different aspects of the products, services, and support.[45] The measurement instrument is presented in Fig. 7.4.

Other approaches do not directly ask whether the customer is satisfied. Rather, they employ the conceptual foundation of satisfaction (dissatisfaction) as expectations that are (are not) met. Questions are then framed in terms of expectations and performance. For example, suppose you were interested in the sound quality of a stereo system. You could begin by asking, "What kind of sound quality did you expect before listening to the system?" Responses might be on a seven-point bipolar (Good sound–Poor sound) scale. Next you could use the same scale to ask how good the sound actually was. The difference between performance and expectation can then be taken as a measure of satisfaction. Alternatively, one could simply ask for one judgment on a bipolar "Much better than expected–much worse than expected" scale. In this mode, no need for a difference score exists.

An example of a performance/expectations difference score scale is SERVQUAL, a multiple-item scale that was developed especially for services.[46] Fig. 7.5 presents the three-part SERVQUAL instrument. The first part contains 22 statements that elicit expectations with respect to five basic service-quality dimensions (tangibles—statements 1 to 4, reliability—statements 5 to 9, responsiveness—statements 10 to 13, assurance—statements 14 to 17, and empathy—statements 18 to 22) identified by the scale's developers. The second part requests information on the relative importance of the five dimensions. Finally, the third part elicits performance perceptions in a manner parallel to the expectations portion. An overall SERVQUAL score can be obtained through the following four steps:[47]

Please tell us how satisfied you were with McDonald's today by writing numbers from 1 to 10 in the spaces to the right of the perforation. If you were extremely satisfied, use a high number. If you were not at all satisfied, use a low number . . . like this:

Not at all Satisfied Today → 1   2   3   4   5   6   7   8   9   10 ← Extremely Satisfied Today

Answer Here

Overall:
- With the service you got during your visit
- With the value we were provided for the money you spent
- With the food you ate
- With how comfortable our restaurant was

About today's service:
- Being able to order quickly
- Getting your food promptly after you order
- Getting your order right the first time
- Welcoming special requests
- Providing salt, pepper, ketchup, sauces, straws and utensils

About the interior of the restaurant:
- Providing a neat and clean dining area
- Keeping the restrooms clean and well stocked
- Having a menu board that is easy to read
- Having plenty of seating available
- Providing a friendly, fun place for children

About the food today:
- Serving you fresh tasting food
- Serving hot things hot and cold things cold
- Offering enough variety for you to visit often
- Offering food choices for everyone's tastes

About the employees today:
- Being friendly and courteous
- Being clean and neatly dressed
- Being available to handle customers' problems or complaints

About prices:
- Having competitive prices every day

Please tell us a few thing about you and your visit to McDonald's today:
How many times have you visited this McDonald's in the past month?
Would you visit this McDonald's again? (Please circle Definitely, Maybe or No) .... D M N
How much money did you spend at McDonald's today? .... $
Who came with you to McDonald's today? (Please circle No one, Family, Friends or Other) ... N Fa Fr O
Did your party include any children under age 10? (Please circle Yes or No) .... Y N
If this McDonald's had been closed, which ONE of the following would you have been most likely
  to visit, instead?: (Please circle only one: Burger King, Wendy's, Hardee's, Taco Bell or Other) ... B W H T O
What ONE thing do you like best about that restaurant? (Please circle only one: Price, Service,
  Employees, Taste or Convenient locations) .... P S E T C
Overall, how satisfied have you been with your visits to that restaurant? (Please use a scale of 1 to 10)

Sign Here _____

May we contact you
in the future?

Name: _____

Phone: (_____) - _____ - _____

FIGURE 7.3A   McDonald's Customer Satisfaction Questionnaire

We Want To Make Your Visit Even Better At

McDonald's
Campus Office Building
Kroc Drive
Oak Brook, IL 60521

Dear Customer,

Your feedback will help make this McDonald's even better.

We want to know how satisfied you were with your visit today. And we want to offer you $1.00 as a "Thank You" for taking the time to tell us.

If you have any questions, please don't hesitate to ask one of our employees.

Thank you again for taking the time to participate in our survey.

For distribution on:

Friday
Lunch (10:30 am - 2:00 pm)
at the Counter

Here's $1.00 For You To Check Us Out

It's Easy:

1. Complete the survey by writing your answers on the back of the check.

2. Remove the check. You may cash it at this McDonald's or wherever you usually cash or deposit checks.

3. After you cash or deposit your check, the bank will return your anwers to us.

DETACH BEFORE CASHING

320-0510

CheckMetrix
CheckMetrix
CheckMetrix
CheckMetrix
CheckMetrix

1512-10799

CheckMetrix, Inc.
500 North Michigan Ave.
Chicago, IL 60611

"Thank You"
Check

0010521649

May 10, 1993
(Void after June 25, 1993)
2-52/710

Pay to the order of BEARER $1.00

One and 00/100   *Dollars*

Boulevard Bank
Member Boulevard Bancorp
Chicago, IL 60611–4181

Stephen Turner, CheckMetrix

⑈071000521⑈ ⑈706204 4⑈

Source: Used with permission from McDonald's Corporation.

FIGURE 7.4   Xerox's Customer Satisfaction Questionnaire

This questionnaire should be completed by the individual who makes decisions about the acquisition of _____ . Please focus on your experiences in the product areas mentioned as you complete the questionnaire.

SECTION 1: GENERAL SATISFACTION

	Very Satisfied	Somewhat Satisfied	Neither Satisfied Nor Dissatisfied	Somewhat Dissatisfied	Very Dissatisfied
1. Based on your recent experience, how satisfied are you with Xerox?	☐	☐	☐	☐	☐

	Definitely	Probably	Might or Might Not	Probably Not	Definitely Not
2. Based on your recent experience, would you acquire another product from Xerox?	☐	☐	☐	☐	☐
3. Based on your recent experience, would you recommend Xerox to a business associate?	☐	☐	☐	☐	☐

	Very Satisfied	Somewhat Satisfied	Neither Satisfied Nor Dissatisfied	Somewhat Dissatisfied	Very Dissatisfied
4. How satisfied are you overall with the quality of:					
a) Your Xerox product(s)	☐	☐	☐	☐	☐
b) Sales support you receive	☐	☐	☐	☐	☐
c) Technical service you receive	☐	☐	☐	☐	☐
d) Administrative support you receive	☐	☐	☐	☐	☐
e) Handling of inquiries	☐	☐	☐	☐	☐
f) Supplies support you receive	☐	☐	☐	☐	☐
g) Xerox user training	☐	☐	☐	☐	☐
h) Xerox supplied documentation	☐	☐	☐	☐	☐

Please complete 4i and 4j only if you are the decision maker for systems products (printers, workstations, personal computers and wordprocessors)

	Very Satisfied	Somewhat Satisfied	Neither Satisfied Nor Dissatisfied	Somewhat Dissatisfied	Very Dissatisfied
i) Your Xerox supplied software	☐	☐	☐	☐	☐
j) Xerox Systems Analyst support	☐	☐	☐	☐	☐
k) Telephone Hotline support	☐	☐	☐	☐	☐

SECTION 2: SALES SUPPORT

	Very Satisfied	Somewhat Satisfied	Neither Satisfied Nor Dissatisfied	Somewhat Dissatisfied	Very Dissatisfied
5. How satisfied are you overall with Xerox Sales Representatives with regard to:					
a) Timeliness of response to your inquiries	☐	☐	☐	☐	☐
b) Frequency of contact to review your needs	☐	☐	☐	☐	☐

(Continued on next page)

FIGURE 7.4 Continued

	Very Satisfied	Somewhat Satisfied	Neither Satisfied Nor Dissatisfied	Somewhat Dissatisfied	Very Dissatisfied
c) Frequency of contact to provide information about new Xerox products and services	☐	☐	☐	☐	☐
d) Product knowledge	☐	☐	☐	☐	☐
e) Application knowledge	☐	☐	☐	☐	☐
f) Understanding of your business needs	☐	☐	☐	☐	☐
g) Accuracy in explaining terms/ conditions	☐	☐	☐	☐	☐
h) Ability to resolve problems	☐	☐	☐	☐	☐
i) Professionalism	☐	☐	☐	☐	☐

SECTION 3: CUSTOMER SUPPORT

6. What was the purpose of your most recent call to Xerox?
   ☐ Inquiry   ☐ Problem
   ☐ Haven't called, can't answer (skip to Question 10)

7. How long ago did you make this call?
   ☐ Less than 3 months   ☐ 3–6 months
   ☐ 6–12 months   ☐ Greater than 12 months

8. What Xerox function did you contact?
   ☐ Sales   ☐ Service   ☐ Supplies   ☐ Systems Analyst
   ☐ Billing   ☐ Collection   ☐ Customer Relations Group
   ☐ Telephone Hotline Support

9. How satisfied are you with the support you received?

	Very Satisfied	Somewhat Satisfied	Neither Satisfied Nor Dissatisfied	Somewhat Dissatisfied	Very Dissatisfied
a) Ability to get to the right person(s) quickly	☐	☐	☐	☐	☐
b) Attitude of Xerox personnel who assisted you	☐	☐	☐	☐	☐
c) Ability to provide a solution	☐	☐	☐	☐	☐
d) Time required to provide a solution	☐	☐	☐	☐	☐
e) Effectiveness of the solution	☐	☐	☐	☐	☐
f) Overall satisfaction with support received	☐	☐	☐	☐	☐

10. What specific things can we do to increase your satisfaction with Xerox, our products and our services? Thank you for your feedback!

Your name _____
Position _____
Tel # _____
Date _____

Account #
123456789

Source: "Xerox Corporation: The Customer Satisfaction Program" (1991), Harvard Business School Case #9-591-055, Boston, MA, 19–20.

FIGURE 7.5 The SERVQUAL Questionnaire

Directions: Based on your experiences as a consumer of _____ services, please think about the kind of _____ company that would deliver excellent quality of service. Think about the kind of _____ company with which you would be pleased to do business. Please show the extent to which you think such a _____ company would possess the feature described by each statement. If you feel a feature is *not at all essential* for excellent _____ companies such as the one you have in mind, circle the number 1. If you feel a feature is *absolutely essential* for excellent _____ companies, circle 7. If your feelings are less strong, circle one of the numbers in the middle. There are no right or wrong answers—all we are interested in is a number that truly reflects your feelings regarding companies that would deliver excellent quality of service.

	Strongly Disagree						Strongly Agree
1. Excellent _____ companies will have modern-looking equipment.	1	2	3	4	5	6	7
2. The physical facilities at excellent _____ companies will be visually appealing.	1	2	3	4	5	6	7
3. Employees at excellent _____ companies will be neat-appearing.	1	2	3	4	5	6	7
4. Materials associated with the service (such as pamplets or statements) will be visually appealing in an excellent _____ company.	1	2	3	4	5	6	7
5. When excellent _____ companies promise to do something by a certain time, they will do so.	1	2	3	4	5	6	7
6. When a customer has a problem, excellent _____ companies will show a sincere interest in solving it.	1	2	3	4	5	6	7
7. Excellent _____ companies will perform the service right the first time.	1	2	3	4	5	6	7
8. Excellent _____ companies will provide their services at the time they promise to do so.	1	2	3	4	5	6	7
9. Excellent _____ companies will insist on error-free records.	1	2	3	4	5	6	7
10. Employees in excellent _____ companies will tell customers exactly when services will be performed.	1	2	3	4	5	6	7

(Continued on next page)

FIGURE 7.5 **Continued**

	Strongly Disagree						Strongly Agree
11. Employees in excellent _____ companies will give prompt service to customers.	1	2	3	4	5	6	7
12. Employees in excellent _____ companies will always be willing to help customers.	1	2	3	4	5	6	7
13. Employees in excellent _____ companies will never be too busy to respond to customers' requests.	1	2	3	4	5	6	7
14. The behavior of employees in excellent _____ companies will instill confidence in customers.	1	2	3	4	5	6	7
15. Customers of excellent _____ companies will feel safe in their transactions.	1	2	3	4	5	6	7
16. Employees in excellent _____ companies will be consistently courteous with customers.	1	2	3	4	5	6	7
17. Employees in excellent _____ companies will have the knowledge to answer customers' questions.	1	2	3	4	5	6	7
18. Excellent _____ companies will give customers individual attention.	1	2	3	4	5	6	7
19. Excellent _____ companies will have operating hours convenient to all their customers.	1	2	3	4	5	6	7
20. Excellent _____ companies will have employees who give customers personal attention.	1	2	3	4	5	6	7
21. Excellent _____ companies will have the customer's best interest at heart.	1	2	3	4	5	6	7
22. The employees of excellent _____ companies will understand the specific needs of their customers.	1	2	3	4	5	6	7

(Continued on next page)

FIGURE 7.5   Continued

Directions: Listed below are five features pertaining to _____ companies and the services they offer. We would like to know how important each of these features is to *you* when you evaluate a _____ company's quality of service. Please allocate a total of 100 points among the five features *according to how important each feature is to you*—the more important a feature is to you, the more points you should allocate to it. Please ensure that the points you allocate to the five features add up to 100.

1. The appearance of the _____ company's physical facilities, equipment, personnel, and communication materials.   _____ points

2. The _____ company's ability to perform the promised service dependably and accurately.   _____ points

3. The _____ company's willingness to help customers and provide prompt service.   _____ points

4. The knowledge and courtesy of the _____ company's employees and their ability to convey trust and confidence.   _____ points

5. The caring, individualized attention the _____ company provides its customers.   _____ points

   TOTAL points allocated   100   points

Which *one* feature among the above five is *most important* to you? (please enter the feature's number)   _____

Which feature is *second* most important to you?   _____

Which feature is *least important* to you?   _____

Directions: The following set of statements relate to your feelings about XYZ Company. For each statement, please show the extent to which you believe XYZ Company has the feature described by the statement. Once again, circling a 1 means that you strongly disagree that XYZ Company has that feature, and circling 7 means that you strongly agree. You may circle any of the numbers in the middle that show how strong your feelings are. There are no right or wrong answers—all we are interested in is a number that best shows your perceptions about XYZ Company.

	Strongly Disagree						Strongly Agree
1. XYZ Co. has modern-looking equipment.	1	2	3	4	5	6	7
2. XYZ Co.'s physical facilities are visually appealing.	1	2	3	4	5	6	7
3. XYZ Co.'s employees are neat-appearing.	1	2	3	4	5	6	7
4. Materials associated with the service (such as pamphlets or statements) are visually appealing at XYZ Co.	1	2	3	4	5	6	7
5. When XYZ Co. promises to do something by a certain time, it does so.	1	2	3	4	5	6	7

(Continued on next page)

FIGURE 7.5 Continued

	Strongly Disagree						Strongly Agree
6. When you have a problem, XYZ Co. shows a sincere interest in solving it.	1	2	3	4	5	6	7
7. XYZ Co. performs the service right the first time.	1	2	3	4	5	6	7
8. XYZ Co. provides its services at the time it promises to do so.	1	2	3	4	5	6	7
9. XYZ Co. insists on error-free records.	1	2	3	4	5	6	7
10. Employees in XYZ Co. tell you exactly when services will be performed.	1	2	3	4	5	6	7
11. Employees in XYZ Co. give you prompt service.	1	2	3	4	5	6	7
12. Employees in XYZ Co. are always willing to help you.	1	2	3	4	5	6	7
13. Employees in XYZ Co. are never too busy to respond to your requests.	1	2	3	4	5	6	7
14. The behavior of employees in XYZ Co. instills confidence in you.	1	2	3	4	5	6	7
15. You feel safe in your transactions with XYZ Co.	1	2	3	4	5	6	7
16. Employees in XYZ Co. are consistently courteous with you.	1	2	3	4	5	6	7
17. Employees in XYZ Co. have the knowledge to answer your questions.	1	2	3	4	5	6	7
18. XYZ Co. gives you individual attention.	1	2	3	4	5	6	7
19. XYZ Co. has operating hours convenient to all its customers.	1	2	3	4	5	6	7
20. XYZ Co. has employees who give you personal attention.	1	2	3	4	5	6	7
21. XYZ Co. has your best interests at heart.	1	2	3	4	5	6	7
22. Employees of XYZ Co. understand your specific needs.	1	2	3	4	5	6	7

Source: Parasuraman, A., Valerie A. Zeithaml, and Leonard L. Berry (1988), "SERVQUAL: A Multiple-Item Scale for Measuring Consumer Perceptions of Service Quality," *Journal of Retailing* 64 (Spring): 12–40.

Step 1: For each customer, compute the average SERVQUAL (performance minus expectations) score for each of the five dimensions.

Step 2: For each customer, multiply the SERVQUAL score for each dimension (obtained in step 1) by the importance weight assigned by the customer to that dimension (the importance weight is simply the points allocated to the dimension divided by 100).

Step 3: For each customer, add the weighted SERVQUAL scores (obtained in step 2) across all five dimensions to obtain a combined weighted SERVQUAL score.

Step 4: Add the scores obtained in step 3 across all *N* customers and divide by *N*.

Customer Franchise

Explicitly recognizing that maximizing short-run financial measures can be nonproductive in the long run, General Electric has developed a variable it calls *customer franchise* or *consumer goodwill.* Although GE's precise definitions of these terms are not available, its measurement procedure is.[48] It involves customer surveys in which the following questions are asked:[49]

1. Do you own the product (category)?
2. What brand do you own?
3. If you were to buy this product, what brands would you consider buying?
4. Which brands would you most likely buy?
5. If your preferred brand was not available in a reasonable length of time, would you wait for it or switch to another brand?

Respondents are assigned values from 1 to 18 depending on their answers to these questions. Table 7.5 contains the explicit assignments. Those respondents assigned the value of 18 are the most "committed" (GE's word) to the brand; those assigned the value 1 are the least.

GE has shown that this measure does relate to purchase probabilities, at least for its brands. GE has also shown that (both their and competitor brands) high in consumer franchise are less price sensitive. While these properties recommend the use of GE's measure of consumer franchise and we applaud their intention, we believe that it should be used only with a great deal of caution. The reason is that the measure is not based on a strong conceptual definition of consumer franchise. Without this definition, one cannot be sure exactly what is being measured. Indeed, GE representatives use the terms *customer franchise, goodwill,* and *loyalty* interchangeably.[50] The measure itself contains components of ownership, consideration, and purchase intention and switching. These are different things. Each is an important variable in itself.

What we would suggest to companies is using the GE measure as a prototype. Develop definitions of exactly what you want to measure and design your measures carefully so that they correspond to the concept you have defined. The determination of critical performance outcomes is essential in this regard. GE's effort is a good starting point, but its limitations prevent it from being the last word.

TABLE 7.5 **General Electric's Consumer Franchise Scale**

Product Owned?	"Brand A" Owned?	Would Consider "Brand A"?	Most Likely to Buy "Brand A"?	Wait for Preferred Brand?	Scale
Yes	Yes	Yes	Yes	Yes	18
Yes	No	Yes	Yes	Yes	17
No	—	Yes	Yes	Yes	16
Yes	Yes	Yes	Yes	No	15
Yes	No	Yes	Yes	No	14
No	—	Yes	Yes	No	13
No	—	Yes	No	No	12
Yes	No	Yes	No	No	11
Yes	Yes	Yes	No	No	10
No	—	Yes	No	Yes	9
Yes	No	Yes	No	Yes	8
Yes	Yes	Yes	No	Yes	7
No	—	No	No	No	6
Yes	No	No	No	No	5
Yes	Yes	No	No	No	4
No	—	No	No	Yes	3
Yes	No	No	No	Yes	2
Yes	Yes	No	No	Yes	1

Source: Reprinted from the Journal of Advertising Research, (c) Copyright 1984 by the Advertising Research Foundation.

MEASURING POSITIONAL ADVANTAGES

As stated earlier, most (if not all) successful strategies involve one of two major categories of positional advantage—low cost or differentiation. Thus it becomes critical for a firm to be able to measure and/or forecast its costs and basis of differentiation. Furthermore, there are two major classes of paths to differentiation—creating quality offerings and building strong brands.[51] In this section we discuss the experience curve, a tool that enables us to forecast costs, as well as the measurement of quality and brand equity.

Cost and Experience

In pursuing a low-cost strategy, a firm strives to achieve a cost advantage in producing or distributing the product or service. This can be accomplished through experience gained from a high market share, favorable access to raw materials, or state-of-the-art production equipment. A low-cost strategy can either be associated with a lower price (thereby providing customer value) or enhanced profits (if the product is perceived as being of equal value), which could potentially be reinvested. Indeed, the prices of laptops and notebooks are constantly falling. The price premiums that notebooks command over comparably equipped desktops are also vanishing.

Given that low cost is an important positional advantage and that every market has a cost leader, a tool that could help managers understand and predict costs would obviously be helpful in assessing the cost positions of a firm and its competitors. The experience curve is such a tool.

The *experience curve* refers to the empirical generalization that costs (net of inflation) decline systematically with increases in accumulated experience in production. In particular, costs tend to decline by a constant fraction, r, each time accumulated production doubles. We call such a relationship a $(1 - r)$ experience curve.

The logic behind it is that experience presents a firm with opportunities to introduce new production technology, learn how to use existing technology faster and better, and redesign the product so that it can be made in a less expensive way. Costs do not decline automatically with experience. Rather their decline is the result of managerial action upon the opportunities that experience provides. Managers must look for technological or efficiency improvements in production, operations, and/or product design. For example, redesigning car door locks reduced the number of parts from 17 in 1954 to 4 in 1974, thereby reducing costs by almost 75 percent.[52] Over the 20-year period, the product was redesigned an average of once a year. Without an active management searching for such opportunities, the experience curve would not be realized.

The experience curve is described by the following model:

$$C_q = C_n \left(\frac{q}{n} \right)^{-b}$$

where q = accumulated production to date, n = accumulated production at a particular (perhaps earlier) time, C_n = the cost of the nth unit (net of inflation), C_q = the cost of the qth unit (net of inflation), and b = a learning constant.

This model can be graphed as a curvilinear function as in the top of Fig. 7.6. The learning constant, b, is uniquely related to the cost reduction fraction, r, by the following expressions:

$$r = 100(2^{-b})$$

and

$$b = \frac{\log 100 - \log r}{\log 2}.$$

Table 7.6 details some of the corresponding values.

In order to apply the experience curve, one needs to calculate b. Then C_q can be computed for any value q. The ingredients for calculating b are the costs at at least two different levels of accumulated experience. The appropriate calculation is now demonstrated.[53]

We begin with the basic expression

$$C_q = C_n \left(\frac{q}{n} \right)^{-b}.$$

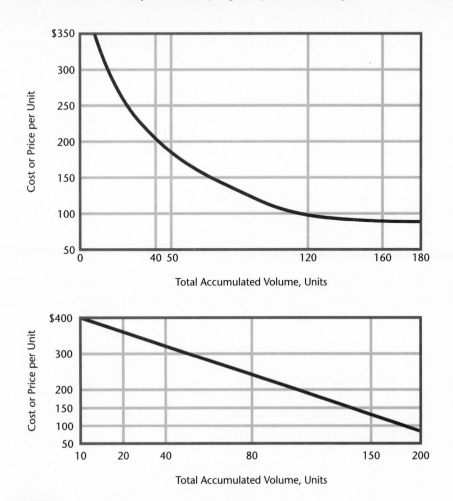

FIGURE 7.6   **The Experience Curve Represented on Linear and Log-Log Scales**

Source: *Perpectives on Experience* (1968), Boston: Boston Consulting Group.

Taking the logarithm of both sides we obtain

$$\log C_q = \log C_n - b(\log q - \log n),$$

which is a straight line in $\log C_q$ and q with slope $-b$. An experience curve can therefore be graphed as a straight line on log-log graph paper as in the bottom of Fig. 7.6. If we know the costs for two levels of accumulated production, we can simply plug them in the above expression for q, n, C_q, and C_n and solve for b. If we know more than two values, we can run a regression on the logs. The negative of the slope of that regression line is then b.

Two issues that arise in practice with the experience curve are what the units of experience and analysis really are. Different industries use different bases for calculating

TABLE 7.6   **Value of Experience Curve Exponent for Various Rates of Cost Decline**

Observed Cost Decline (Percent) with Doubling of Accumulated Production	Elasticity Coefficient of the Response Function (*b*)
0%	0.000
5	0.074
10	0.152
15	0.234
20	0.322
25	0.450
30	0.515

Source: Adapted from Sallanave, J. P. (1976), *Experience Analysis for Industrial Planning*, Lexington, MA: Lexington Books, 18.

cumulative experience. Some industries have found that units produced are not the best measure. For example, making a large engine may provide more experience than making a small engine. Some units of experience for different industries include units for integrated circuits, pounds (not birds) for broiler chickens, conversations for long-distance telephone services, and policy-years (not policies) for life insurance.

With respect to unit of analysis, should costs and the experience curve be analyzed for individual product units (cartons of yogurt)? Units sold to particular segments (low-fat yogurt)? Maybe a company's entire product line (dairy products)? Defining the unit of analysis too broadly does not recognize that specialized experience advantages might exist. For example, different grades of sandpaper have different formulas and so are made of different types of abrasives, bonding agents, paper, and so on. On the other hand, the danger in defining the unit of analysis too narrowly is that experience can be shared between similar products. It would be hard to imagine that production of one sandpaper grade did not have a positive impact on the production costs of others. For example, the same bonding agent can be used in more than one sandpaper grade. If this agent is manufactured, we would expect the bonding agent to have an experience curve of its own. Therefore making the bonding agent for one grade creates experience that can lower the costs for another grade. If the bonding agent is bought, volume discounts and scale economies reduce costs.

The issue of unit of analysis raises the possibility that a particular, perhaps modular, component of the overall product may have an experience curve of its own. It may be a specialized product in its own right, with unique aspects. Indeed, searching for opportunities to use the same component in multiple products, as with the bonding agent, provides an important vehicle for managers to lower costs by creating shared experience. In cases where the components have their own experience curve, the overall product's cost will be the sum of those of its components.

In sum, the basic steps in implementing the experience curve are as follows:[54]

Step 1:   Determine the unit of analysis.

Step 2:   Gather relevant historical cost data for the various cost components over a time period covering many doublings of experience.

Step 3: Determine which of these costs should be actually allocated to the unit of analysis.

Step 4: Group cost components likely to behave similarly with respect to experience, isolating those that have significantly different amounts of prior experience, learning rates, or shared experience.

Step 5: For each group determine and plot (on double log paper) short-run average unit costs at various points in time.

Step 6: Fit a line through the plotted points, judiciously selecting a slope that appears to be most representative of how future costs will behave.

Step 7: Use the fitted line to project future costs of each component, allowing for shared experience with other units of analysis.

Step 8: Combine the projections of the separate cost components.

If a breakdown of costs into components is deemed either unnecessary or impossible, aggregate data must be used and steps 4 and 8 eliminated.

Experience curve analysis makes it possible to estimate the profitability of competitors at prevailing prices. A firm usually knows the slope of its own experience curve and can reasonably estimate the cumulative experience of its competitors from market share data. Unfortunately, the firm cannot take the competitor experience, plug it into its own cost curve, and obtain the competitors' actual costs. The primary reason is because experience curve followers usually have lower initial costs and less steep slopes than market pioneers because they benefit from the pioneer's experience by analyzing their products and hiring some of their personnel. Nevertheless, the costs obtained from the direct translation can provide a reference point (upper bound) for those the competitor actually faces.

Measuring Quality

In his survey investigating the number of competitive advantages managers employ, Aaker found that the thing named most often was "reputation for quality."[55] It was named by 105 of the 248 businesses studied. This is not surprising given the role of quality in the PIMS and Project NewProd studies. What is frustrating, though, and calls all the quality findings into question is that different people mean different things when they use the word. For example, Garvin has identified eight dimensions of product quality: performance, durability, conformance to specifications, features, name, reliability, serviceability, and fit and finish.[56] Is a Porsche a quality car because of its performance? How about a Volvo because of its durability? A Jaguar because of its name? Maybe all of them are quality cars. If so, what meaning does the word have if it represents so many things?

Historically, the word *quality* had a multitude of meanings. Its original significance in the business lexicon referred to quality control—manufacturing processes with low tolerance for error and a constant aim towards zero defects and small variances in the physical characteristics of manufactured products. Today quality means much more. Fortunately, an umbrella concept of quality embraces all the multiple dimensions cited in the previous paragraph.

Today's common business language refers to a product as being of quality if it is built with an eye towards meeting customer expectations and consequently generating customer satisfaction. Quality products are designed, manufactured, and distributed with the customer always in mind. Management systems called Total Quality Management (TQM) have emerged to implement this philosophy. They are characterized by commitment of senior management to TQM values, cross-functional teams that translate customer requirements into product features and engineering characteristics (which are in turn analyzed for production requirements, manufacturing process implications, and parts deployment), and continual monitoring of customer satisfaction. Xerox's "Leadership through Quality" program, discussed earlier, is an example of the TQM approach. Quality and customer satisfaction are considerations that permeate the entire functioning of the organization. They are "total."

Interestingly, a survey conducted by Arthur D. Little found that only 36 percent of executives questioned felt that their quality initiatives had actually made their companies more effective; 38 percent gave their programs a failing grade.[57] One product that seems to have benefited from a TQM perspective is the 1996 Ford Taurus.[58] The Taurus had been the best-selling car in America since its introduction in 1986. It owed much of its success to the low-margin markets of car-rental agencies and corporate fleets. Furthermore, within the consumer market, the Taurus did far better with older buyers than younger ones. Ford chairman Trotman felt that luring baby boomers, who have tended to buy Japanese imports, to America's number one car was critical for the company's survival. Baby boomers wanted a quieter, smoother car. Team Taurus was the cornerstone of the product development process. Engineers, designers, marketers, bean counters, suppliers, and factory-floor workers work together to design and test the vehicle.[59] Costs were often pitted against design features in the process. The result was a car with distinctive elliptical styling; a quiet, comfortable interior; taut precise handling; and a relatively affordable price ($19,300).

Given this background, the question turns to how to measure quality. It should be clear that Garvin's eight dimensions of quality are reconciled by the notion that different groups of customers will have different requirements. (See the discussion of benefit segments in Chapter 2.) Thus, products can have different characteristics and still all be called "quality" if they are constructed to satisfy the varying requirements of different target groups of customers.

The implications for measurement are straightforward. If one knew the requirements of a set of target customers, one could derive (perceived) quality measures simply by asking members of the target group to provide ratings bipolar scales of the extent to which a product (or service) satisfied the requirement in question. However, these measures are potentially contaminated by the impact of the brand's name. (See the discussion of brand equity in the next section.) Furthermore, given the process orientation of TQM, it might be important to measure the entire effort. The Malcolm Baldrige National Quality Award, awarded by the U.S. Department of Commerce, suggests a scheme to do just that.

The Baldrige Award   The Baldrige award, given to Xerox in 1989 for "Leadership through Quality," is based on seven criteria:[60]

Leadership—management's success in creating quality values and integrating them in the company's operations;

Information and Analysis—effectiveness of company's information system for quality improvement;

Strategic Quality Planning—effectiveness of integration of customer requirements into business plans;

Human Resource Use—company's ability to realize full potential of workforce for quality;

Quality Assurance of Products and Services—effectiveness of company systems for assuring quality control and integrating it with continuous quality improvement;

Quality Results—improvements in quality and (quantitative) demonstration of excellence; and

Customer Satisfaction—effectiveness of systems to determine and fulfill customer requirements.

Fig. 7.7 details the subcriteria and weightings for the calculation of the total score. The Department of Commerce scores each applying company with this scheme. However, there is nothing to prevent a company from using this same scheme or some customized variant of it to assess itself. Managers must use their judgment to rate how well they feel their organization has done on each item.

Measuring Brand Equity

A *brand* is a name and/or symbol that distinguishes a product from its competitors. It provides a signal of the product's origin and protects the customer as well as the firm from competitors who would attempt to duplicate it. One of marketers' primary activities these days is to build strong brands. As George J. Bull, the chief executive of Grand Metropolitan, the food and beverage conglomerate, has said, "If you can convince consumers that your product tastes better than your competitor's, that it is made with superior ingredients, then you can command a premium price for it."[61] Hopefully, the brand name conveys the appropriate information to customers. Grand Met practices what its CEO preaches. American consumers pay 15 to 20 percent more for premium brands like J&B Scotch, Smirnoff's Vodka, and Haagen-Dazs ice cream.

Aaker defines brand equity as "the set of assets and liabilities, linked to a brand, its name, or symbol, that add to or subtract from the value provided by a product or service to a firm and/or that firm's customers."[62] Although these assets and liabilities differ from brand to brand, they usually fall into five categories: brand loyalty, name awareness, perceived quality, brand associations in addition to perceived quality (attributes, benefits, user category, price—anything that comes to a consumer's mind when prompted by the brand), and other proprietary brand assets (patents, trademarks, channel relationships, etc.).

FIGURE 7.7   **Categories, Items, and Point Values for Malcolm Baldrige Award**

Examination Categories/Items		Maximum Points
1.0 Leadership		**100**
Senior Executive Leadership	40	
Quality Values	15	
Management for Quality	25	
Public Responsibility	20	
2.0 Information and Analysis		**70**
Scope and Management of Quality Data and Information	20	
Competitive Comparisons and Benchmarks	30	
Analysis of Quality Data and Information	20	
3.0 Strategic Quality Planning		**60**
Strategic Quality Planning Process	35	
Quality Goals and Plans	25	
4.0 Human Resource Use		**150**
Human Resource Management	20	
Employee Involvement	40	
Quality Education and Training	40	
Employee Recognition and Performance Measurement	25	
Employee Well-being and Morale	25	
5.0 Quality Assurance of Products and Services		**140**
Design and Introduction of Quality Products and Services	35	
Process Quality Control	20	
Continuous Improvement of Processes, Products, and Services	20	
Quality Assessment	15	
Documentation	10	
Business Process and Support Services Quality	20	
Supplier Quality	20	
6.0 Quality Results		**180**
Products and Service Quality Results	90	
Business Process, Operational, and Support Service Quality Results	50	
Supplier Quality Results	40	
7.0 Customer Satisfaction		**300**
Determining Customer Requirements and Expectations	30	
Customer Relationship Management	50	
Customer Service Standards	20	
Commitment to Customers	15	
Complaint Resolution for Quality Improvement	25	
Determining Customer Satisfaction	20	
Customer Satisfaction Results	70	
Customer Satisfaction Comparison	70	
TOTAL POINTS		**1000**

Source: Adapted from National Institute of Standards and Technology (1991), Malcolm Baldrige National Quality Award, Application Guidelines by Urban, Glen L., and John R. Hauser (1993), *Design and Marketing of New Products*, 2nd ed., Englewood Cliffs, NJ: Prentice-Hall, 380–381.

Brand equity provides value to the customer by facilitating the interpretation and processing of information about products. Each asset category does this in a different way. Loyalty prevents the need for such processing by giving the customer a simple rule to follow—buy the usual brand. Awareness dictates which brands can be in the consumer's consideration set. The associations (quality and otherwise) provide cues for the consumer to infer characteristics of the brand.

The value brand equity provides to the customer provides value to the firm, in turn, by increasing the effectiveness of its marketing campaigns, enabling it to charge a premium price, helping the firm get leverage with the trade, and providing the basis for potential brand extensions. Providing the basis for extensions may be the most beneficial of these for fostering growth. Fewer and fewer products exist as standalone brands these days. Consider the example of detergents in the United Kingdom.[63] Before Lever introduced the first liquid, Wisk, the market was shared by Persil, a Lever (powdered) brand, and Aerial, a P&G (powdered) brand. Wisk's launch resulted in a 4 percent share. Aerial responded with Aerial liquid and gained nearly 10 percent of the market. Consumers hesitant to try a new product form were less so when there was a recognized name. Lever gained another 7 percent by responding with Persil liquid (which was really the same product as Wisk except for the container!).

These methods of signaling value to both consumers and firms can form the basis of a set of measurement procedures. For example, DDB Needham Worldwide and Landor Associates measure share of mind and esteem, variables that reflect brand name awareness. This can be accomplished by asking a sample of consumers to list the brands of a certain product category that come to their minds in the order that they came to mind.

Another straightforward method would involve simply asking consumers to provide bipolar ratings of overall evaluation, quality (poor-excellent), or value for money (poor-excellent). While this is exceedingly simple and does give the analyst an idea about how consumers see the brand, it does not really address the perceived quality value of the brand name apart from the physical basis for actual quality. Just as direct questions about quality cannot separate out the impact of brand name from a measurement of actual quality, they cannot separate out actual quality from a measurement of the impact of brand name.

In the remainder of this section, we address three more sophisticated approaches to measuring brand equity: the dollarmetric approach, brand-specific constants in choice models, and a new extension-based approach. The first two reflect the sum total of the assets and liabilities that comprise brand equity rather than a specific path of providing value; in contrast, the last one reflects the potential for the brand name to be used in extensions.

Dollarmetric Approach   The dollarmetric method is appropriately named. Its objective is to create a metric (measure) of brand value in dollars.[64] Consider the following experiment. A subject is offered the choice between two brands of chocolate chip cookies, each marked with its "regular" price. After choosing, the subject is asked to indicate the price to which the preferred brand must rise before the subject

TABLE 7.7 Dollarmetric Brand Values for Personal Computers	
IBM	$295
Compaq	232
Apple	195
Digital	129
AST Computer	107
Dell	92
Hewlett Packard	76
Zeos	−$15
NEC	−44
Everex	−47
Packard Bell	−69

Source: "Computers: They're No Commodity" (1993),
The Wall Street Journal, October 15, B1.

would switch his/her original preference. The difference between that price and the original one contains information on how much the subject values the brand.

McKinsey & Co. and Intelliquest Inc. used a variation of the dollarmetric approach to assess the brand values of personal computers.[65] Table 7.7 presents the results in dollar terms.

Research International uses a variant of the dollarmetric approach in its BETA (Brand Equity Trade-Off Analysis) procedure.[66] It uses an experiment along the following lines. Subjects are shown up to five brands of cookies, each at average supermarket prices, and are asked which one they would buy. The price of the chosen brand is increased a few cents and the subjects are asked to reconsider. They can either stay with the (more expensive) preferred brand or switch. Whichever brand they decide on, its price is increased by the same amount and the process is repeated. These trade-off choices provide a complete map of the subject's brand preferences. Research International derives a price preference curve for any brand by using the trade-off data to predict the market shares for that brand at a range of different prices.

Brand-specific Constants   Imagine that you were performing a conjoint analysis for notebook computers. Conjoint analysis allows you to examine the contribution of each of several attributes to consumer preference. One of those attributes may be brand name! Indeed, the part-worth of brand name indicates how much utility is provided by the brand name beyond that provided by the other attributes (processor speed, screen quality, hard disk size, warranty, service policy, etc.). That is certainly a measure of brand value or brand equity. The rank order of the magnitudes of the brand name part-worths would correspond to the order of brand values. Furthermore, since the range of part-worths for an attribute represents the importance of that attribute, we can compute the importance of brand name in the consumer's decision by computing the ratio of the range of brand name part-worths to the sum of the ranges for all the attributes.

Similarly, the brand-specific constants in the multinomial logit model can be taken as a measure of brand equity.

In principle, conjoint analysis or the multinomial logit model could be applied at either the individual consumer or aggregate market levels. However, most of the consumer choice applications of conjoint analysis are performed at the individual level, while most of the applications of the multinomial logit model are at the aggregate market level as discussed earlier. In practice, then, conjoint analysis tends to provide individual measures of brand equity (aggregate measures can be derived by taking the average of the individual measures) and multinomial logit applications tend to provide aggregate measures.

Extension-Based Approach   If one of the ways brand equity provides value to the firm is by giving it the ability to extend the brand successfully, then it stands to reason that brand extensions should provide a suitable context in which to measure brand equity. If a brand is strong, there should be a high likelihood of consumers' trying an extension they perceive to be appropriate. Researchers have used seven-point bipolar perceived quality (Inferior-Superior) and likelihood of trying (Not at all likely-Very likely) scales to evaluate extensions.[67] One of the authors has used this method to evaluate the brand equity in several brands of candy bars.[68]

In applying this approach one must be careful in interpreting negative results. If a potential extension is evaluated poorly, it does not necessarily mean that the brand has low equity or value. It could simply mean that the extension is simply a bad one. For example, consumers are likely to evaluate Levi's business suits negatively despite the fact that the Levi's brand name is well thought of. Therefore it is important to make sure that the extensions are reasonable ones. In the course of the candy bar study we determined that the best way to do this was to use an extension that is a substitute for the original product.

Before leaving our discussion of brand equity, it is worth pointing out that although brand equity is usually thought of as a strength, it can be a weakness as well. For example, Air Canada can be thought of as having negative brand equity.[69] Customers associate the airline with the Canadian government. A recent survey showed that 49 percent of Canadians are "very dissatisfied" with their government. Given the association, this feeling translates to negative brand equity for Air Canada. This association would be bad enough if Air Canada were indeed state owned. It isn't! It's as private as American or United Airlines.

It has also become popular recently to disparage the power of brands. A recent Roper Organization survey found that 37 percent of shoppers judged name brands in premium categories as worth paying more for.[70] In 1988 the figure was 45 percent. Consumers are simply becoming more price conscious. In 1992 Kraft charged 45 percent more than private label brands. Its market share fell three points. It then cut prices 8 percent and share rose five points.[71] Liguori, vice-president for marketing at Frito-Lay, says, "Brand equity is being challenged like never before."[72]

We believe that this phenomenon is not a signal of decreasing importance for brand equity. We believe that it is signaling just the opposite. Phil Dusenberry, vice-chairman of BBDO Worldwide, says, "The brands that will succeed are the

No. 1 and No. 2 in a category, plus a private label. Anything below that will get squeezed right off the shelf."[73] If this is true, that will only make a brand equity–based competitive advantage more difficult to achieve and sustain. Therefore, firms trying to build such an advantage will need an even greater understanding of the concept than before.

MEASURING SOURCES OF ADVANTAGE

The invisibility of skills and resources prevents marketers from going much beyond ad hoc judgment in the assessment of sources of advantage. One exception, the measurement of technology, has been briefly discussed in Chapter 6. Once again we are faced with overcoming the limitations of and biases inherent in managerial judgment. We discuss a framework, Ansoff's Grid of Competences, which can provide structure for these judgments and minimize the threat of biases.

Ansoff's Grid of Competences

Ansoff developed a four-by-four matrix that cross-classifies skills and resources against functional areas. The underlying logic is that each functional area in a fully integrated manufacturing firm has to be successful for the firm as a whole to be successful. The skills and resources are research and development, operations, marketing, and general management and finance. The functional areas are facilities and equipment, personnel skills, organizational capabilities, and management capabilities. Ansoff's intent was to provide a master checklist, within each of the 16 cells, that would reflect the different capabilities found within a great variety of industries. That way most firms could just pick and choose from the lists. The resulting grid is shown in Table 7.8.

Ansoff recognized that the contents of the grid may have to be augmented for some firms. Different industries have different critical success factors. Indeed, since the grid was developed for a fully integrated manufacturing firm, it would have to be modified for analyzing firms in trade, finance, and other services.

Managers would have to complete this grid for both the firm in question and its competitors to gain insight into their sources of competitive advantage. For example, Canon's sources of competitive advantage in its diversification from cameras into business equipment most likely lie in the personnel skills and organizational capabilities of the research and development row of Table 7.8.

PERSPECTIVES ON MEASUREMENT

Measurement can be defined as the assignment of numbers or categories to a set of observations about some set of marketplace conditions.[74] The word *marketplace* is added to reflect the focal interests of this book and its readers. Given this definition, it probably would not be inaccurate to say that most of this book has really been about

TABLE 7.8   **Ansoff's Grid of Competences**

	Facilities and Equipment	Personnel Skills	Organizational Capabilities	Management Capabilities
General Management and Finance	Data processing equipment	Depth of general management	Multidivisional structure	Investment management
		Finance	Consumer financing	Centralized control
		Industrial relations	Industrial financing	Large systems management
		Legal	Planning and control	Decentralized control
		Personnel recruitment and training	Automated business data processing	R&D–intensive business
		Accounting		Capital equipment–intensive business
		Planning		Merchandising–intensive business
				Cyclical business
				Many customers
				Few customers
Research and Development	Special lab equipment	Areas of specialization	Systems development	Utilization of advanced state of the art
	General lab equipment	Advanced research	Product development, industrial, consumer process	Application of current state of the art
	Test facilities	Applied research	Military specifications compliance	Cost-performance optimization
		Product design: industrial, consumer, military, specifications		
		Systems design		
		Industrial design: consumer, industrial		

(Continued on next page)

TABLE 7.8   **Continued**

	Facilities and Equipment	Personnel Skills	Organizational Capabilities	Management Capabilities
Operations	General machine shop	Machine operation	Mass production	Operation under cyclic demand
	Precision machinery	Toolmaking	Continuous flow process	Military specifications quality
	Process equipment	Assembly	Batch process	Tight cost control
	Automated production	Precision machinery	Job shop	Tight scheduling
	Large high-bay facilities	Close tolerance work	Large, complex product assembly	
	Controlled environment	Process operation	Subsystems integration	
		Product planning	Complex product control	
			Quality control	
			Purchasing	
Marketing	Warehousing	Door-to-door selling	Direct sales	Industrial marketing
	Retail outlets	Retail selling	Distributor chain	Consumer merchandising
	Sales offices	Wholesale selling	Retail chain	
	Service offices	Direct industry selling	Consumer service organization	Department of Defense marketing
	Transportation equipment	Department of Defense selling	Industrial service organization	State and municipality marketing
		Cross-industry selling	Department of Defense product support	
		Applications engineering	Inventory distribution and control	
		Advertising		
		Sales promotion		
		Servicing		
		Contract administration		
		Sales analysis		

Source: *The New Corporate Strategy*, H. Igor Ansoff, Copyright (c) 1988. Reprinted by permission of John Wiley & Sons, Inc.

measurement: measurement of segment membership, unmet needs, competitive sets, and future environments. However, the multidimensional nature of the term *competitive advantage,* as reflected in Fig. 7.1, led to a diversity in measurement methods beyond that exhibited by the topics of earlier chapters.

The variety of methods introduced in this chapter presents us with an opportunity to consider some fundamental issues of measurement as they relate to measuring competitive advantage. Specifically, with respect to our opening definition of measurement, we address what information sources provide the basic observations about marketplace conditions, whether the assignment of numbers or categories to these observations is objective or subjective, and the level of the organization and/or market to which the measure applies.

Information Sources

In the early chapters of this book customer input proved critical in determining the conditions (benefits desired, unmet needs) that formed the basis for measurement. Even when we began to discuss competition in Chapter 4, we essentially argued that companies were not competitors unless customers said so with the dollars in their pocketbooks. In the middle chapters, forecasting the market environment was the issue. Sources internal to the company and publicly available secondary sources described the relevant conditions here in either numerical or verbal form.

Information for assessing competitive advantage or strengths and weaknesses is available from a variety of sources. The majority of these fall into four categories: the company itself, its customers, its competitors, and secondary sources. Many common secondary sources are listed in Table 7.9 and discussed in Appendix 5B.

Sources within the firm include both formal records and the collective memories of company personnel. The keys to effective assembly of a firm's internal information resources are the sensitization of its executives, sales force, engineers, and scientists to the need for compiling such information and training them to recognize and transmit it. One way to accomplish this is to have managers, scientists, and the like visit the point of transaction as a customer or customer representative, and visit it often. These personnel should also take regular shopping trips and buy the company's (and competitors') products for their own use. Furthermore, spending time as a customer service representative will enable them to appreciate how customers perceive their products. Indeed, every McDonald's marketing executive must take a customer's cheeseburger order several times a year.[75]

In addition, competitors will often give you a great deal of information without your even asking for it. Speeches and public announcements will often reveal management philosophy, priorities, and company skills (as managers perceive them). Of course, some announcements may be made with the intention of deceiving a competitor and consequently influencing its actions. For example, in 1993, Boeing announced that it was building a 600- to 800-seat plane, larger and more expensive than any other plane in existence. Industry insiders suggested that Boeing's move was a bluff to preempt Airbus from doing that exact thing.[76] One study suggested that while many announcements

TABLE 7.9 **Secondary Sources of Information for Assessing Strengths and Weaknesses**

Source	Types of Information	Location of Source
Information directories	Reference guides providing sources of information about business and government	Library, bookstore
On-line databases	Financial, textual, macroeconomic, and other data	Commercial suppliers of on-line services
Government publications	Various books, pamphlets, and computer tapes providing information about the economy and selected industries	Commerce Department, Census Bureau, Treasury Department, other government agencies, local library
Investment reports	Various industry reports produced by brokerage firms and other financial services companies	Brokerage firms, investment advisors
Industry and trade publications	Industry/trade issues, growth projections, areas of need	Industry and trade associations, library, bookstore
Clipping services	Newspaper and magazine articles on current business trends, target companies and industries, and competitors	Outside market research company, company employees
Employment advertisements	Insights into who's hiring and for what purposes; may indicate a market need or a new competitor direction	Newspapers
Publicly available financial reports	Financial condition and target markets of prospective clients and competitors	Brokerage firms, on-line databases

Source: Adapted from Sultan, Fareena, and Thomas J. Kosnik (1989), "Marketing Situation Assessment," Cambridge, MA: Harvard Business School Case #9-590-006, 17–18.

may not be truthful, firms are best off believing what their competitors say.[77] In the long run, fewer errors will be made that way.

Of course, the choice among information sources must first and foremost depend on the particular component of competitive advantage or the specific strength or weakness being assessed. This is illustrated in Table 7.10, which presents some examples. Performance outcomes can be observed in any of the four categories of information sources. Of course, the firm keeps its own sales records. Many routinely inquire whether their (as well as their competitors') customers are satisfied. Data suppliers such as IRI and Nielsen regularly compile sales and market share data with the aid of supermarket scanners. Publicly held competitors must release financial statements. Finally, industrywide surveys, such as the J.D. Powers survey in the auto industry, compile customer satisfaction ratings for industry participants.

Customers, competitors, and internal sources can all provide data useful in assessing positional advantage. Customers are the best judges of the relative value different products provide them with. Simple surveys that collect perceived attribute ratings for each product along with ideal attribute levels can serve this purpose.

TABLE 7.10 **Typical Information Sources Classified by Component of Competitive Advantage**

	The Firm	Customers	Competitors	Secondary Sources
Sources of Advantage	Managerial memory and intuition Past marketing plans		Public announcements including annual report	
Positional Advantage	Product blueprints and specifications Past marketing plans Cost allocations	Surveys on product attributes	Public announcements including annual report	*Consumer Reports*
Performance Outcomes	Sales records	Customized satisfaction surveys	Public announcements including annual report	Industrywide satisfaction survey services Scanner panel data

Secondary sources can be of some help here too. For example, *Consumer Reports* magazine will formally compare (and rate the "quality" of) the offerings in selected industries. These sources present a more professional view of product value. Consequently, they may be one vehicle for separating out actual quality from brand equity in consumer product ratings. Of course, *Consumer Reports* ratings become closer to perceived quality when consumers read, believe, and act on them.

The customer is not of much help in assessing cost positions. For example, airlines do not know the relative costs of Boeing, McDonnell Douglas, and Airbus. The companies themselves have to use their own resources. Company records should demonstrate a firm's own costs, while company personnel need to have input on assessing competitors'. Perhaps competitors' public announcements can lend insight into the costs of their operations.

Finally, owing to their invisibility, the sources of advantage must be observed within the firm itself. Customers and secondary sources are of no use whatsoever. Presumably, though, a firm's sources of advantage are on record in its archived marketing and strategic plans. Competitors are a different story unless, again, they reveal information through a public announcement or perhaps a cocktail party conversation at a trade convention. Firms must infer the skills and resources of their competitors from the products themselves.

Is the Assignment Objective or Subjective?

Once marketplace observations are made, they must be assigned a number or category. Often the assignment is made by the information source that reported on the observation. Scanner data sources compute market shares; customers respond to bipolar scales with a number; costs are assessed by firm personnel. Other assignments are made by parties other than the one that reported on the observation. A manager infers a competitors' skills from examining laboratory tests on its product. Some of these assignments are objective (sales, market shares); others are subjective (customer product ratings, managerial judgment of competitor skills). Does the distinction matter?

A knee-jerk reaction to this question might be that objective assignment is preferable to subjective assignment. This is not necessarily so. If a customer is making the assignment, as in providing perceptions about a brand, subjectivity is more important than objectivity. You can still have an objective interpretation of a subjective assignment. In terms of assessing customer value, it matters more whether customers think that Stolychinaya is a higher quality vodka than Brand X than whether it really is. Managers can objectively use this information. After all, how much closer to a commodity can you get than vodka, something that is clear, colorless, odorless, and tasteless?

On the other hand, too much subjectivity in managerial judgments of strengths and weaknesses can be a dangerous thing. At several points in this chapter, we have alluded to the inherent limitations of managers' abilities to interpret information and the resulting biases in judgment that emerge. Three avenues to minimizing the negative impacts of these are: structuring judgments, raising the general awareness of particular biases (and in so doing enabling managers to avoid them), and training managers to be more systematic in their decision making. Much of the chapter has been about the first. We now briefly discuss the last two.

Judgmental Biases   In "thinking backwards," managers will tend to avoid evidence that would disconfirm any experience, expectations, or theories they might have.[78] Decision makers tend to focus on a single theory, a unique conclusion, only one interpretation, and a lone hypothesis. Not only will managers avoid information that might disconfirm their ideas, they will interpret it as actually doing so. This type of information is sometimes called *pseudodiagnostic.*[79]

For example, some authors contend that the identities of critical success factors are obvious to those who participate in an industry.[80] The judgment involved in assessing one of these "obvious" factors may well be flawed and biased. Stevenson found that managers' perceptions of strengths and weaknesses of their firms are strongly biased by factors associated with the individual's position in the organization, perceived role, and type of responsibility.[81] These are primary sources of the manager's experience, expectations, and theories. In particular, upper-level managers are biased towards organizational and personnel factors; middle managers are biased towards marketing and technical factors; and entry-level managers are biased towards financial factors.

The positional bias is a manifestation of the more general notion that people pay a disproportionate amount of attention to vivid information and like to have control over their environments. Information related to one's organizational position is both more vivid and controllable by the individual.

The importance of vividness of information can be further illustrated in a study one of us performed with Glazer and Winer.[82] We supplied half of the decision makers in a simulated environment with a perceptual map, vivid by its pictorial nature. The other half did not have access to it. Those that had access to the map made decisions consistent with its implications. However, they did not perform as well in the market. The reason was that the market was extremely sensitive to sales force expenditures—decisions that the map was not relevant for. Decision makers with the information paid more attention to it and did not do as well in the market because it distracted them from the *real* critical success factors. On the other hand, decision makers without the information could not use it and consequently were better equipped to diagnose those decision-making factors actually important for success.

A final bias relevant to thinking backwards is the self-serving bias.[83] The *self-serving bias* is the tendency for individuals to take credit for successes that they achieve yet deny blame for their failures. Such a tendency necessarily clouds a human's judgment about what factors lead to successful performance.[84]

Training　Unfortunately, simply making someone aware of a judgmental bias does not guarantee that it will no longer be a problem. Research has shown that explicitly describing a bias to people does not prevent them from falling prey to it.[85] The only hope is intensive personalized feedback. Bazerman advocates an approach where an individual is given a series of quiz questions designed to elicit a particular bias.[86] The individual will get many of these wrong and want to know why and how to do better. A pure text format or lecture is not likely to achieve as much success as this interactive approach.

Einhorn and Hogarth advocate a more general set of rules designed to minimize the biases inherent in thinking backwards. These include the following:[87]

1. Always generate and test several theories;
2. Never rely on only one piece of information;
3. Be prepared to make judgments counter to those suggested by the information; and
4. Logically work through cause-and-effect mechanisms in detail.

At What Level Does the Measurement Apply?

Sources of competitive advantage reside at several levels of the organization. For example, Sony's *corporate*-level expertise at making intricate tape-spinning mechanisms and optical disk pickups has made it the preeminent video and music brand in the American living room over the past half-century. The Maxwell House *division* of Kraft–General Foods has assembled vast amounts of market intelligence that has proven useful for all of the division's brands (such as Sanka and Brim). The secret formula Coca-Cola uses to make the *product* Coca-Cola Classic has been a basis for the brand's success for most of the twentieth century.

Similarly, positional advantages are manifested at different organizational levels. Harvard University has a reputation as an organization that extends to its individual schools. Pepsico's restaurant business units (Pizza Hut, Taco Bell) have lower beverage procurement costs. Nike provides value to buyers of its Air Jordan basketball shoes by providing an association with Michael Jordan.

In theory, any source of advantage that exists at one level of the organization can be drawn upon to generate positional advantages and, consequently, greater performance outcomes, at all lower levels. That is not necessarily the case in practice, though, if the company participates in a wide variety of businesses. For example, Sony's technological expertise has neither been helpful to its troubled Hollywood entertainment business nor will it necessarily be an asset to its fledgling computer business.[88]

The same is true for firms that serve diverse market segments within a single business unit. Sources of advantage useful for generating positional advantages (and performance outcomes) in one segment may not be useful for another. Reconsider the Philadelphia Chewing Gum Corp., maker of the offensive-tasting Cry Baby gum, first discussed in Chapter 2.[89] The recipe for that gum, developed at the corporate level, generated a positional (taste-based) advantage at the product level for the early teen segment. Such a positional advantage is not likely to be duplicated in any other segment.

Thus, meaningful measurement of strengths and weaknesses and competitive advantage must consider both where the advantage resides and where it is to be applied. Sources of advantage must be assessed at the level at which they reside. Positional advantages must be measured at the level to which they are intended to be applied. Determining whether and how sources and targets of application can be linked remains the major task of the strategy analyst.

AN ILLUSTRATION

The diversity of methods described in this chapter suggests that the choice among them may be quite complex. No single method is going to be applicable in all cases. Fortunately, the last section suggests a set of considerations that should be taken into account in making the appropriate choices. In particular, we should be wary of the component of competitive advantage addressed, the information sources most appropriate for that component, and the degree of bias the measurement is vulnerable to. We illustrate these issues by reexamining the unfortunate situation of the EMI CT scanner alluded to earlier in the chapter.

Fig. 7.1 shows that the components of competitive advantage are connected in a cyclical fashion. In theory, then, one could enter the cycle at any given point and get to all three components. However, we suggest that the assessment of strengths and weaknesses begin with examining positional advantages. We view these as the fundamental drivers of a firm's marketing strategy. Positional advantages provide either the reasons behind customers' purchases and/or the cost structure that makes those purchases profitable for the firm. The firm then develops skills and resources and measures results consistent with this.

Consider now EMI's initial pioneering development of the CT scanner as a device that allowed an X-ray beam to be rotated around the body, thereby creating images of organs that overlap. This suggests that the original marketing strategy was (or perhaps should have been) geared to the provision of visual information that assists in medical diagnoses. In the mid-1970s competition began to emerge and technological developments accelerated. Until then, EMI had a "competitive" advantage in providing consumer value. Now more careful planning and assessment of true competitive advantage was in order. However, EMI's initial reaction was to counter with sales force and production step-ups.

EMI had to either identify what visual information was important to customers in order to guide the development of superior images or determine how to provide equivalent images at a lower cost. Given EMI's overall orientation towards the music business, the latter avenue was probably not feasible. Direct questioning or conjoint analysis could have been used here. If they had been, they probably would have let EMI's management know that customers were more interested in reducing scan time than EMI believed. EMI's (inaccurate) belief was that a 20-second scan-time was practical since patients could typically hold their breath at least that long. Besides, EMI believed that shorter scan times would lead to more blurred images.

Given selected positional advantages, skills and resources need to be developed that will enable the firm to achieve them and to measure their performance. Of course, the question is then, which skills and resources? Table 7.10 suggests that the firm must rely on the collective memories, judgments, and file cabinets of its managers in this task. The value chain and/or CSF method can provide a useful structure, as described in the text. If EMI were to opt for shorter scan times, it would have to (judgmentally) determine what skills and resources would be needed to reduce scan time. Lighter parts? More powerful motors? More efficient design? Better parts or better designers?

It is also important that appropriate performance measures be used. The long selling cycle and continuing development in CT scanners suggest that sales revenues or units sold might not be the best measure of performance for EMI. Customer interest or purchase intent might have been better at this point in time.

Unfortunately for EMI, however, it did not opt for shortening scan time. Consistent with the 20-second belief, the company went for improved picture quality instead. The error here was in not using the best information sources. Customers, not firm personnel, are the best source of information about customer motivations. Furthermore, the firm personnel that made the 20-second judgment were scientists, not managers. They were thus vulnerable to positional and self-serving biases toward scientific and technological, rather than customer-oriented, concerns.

General Electric was able to capitalize on EMI's mistakes by first developing scanners with shorter scan times and then using computers to refine the blurred images.

Not only did EMI misread the market, it misused what was possibly its most productive asset. Instead of spending time in the laboratory, the scanner's inventor, Godfrey Houndsfield, and his staff went on public relations tours trying to reinforce EMI's market leadership reputation. EMI felt that such a reputation could swing many a sale (via brand equity). While EMI was indeed the recognized pioneer, it was not clear whether General Electric's reputation in medical electronics could overcome EMI's leadership status in this one part of the industry. A conjoint analysis with brand name or perhaps a dollarmetric study of the brand names would have indicated that EMI's advantage was probably not as strong as the company thought.

With development going in the wrong direction and without the reputational advantage the company felt it enjoyed, EMI was destined to be overtaken by GE. Not only was it overtaken, its insistence on fighting a losing battle proved to be the downfall of the company. Had the company had a clearer understanding of the basis of competitive advantage, critical success factors, and where it stood with respect to them, it would have either redirected development efforts or perhaps exited the market while it still could (and made a tidy profit from licensing fees besides). Our discussion of EMI suggests that the following steps be invoked in selecting strength and weakness measurement procedures:

Step 1: Identify critical positional advantages.

Step 2: Isolate skills and resources that will produce these advantages as well as a performance measure that both reflects these advantages and an appropriate time horizon.

Step 3: Determine techniques suitable for assessing the particular positional advantages sought.

Step 4: Identify the information sources most suitable for assessing the particular positional advantages sought; determine feasibility of source acquisition.

Step 5: Select techniques from step 3 that process information contained in or obtainable from sources in step 4. Different techniques may have to be used to assess each competitor because of source feasibility.

Step 6: Question the potential for judgmental bias in either the source, processing, or interpretation of the information.

Step 7: If the potential for judgmental bias is large, examine whether either more objective information sources or more objective ways to collect, summarize, or interpret the information exist and if so how costly they are.

Step 8: Repeat steps 3 through 6 for sources of advantage and performance outcomes.

SUMMARY

A complete understanding of competitive advantage involves assessment of the skills and resources that provide the sources of advantage, the positional superiorities obtained by application of these sources (low cost, higher value), and the performance outcomes produced by the positional superiorities. Assessment of competitive advantage begins with the determination of critical success factors—those specific realizations of source of advantage, positional advantage, and performance outcomes that are critical for success in the firm's industry. It continues with the measurement of these factors for all firms in the industry. Different factors require different information as measurement inputs. When managerial judgment is used, the potential for judgmental biases presents a real danger to obtaining correct measures. Care must also be taken to ensure that the correct information sources and measurement tools are used. The desired positional superiority is the best starting point for the selection process.

Review Questions

1. What are the sources of advantage, positional advantages, and performance outcomes for your school or firm?

2. Value chain analysis is based on cost-benefit analysis of the offering as perceived by the consumer. True or false? Why?

3. What is the approximate cost of the 100,000th unit produced when the initial cost was $631 and the cost of the 1,000th unit was $158?

4. Discuss the pros and cons of using managerial judgment in assessing the skills and resources required for success in an industry of your choice.

5. Can brand equity provide a *sustainable* competitive advantage? Discuss your answers with examples.

6. Are there any industries in which consumer satisfaction measures are not appropriate performance measures? Discuss your reasoning.

Notes

1. See the discussion in Day, George S., and Robin Wensley (1988), "Assessing Advantage: A Framework for Diagnosing Competitive Strategy," *Journal of Marketing* 92 (April): 2–4.

2. See Collis, David J., and Cynthia A. Montgomery (1995), "Competing on Resources: Strategy in the 1990s," *Harvard Business Review* 73 (July-August): 118–128 for a complete discussion and some critical references.

3. See "Hot Products" (1993), *Business Week,* June 7, 54–57.

4. See "Saturn: Labor's Love Lost?" (1993), *Business Week,* February 8, 122–123.

5. See "Note on the Motorcycle Industry—1975" (1978), Intercollegiate Case Clearing House, Boston, MA: Harvard Business School; and "EMI and the CT Scanner (B)" (1983), Intercollegiate Case Clearing House #9-383-195, Boston, MA: Harvard Business School.

6. This analysis is taken from Day and Wensley (1988), "Assessing Advantage," 6, who adapted it from MacAvoy, Robert E. (1987), "Establishing Superior Performance Through Competitive Analysis," in *Strategic Planning and Management Handbook,* William R. King and David I. Clelland, (eds.), New York: van Nostrand.

7. See "Laptops Take Off" (1991), *Business Week,* March 18, 118–124.

8. See Aaker, David A. (1989), "Managing Assets and Skills: The Key to a Sustainable Competitive Advantage," *California Management Review* (Winter): 91–106.

9. See "The Hunt for Mr. X: Who Can Run IBM?" (1993), *Fortune,* February 22, 68–71.

10. Rockart, John F. (1979), "Chief Executives Define their Own Data Needs," *Harvard Business Review* 57 (March-April): p. 85.

11. Reprinted with the permission of The Free Press, a Division of Simon & Schuster, from MARKET DRIVEN STRATEGY: Processes for Creating Value by George S. Day. Copyright (c) 1990 by George S. Day.

12. Buzzell, Robert D., and Bradley T. Gale (1987), *The PIMS Principles: Linking Strategy to Performance,* New York: Free Press.

13. Kerin, Roger A., Vijay Mahajan, and P. Rajan Varadarajan (1990), *Contemporary Perspectives on Strategic Market Planning,* Boston: Allyn and Bacon.

14. See *Ibid.,* 168–173, for further discussion.

15. For a more complete discussion, see Levitt, Theodore (1980), "Marketing Success through Differentiation—of Anything," *Harvard Business Review* 58 (January-February): 83–91.

16. See Buzzell and Gale, *The PIMS Principles.*

17. See Cooper, Robert G. (1979), "The Dimensions of Industrial New Product Success and Failure," *Journal of Marketing* 43 (Summer): 93–103 for full details.

18. *Ibid.*

19. See Cooper, Robert G. (1992), "The NewProd System: The Industry Experience," *Journal of Product Innovation Management* 9 (June): 113–127.

20. See Vasconcellos, Jorge Alberto Sousa De (1991), "Key Success Factors in Marketing Mature Products," *Industrial Marketing Management* 20, 1–16.

21. See Aaker, "Managing Assets and Skills."

22. See McFadden, Daniel (1974), "Conditional Logit Analysis of Qualitative Choice Behavior," in *Frontiers in Econometrics,* P. Zarembka (ed.), New York: Academic Press, 105–142.

23. See Guadagni, Peter M., and John D. C. Little (1983), "A Logit Model of Brand Choice Calibrated on Scanner Data," *Marketing Science* 2 (Summer): 203–238.

24. This example is drawn from Buaron, Roberto (1981), "How to Win the Market-Share Game? Try Changing the Rules," *Management Review* 70 (January): 8–19.

25. Porter, Michael E. (1985), *Competitive Advantage,* New York: Free Press, 36.

26. This example is drawn from and described in detail in Solomon, Steven D. (1995), "American Express Applies for a New Line of Credit," *New York Times Magazine,* July 30, 35–47.

27. This example was drawn from and described in more detail in "Texas Instruments' Global Chip Payoff" (1995), *Business Week,* August 7, 64–66.

28. Tully, Shawn (1993), "Can Boeing Reinvent Itself?" *Fortune,* March 8, 66–73, describes the sources of Boeing's cost advantages as streamlined operations, effective inventory management, and interdepartmental design teams.

29. See Prahalad, C. K., and Gary A. Hamel (1990), "The Role of Core Competencies of the Corporation," *Harvard Business Review,* 68 (May-June): 79–91.

30. The Canon-Xerox matchup is drawn from Wang, Clement K., and Paul D. Guild (1995), "The Strategic Use of Organization Competencies and Backcasting in Competitive Analysis," ISBM Report 7-1995, Institute for the Study of Business Markets, Smeal College of Business Administration, Penn State University.

31. See Einhorn, Hillel J., and Robin M. Hogarth (1987), "Decision Making: Going Forward in Reverse," *Harvard Business Review* 65 (January-February): 66–70.

32. *Ibid.,* 66.

33. See Rockart, John F. (1979), "Chief Executives Define their Own Data Needs," *Harvard Business Review* 57 (March–April): 81–93, for a discussion of the method and its background.

34. *Ibid.*

35. These are discussed by Boynton, Andrew C., and Robert W. Zmud (1984), "An Assessment of Critical Success Factors," *Sloan Management Review* 25 (Summer): 17–27.

36. Lieberman, Marvin B., and David B. Montgomery (1988), "First-Mover Advantages," *Strategic Management Journal* 9, 41–58 fully explore the trade-offs between early and late entry.

37. Kerin, Roger A., P. Rajan Varadarajan, and Robert A. Peterson (1992), "First-Mover Advantage: A Synthesis, Conceptual Framework, and Research Propositions," *Journal of Marketing* 56 (October): 33–52 review these studies.

38. Golder, Peter N., and Gerard J. Tellis (1993), "Pioneer Advantage: Marketing Logic or Marketing Legend?," *Journal of Marketing Research* 30 (May): 158–170.

39. Reprinted from "First to Market, First to Fail? Real Causes of Enduring Market Leadership," by Gerard J. Tellis and Peter N. Golder. *Sloan Management Review,*

Issue 37 (Winter), 1996, pp. 65–75, by permission of the publisher. Copyright 1996 by Sloan Management Review Association. All rights reserved.

40. *Ibid.,* 67.

41. See Hammermesh, Richard G., M. Jack Anderson, Jr., and J. Elizabeth Harris (1978), "Strategies for Low Market Share Businesses," *Harvard Business Review* 56 (May-June): 95–102.

42. Karnani, Aneel (1982), "Equilibrium Market Share—A Measure of Competitive Strength," *Strategic Management Journal* 3, 43–51 presents a theoretical justification of market share as a measure of competitive strength.

43. See "Too Many Think the Bunny is Duracell's, Not Eveready's," (1990), *The Wall Street Journal,* July 31, B1.

44. This is discussed by Aaker, "Managing Assets and Skills."

45. See "Xerox Corporation: The Customer Satisfaction Program" (1991), Harvard Business School Case #9-591-055, Boston, MA.

46. See Parasuraman, A., Valerie A. Zeithaml, and Leonard L. Berry (1988), "SERVQUAL: A Multiple-Item Scale for Measuring Consumer Perceptions of Service Quality," *Journal of Retailing* 64 (Spring): 12–40.

47. Reprinted with the permission of The Free Press, a Division of Simon & Schuster, from DELIVERING QUALITY SERVICE: Balancing Customer Perceptions and Expectations by Valarie A. Zeithaml, A. Parasuraman, Leonard L. Berry. Copyright (c) 1990 by The Free Press.

48. Reprinted from the Journal of Advertising Research, (c) Copyright 1984 by the Advertising Research Foundation.

49. *Ibid.,* 11–12.

50. See their use in *Ibid.*

51. See Aaker, David A. (1995), *Strategic Market Management,* 4th ed., New York: Wiley.

52. See Kiechel, Walter (1981), "The Decline of the Experience Curve," *Fortune* 105 (October): 139–146 for a more complete discussion.

53. See Day, George S., and David B. Montgomery (1983), "Diagnosing the Experience Curve," *Journal of Marketing* 47 (Spring): 44–58 for a more thorough discussion of the theoretical structure behind and the empirical evidence for the experience curve as well as its strategic implications.

54. STRATEGIC MARKET PLANNING by Abell/Hammond, (c) 1979. Reprinted by permission of Prentice-Hall, Inc., Upper Saddle River, N.J.

55. See Aaker, "Managing Assets and Skills," p. 94.

56. See Garvin, David A. (1984), "What Does 'Product Quality' Really Mean?," *Sloan Management Review* 25 (Fall): 25–43.

57. "Making Quality More than a Fad," (1992), *Fortune,* May 18.

58. This example is drawn from and described in more detail in "The Shape of a New Machine" (1995), *Business Week,* July 24, 60–66.

59. *Ibid.,* 63.

60. These descriptions are based on the adaptation of National Institute of Standards and Technology (1991), Malcolm Baldrige National Quality Award, Application Guidelines made by Urban, Glen L., and John R. Hauser (1993), *Design and Marketing of New Products,* 2nd ed., Englewood Cliffs, NJ: Prentice-Hall, 379.

61. See "Grand Met's New CEO Emphasizes Premium Brands" (1993), *The Wall Street Journal,* October 7, B4.

62. Reprinted with the permission of The Free Press, a Division of Simon & Schuster, from MANAGING BRAND EQUITY by David A. Aaker. Copyright (c) 1991 by David A. Aaker.

63. This example is taken from "Brand Equity" (1993), *Brandweek,* June 28, 20–24.

64. This concept was introduced into the marketing literature by Pessemier, Edgar, Philip Burger, Richard Trach, and Douglas Tigert (1971), "Using Laboratory Brand Preference Scales to Predict Consumer Brand Purchases," *Management Science* 17 (February): B371–B385.

65. "Computers: They're No Commodity," (1993), *The Wall Street Journal,* October 15, B1.

66. For a more complete description, see "Brand Equity."

67. See, for example, Aaker, David A., and Kevin L. Keller (1990), "Consumer Evaluations of Brand Extensions," *Journal of Marketing* 54 (January): 27–41.

68. See Agarwal, Manoj K., and Vithala R. Rao (1994), "An Empirical Comparison of Consumer-Based Measures of Brand Equity," Working Paper, Johnson Graduate School of Management, Cornell University.

69. See "Ah Canada" (1994), *Forbes,* January 3, 74.

70. See "Brands on the Run" (1993), *Business Week,* April 19, 26–29.

71. *Ibid.*

72. *Ibid.*

73. *Ibid.*

74. *Handbook of Experimental Psychology,* edited by S. Stevens, "Mathematics, Measurement, and Psychophysics," by S. Stevens, Copyright (c) 1951. Reprinted/Adapted by permission from John Wiley & Sons, Inc.

75. See "Customer Conversations: The Benefits of Being a Good Listener" (1993), *Brandweek,* February 15, 30–31.

76. This example is discussed in Rymon, Talia, Jehoshua Eliashberg, and Thomas. S. Robertson (1996), "When Should You Believe Your Competitor's Announcement?," Working Paper, Graduate School of Industrial Administration, Carnegie-Mellon University.

77. *Ibid.*

78. For example, see Anderson, Norman H., and A. Jacobson (1965), "Effect of Stimulus Inconsistency and Discounting Instructions in Personality Impression Formation," *Journal of Personality and Social Psychology* 2, 531–539.

79. See Hoch, Stephen J., and John Deighton (1989), "Managing What Consumers Learn from Experience," *Journal of Marketing* 53 (April): 1–20, for a more complete discussion.

80. See, for example, Hofer, Charles W., and Dan Schendel (1977), *Strategy Formulation: Analytical Concepts,* St. Paul, MN: West Publishing.

81. See Stevenson, Howard H. (1976), "Defining Corporate Strengths and Weaknesses," *Sloan Management Review* (Spring): 51–68.

82. See Glazer, Rashi, Joel H. Steckel, and Russell S. Winer (1992), "Locally Rational Decision Making: The Distracting Effect of Information on Managerial Performance," *Management Science* 38 (February): 212–226.

83. The self-serving bias is discussed extensively in Fiske, Susan T., and Shelley E. Taylor (1991), *Social Cognition,* 2nd ed., New York: McGraw-Hill.

84. The self-serving bias is demonstrated for marketing decision making by Curren, Mary T., Valerie S. Folkes, and Joel H. Steckel (1992), "Explanations for Successful and Unsuccessful Marketing Decisions: The Decision Maker's Perspective," *Journal of Marketing* 56 (April): 18–31.

85. This is demonstrated by Fischoff, Baruch (1977), "Cognitive Liabilities and Product Liability," *Journal of Products Liability* 1, 207–220.

86. See Bazerman, Max (1990), *Judgment in Managerial Decision Making,* 2nd ed., New York: Wiley.

87. Modified from Einhorn and Hogarth (1987), "Decision Making," 68.

88. See Pollack, Andrew (1996), "Remaking Sony, Bit by Bit," *New York Times,* May 19, Section 3, 1.

89. See *Business Week* (1992), "Tastes Yucky, Sells Like Hotcakes," May 18, 56.

Bibliography

Aaker, David A. (1989), "Managing Assets and Skills: The Key to a Sustainable Competitive Advantage," *California Management Review* (Winter): 91–106.

Aaker, David A. (1991), *Managing Brand Equity,* New York: Free Press.

Aaker, David A. (1995), *Strategic Market Management,* 4th ed., New York: Wiley.

Aaker, David A., and Kevin L. Keller (1990), "Consumer Evaluations of Brand Extensions," *Journal of Marketing* 54 (January): 27–41.

Abell, Derek F., and John S. Hammond (1979), *Strategic Market Planning,* Englewood Cliffs, NJ: Prentice-Hall, 131–132.

Agarwal, Manoj K., and Vithala R. Rao (1996), "An Empirical Comparison of Consumer-Based Measures of Brand Equity," *Marketing Letters,* 7: 3, 237–247.

"Ah Canada" (1994), *Forbes,* January 3, 74.

Anderson, Norman H., and A. Jacobson (1965), "Effect of Stimulus Inconsistency and Discounting Instructions in Personality Impression Formation," *Journal of Personality and Social Psychology* 2, 531–539.

Ansoff, H. Igor (1988), *The New Corporate Strategy,* New York: Wiley.

Bazerman, Max (1990), *Judgment in Managerial Decision Making,* 2nd ed., New York: Wiley.

Boynton, Andrew C., and Robert W. Zmud (1984), "An Assessment of Critical Success Factors," *Sloan Management Review* 25 (Summer): 17–27.

"Brand Equity" (1993), *Brandweek,* June 28, 20–24.

"Brands: It's Thrive or Die" (1993), *Fortune,* August 23, 52–56.

"Brands on the Run" (1993), *Business Week,* April 19, 26–29.

Buaron, Roberto (1981), "How to Win the Market-Share Game? Try Changing the Rules," *Management Review* 70 (January): 8–19.

Buzzell, Robert D., and Bradley T. Gale (1987), *The PIMS Principles: Linking Strategy to Performance,* New York: Free Press.

Collis, David J., and Cynthia A. Montgomery (1995), "Competing on Resources: Strategy in the 1990s," *Harvard Business Review* 73 (July–August), 118–128.

"Computers: They're No Commodity" (1993), *The Wall Street Journal,* October 15, B1.

Cooper, Robert G. (1979), "The Dimensions of Industrial New Product Success and Failure," *Journal of Marketing* 43 (Summer): 93–103.

Cooper, Robert G. (1992), "The NewProd System: The Industry Experience," *Journal of Product Innovation Management* 9 (June): 113–127.

Curren, Mary T., Valerie S. Folkes, and Joel H. Steckel (1992), "Explanations for Successful and Unsuccessful Marketing Decisions: The Decision Maker's Perspective," *Journal of Marketing* 56 (April): 18–31.

"Customer Conversations: The Benefits of Being a Good Listener" (1993), *Brandweek,* February 15, 30–31.

Day, George S. (1990), *Market Driven Strategy: Processes for Creating Value,* New York: Free Press.

Day, George S., and David B. Montgomery (1983), "Diagnosing the Experience Curve," *Journal of Marketing* 47 (Spring): 44–58.

Day, George S., and Robin Wensley (1988), "Assessing Advantage: A Framework for Diagnosing Competitive Strategy," *Journal of Marketing* 92 (April): 1–20.

Einhorn, Hillel J., and Robin M. Hogarth (1987), "Decision Making: Going Forward in Reverse," *Harvard Business Review* 65 (January-February): 66–70.

"EMI and the CT Scanner (B)" (1983), Intercollegiate Case Clearing House #9-383-195, Boston, MA: Harvard Business School.

Fischoff, Baruch (1977), "Cognitive Liabilities and Product Liability," *Journal of Products Liability* 1, 207–220.

Fiske, Susan T., and Shelley E. Taylor (1991), *Social Cognition,* 2nd ed., New York: McGraw-Hill.

Garvin, David A. (1984), "What Does 'Product Quality' Really Mean?," *Sloan Management Review* 25 (Fall): 25–43.

Glazer, Rashi, Joel H. Steckel, and Russell S. Winer (1992), "Locally Rational Decision Making: The Distracting Effect of Information on Managerial Performance," *Management Science* 38 (February): 212–226.

Golder, Peter N., and Gerard J. Tellis (1993), "Pioneer Advantage: Marketing Logic or Marketing Legend?," *Journal of Marketing Research* 30 (May): 158–170.

"Grand Met's New CEO Emphasizes Premium Brands" (1993), *The Wall Street Journal,* October 7, B4.

Guadagni, Peter M., and John D. C. Little (1983), "A Logit Model of Brand Choice Calibrated on Scanner Data," *Marketing Science* 2 (Summer): 203–238.

Hammermesh, Richard G., M. Jack Anderson, Jr., and J. Elizabeth Harris (1978), "Strategies for Low Market Share Businesses," *Harvard Business Review* 56 (May-June): 95–102.

Hoch, Stephen J., and John Deighton (1989), "Managing What Consumers Learn from Experience," *Journal of Marketing* 53 (April): 1–20.

Hofer, Charles W., and Dan Schendel (1977), *Strategy Formulation: Analytical Concepts,* St. Paul, MN: West Publishing.

"Hot Products" (1993), *Business Week,* June 7, 54–57.

Karnani, Aneel (1982), "Equilibrium Market Share—A Measure of Competitive Strength," *Strategic Management Journal* 3, 43–51.

Kerin, Roger A., Vijay Mahajan, and P. Rajan Varadarajan (1990), *Contemporary Perspectives on Strategic Market Planning,* Boston: Allyn and Bacon.

Kerin, Roger A., P. Rajan Varadarajan, and Robert A. Peterson (1992), "First-Mover Advantage: A Synthesis, Conceptual Framework, and Research Propositions," *Journal of Marketing* 56 (October): 33–52.

Kiechel, Walter (1981), "The Decline of the Experience Curve," *Fortune* 105 (October): 139–146.

"Laptops Take Off" (1991), *Business Week,* March 18, 118–124.

Lehmann, Donald R., and Russell S. Winer (1991), *Analysis for Marketing Planning,* 2nd ed., Homewood, IL: Irwin.

Levitt, Theodore (1980), "Marketing Success through Differentiation—of Anything," *Harvard Business Review* 58 (January-February): 83–91.

Lieberman, Marvin B., and David B. Montgomery (1988), "First-Mover Advantages," *Strategic Management Journal* 9, 41–58.

MacAvoy, Robert E. (1987), "Establishing Superior Performance Through Competitive Analysis," in *Strategic Planning and Management Handbook,* William R. King and David I. Clelland (eds.), New York: van Nostrand.

"Making Quality More than a Fad" (1992), *Fortune,* May 18.

McFadden, Daniel (1974), "Conditional Logit Analysis of Qualitative Choice Behavior," in *Frontiers in Econometrics,* P. Zarembka (ed.), New York: Academic Press, 105–142.

Mehotra, Sunil (1984), "How to Measure Marketing Productivity," *Journal of Advertising Research* 24 (June-July): 9–15.

National Institute of Standards and Technology (1991), Malcolm Baldrige National Quality Award, Application Guidelines.

"Note on the Motorcycle Industry—1975" (1978), Intercollegiate Case Clearing House #9-578-210, Boston, MA: Harvard Business School.

Parasuraman, A., Valerie A. Zeithaml, and Leonard L. Berry (1988), "SERVQUAL: A Multiple-Item Scale for Measuring Consumer Perceptions of Service Quality," *Journal of Retailing* 64 (Spring): 12–40.

Perspectives on Experience (1968), Boston, MA: Boston Consulting Group, Inc.

Pessemier, Edgar, Philip Burger, Richard Teach, and Douglas Tigert (1971), "Using Laboratory Brand Preference Scales to Predict Consumer Brand Purchases," *Management Science* 17 (February): B371–B385.

Pollack, Andrew (1996), "Remaking Sony, Bit by Bit," *New York Times,* May 19, Section 3, 1.

Porter, Michael E. (1980), *Competitive Strategy,* New York: Free Press.

Porter, Michael E. (1985), *Competitive Advantage,* New York: Free Press.

Prahalad, C. K., and Gary A. Hamel (1990), "The Role of Core Competencies of the Corporation," *Harvard Business Review* 68 (May-June): 79–91.

Rockart, John F. (1979), "Chief Executives Define their Own Data Needs," *Harvard Business Review* 57 (March-April): 81–93.

Rymon, Talia, Jehoshua Eliashberg, and Thomas S. Robertson (1996), "When Should You Believe Your Competitor's Announcement?," Working Paper,

Graduate School of Industrial Administration, Carnegie-Mellon University.

Sallanave, J. P. (1976), *Experience Analysis for Industrial Planning,* Lexington, MA: Lexington Books.

"Saturn: Labor's Love Lost?" (1993), *Business Week,* February 8, 122–123.

Solomon, Steven D. (1995), "American Express Applies for a New Line of Credit," *New York Times Magazine,* July 30, 35–47.

Stevens, S. (1951), "Mathematics, Measurement, and Psychophysics," in *Handbook of Experimental Psychology,* S. Stevens (ed.), New York: Wiley, 1.

Stevenson, Howard H. (1976), "Defining Corporate Strengths and Weaknesses," *Sloan Management Review* (Spring): 51–68.

Sultan, Fareena, and Thomas J. Kosnik (1989), "Marketing Situation Assessment," Cambridge, MA: Harvard Business School Case #9-590-006, 17–18.

"Tastes Yucky, Sells Like Hotcakes" (1992), *Business Week,* May 18, 56.

Tellis, Gerard J., and Peter N. Golder (1996), "First to Market, First to Fail? Real Causes of Enduring Market Leadership," *Sloan Management Review* 37 (Winter): 65–75.

"Texas Instruments' Global Chip Payoff" (1995), *Business Week,* August 7, 64–66.

"The Hunt for Mr. X: Who Can Run IBM?" (1993), *Fortune,* February 22, 68–71.

"The Shape of a New Machine" (1995), *Business Week,* July 24, 60–66.

"Too Many Think the Bunny is Duracell's, Not Eveready's," (1990), *The Wall Street Journal,* July 31, B1.

Tully, Shawn (1993), "Can Boeing Reinvent Itself?," *Fortune,* March 8, 66–73.

Urban, Glen L., and John R. Hauser (1993), *Design and Marketing of New Products,* 2nd ed., Englewood Cliffs, NJ: Prentice-Hall.

Vasconcellos, Jorge Alberto Sousa De (1991), "Key Success Factors in Marketing Mature Products," *Industrial Marketing Management* 20, 1–16.

Wang, Clement K., and Paul D. Guild (1995), "The Strategic Use of Organization Competencies and Backcasting in Competitive Analysis," ISBM Report 7-1995, Institute for the Study of Business Markets, Smeal College of Business Administration, Penn State University.

"Xerox Corporation: The Customer Satisfaction Program" (1991), Harvard Business School Case #9-591-055, Boston, MA.

Zeithaml, Valerie A., A. Parasuaman, and Leonard L. Berry (1990), *Delivering Quality Service: Balancing Customer Perceptions and Expectations,* New York: Free Press.

8 Resource Allocation Methods

INTRODUCTION

The implementation of almost any marketing strategy involves determining the magnitude of the resource commitment and its allocation to competing means of accomplishing the strategy. For example, when a firm decides to introduce a new brand in an existing product category, it needs to determine the marketing budget for the new product as well as the budget allocated to various marketing mix elements such as product design, advertising, and trade support. In a general sense, one may view the task of strategic decision making to be one of allocation of resources.

Typically, a corporation markets several brands, some of which may compete with each other because they are intended to serve similar customers' needs. Such brands may be grouped into a product category. In the case of the Chevrolet division, the product categories may be vans, sedans, coupes, and hatchbacks. Within each product category, the division may market multiple brands of automobiles, such as Corsica and Beretta. In general, such categories are managed as *strategic business units (SBUs).**

A corporation can be thought of as a collection of product categories or strategic business units. Thus, the resource allocation problem generally involves allocating resources among various SBUs of a company and among various brands within each SBU. Further, the problem also involves determining resources for existing versus new projects (that may lead to either new SBUs or new brands within existing SBUs).

To appreciate the complexities involved in resource allocation, consider a hypothetical firm that markets four brands in two product categories, P and Q. We call the category P brands A and B and the category Q brands C and D. We also assume that the two product categories are managed as parts of two divisions within the firm. Given this structure, four decision-making levels will be of interest in the management of these brands within the corporation: top management level, divisional level,

---

*We use the term *strategic business unit* interchangeably with *product category,* although there are some differences between the two. We discuss the concept of SBU more formally in the next section.

middle level (or product category level), and brand level. The procedure may be more complex in a large, multidivisional corporation such as General Motors. Top management at GM may essentially deal with determining the level of resources for each division (Chevrolet, Buick, Cadillac, Saturn, and Pontiac), leaving the responsibility of allocating them within the division to the general manager of each division. The general manager will in turn allocate resources between existing and new businesses.) The major responsibilities of each level follow:

Level	Resource Allocation Responsibility
Top	Determination of the level of resources between existing product categories as a group and research and development for possible new products
Division level	Allocation of funds for the existing product categories between the two divisions
Category level	Allocation of funds for the division between the brands within it
Brand level	Allocation of the predetermined resources among the elements of marketing mix for a given brand

This example illustrates the fact that the unit of analysis (product category or brand) chosen for determining resource allocation will naturally depend on the managerial level at which such decisions are made. While product category is the unit at the division level, the brand is the unit at the category level of management.

At the firmwide level, strategic decisions are made about the specific product/markets the firm wishes to enter, wishes to support in the future, and wishes to reduce its support of or even withdraw from entirely. Decisions at this level define the general constraints within which mid-level marketing managers allocate resources for both the long and short term. Decisions at this level of the firm may also enhance the level of aggregate support for an individual product/market. As an example, one may view PepsiCo's decision to acquire Frito-Lay as enabling PepsiCo to expand its resource base, which helped build its other businesses, such as restaurants.

Once the level of total marketing resources for a particular business (that is, product/market) has been decided upon, the allocation problem becomes one of deciding the amounts to be spent on each of the competing elements in the marketing mix. These include not only advertising, the sales force, trade support, and consumer promotion, but also the expenditures necessary to maintain and improve the product and service quality associated with the business.

Three significant factors need to be included in this allocation task: (1) the interdependence between one product/market and another, (2) the interdependence of the effects of any expenditures over time, and (3) the interdependence of expenditures among the elements of the marketing mix. Consideration of these interdependencies is extremely critical to maintain the strategic advantage of each business.

Further, decisions concerning resource allocation must explicitly take into account the nature and degree of competition for the respective business (product/market). Intense competition is likely to erode the benefits of marketing expenditures. First, the firm ought to consider the overall environment in which the business is likely to operate in the future—an understanding achieved by careful analysis of the threats and opportunities faced. If the threats are serious, the firm may wish to devote a portion of the allocated resource to deal with threats from future entrants, technological developments, and potential supplier and intermediary behavior. For example, Procter & Gamble may need to increase advertising expenditures in the detergent category (for several major brands such as Tide and Cheer) if the competition from Lever Brothers becomes more intense due to either introduction of a new brand of detergent or an expanded advertising campaign for its existing brands (Surf or Wisk). P&G may also need to allocate more resources to its detergents if new private label brands are likely to appear on the market.

Even if the external environment is favorable to the growth of the business, the firm needs to consider the intensity of competition within the industry as well as within various submarkets in which it competes. When Condé Nast acquired the magazine *Architectural Digest* in 1993, it needed to shut down publication of *House and Garden* due to the significant overlap in competing for advertisers.[1] This example illustrates competition within a market segment and its effects on overall resource allocation.

The actual decision-making process may involve negotiations at various levels within the organization. The process is usually iterative. Plans drawn at a lower level (say, at the brand level) may be aggregated bottom up to arrive at the total level of resources called for. After consideration of various constraints, adjustments may be made. Alternatively, the decision-making process may be totally hierarchical. Here, the unit at the lower level may be given a level of resources to be allocated top down among its competing demands. In general, either procedure may be suboptimal for the firm because it may ignore market-level responses. Further, the decision-making process at each level will need to consider any potential synergistic effects associated with any allocation between competing demands.

Resource allocation decisions are also made between existing products and new opportunities within various product markets not currently served by the firm. Furthermore, new opportunities may reside within existing strategic business units or lead to the creation of new SBUs. The procedures for such an allocation are not as precise as those for allocating a given marketing resource among different elements of the marketing mix; this is due to the inherent uncertainties involved in predicting the success of research and development activities.

A streamlined procedure for marketing resource allocation consists of the following steps:

1. The firm needs to determine the total amount of resources that could be expended on all of its current and future businesses in a given time period (for example, one year).
2. The total resources need to be allocated between existing businesses and future businesses under development.
3. The resources determined for existing businesses need to be allocated to each.
4. The expenditure on an existing business needs to be allocated to various marketing mix elements; if the business consists of multiple brands, resources should first be allocated among the brands.

The enormous importance of new products for the continued success of any firm requires management to consider the allocation to future businesses via research and development. The objective is to determine both magnitude and allocation of resources so as to maximize overall profit for the firm. This procedure requires a clear knowledge of the market response function at all levels of the firm. These market responses must ultimately be built up from those of brands to any level in the firm.

Against this background, this chapter will describe several methods of analysis for allocating marketing resources. First, we discuss general principles of resource allocation. Second, we discuss methods for allocating resources among various product categories (or SBUs) of a firm. These include five different approaches: graphical product portfolio approaches; the mathematical portfolio method, STRATPORT; methods based on pooled business experience (PIMS, ADVISOR); methods using the analytic hierarchy process (AHP); and methods that use elasticities computed from market response functions. Third, we consider methods for allocating resources among brands within a SBU. Next, we will consider methods for allocating resources among mix elements for a brand. These methods include the use of elasticities computed from the marketing response function for a brand, techniques based on pooled business experience, and AHP. Finally, we will describe approaches for allocating resources among geographic territories for a brand, a product category, or the firm as a whole.

In principle, the methods for allocating resources among different brands within a SBU are similar to those for allocating resources among different SBUs. In some product categories, the interdependence among brands may be very significant and cannot be ignored. The problem of interdependence is not likely to be critical when allocating resources among different product categories.

PRINCIPLES OF RESOURCE ALLOCATION

The general principle of allocating any resource to competing elements is quite simple. The resources allocated to each competing element should be such that the marginal benefits expected are equal for all. In general, marginal benefits associated with any resource will diminish as more of that resource is invested. Therefore, if the marginal benefits are not equal, the firm may increase or decrease expenditures on those elements with lower (or higher) marginal benefits to increase overall benefit. When the allocation across competing elements results in equal marginal benefits, any departure will necessarily decrease the total benefit, rendering the new allocation suboptimal. Thus, the major task is to determine the marginal benefit after taking into account various factors already identified. When one considers the resource allocation problem at the level of a particular business (say, a brand), marginal benefits are essentially determined by the market response function for that brand.

Fig. 8.1 shows various determinants of market response to a set of marketing mix decisions (which are effectively the result of allocation of resources) for one brand. The relationship between market response and its determinants (marketing

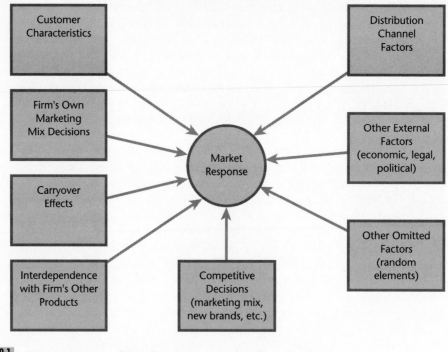

FIGURE 8.1   **Determinants of Market Response for One Product**

mix decisions for the brand and competing brands, customer characteristics, other environmental factors, and so on) is called the *market response function*. Response functions can be conceptualized at three levels of aggregation: for a single brand in a product category, for all brands marketed by the firm in a particular category, and for all product categories marketed by the firm. The specific response for a brand depends not only on the firm's actions, but also on competitors' and conditions in the environment. The total amount of marketing resources and their optimal allocations will thus be contingent on the firm's expectations of competitive behavior and assumptions regarding other determinants of market response.

The foregoing discussion should indicate that the task of determining optimal resource levels and allocations is quite intricate, particularly when the firm has no specific knowledge of market response functions. The methods discussed in this chapter range from rules using market response functions (if the firm has them) to heuristic methods that provide approximate solutions. These include product portfolio methods and pooled experience rules. Further, the analytic hierarchy process (AHP) methodology, which tackles large-scale decision problems using judgmental data collected from decision makers, can be adapted to this problem. We offer a taxonomy of these methods in Table 8.1. The methods fall into five broad categories:

TABLE 8.1   **A Taxonomy of Different Methods for Allocating Marketing Resources**

Task of Allocating	Market Response Functions Are	
	Not Used	Used
I. Resources among different product categories	• Several graphical product portfolio methods • AHP	• Methods based on elasticities • STRATPORT
II. Resources among multiple brands of a product category	• AHP • Conjoint analysis	• Methods based on elasticities
III. Resources among marketing mix elements for one brand	• AHP • Conjoint analysis	• Methods based on elasticities • Based on pooled business experience
IV. Resources among different geographical territories for a brand		• Methods based on elasticities

- Optimal methods that use elasticities* calculated from market response functions.
- Several graphical product portfolio methods that attempt to simplify the problem, usually to two composite dimensions.
- STRATPORT, a mathematical portfolio method that uses market response functions and mathematical programming techniques.
- Methods that use the analytic hierarchy process, which attempts to decompose and synthesize executive judgments on various relevant dimensions of the allocation problem.
- Methods that use conjoint analysis of selected judgmental data.

Further, Table 8.1 identifies four major tasks in the allocation problem: allocating resources at the firm level among different product categories; allocating resources among multiple brands of a product category; allocating resources among marketing mix elements for one brand; and allocating resources among different geographic territories for a brand, product category, or number of categories. We have indicated how suitable these methods are for each of the tasks depending on the use or nonuse of market response functions. We must also note that even the

---

*When one marketing mix variable, x (price), affects the market response, y (sales in units), price elasticity of sales measures the percent change in sales for 1 percent change in price; it is usually negative. Similarly, advertising elasticity of sales measures the percent change in sales for a 1 percent change in advertising expenditures and is usually positive. Because it is a ratio of two percent changes, elasticity is a "unit-free" measure. It can be used to compare responses of expenditures of two different marketing mix variables, such as advertising and sales force expenditures.

optimal methods that use elasticities may require some adjustments to accommodate additional (usually conjectural) available information on competitive behavior and other environmental factors.

For a given level of resources, these methods provide guidance on how to allocate resources among competing means. But the allocation process can be repeated for various levels of total resources, and the level for which the corporate objective (profit) is the highest can be deemed the appropriate level for consideration. Of course, financial and other constraints on the firm will have a major influence on the ultimate level of resources to be devoted to a brand or product category.

METHODS FOR ALLOCATING RESOURCES AMONG SBUs

In this section, our focus will be on techniques for allocating resources among a firm's various SBUs. These methods can also be used for allocating resources for both existing and new opportunities. The general premise is that a firm is better off seeking a balance among the competing demands on its resources.

At the outset, we should note that the problem of allocating resources among various SBUs can also be handled using finance-oriented models such as the risk-return model.[2] But this approach requires additional data on discount rates and market indexes and requires calculation of financial return for each SBU. These details are not easy to compile and are normally inaccessible to a marketing member of a corporation. It is also not clear whether the assumptions of finance theory required for diversification of stocks in an individual's portfolio are satisfied when the risk-return model is applied to the case of SBUs of a particular firm. Given these considerations, we will not delve into this set of methods for resource allocation.

As noted earlier, we describe methods for allocating resources among the various SBUs of a corporation: graphical portfolio methods, mathematical portfolio methods, and the analytic hierarchy process. The firm may not have knowledge of the market response functions for each SBU or product category and that this lack of knowledge calls for the use of other methods to yield approximate answers.

While portfolio methods attempt to compare the demands on resources of one SBU versus another in the same firm, the methods based on pooled business experience try to compare an SBU of a firm with corresponding SBUs in a large number of firms. They attempt to measure how the firm's SBU is performing versus a standard or par developed from the experience of other companies. This approach does not assume that the behavior of the various firms whose experience is pooled is necessarily optimal, although it does assume that it is reasonable. Also, both methods try to use objective data on sales and costs.

The AHP methodology determines the relative attractiveness of competing resources from judgmental data provided by key managers of the firm; these judgments relate to the general objective of maximizing overall profitability of the firm. The portfolio methods and pooled business experience methods can be thought of as standardized approaches, while AHP can be thought of as a customized approach.

Criteria for Defining SBUs

It should be quite clear that the methods of portfolio analysis require a clear definition of a strategic business unit (SBU). The following criteria are relevant for defining an SBU:

- An SBU must serve an *external* rather than internal market. The profitability of the SBU must be able to be measured in real income rather than in artificial dollars posted as transfer payments.

- An SBU should serve distinct groups of *customers* different from those served by other SBUs and should have a distinct set of external competitors it is trying to equal or surpass.

- The managers of an SBU should have control over the key factors that determine success in their served market and utilize shared resources.

- An SBU should be *strategically autonomous.*

GRAPHICAL PORTFOLIO METHODS

The problem of allocating resources among several SBUs of a firm has received the attention of managers for several years.[3] Several consulting companies have developed techniques for this. Whether these methods will stand the scrutiny of rigorous analysis is debatable; but the methods seem to have significant face value and appear to give reasonable direction to management for allocating resources.

Fundamentally, these methods are based on two criteria: attractiveness of the market in which a SBU is located and relative market position of the SBU in the industry. The premise is that those SBUs in more attractive industries and weaker market positions should receive higher allocation of resources, while the SBUs operating in less attractive industries with stronger market positions should get the level required to maintain the existing market position. Many of the methods make recommendations to withdraw or reduce support for those SBUs with weaker market positions in less attractive industries.

Two empirical phenomena are used to generally support these guidelines: the product life cycle for a given industry or SBU and the experience curve for cost reduction over time due to accumulated production. These ideas were initially formulated by the Boston Consulting Group (BCG) using simpler operationalizations of the two constructs: market attractiveness was measured by growth rate and market position by relative market share. Refinements to this simpler approach have been made over the years, resulting in several paradigms for allocating resources.[4] We delve into these in this section.

Assumptions

Graphical portfolio methods are based on the following critical assumptions. In reality, all of these assumptions may not be satisfied in a specific situation:

- All managers of various products/divisions share the same corporate goals. In fact, any manager is willing to make his or her business goals subservient to the overall corporate goals.
- All managers agree that opportunities in various product markets vary at any one point in time and over time.
- There is sufficient information on the major competitors to each business, and the respective market structures have been clearly identified. Presumably, various methods we described in the previous chapters have been utilized to obtain a clear picture of competition and market structure.
- Production cost functions for the products are known and fixed costs have been allocated in an amicable manner across the various products.

We focus on four representative approaches: the BCG; Business Assessment Array—also called GE's Business Screen (industry attractiveness/competitive business position matrix); Shell's Directional Policy Matrix; and the Life Cycle Portfolio Matrix. We now turn to a brief description of these approaches.

Measuring Market Share

A significant question in using portfolio methods is how to define market share for the SBU in question. The measurement of market share depends critically on the definition of the particular market or segment in which the SBU competes. This impacts the denominator in:

$$\text{market share} = \frac{\text{company sales}}{\text{market sales relationship}}.$$

Actual measure will vary according to the units of measurement and definition of product.

As an example, consider the following 1986 U.S. soft-drink data.[5]

Rank	Brand	Market Share (based on quantity consumed)
1	Coke Classic	18.9%
2	Pepsi	18.5
3	Diet Coke	7.1
4	Diet Pepsi	4.3
5	Dr. Pepper	4.1
6	Sprite	3.6
7	7-Up	3.5
8	Mountain Dew	2.6
9	Coke	2.3
10A	RC	1.7
10B	Cherry Coke	1.7
	Other brands	31.7

From these data, it is clear that the total share of all brands marketed by the Coca-Cola Company in the soft drink market is 33.6 percent (= 18.9 + 7.1 + 3.6 + 2.3 + 1.7), the share of the cola submarket is 54.5 percent (18.9 + 18.5 + 7.1 + 4.3 + 2.3 + 1.7 + 1.7), and the share of the Coke brand in the cola submarket is 55 percent (= 30.0 ÷ 54.5). Similarly, the share of Coca-Cola in the direct diet segment of the market is 62 percent [= 7.1 ÷ (7.1 + 4.3)]. Thus, the actual value of market share depends on the base used.

The BCG Business Portfolio Matrix (Growth-Share Matrix)

This approach involves computing two indices for each SBU: its relative market share and the growth rate of its market.

The SBUs can be classified into one of four cells: stars—high market growth and high relative share; question marks—high market growth and low relative market share; cash cows—low market growth and high market share; and dogs—low market growth and low market share. Given this classification, some prescriptions are given the allocation of resources; for example, injection of new resources, withdrawal of support, or even withdrawal of the SBU itself from the market. Our view of these prescriptions is shown in Fig. 8.2.

From the firm's perspective, all SBUs are plotted in a graph that looks like the two panels shown in Fig. 8.3. The portfolio of products for the firm depicted in the first panel is more balanced than that in the second panel. Although both of these firms have ten products each, the firm in the top panel has four products—A, B, C, and D—in the star category compared with two products—a and b—for the second firm. Also, each of the four products of the first firm seems to offer greater potential than the two corresponding products for the second firm. Further, the second firm has more products (four versus two) in the cash cow category, which implies that it could generate cash to improve its position in the two question mark products—g and h. But the possibility of improving the position of the question mark products of the first firm—G and H—is greater because they are in relatively more attractive (higher growth) markets. Also, the second firm may find it more difficult to divest its two dogs because of the less attractive market growth rates may reduce the number of potential buyers. All of these judgments imply that the first firm is likely to have more significant growth in the longer term than the second. One may conclude that the first firm's product portfolio is more balanced than the second firm's.[6]

Business Assessment Array

This approach is also known as GE's Business Screen. It is also based on two factors: industry attractiveness and competitive business position. Industry attractiveness is an expanded version of the BCG relative market growth concept. The competitive business position factor measures the firm's ability to compete in the market, a notion much broader than simple relative market share. The score for each factor is computed using a number of variables. For industry attractiveness, the variables include market growth, market size, market cyclicity, market concentration, technological maturity, and competitive concentration. For business position, such variables as advantage in technology,

	Relative Market Share	
	High	Low
High **Market Growth Rate** **Low**	**Stars:** Maintain share by reinvesting earnings in price reductions, product refinement, advertising, and personal selling to discourage competitive entry. Stars become cash cows as the product matures. *	**Question Marks:** Invest in market-segmentation strategies, thereby reducing competition and increasing share or reduce further marketing investment and let the product drop to the dog category. ?
	Cash Cows: "Milk" the cash out of the product by investing in marketing only enough to maintain market share. The product is now too late in its life cycle for a strong competitive entry. $	**Dogs:** Move the dogs into the cash cow category if the returns exceed the coast of an effective segmentation strategy or prepare to drop the product. Drop the product. X

FIGURE 8.2   **Classification of Products and Recommendations according to the BCG Matrix**

advantage in marketing, advantage in production, size, and market share are used. Specific variables to be included will naturally depend upon the industry context. The complete lists of variables for computing the two factors are shown in Table 8.2.

The matrix is applied as follows. The analyst computes values of these two factors for each of the firm's products by taking the weighted sum of scores given on the relevant variables. The analyst then classifies them into the 3×3 table shown in Fig. 8.4. The range of each factor is divided into three equal intervals; these intervals determine the high, medium, and low categories for the industry attractiveness factor and the strong, medium, and weak categories for the competitive business position. The SBUs falling into the (high/strong) cell are recommended for additional investment and growth of the corresponding businesses. The SBUs in the medium/strong or high/medium cell are carefully considered for growth; therefore, they are called the selective growth category. The SBUs in the diagonal cells—high/weak, medium/medium and low/strong—are recommended for careful analysis of their market segment, and investments are recommended for strengthening the firm's position in some segments and letting it weaken in others. It is recommended that the SBUs in the three

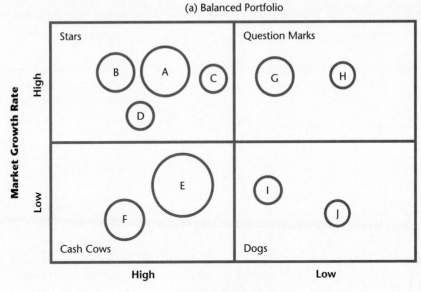

(a) Balanced Portfolio

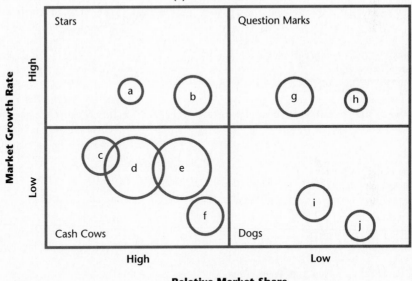

(b) Unbalanced Portfolio

FIGURE 8.3 **Examples of Balanced and Unbalanced Portfolios**

other cells—medium/weak, low/medium, and low/weak—either be harvested (by withdrawing current investments or not increasing current rates of investment) or be divested altogether. These resource allocation prescriptions are also shown in Fig. 8.4.

| TABLE 8.2 | **Factors Contributing to Market Attractiveness and Business Position** |

Attractiveness of Your Market	Status Position of Your Business
Market Factors	
Size (dollars, units, or both)	Your share (in equivalent terms)
Size of key segments	Your share of key segments
Growth rate per year:	Your annual growth rate:
Total	Total
Segments	Segments
Diversity of market	Diversity of your participation
Sensitivity to price, service features, and external factors	Your influence on the market
Cyclicity	Lags or leads in your sales
Seasonality	
Bargaining power of upstream suppliers	Bargaining power of your suppliers
Bargaining power of downstream suppliers	Bargaining power of your customers
Competition	
Types of competitors	Where you fit: how you compare in terms of
Degree of concentration	products, marketing capability, service,
Changes in type and mix	production strength, financial strength,
Entries and exits	management
Changes in share	Segments you have entered or left
Substitution by new technology	Your relative share change
Degrees and types of integration	Your vulnerability to new technology
	Your own level of integration
Financial and Economic Factors	
Contribution margins	Your margins
Leveraging factors, such as economies of scale	Your scale and experience
and experience	
Barriers to entry or exit (both financial and nonfinancial)	Barriers to your entry or exit (both
Capacity utilization	financial and nonfinancial)
	Your capacity utilization
Technological Factors	
Maturity and volatility	Your ability to cope with change
Complexity	Depths of your skills
Differentiation	Types of your technological skills
Patents and copyrights	Your patent protection
Manufacturing process technology required	Your manufacturing technology
Sociopolitical Factors in Your Environment	
Social attitudes and trends	Your company's responsiveness and flexibility
Laws and government agency regulations	Your company's ability to cope
Influence with pressure groups and government	Your company's aggressiveness
representatives	Your company's relationships
Human factors, such as unionization and community	
acceptances	

Source: Abel, Derek F., and John S. Hammond (1979), *Strategic Market Planning*, Englewood Cliffs, NJ: Prentice-Hall.

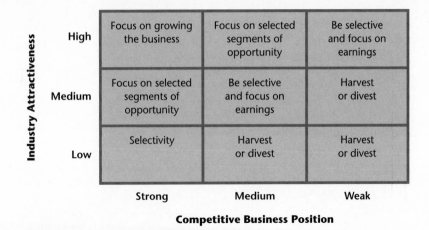

	Strong	Medium	Weak
High	Focus on growing the business	Focus on selected segments of opportunity	Be selective and focus on earnings
Medium	Focus on selected segments of opportunity	Be selective and focus on earnings	Harvest or divest
Low	Selectivity	Harvest or divest	Harvest or divest

Industry Attractiveness (vertical axis)

Competitive Business Position

FIGURE 8.4   **Business Assessment Array**

As can be seen, this approach uses more variables than the BCG approach. (We illustrate this approach in Appendix 8A.)

The Directional Policy Matrix (Shell)

This approach, developed by Shell Chemical Companies, is quite similar to the business assessment array.[7] It uses two composite factors: business sector prospects and the company's competitive capabilities. In a manner analogous to the business assessment array, these two factors are weighted sums of ratings given on several variables. Fig. 8.5 shows the components included in each composite factor. The procedure for computing these factor scores is similar to that of the business assessment array. Each variable of the factor is given from 1 to 5 stars (instead of numbers). The stars given are as follows:

Business Sector Prospects

Market Growth:
This variable is intended to measure the business sector's profit potential in the future. However, high market growth rates are not always regarded as those with high profit growth. Various other criteria that affect profit are included in this measure. The center point or average rating (three stars) is given to a business sector that is average for the broader industry in which the sector is located. The rating is adjusted using this as the benchmark.

Market Quality:
The rating on this variable uses answers to such questions as: "Has the sector a record of high, stable profitability? Can the margins be maintained when manufacturing capacity exceeds demand? Is the product resistant to commodity pricing behavior? Is the

technology of production freely available or is it restricted to those who developed it? Is the product free from the risk of substitutes of an alternative synthetic or natural product?"

Industry Feedstock Situation: This variable is an attempt to consider whether the supply of raw materials (feedstock) is likely to be stable or whether there are alternative demands from other industries for such a supply. Based on this assessment, a rating is given. In some industries, this variable is not that relevant.

Environmental (Regulatory) Aspects: This variable assesses the extent of restrictions from government on manufacture, transportation, or marketing that will affect the prospects for the business sector.

Company's Competitive Capabilities:

Market Position: Market share leader, five stars; major producer, four stars; strong and viable position, three stars; minor market share, two stars; and one star for negligible market share.

Production Capability: This variable is a combination of process economics, capacity of hardware, location and number of plants, and access to feedstock. Stars are assigned to this variable depending upon the answers to questions such as, "Does the producer employ a modern economic production process? Is it his or her own process or licensed? Has the producer secured access to enough feedstocks to sustain present market share?"

Product Research and Development: This variable is intended to measure how a customer will judge the technical package offered by the business. The five-star rating is judged on whether the company's product R&D is better than, commensurate with, or worse than its position in the market.

After each variable has been rated using the five-star scale, the total score for each factor is computed as a weighted sum of the scores on the variables. The weights are determined by the strategy analyst and are specific to the organization. Each factor is divided into three intervals as shown in Fig. 8.5. After scores for all the products of the firm have been computed, they are located in the 3×3 matrix. The approach offers prescriptions for resource allocation, as shown in the figure. For example, if a product is classified in the cell of unattractive business prospects and strong competitive capabilities for the firm, the prescription is to use the product to generate cash, some of which may be used to support products in other cells such as those with attractive business prospects and average competitive capabilities of the firm.

Business Sector Prospects

		Unattractive	Average	Attractive
Company's Competitive Capabilities	**Weak**	Disinvest	Phased withdrawal Custodial	Double or quit
	Average	Phased withdrawal	Custodial Growth	Try harder
	Strong	Cash generation	Growth Leader	Leader

Variables Included in the Dimensions

Business Sector Prospects	Company's Competitive Capabilities
Market growth rate	Market position (primarily market share)
Market quality	Production capability
Industry feedstock situation (supply of raw materials)	Product research and development
Environmental (regulatory) aspects	

FIGURE 8.5   **Directional Policy Matrix**

Source: Reprinted from *Long Range Planning,* Vol. 11, June, by S. J. Q. Robinson, R. E. Hichen, and D. P. Wade, "The Directional Policy Matrix—Tool for Strategic Planning," Copyright 1978, with kind permission from Elsevier Science Ltd, The Boulevard, Langford Lane, Kidlington OX5 1GB, UK.

Life Cycle Portfolio Matrix

The premise of A. D. Little's Life Cycle Portfolio Matrix[8] is that industries, like products, have life cycles and that the level of maturity of the business unit's industry should be important in portfolio analysis. Accordingly, this approach reduces different variables into two composite dimensions: industry maturity and competitive position. This approach distinguishes between four phases of industry maturity—embryonic, growing, maturing, and aging—and five levels of competitive position—dominant, strong, favorable, tenable, and weak. All business units of a firm are classified on these two factors and positioned in a 4×5 matrix, as shown in Fig. 8.6.

Variables included in the industry maturity factor are market growth rate, growth potential, market share distribution among the participants, stability of market share, breadth of product line in the industry, number of competitors, customer stability, ease of entry, and technological stability. Each variable is measured, and a weighted score is computed to classify industries into the four maturity categories. A similar procedure is applied to classify a business unit on a competitive position. While the specific coding scheme is not publicized, the industry maturity and competitive position categories may be described as follows:[9]

Competitive Position	Stage of Industry Maturity			
	Embryonic	Growth	Mature	Aging
Dominant	All-out push for share / Hold position	Hold position / Hold share	Hold position / Grow with industry	Hold position
Strong	Attempt to improve position / All-out push for share	Attempt to improve position / Push for share	Hold position / Grow with industry	Hold position or Harvest
Favorable	Selective or all-out push for share / Selectively attempt to improve competitive position	Attempt to improve position / Selectively push for share	Custodial or maintenance / Find niche and attempt to protect	Harvest / Phased withdrawal
Tenable	Selectively push for position	Find niche and protect it	Find niche and hang on or Phased withdrawal	Phased withdrawal or Abandon
Weak	Up / or / Out	Turnaround or Abandon	Turnaround or Phased withdrawal	Abandon

FIGURE 8.6 **The Life Cycle Portfolio Matrix**

Source: Reprinted from *Long Range Planning*, Vol. 11, April, "A Frame of Reference for Strategy Development," by P. Patel and M. Younger, Copyright 1978, with kind permission from Elsevier Science Ltd, The Boulevard, Langford Lane, Kidlington OX5 1GB, UK.

Industry Maturity

Embryonic Industry: Rapid growth, changes in technology, vigorous pursuit of new customers, and fragmented and unstable market shares

Growth Industry: Continues to exhibit rapid growth, established trends in customer purchase patterns, better-known competitors and technology, and difficulties in entering the industry

Mature Industry: Exhibits stability in customers, technology, and market shares (although the industry may still be highly competitive)

Aging Industry: Characterized by falling demand, declining number of competitors, and a narrowing of product line

Competitive Position

Dominant: This situation is extremely rare. Dominance results from a quasi-monopoly or from a strongly protected technological leadership. (An example is Intel in the microprocessor chip industry.)

Strong: Exhibited by the firm's ability to follow strategies of its choice, irrespective of its competitors. (An example may be Kellogg in the cereal industry.)

Favorable: This category is assigned to a leader in an industry that is quite fragmented, with no significant competitor.

Tenable: This category is applied to a business whose profitability can be maintained through product specialization or a niche strategy.

Weak: A position that cannot be sustained in the long term given the competitive economics of the industry. The business may be suffering from past mistakes or from a critical weakness.

Fig. 8.6 also shows proposed guidelines for resource allocation and strategies for various cells of the product life cycle matrix. For example, if the competitive position in an embryonic industry is weak, the firm has essentially two options: significantly investing to grow or divesting the business. If the position in a growing industry is strong, a selective push for market share is recommended. The recommendations in general imply changes in the resource allocations to various businesses.

An Empirical Comparison of Portfolio Models

Wind, Mahajan, and Swire examined the consistency of four standardized portfolio models in classifying 15 SBUs of a large Fortune 500 firm.[10] The models were BCG's Growth-Share Matrix; the Business Assessment Array; Shell's Directional Policy Matrix; and Modified A. D. Little (Market Share and Stage of Life Cycle), or what we called the Life Cycle Portfolio Matrix.

The authors operationalized the different constructs in these portfolio approaches using data collected from the company on its 15 businesses. First, four different definitions were used for the market growth variable: (1) average annual rate of growth, in real terms, of the served market over the past four-year period; (2) same rate as 1 but in nominal terms; (3) company's own forecast of average annual growth in real terms over the next four years; and (4) average of company's forecasts of growth in real terms over next four years and six years after that (used as an approximation of the outlook for a 10-year period).

Next, four different definitions were used for measuring market share of each business: (1) the ratio of the company's sales to the total sales of the served market; (2) the ratio of the company's sales to the total sales of the three largest competitors; (3) the ratio of the company's sales to the sales of the largest competitor; and (4) a market share index computed as the sum of the two normalized market shares—normalized market share in the served market and the normalized market share of the firm versus three leaders in the market. The result of normalization is that the mean of all market shares in the corresponding set is zero. (In the case of market share in the served market, the average of market shares of all the companies in the served market is adjusted to zero by subtracting each share from the mean. A similar procedure is followed for the second normalization.) The effect of normalization is that a market share index of zero implies that the business is pretty much like the industry, and values above zero imply that the firm is doing better than the industry.

Three other issues need to be resolved. First, some approaches are stated in terms of three or four categories on each composite dimension, while the rest are stated in terms of two categories for each. To ensure comparability, the authors used two dimensions for all approaches. The second issue deals with the rule to be used for dividing a dimension (or composite score) into high and low categories. The authors had used two methods: (1) an internal rule of classifying businesses as high (or low) on a dimension depending on whether the business is above (or below) the mean of all 15 businesses of the company; and (2) an external rule in which the cut point is the mean of all businesses in the PIMS database.* The third issue is deciding the weights to be used for computing the composite scores for the dimensions, such as industry attractiveness. The authors used two options: no weights at all and the weights determined in a PIMS PAR ROI model (which involves estimating the future ROI for a business according to the characteristics of an average or PAR business in the PIMS database).

Thus, this comparison involves a variety of ways of implementing the four approaches of portfolio analysis: all combinations of the market growth and market share computation, two ways of determining the categories on a dimension, and two options for weights. The authors compared how the 15 businesses would be classified into the four quadrants of the 2×2 matrix for each portfolio analysis approach.

This study brought out several important concerns about the standardized product portfolio models:

- Classification of an SBU depends on the operational definition used for market share and market growth.
- The rule for dividing a dimension into high or low *or* high, medium, or low is critical.
- The weighting schemes used in building a composite score can change the classification of an SBU.

Fig. 8.7 shows the results of classifying the 15 businesses for one particular way of implementing each of these four portfolio approaches. The details used in these classifications are as follows:

BCG Growth-Share Matrix: Market share versus leading competitor and real growth rate for the market over the last four years.

Business Assessment Array: Weights from the PIMS PAR ROI model for computing the two composite dimensions and mean for each dimension as the cutoff for classifying into high or low.

Directional Policy Matrix: Weights from the PIMS PAR ROI model used to compute the two composite dimensions, prospects for profitability and company's competitive capabilities. The cutoff was the mean on each dimension.

Modified A. D. Little Matrix: Market position was determined by market share (similar to the BCG matrix) and two stages of life cycle—maturity and growth—were used to describe the life cycle dimension. Using the means as the cutoff for market share, this approach also yielded a 2×2 matrix.

---

*The PIMS database consists of over 600 businesses that provided periodic data on their characteristics. We will discuss this database later in the chapter.

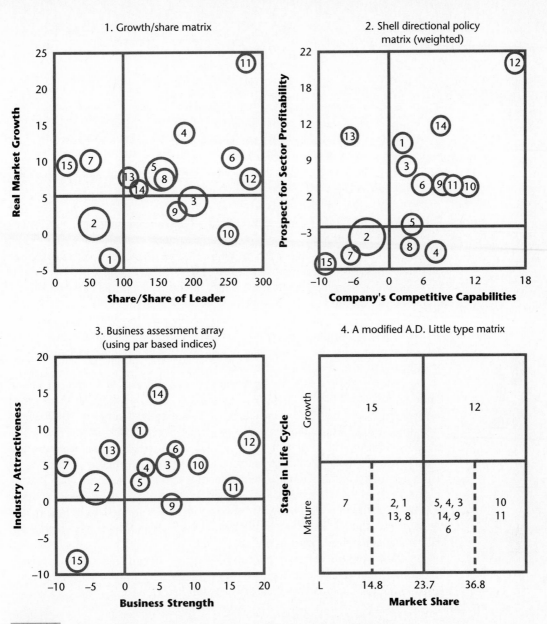

FIGURE 8.7   **A Comparison of Four Standardized Portfolio Models**

Source: From Yoram Wind, Vijay Mahajan, and Donald J. Swire, "An Empirical Comparison of Standardized Portfolio Models," *Journal of Marketing,* Vol. 47, Spring 1983, pp. 89–99. Reprinted with permission of the American Marketing Association.

The comparison of the classifications of the 15 businesses based on these four portfolio approaches showed that only one business (#12) was classified consistently. Of the remaining 14 businesses, different patterns of classification emerged as follows:

Number of Businesses	Patterns	Specific Businesses
7	high/low and high/high	3,4,5,6,9,10,11
3	low/low and low/high	2,7,15
2	low/low, high/low and high/high	8,14
1	low/low, low/high and high/high	13
1	low/low and high/high	1

Based on these, the authors concluded that each portfolio model yields classifications highly specific to it; thus it is almost impossible to replicate the results from any one approach with another approach. This means the recommendations for resource allocation will differ from one approach to another.

Evolution over Time   Suppose that a firm utilizes one portfolio approach consistently over time. In that case, it may be possible to study changes in the positions of businesses due to various resource allocation decisions. A pictorial way to depict the expected impact of specific allocations of resources to various business units is shown in Fig. 8.8 for the growth/share matrix. In this example, the likely movement of an SBU's position is well illustrated. A log-scale is used for the relative market share axis.

First, it is important to recognize that this figure represents products (or businesses) by circles and that the diameter of each circle is proportional to the product's contribution to total company sales volume.

It is interesting to see in this figure that product A, a star, was forecasted to be quite prominent. Similarly, SBU D, a question mark, is expected to grow much larger, presumably with heavy injections of marketing resources. By withdrawing investment from SBU E, the figure forecasts that it will shrink considerably. The released resources will presumably be used for developing A and D in the future. The market growth of SBU B's industry is expected to be slower, which is reflected in its being demoted from star to cash cow, although the investments are such that its market share is expected to remain stable. SBU C's industry is also expected to grow slower, indicating that it is better for the firm to milk it in the future. Finally, the figure depicts that the firm is currently better off divesting SBU G, which is essentially a dog in the firm's portfolio.

In closing this discussion of portfolio dynamics, we must caution that a considerable amount of data is necessary to develop forecasts. Our discussion of the mathematical portfolio approach indicates these requirements.

Some Developments in Portfolio Analysis

The foregoing discussion indicates the lack of consistency of results obtained from a graphical approach to portfolio analysis. This situation could be due to such factors as the reliance on at most two dimensions to describe a product or a business; relatively simple operationalizations of the dimensions chosen and limited number of variables (in most cases only one), inappropriate weights in determin-

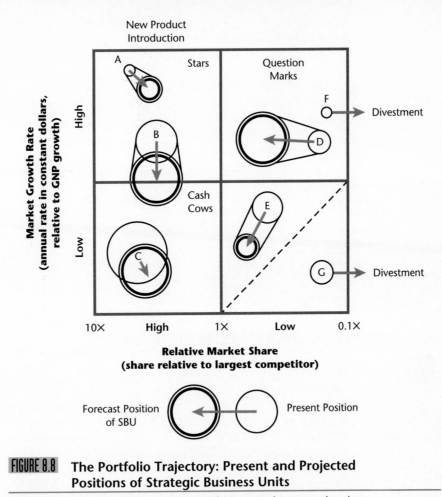

FIGURE 8.8 **The Portfolio Trajectory: Present and Projected Positions of Strategic Business Units**

Diameter of circle is proportional to product's contribution to total company sales volume.

Source: From George S. Day, "Diagnosing the Product Portfolio," *Journal of Marketing,* Vol. 41, April 1977. Reprinted with permission of the American Marketing Association.

ing the composite dimensions; relying on historical data; and treating each business as a composite unit, not in terms of several submarkets or segments. When historical data are not available, the tendency is to rely on the judgment of one manager in the firm. These graphical approaches will lead to a high degree of uncertainty for a firm.

To correct these problems, product portfolios can be developed on a situation-by-situation basis. This customized approach supplements existing objective data with judgments from several managers who have some experience with the product. Management's input is solicited to help decide the specific variables to use in describing a business and deriving appropriate weights for the variables. Further, the trend is to think in terms of future situations (projected data) rather than to use historical data alone. Another trend is to consider resource allocation at multiple levels and at smaller units, such as product segments. These customized approaches include the analytic hierarchy process and the use of conjoint analysis, which we discuss in a later section.

Trends in the graphical approaches of portfolio analysis are summarized below. The general trend is toward the use of customized methods, which utilize managerial judgment to a considerable extent.

From Analysis Based on:	To Analysis Based on:
• One or two specified dimensions	Management-selected dimensions
• Single-measure dimensions	Composite dimensions
• Unweighted dimensions	Weighted dimensions
• Single respondent's objective data	Multiple respondents', and integrative and objective data
• Historical data	Projected data
• Single-level analysis	Multilevel hierarchical analysis

Source: From Yoram Wind, Vijay Mahajan, and Donald J. Swire, "An Empirical Comparison of Standardized Portfolio Models," *Journal of Marketing,* Vol. 47, Spring 1983, pp. 89–99. Reprinted by permission of the American Marketing Association.

METHODS BASED ON RESPONSE FUNCTIONS

The standardized product portfolio approaches give descriptive recommendations for the actual allocation of resources across various SBUs of a firm. The procedures are quite intuitive and compute factors that determine the pictorial representation of the positions of each SBU on a product portfolio chart. But the methods do not explicitly involve any optimization of an objective of the firm, and thus the recommended allocations of resources are likely to be suboptimal.

One procedure that attempts to accomplish optimization is STRATPORT, developed by Larreche and Srinivasan.[11] They developed a decision support system that extends and operationalizes standardized product portfolio approaches. It is designed for managers to evaluate and formulate various business portfolio strategies (resource allocation schemes). The system is based on a mathematical model that utilizes existing data on SBUs as well as judgmental data obtained from managers.

STRATPORT

The basic structure of STRATPORT for a single business unit is shown in Fig. 8.9. The system begins with a decision made on the marketing investment for the business unit in the planning period. The STRATPORT system uses six main functional relationships at the level of the business unit (product category) as indicated in Fig. 8.9. These are (1) the market response function, (2) the maintenance marketing function, (3) the capacity expenditures function, (4) the working capital function, (5) the cost function, and (6) the price function. The authors utilize well-established functional forms and estimate their parameters either from past data or from judgmental data collected from managers.

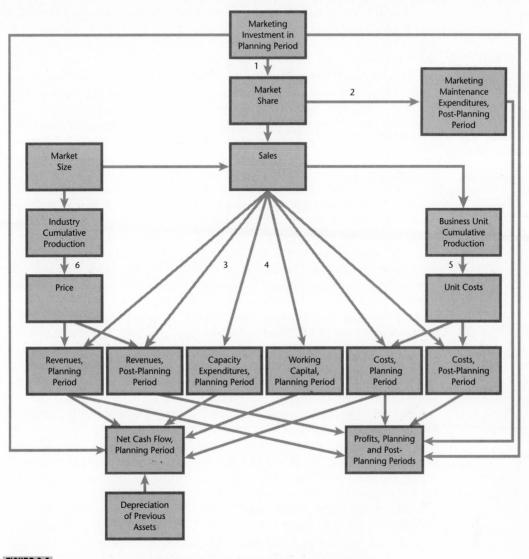

FIGURE 8.9   **Structure of STRATPORT for a Single Business Unit**

Source: Larréche, Jean-Claude, and V. Srinivasan (1981), "STRATPORT: A Decision Support System for Strategic Planning," *Journal of Marketing* 45 (Fall): 39–52.

As can be seen, the STRATPORT system incorporates the relationships between marketing investment (resources devoted to a SBU) and the expected market share at any given time in a planning period (this relationship is marked 1 in the figure). Further, it determines the expenditure needed to maintain market share beyond the planning period (called the post-planning period); this is marked 2 in the figure.

The experience-curve effects on the production costs are also incorporated, as shown by the arrow marked 5. The STRATPORT model assumes that unit costs, expressed in constant dollars, decline as a function of the business unit's cumulative production. In this model, however, unit costs incorporate all costs (including depreciation) with the exception of marketing investments, which are accounted for separately. Many discussions of experience curve only consider value-added costs. The model also utilizes a relationship between the total size of the category and the cumulative production of the industry, which determines the competitive price level for the firm (as shown by relationship 6). The price function also assumes that average industry price per unit declines as a function of cumulative production similar to unit costs.

The cash flows during the planning period for the SBU are computed as the after-tax profits from the business unit (revenues minus costs minus marketing investments, adjusted by the appropriate tax rate) minus the portion of the increase in working capital not expensed during the planning period, minus the portion of additional capacity investment not depreciated during the planning period, plus the depreciation during the planning period of assets acquired beforehand. (The effects on capacity expansion and working capital are shown by the numbers 3 and 4, respectively, in the figure.) In other words, the computation for the cash flows is made as precise as possible, taking into account all of the relevant factors, including taxes and depreciation. The level of risk associated with any SBU is incorporated into the STRATPORT system by computing the present value of the cash flows using a discount rate higher than the expected rate of return for risk-free assets. STRATPORT uses a rate of return model using the financial beta coefficients computed for closely related industries.

The authors utilize an efficient algorithm to optimize the allocation of resources among the SBUs so as to maximize the present value of the sum of SBU profits subject to a constraint on the discounted cash flow during the planning period. The effects of the allocation can also be evaluated for various levels of the cash constraint of the firm, which represent the firm's ability to borrow or lend during the planning horizon.

Table 8.3 illustrates the use of STRATPORT. This illustration shows a firm with four existing business units—BU1, BU2, BU3, and BU4 (which are respectively a cash cow, a star, a dog, and a question mark in the terminology of the Boston Consulting Group)—with current market shares of 20, 30, 5, and 5 percent, respectively. The first portion of the table shows the projections of the model for the status quo strategy for the planning and post-planning period (with no optimization used). These projections show that the four business units require $45 million, $150 million, $40 million, and $30 million, respectively, to maintain their current market shares. Also, the status quo strategy implies that the firm does not make any investments into two new business units, labeled 5 and 6. This status quo strategy would generate cash needs of −$297 million or, equivalently, a net cash flow of $297 million over a three-year planning period and profits of $1367 (= 665 + 550 + 37 + 115) million over the eight-year time horizon considered in the analysis (planning period plus post-planning period). Further, during

TABLE 8.3 **An Illustrative Run of the STRATPORT Model**

Indicate Marketing Investment for

  Business Unit 1: 45

  Business Unit 2: 150

  Business Unit 3: 40

  Business Unit 4: 30

  Business Unit 5: 0

  Business Unit 6: 0

Output Saved in File for Off-Line Printing

Do You Want to Proceed (0), or to Display Results (1)?   1

Evaluation of Portfolio Strategy

Cash Needs   −297

Profit Level   1367

Market Share

  BU 1   0.202

  BU 2   0.300

  BU 3   0.050

  BU 4   0.050

  BU 5   0.000

  BU 6   0.000

Sources and Uses of Funds

BU Number	1	2	3	4	5	6
Cash Needs						
Revenue PL	824	1372	345	190	0	0
Costs PL	551	1082	295	127	0	0
Mktg. IN PL	45	150	40	30	0	0
Capa. IN PL	25	79	−11	23	0	0
Total	−204	−61	−21	−10	0	0
Profits						
Revenue PL	824	1372	345	190	0	0
Costs PL	551	1082	295	127	0	0
Mktg. IN PL	45	150	40	30	0	0
Revenue PP	1623	3838	623	468	0	0
Costs PP	1089	2969	530	302	0	0
Mktg. IN PP	98	460	67	84	0	0
Total	665	550	37	115	0	0

Input minimum and maximum levels of external cash availability: −600.200

Output saved in file for off-line printing

Do you want to proceed (0), or to display key results (1)

Profit contributions (2), or cash flows (3) 1

(Continued on next page)

TABLE 8.3   Continued

Key Optimization Results

	Option 1	Option 2	Option 3	Option 4	Option 5	Option 6
Cash Needs	206	195	185	175	165	106
Profit Level	2911	2894	2877	2860	2842	2735
Marg. % Yield	19.53	20.26	21.00	21.73	22.46	23.19
Market Share						
BU 1	0.203	0.201	0.198	0.195	0.193	0.150
BU 2	0.394	0.393	0.391	0.390	0.389	0.387
BU 3	0.010	0.010	0.010	0.010	0.010	0.010
BU 4	0.171	0.170	0.170	0.169	0.169	0.168
BU 5	0.360	0.358	0.355	0.353	0.351	0.349
BU 6	0.000	0.000	0.000	0.000	0.000	0.000

	Option 7	Option 8	Option 9	Option 10	Option 11
Cash Needs	−383	−386	−389	−393	-609
Profit Level	1813	1807	1801	1793	1330
Marg. % Yield	23.92	24.66	25.39	26.12	26.85
Market Share					
BU 1	0.150	0.150	0.150	0.150	0.150
BU 2	0.050	0.050	0.050	0.050	0.050
BU 3	0.010	0.010	0.010	0.010	0.010
BU 4	0.168	0.167	0.167	0.166	0.166
BU 5	0.346	0.344	0.342	0.339	0.000
BU 6	0.000	0.000	0.000	0.000	0.000

PL = Planning Period   BU = Business Unit

PP = Post-Planning Period   IN = Investment

Source: From Jean-Claude Larreche and V. Srinivasan, "STRATPORT: A Decision Support System for Strategic Planning," *Journal of Marketing,* Vol. 45, Fall 1981. Reprinted by permission of the American Marketing Association.

the planning period, business unit 1 contributes $204 million to the net cash flow of the firm (or about 69 percent of its total profit). Over the long run, business units 1 and 2 contribute over 90 percent of the firm's total profits.

The second part of Table 8.3 shows the optimization results for 11 different portfolio strategies (labeled options 1 through 11) for different cash constraints, ranging from a net cash generation of $609 million to a net cash need of $206 million. These strategies produce widely varying results. At one extreme, option 1 would require a net cash injection of $206 million and would generate a total profit of $2911 million. At the other extreme, option 11 would generate a net cash flow of $609 million (or a cash need of −$609 million) and a total profit of $1330 million. Under each of the options, business unit 6 does not achieve any market share. Also, the most appropriate strategy for business unit 3 in all options is minimum investment, while business unit 4 appears to warrant a substantial marketing investment to increase its market share. The optimum business strategies for the remaining three business units differ widely under the 11 options.

METHODS BASED ON AHP

Consider a firm that seeks to invest additional resources in product modification, market development, or new product development as opposed to just continuing an existing investment strategy. (These decisions are equivalent to allocating resources across various SBUs of a firm.) The firm may have multiple objectives such as growth of sales, increased market share, high profitability, and reduced of vulnerability to external forces. Further, the firm needs to make these decisions without knowing how the environment will change during the planning horizon. The problem here is to judgmentally integrate several factors in some manner and reach a final allocation.

The Analytic Hierarchy Process (AHP) developed by Saaty offers a natural tool to facilitate such integration.[12] First, it breaks down a large problem into smaller problems, each of which are hierarchically organized by the decision maker. Fig. 8.10 shows a hierarchical decomposition for this problem of allocation for new product activities. This hierarchy implies that environment is the overriding factor affecting the overall well-being of the firm. It is, therefore, placed at the top of the hierarchy. The next two levels show various objectives and the competing strategies to reach them. Various objectives of the firm need to trade the objectives off against each other to accomplish the overall objective of corporate well-being. The trade-offs are assessed for each environmental scenario. This example considers four objectives:

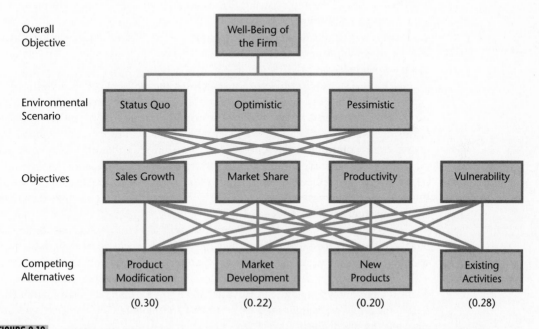

FIGURE 8.10   **A Hypothetical Hierarchy for Allocation Decisions for Growth Strategies**

increasing sales growth, market share, and productivity and reducing vulnerability to competitive pressures.

The competing strategies are existing product modification, market development, creating new products, and other nonmarketing activities. Further, one needs to consider all four objectives under each of the scenarios in the process of allocating resources among the four alternatives. The AHP methodology offers a way to accomplish this difficult task using judgmental data obtained from executives. The AHP exercise results in percentage allocations of a budget to competing alternatives. As shown in Fig. 8.10, the judgments of the executives indicate that 32 percent of resources should be allocated to modifying products, 22 percent to developing markets, 20 percent to developing new products, and 28 percent to existing plans of the firm.

In implementing AHP, in general, the decision problem is decomposed into a hierarchy with several layers, each consisting of a subgroup of related factors relevant to the main problem. Using a simple data collection procedure and analysis, weights are developed for each factor in any layer. In this process, judgmental data are collected from the decision maker. If the decisions are to be made by a group, this procedure can be repeated for every member of the group. The methodology provides for combining data from each decision maker in a group. We illustrate this methodology for the case of one and multiple decision makers.

An Illustration of AHP with One Decision Maker

The AHP methodology has been applied to resource allocation at the Colonial Penn Insurance Company, a fast-growing firm specializing in developing and marketing auto and homeowner's policies to the over-50 market segment.[13] The AHP helped guide the selection of a desired portfolio of products/markets and distribution outlets and the allocation of resources among them. The hierarchy developed for handling this is shown in Fig. 8.11.

In this hierarchy, the objective of increasing the well-being of the company is evaluated under three possible environmental scenarios describing the growth of the economy. Five specific objectives are considered relevant to the well-being of the company: profit level, sales growth, market share, volatility, and demand for resources. The three activities highlighted here are distribution, customers, and products. Once the data on the relative priorities are obtained and combined, the AHP will yield recommended allocations of resources across the three activities. In this situation, the chief executive of the company provided the input data. The results are shown in Fig. 8.12.

According to Fig. 8.12, the chief executive considers the pessimistic scenario to be more likely (with a weight of 0.5) than the optimistic scenario (weight of 0.2) and continuation of status quo (weight of 0.3). Further, the five objectives leading to the well-being of the company differ in relative importance. For example, volatility is deemed more important, with a relative weight of 0.250, than the profit-level objective, with a relative weight of 0.242. The final weights for the three activities as estimated by this analysis are as follows for each scenario:

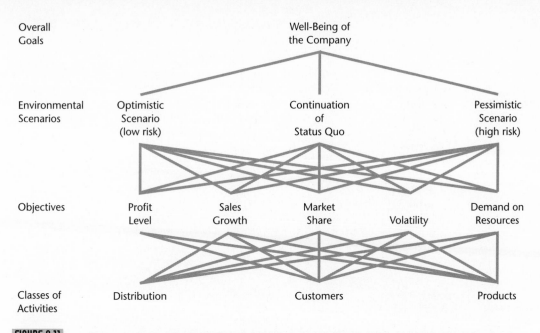

FIGURE 8.11   **A Disguised Analytical Hierarchy for the Colonial Penn Insurance Company**

Source: Wind, Y., and T. L. Saaty (1980), "Marketing Applications of the Analytic Hierarchy Process," *Management Science* 26 (July).

Activity	Optimistic	Continuation	Pessimistic	Total
Distribution	0.101	0.143	0.210	0.454
Customers	0.065	0.098	0.160	0.323
Products	0.034	0.059	0.134	0.223
Total	0.2	0.3	0.5	1.000

According to this analysis, based on the judgments of the chief executive, the firm should allocate 45.4 percent of its resources to developing and maintaining its distribution outlets. Further, 32.3 percent should be allocated to identifying and targeting current and new customers, and 22.3 percent should be allocated to developing and maintaining the firm's products.

The interactive software EXPERT CHOICE can be used to implement AHP.[14] By posing a set of questions to the user, the software develops a hierarchy for the problem and collects necessary judgmental data to compute weights for the alternatives.

The essential details of how to implement the AHP method are described in Appendix 8B.

An Illustration of AHP with Multiple Decision Makers

The setting for this application was an industrial manufacturing firm, an internationally known and highly diversified firm with annual sales revenue in excess of $3 billion. It shows how judgments of different decision makers can be integrated via AHP.

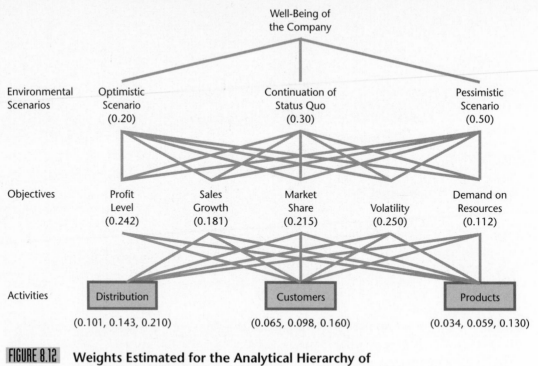

Well-Being of
the Company

Environmental
Scenarios

Optimistic
Scenario
(0.20)

Continuation of
Status Quo
(0.30)

Pessimistic
Scenario
(0.50)

Objectives

Profit
Level
(0.242)

Sales
Growth
(0.181)

Market
Share
(0.215)

Volatility
(0.250)

Demand on
Resources
(0.112)

Activities

Distribution

Customers

Products

(0.101, 0.143, 0.210)   (0.065, 0.098, 0.160)   (0.034, 0.059, 0.130)

FIGURE 8.12 **Weights Estimated for the Analytical Hierarchy of Colonial Penn Insurance Company**

Source: Wind, Y., and T. L. Saaty (1980), "Marketing Applications of the Analytic Hierarchy Process," *Management Science* 26 (July).

In the midst of a severe recession, several of the firm's SBUs were operating at less than half their capacity. Earnings were sharply reduced, and the number of lay-offs was substantial.

The transportation equipment SBU was perhaps the hardest hit. The general manager of this SBU was determined to improve the profitability of his products. He believed the key to better profits was "smarter" resource allocation. Consequently, he commissioned an external consulting team to study his SBU and recommend a resource allocation scheme that would improve long-term profitability and gain consensus among his top managers.

Transportation Equipment Division Market Position   The transportation equipment division manufactures and markets a wide variety of industrial components such as sprockets, industrial timing belts, and couplings. Since its formation, this division generally operated with acceptable efficiency, especially in solving short-term problems, but paid almost no attention to long-term planning issues. Product development, market expansion, and facilities expansion were sacrificed to maintain current dividends and high employee bonuses. Due to the cyclical nature of the transportation industry, the division had been through some challenging periods, but the current recession, coupled with increased foreign competition, had made management eager to implement an effective planning and resource allocation system.

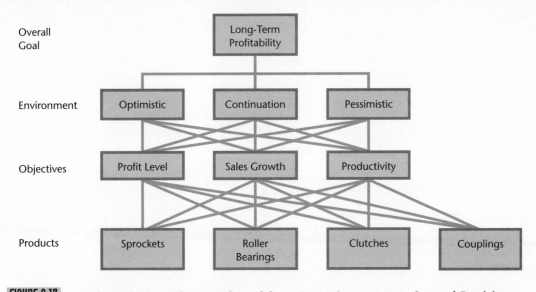

FIGURE 8.13   **Analytical Hierarchy Developed from Interviews among Several Decision Makers for an Industrial Manufacturing Firm**

Resource Allocation Study   The consulting team was charged to "get more with less" and assigned to develop a plan for allocating resources among the division's four major products (sprockets, roller bearings, clutches, and couplings) based on the inputs of several key managers. The consulting team conducted the study using AHP.

The model addresses the allocation of limited resources within a given product mix. Unlike other portfolio models such as the Boston Consulting Group's growth/share matrix or PIMS, AHP focuses on multiple objectives (in this study, profitability, sales, growth, and productivity).

Research Design   Eight executives from various levels and functional areas of the organization were interviewed. During the interviews, a questionnaire was administered to the managers. If a completed questionnaire contained ambiguities with respect to legibility, completeness, consistency, or accuracy, a second interview was conducted.

Current Allocation Scheme   A recent organizational audit showed that 10 percent of the transportation equipment division's resources were allocated to sprockets, 30 percent to roller bearings, 25 percent to clutches, 25 percent to couplings, and 10 percent to various other products within the division. Thus, the allocation of resources among the four product groups (excluding other products) was 11 percent to sprockets, 33 percent to roller bearings, 28 percent to clutches, and 32 percent to couplings. All eight managers indicated they were not satisfied with the current allocation, feeling that the plan was too "middle of the road" to be anything other than "suboptimal." Based on several interviews, the researchers developed the hierarchy shown in Fig. 8.13.

Table 8.4 shows the detailed results for one manager, Manager A, as well as the computed allocations for all eight managers interviewed in this study. An important

TABLE 8.4   **Estimated AHP Weights for the Managers of the Industrial Firm**

Manager A Environment		Objectives		Products	
Optimistic	0.101	Profit level	0.46	Sprockets	0.2581
Continuation	0.799	Sales growth	0.055	Roller bearings	0.0916
Pessimistic	0.099	Productivity	0.48	Clutches	0.4508
				Couplings	0.1991

Computed Resource Allocation Weights for the Four Products for Eight Managers

Managers	Position and Background	Sprockets	Roller Bearings	Clutches	Couplings
A	Product Manager, MBA, 7 yrs	0.26	0.09	0.45	0.20
B	Industrial Marketing Manager, BS, 14 yrs	0.05	0.49	0.31	0.15
C	General Manager, BS, 20 yrs	0.04	0.54	0.30	0.12
D	Division Manager, BS, 16 yrs	0.10	0.43	0.17	0.30
E	Marketing Manager, MBA, 6 yrs	0.08	0.52	0.10	0.30
F	Vice-President Operations, BS, 17 yrs	0.03	0.28	0.28	0.41
G	Field Sales Manager, MBA, 10 yrs	0.14	0.62	0.15	0.08
H	Vice-President Marketing and Sales, MBA, 10 yrs	0.03	0.14	0.45	0.38
Average		0.09	0.39	0.28	0.24
Current Allocation		0.11	0.33	0.28	0.32

question in this situation is how to arrive at consensus for the resource allocation scheme for this unit. The estimated allocations for each manager can be weighted in proportion to their expertise with the various businesses or their experience with the company. Another weighting scheme could be on the basis of internal consistency of their judgments. For ease, we simply show the average allocation for the eight managers. Compared to the current allocation of resources to the four product groups, the average scheme based on AHP suggests a reduction in emphasis on couplings in preference to roller bearings.

METHODS BASED ON CONJOINT ANALYSIS

Conjoint analysis can be employed to determine the appropriate allocation of resources to a set of businesses. (The essentials of conjoint analysis were described in Chapter 2.) The method works as follows. The analyst first determines both the range of resource allocation feasible for each business and a small number of levels for each; for example, the range for any business could be between $10 and $25 million, with levels of $10, $15, $20, and $25 million. Using this information, the analyst develops a number of potential resource allocations to the businesses under consideration. In a situation with four businesses—A, B, C, and D—these profiles may be as follows:

Allocation Profile	A	B	C	D
1	10	15	20	12
2	20	18	15	15
etc.	etc.			

Along with detailed descriptions of the industries and current business situations, the profiles are presented for evaluation by a number of managers. Each resource allocation profile will be judged on such criteria as growth of profits for the firm and feasibility. Using this information, the analyst estimates each respondent's utility functions for allocations to each business. This information is then used to simulate a number of potential allocation plans.

This approach is fully adaptable to any specific situation. The levels of resources used in profiles, the businesses selected, and the criteria of evaluation can be adjusted to the particular needs of management. Although it is judgmental, conjoint analysis is in the same spirit as the different portfolio approaches described earlier. It enables one to synthesize managerial experience in resource allocation decisions. The results do not yield optimal allocations, but they can be used in a computer simulation to evaluate how a number of suggested allocations will fare on the criteria used in the conjoint study. Only limited applications of this method exist.

ALLOCATING RESOURCES ACROSS MULTIPLE PRODUCTS WITHIN AN SBU

Methods Based on Conjoint Analysis and AHP

Given the versatility of the conjoint and AHP methods, they can be applied to the problem of determining appropriate allocation of a given resource for an SBU to various brands. The procedures are the same as those described for allocation among various SBUs. The difference will be in terms of detailed descriptions of the positions of various products within the SBU where the allocations will be made. Further, the analyst should design the study to ensure determination of any potential interactions between the allocations to the brands. This issue is important because of the potential (positive and negative) synergy between the brands of an SBU. The conjoint design will accordingly be more complicated, but the corresponding AHP hierarchy will be much simpler.

Methods Using Market Response Functions

Rules for optimal allocation of marketing resources among different products or SBUs can be developed using their market response functions. One needs to estimate the elasticity of sales response to changes in the total marketing expenditure for any product. The optimal allocation for a given product category will depend on its degree of interdependence with other products. Products are interdependent if expenditures on one product influence the sales of another. We will consider the cases of absence and presence of interdependence separately.

Methods for estimating market response functions* include econometric methods, the judgmental approaches such as STRATPORT, and experimental methods such as conjoint analysis.

No Interdependence   Once a market response function has been estimated, the rule for optimal allocation across products (assuming no interdependence among products) is as follows:

$$X_i^* = \frac{(P_i - c_i)e_{ii}S_i}{\sum_{i=1}^{n}(P_i - c_i)e_{ii}S_i} \times B$$

where

B = budget for all n products

n = number of products

S_i = sales (units) for the ith product

X_i^* = optimal allocation for the ith product

P_i = price per unit for the ith product

c_i = cost per unit for the ith product

e_{ii} = self-elasticity of ith product's sales with respect to amount of resources devoted to it.

This rule indicates that a product will receive higher optimal allocation of resources if its margins are higher, the market is more responsive to such expenditures (shows higher elasticity), and its sales are larger. Such a determination is quite intuitive.

Interdependence   When demand functions of products interact, the rule for optimal allocation across products is

$$X_i^* = \frac{\sum_{j=1}^{n}(P_j - c_j)e_{ji}S_j}{\sum_{i=1}^{n}\sum_{j=1}^{n}(P_j - c_j)e_{ji}S_j} \times B,$$

---

*These functions are used to compute the elasticity of sales of a product with respect to the marketing expenditures devoted to it. In addition to this self-elasticity, one may also compute a cross-elasticity for one product with respect to the marketing expenditures for another product to determine the cross-effect.

where the new term, e_{ji}, = cross-elasticity of jth product sales with respect to the amount of resources devoted to ith product; $i,j = 1, 2, \ldots, n$. Other terms are the same as before. If the cross-elasticities are zero, and the products do not interact, this formula reduces to the one for the case of no demand interdependence.

The impact of demand interdependence among products can be observed in several situations. Examples include the Gillette Sensor and Gillette Sensor Prestige series of men's razors, the American Express Green, Gold, and Platinum credit cards, and various brands of laundry detergents of Procter & Gamble. The effects of interdependence on the optimal allocation of resources depend on the magnitudes of the cross-elasticities among the products, as shown in the formula. We will illustrate these effects with hypothetical data.

Assume that a firm marketing a brand of men's personal use item has developed a more expensive version of the same product (perhaps made with better materials and packaged more elegantly). We call these "regular" and "elite." Also, assume that experience with the promotion of the elite version indicates that it has a pronounced effect on the demand for the regular. But the regular version has almost no effect on the demand for elite. Essentially, the regular version is aimed at the mass market. This situation could be due to various factors such as the exclusive distribution achieved for the elite version or the way it is promoted. As could be expected, sales of the regular version are many times larger than those of the elite version. Assume that sales of the regular version are $1400 million versus $30 million for the elite. A total resource of $250 million is to be allocated between these two products. Further, assume that the average prices per unit of the regular and elite versions were approximately $4 and $40, with respective margins of 50 percent and 70 percent. Assume that the self- and cross-elasticities of sales with respect to the marketing expenditures on the two versions were as follows:

	Sales of	
Expenditure on	**Regular**	**Elite**
Regular	0.4	almost zero
Elite	0.05	0.2

Optimal allocations of marketing expenditures to the two products under different assumptions of product interdependence are shown in Table 8.5; these are labeled Cases I, II, and III. Under Case I, the elite version would receive a budget of $30.7 million, while the regular version would receive $219.3 million, using the elasticities just shown. However, if the products are deemed independent, the elite version would receive only $3.7 million, and the lion's share would be spent on the regular version. Presumably, the image of the elite version would have a considerable impact on sales of the less expensive brand.

Cases II and III demonstrate that even if the judgments on self-elasticities were changed, the impact of interdependence is quite dramatic. If both products are judged to have equal self-elasticities, the elite version would receive higher allocations than Case I. If, on the other hand, regular version expenditures are not as effective as elite version expenditures (compare 0.2 with 0.4), regular would receive a smaller allocation. But the

TABLE 8.5   Illustrative Allocation of Budget under Demand Interdependence

Product	Price	Margin (P-C)	Sales ($ millions)	Sales Units (millions)
Regular	$ 4.00	2.00	$1,400	350
Elite	$40.00	28.00	$ 30	0.75

Cross-Elasticity Matrix

		Effect on Sales of	
Expenditure on		Regular	Elite
X_1	Regular	e_{11}	$e_{21} = 0$
X_2	Elite	e_{12}	e_{22}

		Optimal Allocation	
Case	Interdependence	X_1^* (Regular)	X_2^* (Elite)
Case I			
$e_{11} = 0.4$	Yes	219.30	30.7
$e_{12} = 0.05$	No	246.30	3.7
$e_{22} = 0.2$			
Case II			
$e_{11} = 0.4$	Yes	216.50	33.5
$e_{12} = 0.05$	No	242.72	7.28
$e_{22} = 0.4$			
Case III			
$e_{11} = 0.2$	Yes	190.84	59.16
$e_{12} = 0.05$	No	235.85	14.15
$e_{22} = 0.4$			

impact of interdependence continues to be high. The procedure just described is directly applicable to allocating a given level of marketing resources across multiple brands of a product category. Various brands in a multibrand corporation are likely to be interdependent. Thus, the market response functions for any brand should include self-elasticities as well as cross-elasticities. Once these elasticities are estimated, allocations can be made using the formula shown earlier.

METHODS FOR ALLOCATING MARKETING EXPENDITURES FOR A SBU

Methods Based on Pooled Business Experience

In this section, we briefly discuss methods for allocating resources that are based on pooled business experience. *Pooled business experience* refers to the accumulation of business decisions made and the resulting performance of several businesses in different industries at one or more points in time. It is clear that any one business can yield only a limited number of data points from which a statistical model relating decisions to results can be built. Researchers, therefore, to collect data on pooled business experience for developing such statistical relationships.

The principle involved is that a model can be developed using cross-sectional experience of several businesses and used to determine the expected performance of a business under various contingent assumptions about resources and other business characteristics. The idea is that managers dealing with similar problems over a period of time may develop decision rules that appear reasonable. Thus a model developed using data on several businesses may be applicable to a separate business, once we account for variables specific to it.

Relevant data for building these models are obtained through surveys administered in a sample of businesses. One of the major efforts for collecting such data is the PIMS system of the Strategic Planning Institute (SPI), which grew out of an internal project of the General Electric Corporation. The SPI was created in 1975 as a nonprofit, autonomous corporation. The PIMS database has grown steadily over the years and included over 2600 businesses by mid-1986.[15] It covers various industry categories (durable, nondurable, consumer, industrial, and service and distribution).

The second major effort is the ADVISOR project, which focuses on industrial products and collects more detailed data on products than does PIMS, which emphasizes businesses.[16] Further, the definition used by PIMS for an industrial product is much less stringent than that used for ADVISOR (for example, less than 50 percent of the business's sales could be to households). The second phase of this project, ADVISOR 2, involved 22 companies and 131 products. A firm can also build a database for its brands from internal records and develop a model for use in allocating resources across products.

The PIMS PAR Approach   The PIMS data were used to build a regression model to predict a business's profit performance (as measured by ROI, return on investment) in terms of various product, market, and customer characteristics. In this regression model, several variables are statistically significant. Importantly, the variables of market growth and market share (which are the core of the graphical portfolio approaches) are significant and influence the ROI in a positive direction. Other variables included in these models capture various characteristics of the product (relative quality and percent of new products), the market (degree of vertical integration), and the customer (average purchase amount and customized products). Business characteristics such as R&D as a percent of sales and marketing as a percent of sales are also included in this model.

The SPI produces several reports from the PIMS data; one significant for resource allocation is the "PAR Report." The "PAR Report" specifies the return on investment that is normal (or "par") for a business, given the characteristics of its market, competition, position, technology, and cost structure. The experience of similar businesses is used in computing the par for a business. The par then refers to an estimate of the normal return of a business similar to the one under consideration. It also indicates what strategic changes in the business have the most promise of improving ROI.

Armed with this knowledge, the strategy analyst will be in a position to determine which should be changed to realize higher than par returns. The "PAR Report" also includes strategy-sensitive reports that show how the rate of return for the business would change under various assumed environments and strategies (such as a strategy to build market share). In addition, the report indicates the combination of strategic moves that promises optimal results for a business. The combination of strategic moves is translated into a specific allocation of resources.

Consider a summary of a "PAR Report" for a hypothetical business 12345; it has a pretax par ROI of 34.0 percent compared to its actual ROI of 39.5 percent. Thus, the business performs above par. A summary of the effects of various strategic moves (and associated resource allocations) on the average ROI follows.

Strategic Move	Associated Investment ($ millions)	Average ROI (5 years)	Net Sales ($ millions)	Market Share
Major decrease in market share	$221	49%	$1144	16%
Small decrease in market share	240	45	1364	20
No planned change in market share	290	41	1603	23
Small increase in market share	343	36	1863	27
Major increase in market share	399	32	2147	31
Strategy to optimize discounted net income	226	48.8	1142	15.5

Source: Extracted from S. J. Aguilar (1979), "Norton Company: Strategic Planning for Diversified Business Operations," the Appendix in the Harvard Business School Case, #377–044, Boston, MA.

This example highlights several aspects of PIMS analysis. First, there is a trade-off between ROI and market share. Second, optimizing discounted net income is quite distinct from seeking increases in market share. Finally, different strategies require different levels of investment. Once management decides on the specific objective to be realized (for example, a major decrease or a small increase in market share), these analyses will identify the total amount of investment (or resource) called for to achieve that objective. The particular utilization of the investment (for example, allocations to marketing and R&D as determined by the marketing/sales ratio and R&D/sales ratio) will also be part of the "PAR Report" for the business. In this example, percent marketing/sales is 8.6 for the objective of major increase in market share, compared with 7.2 optimizing discounted net income—or $185 million (= 2,147 × 8.6%) versus $82 million for the two strategic moves.

ADVISOR   In contrast to the PIMS approach, the ADVISOR models are specific to industrial products. They involve estimation of "norm" regression models for advertising expenditures, marketing expenditures (defined as advertising, personal selling, and technical service spending), and the proportion of the marketing budget allocated to advertising for a product in the sample. Table 8.6 shows the actual regression models. Definitions of the variables are given in Table 8.7 on page 365. ADVISOR results can also be used to produce a "norm" report for a product. A sample portion of a norm report for a hypothetical product is shown as follows.

TABLE 8.6 Regression Models of Advisor 2

Dependent Variable	Continuous Variables						Dichotomous Variables			Constant	R^2 / F	SEE / N
	Sales (LSLS)	No. of Users (LUSERS)	Customer Concentration (LCONC)	Fraction of Sales Made to Order (LSPEC)	Prospect Customer Product Attitude Difference (DIFF)	Sales Direct to Users (LDIR-USER)	Stage in Life Cycle (LCYCLE)	Product Plans (PLANS)	Product Complexity (PROD)			
Advertising (LADV)	+0.618 (9.1)	+0.104 (3.6)	−1.881 (3.1)	−1.989 (4.4)	*	*	−0.892 (3.7)	+1.903 (6.0)	*	−0.651	0.39 / 25.0	1.12 / 110
A/M (Logit (A/M))	−0.232 (4.5)	*	*	*	+0.383 (2.0)	−0.255 (2.1)	*	*	−0.230 (1.2)	+0.544	0.24 / 7.5	0.91 / 100
Marketing (LMKTG)	+0.712 (12.6)	+0.082 (3.1)	−1.633 (3.1)	−0.993 (2.8)	−0.305 (1.7)	+0.194 (0.6)	−0.424 (2.0)	+0.809 (3.9)	+0.528 (2.5)	+0.185	0.72 / 28.2	0.91 / 110

*Variable insignificant

Notes: t–statistics in (·)

• variable names, keyed to Appendix 8A, in (·)

• all equations significant at < 0.001

Source: Adapted from Lilien, G. L. (1979), "ADVISOR 2: Modeling the Marketing Mix Decision for Industrial Products," *Management Science 25* (February): 191–204.

	Actual Budget	Center	Industry Norms Range
Advertising (K$)	$20.00	$24.00	$19.20–$28.80
Advertising/Marketing	0.020%	0.025%	0.020%–0.030%
Marketing (K$)	$1000.00	$950.00	$760.00–$1140.00

In addition, the ADVISOR results can be used to determine spending levels for an existing product or even for a product with no sales history.

The ADVISOR approach is used as follows. First, measurements are made for all the variables included in the norm model for marketing expenditure (i.e., using the estimated equation for LMKTG or logarithm of marketing expenditures) for the product in question. Then, the norm of marketing expenditure for the product is estimated. Because this is a statistical model, we can compute a range for the norm expenditure. Further, the same model is also used to estimate the spending level for an average product in the ADVISOR database; this estimate is called the *base*. A ratio of the norm for the product and base can be decomposed into a number of terms as follows:

$$\text{Norm} = \text{Base } (1 + \text{Effect of Customers}/100) \times$$

$$(1 + \text{Effect of Special Order}/100) \times$$

$$(1 + \text{Effect of Life Cycle}/100) \text{ etc.}$$

The values of the effects coefficients are used for diagnostic purposes. Each effect coefficient will indicate the percentage change in the spending level due to a unit change in the variable.

An illustration of an ADVISOR report is shown in Table 8.8 for Flowclean Sootblowers, a product of the Convection Corporation. (ADVISOR was implemented for three of this firm's brands.) This brand reduced the need for cleaning in a large-scale fossil fuel steam boiler, resulting in less boiler downtime.

The estimated norm spending level for this product was $1.813 million with a range of $1.178 to $2.774. Current spending was $2.9 million. The marketing spending base corresponding to Flowclean was estimated to be $2.226 million. Analysis of diagnostics indicated that the spending norm will be lower for increases in the fraction of customers with special orders and as the product matures in its life cycle (from growth to maturity). Further, the norm will increase if the manager's objective was to increase the market for the product.

Table 8.8 also shows norms and ranges for expenditures on personal selling/technical service and advertising for Flowclean as well as the corresponding diagnostics.

This example illustrates how ADVISOR can be used in determining marketing expenditures for an industrial product. The analysis estimates norm and diagnostic effects, which become a valuable input into the resource allocation process.

Methods Based on AHP

The AHP methodology is also applicable to allocating marketing resources among competing mix elements for a given product. The procedures are very similar to

TABLE 8.7   Variable Definitions in the ADVISOR Model

Variable Name	Description	Models
1. ADV	Total amount of money spent on advertising and sales promotion for this product, including production, in 1000s.	
2. ADVDUM	= 0 if advertising budget < sample median; 1 otherwise.	
3. CCOM	$\dfrac{\text{No. of major competitors (over 1\% market share) year 1} - \text{No. of major competitors year 2}}{\text{No. of major competitors year 2}}$	CHANGE-ADV
4. CONC	Fraction of industry dollar sales purchased by industry's three largest customers.	CHANGE-ADV
5. CPLANS	Change in product plans from current year to year 1. (Variable constructed from change in weighted average of possible product plans possibilities in original questionnaire.)	CHANGE-ADV
6. CSHARE	$\dfrac{\text{Dollar Market Share}_{t-1} - \text{Dollar Market Share}_{t-2}}{\text{Dollar Market Share}_{t-2}}$	CHANGE-ADV
7. DIFF	Difference between how current customers and prospective customers perceive product quality relative to industry average. = 0, prospective customers perceived quality higher than current customers = 1, otherwise	NORM-A/M MKTG
8. DIRUSER	Fraction of sales volume made direct to users + fraction of sales volume made to users via company-owned resellers + 1.	NORM-A/M
9. LADV	LN(ADV)	
10. LCONC	LN(1 + CONC)	NORM-ADV, MKTG
11. LCUSER	LN (No. of industry downstream specifiers year 1 + No. of industry users year 1 + No. of industry independent resellers year 1)	CHANGE-ADV
12. LCYCLE	Stage in product life cycle = 0, growth = 1, maturity Missing, introduction or decline	NORM-ADV, MKTG
13. LDIRUSER	LN(DIRUSER + 1)	NORM-MKTG
14. LMKTG	LN(MKTG)	
15. LSLS	LN (Product $ sales) (Lagged 1 year in 1000)	NORM-ADV, A/M MKTG
16. LSPEC	LN (SPEC + 1) (see definition of SPEC)	NORM-ADV, MKTG

(Continued on next page)

TABLE 8.7	Continued		
Variable Name	**Description**		**Models**
17. LUSERS	LN (No. of industry downstream specifiers + No. of industry users × No. of usual decision makers in user's organization + No. of industry independent resellers × No. of usual decision makers in reseller's		NORM-ADV, MKTG
18. MKTG	PSTS + ADV		
19. PLANS	= 1, if product plans are "positive," i.e., if respondent indicated increase in market as an objective, say = 0, otherwise		NORM-MKTG, ADV
20. PROD	Product complexity = 1, if the product is machinery and equipment, or component part, = 0, otherwise		NORM-MKTG, A/M
21. PSTS	Total amount of money spent on Personal Selling and Technical Service for the product (including applicable overhead) in the current year, in 1000s.		
22. SPEC	Fraction of product's volume sales produced to order		

Source: Lilien, Gary L. (1979), "ADVISOR 2: Modeling the Marketing Mix Decision for Industrial Products," *Management Science* 25 (February): 191–204.

those described earlier. The hierarchy relevant to increasing the long-term profitability of a brand will consist of two layers: one describing the subobjectives for the brand such as profitability, market share, and competitive retaliation and the other describing the alternative marketing mix elements such as media advertising, temporary price promotions to consumers, trade promotions, expanding distribution, use of direct marketing, and so on.

Methods Based on Conjoint Analysis

Again, the problem of allocating a given resource to different marketing mix elements can be tackled by conjoint methods. The approach is essentially the same as that described for allocating resources across SBUs. The only difference will be in terms of the attributes and levels.

Levy, Webster, and Kerin applied conjoint analysis to determining marketing mix strategies (or marketing mix allocations) for one product.[17] Their objective was to determine the profit function for alternative push strategies for a margarine manufacturer. Each push strategy was described in terms of four marketing mix variables: cooperative advertising, coupons in local newspapers, financial terms of sale, and

TABLE 8.8   **ADVISOR Report for Flowclean**

		Marketing Spending ($000s)	Personal Selling/ Technical Service ($000s)	Advertising Spending ($000s)
Norm		1,813.3	1,712.2	101.1
Range	Low	1,178.6	1,112.9	65.7
	High	2,774.3	2,619.6	154.6
Current spending		2,900	2,652.0	248.0
Diagnosis Spending Base		$2,226.2	$1,882.4	$343.8
Number of customers		1.7	−0.4%	2.3%
Fraction of special orders	-	−27.6	−25.1	−50.1
Customer concentration		−35.6	−35.1	−46.2
Fraction of direct sales		−0.5	−2.6	
Plans		41.4	51.5	
Customer/prospect attitude	-	5.8	−8.8	
Product complexity		59.1	−66.4	81.9
Life cycle		−18.5	−16.2	−41.1

Product Description Variables

Product category:	Fabricated metal	Customer/prospect attitude difference of product quality relative to industry average	0 (Prospects not higher than current customers)
Number of customers last year (end users, resellers, and downstream specifiers):	1,049	Product complexity (1 = machinery or component; 0 = otherwise)	0
Fraction of special orders:	1.00	Stage in product life cycle:	Mature
Customer concentration (fraction of sales by three largest customers)	0.63	Product sales ($ mil) to users plus independent resellers	
		Last year	24.1
Fraction of direct sales:	0.55	Year before last	23.5
Plans:	Maintain market share; improve image; retaliate against competitive action	Industry sales ($ mil) to users and independent resellers	
		Last year	48.2
		Year before last	47.0

Source: Adapted from Convection Corporation Case in Clarke, Darral G. (1993), *Marketing Decision Making: Text and Cases with Spreadsheets*, 2nd ed., San Francisco, CA: The Scientific Press.

service level (defined as percentage of orders shipped). While costs for a push strategy could be computed from the firm's internal records, sales response could not. The authors utilized conjoint analysis to determine the retailers' sales response to different push strategies. Nine profiles, developed using a fractional factorial orthogonal design, were presented to a sample of 68 buyers and merchandising managers. Details of the levels for the four marketing mix variables, profiles developed, and the data collection instrument are shown in Table 8.9. The part-worth functions were estimated for each segment of retailers (defined by the size of their past purchases). These functions were used to estimate the sales response and profit for each of the 54 possible marketing mixes.

Determining the Profit Function   To determine the total sales response function, the part-worths for the individual variable levels for each segment derived above were combined into 54 unique marketing mixes using the model

$$S_i = N \left[a + \sum_{j=1}^{m} B_{ji} s_{ji} \right],$$

where

S_i = the overall sales estimate of the ith marketing mix,

a = the sales constant,

N = the number of customers adjusted for size,

B_{ji} = the value 1 or 0, depending on whether or not a particular marketing mix variable j is included in the ith marketing mix,

s_{ji} = the sales dollar estimate contributed by a particular marketing mix variable level j, in the ith marketing mix, and

m = the number of different variable levels.

The total cost for each marketing mix is the sum of the costs for the component variables:

$$C_i = \sum_{j=1}^{m} B_{ji} c_{j.}$$

where

C_i = the overall cost estimate of the ith marketing mix, and

c_{ji} = the cost estimate contributed by a particular marketing mix variable level in the ith marketing mix.

Based on this analysis, the authors conclude that the least profitable marketing mix is cooperative advertising offered three times a year at 15 cents per pound, coupons in newspapers offered two times a year at 25 cents per pound, terms of sale of 2 percent/10 days/net 30, and 96 percent level of service. The most profitable marketing mix consisted of cooperative advertising six times a year at 7 cents per pound,

TABLE 8.9   **Use of Conjoint Analysis for Allocating Marketing Mix Expenditures for a Brand**

Panel A

Sales Dollar Estimates of Various Levels of Marketing Mix Variables

Marketing Mix Variable Level		Sales
Cooperative Advertising		
(0)	3 times at 15¢/lb	$2477
(1)	4 times at 10¢/lb	873
(2)	6 times at 7¢/lb	0
Coupons in Local Newspapers		
(0)	2 times at 25¢/lb	0
(1)	4 times at 10¢/lb	481
(2)	3 times at 15¢/lb	913
Financial Terms of Sale		
(0)	2%/10 days/net 30	0
(1)	2%/30 days	1366
"Service Level" Percentage of Items Shipped That Were Ordered		
(0)	96%	0
(1)	98%	1283
(2)	99.5%	1173

Panel B

Partial Factorial Orthogonal Design*

Package	Cooperative Advertising	Coupons in Local Newspapers	Financial Terms of Sale†	Service Level
1	0	2	1	0
2	1	0	0	0
3	2	1	1	0
4	0	0	1	1
5	1	1	1	1
6	2	2	0	1
7	0	1	0	2
8	1	2	1	2
9	2	0	1	2

* Numbers in table correspond to descriptions in Panel B.

† Only 2 levels are defined for this variable.

(Continued on next page)

TABLE 8.9 **Continued**

Panel C

Typical Question in the Data Collection Instrument	
Profiles:	**Activities**
1. Cooperative advertising:	3 times a year at 15¢
2. Manufacturers' ROP coupons in newspapers:	3 times a year at 15¢
3. Financial terms of sale:	2%/30 days
4. Percent of total cases ordered that were shipped:	96%

24-lb
cases
(000)

| 15 | 18 | 21 | 24 | 27 | 30 | 33 | 36 | 39 | 42 | 45 |

%
Change

| – 50 | – 40 | – 30 | – 20 | – 10 | 0 | +1 0 | +2 0 | +3 0 | +4 0 | +5 0 |

Scale for
Response

Source: Adapted from Michael Levy, John Webster, and Roger A. Kering, "Formulating Push Marketing Strategies: A Method and Application," *Journal of Marketing,* Vol. 47, Winter 1983. Reprinted by permission of the American Marketing Association.

coupons four times a year at 10 cents per pound, 2 percent/30-day terms, and a 98 percent service level. Although the results are specific to the situation considered, the application shows how conjoint analysis can help allocate the marketing mix budget for a brand.

Methods Using the Market Response Function

The optimal allocation rule for one product is:

$$X_j^* = \frac{e_j}{\sum e_j} \times B$$

$$j = 1, 2, \ldots, n$$

where

$B =$ Budget allocated to the product

$X_j^* =$ Optimal allocation to the jth mix element for the product

$e_j =$ Elasticity of sales response with respect to the jth mix element.

Montgomery and Silk estimated the market response function for an ethical drug using econometric methods.[18] They used 54 monthly observations of current and lagged expenditures for journal advertising, direct mail, and sampling and literature used for promoting the drug. The dependent variable in this analysis was the drug's market share of the new prescriptions. The estimates for both the short-run and long-run elasticities* for these marketing mix elements are shown in Table 8.10. Also shown are actual monthly expenditures and optimal expenditures according to the previous rule for both the short run and long run.

These results indicate that the ethical drug market share was highly responsive to journal advertising and moderately responsive to expenditures on sampling and literature and direct mail. Also, long-run effects are much higher than short-run effects for each marketing element. The actual monthly expenditures were $1.209, $1.630, and $1.355 for journal advertising, direct mail, and sampling and literature (these were disguised to preserve confidentiality, while maintaining their actual relative values).

But when compared to the average monthly expenditures made by the firm for each communication method, it appears that the firm is allocating expenditures inversely to the estimated elasticities! While the optimal allocation among journal advertising, direct mail, and sampling and literature using the short-term elasticities should be 90, 1, and 9 percent, actual allocations were 29, 39, and 32 percent. Also, the allocations based on long-run elasticities are higher for direct mail and sampling and literature than those based on short-run effects. The reverse is true for the allocation to journal advertising. This example illustrates how one could compute the optimal expenditures using rules based on the market response function and examine how far the current practice is from the optimal allocation.

METHODS FOR ALLOCATING RESOURCES ACROSS GEOGRAPHIC MARKETS

Methods Based on Market Response Function

Once a total budget has been decided for a marketing mix element (say, sales force expenditure) for a product, sometimes it is necessary to allocate it across the different geographic territories in which the product is marketed. This allocation requires knowledge of the market response functions for each territory. The rule for optimal allocation is essentially the same as that for allocating across different marketing mix elements for a brand: allocate the total budget in proportion to the elasticities for the

---

*A short-run elasticity measures the influence of a marketing element in the period in which expenditures were incurred. However, because of carryover effects, the short-run elasticities underestimate the influence of marketing expenditures. Long-run elasticities account for these carryover effects and measure the influence of a marketing element on response over a long period.

TABLE 8.10   **Actual and Optimal Marketing Mix Allocations for a Prescription Drug**

| Marketing Element | Estimated Elasticities | | Actual Monthly Expenditures | | Optimal Expenditures | | | |
| | Short Run | Long Run | % | Amount | Short Run | | Long Run | |
					%	Amount	%	Amount
Journal advertising	0.157	0.303	29%	$1.209	90%	$3.784	78%	$3.187
Direct mail	0.002	0.019	39	1.630	1	0.048	5	0.210
Sampling and literature	0.015	0.076	32	1.355	9	0.362	19	0.797
Total			100%	$4.194	100%	$4.194	100%	$4.194

different areas. A geographic area that is more responsive to the expenditure will receive a higher budget than the less responsive area.

SUMMARY

This chapter covered a number of approaches for allocating resources in a multi-product firm. Any strategic decision involves determination of the magnitude of resources and their allocation.

We have considered allocation of resources among several SBUs of the firm, among different brands within a particular SBU, among various marketing mix elements for a brand, and across different geographic territories for a product. Methods include product portfolio approaches and methods based on the analytic hierarchy process, conjoint analysis, and market response functions. While methods using market response functions provide optimal solutions, their estimation is quite difficult, particularly for aggregation of brands and products such as a business (or a SBU). Owing to this, different product portfolio methods have been proposed by various consulting organizations. These portfolio approaches develop composite dimensions from a large number of relevant variables and classify businesses into matrices of various sizes (2×2, 3×3, or 4×5). Based on such classifications, each approach makes prescriptions for the direction of allocation of resources. Research comparing how these approaches analyze one situation indicates there is almost no consistency in the way businesses are classified according to the product portfolio methods. This is most disturbing in practical applications.

To contend with the problems of portfolio methods, various customized approaches have evolved in the literature. These include methods based on AHP and conjoint analysis. We described how they can be used for several resource allocation situations.

Review Questions

1. What are the advantages and disadvantages of the graphical and mathematical approaches to portfolio analysis? Assume that you are the vice-president for marketing of a firm that markets various sporting goods. Which approach would you favor and why?

2. Consider a typical large supermarket in the United States (more than 60,000 sq ft in area). Reflecting upon your experiences shopping in such a store, identify the various SBUs for such a supermarket.

3. What are the implications of the Wind, Mahajan, and Swire study on comparisons of portfolio models? Would the use of a portfolio model over time impact the conclusion of this study?

4. Consider the illustration in the chapter of the use of AHP with multiple decision makers. Instead of the computed average allocation (next to the last row of Table 8.4), suppose you wish to compute a weighted average. How might you determine such weights? What are the implications of a weighted average rather than a simple average in this context?

5. Assume that you need to allocate a total budget of $300,000 across two products X and Y. The relevant data are given below.

Product	Margin ($)	Sales Units (000s)
X	14	400
Y	30	300

Expenditures	Sales of	
	X	Y
X	e_{11}	e_{21}
Y	e_{21}	e_{22}

	e_{11}	e_{12}	e_{22}	e_{21}
Case I	0.3	0.05	0.5	0.1
Case II	0.3	0.1	0.5	0.02
Case III	0.7	0	0.5	0.15

Using this information, compute the allocations of budget called for in the table below.

Interdependence	X	Y
Yes		
No		

Notes

1. See Carmody, Deirdre (1993), "In a Reversal, Condé Nast closes HG," *New York Times,* April 21, D1.
2. See, for example, Myers, Stuart (1984), "Finance Theory and Financial Strategy," *Interfaces* (January-February): 126–137; Rappaport, Alfred (1986), *Creating Shareholder Value,* New York: Free Press; and Naylor, Thomas H., and Francis Tapon (1982), "The Capital Asset Pricing Model: An Evaluation of its Potential as a Strategic Tool," *Management Science* (October): 1166–1173.
3. For a comprehensive discussion of portfolio methods, see Kerin, Roger A., Vijay Mahajan, and P. Rajan Varadarajan (1990), *Contemporary Perspectives on Strategic Market Planning,* Needham Heights, MA: Allyn and Bacon.
4. See Wind, Yoram, and Vijay Mahajan (1981), "Designing Product and Business Portfolios," *Harvard Business Review* 59 (January-February): 155–165.
5. Data from Morris, Betsy (1987), "Coke vs. Pepsi: Cola War Marches on," *The Wall Street Journal,* June 3, 31.
6. This judgmental analysis can be complicated if the firms have unequal numbers of products. One may require a multi-attribute model to determine the degree of balance among a set of products; see Farquhar, Peter H., and Vithala R. Rao (1976), "A Balance Model for Evaluating Subsets of Multiattributed Items," *Management Science* 22 (May): 528–539.
7. Robinson, S. J. Q., R. E. Hichens, and D. P. Wade (1978), "The Directional Policy Matrix—Tool for Strategic Planning," *Long Range Planning* 11 (June): 8–15.
8. See Patel, Peter, and Michael Younger (1978),"A Frame of Reference for Strategy Development," *Long Range Planning* 11, (April): 6–12. See also Osell, Roger R., and Robert V. L. Wright (1980), "Allocating Resources: How to Do It in Multi-Industry Corporations," in Kenneth J. Albert, (ed.), *Handbook of*

Business Problem Solving, New York: McGraw-Hill, 1-89-1-109 for a comprehensive application of this approach.
9. See Hax, Arnoldo C., and Nicholas S. Majluf (1984), *Strategic Management: An Integrative Perspective,* Englewood Cliffs, NJ: Prentice-Hall.
10. See Wind, Yoram, Vijay Mahajan, and Donald J. Swire (1983), "An Empirical Comparison of Standardized Product Portfolio Models," *Journal of Marketing* 47 (Spring): 89–99.
11. See Larreche, Jean-Claude, and V. Srinivasan (1981), "STRATPORT: A Decision Support System for Strategic Planning," *Journal of Marketing* 45 (Fall): 39–52.
12. See Saaty, Thomas L. (1980), *The Analytic Hierarchy Process,* New York: McGraw-Hill.
13. See Wind, Yoram, and Thomas L. Saaty (1980), "Marketing Applications of the Analytic Hierarchy Process," *Management Science* 26 (July): 641–658.
14. Expert Choice, Inc. (1995), EXPERT CHOICE, Version 9.0, McLean, VA: Decision Support Software, Inc.
15. See Buzzell, Robert D., and Bradley T. Gale (1987), *The PIMS Principles: Linking Strategy to Performance,* New York: The Free Press.
16. See Lilien, Gary L. (1979), "ADVISOR 2: Modeling the Marketing Mix Decisions for Industrial Products," *Management Science* 25 (February): 191–204.
17. See Levy, Michael, John Webster, and Roger A. Kerin (1983), "Formulating Push Marketing Strategies: A Method and Application," *Journal of Marketing* 47 (Winter): 25–34.
18. See Montgomery, David B., and Alvin J. Silk (1972), "Estimating Dynamic Effects of Market Communication Expenditures," *Management Science* 18 (June): B-485–B-501.

Bibliography

Abell, Derek F., and John S. Hammond (1977), *Strategic Market Planning,* Englewood Cliffs, NJ: Prentice-Hall.
Ansoff, Igor, and Edward McDonnell (1990), *Implanting Strategic Management,* Englewood Cliffs, NJ: Prentice-Hall.
Buzzell, Robert D., and Bradley T. Gale (1987), *The PIMS Principles: Linking Strategy to Performance,* New York: Free Press.
Caroll, J. Douglas, Paul E. Green, and Wayne S. DeSarbo (1979), "Optimizing the Allocation of a Fixed Resource: A Simple Model and Its Experimental Test," *Journal of Marketing* 43 (January): 51–57.
Chakravarti, Dipankar, Andrew Mitchell, and Richard Staelin (1981), "Judgment Based Marketing Decision

Models: Problems and Possible Solutions," *Journal of Marketing* 45 (Fall): 13–23.
Kerin, Roger A., Vijay Mahajan, and P. Rajan Varadarajan (1990), *Contemporary Perspectives on Strategic Market Planning,* Needham Heights, MA: Allyn and Bacon.
Larreche, Jean-Claude, and V. Srinivasan (1981), "STRATPORT: A Decision Support System for Strategic Planning," *Journal of Marketing* 45 (Fall): 39–52.
Levy, Michael, John Webster, and Roger A. Kerin (1983), "Formulating Push Marketing Strategies: A Method and Application," *Journal of Marketing* 47 (Winter): 25–34.

Lilien, Gary L. (1979), "ADVISOR 2: Modeling the Marketing Mix Decision for Industrial Products," *Management Science* 25 (February): 191–204.

Little, John D. C. (1970), "Models and Managers: The Concept of a Decision Calculus." *Management Science* 16 (April) B466–B485.

Lodish, Leonard M. (1986), *The Advertising and Promotion Challenge: Vaguely Right or Precisely Wrong?* New York: Oxford.

Montgomery, David B., and Alvin J. Silk (1972), "Estimating Dynamic Effects of Market Communication Expenditures," *Management Science* 18 (June): B-485–B-501.

Pessemier, Edgar A. (1982), *Product Management,* 2nd ed., New York: Wiley, Chapter 4.

Rao, Vithala R., and Darius Sabavala (1986), "Measuring and Use of Market Response Functions for Allocating Marketing Resources," Marketing Science Institute Technical Working Paper, 86–105.

Rao, Vithala R., Jerry Wind, and Wayne S. DeSarbo (1988), "A Customized Market Response Model: Development, Estimation, and Empirical Testing," *Journal of the Academy of Marketing Science* 16 (Spring) 128–140.

Saaty, Thomas L. (1980), *The Analytic Hierarchy Process,* New York: McGraw-Hill.

Srinivasan, V. (1985), "Computer-Aided Decision Making for Strategic Business Portfolio Decisions," in *Marketing in an Electronic Age,* R. D. Buzzell (ed.), Boston: Harvard Business School Press, 329–343.

Wind, Yoram, and Vijay Mahajan (1981), "Designing Product and Business Portfolios," *Harvard Business Review* 59 (January–February): 155–165.

Wind, Yoram, Vijay Mahajan, and Donald J. Swire (1983), "An Empirical Comparison of Standardized Portfolio Models," *Journal of Marketing* 47 (Spring): 89–99.

Wind, Yoram, and Thomas L. Saaty (1980), "Marketing Applications of the Analytic Hierarchy Process," *Management Science* 26 (July): 641–658.

Appendix 8A

Illustration of the Use of Business Assessment Array

This illustration is based on the "General Electric—Clock and Timer Market Strategy" case (Harvard Business School Case #9-582-031, rev. 5/84) prepared by Jeffrey Hunker under the supervision of John F. Cady. This illustration uses only some of the attributes described in the chapter. Nevertheless, the process of using the business assessment array should be clear.

The problem here is how General Electric should view its various products (businesses or SBUs) in the electric clock and timer industry in 1977. The firm had seven products with sizes, growth rates, shares, and margins presented in Table A8.1.

Computation of Scores on the Two Factors

First, the analyst obtains relative weights for the attributes included in the two factors. Then, she or he evaluates each product on these attributes. In this illustration, a three-point scale (1 = Low, 2 = Medium, and 3 = High) was used for the weights. Each attribute of the factor was also rated on a three-point scale, using the codes shown in Table A8.2. Actual ratings and weights are shown in Table A8.3.

TABLE A8.1 Data Used in Analysis

Product (Business)	Market Size 1977 ($ millions)	Growth Rate 1977–1981 (%)	GE's Share in 1977 (%)	GE's Variable Margin in 1977 (%)
Digital electronic alarms	$7.02	64.0%	8.3%	30.0%
Digital electromechanical alarms	21.06	−17.5	27.8	42.4
Analog clocks	21.2	~2.5	35.0	30.0
Wall clocks	48.6	7.0	7.0	38.0
Commercial wall clocks	4.2	9.4	38.0	46.0
Electro-mechanical timers	19.1	−10.0	18.7	45.0
Electronic timers	—	61.0	—	—

TABLE A8.2 **Codes Used for Ratings**

(a) Industry Attractiveness

Item	Weight	High = 3	Medium = 2	Low = 1
			Rating	
Market segment size in 1977 (end products)	2	Over $100 million	$100 million to $50 million	Below $50 million
Market segment growth 1977 to 1981	3	Over 20%	20% to 10%	Below 10%
Profitability: variable margins	3	Over 40%	40% to 25%	Below 25%
Market share vulnerability	2	Easy to defend	Stable market shares	Share is vulnerable
Competitive environment	2	Very stable competitive environment	Moderately stable	Very unstable

(b) Competitive Business Position

Item	Weight	High = 3	Medium = 2	Low = 1
			Rating	
Product parity	3	Ahead of competition	About equal	Behind competition
Profit relative to industry	2	More than 1.1	1.1 to 0.9	Less than 0.9
Market share percent in 1977	2	Over 20%	20% to 10%	Below 10%
Unique strengths	2	Several with impact	One with impact	None
Market share relative to leader in 1977	1	Above 1.0	1.0 to 0.5	Less than 0.5

A summary rating on each factor was computed as the weighted average of the ratings for each of the seven products. The formula used was as follows:

$$\frac{\sum (\text{Weight}) * \text{Ratings}}{\sum \text{Weight}}.$$

The results are shown in Table A8.4.

The intervals used for forming the three groups of high, medium, and low for the industry attractiveness factor were 2.3–3.0, 1.6–2.3, and 1–1.6, respectively. The range

TABLE A8.3 Weights and Ratings for the Seven Products

(a) Industry Attractiveness

Attribute	Weight	Digital Electronic Alarms	Digital Electromechanical Alarms	Analog Clocks	Wall Clocks	Commercial Clocks	Electromechanical Timers	Electronic Timers
Market segment size in 1977	(2)	1	1	1	1	1	1	1
Market segment growth 1977–1981	(3)	3	1	2	1	1	3	3
Profitability: variable margins	(3)	3	2	1	2	3	3	1
Market share vulnerability	(2)	1	1	1	2	3	1	1
Competitive environment	(2)	2	1	1	1	2	1	1

(b) Competitive Business Position

Attribute	Weight	Digital Electronic Alarms	Digital Electromechanical Alarms	Analog Clocks	Wall Clocks	Commercial Clocks	Electromechanical Timers	Electronic Timers
Product parity	(3)	2	1	1	2	3	2	2
Profit relative to industry	(2)	3	2	1	2	2	2	2
Market share percent in 1977	(2)	2	3	3	1	3	2	3
Unique strengths	(2)	2	1	1	1	1	1	2
Market share relative to leader in 1977	(1)	1	2	2	1	3	2	3

TABLE A8.4   **Scores for the Seven Products on the Two Factors**

| | Factor | |
Product	Industry Attractiveness	Competitive Business Position
Digital electronic alarms	2.2	2.7
Digital electromechanical alarms	1.25	1.7
Analog clocks	1.0	1.5
Wall clocks	1.5	1.4
Commercial wall clocks	2.0	2.5
Electromechanical timers	2.0	1.8
Electronic timers	1.5	2.3

TABLE A8.5   **Computed Business Assessment Array**

| | Competitive Business Position | | |
Industry Attractiveness	High 3.0 to 2.3	Medium 2.3 to 1.6	Low 1.6 to 1.0
High 2.3 to 3.0	Investment and growth	Selective growth • Digital electronic alarms • Commercial wall clocks	Selectivity
Medium 1.6 to 2.3	Selective growth	Selectivity • Electro-mechanical timers	Harvest/divest • Digital electromechanical timers • Electronic timers
Low 1.0 to 1.6	Selectivity	Harvest/divest	Harvest/divest • Analog clocks • Wall clocks

for each factor was 1–3. The same intervals were used for the competitive business position. The seven products were classified into the 3×3 matrix. The results are shown in Table A8.5. The corresponding investment recommendations are also shown.

This analysis was important in General Electric's decision to divest these product lines. The company sold its product lines to Timex in 1978.

Appendix 8B

AHP Methodology

The philosophy of this method is as follows:

- The decision problem can be structured as a hierarchy of various relevant factors (Environmental constraints—Perspectives/Actors—Objectives—Policies—Outcomes).
- The decision process can be decomposed into various attributes at each level of the hierarchy.
- Pairwise judgments on levels of any factor encompass all its relevant aspects.

The method is based on the following assumptions:

- The relative importances of levels within a factor are unidimensional and are ratio scaled.
- The judgments are ratio scaled.
- The judgments are consistent; that is,

$$A_{ik} = A_{ij} \times A_{jk}$$

If these assumptions hold, the weights can be estimated. If the true weights (w_1, w_2, ..., w_n) are known, then

$$A_{ij} = \frac{w_i}{w_j}, \quad i, \ j = 1, \ \ldots, \ n$$

For example, for the weights of (.4, .5, .1),

$$A_{12} = \frac{w_1}{w_2} = \frac{.4}{.5} = .8; \quad A_{13} = 4; \quad A_{23} = .5$$

Therefore, the third assumption holds; that is,

$$A_{13} = A_{12} \times A_{23}.$$

Let A be the matrix of pairwise judgments and w be the vector of true weights. The true weights can be shown to be the solution of the matrix equation

$$Aw = nw.$$

One can recognize w as the first eigenvector of A.

The method can be described by the following steps:

Step 1:   Define the problem in a broad context and specify the solution desired.

Step 2:   Structure the hierarchy from the overall managerial purposes (the highest levels) through relevant intermediate levels to the level where control would alleviate—or solve—the problems.

Step 3:   Construct a pairwise comparison matrix for the relative contribution, impact, or importance of each element to each governing objective or criterion in the adjacent upper level.

Step 4:   Obtain all $n(n-1)/2$ judgments (Step 2) specified by the set of matrices developed in Step 3.

Step 5:   Having collected the pairwise comparison data and entered the reciprocals together with n unit entries down the main diagonal, solve the eigenvalue problem* and test for consistency.

Step 6:   Repeat Steps 3, 4, and 5 are for all levels in the hierarchy.

Step 7:   Hierarchical composition is now used to weight the eigenvectors by the weights of the criteria, and the sum is taken over all weighted eigenvector entries corresponding to those in the next lower level, and so on, resulting in a composite priority vector for the lowest level of the hierarchy. The calculation of the priorities does not require judgment on all possible pairs. Various shortcuts can be taken.

Step 8:   Evaluate consistency of the entire hierarchy.

Determination of Weights

The following are five alternative methods to solving the eigenvector problem:

1. *The Crudest:* Sum the elements in each row and normalize by dividing each sum by the total of all the sums; the results now add up to unity. The first entry of the resulting vector is the priority of the first activity, the second of the second activity, and so on.
2. *Better:* Take the sum of the elements in each column and form the reciprocals of these sums. Normalize these numbers to add to unity, divide each reciprocal by the sum of the reciprocals.
3. *Good:* Divide the elements of each column by the sum of that column (that is, normalize the column). Add the elements in each resulting row and divide this sum by the number of elements in each row.
4. *Good:* Multiply the n elements in each row and take the nth root. Normalize the resulting numbers.
5. *Best:* Eigenvalue/eigenvector computation.

These methods can be compared for one set of of judgmental data on the brightness of four chairs, A, B, C, and D, placed at different distances from a light source.

---

*The calculation of the weights does not require judgment on all possible pairs. Various shortcuts exits.

	A	B	C	D
A	1	5	6	7
B	1/5	1	4	6
C	1/6	1/4	1	4
D	1/7	1/6	1/4	1

Solutions for weights given by the five methods are as follows:

	Method 1	Method 2	Method 3	Method 4	Method 5
					(Eigenvector)
A	0.51	0.68	0.590	0.61	0.61
B	0.30	0.16	0.245	0.24	0.24
C	0.15	0.09	0.115	0.10	0.10
D	0.04	0.06	0.050	0.04	0.05

It is interesting to note that the relative weights should be 0.61, 0.22, 0.11, and 0.06 according to the inverse square law of optics in physics.

Actual Case Examples

Analyses in Action

INTRODUCTION

Marketing strategy is a simple concept. As argued in Chapter 1, it essentially boils down to where and how to compete. One of the premises of this book, however, is the notion that, despite the simplicity of the concept, *formulating* marketing strategy is a very difficult task. In so doing, firms need to be sensitive to their ever-changing marketplaces. This involves a thorough understanding of customers, competitors, and the various other external political, economic, social, and technological forces that impact the behavior of present and future customers and competitors. Required information is either unavailable or difficult to interpret—partly because it relates more to the future than the present.

This book has presented a cornucopia of techniques useful for the collection and/or analysis of information to make appropriate decisions. We have presented techniques for identifying market segments and consumer needs, identifying competitors, analyzing a firm's strengths and weaknesses relative to competitors, forecasting environmental scenarios, and allocating resources.

Having read the text up to this point does not necessarily allow the practicing manager to implement these techniques with total confidence. To fully appreciate these tools, the reader has to actually use them in practice. Unfortunately, it is not within the scope of this book to provide the reader with such opportunities. They can only be provided in either the workplace or a practical component of classroom experience. The closest we can come within these pages is to show how other people have applied some of these tools in their own workplaces.

Towards that end, we present four real-life case studies, summarized in Table 9.1. The first, a sports apparel industry study, is a study sponsored by a trade association. The second, the Victoria Moore activewear line study, was performed for a high-profile fashion designer interested in that very same market. The third one, the Citibank photocard study, was conducted by Citibank personnel themselves. The fourth, a study performed for Holdzer Catering, related to institutional catering facilities in Finland.

These studies represent a variety of products, research objectives, and research methodologies. The sports apparel industry study and the Victoria Moore

TABLE 9.1   **Overview of Chapter 9 Studies**

Study	Research Objectives	Relevant Techniques	Chapter with Relevant Material
Sports apparel	Identify benefit segments	Focus groups; factor analysis; perceptual mapping	2, 3, 4
	Identify competition across conventional product lines		
Victoria Moore	Identify unmet needs	Standard surveys	2, 3, 4, 5, 7
	Identify target customers, assess potential, determine benefits required		
Citibank	Assess solution to unmet need	Focus groups	3, 5, 7
	Evaluate basis for differentiation		
Holdzer Catering	Determine value customers place on the Holdzer brand name	Conjoint analysis	2, 7
	Determine service components customers require		

study are about consumer products; the Citibank photocard study is about a service; and the Holdzer Catering study relates to business-to-business marketing. The sports apparel industry study was conducted to find growth opportunities within an industry for firms participating in that industry; the objective of the Victoria Moore study was to investigate growth opportunities within an industry for a firm outside that industry; the Citibank photocard study was conducted to examine the viability of a specific basis of differentiation in a market in which it is difficult to differentiate; and the Holdzer Catering study was conducted to identify customers most favorably disposed to the company and to provide insight into how to design their service offerings. With respect to methodologies, the sports apparel study uses many of the sophisticated computer-intensive techniques presented in Chapters 2 and 4; the Victoria Moore study uses much simpler approaches to survey and questionnaire design; the Citibank study uses the focus group approaches described in Chapter 3; and the Holdzer Catering study uses a modified form of conjoint analysis.

After digesting these four, the reader should have a good feel for the spectrum of market analyses and appreciate their potential contribution to the corporate enterprise.

SPORTS APPAREL INDUSTRY STUDY*

The sports apparel industry can be characterized as large, omnipresent, and extremely diverse. Spearheaded by Nike, Reebok, L.A. Gear, Champion, and Adidas, the industry accounts for close to $50 billion in retail sales annually. It grew about 10 percent from 1991 to 1992. Many of the competitors in this market began as shoe companies. Looking for growth avenues, they followed the prescriptions of Ansoff's product-market matrix (see Chapters 3 and 4) and asked themselves the question, "What else can we sell in our markets?" The answer was sports apparel.

Most Americans (86 percent of the population) own some sports apparel item. The category has equal penetration among both men and women. Women spend even more on sports apparel than men. The industry produces a wide variety of products (shirts, shorts, socks, sweats, hats, apparel with team logos, etc.[1]) made for an even wider variety of activities (running, walking, tennis, aerobics, biking, swimming, soccer, etc.). The increasing diversity of such activities has helped to fuel recent growth in the industry. Growth has been further fueled by the use of sports apparel for things other than sports. In particular, approximately 91 percent of the people who own sports apparel also commonly use it as casual wear. In fact, over one-third of the people who own sports apparel use it *only* as casual wear.

Despite this rosy picture, dark clouds have begun to appear on the horizon. In 1993, for the first time in a long time, the industry saw essentially no growth at all. Sales to women actually declined. Furthermore, new competitors entered the arena. The importance of casual use has left the industry vulnerable to fashion companies like Donna Karan, Liz Claiborne, and Pierre Cardin that have not traditionally marketed sports apparel but *have* marketed casual wear. Doubtlessly, this contributed to the decline in sales to women in 1993.

In response to these circumstances, the Sports Apparel Products Council of the Sporting Goods Manufacturers Association, a trade association, recognized the need to devise strategies to not only defend the markets of its participating companies, but establish new directions in which its participating companies could grow. Towards this end the council commissioned Directions for Decisions, a New York–New Jersey–based survey and market research consulting firm, to perform a study with the following objectives:

1. to uncover whatever benefit segments exist in the marketplace, and
2. to examine how consumers perceive the different items in the sports apparel category.

Satisfying the first objective will enable manufacturers to discover exactly what consumers want in their sports apparel and who wants it. This will reveal potential

*The authors would like to thank Elliot Savitsky of Directions for Decisions, Inc., 10 Exchange Place, 17th floor, Jersey City, NJ 07302, (201)413-9000, and Maria Stefan of the Sporting Goods Marketing Association, 200 Castlewood Dr., North Palm Beach, FL 33408, (407)840-1150, for permission to use this research.

growth opportunities by either uncovering desired benefits that are not being provided (unmet needs) or suggesting how and to whom manufacturers might promote their products that provide specific benefits. Satisfying the second objective could lead to a customer-oriented understanding of the competitive structure of the industry, thereby leading to an understanding of how potential competitors (either existing firms or new entrants) might compete with current ones.

The study centered around a survey developed after a series of focus groups conducted to refine issues and test preliminary questions. A 36-page interviewer-administered questionnaire was developed and administered to 1,107 consumers in 60 U.S. locations during June of 1993. The respondents included men and women ranging in age from 10 to 75. The interview took about 45 minutes. During the interview, respondents filled out worksheets and studied photographs of different types of sports apparel. After the interview, respondents completed a leave-behind booklet containing questions about their lifestyles, hobbies, and media habits. This booklet was picked up later the same day.

Benefit Segments

Data Collection and Procedures In the interview, respondents were asked to rate the importance (on a five-point scale) of several characteristics they might consider in the purchase of sports apparel. These characteristics are listed in the page from the interviewer's script presented in Fig. 9.1. (This page includes only the first 22 of the 29 benefit items asked about.) The percentage of the sample that rated the importance of a given characteristic when being used for sports activity as "extremely important" is shown in Fig. 9.2. A similar question was asked for casual activity with similar results. The individual respondents' sports and casual use importance ratings were pooled and factor analyzed and the factor scores were clustered into seven groups. The demographics, spending patterns, and media habits of each group (segment) were then summarized.

Results Fig. 9.3 shows the seven benefit segments and their relative sizes. The segment names were chosen by the firm that conducted the research to correspond to the segment's benefits desired, demographics, lifestyles, and media habits. It is noteworthy that these segments were formed to maximize the differences across and similarities within segments with respect to benefit importances. This does not guarantee that there will be any differences with respect to demographics, lifestyles, spending patterns, and media habits. Fortunately, in this study there were. Many of these differences are profiled in Table 9.2. The table only presents benefit requirements that differ from the population as a whole. For example, all segments consider "comfortable fit" to be the most important benefit, so it is not mentioned in the table; however, the *Inner City–Influenced* have a greater than average desire to wear clothes that "all their friends are wearing."

The *Self-Oriented* segment is puzzling in that the only benefit it rated greater than average in importance is that the apparel be "old." However, this value is so low on the average (see Fig. 9.2) that it is not useful here. These people's responses to

20. Let's talk for a few minutes about how you decide to buy your sports apparel.

First, I'd like to know what is important to you when deciding to buy sports apparel. To do this, I'm going to read several characteristics. For each one I read, I'd like you to rate how important you feel that characteristic is in your decision to buy sports apparel. Please use any number from 1 to 5, where 1 means the characteristic is "not important at all" and 5 means the characteristic is "extremely important."

Let's start with (<u>INSERT CIRCLED CHARACTERISTICS</u>). How important is (<u>CHARACTERISTIC</u>) in your decision to buy sports apparel? (RECORD RATING # BELOW)

How important is (<u>INSERT NEXT CHARACTERISTIC</u>)? (CONTINUE FOR ALL CHARACTERISTICS)

1	5
Not At All Important	Extremely Important

a. The look or style	_____	(92)
b. Good value for the money	_____	(93)
c. Fits comfortably	_____	(94)
d. Advertising	_____	(95)
e. It performs the way you want it to	_____	(96)
f. Brand name	_____	(97)
g. Knowledgeable salespeople	_____	(98)
h. The color	_____	(99)
i. Can be used for casual use as well as for sports	_____	(100)
j. The quality	_____	(101)
k. The fabric it's made of	_____	(102)
l. Durability	_____	(103)
m. All your friends have it	_____	(104)
n. Is in style	_____	(105)
o. Playing the sport for which it is intended	_____	(106)
p. Won't shrink	_____	(107)
q. Being easy to care for	_____	(108)
r. Being endorsed by a celebrity	_____	(109)
s. Having good stitching	_____	(110)
t. Made in USA	_____	(111)
u. Can be used for a number of different sports	_____	(112)
v. Having a team logo that you want	_____	(113)

BE SURE ALL CHARACTERISTICS HAVE BEEN RATED BEFORE PROCEEDING.

FIGURE 9.1 **Page from Sports Apparel Interview Script**

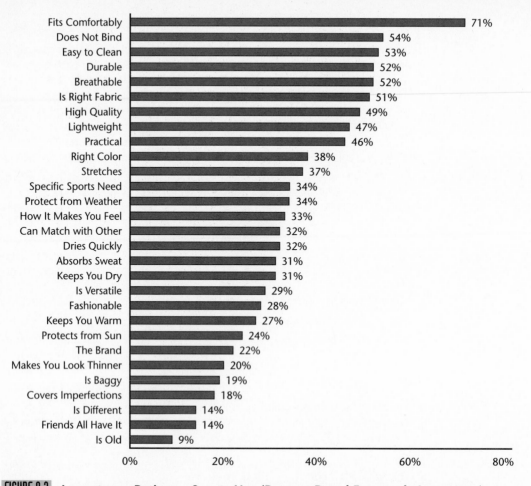

FIGURE 9.2 **Importance Ratings—Sports Use (Percent Rated Extremely Important)**

lifestyle questions in the leave-behind booklet indicate that their motives for participating in sports were to attract the opposite sex, experience the feeling of competition, improve their skills, and make new friends. Their name comes from the fact that they have a low level of concern for today's social issues.

More than any other segment, the *Tough Customer* demands an extraordinary number of benefits for sports apparel. Their importance ratings are higher than average on almost every benefit. Their "comfortable fit" rating is even 14 percent higher than the average for the population as a whole. They walk for exercise to control their weight. They are old fashioned in that they do not believe women with children should work. Finally, they do not like to be in public unless they look their best, probably because they feel you can tell a lot about a person by the way he or she dresses.

The primary benefit desired by the *Inner-City Influenced* segment (relative to the population) is that "all their friends have it." They jog, lift weights, and play basket-

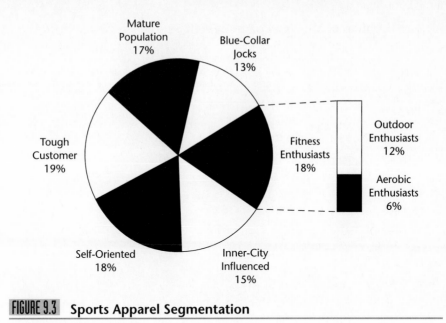

FIGURE 9.3 **Sports Apparel Segmentation**

ball more than the average and exercise for the competition it provides and to be with their friends. They like to spend money on their appearance and are fashion conscious. They tend to be single and live in urban areas.

Blue-Collar Jocks require sports apparel that is versatile and used for the sport for which it is intended. They own a higher than average amount of outdoor wear and would like to be able to spend more on clothes. Blue-collar jocks lift weights, bowl, fish, and play a lot of football and softball. They have little concern for politics and place a greater than average emphasis on sports.

The *Mature Population* segment tends to be a bit older. Its primary activities are exercise and fitness walking. Health is more important than appearance. These people tend to be conservative and like to garden, spend time with their spouse, and participate in church and religious activities. This is one of the few segments that does not expect its income to increase.

The *Aerobic Enthusiasts* segment consists primarily of housewives and participates heavily in aerobics. Its members have the highest household income of all the segments and are impulse purchasers. They feel that the way one looks strongly impacts the way one feels.

The *Outdoor Enthusiasts* are heavy spenders (12 percent of the people, 17 percent of the dollars). More than the average, they desire sports apparel that is nonbinding, durable, provides protection from the weather, and is breathable. They participate in camping, biking, boating, fishing, and weight lifting. They are liberal, progressive thinkers who are down to earth. They place a great deal of emphasis on career.

Implications A comfortable fit is clearly the most important benefit in sports apparel across all segments. Therefore it becomes crucial to communicate fit in advertising.

TABLE 9.2   **Profiles of Sports Apparel Benefit Segments**

	Market Segments						
	Self-Oriented	Tough Customers	Inner City–Influenced	Blue-Collar Jocks	Mature Population	Aerobic Enthusiasts	Outdoor Enthusiasts
Male	X		X	X	X		X
Female	X	X	X		X	X	X
Age (mean)	35.0	41.0	33.0	35.0	45.0	38.0	40.0
% Married	56%	69%	36%	44%	65%	59%	54%
Income (mean) in thousands	$44.0	$43.0	$40.0	$40.0	$36.0	$45.0	$40.0
% of Sample	18%	19%	15%	13%	17%	6%	12%
$ spent past year	$76.7	$59.6	$73.0	$71.5	$53.7	$53.7	$75.5
Media							
Television							
Sports	X		X	X			X
Drama						X	
News					X	X	
Talk shows		X					
MTV	X		X	X			
Cartoons		X	X				
Sitcoms		X					
Variety							
Documentaries					X		
Soaps		X					
Magazines							
General sports	X		X	X			X
Women's		X					
General interest		X	X				
TV Guide			X				
African-American			X				
Teen Magazines							
Men's lifestyle			X				
Benefits Sought	Old	Higher on most	All friends have it	Authentic use	Protects from weather Easy care	Non-binding Breathable Stretches Practical Need for sport	Non-binding Durable Protects from weather Breathable

X = Important to market segment.

TABLE 9.3 **Sports Apparel Segments' Market Spending**

	Total	Self-Oriented	Tough Customers	Inner City–Influenced	Blue-Collar Jocks	Mature Population	Aerobic Enthusiasts	Outdoor Enthusiasts
Mean amount spent past year	$44.5	$76.7	$59.6	$73.8	$71.5	$53.7	$41.7	$75.5
Mean amount willing to spend next year	$68.5	$35.9	$67.1	$76.5	$79.1	$52.8	$44.1	$73.9
Mean % increase/decrease	+6%	+12%	+13%	+5%	+11%	–2%	+6%	–2%

We identified a wide variety of market (benefit) segments that could be developed. The decisions related to which segments to pursue would involve a trade-off between the magnitude of the opportunity the segment represents and the expenditures necessary to develop and exploit a competitive advantage in that segment.

In assessing the opportunity each segment provides several factors should be considered. These include segment size, expenditures per customer, and projected growth. Size and expenditures per customer are found in Table 9.2. To get a handle on projected segment growth, the leave-behind booklet included questions directed at expected expenditures as well as current ones. The mean values for these, as well as the resultant growth, are given in Table 9.3.

The three segments with the greatest growth are the Self-Orienteds, Tough Customers, and Blue-Collar Jocks. The Self-Orienteds and Tough Customers are especially attractive because not only do the data indicate that their expenditures will increase the most, but they are the largest segments too (see Figure 9.3 on page 389). Thus, the expenditure increase will occur over more people! However, marketing to these groups could be quite competitive. Some companies might be better off choosing a target, like the Mature Population, that represents a growing group in terms of population size. The Mature Population of the future will be filled with today's baby boomers, who will probably bring many of their attitudes and habits with them.

Consumer Perceptions

Data Collection and Procedures   A portion of the interview was devoted to a card-sorting task. Respondents were given 62 different photographs of sports apparel items. Different sets were used for men and women. In each case, respondents were instructed to sort into groups the items that were "similar" to each other and "different" from those in other piles. Respondents were free to choose any number of piles up to 62 with as many photos in a pile as they wished. The frequency with which two items were put into the same pile across the entire sample served as a measure of similarity between them.

Results   Separate perceptual maps were created from these data for men and women. These are presented in Figs. 9.4 and 9.5, respectively.

As is evident from the figures, there are several qualitative similarities to the ways men and women view the market. First, both maps have garments of similar categories (jackets, shirts, shorts, hats, etc.) positioned close to each other. Nike shirts appear to compete more with Reebok shirts than they do with Nike shorts. Second, within categories, items associated with the same sport are located in close proximity. Finally, it seems that other distinguishing features (such as color, brand, and presence of a team license, etc.) determine precise locations.

Implications   The category-primary nature of the way consumers view the market suggests that extensions to other categories provide greater opportunities than line extensions within a category. Within-category line extensions will simply be seen as substitutes and are likely to cannibalize a firm's current offerings to current customers. Recall that the penetration of sports apparel is so high that new category customers are rare. The dominant mode of sales increase, then, is likely to be capturing customers from other firms.

Thus, different apparel categories should be added before new styles are added to a currently manufactured category. If L.A. Gear, for example, invested in the design and production of more tennis shirts, it could avoid competing with (and cannibalizing) its tennis shoes. Consistent with this, licensing could be done in several categories. Furthermore, manufacturers trying to attract attention to their entire line should encourage retailers to merchandise and display combinations of separates. This could overcome the brand-primary perception and suggest that someone buying a shirt consider a pair of pants as well.

THE "VICTORIA MOORE" ACTIVEWEAR LINE*

The Victoria Moore Company is a multifaceted, upscale clothing design firm. It designs and manufactures women's dress and casual clothing, shoes, jeans, accessories, menswear, and children's wear. The vast majority of its business is in women's clothing, the area in which the company began. One day, while in an airport readying for vacation, the company president saw that a few of her fellow passengers were dressed in warm-up suits and sweatpants. She had the inspiration for the Victoria Moore activewear line. She wondered whether there was a market for

---

*Victoria Moore is a disguised name. The real company featured in this example preferred to remain anonymous. The authors wish to thank the Victoria Moore Company for permission to use this study. They further wish to thank the research team of Kimberly Banks, Gina Lee Plaia, Tracy Pollastri, and Joseph Weglein.

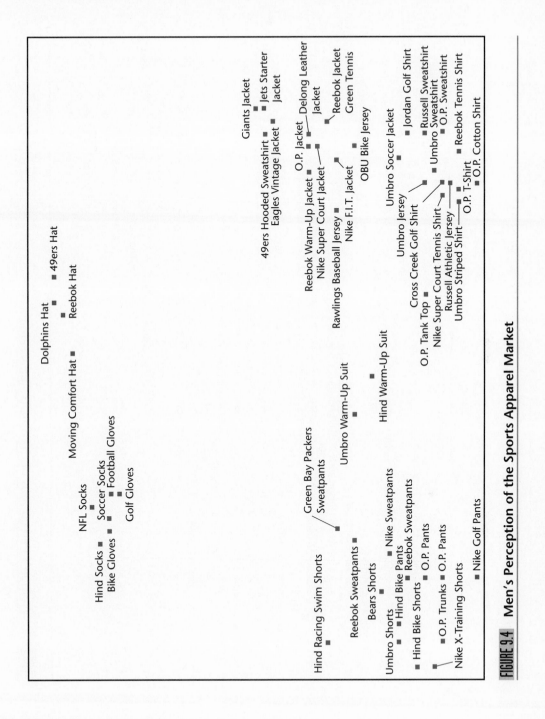

FIGURE 9.4 Men's Perception of the Sports Apparel Market

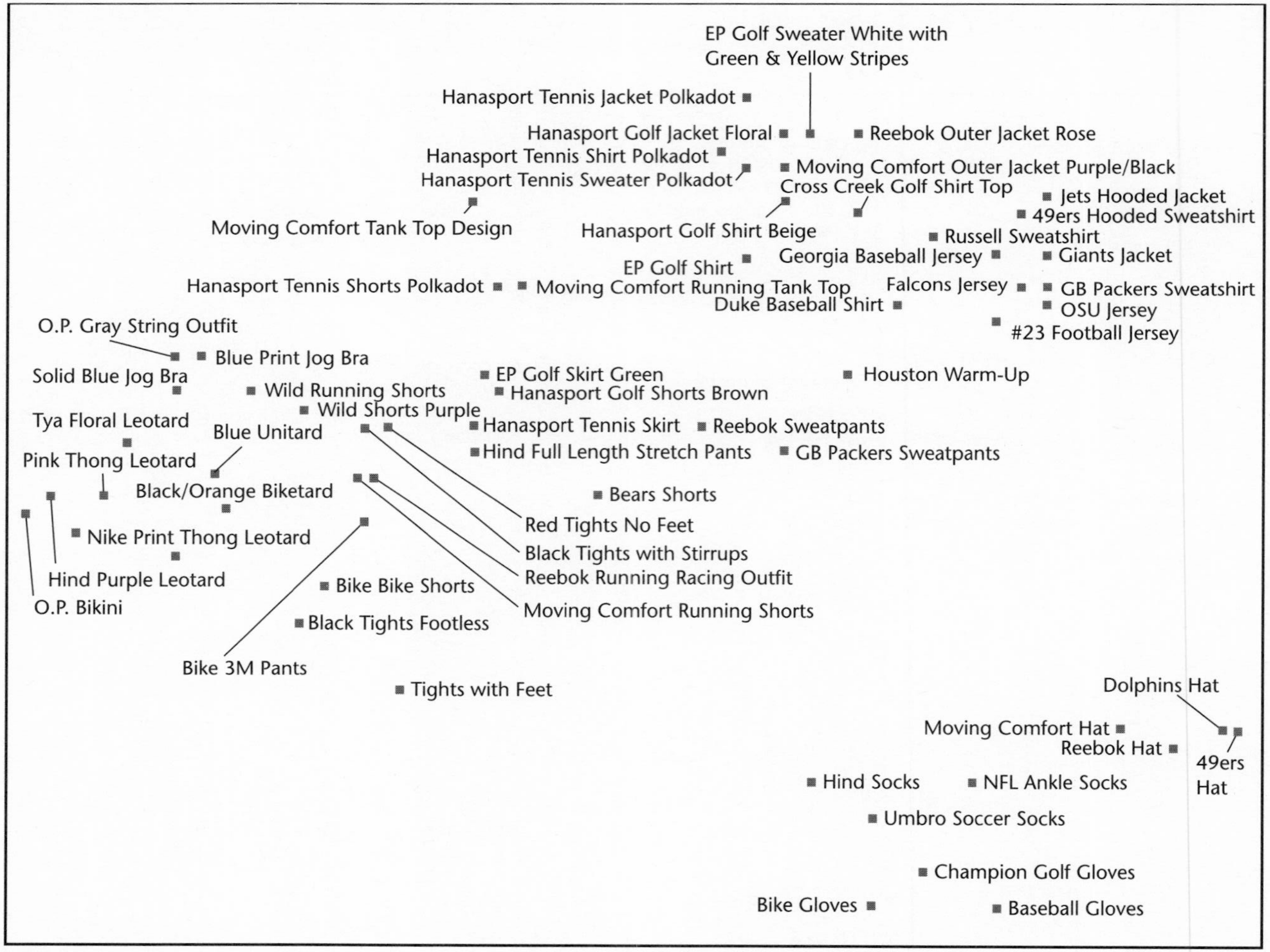

EP Golf Sweater White with
Green & Yellow Stripes ■

Hanasport Tennis Jacket Polkadot ■

Hanasport Golf Jacket Floral ■   ■ Reebok Outer Jacket Rose
Hanasport Tennis Shirt Polkadot ■   ■ Moving Comfort Outer Jacket Purple/Black
Hanasport Tennis Sweater Polkadot ■   Cross Creek Golf Shirt Top ■   ■ Jets Hooded Jacket
                                                                     ■ 49ers Hooded Sweatshirt
Moving Comfort Tank Top Design ■   Hanasport Golf Shirt Beige ■   ■ Russell Sweatshirt
                                      EP Golf Shirt ■   Georgia Baseball Jersey ■   ■ Giants Jacket
Hanasport Tennis Shorts Polkadot ■   ■ Moving Comfort Running Tank Top   Falcons Jersey ■   ■ GB Packers Sweatshirt
                                         Duke Baseball Shirt ■   ■ OSU Jersey
O.P. Gray String Outfit ■   ■ #23 Football Jersey
                          ■ EP Golf Skirt Green   ■ Houston Warm-Up
Solid Blue Jog Bra ■   ■ Blue Print Jog Bra   Hanasport Golf Shorts Brown ■
                    ■ Wild Running Shorts   Hanasport Tennis Skirt ■   ■ Reebok Sweatpants
Tya Floral Leotard ■   ■ Wild Shorts Purple   Hind Full Length Stretch Pants ■   ■ GB Packers Sweatpants
Pink Thong Leotard ■   Blue Unitard ■
                      ■ Black/Orange Biketard   ■ Bears Shorts
                                              ■ Red Tights No Feet
                   ■ Nike Print Thong Leotard   ■ Black Tights with Stirrups
Hind Purple Leotard ■   ■ Bike Bike Shorts   ■ Reebok Running Racing Outfit
O.P. Bikini ■   ■ Black Tights Footless   ■ Moving Comfort Running Shorts

Bike 3M Pants ■   ■ Tights with Feet

                              Dolphins Hat ■

                    Moving Comfort Hat ■   ■ 49ers
                              Reebok Hat ■   Hat

                ■ Hind Socks   ■ NFL Ankle Socks

                    ■ Umbro Soccer Socks

                    ■ Champion Golf Gloves
Bike Gloves ■   ■ Baseball Gloves

FIGURE 9.5   **Women's Perceptions of the Sports Apparel Market**

another upscale, high-fashion, prestige line of sports apparel. Other designers have recognized this potential opportunity. Recent entrants include the Ralph Lauren active line, Evan Picone's EP Sport line, and the Liz (Claiborne) Sport line. However, Victoria Moore had a more upscale image than these designers. In contrast, Ellesse, traditionally an upscale activewear line, has been contemplating entry into the fashion casual wear segment, further signaling a potential blurring of market boundaries.

The company president needed answers to several questions before going forward with Victoria Moore activewear:

1. How could she identify her target customers? What potential do they represent?
2. Who would her competitors most likely be—other fashion designers of casual wear or sports apparel manufacturers?
3. What benefits do potential customers look for in leisure sports apparel: fit, fashion, comfort?
4. Is the Victoria Moore brand name an advantage in this category? And if so, what is its value?

To answer these questions, the president authorized a mail survey to be conducted by a team of students from New York University's Stern School of Business. The survey questionnaire, developed by the team, and a summary of the responses received can be found in Appendix 9A. The questionnaire was the result of pretesting an earlier version on 50 women to ensure self-administration and low levels of difficulty. Two thousand questionnaires were mailed, 1,600 to female American Express Gold Card holders and 400 to female NYU business school alumni who had graduated five to ten years earlier. (The responses of the two subsamples proved to be indistinguishable.) To increase the response rate, a drawing for Victoria Moore accessories was promised to all who returned the questionnaire in a self-addressed, stamped envelope. The eventual response rate was 30 percent.

The sample was clearly skewed towards upper-income respondents. This was done because targeting lower-income households would likely damage the Victoria Moore image. Furthermore, the market would be too unfamiliar to the company to enter with a brand new product.

Target Customers   Two steps were implemented in the identification of potential customers. First, question 12 provided information on the proportion of the sample interested in buying Victoria Moore activewear. This group was identified as potential customers. Second, descriptive characteristics of this subgroup were compared with those of the sample at large and those of activewear customers in general (from question 1 in the survey) to isolate the distinguishing characteristics of this target population.

Consistent with the trade association study described in the last section, 79 percent of the sample indicated that they were activewear buyers; 26 percent of these indicated that they would consider buying Victoria Moore activewear.

The largest share of activewear consumers (28 percent) report a household income of less than $50,000 (question 17). However, 30 percent of Victoria Moore's potential customers came from households with incomes in excess of $100,000. Furthermore, 40 percent of all activewear customers with incomes exceeding $100,000 were interested in Victoria Moore activewear. Thus, Victoria Moore's customer base could be characterized as high income.

Further, 80 percent of all activewear consumers are employed full time, while only 66 percent of those interested in Victoria Moore are. Thus the potential Victoria Moore customer appears to have more time for leisure activity than the average activewear customer. In addition, it was found that while the overall activewear customer was most likely to be between 35 and 44 years old, the potential Victoria Moore customer was more likely to be between 25 and 34 years old.

In addition, 60 percent of Victoria Moore's potential customers said that they spend between $100 and $500 annually on activewear. Given that many customers spend in excess of $1000 annually and the distribution of annual expenditures is therefore asymmetric, it was assumed that $350 per year (not $300, the midpoint of the $100–$500 range) was the average amount the Victoria Moore prospect spends. Taking these figures together with the incidence of Victoria Moore prospects in the sample and making the assumption that the target market includes women residing in households with incomes greater than $75,000,[2] we conclude that the maximum market potential for Victoria Moore activewear is in the healthy neighborhood of *one billion dollars!* This is seen as follows:

15 million women in target market

> × *79% of population who are activewear buyers*[3]
> 11,850,000 market potential customers
>
> × *26% would consider Victoria Moore*[4]
> 3,081,000 potential customers for Victoria Moore
>
> × *$350 expenditures per customer*
> *$1,078,350,000 sales from potential Victoria Moore customers!*

Competition   In Chapter 4, we emphasized that the identification of competitors rested on how customers viewed a product. Question 14 of the survey asked respondents whether they would wear Victoria Moore activewear for sports purposes, leisure activities, or both. *No respondent in the group of potential Victoria Moore customers indicated that she would purchase Victoria Moore for sports alone!* Of the respondents who were potential Victoria Moore customers, 36 percent did not answer this question; perhaps it was too complicated. Nevertheless, 14 percent said they would use Victoria Moore activewear for leisure alone; 50 percent said that they would use it for both. These results indicate that women expect Victoria Moore activewear to be too nice to use only for exercising. It seems then that Victoria Moore could potentially draw from both traditional sports apparel manufacturers and other high-fashion designers. In any event, given the universality of leisure use, the latter certainly cannot be ignored.

Benefits Required   Question 6 of the survey asked respondents to rank six factors in order of importance in the purchase decision for both sports and leisure activities.

In both categories, comfort was rated the number one criterion; 69 percent ranked it in the top two for sports activities and 71 percent did so for leisure activities. This is consistent with the results of the sports apparel industry study described in the last section. In this study, fashion ranked a clear second for leisure or casual activities; 46 percent had it in the top two. There was no clear second for sports. Nevertheless, since Victoria Moore's customers are more interested in leisure activities, the comfort first–fashion second benefit priorities seem paramount.

Brand Equity   The amount of equity built into the Victoria Moore name can be determined by the amounts customers are willing to pay for the brand relative to those of other designers. The responses to question 13 on the survey generally indicate that activewear consumers are willing to pay at least as much for Victoria Moore activewear (or a sweatshirt, to be specific) as for other designer activewear. They are also willing to pay approximately a 10 percent premium for Victoria Moore over Liz Claiborne and Leslie Fay. This can be seen in the following table, extracted from the comprehensive data tabulated in Appendix 9A.

	Amount Consumers Are Willing to Pay		
Sweatshirt Designer	All Activewear Consumers	Victoria Moore Activewear Potential Customers	Current Victoria Moore Customers
Victoria Moore	$48	$51	$53
Leslie Fay	41	46	47
Liz Claiborne	42	45	48

One possible caveat to these findings is that current owners of Victoria Moore clothing are willing to pay more for all brands than are potential Victoria Moore customers.[5] This implies that current customers place a higher value on brand name than noncustomers do. Furthermore, Victoria Moore should consider marketing its activewear in distribution outlets at which current customers shop.

Implications   The implications of this research are quite straightforward. There is a demand for designer activewear, as 75 percent of respondents said they would purchase it. None, however, would buy it for sports alone. Thus it is important that the items be comfortable and fashionable. The Victoria Moore name carries a lot of value, so the company can command its usual price premium. All signs point to Victoria Moore entering this market. The appropriate target seems to be higher-income households with a female head between 25 and 34 years of age.

CITIBANK PHOTOCARD FOCUS GROUP PROJECT*

The credit card industry is a difficult one in which to compete. Market penetration approaches 90 percent. Furthermore, new, nontraditional competitors (AT&T, Ford, GM) are entering the market. This has led consumers to carry more and more credit

*The authors would like to thank Betty Hoople of Citibank for permission to use this research in this book.

cards and use each card already held less and less. Most of the major attributes of credit cards (annual fee, interest rate, length of grace period) are immediately duplicatable. Thus suppliers are compelled to continually search for new and unique ways to differentiate their offerings. If they succeed, they get to keep a share of the customer's business. Nevertheless, credit cards reflect a very profitable business, so there is no shortage of companies and institutions willing to participate in this extremely competitive arena.

In the early 1990s Citibank attempted to differentiate its classic Visa and MasterCard by placing a photograph of the customer on them.[6] The intent was to reinforce the Citibank Bankcard Division's positioning statement, "No other credit card gives you the security and confidence of Citibank MasterCard and Visa because no one is as responsive to your needs." Like the bank's price-protection plans, the photo was to appeal to security-conscious consumers who might be afraid of fraudulent charges made with a lost card. It also reinforced Citibank's image as a leader in card products and technology, as it had pioneered several banking innovations. Citibank was among the first to use ATMs on a large scale, issue a preferred Visa, institute usage incentives (Citidollar$ and free gifts), and offer emergency credit line increases.

Before the photocard was introduced on a wide scale, Citibank was interested in obtaining customers' reactions to various aspects of acquiring and using their cards. In particular, the bank wanted some insight into the relative importance of the photo in acquiring and using the card. As a first step, Citibank conducted three focus groups on October 1, 1990, in the Las Vegas test market, where the card was introduced before national rollout. The three groups were made up of recent acquirers of a Citibank Visa photocard who had used it at least once. One group consisted of cardholders who were 55 to 66 years old and the other two consisted of cardholders between the ages of 21 and 54. Each group was approximately half male and half female. Reflecting population norms, two-thirds of the participants revolved their balances while one-third paid their balance off each month. All had at least a high school education and household incomes of $15,000 or more. In the two younger groups, all males and at least three-fourths of the females were employed full time. Several participants in the older group were retired.

It is important to recognize that the results of this study should be considered qualitative aids for management judgment only and not generalized to the total U.S. population. A copy of the focus group moderator's discussion guide can be found in Appendix 9B.

This small-scale research suggested that the photocard appeared to be a promising vehicle for both retaining current customers and increasing their Citibank Visa usage. Members of the focus groups were quite positive about the Citibank photocard. Transcripts of the focus group sessions reflected two categories of reasons for acquisition and usage, practical and emotional.

Practical Reasons   Although older cardholders appeared to be more concerned about the practical reasons for owning and using a photocard, these issues surfaced in all groups to some degree. Convenience and positive identification were cited most frequently as reasons for obtaining the card. A photocard was viewed as more convenient in that it saved time in the purchase transaction. Customers no longer had to dig through their wallets for additional identification when using the card. Quotes from the transcript include the following:

"With this card, a clerk has no reason to ask you any questions."

"It's convenient . . . a time saver. It's a positive ID so I only have to pull one thing out of my wallet."

"I don't get asked for other ID's. It's 'no hassles'."

"It's easy to use because the picture is so good [clear]."

"They can verify that it's you right away."

Several participants also noted that they could use (and some had already used) their photocard as "proof of identity." These participants noted that this would be valuable when cashing a check or when a merchant asked them for identification when using another credit card. One respondent said she favored using the photocard as an ID over her driver's license because:

"People don't have to know personal information about me like how old I am or where I live."

Emotional Reasons   The perceived safety and security that the photocard offers were seen as key reasons for having one. Both older and younger cardholders were greatly concerned about losing their cards or having them stolen. The photo would be a deterrent to anyone else's using it. Some of the comments made were the following:

"I keep this card with me because it's a 'sure thing.' Even if I lose it, no one else can use it."

"Even if someone steals it, they're likely to throw it away."

"You don't have to worry if it's stolen because the chances of someone else using it are slim to none."

The focus groups seemed to agree that while they would be liable for the first $50 of fraudulent use of their cards, a photocard should limit the possibility of this because of its difficulty of use. Some also felt that the burden should fall on the merchant who accepts a fraudulent card. Additional comments included these:

"All cards should have this [photo] on it for safety. . . . I feel better having my picture on it. I feel safer."

"If my picture's on it, the merchant should be held liable if it's misused."

Furthermore, given the reduced likelihood of fraudulent use, many felt that there would be minimal hassles associated with card replacement.

In addition, the newness and uniqueness of the photocard led some cardholders to associate the card with status and prestige. The photocard differentiated them from the crowd and made them feel special, as illustrated in the following transcript excerpts:

"It makes me feel 'preferred'."

"It makes you feel good in a store because you know they noticed you."

"I feel superior to the merchant [when I use the card]."

Finally, some participants liked the idea that Citibank was "nurturing" them. The photocard communicated that Citibank was taking care of them and looking out for their best interests. This is reflected by these comments:

"They [Citibank] look at me as a person, not just as a number."

"[Citibank is saying] 'you're important. That's why we want your picture, not just your signature'."

"Citibank is working for you, not just for themselves, so that you'll be more secure."

Summary and Implications   The overall findings of the focus groups were overwhelmingly positive. Having their photo on a credit card caused some participants to increase their usage of the Citibank Visa card over other cards. This can be traced to a combination of convenience, safety, security, and status. The positive image created by the Citibank photocard appears to reflect back on Citibank in general. Participants felt that a bank that takes the extra step of putting photos on credit cards is innovative and caring.

HOLDZER CATERING*

Holdzer Catering was the market leader in Finnish employee catering in 1986 with a 10 percent market share. Management essentially decided that the company's intended growth direction would be, in the terms of Ansoff's product-market matrix, that of market penetration (increasing share of current products in current markets). Specifically, managers issued an objective to increase company market share to 16.5 by 1991. The market was expected to grow only about 5 percent between 1986 and 1991, which made the objective extremely demanding. If all of the new customers went to Holdzer, the objective would still not be reached. The difficulty is further highlighted by the fact that Holdzer's two major competitors grew faster than Holdzer in the years immediately preceding 1986. If Holdzer had any hope of reaching its objective, it had to truly understand first, which classes of potential customers perceived the company in a most favorable light and second, the criteria used by corporate and association executives for selecting employee catering arrangements for their organizations and how they traded off these criteria against price.

Holdzer therefore conducted a study with an eye towards answering the following four questions:

1. How do potential customers value the Holdzer name in employee catering?
2. Does this value vary at all with customer requirements (such as number of employees, preference for service style)?
3. What is the relative importance to the customer of different components of the assortment of menu items Holdzer could offer?

---

*At the request of the company, Holdzer Catering is a fictitious name. It was used to disguise the company's true identity. Other aspects of the study are also disguised. The study reported here was conducted by SCIENMAR: Scientific Marketing Consultants, 318 Blackstone Avenue, Ithaca, NY 14850.

4. What is the relative importance to the customer of different aspects of the price and bid mechanisms?

Pricing mechanisms are very complicated in this market. Potential suppliers submit competitive bids that propose a fixed (one-time) payment. In addition, there is a fee schedule that includes prices for each item sold at normal meals in the standard company facility as well as prices for office catering and banquets. Understanding how customers make the trade-offs implicit in these price components was critical for Holdzer to achieve its objectives in market penetration.

Research Approach and Variables Employed Given the role that understanding customer preferences played in Holdzer's research objectives, the company commissioned a conjoint analysis study to answer the previous questions. Conjoint analysis was discussed in Chapter 2 as a method for uncovering the benefits consumers look for and how they trade them off against each other.

Preliminary qualitative interviews and focus groups revealed that the components of daily and weekly assortment that customers paid attention to were the following:

- the number of hot entrees available for employees;
- whether an entree was available a la carte;
- whether a salad table was available;
- whether sandwiches were available;
- whether hot cereals were available;
- whether desserts were available; and
- whether the weekly menu was repeated.

Table 9.4 presents a set of dummy variables that operationalize these seven assortment components. (See the appendix to Chapter 2 for an illustration of how dummy variables are used in conjoint analysis.) It also describes four price and five bid variables used in the study.

Model Development We begin with the following model formulated as a regression equation:

$$\text{Utility} = b_0 + b_1 Z_1 + b_2 Z_2 + \cdots + b_{17} Z_{17}.$$

In this equation, b_0 is an additive constant and does not matter because of the reasons mentioned in the appendix of Chapter 2; b_1 is the part-worth for the brand name Holdzer; b_2 to b_7 are the part-worths for the higher levels of the daily assortment variables; b_8 is the part-worth for weekly menu repetition, b_9 to b_{12} are the coefficients of price variables (lunch, company subsidy, catering costs, and banquet costs).

Using the actual price variables, Z_9 to Z_{12}, implicitly assumes that response to the price variables is linear; that is, raising the price by two dollars has twice the effect on utility of raising the price by one dollar. Holdzer could have allowed for nonlinear response to price by using multiple dummy variables as in the credit card example in Chapter 2. However, this would have increased the number of independent variables

TABLE 9.4   Variables and Coding for Holdzer Catering Conjoint Study

Brand Name	Z_1
Holdzer	1
Other	0

Daily Assortment Variables

Number of Warm Entrees	Z_2
Two or three	1
One	0

A La Carte Entree Available	Z_3
Yes	1
No	0

Salad Table	Z_4
Yes	1
No	0

Sandwiches	Z_5
Yes	1
No	0

Hot Cereals	Z_6
Yes	1
No	0

Dessert	Z_7
Yes	1
No	0

Weekly Menu Repetition	Z_8
Yes	1
No	0

Price Variables

Lunch Price	Z_9 = actual price in marks
Company Subsidy	Z_{10} = actual subsidy in marks
Catering Costs	Z_{11} = costs in 100,000 marks units
Banquet Costs	Z_{12} = costs in 100,000 marks units

Bid Variables

Z_{13} to Z_{17} = variables reflecting the relative bids of the five major competitors to some reference or expectation: Holdzer, Fazer, Polarkesti, Lounasrengas, and Yrityksen Oma Toiminita. The potential values were 5% increments above or below the reference (up to 20%). The reference price is assumed to be 100. Thus, the potential values for these variables are 80, 85, 90, 95, 100, 105, 110, 115, and 120.

Customer Requirement Variables

X_{a1} = Number of employees (in 100s)
X_{a2} = Number of managers and white-collar employees (in 100s)
X_{a3} = Percent of women employees
X_{a4} = Preference for dining environment (six-point scale; 1—cozy, 6—elegant)
X_{a5} = Preference for service style (six-point scale; 1—effective and neutral, 6—courteous and high standard)
X_{a6} = Preference for food type (six-point scale; 1—institutional type, 6—home-cooked type)

in the equation, and more independent variables require more data to make any estimation reliable. Data collection for this problem was already thought to be cumbersome enough. The actual bid indices, Z_{13} to Z_{17}, were also used in the model. Similar comments apply to the trade-offs between data collection and incorporating nonlinearities in the competitive bid independent variables.

The model as presented does not allow for the variation of the value of the Holdzer name with customer requirements, as stated in question 1. The basic model can be extended to allow for this by modeling b_1 as a function of customer requirements as follows:

$$b_1 = b_{a0} + b_{a1}X_{a1} + \cdots + b_{a6}X_{a6},$$

where b_{a0} is an additive constant, X_{a1} to X_{a6} are variables that reflect customer requirements, and b_{a1} to b_{a6} reflect the impact of the associated variable on the part-worth value for Holdzer. The customer requirement variables that management felt important enough to examine are also detailed in Table 9.4.

Substituting b_1 from the previous equation into the one before that leaves us with the final model

$$\text{Utility} = (b_0 + b_{a0}) + b_{a1}X_{a1}Z_1 + b_{a2}X_{a2}Z_1 + \cdots b_{a6}X_{a6}Z_1 + b_2Z_2 + b_3Z_3 + \cdots b_{17}Z_{17}.$$

This approach of modeling variation in part-worths as a function of other characteristics draws its inspiration from the work of Green and DeSarbo.[7]

Data Collection   The 17 assortment, price, and bid attributes were used to form an appropriate orthogonal fractional factorial design. A design that would accommodate so many attributes (variables) would be so large that it would present a tremendous burden to any single respondent. Therefore portions of it (nine profiles) were given to each respondent in the study. All the data were then pooled and one aggregate model was estimated. This approach treats the population as if it were homogeneous except in that it may vary with respect to the value it places on the Holdzer brand name. That variation is dictated by the customer requirement variables. An alternative approach would have been to reduce the variables to a more manageable number. This would have allowed the researcher to construct a data collection task that would in turn have allowed derivation of a utility model for each respondent. There is an obvious trade-off here between accounting for a comprehensive set of decision criteria and accounting for individual variation in how those criteria are weighed.

A questionnaire designed to collect utility measures for nine hypothetical profiles and the customer requirement variables in Table 9.4 was administered to 207 respondents: 123 from manufacturing firms, 34 from retail companies, 25 from financial services, and 25 engaged in business-to-business marketing.[8] Utility was measured through a seven-point "likely to consider" scale. Of course, each respondent reacted to a different set of nine profiles. This enabled the analysts to collect sufficient data for all combinations in the master orthogonal design.

Results   The confidentiality of the study allows us to present only a portion of the results and those results are disguised. In particular, we do not have the bid variable coefficients available to us. The results we do have can be found in Table 9.5. The different units for each of the variables make the coefficients difficult (if not impossible) to compare. Furthermore, the aggregate level of the analysis renders any conclusions that we draw tentative. Nevertheless, the statistically significant results in the table can be used as a rough guide for preparing offers to potential clients.

These results include the following:

a. Firms with more managers have a lower image of Holdzer.
b. Clients where the decision makers prefer a cozy environment with effective and neutral service and home-cooked-style food are more likely to have a more favorable impression of Holdzer.

TABLE 9.5	Effects of Selected Variables on Likelihood of Considering Holdzer
Variable	**Magnitude of Impact**
Number of employees in units of 100 (b_{a1})	1.7
Number of managers and white collar workers in units of 10 (b_{a2})	−1.5*
Percentage of women in company (b_{a3})	−0.4
Rating on dining environment preference (b_{a4})	−11.2*
Rating on service style (b_{a5})	−14.4*
Rating on food preference (b_{a6})	4.7*
Number of warm entrees (b_2)	8.8
A la carte entree available (b_3)	24.9
Salad table available (b_4)	−3.5
Sandwiches available (b_5)	7.1
Hot cereals available (b_6)	−40.0*
Dessert available (b_7)	−23.8*
Repetition of weekly menu (b_8)	5.3*
Lunch price in Marks (b_9)	1.8*
Company subsidy in marks (b_{10})	0.6
Catering costs in 1000-mark units (b_{11})	0.8
Banquet costs in 1000-mark units (b_{12})	5.6

* Statistically significant at 0.05 level.

c. While a la carte entrees generally increase the chances of Holdzer being chosen, offering hot cereals and dessert dramatically decreases the chances of Holdzer being chosen.

d. Holdzer's chances of being chosen go up for various financial variables.

Implications   These results have several market selection and product offering implications for Holdzer in its attempts to reach its market share goals. First, Holdzer should target potential clients that have a lower concentration of white-collar workers relative to blue-collar workers. This is a particularly fertile segment, as it has favorable impressions of Holdzer. Second, the company should position itself as supplying home-style cooked food in an efficient manner. Finally, it should stress the simplicity of its menus (no desserts, hot cereals, single items). It should offer just full meals and a la carte entrees.

Utilization   The researchers used the results to develop an interactive software to assist Holdzer in preparing bids for potential customers. The software used the part-worth function shown in Table 9.5 along with information on customer requirements and anticipated competitive bids. With this software, the company experienced great success in landing new accounts.

PRINCIPLES OF ANALYSIS

We conclude this chapter (and this book) with a collection of general principles we have found desirable in conducting studies of the type presented in this chapter. The first two of these principles often require the firm to incur substantial additional costs. Therefore they are often not implemented. Nevertheless, they should be kept in mind for those circumstances in which the expected benefit exceeds the cost.

1. *Use multiple methods for convergence.* Back in Chapter 1, we argued that research and analysis cannot eliminate uncertainty. They can only reduce it. However, if research and analysis using several different approaches all point in the same direction, the uncertainty is reduced even more.

   For example, despite the overwhelmingly positive reaction they indicate, the transcripts of the Citibank photocard focus groups may be misleading. After all, the participants were already users and were asked to focus on the photo aspect. Suppose that, in addition to focus groups, Citibank performed a conjoint analysis on general cardholders with picture (yes-no), interest rate on revolved balances (percentage), annual fee (amount), and retail acceptability as the attributes, all presented in an equal manner, and then found that picture was more important than, say, interest rate and annual fee. It would then have greater confidence in the results of the focus groups.

2. *Develop internal databases to accumulate experience.* The results of any study become part of the "internal memory" of the organization and, as such, provide information that may be useful in other decisions as well. Firms should look for ways to systematically organize the libraries of information that they accumulate to maximize its usefulness.

   Chapter 6 discussed the use of intentions data to forecast product (or business) performance. We used such data to estimate the market potential of Victoria Moore activewear. However, it is well known that intentions overstate purchase behavior. The question is, by how much? If, in a shopping mall, 40 percent of people stopped and asked to taste a new flavor of Haagen Dazs ice cream indicated that they would buy it, the eventual trial rate is likely to be lower than that. If Haagen Dazs kept a library of product tests on past flavors, it could predict trial rate for the new flavor by building a regression of trial as a function of intention on the past data or even just drawing a scatter plot of the same data and making a visual inference. Victoria Moore could begin to build a similar database with the results of the study described in this chapter.

3. *Analysis complements and does not substitute for judgment.* Again we begin with the point that analysis reduces but does not eliminate uncertainty. Ultimately, any decision comes down to judgment. If research and analysis alone could provide all the answers, managers would not be needed. Computers could make all the decisions with research findings as input. Therefore, a decision maker's information base consists of research findings and his/her memory and/or judgment. The manager has to determine how to integrate findings into judgment. Another way to frame the task is to identify the appropriate weight to give to new findings. This is especially important in cases where the findings disconfirm prior expectations. When findings confirm expectations, this is not an issue.

   There is no simple answer to the question of appropriate weights. Most people are tempted to either give new findings no weight and ignore them as irrelevant or give them too much weight and take them as gospel. Both are wrong. The right weight lies somewhere in the middle and depends on the reliability of the findings and the foundation of the manager's expectations.

SUMMARY

This chapter has presented a series of examples that should place the reader on firmer footing with respect to applying the techniques described in this book. The applications covered a wide variety of industries (consumer products, consumer services, industrial services), managerial objectives (benefit segmentation, identification of unmet needs, identification of competitors, target market identification, brand name assessment), and tools and techniques (focus groups, perceptual mapping, conjoint analysis). This variety goes a long way towards providing the reader with a foundation to initiate applications that may not perfectly match any of those presented here, but have elements of each.

With the exception of the sports apparel trade study, which was not performed for or by a single, specific company, each of these studies had an impact on the companies involved. Victoria Moore introduced a line of activewear; the photocard has been a major impetus for Citibank's credit card division; and Holdzer Catering increased its market share. Analysis is done for a reason. That reason is that it impacts decisions. Even if this book affects only one important decision for each reader over the course of a lifetime, it will have been worth its weight in gold.

Notes

1. Nike, for example, has over 5,000 SKUs of sports apparel.
2. There are approximately 15 million U.S. households with income greater than $75,000 according to the *Statistical Abstract of the U.S.: 1992,* Washington, DC: U.S. Department of Commerce.
3. Seventy-nine percent of the sample were activewear buyers. This figure was projected to the population.
4. Again, the sample figure was projected to the population.
5. The last column in this table as well as in the complete table in the appendix to this chapter is universally higher than the next-to-last column.
6. Photocards were available in the early 1980s from some regional banks, such as Baybank in Boston. These cards were abandoned because of excessive production costs. In the early 1990s technology had advanced to a point where cost was no longer an issue.
7. See Green, Paul E., and Wayne S. DeSarbo (1978), "Componential Segmentation in the Analysis of Consumer Trade-Offs," *Journal of Marketing* 43 (Fall): 83–91.
8. The responses from each of these segments did not differ significantly. Thus, this categorization does not appear to be useful in segmenting this market.

Appendix 9A

1. Customer Survey and Detailed Results for Victoria Moore Study

January 29, 1993

Dear Female Head of Household:

As MBA students at the Leonard N. Stern School of Business at New York University, we are participating in a consulting assignment called the Management Advisory Project. We are currently conducting a market research study for a major fashion designer considering the launch of a new activewear division.

The information we gather from the following survey will allow us to recommend the correct direction and focus on our client's new line. This will also allow our client to better service your needs. This information will be used only for research purposes and will not be forwarded to our client for any reason.

Your time and support in completing this survey will be greatly appreciated. In exchange, we will enter your name in a contest to win one of several prizes including a designer leather agenda with a retail value of $105 and a designer signature scarf with a retail value of $115. The grand prize will be a designer leather handbag with a retail value of $230. This survey is being distributed throughout the United States with all respondents eligible for the drawing. The drawing will be held on March 1, 1993 so please return your survey and entry form by February 26, 1993.

Thank you again for your help. Good luck!

Sincerely,

Kimberly Banks   Gina Plaia

Tracy Pollastri   Joseph Weglein

Please complete and return with questionnaire:

Name: _____

Address: _____

          _____

First, we would like to ask you a few questions about your lifestyle and your activewear purchase. For the purpose of this survey, activewear is defined to incorporate items such as sweatshirts, leggings, and t-shirts. More sports-specific items including tennis skirts, ski pants, and biking shorts would also be represented. This category does NOT include sports equipment or footwear.

1. Do you wear activewear?
   _____ Yes
   _____ No (Please skip to Question 11)

2. When do you wear activewear?
   _____ For sports-related activities only
   _____ For leisure activities only
   _____ For both sports-related and leisure activities

3. How often do you participate in the following activities? (If you do not participate in any of the sports-related activities listed below, please skip to Question 5.)

	Frequently	Occasionally	Rarely	Never
Aerobics/Step Aerobics	_____	_____	_____	_____
Biking	_____	_____	_____	_____
Golf	_____	_____	_____	_____
Rollerblading™	_____	_____	_____	_____
Running	_____	_____	_____	_____
Sailing	_____	_____	_____	_____
Skiing	_____	_____	_____	_____
Swimming	_____	_____	_____	_____
Tennis	_____	_____	_____	_____
Using exercise equipment	_____	_____	_____	_____
Weightlifting	_____	_____	_____	_____
Other	_____	_____	_____	_____

4a. Please indicate your FAVORITE activity of those listed above. Please list the types of clothing you wear for this activity and, if possible, their brands.

   e.g., Skiing   Overalls (CB), down ski jacket (Bogner), ski sweater (Bogner).
   Favorite: Types and brands of clothing

   _____   _____

                 _____

4b. If the activity which you engage in MOST OFTEN is not your favorite, please indicate which it is and the clothing you wear for this activity.

   Most
   Frequent: Types and brands of clothing

   _____   _____

                 _____

5. Approximately, how much do you spend annually on activewear? Please do not include equipment or footwear in your estimate.

    _____ Under $100
    _____ $100 –$499
    _____ $500 – $999
    _____ $1,000 or more

6. Please rank the following factors from "1" to "6" in order of importance in your decision to purchase activewear for both sports-related and leisure activities. Let "1" represent the most important factor and "6" the least

	Sports-related activities	Leisure activities
Brand Name	_____	_____
Comfort	_____	_____
Durability	_____	_____
Fashion/Look	_____	_____
Functionality	_____	_____
Price	_____	_____

7. How do you rate the quality of the following brands of clothing? Please indicate with an "X" the level of quality you associate with the following brands. If you have no experience with a particular brand, please check N/A.

	Lowest Quality 1	2	3	4	5	6	Highest Quality 7	N/A
Adidas	____	____	____	____	____	____	____	____
Bogner	____	____	____	____	____	____	____	____
CB Sports	____	____	____	____	____	____	____	____
Champion	____	____	____	____	____	____	____	____
Ellesse	____	____	____	____	____	____	____	____
Fila	____	____	____	____	____	____	____	____
Head	____	____	____	____	____	____	____	____
Lacoste	____	____	____	____	____	____	____	____
Le Coq Sportif	____	____	____	____	____	____	____	____
Nike	____	____	____	____	____	____	____	____
Reebok	____	____	____	____	____	____	____	____
Sergio Tacchini	____	____	____	____	____	____	____	____
Skyr	____	____	____	____	____	____	____	____
Spider	____	____	____	____	____	____	____	____
Other_____	____	____	____	____	____	____	____	____

8a. What characteristics do you LIKE most about currently available activewear?

_____

_____

_____

_____

8b. What characteristics do you DISLIKE most about currently available activewear?

_____

_____

_____

_____

9. Are there any activewear items or attributes you have been looking for but have been unable
to locate?

_____

_____

_____

_____

I0. Where are you most likely to shop for activewear? Please check all that apply.

_____   Department Store (e.g., Saks, Macy's, Bloomingdales)
_____   General Sporting Goods Store (e.g., Herman's)
_____   Pro Shop at my Gym/ Health Club
_____   Sport Specific Store (e.g., Golf Store, Tennis Shop, Ski Outlet)
_____   Discount Store (e.g., Marshalls, Filene's Basement)
_____   Dance Supply Store (e.g., Parklane, Capezio)
_____   Specialty Store/Boutique
_____   Catalog (e.g., Road Runner Sports)
_____   Other (please specify)

Questions on the following page deal with major fashion designers.

	11. Please indicate all of the designer(s) that you currently wear.	12. If available, which designer activewear line(s) would you consider purchasing? Please check all that apply. (Note: Not all of the designers listed below currently offer activewear.)	13. Please indicate the highest price you would be willing to pay for a sweatshirt by the designer(s) you chose in question 12.	14. Please indicate the activities for which you would purchase this activewear. Circle "S" for sports activities only "L" for leisure only "B" for both activities "NP" for would not purchase
Adrienne Vittadini				S L B NP
Anne Klein				S L B NP
Calvin Klein				S L B NP
Carole Little				S L B NP
Chanel				S L B NP
Christian Dior				S L B NP
Dana Buchman				S L B NP
Donna Karan				S L B NP
Ellen Tracy				S L B NP
Jones New York				S L B NP
Leslie Fay				S L B NP
Liz Claiborne				S L B NP
Ralph Lauren				S L B NP
Saint Gillian				S L B NP
Victoria Moore				S L B NP
Other				S L B NP

Now a few questions about yourself.

15. Where did you take your last two vacations?

_____

_____

16. Please indicate Your age.
    _____ Under 25
    _____ 25–34
    _____ 45–54
    _____ 55 and above

17. Please indicate your household income.
    _____ under $50,000
    _____ $50,000–$59,999
    _____ $60,000–$74,999
    _____ $75,000–$100,000
    _____ over $100,000

18. Please indicate your employment status.
    _____ Full-time
    _____ Part-time
    _____ Not employed (outside the home)

19. Please indicate your marital status.
    _____ Never married
    _____ Married
    _____ Separated/divorced/widowed

Thank you for your time and effort.

	# of Activewear Consumers[1]	% of Activewear Consumers[2]	% of Victoria Moore Active Potential[3]
Region of Country			
Northeast	200	42%	50%
East Central	40	8	8
West Central	69	14	12
South	93	19	15
Pacific	50	10	11
When Wear Activewear			
Sports Only	13	3%	2%
Leisure Only	75	16	11
Sports & Leisure	385	80	87
Activities*			
Aerobics	217	45%	55%
Biking	200	42	52
Golf	76	15	15
Running	117	24	34
Sailing	53	11	14
Skiing	104	21	24
Swimming	287	60	64
Tennis	147	28	33
Exercise Eqpmt	289	60	70
Walking	104	22	18
Weights	136	28	40
Annual Expenditures			
<$100	176	37%	30%
$100–$500	257	54	60
$500–$1,000	35	7	5
$1,000+	5	1	3
Where Shop for Activewear*			
Dept. Store	322	67%	74%
Sporting Goods	229	48	61
Pro Shop	54	11	14
Sports Specific	111	23	30
Discount	289	60	57
Dance supply	65	14	16
Boutique	84	18	21
Catalog	205	43	47

*Respondents were free to check more than one option.

	# of Activewear Consumers[1]	% of Activewear Consumers[2]	% of Victoria Moore Active Potential[3]
Designers Currently Owned*			
(Question 11)			
A. Vittadini	84	18%	30%
Anne Klein	177	37	62
Calvin Klein	203	42	51
Carole Little	75	16	22
Chanel	30	6	8
Christian Dior	115	24	34
Dana Buchman	26	5	14
Donna Karan	55	11	29
Ellen Tracy	82	17	31
Jones NY	165	34	46
Leslie Fay	129	27	33
Liz Claiborne	303	63	72
Ralph Lauren	135	28	37
Victoria Moore	85	18	40
Intend to Buy Activewear*			
(Question 12)			
A. Vittadini	83	17%	42%
Anne Klein	124	26	58
Calvin Klein	147	31	56
Carole Little	58	12	28
Chanel	48	10	26
Christian Dior	88	18	36
Dana Buchman	34	7	23
Donna Karan	87	18	70
Ellen Tracy	67	14	35
Jones NY	93	19	42
Leslie Fay	82	17	41
Liz Claiborne	203	42	63
Ralph Lauren	118	25	45
Victoria Moore	86	18	69

*Respondents were free to check more than one option.

Price Would Pay for Sweatshirt (in $)[4]

A. Vittadini	$49	$54
Anne Klein	44	46
Calvin Klein	42	46
Carole Little	48	51
Chanel	47	52
Christian Dior	43	48
Dana Buchman	50	53
Donna Karen	46	48
Ellen Tracy	48	53
Jones NY	45	50
Leslie Fay	41	46
Liz Claiborne	41	45
Ralph Lauren	45	51
Victoria Moore	48	51

	# of Activewear Consumers	% of Activewear Consumers	% of Victoria Moore Active Potential[1]
When Would Wear Activewear (Sports/Leisure/Both)			
A. Vittadini	3/40/57	1%/8%/12%	2%/16%/26%
Anne Klein	3/59/92	1/12/19	1/22/39
Calvin Klein	7/64/111	1/13/23	4/17/35
Carole Little	5/29/52	1/6/11	1/9/25
Chanel	1/33/46	0/7/10	0/15/22
Christian Dior	3/37/74	1/8/15	1/10/28
Dana Buchman	1/19/32	0/4/7	0/8/21
Donna Karan	4/42/57	1/9/12	2/26/40
Ellen Tracy	1/36/47	0/8/10	1/12/24
Jones NY	2/46/68	0/10/14	0/13/31
Leslie Fay	0/32/87	0/7/18	0/9/34
Liz Claiborne	6/80/154	1/17/32	1/18/44
Ralph Lauren	3/48/102	1/10/21	0/14/34
Victoria Moore	1/26/79	0/5/16	0/14/50
Age of Consumer			
<25	24	5%	5%
25–34	137	29	44
35–44	161	34	31
45–54	109	23	13
55+	44	9	9

	# of Activewear Consumers[1]	% of Activewear Consumers[2]	% of Victoria Moore Active Potential[3]
Household Income			
<$50,000	125	26%	21%
$50,000–$59,999	79	16	14
$60,000–$74,999	76	16	15
$75,000–$99,999	75	16	18
$100,000+	90	19	29
Employment			
Full Time	297	62%	66%
Part Time	64	13	17
Not Employed	111	23	18
Marital Status			
Single	89	19%	26%
Married	328	68	64
Separated, etc.	55	11	10
Most Frequent Activities*			
Aerobics	80	17%	18%
Biking	34	7	6
Golf	14	3	2
Running	29	6	6
Sailing	3	1	2
Skiing	21	4	7
Swimming	58	12	11
Tennis	37	8	6
Exercise Eqpmt	41	9	11
Walking	46	10	11
Weights	10	2	4
Clothes Worn*			
Sweatshirt	101	21%	20%
Sweat Pants	93	19	24
T-shirt	147	31	33
Leggings	83	17	17
Shorts	92	19	21
Bodysuit	41	9	11
Tights	30	6	8
Ski Sweater	6	1	2

*Respondents were free to check more than one option.

Important Features/Sports (Median Score)[5]

Brand	6	6
Comfort	1	1
Durability	4	4
Fashion/Look	4	4
Function	3	3
Price	4	4

Important Features/Leisure (Median Score)[6]

Brand	6	5
Comfort	1	1
Durability	4	4
Fashion/Look	3	3
Function	4	4
Price	4	4

	# of Activewear Consumers[1]	% of Activewear Consumers[2]	% of Victoria Moore Active Potential[3]
Available Features Like			
Easy to Wash/Dry	48	10%	14%
Comfortable	210	44	46
Durable	65	14	10
Color Variety	144	30	34
Style Variety	113	24	22
Fabric	79	16	20
Fashionable	73	15	16
Versatile	32	7	8
Available Features Dislike			
Durability	37	8%	9%
Colors	57	12	14
Lack of Sizing	46	10	13

[1]People who answered that they wear activewear (Question 1).

[2]These numbers may not add up to 100 because of rounding error, missing data, or multiple responses.

[3]People who expressed interest in Victoria Moore Activewear (Question 12)

[4]The values are ALL average $ amounts, not percents.

[5]The values given are the median of a scale of 1 to 5, where 1 represents most important and 6 represents least important.

[6]The values given are the median of a scale of 1 to 6, where 1 represents most important and 6 represents least important.

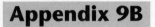

Appendix 9B

2. Discussion Guide Outline for Citibank Photocard Focus Groups

**CITIBANK CLASSIC VISA PHOTOCARD
EXPLORATORY RESEARCH**

DISCUSSION GUIDE OUTLINE

OCTOBER 1990

Prepared for: CITIBANK. Prepared by: MCC QUALITATIVE CONSULTING, MEADOWLANDS CONSUMER CENTER INC., 700 Plaza Drive, Secaucus, New Jersey 07094, (201) 865-4900

WARM UP
- Companies are interested in what people have to say about their products or services.
- Independent market research—no vested interest.
- Individual opinions are key—no right or wrong answers.
- Tape/mirror/For marketing research purposes only.
- Any questions.

1. INDIVIDUAL INTRODUCTIONS
- First name, where you live.
- Family composition.
- Occupation.
- What credit cards you currently have, what banks.

2. PHOTOCARD OVERVIEW
- You all mentioned you have a Citibank Photocard, what I'd like you to do now is WRITE an informal letter to a friend of yours about your Citibank Photocard. Tell them whatever it is you think they should know. Assume that this friend doesn't live around here and doesn't know anything about this card.
- [EACH RESPONDENT WILL SHARE HIS/HER LETTER] Probe key points as necessary listening for salient benefits/drawbacks.

3. ACQUISITION PROCESS
- Now I'd like to track through the process you went through in acquiring your Photocard and how you felt about it. First of all . . .
- How did you FIRST HEAR about the Citibank Photocard?
   ___What was your initial reaction?
   ___Why did you feel that way?
- Initially, what BENEFITS did you see in this card?
   ___How is that important to you?
- What would you say was the key REASON you accepted the offer for the Photocard?
   ___How was that important to you?
- Thinking back, what QUESTIONS, if any, did you have?
   ___What drawbacks, if any, did you think about?
   ___How did you feel about those?
- Prior to applying, did you talk to anyone about it or not? Who? Why?
- What were the STEPS involved? Walk me through the whole process.
   ___Probes: Application
                Picture-taking process
                How long to receive, etc.
   ___How did you feel about each of these steps?

4. USAGE
    - Now let's talk about what it's LIKE HAVING THIS CARD. What thoughts went through your mind when you FIRST RECEIVED the Photocard?
      ___What was your initial reaction?
      ___How did it compare to what you EXPECTED?
      ___How did you feel about that?
    - How often have you used the card?
    - I'd like you to think back to the first time you used the card. What did you use it for? Where? Why that?
    - How did this initial use compare to what you expected?
    - What were your experiences with merchants when you gave them the card? Did they examine the card? What comments did they make?
    - How did using the card/having the card make you FEEL?
      ___Why would you say that?
      ___Listen for end benefits: i.e., Security, safety, prestige, etc.
    - How has having this card CHANGED the way you use other credit cards? (any canceled or usage reduction)
      ___Why would you say that?
      ___What is the KEY reason you say that?
        Any other reasons?
    - Did you show the card to your family? How did they react to it? How about your friends?
    - If you were trying to convince someone to apply for this card, what would you say to them?
      ___What part would the Photo play? How strong do you feel about that? Why?
    - You mentioned a number of reasons why you applied for the Citibank Photocard and why others should [REITERATE REASONS BEYOND JUST THE PHOTO—assuming other mentioned].
      ___Of all these reasons to get this card, how important is the Photo?
      ___Why would you say that?
    - Are there any DISADVANTAGES you see associated with this card?
      ___Probe any mentions.
    - What does it say about a COMPANY that would OFFER a card such as this?
    - If you could, would you CHANGE anything about the process of obtaining the Citibank Photocard or anything else about it?
      ___Why that? How would that be a benefit?
    - What CONCERNS, if any, do you have that you haven't mentioned?
    - As you can imagine, there are ADDITIONAL COSTS to produce a credit card with a picture on it. We've talked a lot about the advantages in and benefits of having this card. Suppose the annual fee for this card was $__ above what other nonpicture cards are charging?
      ___How do you feel about that?
      (Alternatively pricing question will be phrased in an open ended manner.)
    - Tie up any loose ends.
    - Thank you very much.

Cases

Regent Rubber Company*

The Regent Rubber Company was a leading manufacturer of a wide range of rubber products. Until March 1969, it evinced a steady rate of growth. Since then, growth had slowed tremendously and the president, Mr. Daniel Norris, looking for new products, was considering adding automobile tires to the company's range of products. At his request, the Design Engineering Department had come up with a number of possible design options and submitted to him data on relevant production costs. In February 1973, Mr. Norris assigned the Marketing Department the task of determining which options, if introduced, would yield the highest profit.

The marketing research staff had recently been exposed to the use of simulation techniques and decided to build a simulation model to solve this problem. The simulation approach offered the advantage of being much faster and cheaper than a market survey. The model would enable the manager to incorporate the several microbehavioral aspects of the buyer's decision process and provide aggregate estimates of the market performance of the company's brands of tires under consideration. The research staff had surveyed the business literature and other related documents to obtain some basic data on the tire market and its competitors. (See the Bibliography for the list used.) This was supplemented by an exploratory survey among several customers to develop a quick consumer profile as well as salient brand attributes. This phase did not take any more than three weeks. This information was utilized in the development of the simulation model, which was completed by June 1973.

The Automobile Tire Market

The auto tire market could be broadly classified into three segments: the original equipment manufacturers (OEM) market, the replacement tire market, and the export market. The OEM segment was served by five major tire companies and was impossible to break into, at least at the outset. The export market accounted for a nominal (5 percent) share of the total market. Thus, the management decided to concentrate on the replacement tire market, which made up 67 percent of the total. The demand in this segment alone was expected to be 150 million units in 1973. Tires marketed in 1972 could be classified into three types: the conventional bias-ply, the belted bias,

---

*This case was prepared by Vithala R. Rao, with the assistance of Anil Sood, as a basis for class discussion rather than to illustrate either effective or ineffective handling of an administrative situation.

and the radial. The latter two, though almost twice as expensive as the bias-ply, offered numerous advantages with regard to mileage, safety, and other performance factors. Within each type, different modifications were possible; that is, different materials could be used, and trimmings such as whitewalls could be added. Regent was considering all possibilities, as it was felt that all types would continue to maintain the large growth rates they were experiencing.

The Model

The PRODSIM model was developed around a particular version of the buyer's purchase decision process.[1] Briefly, the process was as follows. All buyers have a certain perception of the brands on a number of relevant tire attributes, as measured by the relative attractiveness of the brands on these attributes. Each customer then weighs these attributes according to individual priorities. The weights given the attributes depend on the market segment of the customer. Each segment is represented by a uniformly distributed set of weights for each attribute. The weighting process yields a set of probabilities that the customer would consider buying each brand. Final selection is made from among the consideration class. The flow diagram (Exhibit 1) shows this process.

The Inputs

The model requires several inputs. These are quantified as shown in Exhibit 2. The eight brands[2] currently in the market are described with respect to the decision variables (design parameters, their price, and the advertising effort behind them). See Exhibit 3. Except for those directly quantifiable, such as the price, the parameters are measured on a scale that would easily lend itself to translation into salient attributes. On the basis of reports published in the near past and the results of exploratory interviews, the buyers were divided into three segments (namely, Thrifty, On-the-go, and Enthusiast). Each segment was distinguished by its own distributions of weights for the attributes. On the basis of the survey, four attributes were found to be most significant in the choice of an auto tire. These are price, mileage and tread life, stopping and cornering ability and rupture resistance, and brand image and the trimmings available (for example, whitewalls). The research group, upon consulting with the marketing executives, developed transformation functions to translate the design and other parameters into values for brands on these four attributes (price, mileage, performance, and brand image). The production cost functions developed independently were also incorporated into the simulation model. The brands that the company was considering for introduction were quantified in the same way. It was felt that two brands would have to be introduced at the same time to make any impact on the market. The model takes this aspect into account. The model develops estimates of market shares after the effects of the introduction of brands have leveled off.

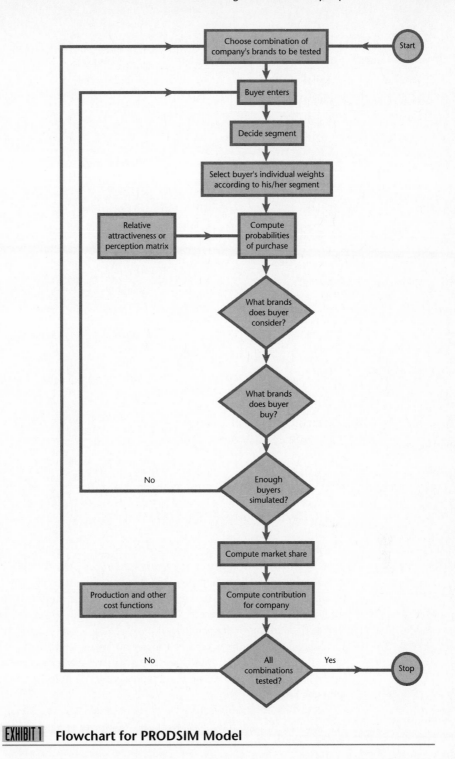

EXHIBIT 1 **Flowchart for PRODSIM Model**

EXHIBIT 2   Scaling Used for Decision Variables

Decision Variable	Codes Employed in the Program		Possible Values
Price:	Dollars		No restriction
Advertisement:	Millions of dollars		No restriction
Trimmings:	Whitewalls only	1.0	
	Whitewalls and other trimmings	1.5	No restriction
	Just trimmings	0.5	
Type:	Radial	2.0	Only one of these three values is permissible for this variable.
	Belted bias	1.5	
	Bias-ply	0.5	
Materials:			
Sidewalls	Polyester	1.5	Variable can be continuous in the range (0.5, 1.5).
	Rayon, nylon	1.0	
Belts	Steel	1.5	
	Rayon/fiberglass	1.0	Variable can be continuous in the range (0, 1.5).
	None	0.0	
Tread quality:	High	2.0	Variable can be continuous in the range (1,2).
	Low	1.0	
Engineering:	High	2.0	Variable can be continuous in the range (0,2).
	Low	0.0	
Width:	Normal	0.0	
	Wide	0.5	Only these values are permitted.
	Super wide	1.0	

Actual Working of PRODSIM

The model simulated a buyer sample of given size, simulating each buyer's decision process when faced with (up to) ten brands. These ten brands comprised the eight existing brands and two options under consideration by Regent. Once the market share of each brand was determined on the basis of the purchase behavior of this sample, actual market size and the company's cost functions were used to determine the profit accruing to the company.

The model can be used to estimate the impact (on shares and profits) for any one or any two of the brands under consideration by Regent. A display of the impact of several alternative combinations would help in the new product decisions of Regent.

As a first cut, complicating factors such as deals being offered, the different outlets at which the purchase was made, and the interaction between attributes were left out in this model.

EXHIBIT 3   Market Data

A. Brands and Attributes

Brand	Price	Advertising Budget	Trimmings	Type	Side-walls	Belts	Tread Quality	Engineering	Width	
Kings	$50.00	$4.90	1.50	2.00	1.50	1.50	2.00	2.00	0.0	
Safety	32.00	4.50	1.50	1.50	1.50	1.50	1.00	1.00	0.0	
Super	45.00	5.00	1.50	2.00	1.00	1.00	2.00	1.50	0.50	
Hi-Value	28.00	2.00	0.50	1.50	1.50	1.50	1.80	2.00	0.0	*
Traveler	36.50	5.00	1.00	2.00	1.00	1.00	2.00	2.00	0.0	
Commoner	29.00	4.50	1.50	0.50	1.50	0.00	2.00	1.00	0.0	
Racer	39.50	4.50	0.50	1.50	1.50	1.50	2.00	2.00	1.00	
Economy	23.00	1.50	0.00	0.50	1.00	0.00	1.50	0.50	0.0	
Regent	51.00	5.00	1.50	2.00	1.50	1.50	2.00	2.00	0.0	
Apollo	38.00	4.00	1.50	1.50	1.50	1.00	2.00	2.00	0.0	**
Longlast	39.00	4.50	0.00	1.50	1.50	1.50	2.00	2.00	1.00	
Moneysaver	22.00	1.50	0.00	0.50	1.00	0.00	1.50	0.0	0.0	

*Existing brands.

**New brands under review by Regent.

Note: Advertising budget in millions of dollars, price in dollars; all other parameters on scales defined in the *User's Manual*.

B. Segments and Weights

Segment	Percentage	Attribute 1		Attribute 2		Attribute 3		Attribute 4	
Thrifty	0.50%	0.60	0.30	0.30	0.00	0.10	0.00	0.15	0.00
On-the-go	0.25	0.45	0.15	0.35	0.05	0.20	0.10	0.10	0.05
Enthusiast	0.25	0.30	0.00	0.25	0.05	0.45	0.15	0.10	0.00

Upper and Lower Limits of Weights for columns above.

C. Model Applied to Current Situation

Brand Perception Matrix

Attribute	Kings	Safety	Super	Hi-Value	Traveler	Commoner	Racer	Economy
1	0.0834	0.1303	0.0926	0.1469	0.1142	0.1438	0.1055	0.1813
2	0.1598	0.1256	0.1332	0.1438	0.1370	0.0913	0.1408	0.0685
3	0.1481	0.0926	0.1461	0.1296	0.1481	0.0926	0.1667	0.0741
4	0.1507	0.1518	0.1513	0.0844	0.1296	0.1518	0.1084	0.0720

Note: Sample size = 1000

(Continued on next page)

Performance of the Model

To test the validity of the model, it was first run on only the existing brands. The results obtained compared extremely well with actual market data (see the following table).

| EXHIBIT 3 | **Continued** |

Purchase Decision Data

	Thrifty		On-the-go		Enthusiast	
	# Considering	# Buying	# Considering	# Buying	# Considering	# Buying
Kings	9	4	67	20	142	47
Safety	86	52	66	19	8	2
Super	16	4	50	14	97	30
Hi-Value	238	181	104	99	66	29
Traveler	69	22	65	39	95	46
Commoner	84	59	47	12	1	1
Racer	23	10	76	34	105	93
Economy	405	164	17	9	0	0

Market Shares (%)

Kings	7.26%
Safety	7.42
Super	4.91
Hi-Value	31.03
Traveler	10.82
Commoner	7.29
Racer	13.69
Economy	17.37

	Market Share	
Brand	**Model Estimate (%)**	**Actual (%)**
Kings	7.26%	7.50%
Safety	7.42	7.40
Super	4.91	5.00
Hi-Value	31.03	31.80
Traveler	10.82	11.00
Commoner	7.29	7.50
Racer	13.69	12.50
Economy	17.37	17.30

Brands under Review

The company reduced the set of alternative concepts to four new brands, tentatively named Regent, Longlast, Apollo, and Moneysaver. The physical design parameters for these are also described in Exhibit 3. The management needs your advice on which of these brands should be introduced, and at what prices and at what advertising support.

Some Results

Results from selected simulation runs are shown in Exhibit 4 for Regent and Moneysaver, Apollo and Longlast, and Regent and Longlast. These are based on the choices made by the management.

EXHIBIT 4   Model Applied to Current Situation

Trial #1
Brand Perception Matrix

					Brand					
Attribute	Kings	Safety	Super	Hi-Value	Traveler	Commoner	Racer	Economy	Regent	Moneysaver
1	0.0656	0.1025	0.0729	0.1171	0.0898	0.1131	0.0830	0.1426	0.0643	0.1491
2	0.1301	0.1022	0.1084	0.1171	0.1115	0.0743	0.1146	0.0558	0.1301	0.0558
3	0.1231	0.0769	0.1231	0.1077	0.1231	0.0769	0.1385	0.0615	0.1231	0.0462
4	0.1232	0.1241	0.1237	0.0690	0.1059	0.1241	0.0886	0.0589	0.1237	0.0589

Purchase Decision Data

	Thrifty		On-the-go		Enthusiast	
	# Considering	# Buying	# Considering	# Buying	# Considering	# Buying
Kings	10	4	54	20	67	42
Safety	126	43	43	16	2	1
Super	11	4	50	13	40	24
Hi-Value	287	127	198	89	59	23
Traveler	31	19	117	35	89	36
Commoner	45	44	27	10	0	0
Racer	28	8	37	31	230	79
Economy	233	95	10	7	0	0
Regent	16	4	21	18	70	41
Moneysaver	203	147	16	6	0	0

Market Shares (%)

	Previous	Present
Kings	7.26%	6.76%
Safety	7.42	6.15
Super	4.91	4.15
Hi-Value	31.03	24.09
Traveler	10.82	9.13
Commoner	7.29	5.59
Racer	13.89	12.00
Economy	17.37	10.27
Regent	0.00	6.41
Moneysaver	0.00	15.46

	Regent	Moneysaver
Price/unit	$ 51.00	$ 22.00
Advertising cost/unit	7.80	0.97
Variable cost/unit	36.50	17.00
Distribution cost/Unit	4.00	1.00
Contribution to overheads/Unit	2.70	3.03
Total contribution for brand	$1,733,363.00	$4,584,220.00
Total contribution for trial	$6,417,583.00	

(Continued on next page)

EXHIBIT 4 Continued

Trial #2
Brand Perception Matrix

					Brand					
Attribute	Kings	Safety	Super	Hi-Value	Traveler	Commoner	Racer	Economy	Apollo	Longlast
1	0.0685	0.1071	0.0762	0.1224	0.0939	0.1182	0.0868	0.1490	0.0902	0.0879
2	0.1251	0.0983	0.1042	0.1126	0.1072	0.0715	0.1102	0.0536	0.1072	0.1102
3	0.1143	0.0714	0.1143	0.1000	0.1143	0.0714	0.1286	0.0571	0.1000	0.1286
4	0.1217	0.1225	0.1221	0.0682	0.1046	0.1225	0.0875	0.0581	0.1225	0.0700

Purchase Decision Data

	Thrifty		On-the-go		Enthusiast	
	# Considering	# Buying	# Considering	# Buying	# Considering	# Buying
Kings	14	5	42	19	96	33
Safety	121	53	33	15	2	1
Super	20	5	29	12	39	20
Hi-Value	367	173	174	79	69	24
Traveler	31	24	56	32	89	33
Commoner	115	58	18	8	0	0
Racer	35	11	31	29	110	65
Economy	305	139	21	5	0	0
Apollo	45	20	48	21	36	13
Longlast	19	9	65	24	106	55

Market Shares (%)

	Previous	Present
Kings	7.26%	5.90%
Safety	7.42	7.01
Super	4.91	3.84
Hi-Value	31.03	27.80
Traveler	10.82	9.10
Commoner	7.29	6.77
Racer	13.89	10.68
Economy	17.37	14.48
Apollo	0.00	5.49
Longlast	0.00	8.92

	Apollo	Longlast
Price/unit	$ 38.00	$ 39.00
Advertising cost/unit	7.29	5.04
Variable cost/unit	28.00	30.50
Distribution cost/unit	3.00	3.00
Contribution to overheads/unit	−0.29	0.46
Total contribution for brand	−$158,580.00	$406,324.30
Total contribution for trial	$247,744.30	

EXHIBIT 4 Continued

Trial #3
Brand Perception Matrix

					Brand					
Attributes	Kings	Safety	Super	Hi-Value	Traveler	Commoner	Racer	Economy	Regent	Longlast
1	0.0701	0.1096	0.0779	0.1253	0.0961	0.1209	0.0888	0.1525	0.0688	0.0899
2	0.1229	0.0965	0.1024	0.1106	0.1053	0.0702	0.1083	0.0527	0.1229	0.1083
3	0.1127	0.0704	0.1127	0.0986	0.1127	0.0704	0.1268	0.0563	0.1127	0.1268
4	0.1218	0.1226	0.1222	0.0682	0.1047	0.1226	0.0876	0.0582	0.1222	0.0701

Purchase Decision Data

	Thrifty		On-the-go		Enthusiast	
	# Considering	# Buying	# Considering	# Buying	# Considering	# Buying
Kings	13	3	56	16	72	26
Safety	50	50	52	16	7	2
Super	8	3	37	11	35	17
Hi-Value	414	154	93	88	91	31
Traveler	37	19	45	31	106	33
Commoner	169	64	24	11	4	1
Racer	28	8	86	27	171	59
Economy	322	186	33	9	0	0
Regent	7	2	31	14	27	25
Longlast	11	6	45	22	149	51

Market Shares (%)

	Previous	Present
Kings	7.26%	4.62%
Safety	7.42	6.96
Super	4.91	3.29
Hi-Value	31.03	27.48
Traveler	10.82	8.45
Commoner	7.29	7.70
Racer	13.89	9.51
Economy	17.37	19.64
Regent	0.00	4.32
Longlast	0.00	8.04

	Regent	Longlast
Price/unit	$ 51.00	$ 39.00
Advertising cost/unit	11.58	5.59
Variable cost/unit	36.50	30.50
Distribution cost/unit	4.00	3.00
Contribution to overheads/unit	−1.08	−0.09
Total contribution for brand	−$467,594.20	−$76,215.44

Notes

1. See Rao, V. R. (1973), "A View of the Competitive Marketing Mix Model," AMA Proceedings, Fall.

2. The several brands in the market have been grouped and renamed in this case. These eight account for practically all of the replacement market.

Bibliography

Consumer Reports (1971), August.
Consumer's Bulletin Annual (1972).
Staff Report to the Federal Trade Commission (1966), *Economic Report on the Manufacture and Distribution of Automotive Tires,* Washington, DC: Federal Trade Commission, March.

Stykolt, Stefan (1965), *Economic Analysis and Combines Policy,* Toronto: University of Toronto Press.
The Twenty-Fourth Look National Automobile and Tire Survey (1960), New York: Cowles Magazine, Inc.

The U.S. Athletic Footwear Industry (A)*

Market Structure and Growth

In 1991 about 1.1 billion pairs of shoes (excluding rubber and plastic footwear) were sold in the United States. This footwear market can be divided into three major shoe types—dress, casual, and athletic shoes—that represent different uses. Dress shoes are designed for formal occasions such as business and ceremonies, casual shoes for everyday wear, and athletic shoes for sports use. During the 1980s, when the latter category experienced high growth, the use of athletic shoes was extended into all occasions of daily life by offering comfort and fashion. Casual shoes such as loafers lie between the two other categories and offer the benefits of both: they can be worn on more formal occasions than athletic shoes but are more comfortable than dress shoes. As athletic footwear has expanded into everyday use, these two markets are beginning to compete for the same customers.

During the 1970s, the U.S. footwear market was stable, with about 800 million pairs sold each year (Exhibit 1).[1] The use of athletic footwear was limited to sports participants, who were not the majority of the U.S. population. Throughout the decade the brand athletic footwear industry was characterized by relatively few companies with niche market orientations. Sneakers were seen as somewhat generic and no real lead brand emerged. In the late 1970s and early 1980s athletic footwear sales grew rapidly as national interest in running, aerobics, and fitness increased. By 1984 more than 70 percent of the U.S. population participated in a sport or fitness activity at least once a week,[2] and physical health and well-being had become a common value among the U.S. population. Because this created a new market for footwear, the athletic footwear category expanded without cannibalizing other footwear segments. Many new companies such as Reebok and L.A. Gear took advantage of this rapidly growing market. In 1982, 185 million pairs of athletic shoes were sold, and this increased to more than 300 million pairs by 1986.[3] The total footwear market also expanded from 830 million pairs in 1981 to 1170 million pairs in 1986 (Exhibit 1). The 1981 expiration of orderly marketing agreements with South Korea and Taiwan, which limited import volume from these countries, also helped the expansion of the footwear market.[1] Since then these countries have become the major product source of athletic footwear.

The athletic footwear market continued to grow, although at a decreased rate, during the latter half of the 1980s. The average growth of retail value between 1982 and 1990 was 16 percent with the peak of more than 30 percent growth between 1985 and 1986.[3] Branded athletic footwear grew even more quickly, over 20 percent per year on average in wholesale value, by taking a share from nonbranded

---

*©1993 This case was prepared by Mr. Tetsuo Yamada, Cornell MBA 1993 under the general direction of Professor Vithala R. Rao.

EXHIBIT 1 U.S. Footwear Market Size and Growth

Total Nonrubber (million pairs)

	1972	1973	1974	1975	1976	1977	1978	1979	1980	1981
Shipment	561	488	453	419	425	431	413	403	385	375
Import	297	307	267	286	370	368	374	405	366	375
Export	2	4	4	5	6	5	7	9	13	11
Consumption	855	791	716	700	789	794	780	798	738	738
Growth		−7.5%	−9.5%	−2.2%	12.6%	0.6%	−1.7%	2.3%	−7.6%	0.1%

	1982	1983	1984	1985	1986	1987	1988	1989	1990	1991	CAGR(1982–1991)
Shipment	357	343	307	270	244	226	237	228	197	181	−7.3%
Import	480	582	726	843	941	938	903	860	898	937	7.7%
Export	9	7	7	11	13	15	18	14	15	18	8.1%
Consumption	828	917	1,024	1,102	1,173	1,149	1,122	1,074	1,079	1,100	3.2%
Growth	12.1%	10.8%	11.6%	7.6%	6.4%	−2.0%	−2.4%	−4.2%	0.5%	1.9%	

Source: *U.S. Industrial Outlook 1983–1993*, International Trade Administration, U.S. Department of Commerce (includes estimates by the author due to lack of consistent data).

Athletic Footwear (million pairs)

	1982	1983	1984	1985	1986	1987	1988	1989	1990	1991	CAGR(1982–1991)
Total	185	214	235	258	304	349	377	389	393	381	8.4%
Growth		15.9%	9.6%	9.8%	18.1%	14.7%	8.0%	3.1%	1.1%	−3.0%	
Men	61	69	78	87	104	113	129	124	122	115	7.3%
Growth		12.5%	13.0%	12.1%	19.6%	7.9%	14.2%	−3.3%	−1.8%	−5.8%	
Women	59	71	75	85	104	130	139	157	163	169	12.5%
Growth		21.1%	5.9%	13.5%	22.2%	24.8%	6.7%	12.9%	3.6%	3.7%	
Juvenile	65	74	82	85	96	106	109	107	108	98	4.7%
Growth		14.4%	9.9%	4.2%	12.5%	11.2%	2.9%	−1.9%	0.8%	−9.8%	
% of total footwear	22.3%	23.3%	22.9%	23.4%	26.0%	30.4%	33.6%	36.2%	36.4%	34.7%	

(Retail $MM)	1982	1983	1984	1985	1986	1987	1988	1989	1990	1991	CAGR(1982–1991)
Total	$3,558	$4,234	$4,528	$5,147	$6,758	$8,061	$9,737	$10,885	$11,941	$11,929	14.4%
Growth		19.0%	6.9%	13.7%	31.3%	19.3%	20.8%	11.8%	9.7%	−0.1%	
Men	$1,454	$1,743	$1,956	$2,237	$2,932	$3,421	$4,350	$4,640	$5,122	$5,008	14.7%
Growth		19.9%	12.2%	14.3%	31.1%	16.7%	27.2%	6.7%	10.4%	−2.2%	
Women	$1,161	$1,391	$1,447	$1,747	$2,369	$2,988	$3,554	$4,265	$4,688	$4,907	17.4%
Growth		19.8%	4.1%	20.7%	35.6%	26.2%	18.9%	20.0%	9.9%	4.7%	
Juvenile	$942	$1,100	$1,124	$1,163	$1,457	$1,652	$1,834	$1,980	$2,131	$2,014	8.8%
Growth		16.7%	2.2%	3.5%	25.3%	13.4%	11.0%	8.0%	7.6%	−5.5%	

Source: Sporting Goods Manufacturers Association/SMI Footwear Market Insights.

sneakers.[4] More people began to wear athletic footwear for casual use, and athletic footwear had even become a fashion item with the elevation in conspicuous consumption of status names such as Reebok and Nike. During this same period, the battle between athletic footwear marketers became intense, and the winners and losers became clear by the end of the 1980s. Because the total footwear market declined slightly during this period, athletic footwear had become the largest segment of the footwear market by the end of the decade, taking a share from other footwear segments. According to Footwear Market Insights (FMI), 420 million pairs of athletic shoes were sold in 1990, representing 40 percent of the total footwear market measured in pairs. In comparison, dress and casual shoes represented 23 percent (240 million pairs) and 12 percent (130 million pairs) of the market, respectively (Exhibit 2).[5]

Beginning in 1990, however, the athletic footwear industry entered its mature stage. The growth in sales flattened substantially as the number of people participating in exercise and fitness activities peaked and the domestic economy began to falter. Consumers began to shift toward value consciousness. Some marketers are considering the shift toward lower-end shoes.[4] In 1990, domestic sales grew by roughly 10 percent to $11.9 billion retail sales value (Exhibit 1).[3] The growth of total athletic footwear sales stopped in 1991 (no growth in retail value and 3 percent decline in pairage), although branded athletic footwear grew at a lower rate (4 percent in wholesale value) to $5.8 billion wholesale value, taking market share from nonbrand sneakers.[4] In 1991 branded athletic footwear accounted for about 70 percent of the total athletic footwear market in pairs[6] and about 80 percent in value. According to the Sporting Goods Manufacturers Association, unit sales in mid-1992 were level with those in mid-1991. FMI forecasts that the athletic footwear market will remain almost flat (0.4 percent growth per year in pairage) during the 1990s, while the dress and casual shoe market will grow at a relatively higher rate (0.8 percent per year for both in pairage) (Exhibit 2).[5] This situation has already resulted in significant price pressure within the athletic footwear industry as companies try to liquidate inventory and maintain market share. Although no evidence exists yet, this situation suggests that the industry may consolidate throughout the early 1990s.

Nonetheless, several areas of unrealized potential still seem to exist in the U.S. market. In fact, if we examine more detailed market segments within athletic footwear, the growth during the 1980s was not uniform across all the categories but rather an aggregate of different trends toward different types of products. At the beginning of the 1980s the growth came from the running craze. After a few years, however, aerobic shoes led the growth of the industry. They were in turn replaced by other types of shoes such as basketball, cross-training, and walking shoes in the late 1980s.[7,8] In the early 1990s, the running, aerobics, and tennis categories have begun to decline; basketball and cross-training categories, the two dominant product categories in athletic footwear, have begun to flatten; and walking and golf shoes still show high growth (Exhibit 3).[6] It is expected that the walking category will be the next important growth segment, driven especially by an aging population's need to find less strenuous ways to keep fit. The market size of product categories intended by the shoe manufacturers does not match the actual use of athletic shoes for each

EXHIBIT 2   Footwear Market Breakdown by Segment (Current and Forecast)

	(Millions of Pairs Sold)		
	1990	2000	Change
Athletic footwear	420	435	3.4%
Men's	140	148	5.3%
Women's	172	182	5.7%
Boys'	50	50	−0.8%
Girls'	28	28	−1.7%
Infants'	29	27	−7.8%
Dress	240	260	8.1%
Men's dress	65	71	9.1%
Women's dress	175	189	7.7%
Casual	31	142	8.4%
Men's casual	29	32	8.1%
Women's casual	101	110	8.5%
Other	187	203	8.6%
Men's other	62	66	7.8%
Women's sandals	57	63	10.6%
Women's other	69	74	7.7%
Children (Nonathletic)	47	46	−1.5%
Boys' dress casual	11	11	−1.0%
Boys' other	6	6	−0.4%
Girls' dress/casual/sandal	23	23	−2.0%
Girls' other	6	6	−1.5%
Infants' (nonathletic)	29	27	−7.8%
Total footwear	1,054	1,112	5.5%
Men's	296	316	6.9%
Women's	574	617	7.5%
Boys'	68	67	−0.8%
Girls'	58	57	−1.8%
Infants'	59	54	−7.8%

Source: *Footwear Market Insights.*

type of activity (compare Exhibit 3 and Exhibit 4).[9] Although the product category volume for walking is small (10.8 percent of total athletic footwear in pairage), walking shoes constitute the most popular category based on consumers' responses. These statistics suggest that consumers use shoes for purposes different from those intended by the marketers. Thus, if a product is appropriately positioned, it can gain the potential consumers who otherwise will buy substitute products. The increasing popularity of sporty casual shoes (athletic construction with traditional styling) may also offer another area of growth.[10] To respond to these opportunities,

EXHIBIT 3   **Athletic Footwear Market by Category**

	1991 Wholesale Value ($MM and %)		Historical Growth		
			1990–1991	1988–1989	1987–1988
Basketball	$1,675	26.2%	0%	20%	44%
Cross-training/fitness	1,125	17.6	2	48	72
Tennis	725	11.3	–9	14	21
Walking	690	10.8	15	26	61
Running/jogging	635	9.9	–16	11	–2
Aerobics	425	6.6	–17	0	–10
Golf	390	6.1	30	29	32
Cleated	250	3.9	4	24	23
Other court	40	0.6	0	44	17
Other	440	6.9	73	18	83
Total adult	$6,395	100.0%			
Children's	$1,235				
Athletic total	7,630				

Source: Sporting Goods Manufacturers Association/SMI Footwear Market Insights.

some athletic footwear companies such as Reebok and L.A. Gear have introduced casual product lines using subbrands under their own brand umbrellas.[11,12,13]

Trends in Physical Fitness and Exercise

The boom in exercise and health consciousness that swept the United States in the late 1970s and early 1980s expanded the market for athletic and exercise equipment dramatically, and it is anticipated that this lifestyle trend will continue into the future. This new lifestyle has been accepted more widely as a status symbol by white-collar people with higher education and income.[2] During this same period women's participation in all kinds of fitness activities increased significantly. The types of sports activities that attract Americans changed during the 1980s from team to individual sports such as aerobics, jogging, and walking.[2] Much of this exercise and physical fitness trend was focused on indoor activities and, consequently, the home exercise equipment market experienced significant sales growth. In the coming decade, it is anticipated that the desire for fitness will not diminish, but the location of these activities will move from indoors to outdoors.[14]

Some of the more popular athletic pursuits are running, aerobics, bicycling, tennis, and skiing. People interested in these sports also show a higher involvement in camping, hiking, and other wildlife or environmentally related pastimes than average people. Walking is also very popular among the U.S. population. Seventy million people walk for exercise in the United States.[15] In the *Lifestyle Market Analyst* by Standard Rate and Data Service, 36.8 percent in household count answered that they enjoy walking as a recreational form of exercise. Although the other athletic activities are enjoyed by

EXHIBIT 4   Market by Product Category (categorization by customer)

Millions (and percent) Who Own

	U.S. Adults	Any Athletic Shoes		Exercise Walking Shoes		Tennis Shoes		Jogging/Running Shoes		Golf Shoes		Aerobic Shoes		Cross-Basketball Shoes		Training Shoes	
Total	182	N.A.		18.2	(10%)	17.6	(10%)	17.4	(10%)	12.0	(7%)	9.8	(5%)	6.9	(4%)	5.8	(3%)
Male	87			7.0	(8%)	8.7	(10%)	9.5	(11%)	8.5	(10%)	2.6	(3%)	5.4	(6%)	3.4	(4%)
Female	95			11.2	(12%)	8.9	(9%)	7.9	(8%)	3.5	(4%)	7.3	(8%)	1.5	(2%)	2.4	(3%)
18–24	26			2.1	(8%)	2.9	(11%)	3.7	(15%)	1.1	(4%)	1.8	(7%)	1.5	(6%)	1.4	(5%)
25–34	44			3.7	(8%)	5.3	(12%)	5.4	(12%)	2.7	(6%)	3.0	(7%)	2.4	(5%)	2.1	(5%)
35–44	38			4.4	(12%)	4.6	(12%)	4.0	(11%)	3.5	(9%)	2.5	(7%)	1.6	(4%)	1.3	(4%)
45–54	25			3.0	(12%)	2.5	(10%)	2.1	(8%)	1.8	(7%)	1.3	(5%)	0.9	(3%)	0.6	(2%)
55–64	21			2.8	(13%)	1.3	(6%)	1.3	(6%)	1.5	(7%)	1.0	(5%)	0.3	(2%)	0.2	(1%)
65 or older	29			2.3	(8%)	1.0	(3%)	0.8	(3%)	1.4	(5%)	0.3	(1%)	0.2	(1%)	0.2	(1%)

Millions (and percent) Who Bought in the Last 12 Months

	U.S. Adults	Any Athletic Shoes		Exercise Walking Shoes		Tennis Shoes		Jogging/Running Shoes		Golf Shoes		Aerobic Shoes		Cross-Basketball Shoes		Training Shoes	
Total	182	125.2	(69%)	9.2	(5%)	7.1	(4%)	8.0	(4%)	2.2	(1%)	4.6	(3%)	2.8	(2%)	2.9	(2%)
Male	87	58.3	(67%)	3.1	(4%)	3.3	(4%)	4.4	(5%)	1.3	(1%)	1.1	(1%)	2.4	(3%)	1.6	(2%)
Female	95	66.9	(70%)	6.0	(6%)	3.9	(4%)	3.6	(4%)	0.9	(1%)	3.5	(4%)	0.5	(0%)	1.3	(1%)
18–24	26	19.2	(75%)	0.7	(3%)	1.2	(5%)	2.0	(8%)	0.0	(0%)	0.8	(3%)	0.7	(3%)	0.5	(2%)
25–34	44	34.2	(78%)	1.8	(4%)	2.1	(5%)	2.4	(5%)	0.6	(1%)	1.3	(3%)	1.2	(3%)	1.1	(3%)
35–44	38	29.2	(78%)	2.5	(7%)	1.8	(5%)	1.7	(4%)	0.8	(2%)	1.2	(3%)	0.5	(1%)	0.7	(2%)
45–54	25	18.0	(71%)	1.6	(6%)	1.2	(5%)	0.9	(4%)	0.3	(1%)	0.7	(3%)	0.3	(1%)	0.3	(1%)
55–64	21	12.9	(61%)	1.5	(7%)	0.5	(2%)	0.7	(3%)	0.2	(1%)	0.4	(2%)	0.1	(1%)	0.1	(1%)
65 or older	29	11.7	(40%)	1.1	(4%)	0.3	(1%)	0.3	(1%)	0.2	(1%)	0.2	(1%)	0.1	(0%)	0.1	(0%)

Source: *1991 Study of Media & Markets*, Simmons Market Research Bureau, Inc.

mostly younger people between 18 and 45 years of age (representing 60–70 percent), more than 45 percent of all fitness walkers are 55 or over, and 25 percent are grandparents.[16] The emerging lifestyle concepts in the 1990s of moderation and wellness are extending beyond eating to exercise as well. Consequently, low-impact sports activities are expected to show high growth.[15] As baby boomers age, it is expected that they will select walking as their major fitness activity.

Exercise habits in recent years have become varied and unpredictable. Consumers show a tendency to move from activity to activity.[7] These are important implications for marketers of athletic footwear. First, there is a market for a wide range of shoe designs to accommodate consumer needs for shoes that are appropriate for each specific activity. Second, an opportunity exists to market shoes with flexible and versatile designs that allow users to move between activities without having to purchase several pairs of shoes. Certainly the rapid growth of the cross-training category during the late 1980s validates this assessment.

Customer Profile and Needs

Athletic footwear has penetrated virtually all segments of U.S. consumers. According to the 1991 national survey by the Athletic Footwear Association,[17] about 85 percent of consumers between ages 13 and 75 wear athletic shoes, and more than 70 percent bought at least one pair in the past year. These numbers are fairly consistent between sexes. Teenagers (ages 13–17), most of whom are avid athletes, are more enthusiastic buyers than adults, who are mostly moderate sports participants. The wearer of athletic shoes owns 2.9 pairs on average; teens, slightly more.[17] These statistics have not changed significantly since 1988, and although this indicates that the athletic footwear market is now at the mature stage, consumers are not turning away from athletic footwear: 85 percent indicated that they plan to wear athletic footwear with the same frequency the next year, and 10 percent planned to wear it more often (Exhibit 5).[17]

In 1990, 40 percent of the total footwear purchase in pairage was athletic footwear. This number was higher for men (47 percent) than for women (33 percent) because the dress shoe market is still the largest segment for women.[5] Although AFA's research shows similar market penetration by male and female customers, the market size in pairage is significantly larger for the female market (140 million pairs for men versus 170 million pairs for women in 1990), probably reflecting high replacement by female consumers (Exhibit 2). This difference is canceled out by the lower average price of women's shoes, and market sizes in value are almost the same.[3] In the children's market, athletic shoes have higher market penetration among boys (75 percent) than girls (49 percent), and the boys' market is almost twice as large as the girls' market.[5] Reflecting this, male purchasers are younger than female purchasers (on average 28 versus 33 years of age). More than 33 percent of male purchasers are under 18 compared with 25 percent of females (Exhibit 6).[3]

This high penetration was achieved by the expansion of athletic footwear usage into all aspects of everyday wear. According to the 1991 AFA national survey, 35 percent of the respondents mention sports and fitness activities as the primary

EXHIBIT 5   Penetration of Athletic Footwear

	Percent Who Wear Athletic Footwear		Percent Who Bought in Past Year	
	1988	1991	1988	1991
Total	87%	84%	67%	72%
Male	87%	84%	67%	74%
Female	86%	84%	66%	71%
Teens (13–17)	91%	95%	92%	92%
Adults (18–75)	87%	81%	66%	69%

Source: Athletic Footwear Association national surveys.

Ownership and Wearing Plans among All Wearers, 1991	Total	Males	Females	Teens	Adults
Pairs owned	2.9	2.8	2.9	3.2	2.8
Percent owning 4 or more pairs	25%	24%	27%	31%	24%
Percent planning to wear next year					
Same amount	85%	84%	86%	91%	88%
More often	10%	9%	10%	9%	8%
Less often	4%	5%	3%	1%	4%

Source: Athletic Footwear Association national survey, 1991.

EXHIBIT 6   Demographic Breakdown of Athletic Shoe Purchasers

Age	Percent Male	Percent Female
Under 18	33%	25%
18–34	39	37
35–55	18	25
56+	10	13
Total	100%	100%

Source: Sporting Goods Manufacturers Association/SMI Footwear Market Insights.

reason for wearing athletic footwear, and for the rest the primary purposes are occasions such as around the house, work, school, shopping, and social activities.[17] SGMA's research also indicates that only 10.5 percent of athletic shoes are purchased for only sports or fitness participation.[3] Older consumers are more likely to purchase footwear for active sports use than are young consumers. Active sports usage is higher for men (15.6 percent) than for women (9.4 percent). Younger female consumers are more likely to purchase athletic footwear for fashion reasons (Exhibit 7).[17]

EXHIBIT 7   **Primary Use of Athletic Footwear**

Sports and fitness activities	35%
Other activities	65%
Around the house	23%
Work	13%
School	13%
Shopping	12%
Social activities	10%

Source: Athletic Footwear Association national survey, 1991.

Active Sports Use Share of Market (percent)	1990	1991
Total	9.0%	10.5%
Men	13.9%	15.6%
Women	7.8%	9.4%
Boys	3.7%	5.5%
Girls	3.4%	3.9%

Source: Sporting Goods Manufacturers Association/SMI Footwear Market Insights.

Therefore, consumers expect more from athletic footwear than simply high performance for sports or fitness. By far the most important characteristic is comfortable fit and feel. Eighty-three percent of consumers say this is very important in their decision to buy athletic footwear.[17] Indeed, this is what branded athletic footwear has achieved since the 1980s through product improvement. However, because all top brands already satisfy this requirement sufficiently, product improvement alone can not offer a differential advantage. The next important characteristics are "suits active lifestyle," "has performance advantage," and "has fashion advantage," all of which more than half of the consumers rated as important. Emphasis on "active lifestyle" has grown significantly since 1988, and it is also becoming an important customer need that "the shoe is good for a variety of sports and activities," indicating the need for more cross-over types of shoes (Exhibit 8).[17]

The price per pair of athletic footwear varies widely, from less than $15 to more than $100. Although high-price, high-performance shoes attract people's attention in advertisements, 75 percent of athletic footwear was purchased at less than $44.50 per pair in 1991 according to FMI.[17] If we examine only the adult market (including teens), the average price is $42.60 in 1991. Male consumers spend significantly more ($49.50 per pair) than female consumers ($35.80). This average price increased significantly between 1988 and 1991, indicating that marketers have been successful in upgrading customers to higher priced products.[17] This will become especially important during the 1990s because the unit sales are expected to stay flat. It is encouraging that the maximum amount consumers are willing to pay is still significantly higher ($61.60) than the average price.[17] This suggests the potential of upgrading if the marketers can meet consumers' unmet needs. In addition, teens (ages 13–17) spend significantly more for a pair

EXHIBIT 8   Consumer Needs

**Characteristics Consumers Say Are Very Important in
Their Decisions to Buy Athletic Footwear**

Comfort, fit, and feel	83%
Suits active lifestyle	63%
Has performance advantages	56%
Has fashion advantages	54%
Meets basic needs	50%
Good for everyday wear	41%
Has conservative appearance	29%
Has good brand aura	27%
Is "hot" with friends, celebrities	13%

Source: Athletic Footwear Association national survey, 1991 (composite of
37 separate characteristics grouped by factor analysis).

EXHIBIT 9   Retail Price

**1991 Athletic Footwear Market by Retail Price Point
(percent of total pairs)**

Less than $12.50	22.5%
$12.50–$24.49	23.6%
$24.50–$34.49	15.0%
$34.50–$44.49	13.6%
$44.50–$54.49	10.0%
$54.50–$74.49	10.7%
More than $74.50	4.6%

Source: *Footwear Market Insights*.

Average Amount Purchasers Spent and Are Willing to Spend

	Amount Spent		Most Would Spend	
	1988	**1991**	**1988**	**1991**
Total	$30.10	$42.60	$42.00	$61.60
Male	$33.60	$49.50	$45.30	$68.30
Female	$26.90	$35.80	$38.80	$55.00
Teens (13–17)	$35.30	$54.20	$52.50	$76.10
Adults (18–75)	$29.80	$40.20	$41.30	$58.70

Source: Athletic Footwear Association national surveys.

and also are willing to pay more than adults.[17] Together with high volume, especially for men's athletic shoes, this market is a critical segment for marketers (Exhibit 9).

Because of differences in consumer attitudes for the purchase and use of athletic footwear by different age and gender groups, the change in consumer demographics during the coming decade will have a significant influence on the athletic footwear industry. The most notable change is the aging of the baby boom generation and the growing percentage of senior citizens, and the expected decrease in the population under 35 years of age. The purchase of shoes by each age group is expected to correlate closely with population growth. FMI forecasts that purchases by the 18–24 and 25–34 age groups will decrease respectively by 3.3 percent and 15.4 percent while those by the age groups 35–44, 45–54, 55–64, and 65 and over will increase by 15.5 percent, 45.5 percent, 12.6 percent, and 10.4 percent, respectively.[5]

AFA has recently developed a segmentation based on consumer attitudes toward athletic footwear and their lifestyles. AFA proposes the following five segments: Sports Involved, Trendsetters, Impressionables, Conformists, and Practicals. While Sports Involved, 26 percent of wearers, consider performance most important, the other four segments are fashion oriented. Trendsetters, the youngest group, spend or are willing to spend the most money to be fashionable. Although the group is small, it is important because it influences other segments, especially Impressionables and Conformists, who are fashion conscious but look to others for guidance on what to wear (see Exhibit 10 for details).[17]

Consumers' Purchasing Decisions

Intensive advertising through consumer media such as network television has characterized the athletic footwear industry since the late 1980s. The industry's media spending expanded more than 10 times from $20 million to $250 million between 1983 and 1991, much larger growth than that of the market itself, and it is still expected to increase even after the market growth has hit the plateau[18] (Exhibit 11). Although advertising is the primary source of information for consumers, there are other important ways to address marketers' message to consumers. Store displays and word of mouth are two important information sources cited by athletic shoe wearers (Exhibit 12).[17] Compared to advertising, these are still underdeveloped areas for most marketers. One effort to increase customer communication is showcase stores operated by marketers themselves. One example is Nike Town, which works not only as a showcase to consumers but also gives Nike feedback about the latest methods of displaying merchandise, which in turn can be shown to retailers.[19,20]

The most common advertising method among top athletic footwear marketers such as Nike, Reebok, and L.A. Gear is campaigns featuring top sports figures. Although it is generally believed that this is the most effective way to enhance the high-performance image, and it has been proved by the success of Nike and Reebok's past endorsement campaigns, the response of athletic shoe wearers to the survey by AFA is contradictory. Eighty-eight percent of adults and 63 percent of teens state that the celebrity endorsement has no effect on their buying decision. Similarly, 94 percent of adults and 74 percent of teens say that they learn nothing about new sneakers from seeing what celebrities wear.[17] Nevertheless, AFA concludes that "celebrity endorsements are effective in attracting attention to a new brand or style through advertising and store displays." It is at least true that

EXHIBIT 10   **Consumer Profiles/Segmentation**

Sports Involved is the largest segment. Predominantly male, they most often choose footwear for a specific sport but are not particularly brand conscious.

Trendsetters, a youthful group, closely follow all marketing efforts but consider themselves independent, smart shoppers.

Impressionables, also very fashion conscious, look to others for guidance on what to wear.

Conformists, oriented to the home, are fashion conscious but conservative.

Practicals are career-oriented, smart shoppers who seek low prices.

	Sports Involved	Trendsetters	Impressionables	Conformists	Practicals
Percent of wearers	26%	15%	22%	19%	17%
Sex	61% male	54% male	55% male	66% female	65% female
Age	36 (17% teens)	28 (31% teens)	31 (25% teens)	42 (2% teens)	35 (13% teens)
Household income	$38,300	$34,700	$33,600	$38,400	$39,100
Preferred sneaker attributes	Performance	Fashion	Brand aura	Conservative but in fashion	Multi-use/ conservative
Amount paid for last pair	$46.40	$48.30	$47.60	$40.20	$31.80
Most would pay	$66.90	$71.30	$66.50	$56.90	$50.60
Distinguishing shopping habits	•Shops equally at department stores/ athletic footwear chains •Often buys for specific sport	•Prefers national athletic footwear chains	•Prefers national athletic footwear chains •Likes multicolor shoes	•Prefers department stores •Strong preference for 1-color shoes	•Prefers department and discount stores

Notes: The qualitative sections above dramatize differences. All segments, for example, rate fit and feel as the most important characteristic in athletic footwear. All spend about 18 hours a week watching TV and say movies are their favorite program. None spends more than 27% of their viewing time watching sports.

Source: Athletic Footwear Association.

celebrity endorsements work more effectively on teenagers and particularly "Impressionables." Twenty-nine percent of teens say they are more likely to buy the shoes with celebrity endorsement compared with only 7 percent of adults.[17] Teenagers are important in the marketing of athletic footwear because they drive the fashion segment as trendsetters. Also, the number of people affected by the celebrity endorsement is increasing. In 1991, 26 percent of teens said they learn about new sneakers from seeing what celebrities wear compared with 10 percent in 1988 (Exhibit 12).[17]

EXHIBIT 11 Media Spending by Company ($MM)

		1984	1985	1986	1987	1988	1989	1990	1991	1992(1–6)
Nike Inc.	Total	$9.7	$6.2	$9.2	$14.2	$35.9	$50.9	$87.7	$109.5	$54.4
	Network TV	1.1	1.9	1.6	5.6	14.5	24.2	42.8	53.0	27.7
	Other TV*	4.6	2.5	0.6	2.4	4.1	7.1	19.4	24.4	7.4
	Magazines	2.8	1.1	6.9	6.0	16.7	18.9	24.9	31.4	19.0
	Other	1.2	0.7	0.1	0.2	0.7	0.6	0.7	0.7	0.3
Reebok Int'l	Total	N.A.	$3.8	$8.5	$18.7	$41.4	$45.0	$48.5	$75.7	$49.5
	Network TV		0.0	0.6	1.3	20.3	16.4	18.4	29.4	24.1
	Other TV*		0.0	0.4	4.0	8.6	14.3	10.9	16.5	11.6
	Magazines		3.7	7.4	12.8	11.4	13.3	16.9	22.9	11.0
	Other		0.1	0.2	0.6	1.2	1.1	2.3	6.9	2.9
L.A. Gear	Total	N.A.	N.A.	N.A.	$3.0	$10.2	$23.6	$36.1	$24.9	$8.7
	Network TV				0.0	0.0	3.3	12.8	6.4	1.7
	Other TV*				2.6	8.7	16.3	17.1	13.8	5.9
	Magazines				0.3	1.4	3.8	4.2	3.0	1.1
	Other				0.1	0.1	0.2	1.9	1.7	0.0

*Other TV: Spot, syndicated, and cable networks.

Athletic Footwear Only

	1980	1981	1982	1983	1984	1985	1986	1987	1988	1989	1990	1991	1992(1–6)
Nike	$0.1	$0.1	$0.7	$1.3	$8.8	$5.3	$8.1	$13.4	$31.9	$44.1	$77.5	$97.8	$50.4
Reebok	—	—	—	0.1	0.7	3.8	8.5	12.1	25.7	33.1	38.8	59.4	40.1
L.A. Gear	—	—	—	—	0.0	0.1	0.7	0.5	9.7	21.9	35.8	24.1	8.6
Easy Spirit (US Shoe Corp)	—	—	—	—	—	—	—	1.4	3.1	3.8	11.6	13.6	5.4
Converse	0.3	0.9	3.0	3.3	4.5	3.1	2.7	2.8	4.9	3.7	10.0	10.4	6.4
Keds	0.8	0.5	0.2	0.4	0.7	0.1	0.5	1.1	3.5	5.6	9.7	10.1	5.7
Side 1 (Nike)	—	—	—	—	—	—	—	—	—	2.0	1.4	5.2	—
Avia	—	0.0	0.0	—	0.2	0.5	1.5	3.6	10.1	7.9	4.3	4.2	2.8
Adidas	0.6	0.5	0.7	0.9	4.3	0.7	1.4	0.9	0.0	5.3	0.5	3.3	0.4
British Knight	—	—	—	—	—	—	0.0	0.2	0.7	0.4	1.0	3.2	1.0
Etonic Sporting Footwear	0.4	0.8	0.8	1.5	3.0	0.8	0.4	0.9	1.2	2.3	2.1	2.9	3.3
Asics Tiger	—	—	—	—	—	—	0.4	0.8	0.8	0.8	2.2	2.8	1.9
Foot-Joy	0.5	1.0	1.0	1.2	1.6	1.5	1.2	2.3	1.9	1.3	1.6	2.6	2.4
K-Swiss	0.1	0.1	0.1	0.2	0.1	0.2	0.3	0.4	0.9	1.2	1.3	1.7	0.9
New Balance	0.0	0.2	0.3	0.8	0.9	0.6	0.8	1.0	1.8	1.3	0.8	1.6	2.4
Industry Total	$12.9	$19.7	$14.3	$20.2	$31.9	$28.9	$42.2	$57.3	$113.1	$135.6	$210.0	$247.2	N.A.

Source: AD $ Summary, LNA Arbitron Multi-Media Service.

EXHIBIT 12   Information Sources

Most Important Source of Information about New Sneakers: Athletic Footwear Wearers Aged 13–75

All advertising	69%
TV commercials	53%
Store displays	57%
Friends	48%
Observing others	41%
Magazine articles	19%
Salespeople	19%
Newspaper articles	13%
Mail-order catalogs	11%
Celebrities	10%

Source: Athletic Footwear Association national survey, 1991.

Influence of Celebrity Endorsement

"If a sports star or celebrity endorsed a sneaker brand, how would that affect your decision to buy?"

	Adults (18–75)	Teens (13–17)
No influence	88%	63%
More likely to buy	7%	29%
Less likely to buy	5%	6%

Percent of wearers saying they learn about new sneakers from seeing what celebrities wear:

	Adults (18–75)	Teens (13–17)
1988 survey	3%	10%
1991 survey	6%	26%

Source: Athletic Footwear Association national surveys.

EXHIBIT 13   Importance of Brand

Planning for Last Sneaker Purchase: Athletic Footwear Wearers Aged 13–75	1988	1991
Essentially undecided	71%	56%
No Plans/decided while shopping	34%	26%
Just planning to buy sneakers	37%	30%
Wanted specific brand	14%	29%

Source: Athletic Footwear Association national surveys.

The importance of brand in the selection of athletic footwear is also increasing, although more than half of wearers are still undecided about which brands to buy before they enter the stores. In 1991, 29 percent of wearers had a specific brand in mind when they bought athletic shoes compared to 14 percent in 1988.[17] While this trend emphasizes the importance of the establishment of brand equity, it also suggests that efforts at the retail level are still important (Exhibit 13).

EXHIBIT 14 Market Share

Brand	U.S. Athletic Shoe Market Share (percent)		
	1990	1991	1992
Nike	28.7%	29.3%	30.0%
Reebok	21.4	23.1	24.4
L.A. Gear	11.8	8.5	5.0
Keds	5.1	6.0	6.1
Converse		3.5	
Adidas		3.1	
Asics		2.9	
Avia	33.0%	2.3	34.5%
British Knights		1.9	
Etonic		1.8	
New Balance		1.6	
K-Swiss		1.6	
28 other brands		14.4	

Source: *Sporting Goods Intelligence.*

Domestic Athletic Footwear Revenue (branded only, $MM)	1989	1990	1991	1992
Industry total (January–December)	$5.00	$5.55	$5.80	N.A.
Nike (year ended May)	1.06	1.37	1.68	$1.75
Reebok (year ended December)	1.15	1.17	1.34	N.A.
L.A. Gear (year ended November)	0.53	0.66	0.49	N.A.

Sources: Annual Reports and 10Ks of Nike, Reebok, and L.A. Gear.

Competition

The athletic footwear market is characterized by the dominance of the two giants, Nike and Reebok, and a number of smaller players focusing on their niches. In 1991, Nike and Reebok together controlled 52.4 percent of the market (Nike, 29.3 percent, and Reebok, 23.1 percent),[21] with more than 40 other athletic footwear brands in the domestic market. L.A. Gear, the number three brand, tried to move from being a niche marketer into the mass market and attained 11.8 percent of the market in 1990, but its share declined significantly to 8.5 percent in 1991 even after it reduced its price to maintain market share.[22] Meanwhile, Reebok, the number two brand, gained share through the revitalization of its entire brand. Thus the gap between the top two brands and the others widened significantly (Exhibit 14). The media spending for each of the top two brands grew to about $100 million a year in 1992 from less than $10 million in 1986, resulting from the advertisement battle between them (Exhibit 11).[18] Thus it is now considered almost impossible for the smaller brands to beat them in the near future. Smaller brands such as Keds, Converse, Adidas, and Asics Tiger are competing for the third position with L.A. Gear, while others are satisfied with their niche positioning.[22,23,24] In spite of the high market share concentration of a few companies, the fashion segment of consumers secures the existence of markets for niche players. In fact, market share concentration is significantly lower for the fashion segment than for the performance segment.[25]

There have been two different approaches to address product identity to consumers: performance and fashion. While Nike, Converse, and Avia focus on high-performance footwear for serious athletes, Reebok and L.A. Gear have had a fashion focus.[26] They have used bright colors and fashion-conscious styling to attract a market heavily dominated by women. This difference has created a different customer base[9] and different market penetration by product type (Exhibit 15). Reebok and L.A. Gear have recently realized that to cover the whole segment, especially the men's market, it is essential to establish a high-performance image. Thus they have signed up top sports figures and developed high-performance technologies such as Reebok's Pump. Besides the difference of performance versus fashion, niche players target a specific age group or specific sport use. Avia focuses on women's fitness, Keds on women's casual wear, Converse on basketball shoes for young males,[27] Foot Joy and Wilson on the golf and tennis market, and New Balance and Brooks on running shoes.

The following is a brief description of the top three players.

Nike

Nike, the market leader with a share of almost 30 percent, was started by Phil Knight in 1964 in his garage. From its early days in the 1970s, Nike has consistently positioned itself as a marketer of high-performance and product technology. Nike experienced significant growth with its high-tech running shoes by riding on the running craze that began in the late 1970s. In 1982, Nike replaced Adidas as the market leader.[28] In 1984, however, Nike's attempt to enter the casual shoe market failed, and it missed the trend toward aerobic shoes that was successfully captured by Reebok.[29] Nike had been focusing on the men's market and neglected the women's market. Nike continued its focus on technology. The Air Jordan basketball shoe, named after NBA star Michael Jordan, used the air technology that had been improved since the late 1970s. Although this shoe, by itself, contributed more than $100 million sales to Nike in 1985, its sales declined rapidly when Michael Jordan broke his foot and had to stay out for the season in 1986.[28] Nike's overall revenue declined that year and Nike lost its leadership position to Reebok by its market share declining from 25 percent to 18.6 percent. But Nike recovered quickly. After the improvement of the air technology, Nike introduced the Nike Air line of 10 performance athletic shoe models unified by a patented system of air cushioning. This system consists of "special gas" shot inside the sole and is marketed as an injury-reduction device.[28] Nike regained its leadership position in 1988.

Nike's greatest strength is its consistent use of a performance-oriented strategy.[26] Nike's footwear is designed primarily for specific athletic use. Basketball, running, and racquet sports are all categories where Nike has excelled both in the past and present. Nike currently supplies between 60 and 70 percent of all high school and college basketball teams with their footwear. This focus on specific sport use, and on serious athletes, is apparent throughout Nike's positioning, distribution, and advertising.

EXHIBIT 15 **Customer Base for Each Brand**

	U.S. Adults (in millions)	Any Athletic Shoes	Reebok	Nike	L.A. Gear	Keds	Converse	Adidas
			Millions (and percent) Who Bought in the Last 12 Months					
Total	182	125.2 (69%)	45.7 (25%)	33.4 (18%)	25.4 (14%)	12.6 (7%)	8.5 (5%)	8.2 (4%)
Male	87	58.3 (67%)	19.9 (23%)	16.6 (19%)	9.2 (11%)	3.5 (4%)	4.8 (6%)	4.3 (5%)
Female	95	66.9 (70%)	25.8 (27%)	16.8 (18%)	16.2 (17%)	9.1 (10%)	3.7 (4%)	3.9 (4%)
18–24	26	19.2 (75%)	6.7 (26%)	5.5 (21%)	4.2 (16%)	1.5 (6%)	1.2 (5%)	1.5 (6%)
25–34	44	34.2 (78%)	12.1 (28%)	8.5 (19%)	7.5 (17%)	3.4 (8%)	2.7 (6%)	1.9 (4%)
35–44	38	29.2 (78%)	12.0 (32%)	9.6 (26%)	7.1 (19%)	3.5 (9%)	2.2 (6%)	2.3 (6%)
45–54	25	18.0 (71%)	7.4 (29%)	5.3 (21%)	3.5 (14%)	1.9 (7%)	1.1 (4%)	1.2 (5%)
55–64	21	12.9 (61%)	4.5 (21%)	2.8 (13%)	1.8 (9%)	1.2 (6%)	0.8 (4%)	0.6 (3%)
65 or older	29	11.7 (40%)	3.1 (11%)	1.8 (6%)	1.3 (4%)	1.1 (4%)	0.6 (2%)	0.7 (2%)

Source: Simmons Market Research Bureau, Inc., 1991.

Advertising is Nike's second forte. In 1991, Nike spent $110 million on consumer media,[18] gaining a 40 percent share of voice in the athletic footwear advertising. The total advertising expenditure in all media combined was even higher. Nike's advertising has been further reinforced through consistency of message: high-performance shoes for serious athletes, as noted by its slogan "Just do it." Nike has also made considerable use of professional sports figures to endorse its products,[14] aiming to create a strong emotional tie with customers by using these athletes to present their shoes. Contracts currently exist with Bo Jackson, Andre Agassi, and Michael Jordan. Although historically Nike's target market was male, Nike has recently introduced its "Dialogue" print campaign to capture the female market. Still, women represent only 17 percent of Nike's total domestic sales.[27]

Other factors also enhance Nike's strength in the marketplace. Nike's distribution network is large and diverse, with its retail base exceeding 16,000 accounts. Nike Town, a showcase store of Nike products, not only provides customers with product information but also works to provide the marketer vivid feedback about consumer needs.[20] Finally, Nike's dominance in outfitting school teams ensures that its products are tested by lead users and trendsetters in the important 14–22 age group.

Reebok

The founder of Reebok, Paul Fireman, also its current chairman, began in 1979 as sole distributor of a small British running shoe manufacturer, J.W. Foster and Sons.[29] In 1984, he bought the parent company and created Reebok International backed by Pentland Industries.[30] Compared to Nike, which was already a $700 million company in 1982, Reebok's presence in this market was limited, with a $4 million revenue. Reebok achieved a surprising growth throughout the 1980s, however, by first targeting women's aerobics shoes. Its shoe using garment leather was different from the traditional sneakers in comfort and fashion. In the early 1980s, Reebok's product was principally aerobic shoes and 75 percent of its customers were women.[29] As the aerobic boom withered, Reebok expanded its product categories and directly competed with performance athletic footwear marketers such as Nike. But Reebok's theme was "freedom of expression," which contrasted with Nike's straight focus on performance. Reebok achieved the number one position in 1986. Two years later, however, the position was reclaimed by Nike.[28,31]

Reebok's advertising campaign has not been very successful. It has struggled to tie its "freedom of expression" theme to purchase of the product. Although the majority of customers buy athletic shoes for nonsports use, they still care about performance in their selection of shoes. Fashion is transient. In 1988 Reebok launched the disastrous "Reebok Lets U.B.U." campaign, spending $35 million.[29] Although the ad was innovative and stressed freedom of expression, it had no sales impact because the ad placed style over content. After this failure, Reebok has been striving to focus on performance. Reebok has reorganized its U.S. operation into two units: performance and lifestyle. However, its next campaign, "Physics Behind the Physique," which was performance-oriented, was again unsuccessful. The simultaneous fashion-oriented ad featuring Paula Abdul confused customers about the message Reebok was trying to convey.[32]

The introduction of the air-inflatable Pump shoe in 1990 was a turning point for Reebok.[4,29] The innovation, initially designed for use in basketball shoes, was widely approved by professional and amateur athletes. Through the success of this line Reebok succeeded in establishing the performance image. Another success was "Blacktop," a basketball shoe designed for outdoor city play. The concept was unique, and the product satisfied fashion-oriented consumers as well as performance seekers.[33,34] These breakthrough products not only increased sales, they also revitalized the entire brand image, thus increasing the sales of other Reebok products. Reebok's share rose by 2 points to 23 percent in 1991.

L.A. Gear

L.A. Gear is also a young company, founded in 1979 by Robert Y. Greenberg. It has shown phenomenal growth since 1987 from 2 percent market share to 11.8 percent in 1990. The original strategy of L.A. Gear was to focus on the female fashion segment rather than performance and innovation and it competed directly with Reebok.[26] With brightly colored shoes and sexy ads it established a strong position in the teenage girl market. Since 1989, L.A. Gear has held the number three position in the market. In 1990, however, the company underwent a major shift in strategy. L.A. Gear realized that to maintain its high growth it had to enter the men's performance market, and tried to compete directly with Nike.[26] To enhance its performance message, it used celebrity marketing featuring Joe Montana for its "Unstoppable" campaign. However, it was difficult to change its established women's fashion brand image, and not only was it unsuccessful in attracting the men's performance market, it also lost support from fickle teenagers.[35] At the same time L.A. Gear tried to maintain its fashion segment by introducing the Jackson line of black, silver-buckled shoes featuring popstar Michael Jackson. This campaign was unsuccessful from the start.[35,36] To maintain its market share and decrease its accumulated inventory, L.A. Gear had to make heavy discounts. The company was weakened as its margins were significantly eroded, and in September 1991 the company called in Trefoil Capital Investors for its rescue.[27]

In 1991, L.A. Gear split its athletic shoe business into two divisions—Lifestyle Footwear and Athletic Footwear. The former continues to focus on fashion and style, while the latter attempts to compete more effectively in the market for performance shoes. The danger of this dual focus lies in the inability to project a consistent image. As L.A. Gear spent time on restructuring and regaining focus, several niche marketers stole its share. Its share declined to 8.5 percent in 1991 and the decline continued through 1992. As a part of its turnaround strategy, it has recently introduced a new advertising campaign, "Get in Gear," which combines the separate images of its fashion, performance, and children's lines under one umbrella.[22]

L.A. Gear's main strength lies in its popularity with the female and youth segments of the market. By contrast, its weaknesses are heavy dependence on one distribution channel, department stores, and a weak financial position.

Other Competitive Threats

In addition to the direct competition, the athletic shoe industry faces competitive pressure from potential entrants into the market. These threats come from essentially three areas. The first is firms expanding into new geographical markets. Examples include Adidas and Puma, both of which have strong positions in European markets. Adidas, which was the market leader in the United States during the 1970s, is currently in the fifth position with a marginal market share of 3.1 percent. But it is still the number one brand outside the United States.[23] Either of these companies could attempt to replicate their strength in the U.S. market.

The second threat is from casual and dress shoe companies. Although it is not likely that they will introduce mass athletic shoe lines in this maturing market, they can introduce their current customer needs for comfort. In fact, casual shoes are comfortable and competing directly with athletic shoes for the fashion segment of consumers. On the performance product side, sporting equipment companies are trying to move into the athletic shoe industry. Examples of this include several tennis racquet manufacturers; possible future candidates include companies such as Salomon, the ski manufacturer, and Ping, the golf club maker.

The third area is companies that are integrating vertically—either forward or backward. More than 95 percent of the athletic footwear sold in the United States is manufactured abroad, mainly in Asia because of its cheap labor.[1] As countries such as Korea and Taiwan have begun to prosper and the labor cost has increased, the U.S. marketers have shifted their production to China and Southeast Asian countries in search of cheaper labor. Many shoe makers in Korea and Taiwan went bankrupt because of the decline of orders from foreign buyers, and they have learned the importance of developing their own brand.[37] It is therefore possible that several of these manufacturers could begin marketing their own brands, although the threat is a few years away. It is also possible that large retailers such as Foot Locker could integrate backward into marketing, manufacturing, or both.

Distribution Channel

Athletic footwear is sold through department stores, specialty athletic shoe stores, shoe stores, sporting goods/pro shops, and discount stores. Although top branded athletic shoe marketers focus on the high-end channel such as specialty athletic shoe stores, sporting goods stores, and department stores and avoid lower-margin mass merchandisers and discounters,[11,12,13] the importance of these low-end mass retailers is growing. According to SGMA's latest study on athletic footwear purchases, the percentage of athletic shoes sold through discount outlets such as Target, Wal-Mart, and K-Mart grew from 25.6 percent in 19% to 27.2 percent in 1991 (Exhibit 16).[3] This is the single largest outlet type (although unbranded and private-label shoes dominate this market). The percentage sold through athletic shoe stores also increased significantly, from 6.9 percent in 1990 to 10 percent in 1991. On the other hand, department stores, shoe stores, and sporting goods stores lost their share. In addition to the share increase in discount stores and athletic shoe stores, the aver-

EXHIBIT 16 Distribution Channel

Retail Outlet–Type Share of Market (in pairs, by percent)

	1990	1991	Change
Discount stores	25.6%	27.2%	+1.6%
Department stores	11.5%	10.6%	−0.9%
Athletic shoe stores	6.9%	10.0%	+3.1%
Other shoe stores	10.6%	9.7%	−0.9%
Sporting goods/pro shops	11.6%	9.3%	−2.3%

Note: Includes unbranded and private-label shoes

Source: Sporting Goods Manufacturers Association/SMI Footwear Market Insights.

age price paid increased by a few percent, reflecting their success in attracting customers without merely lowering prices. There is still a huge difference in the price range between the two types of outlets. The average price paid in an athletic shoe store was $58.80 per pair compared to $17.40 in discount outlets. It is uncertain whether the strategy of the marketers can be sustained when mass merchandisers become more and more powerful in the retail industry. In fact, the top marketers' products can be seen on discount shelves at significantly lower prices because some dealers sell some lines to unauthorized retailers. This has drawn complaints from other retailers who keep the price guidelines given from the marketers. Reebok, Keds, and New Balance have recently implemented trade policies stating that unless retailers follow their price guidelines, they will stop the supply. These policies prompted antitrust lawsuits from discounters.[38]

Product Development and Manufacturing

During the 1980s there was a push toward the more advanced technological athletic shoe with innovations such as air cushioning and inflatable chamber. The product and material innovation brought new levels of comfort and performance to athletic shoes. These innovations were first introduced in high-priced shoes and eventually found their way into the lower-end categories. During the 1990s there have been few radical changes in material, design, and technology used. Compared to the advertising spending of more than $100 million a year, the R&D spending was as low as $8 million in 1990 even for Nike, which spends more on R&D than any competitor.[39] The industry is entering a mature phase with barriers from material limitations (e.g., fiber strength and durability) that prevent major strides forward.

Industry analysts predict that the recession will drive out the expensive shoes with peculiar gimmicks, at least temporarily. Many companies are considering a shift in focus to the lower-end of the market. Nike is also promoting high-technology shoes in the mid-price range. On the other hand, Reebok is introducing advanced technology for its premium-priced Pump line in 1993. These are Insta-Pump and Pump Custom Cushioning, which are aimed at making the shoes fit more precisely using cushions filled with carbon dioxide.[4,40]

Almost all athletic footwear is manufactured in developing nations, especially in Asia, where labor is inexpensive. The economies of these countries have grown significantly in the past decade with a corresponding rise in prosperity. This has been accompanied by a rise in wages as well as an increased exchange rate with the U.S. dollar, thus production costs have risen and profit margins have been squeezed. The strong economic growth in these countries, as well as continued political instability in some countries such as China, have increased the need for the flexibility of sourcing to maintain cost competitiveness. The last few years have seen the rise of a highly mobile and specialized global footwear industry with low-end rubber shoes made in Brazil and the more difficult-to-make leather athletic shoes made in South Korea, Taiwan, and China. The rapid improvement in all these countries' infrastructures has made it easier for the more technically difficult products to be shifted from country to country. While imports from China and Indonesia rose significantly in 1991 because of lower costs, imports from South Korea and Taiwan declined significantly because of the cost in these countries.[1] Thus footwear marketers are continuously shifting their production base as relative cost advantages in these countries change. Recently the Caribbean has become an important base for U.S. manufacturing in general because of its proximity and cheap labor. Although the quality of products varies and consistency has yet to be achieved, this may offer an important cost advantage for the marketers in the United States.

Because of its reliance on the imports, the athletic shoe industry as a whole has been plagued by uncertainty regarding the imposition of duties and quotas.[12] As of 1991 there was 8.5–10 percent duty on leather goods and 6–8 percent for synthetics. There has been increased concern within the shoe industry as the U.S. balance of payments has worsened and stronger calls for tighter restrictions on imported footwear have been heard. In 1985, 1988, and 1989 Congress passed the Textile Act to provide quotas of 1 percent above the previous year for rubber products and fixed at 1989 levels for nonrubber products. Both acts were vetoed, first by President Reagan and then by President Bush. The industry should wait and see how President Clinton will act on this issue.

Notes

1. "U.S. Industrial Outlook" (1983–1993), International Trade Administration, U.S. Department of Commerce.

2. "A Long Race for Fitness Marketers" (1984), *Marketing & Media Decisions,* March, 60–61.

3. Data from Sporting Goods Manufacturers Association (SGMA).

4. "Reebok, Pumping Up" (1992), *The Economist,* February 15.

5. *Footwear News* (1990), 46, No. 53, December 31.

6. SGMA Recreation Market Report, 1988–1991.

7. *USA Today* (1989), September. 27, B1-2.

8. "Stalking Walking" (1986), *Marketing & Media Decisions,* November, 74–80.

9. "1991 Study of Media & Markets," Simmons Market Research Bureau, Inc.

10. "Shoe Marketers Prep for Workout" (1991), *Advertising Age*, March 11, 12.

11. Annual Reports and 10Ks of Reebok.

12. Annual Reports and 10Ks of L.A. Gear.

13. Annual Reports and 10Ks of Nike.

14. "Superbrands 1990" (Supplement to *Adweek Magazines*), 172–173.

15. "Everything in Moderation" (1992), *Adweek*, August 17, 34–35.

16. *The Lifestyle Market Analyst 1992,* Standard Rate and Data Service.

17. "The U.S. Athletic Footwear Market Today" (1991), Athletic Footwear Association.

18. *AD $ Summary,* LNA Arbitron Multi-Media Service, 1980–1992.

19. "Art for Shoes' Sake" (1992), *Forbes,* September 28, 128–130.

20. "Marketers Learn to 'Just Do It'" (1920), *Advertising Age,* January 27, S7-8.

21. "K-Swiss Dips a Toe in Europe" (1992), *Los Angeles Times,* November 3, 3 (original data from Sporting Goods Intelligence).

22. "Small Rivals Leap as L.A. Gear Stumbles" (1992), *Advertising Age,* June 8, 12.

23. "Adidas on the Rebound" (1991), *CFO* 7, No. 9, September, 48–56.

24. The Shoe as Hero" (1990), *Forbes,* August 20, 76–77.

25. "The Numbers Game" (1991), *Footwear News,* January, 22.

26. "Brand Report: Shoeboom!" (1990), *Marketing & Media Decisions,* June, 61–65.

27. Superbrands 1992 (Supplement to *Adweek Magazines*), 43.

28. "Running on Air" (1988), *Marketing & Media Decisions,* March 55–58.

29. The Sneaker Game" (1990), *Forbes* 400, October 22, 114–115.

30. "Setting the Pace" (1986), *Marketing & Media Decisions,* Winter, 34–39.

31. "Treading on Air" (1989), *Business Month,* January, 29–34.

32. "Nike Edges Reebok; L.A. Gear Sprinting" (1989), *Advertising Age,* September 25, 93.

33. "The "Blacktop" is Paving Reebok's Road to Recovery" (1991), *Business Week,* August 12, 27.

34. "Flat-Footed" (1991), *Stores,* August, 67, 82.

35. "L.A. Gear Calls in a Cobbler" (1991), *Business Week,* September 16, 78, 82.

36. "L.A. Gear is Tripping Over Its Shoelaces" (1990), *Business Week,* August 20, 39.

37. "Footwear: Between a Rock and a Hard Place" (1991), *Business Korea,* October 34.

38. "Athletic-shoe Makers Pressure Retailers on Prices" (1992), *USA Today,* December 10, 4B.

39. "Step by Step with Nike" (1990), *Business Week,* August 13, 116–117.

40. "What Recessions? Reebok Introduces High-Priced Pumps for the 'Serious Athletes'" (1992), *Marketing News,* March 16, 3.

Reebok's Marketing Strategy for the 1990s (B)

1. Introduction

As predicted by many analysts, 1992 was a difficult year for all athletic footwear marketers in the United States. The domestic athletic shoe market experienced its second consecutive year of decline in pairs sold. Footwear Market Insights estimates an overall decline of 2 percent for the year ending August 1992.[1] Now it is clear that the industry has entered the mature stage after the double-digit annual growth of the 1980s.

This brings a new challenge for Paul Fireman, chairman of Reebok International. Fireman understands that Reebok's marketing strategy must be adjusted to the new environment, but is not sure how to proceed. The only thing that is clear to him is that in the new market environment, Reebok should have a consistent strategy for all of its products, and each marketing plan should be developed along with the strategy. As of the end of 1992, Reebok was still in the number two position after Nike. During 1992 Reebok gained a market share of about 1 percentage point, yet leaving the gap with Nike intact.[2] In light of these market share trends, the specific strategies are still unclear for Fireman in order to achieve his goal, "become the number one sports and fitness brand."[3]

He recalls the major strategic change in 1990, where Reebok first stressed performance of the shoe for serious athletes by introducing the technology-oriented "Pump." The Pump was very successful, enabling Reebok to regain its market share from Nike and narrow the gap by capturing the performance-oriented segment of customers and by revitalizing all of its shoe lines.[4] But the growth of the Pump has already slowed down as shown by increasing discounting and higher inventory levels at retail stores.[5] Fireman believes that the performance focus was the correct decision but wonders whether Reebok should pursue further performance improvement or whether a different approach is needed to succeed under the new market structure. Probably it is time for Reebok to review its market opportunities and develop a long-term strategy. Fireman sees this as his task because it requires perspective beyond each product division, the marketing unit of Reebok's organization. He has decided to develop his new strategy for the domestic market and present it at the first executive meeting held at the beginning of January 1993.

Reviewing the current marketing plan would be a good starting point. Currently Reebok has three distinct marketing plans. The first is the extension and improvement of the Pump technology. Reebok plans to sell tennis shoes using this new technology beginning in April 1993 and to extend it to other categories later on.[6] The retail price is planned at about $140. But when competitors, including Nike, start to promote their high-tech shoes with a middle-range price, will the new Pump shoe be accepted by the market? How much should Reebok stress performance when most of its customers are not serious athletes? Would this be considered unnecessary gimmicks by the fashion-oriented women, who have been the major purchasers of Reeboks? Is upscaling the correct strategy under the declining market growth and growing importance of mass merchandisers?

The second plan is a product segment approach. Reebok's focus for the coming few years is walking shoes. Reebok plans to introduce the Reebok Bodywalk Program in Spring 1993, aiming at cultivating the still immature walking shoe market and taking more share from the growing product segment.[7] Is the approach of product segmentation by sport the right way to capture underserved customer needs? If so, is walking the only segment Reebok should target or do other segments also offer growth potential?

Are there any other effective ways to segment customers? How can Reebok identify the customers whose needs are not met with its current product lines? For example, what should be Reebok's strategy for the low-end market of cost-conscious customers? Should Reebok simply neglect this segment of the market, or introduce or acquire a different brand to serve it because mass merchandisers are becoming more important?

The third plan is diversification into the casual shoe category. Reebok recently developed a new subbrand, "Boks by Reebok," for its casual footwear and formed a new marketing division that manages Reebok's casual category.[3,8] This division operates separately from other Reebok divisions. The boundary between athletic shoes and casual shoes is disappearing as more people wear athletic shoes for everyday purposes and casual shoes offer more comfort. And this comfort shoe category is expected to have opportunity for future growth. Is this the best category into which Reebok can diversify? If so, is this the correct arrangement to target this market? Should Reebok establish a new division and sell casual shoes under the Reebok brand when its Rockport brand, acquired in 1986, is the number one brand in this category? How can Reebok differentiate the Rockport and Boks brands to avoid cannibalization and waste of marketing expenditure?

2. Reebok International Ltd.

Brief History

Reebok International Ltd., a Massachusetts corporation, designs and markets branded footwear and apparel worldwide. The founder of Reebok, Paul Fireman, also its current chairman, began in 1979 as sole distributor of a small British running shoe manufacturer. In 1984, he bought the parent company and created Reebok International backed by Pentland Industries. In the early 1980s, Reebok marketed principally aerobic shoes, and 75 percent of its customers were women.[9] As the aerobic boom withered, Reebok expanded its application to compete directly with performance athletic footwear marketers such as Nike. But Reebok's theme had been "freedom of expression," which contrasted with Nike's straight focus on performance. Through high growth during the mid-1980s, Reebok achieved the number one position in 1986 in the domestic athletic footwear market, but two years later lost the position to Nike again (Exhibit 1). The introduction of the Pump in 1990 was a turning point for Reebok. The shoe, initially designed for basketball, was widely received by professional and amateur athletes and the concept was extended to other sports. Under the tough market conditions for any business in 1991, Reebok's sales grew significantly, narrowing Nike's lead.[4]

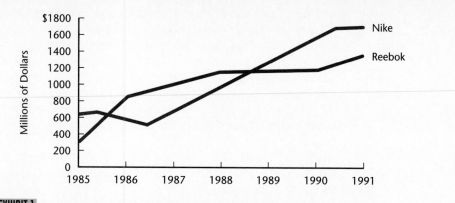

EXHIBIT 1 **Domestic Athletic Footwear Sales: Nike versus Reebok**

Sources: Reebok annual reports, Nike 10Ks; Esquivel, J. et al (1992), "Nike, Inc.—Company Report," Shearson Lehman Brothers, Inc., January 7.

EXHIBIT 2   **Acquisition of Footwear and Other Branded Product Companies**

1986 October 3	The Rockport Company, Inc. (Highland Import Corporation)
1987 April 2	Avia Group International, Inc.
1988 January 20	Ellesse U.S.A., Inc.
1989 October 19	Boston Whaler, Inc.

Acquisition of Distributors Outside of the United States

1987 June 12	Reebok Canada (ESE Sports Co. Ltd.)
1989 December 28	Reebok U.K. (Fleetfoot Ltd.)
1991 January 7	Reebok Italia (Divarese International Sport Diffusion S.P.A.)
April 1	Reebok Japan (total shareholding 51%)

Source: Reebok annual reports.

During the 1980s, Reebok actively acquired other footwear and apparel brands (Exhibit 2). These included Rockport, a leader in casual shoes, and Avia, the number eight athletic footwear brand, which targets the niche market segment of serious women athletes. After these acquisitions, Reebok left these brands and their concepts unchanged. These divisions are operated individually and marketing for these brands is developed separately from the Reebok brand. Therefore Reebok has not used its Reebok brand equity on these newly acquired brands. For the 1990s, Reebok has decided to focus on extending its own business without acquiring other businesses.[10]

International expansion has been another important area for growth. The importance of international business is increasing every year. In 1991, 30 percent of the revenue came from the international market compared to 22 percent in 1990.[3] It is expected to increase to 35 percent in 1992.[10] Reebok's strategy for international markets is a share increase in each market and tighter control through acquisition of independent distributors (Exhibit 2). Compared to the domestic market, the international market is still underdeveloped and offers a high-growth opportunity for

Reebok. Reebok's growth in this market is remarkable, and Fireman is confident about the current growth strategy.

Product

In 1991, 91.1 percent of Reebok's revenue came from its core business, athletic footwear.[3] Other products included sportswear and casual clothes designed primarily for sports use, and recreational boats sold through its Boston Whaler Division, which was acquired in 1989. Reebok has three categories of footwear: sports, fitness, and casual for each of which a distinct marketing group has been formed.[3] The sports category includes shoes for basketball, running, cleated, soccer, tennis, track and field, children's, and volleyball. Most of Reebok's high-technology products, such as the Pump, fall into this category. The fitness category includes aerobics, cross-training, walking, step training, outdoor, and classics. This is Reebok's original domain, but also includes newer market segments such as walking and outdoor shoes. The casual category is sold under the "Boks by Reebok" brand, which was introduced in 1992, and the "Rockport" brand, which was acquired in 1986.

Target Customer

Today Reebok's customers include a much broader base than those in the early 1980s when the company focused on women who seek fashionable sneakers as a means of expressing individuality. The applicable types of sports have been expanded significantly through aggressive line extension. Especially since the introduction of the Pump technology, Reebok's focus has shifted toward more professional use of athletic shoes. Today its customers can be grouped into two categories.[3]

1. Serious athletes—athletes and other sports players who believe that technical and other performance features are critical.
2. General consumers for whom fashion and comfort are the key product attributes.

Although customers in the second category are the majority, Reebok states that the first category constitutes its primary target customers in its 1991 10K.

Function

Reebok is a marketing company that designs product concepts and develops marketing plans. All the manufacturing is contracted out to independent manufacturers in South Korea, Taiwan, Indonesia, China, and Thailand where cheap labor is available.[3] Reebok keeps its high-quality standard, however, by providing detailed product specifications and strict quality control. Its products are sold through specialty retailers, sporting goods stores, and department stores promoted by its own sales force and promotional personnel. Recently a few self-owned "showcase" stores were opened to get direct feedback from customers on their acceptance of product concepts.[11] For Reebok's international operations, both independent distributors and joint ventures, amounting to 40, are used to sell in 129 countries.[3]

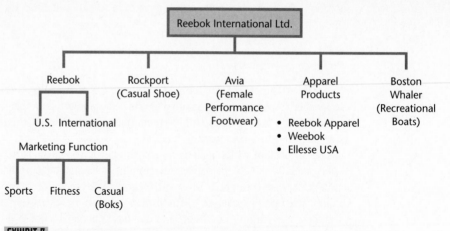

EXHIBIT 3   Organizational Structure: Reebok International Ltd.

Source: Reebok, 10K, 1991.

Internal Organization

The years 1987 to 1990 were a period of "transformation from a marketing phenomenon into a professional organization".[3] Reebok installed systems, structures, and tools needed to manage a large organization professionally. This organization-building was essentially completed by the end of 1990. It was also a period of recovery of strong management and revitalization of the organization. The current chairman and founder of the company, Paul Fireman, returned to take charge of the company in 1989. Emphasis was placed on challenge and creativity, which is now the prevailing philosophy of the entire organization.

Reebok has a decentralized organization divided by brand and type of products (Exhibit 3). Reebok, Rockport, Avia, Apparel products, and Boston Whaler are the divisions that are operated autonomously. Reebok Division, which accounts for 80 percent of Reebok's total business,[3] is divided further into two profit centers, U.S. and international operations, while its product marketing function is organized globally into few product groups: Sports, Fitness, and Casual.

Sales*

The sales of the entire company have been growing rapidly and steadily since the company was started. The compound annual growth between 1986 and 1991 is 24.4 percent. However, the cause of this growth has changed over time. The period until 1988 can be described as the athletic boom and growth of the entire industry in the United States. Reebok's focus on fitness and fashion was well accepted by customers, and its U.S. sales expanded. Acquisition of businesses such as Avia and Rockport also contributed to the sales growth (Exhibit 4).

---

*Note: Numbers in this section are from Reebok annual reports unless otherwise noted.

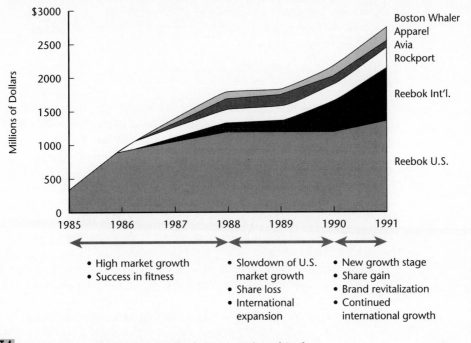

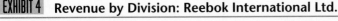

Growth between 1988 and 1990 was supported by international expansion and diversification into casual shoes under the Rockport brand. The growth of the international division during these two years was more than 60 percent annually (40 percent after adjustment for the accounting effect due to acquisition of distributors). The U.S. market growth began to slow down, and Reebok also lost its share to Nike because of its unfocused message to customers. The sales of Reebok's U.S. division stayed flat during this period.

The year 1991 was the start of new growth for Reebok. Its total revenue increased by 26.6 percent through positive growth across all divisions. The significant difference is the high growth of Reebok's U.S. division, which grew 14 percent under the market of only 4 percent growth. Reebok recovered its share by 2 points to 25 percent (including Avia) and narrowed the gap from Nike to 4 points.[4] Where did this growth come from? The success of high-performance, upmarket products seems to have played a significant role here. The Pump increased its sales from 3 million to 5 million pairs,[3] increasing its contribution to revenue from $150 million to $250 million. The Blacktop basketball shoes, which were introduced in 1991, sold 2.2 million pairs, earning $100 million.[12] The increase of $200 million from these products alone exceeds the increase of total U.S. sales of $163 million, although it is highly possible that these cannibalized some of the other Reebok sales. The more significant effect of the successful performance products is that it also revitalized the entire Reebok brand including its relatively low-priced and very profitable Classic lines.[10] There were also some emerging segments such as walking and outdoor shoes. The international division continued its strong performance, growing at 75 percent (40 percent after adjustment for accounting effect).

Profitability*

It was an issue for Reebok until 1990 that its profits had shown very slow growth since 1987 (2.3 percent CAGR) while sales were growing 16 percent annually. Selling expenses rose from 11.9 percent of sales in 1987 to 16.4 percent in 1990, and general and administration expenses rose from 7.4 percent to 9.4 percent. The return on sales of Reebok in 1990 was 8.2 percent and was below Nike's 9.6 percent.[13]

In 1991, however, Reebok saw a remarkable increase in profit, 32.9 percent. The selling, general, and administration cost in terms of percentage of sales decreased from 25.8 percent to 24.4 percent, and return on sales increased to 8.6 percent although it is still 1 percent lower than Nike's. This is attributed to Reebok's successful cost reduction plan focusing on SG&A expenses.

Another of Reebok's strengths is its strong cash flow since the 1980s. Reebok has kept its debt ratio low and used generated cash for the acquisition of brands and its international distribution channel. This excess cash can be used for R&D or marketing spending in the future as well as for buying back common stocks.

3. Marketing Strategy

Traditionally Reebok has focused on comfort and fashion for its shoes. After achieving a worldwide leadership position in fitness shoes, it has committed itself to expanding its sports focus, aiming at the number one position in all major sports categories.[3] To achieve this goal, it has introduced high-technology, performance-oriented products based on its core technology, the Pump, which features inflatable chambers that are adjustable and help provide custom fit and support in footwear. Reebok has extended this original concept for basketball shoes to tennis, aerobics, cross-training, running, golf, and walking shoes.

Another development, which involves a concept rather than a technology, is "Blacktop," a basketball shoe designed for outdoor city play with a tough sole and heavy leather uppers. The concept was unique, and the product satisfied fashion-oriented consumers as well as performance seekers. The product has been so successful that it sold out of many stores in 1991.[12] But, as with the Pump, it is uncertain how long consumers' enthusiasm will continue.

The Pump technology is currently heading in two directions. One is further refinements of the Pump, Insta-Pump, and Pump Custom Cushion, which were introduced at the 1992 Summer Olympics.[14] A tennis shoe using Insta-Pump technology was introduced at the 1992 U.S. Open.[6] Insta-Pump technology employs three separate bladders in the shoe—tongue, central, and rearfoot—and these bladders are

---

*Note: Numbers in this section are from Reebok annual reports unless otherwise noted.

inflated with a handheld carbon dioxide cartridge, the Insta-Pump Activator, a trigger-activated holder that can hold any type of CO_2.[6] One of the running shoes with Custom Cushioning, the Dual Chamber, has tiny electric pressure gauges with digital readouts.[4] Reebok plans to retail a tennis shoe using Insta-Pump technology beginning in April 1993 and extend it to other categories later on. The retail price is planned at about $140, the highest end for athletic footwear. These products target serious athletes.

The other direction is cheaper shoe models using the Pump technology to increase market penetration. Reebok believes both directions are important to extend life of this technology. The growth of the Pump line has already slowed down as is shown by the emergence of product discounting and increased inventory at retail stores.[5]

Although the Pump played an important role in revitalizing the Reebok brand from its share decline due to the misfocus of its advertising programs, it is uncertain whether further emphasis on technology will be accepted positively by general consumers because the new technology is useful only to limited users and the price is too high. Most customers may feel these technologies are unnecessary gimmicks. It should be noted that the competitors are heading toward simpler, more basic shoes.[4] Even Nike is promoting mid-price performance shoes. Nike says that Reebok has failed to realize that the market of the expensive sneaker is temporarily stagnant.[14]

Reebok's dual focus on fashion and performance is another issue. Reebok continues to address these two different themes under the same brand name. In the past this dual focus confused customers as to what the Reebok brand stood for. L.A. Gear's failure to address these two themes for the same brand indicates the risk of this strategy. Although it is possible that the performance focus enforces the fashion image as the Pump did for the Classic line, the benefits and costs of having two different themes under the same brand name should be examined. Further advancement in technology may confuse the original customers who seek comfort and fashion from shoes. Differentiation from the strategy of Nike, which has consistently focused on performance, should also be explored.

As the growth of the entire athletic footwear industry has slowed down, it is becoming more important to identify the growing market segments within the industry. In 1991, Reebok introduced its first line of outdoor hiking and mountain biking shoes.[3] These line extensions will continue to be necessary to respond to changing consumer needs and take a preemptive move to fill the unmet needs with current products. Reebok's major target for the next few years is fitness walking where it sees high growth potential because this market is still immature. According to the National Sporting Goods Association, 77 million Americans engage in fitness walking. The market size of fitness walking shoes is estimated at $1.5 billion by 1992, a tremendous growth from $300 million five years ago. Reebok currently holds the number one position in this segment with 31 percent segment share, while Nike holds about 10 percent.[7]

In spring 1993, Reebok plans to launch its Bodywalk Collection together with a multimedia campaign and the Reebok Bodywalk Program, an educational program introducing a three-level system to maximize the walking workout by using more of the body's muscle groups. Reebok expects that this campaign will further enhance the enthusiasm for walking for fitness. Reebok's worldwide director of marketing for walking says, "We're injecting fun and excitement into the category and really defining it."[7] This promotional campaign is planned to include a $10 million marketing budget, a heavy point-of-purchase campaign at the retail level, and tie-ins with Warner Records and Evian Water. The tie-ins will include cross-promotion with Evian at retail outlets and sales of a workout instruction audiotape from Warner, featuring its latest artists.[7,15]

Another area where Reebok sees future potential is casual shoes—stylish shoes with comfort—which is different in terms of product but shares the same customers and use occasions with athletic shoes. It is expected that after the high growth of the athletic segment, the growth will shift to casual and dress shoes for the coming decade. To build its foothold in this segment, Reebok acquired the Rockport Company, Inc., in 1986, which was and still is the market leader in this segment. To capture this segment with the Reebok brand name, Reebok further developed a new subbrand, "Boks by Reebok," and formed a new autonomous marketing division in summer 1992. This line is similar to Rockport but has more athletic flavor. The collection ranges from street hikers to bucks with lug soles. The target segment for Boks is men and women 18–34 years old. The typical price range for the men's line is $60–$80.[8] Because Boks competes directly with Rockport and the distribution of casual shoes requires different channels from those for athletic shoes, it is uncertain whether spending the marketing money on promotion of Boks is the best arrangement to capture this market, especially when Reebok already has an established Rockport brand with an established channel. The same problem also exists with the walking category because Rockport is also number two in the walking segment with a 10 percent segment share.[7]

In terms of distribution, Reebok, as well as other branded athletic shoe marketers, focuses on specialty athletic retailers, sporting goods stores, and department stores, and avoids lower-margin mass merchandisers and discount outlets to maintain its prestigious image and high profit margins.[3] Reebok also works closely with retailers to reflect consumer feedback into its product development. It is uncertain whether this strategy can be sustainable when mass merchandisers become more and more powerful in the retail industry. They account for about 27 percent of the athletic shoe sales in pairs and this percentage is increasing.[16] Neglecting these markets may imply losing a large segment of customers who are value seekers. In the near future, Reebok will have to determine its strategy on this growing segment.

Notes

1. "Women's Footwear Sales Step Up" (1993), *Discount Store News,* January 4, 41.

2. "Can L.A. Gear's Gold Put It Back in the Race?" (1993), *Los Angeles Times,* February 15, 2 (original data from Sporting Goods Intelligence).

3. 1989, 1990, and 1991 annual reports and 10K reports of Reebok.

4. "Reebok, Pumping Up" (1992), *The Economist,* February 15.

5. Esquivel, J. (1991), "Reebok International Ltd.—Company Report," Shearson Lehman Brothers, Inc.

6. *Footwear News* (1992), August 31, 8.

7. "Deft Reebok Strides into Women's Walking" (1992), *Brandweek,* August 24, 4.

8. "Boks to Feature Casual Line with Performance Influence; Reebok International Ltd." (1992), *Footwear News,* February 3, 63.

9. "The Sneaker Game" (1990), *Forbes,* October 22, 114–115.

10. De Lucia, M. J., A. Tucker, and R. D. Day (1991), "Reebok International Ltd.—Company Report," October 28.

11. "Marketers Learn to 'Just Do It'" (1992), *Advertising Age,* January 27, S7-8.

12. "The 'Blacktop' Is Paving Reebok's Road to Recovery" (1991), *Business Week,* August 12, 27.

13. Industry Surveys, Standard & Poor's Compustat Service, Inc., November 28, 1991.

14. "What Recession? Reebok Introduces High-Priced Pumps for the 'Serious Athlete'" (1992), *Marketing News,* March 16, 3.

15. "Reebok, Evian and Warner Team to Put More Power in Walking" (1992), *Brandweek,* September 14, 73–76.

16. Data from Sporting Goods Manufacturers Association (SGMA).

The Compact Disc Market (A)

It was the summer of 1985 and Leah Springer, vice-president of strategic planning, faced the task of putting together a five-year strategic plan for the Records Division of RCA. RCA is a diversified company with business in several areas including entertainment and consumer electronics. The Records Division was one of several major operations within RCA. With a market share of over 15 percent, RCA is one of the major labels in the recording industry. Currently it is involved in the manufacturing of LP records and cassette tapes, as well as the selling of prerecorded music. She and Don Press, manager of strategic planning, were concerned about the future of the recording industry, especially in light of the fact that a new technology had recently been introduced to consumers. The compact disc format has taken off and practically caught the audio industry by surprise. Of immediate importance to her were reliable forecasts of compact disc sales for the next five years. Forecasts were available from various industry sources, but each source reported widely different numbers, and industry analysts were constantly revising their forecasts as new sales data became available.

Springer and Press believed that a more in-depth analysis of this market was warranted. They knew that the managerial climate at RCA would require a detailed set of analysis and marketing research to back up any recommendations they might make.

The Corporate Operations Research Group of RCA was asked for assistance in developing compact disc sales forecasts. This group acted as internal consultants to the various divisions within RCA. Peter Fowler, manager of operations research, and Terry Bailey, a senior analyst, met with Springer and Press in August to decide on an appropriate approach. Expedient completion of this forecasting project was also critical, as the deadline for the final presentation of recommendations to upper management was quickly approaching.

The Compact Disc Marketing Environment

After several years of research by many major companies in the consumer electronics industry, the compact disc (CD) player was publicly introduced in the United States during March 1983. The CD player was widely available in retail outlets by September of that year. A CD player is a special electronic component using laser technology that can be connected to stereo equipment. This hardware allows prerecorded music to be played through the stereo system. The CD software is a 4.7-inch round piece of plastic with an aluminum coating. Excitement has been generated over

This case was prepared by Professor Barry L. Bayus (Kenan-Flagler Business School, University of North Carolina at Chapel Hill) as a basis for discussion, and is not meant to illustrate either effective or ineffective handling of an administrative situation (March 1997).

this product because the sound quality is reputed to be as good, and in many cases, better than the sound quality of LP records and cassette tapes. In addition, the business market for CD technology looks appealing. Uses of this technology in the computer information industry have only scratched the surface.[1]

Early speculation by industry analysts was that compact disc technology would revive the faltering home-audio business. Tables 1 and 2 show the declining trend in sales of stereo equipment and software. While actual sales figures vary depending on the source, around 35,000 players and 1 million discs were sold in the United States during 1983. Spurred by price reductions (on players, from a suggested retail price of $1000 to around $400 and on software, from a suggested retail price of $22 to around $14), these figures were around 250,000 players and 4 million discs in 1984. In 1983 around 500 different titles were available; in 1984 this number was around 800, and by 1985 there were over 2500 titles available (compared with about 50,000 LP offerings).

Manufacturers have lauded the CD player as the hottest product in the consumer electronics industry, surpassing the early consumer and retailer acceptance observed for other recent products such as cassette tapes, videocassette recorders, and video laser discs. Many industry executives expect this format to eventually replace the current 33-rpm record technology.

Despite the apparently booming market for CDs, the U.S. recording industry has been proceeding cautiously in trying to solve production and distribution problems. The overwhelming majority of blank discs are manufactured overseas. The foreign high-tech factories can turn out a compact disc for $3 (compared to a record for 80 cents). Optimists think higher yields and improved production techniques could cut $1 from the manufacturing cost of $3 over the next few years. With a new disc manufacturing plant costing $20 million to $25 million, the major U.S. recording industry players have been wary about investing heavily in domestic product capacity. As a result, some disc supply problems existed for the major recording companies.

The Operation Research Group's Model

In order to forecast annual sales of CD players and software, a two-step approach was used by the OR group. First, player sales forecasts were developed using a well-known mathematical model of sales growth that has performed well for several other durable products (color TVs, dishwashers, washing machines, etc.). The general structure of this type of diffusion model is pictured in Fig. 1 on page 468. Of the total market available, some smaller proportion can be considered the potential market. (For example, of all households that may be considered the market, only those households that are aware of the product can be considered potential buyers.) From this potential market, some number will eventually buy the product. Buyers are then assumed to positively influence the potential market through word of mouth (the "diffusion" process). Thus, the magnitude and speed of sales growth is dependent on the sizes of these populations, the flow between these groups, and the impact of the populations on each other.

TABLE Consumer Audio/Hi-Fi Hardware Market Unit Shipments/Retail Value

	1984		1983		1982		1981		1980	
	Units	Retail $	Units	Retail $	Units	Retail $	Units	Retail $	Units	Retail $
Total (millions)	*101.6*	*$6359.6*	*102.4*	*$6471.0*	*98.4*	*$6356.2*	*93.7*	*$6589.0*	*87.4*	*$6682.1*
Portable tape equipment	27.5	1335.6	28.9	1441.2	28.1	1474.1	28.1	1587.5	23.4	1447.2
Radios	27.4	822.7	28.2	863.3	26.5	819.1	27.9	863.5	27.0	867.7
Auto players/speakers/radios*	21.8	1953.3	21.2	1850.9	20.7	1772.9	19.8	1655.6	18.4	1486.8
Component Audio	*8.4*	*$1509.8*	*8.6*	*$1518.1*	*8.2*	*$1474.7*	*8.4*	*$1561.2*	*8.9*	*$1704.2*
Speakers	3.3	464.9	3.2	452.1	3.0	418.2	3.2	453.8	3.7	623.6
Turntables	1.7	213.0	2.1	280.3	2.2	314.2	2.3	321.8	2.3	310.7
Tape decks	0.9	161.3	0.9	172.2	0.8	175.3	0.8	173.4	0.7	178.0
Receivers/tuners/other	2.3	567.0	2.4	580.2	2.2	567.0	2.1	612.2	2.2	591.9
Compact disc players	0.2	103.6	0.045	33.3	—	—	—	—	—	—
Personal portable stereos/radios	7.2	NA	6.3	NA	5.7	NA	NA	NA	NA	NA
Accessories (cart./headphones)	6.7	247.6	6.6	247.7	6.2	231.6	5.9	228.4	5.8	292.5
Compact radio/player comb.	2.6	490.6	2.7	549.8	3.0	583.8	3.6	692.8	3.9	883.7

*Excludes OEM.

Note: May not add to totals due to rounding. Total retail $ volume does not include personal portable stereos/radios.

Source: 63rd Annual Statistical and Marketing Report, *Merchandising*, March 1985. Based on EIA data.

TABLE 2 Consumer Prerecorded Audio Software Market Unit Shipments/Retail Dollar Volume

	1984		1983		1982		1981		1980	
	Units	Retail $	Units	Retail $	Units	Retail $	Units	Retail $	Units	Retail $
Total (millions)	679.8	$4,370.4	578.0	$3,814.3	577.7	$3,641.6	635.4	$3,969.9	683.7	$3,862.4
Records	336.1	$1,847.5	334.4	$1,958.3	381.1	$2,208.1	449.9	$2,598.1	487.1	$2,559.6
Long/ext. play	204.6	1,548.8	209.6	1,689.0	243.9	1,925.1	295.2	2,341.7	322.8	2,290.3
Singles	131.5	298.7	124.8	269.3	137.2	283.0	154.7	256.4	164.3	269.3
Cassettes	332.0	2,383.9	236.8	1,810.9	182.3	1,384.5	137.0	1,062.8	110.2	776.4
8-Tracks	5.9	35.7	6.0	27.9	14.3	49.0	48.5	309.0	86.4	526.4
Compact discs	5.8	103.3	0.8	17.2	—	—	—	—	—	—

Note: Net unit shipments by manufacturers after returns. Retail dollar volume based on suggested list price.

Source: Recording Industry Association of America (RIAA) press release, April 1, 1985.

FIGURE 1   The Diffusion Model Structure

Software sales forecasts were then calculated as a function of the hardware values. In this way, total accessory sales are the sum of current and future software purchase streams of player owners. Details of this model are in the appendix.

The sales curve of first-time buyers of CD players is expected to follow the general pattern shown in Fig. 2, with sales declining as the market reaches saturation. This model is a function of three parameters: (1) the initial sales level, which "starts" the process; (2) the product growth rate, which impacts the timing of peak sales; and (3) the market potential, which affects the magnitude of peak sales. Cumulative sales exhibit the familiar, symmetric *S*-shape.

Parameter Estimates

For the model discussed in the appendix, the following information is required:

- the initial hardware sales level
- the growth rate parameter for hardware sales
- product awareness over time
- hardware purchase intentions over time
- software purchase rates over time.

As reported by the Electronics Industry Association, 1983 sales of CD players were 35,000 units. However, since the retail availability of players was not widespread until September, it was felt that this value actually represented only between three and four months of sales. Assuming proportional sales over the year, hardware sales for the first year were estimated at 140,000.

With regard to the growth rate parameter, values for related electronic home entertainment products can be used as a benchmark. These values have been calculated by fitting the basic diffusion model to historical sales data for numerous products. In this way, growth rate values have been estimated for LP record players (0.43), reel tape recorders (0.5), color TVs (0.59), and video games (1.0). A value of

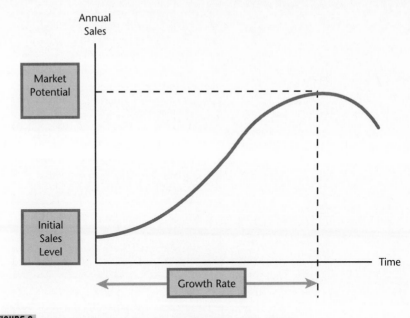

FIGURE 2 The Typical Sales Curve for New Products

0.6 for CD hardware was found to provide results consistent with initial sales estimates and with what industry analysts believed was happening in the market.

An estimate for market potential was obtained as diagrammed in Fig. 3. Of the total number of U.S. households (around 86 million in 1985), it was felt that component stereo households (households that own separate stereo components such as a turntable, receiver, tape deck, etc.) were more representative of the potential market for initial sales since these people could easily connect the CD player to their existing stereo system. From these households (around 32 percent of all households), only individuals who are aware of CDs and have purchase intentions are considered to be potential buyers. Households were also assumed to grow at a rate of 1 million new households per year.

Furthermore, a study conducted in spring 1985 and sponsored by *Newsweek*[2] revealed that four market segments exist among the stereo component households:

1. *Equipment oriented:* upscale individuals, knowledgeable about stereo equipment, heavy music listeners, about 24 percent of the market.
2. *Socially oriented:* status-oriented people, listen to music only in social situations, about 25 percent of the market.
3. *Appliance oriented:* treat stereo system as another household necessity, frequent music listeners, about 22 percent of the market.
4. *Music oriented:* more concerned with music quality than the stereo system, infrequent music listeners, about 29 percent of the market.

A brief demographic profile of the four segments is shown in Table 3.

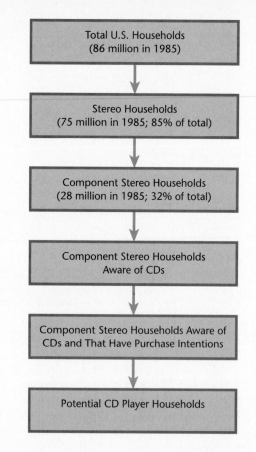

FIGURE 3   **A Model of the Potential Market for CD Players**

These segments allowed additional detail to be incorporated into the sales fore-casts, since different hardware and software purchasing behaviors can be consid-ered. The fact that these segments have different music buying behaviors is supported by the range in record and tape ownership, as shown in Table 4.

Based on 1985 values from the *Newsweek* study and discussions with industry analysts, awareness curves for each segment were judgmentally developed. In this way, the equipment oriented start with an awareness level of 60 percent, the socially oriented start at 35 percent, the appliance oriented start at 40 percent, and the music oriented start at 30 percent. By 1989, the entire potential market is assumed to be aware of CD technology.

CD player purchase intentions were developed by considering the impact of prices. As part of the *Newsweek* study, respondents were asked their purchase intentions of players at three different price levels. The relationship between intentions and prices was then statistically analyzed using the form INTENT = $a \exp(b$ PRICE$)$ + error. As expected, the coefficient b was negative for all segments. Although rigorous statistical

TABLE 3 **Demographic Characteristics of CD Market Segments**

	Total Sample	Equipment Oriented	Socially Oriented	Appliance Oriented	Music Oriented
Male (%)	59	79	58	49	50
Some college or more (%)	54	68	42	45	58
Professional/manager (%)	42	48	39	43	36
Median income ($000)	$30.3	$37.6	$28.6	$29.3	$29.8
Median age (years)	38	31	39	39	43
(Base)	(1045)	(255)	(259)	(230)	(301)

Source: *Newsweek*, "The Compact Disc Market," A Newsweek study conducted by ASK Associates, New York, NY, 1985.

TABLE 4 **Number of Records and Cassette Tapes Owned by Market Segment**

	Total Sample	Equipment Oriented	Socially Oriented	Appliance Oriented	Music Oriented
<50	24%	11%	31%	21%	32%
50–99	29%	22%	28%	38%	28%
100–299	31%	38%	27%	30%	29%
300–499	8%	13%	6%	8%	6%
≥ 500	8%	16%	8%	3%	4%
Median number	94	190	84	88	80

Source: *Newsweek*, "The Compact Disc Market," A Newsweek study conducted by ASK Associates, New York, NY, 1985.

conclusions could not be made because of the small number of data points, this exercise did produce useful purchase intention curves that were felt to be appropriate for this market. The average retail price of CD players was estimated to be $325 in 1985 and assumed to level off to $250 in 1988. Using these values, appropriate intention curves were developed.

Software purchase rates for each segment are presented in Table 5. Lacking explicit marketing research data relating software purchases and promotion efforts (e.g., prices), these rates were developed based on current record and tape ownership (Table 4) and estimated average annual purchase rates of records and tapes by these segments. Initial purchases of software were assumed to be higher than average due to product novelty and the desire to replace existing record and tape libraries. New equipment-oriented consumers were assumed to buy relatively less in later years due to an increase of teenagers (and thus less buying power) in the mix. Other segments were assumed to buy relatively more as software prices decrease.

TABLE 5   **CD Software Purchase Rates by Market Segment (managerial estimates)**

		Equipment Oriented	Socially Oriented	Appliance Oriented	Music Oriented
Time After Purchase of CD Player	1st year	35	25	25	11
	2nd year	19	8	9	7
	≥3rd year	11	8	7	7

1984 price = $14 per disc

		Equipment Oriented	Socially Oriented	Appliance Oriented	Music Oriented
Time After Purchase of CD Player	1st year	31	27	30	14
	2nd year	18	9	10	8
	≥3rd year	10	9	8	8

1989 price = $10.30 per disc

		Equipment Oriented	Socially Oriented	Appliance Oriented	Music Oriented
Time After Purchase of CD Player	1st year	29	28	30	16
	2nd year	17	9	11	9
	≥3rd year	10	9	8	9

1993 price = $8.40 per disc

Forecasting Results

Figs. 4 and 5 show the results obtained by the OR analysts for hardware and software sales forecasts to 1993. First-time-buyer sales of CD players rise to 2.74 million units by 1993. Software sales follow a general S-shaped growth curve, generally leveling off around 1993 at an annual sales rate of 210 million units.

From Figs. 4 and 5 projected sales for 1984 are around 192,000 hardware units and 5.7 million software units. Although not a rigorous test of validity, Fowler and Bailey were encouraged by the model and its results since these forecasts were within the ranges of reported actual sales during 1984. Furthermore, the projected penetration level of CDs into U.S. households by 1993 compared favorably with the penetration of videocassette recorders after 10 years (25 percent for CDs vs. 30 percent for VCRs).

Soon after the forecasting results were obtained, Peter Fowler and Terry Bailey held a meeting in mid-September with Leah Springer and Don Press. Although impressed with the modeling effort, Springer was concerned about the reliability of the forecasts. She was well aware of previous forecasting errors for other entertainment products, which had cost RCA several million dollars. She questioned the accu-

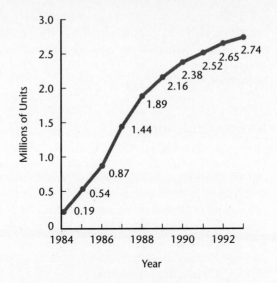

FIGURE 4   **Annual First-Time-Buyer Sales for CD Players**

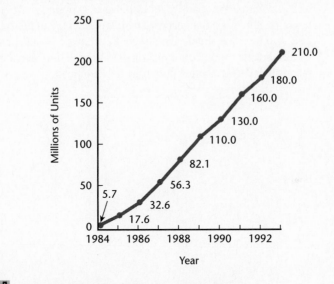

FIGURE 5   **Annual Industry Sales for CD Software**

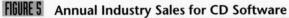

racy of the model, especially since only one data point was available to test the forecasting performance.

Press and Springer also added more uncertainty to the problem by mentioning the anticipated introduction of a new, competing technology. Industry reports indicated that a new format, digital audiotape (DAT), was expected to be marketed in late 1986. Basically, DAT looks and acts like a strangely shaped cassette. Sound quality should be comparable to CDs, with the added attraction of recording capability. Press wondered if the model framework already developed could be used to generate some insight into the possible impact of DAT on the CD forecasts initially obtained.

Recommendations

Before the strategic plan was finalized in late October, the OR analysts developed along with Spring and Press several different scenarios involving various assumptions for player price trends, awareness curves, and DAT acceptance levels. These analyses confirmed the general optimism found from the base case forecasts. Based on these forecasts, CDs were expected to account for close to 50 percent of the total prerecorded audio industry by 1993. Furthermore, sensitivity analyses revealed that player purchase intentions and the software purchase rates were the most critical variables in terms of CD industry sales levels.

Leah Springer knew that any recommendations would be carefully considered by her management. Based on her available information and research, she could recommend that RCA (1) commit to enter into the manufacture of compact discs; (2) continue to source the blank CDs from other suppliers; or (3) conduct further market research. She was still concerned over the accuracy of the sales forecasts and the specific numbers she should include in the strategic plan. The final decision, however, would include input from functional areas including finance, marketing, and manufacturing, as well as other corporate decision makers.

APPENDIX
A Model for New Product Software Sales

Sales of accessory products are clearly tied to hardware sales. How many and how often accessories are purchased by hardware owners is, of course, a function of product availability as well as marketing activities such as prices, advertising, and promotion. In addition, consumer characteristics will play an important role in determining the total market potential. Market segments with different buying behaviors are thus expected to exist.

A straightforward method for calculating software sales is the following:

$$ASALES(t) = \sum_{j=1}^{J} \sum_{i=1}^{t} H_j(i) \times S_j(t - i + 1) \tag{1}$$

where

$ASALES(t)$ = accessory sales (software) at time t

$H_j(k)$ = hardware sales to segment j at time k (measured as hardware unit sales)

$S_j(k)$ = segment j's software purchase rate k time periods after the hardware was purchased (measured as software unit sales per unit time per hardware unit sales)

J = number of market segments.

The key data element in the above equation is software purchase rates. These rates are dynamic functions of marketing efforts and segment characteristics. Total accessory sales are thus the sum of current and future software purchase streams of hardware owners.

For purposes of forecasting software sales, first-time buyers of hardware are the consumers of interest. Replacement sales and multiple-unit ownership of hardware are assumed to not in themselves generate significant additional software sales.

To obtain hardware sales, a model described by Lawrence and Lawton[3] can be used. This model contains only a few parameters and has given excellent fits to historical data for first purchases of several consumer and industrial products. The model formulation is as follows:

$$HCUM(t) = \{[M + N_0] \, / \, [1 + (M/N_0) \exp(-rt)]\} - N_0 \tag{2}$$

where

$HCUM(t)$ = cumulative hardware sales up to time t

N_0 = "effective" number of prior users (not part of M)

M = potential market size

r = growth rate parameter.

Sales at any point in time can of course be calculated as the difference between $HCUM(t)$ and $HCUM(t-1)$. As noted by Lawrence and Lawton, this equation can generate other well-known diffusion models by approximately transforming the parameter values.

It can also be shown that N_0, the number of effective users created at time 0 through advertising (and possibly distribution of free samples), can be found by using (2) with $t=1$ and solving for N_0. In this way,

$$N_0 = M \times HCUM(1) \exp(-r) / [M(1 - \exp(-r)) - HCUM(1)] \qquad (3)$$

where

$HCUM(1)$ = hardware sales in the first time period.

This particular formulation has a number of advantages. One important property of this function is that the growth process can be "interrupted" at any point during the planning horizon. Thus we can, for example, stop the process in the third year of calculations, change a parameter value, and consider the calculations for the remainder of the planning horizon with the new values. These equations can also be easily implemented using any of several computer packages, including microcomputer spreadsheets.

We can extend the general formulation of Lawrence and Lawton by modeling the potential market size as an implicit function of segment characteristics, marketing efforts, and prices:

$$M(t) = \sum_{j=1}^{J} HH(t) \times SEG_j(t) \times AWARE_j(t) \times INTENT_j(t) \qquad (4)$$

where

$M(t)$ = potential market size at time t

$HH(t)$ = total number of households at time t
$\quad = f$ (economic conditions, housing starts, etc.)

$SEG_j(t)$ = proportion of market that is segment j at time t

$AWARE_j(t)$ = proportion of segment j that is aware of the product at time t
$\quad = f$ (marketing efforts, availability, word-of-mouth, etc.)

$INTENT_j(t)$ = proportion of segment j that is aware of the product and has
$\qquad$ positive purchase intentions at time t
$\quad = f$ (marketing efforts, promotions, prices, word-of-mouth, etc.).

The number of total households is used as a starting base. Of the total households, some proportion will be aware of the product. Of the people that are aware of the product, some will have positive purchase intentions. It is these individuals who are aware of the product and have purchase intentions that can be considered potential buyers. Data on consumer awareness and purchase intentions can be collected over time through market research. With appropriate data, statistical relationships between marketing mix variables, awareness, and intentions can also be developed.

The various market segments are also allowed to interact, since total hardware sales is calculated on the basis of one aggregate market potential value, $M(t)$. Sales to each segment can then be found by spreading the calculated value of total sales according to relative segment size.

New product accessory sales over time can thus be calculated as a dynamic function of several variables. With appropriate data, effects due to different segment characteristics, general economic conditions, marketing and promotion efforts, and pricing can be considered in estimating sales. In practice, these calculations can be done at discrete time intervals using equations (1) through (4).[4]

Notes

1. For a discussion, see Dumaine, B. (1985), "The Compact Disk's Drive to Become King of Audio," *Fortune,* July 8, 104–107.

2. Described in Shapiro, A., and J. Schwartz (1986), "Research Must be as Sophisticated as the Products it Studies," *Marketing News,* January 3, 2.

3. Lawrence, K. D., and W. H. Lawton (1981), "Applications of Diffusion Models: Some Empirical Results," in Y. Wind, V. Mahajan, and R. N. Cardozo, eds., *New-Product Forecasting,* Lexington, MA: Lexington Books, 529–541.

4. See also Bayus, B. (1987), "Forecasting Sales of New Contingent Products: An Application to the Compact Disc Market," *Journal of Product Innovation Management,* (December): 243–255.

The Compact Disc Market (B)

In the spring of 1989, Leah Springer asked Peter Fowler and Terry Bailey to reevaluate the compact disc market. Several years had passed since they had made the forecasts that had contributed to the formulation of RCA's five-year strategic plan for entering the CD market. Springer wanted a full report from them on (1) what had happened since 1985, and (2) what could happen in the future.

Fowler and Bailey were able to put together some reliable numbers for both compact disc software sales (Table 1) and compact disc player sales (Table 2) from industry sources. These figures could be compared with the projections they had made four years earlier.

What they found did not really surprise Springer. While the specific projections they had made deviated from actual figures, the overall shape of the actual sales curves, for both software and players, were well preserved. Furthermore, other data that Fowler and Bailey had collected on the CD market reaffirmed her belief in the efficacy of pursuing compact discs:

- As of early 1989, CD penetration of the U.S. market was estimated at 12 percent to 15 percent, well on its way to the 25 percent that had been predicted by 1993.

- Consumer research indicated that "early adopters" of the CD format bought an average of 26 CDs per year, and "average" CD owners bought 16 discs the first year and from 9 to 10 in successive years, suggesting that the purchase rates originally developed for the four consumer segments were generally accurate.

- All of RCA's competitors had entered the market and were producing CDs, to the point where yearly industry capacity was outstripping demand by 60 to 70 percent.

Springer was not bothered that Fowler and Bailey's projections had underestimated total sales. Since 1985, several unanticipated factors had influenced the acceptance of CDs, spurring CD sales beyond the earlier predictions.

Consumer Acceptance   The high level of consumer demand clearly had exceeded expectations. With CD player prices falling below $200 and regular disc prices declining into the $10.99–$11.99 range by 1989, increasing numbers of consumers were finding it feasible and desirable to step up to CDs. Moreover, sales had not yet peaked; led by CBS, the industry was continually lowering profit margins, reducing wholesale prices to $7.50 or below for "discounted" material, and thereby giving consumers even more reason to switch.

_____

This case was prepared by Steve Fontana, under the supervision of Professor Barry L. Bayus, as a basis for class discussion, and is not meant to illustrate either effective or ineffective handling of an administrative situation (March 1997).

TABLE 1   Compact Disc Sales, 1983–1988

	1983	1984	1985	1986	1987	1988
Actual sales, units (millions)*	0.8	5.8	22.6	53.0	102.1	149.7
Actual $ value (millions)*	$17.20	$103.30	$389.50	$930.10	$1593.60	$2089.90
Projected sales, units (millions)†	—	5.7	17.6	32.6	56.3	82.1

*Figures are taken from *Marketing & Media Decisions*, September 1987, 52, and *Billboard*, March 18, 1989, 82.
†See "The Compact Disc Market, Part A."

TABLE 2   Compact Disc Player Sales, 1983–1988

	1983	1984	1985	1986	1987	1988
Actual sales, units (millions)*	0.035	0.208	0.97	1.69	2.49	2.86
Projected sales, units (millions)†	—	0.19	0.54	0.87	1.44	1.89

*Figures are taken from *Appliance's* annual statistical reviews. Portable units are not included.
†See "The Compact Disc Market, Part A."

This rise in demand primarily came at the expense of albums, whose sales dropped over 50 percent during the period. This shift away from LPs was exacerbated by the record companies who, while denying they were hastening the LP's demise, nevertheless created severe disincentives for stores to order LPs. "Retailers who return unsold records to manufacturers, for example, now must pay as much as 15 percent of the wholesale cost of the record as a penalty."[1] Even though many companies, most notably CBS, maintained that they were still committed to LPs, the decrease in stores willing to carry LPs suggested to industry analysts that they would be as extinct as the 78-rpm record and 8-track cassette by 1992.

New Formats   The CD explosion had prompted exploration of the technology's applicability to other situations. In 1987, record companies introduced CD-3, a smaller version of the CD, intended as a replacement for the 7-inch single album. With room for up to 20 minutes of music, these "CD-singles" also were being packaged as classical, jazz, and New Age samplers by small, independent companies. CD-3 sales, while a modest 1.6 million units in 1988, were expected to grow, perhaps to as much as 45 million by 1992.

Following on CD-3's heels in development were CD-V, for "CD-video," thought to be competition for VCRs in movies, and CD-I, for "CD-interactive," for use in archival systems and learning environments.

Threats

Despite this data, Springer realized that she had reason to be concerned for CDs' future. Two new developments had the potential to impact the CD's popularity.

DAT   In 1985, DAT (digital audiotape) had appeared to be an imminent threat to the CD format, but by 1989 it had yet to materialize; it had not even been introduced in the United States. Was it still a danger? What had happened?

DAT was developed by the Japanese in the early 1980s as an outgrowth of video technology. It is a very different form of consumer music product:

> Digital audio tape machines work more like VCRs than standard tape recorders. In a conventional analog deck, sound waves are recorded onto magnetic tape. . . . By contrast . . . when a DAT cassette is loaded into the recorder, the tape surface engages a drum that contains one or more heads. As the drum spins, the rotating heads cram onto the tape billions of tiny digitized bits of information. . . . Analog sound waves are not picked up, so tape hiss is absent in playback, and even if the tape becomes worn the computer reading the data can interpolate any missing bits of sound.[2]

DAT thus represents a breakthrough in consumer recording that also is incompatible with conventional consumer technology.

DAT became immediately available in Europe and Japan, and soon was a reasonable success there. Yet, by 1989, it still had not appeared in any meaningful way in the United States. Why? Possible reasons include the following:

1. *Informal disapproval of DAT by Philips, the Dutch conglomerate that coinvented the CD with Sony.* Rumor has it that Philips discouraged DAT's introduction into the United States in order to extend the growth and development of the CD hardware and software markets. Since Philips has incredible political clout in Europe, a market larger than the United States, Japanese manufacturers have acceded to Philips' preference to avoid potential damage to their efforts there.
2. *Record industry opposition, in the form of threatened lawsuits.* U.S. record companies are afraid not only that competitive pressure from prerecorded DAT could force down the price of CDs, thereby cutting their profit margins, but blank DAT tape could also encourage people to tape CDs, rather than purchase them, thus pirating their market. Despite some evidence that the introduction of new music formats actually increases consumption of the established product, the record companies do not want to take any chances: their stance effectively has prevented DAT machines, except high-priced, play-only units for cars, from entering the United States.
3. *U.S. record company "delaying tactics."* Early on, and separate from their lawsuit activities, record companies sought legislative help from the government that would effectively prevent DAT's entrance. At first, they asked for a "royalty" on the sale of each DAT blank tape. When Congress declared this unfair, the record industry then supported a proposal by CBS to put a "copy-code" computer chip into all DAT units. This chip was intended to be able to detect a certain frequency in prerecorded music that would defeat the "record" function. This system proved unworkable, and it was discarded. Currently, the record companies are pushing the development of Unicopy, an undisclosed Philips technology that would allow only one copy of a prerecorded source to be made.
4. *The high initial cost of DAT hardware.* In contrast to CD players, DAT mechanisms are more complex, mandating much higher base prices for DAT hardware units (from $1000 to $3000) than originally was charged for CD players. This sit-

uation, combined with the unfavorable exchange rate between Japan and the United States, may erect functional entry barriers high enough to disinterest Japanese manufacturers in entering the U.S. market.

What may be the most likely reason, however, was put forward in the March 1989 issue of *Stereo Review:* "Perhaps DAT will serve as a trial balloon, testing the technical and legal aspects of digital recording in the American market, testing the waters for the real recording medium of the future, [CD-R]."

CD-R   CD-R ("recordable-CD") may well be the "technology of the future" that makes DAT obsolete. While not likely to be available in the United States before 1991, its arrival appears inevitable.

The development of CD-R started in the mid-1980s by the Tandy Corporation in the United States, by France's Thomson in Europe, and by Sanyo (among others) in Japan. These companies asked the following "simple" theoretical question: Was there a way to create erasable digital information on a standard compact disc that could be read by a CD player laser? The answer was yes, and two methods are in development:

1. that of Thomson and Sanyo, which utilizes a disc with a magnetic layer, sandwiched between two plastic layers, that can be patterned magnetically with digital "pits" by the recording laser; and
2. that of Tandy, which utilizes a disc with a pair of special dye-polymer layers between the outer plastic layers, to create physically readable "pits" in response to heat generated by the recording laser.

CD-R has several advantages over DAT. By being recordable on both sides, it can conceivably hold as much as 2 1/2 hours of music. Since CD-R is a "programmable" medium, it can allow faster access to music on it, and can allow programmable or random listening sequencing (as opposed to DAT, which would have to be rewound and forwarded constantly). By being "read" by a laser, instead of by physical contact, CD-R could be more durable than DAT. Since it is cheaper to produce, recordable CDs also could be less expensive than blank DAT.

CD-R is seen as inevitable because, rather than being a new, expensive product, it will be a less expensive ($500 to $1000 per unit initially) extension of an established and accepted product. Moreover, it is being developed by increasing numbers of electronics manufacturers. (Sony, Matsushita, Donon, and Philips reportedly are working on CD-R systems now.) While the record companies still plan to sue makers that introduce digital recording products that do not provide them with compensation for potential piracy, the sale of CBS to Sony in 1988 indicates to analysts that some compromise or accommodation will be reached. Most people predict that CD-R units will debut in the United States between 1991 and 1993.

Leah Springer was not sure what would happen in the next several years, and had several questions for Fowler and Bailey:

1. Was the sales forecasting model used earlier reliable? Can the judgmental inputs for this model be appropriately modified to generate the observed sales figures?

2. Would DAT and/or CD-R enter the United States? How would they affect CD player sales?
3. What would happen to compact disc sales as a result?
4. Were there any factors she was failing to consider?

Notes

1. *Washington Post,* March 1, 1989.

2. *Fortune,* June 9, 1986, 89.

CASE 4

Xerox Corporation: The Customer Satisfaction Program

We achieve customer satisfaction through dedication to quality in everything we do.
—Xerox Corporation 1987 Annual Report Cover

In both our businesses, customer satisfaction is the key to our success.
—Xerox Corporation 1988 Annual Report Cover

The Malcolm Baldrige National Quality Award.
—Xerox Corporation 1989 Annual Report Cover

Xerox people are on a crusade to be the industry leader in all aspects of customer satisfaction. And we're making good progress. We have improved customer satisfaction by 35%. Dataquest now rates our products as number one in five out of six market segments. Datapro has named our 1090 copier the "best overall copier in the world."
—President Paul Allaire, Xerox 1989 Annual Report

Xerox embarked on an ambitious program in the early 1980s to regain its eroded leadership in the copier industry—an industry it virtually created with the introduction of its model 914 in 1959. During the 1970s, Xerox customers had become disappointed with Xerox quality and service, and the company lost significant market share to domestic and Japanese competitors.

An obsession with quality and customer satisfaction, cost reductions, restructurings, and new products helped Xerox stem its eroding market share and regain market leadership in multiple markets and multiple market segments. Xerox gained 1 to 1.5 points in market share every year since 1983.

The "Leadership Through Quality" strategy had been in place since 1983 and customer satisfaction had become the first corporate priority since 1987. All this appeared to have paid off with Xerox Business Products and Systems' winning of the prestigious "Malcolm Baldrige National Quality Award" in 1989, the nation's highest award for quality. Established by an Act of Congress in 1987, this highly competitive award was given annually to outstanding American companies that had implemented total quality strategies and had significantly improved customer satisfaction.

In July 1990, President Paul Allaire and Wayland Hicks, executive vice president and head of Xerox Marketing and Customer Operations, decided to take some

Copyright © 1991 by the President and Fellows of Harvard College. Harvard Business School Case 591-055.

This case was prepared by Professor Melvyn A. J. Menezes and Research Associate Jon Serbin as the basis for class discussion rather than to illustrate either effective or ineffective handling of an administrative situation. Reprinted by permission of Harvard Business School.

TABLE A	Estimated Revenues in the U.S. Copier Industry (in billions of dollars)		
	1984	1989	1994 (Expected)
Sales	$ 3.9	$ 4.7	$ 4.6
Rentals	3.3	3.6	4.6
Service	3.1	5.4	5.8
Supplies	3.0	4.3	4.9
Total	$13.3	$18.0	$19.9

time off from their otherwise hectic schedule to review the progress on customer satisfaction. They wondered whether it needed any changes or the introduction of some new programs.

The Copier Industry

The worldwide copier market was mature and intensely competitive. In the United States, copier placements (sales and rentals) had grown at a slow rate of 2.9% CAGR (compound annual growth rate) between 1984 and 1989; service and supplies were the rapidly growing sources of revenue in the industry (see Table A).

Low-Volume Market   Copiers in this market were designed to make fewer than 5,000 copies per month and cost less than $4,000. Over time these machines were becoming more reliable and users were performing more of their own maintenance. This market witnessed explosive growth in the late 1970s and was the fastest-growing market until the late 1980s. By 1990, that growth flattened. Due to intense competition, copier prices and margins in most markets declined steadily through the 1980s, but especially in this low-volume market. Canon, Sharp, Xerox, Mita, and Ricoh were the major players.

Mid-Volume-Market   These copiers were designed to make up to 100,000 copies per month and cost between $4,000 and $60,000. This market, which had the highest overall growth in 1989, was where Xerox had always earned the most revenue and profit. At the lower end, there was intense price pressure, while at the top end, there was relatively less price cutting. Xerox, Canon, Mita, Ricoh, and Konica were the major players.

High-Volume-Market   These copiers cost over $60,000. This market, primarily because of the high product-development costs, was a high-margin business. As you moved from the low-volume to the high-volume market, more machines were leased and fewer bought outright. In the high-volume market, the lease to sale ratio, although declining, was 80:20 in 1990. Competition was based primarily on service and product features. Xerox and Kodak (which purchased IBM's copier business in 1988 when IBM retreated from the business) were the major competitors; Canon, Konica, and Lanier competed in the lower end of this market.

The major producers were developing new products that utilized digital copying technology as opposed to light/lens technology. Some analysts expected that market growth in the nineties would be driven by "smart" multifunction devices that combined copying, faxing, scanning, and electronic printing functions. Competitors with direct sales forces would have an advantage because the complexity and pricing of these machines was too high for effective dealer distribution. Color copying represented another potential growth area. The color copier market was expected to grow from about 6,000 units ($354 million in revenues) in 1989 to almost 60,000 units ($2 billion in revenues) by 1994.

Competition

The copier market was extremely competitive, with 23 companies battling for market share. However, Xerox was the only full-line supplier with products ranging from the low end of the low-volume to the high end of the high-volume. Based on total number of unit placements, Canon was the market leader, followed by Xerox and Sharp (see Exhibit 1). Canon's placements were primarily low-volume, low-priced personal copiers, though Canon did have a presence in the mid- and high-volume markets. In terms of copier industry revenues, Xerox was the market leader with a high market share in the higher-priced mid- and high-volume markets, which also provided significant service and supplies revenues. Xerox had by far the

EXHIBIT 1   **Placement of Copiers (in units), 1989**

	Product Market			
	Low-Volume	**Mid-Volume**	**High-Volume**	**Total**
Canon	28.6%	9.7%	12.5%	23.0%
Xerox	11.3	26.5	45.1	15.2
Sharp	18.6	7.4	—	14.6
Mita	8.4	9.0	—	8.4
Ricoh	5.0	8.5	—	5.7
Konica	4.8	8.0	7.7	5.3
Minolta	3.3	2.7	—	5.1
Lanier	4.8	3.7	3.7	4.4
Savin	1.6	7.3	—	3.2
Kodak	—	2.2	31.0	1.1
Others	13.6	15.0	—	14.0
Total	**100.0%**	**100.0%**	**100.0%**	**100.0%**
Proportion of total units	80.5%	17.0%	2.5%	100.0%
Proportion of revenues	38.7%	31.3%	30.0%	100.0%
Proportion of total copiers	28.9%	31.1%	40.0%	100.0%

largest service organization in the industry and was the largest paper and supplies distributor as well.

Company Background

In 1989, Xerox Corporation, headquartered in Stamford, Connecticut, had revenues of $17.6 billion and net income of $704 million. It had two divisions: (1) Business Products and Systems, which handled all document-processing businesses (1989 revenues: $12.4 billion; net income: $488 million); and (2) Xerox Financial Services, which handled insurance and other financial services (1989 revenues: $5.2 billion; net income: $216 million).

History

In 1959, the Haloid Company launched its model 914 office copier, the first viable xerographic office copier and considered by many to be one of the most successful single products ever made. Haloid renamed itself Xerox in 1961.

Protected by a ring of patents, Xerox achieved phenomenal growth and completely dominated the world copier market through the 1960s and into the early 1970s. After settling antitrust actions with the FTC, Xerox agreed to license its technology to competitors and to end pending patent suits. IBM and Kodak entered the business in 1970 and 1975 respectively, focusing on the high-margin, high- and mid-volume markets. Japanese companies concentrated on mass producing low-volume machines. By the early 1980s, IBM and Kodak gained significant market share in the high-volume market, and Japanese companies created and began to dominate the emerging low-volume market. Also, Japanese producers began to compete in the mid-volume market, and, by 1990, some of them were offering or announcing products to compete in the high-volume market.

During the 1960s and 1970s Xerox diversified into a number of new businesses. It purchased mainframe-maker Scientific Data Systems in 1969. A decade later, the business, a large-scale failure, was sold. Other diversification efforts included entry into a range of office computing businesses, including word processors and document-processing workstations, networks, facsimile equipment, electronic typewriters, scanners, impact and laser printers, software, and medical imaging systems. In the early eighties, Xerox diversified in a new direction through its financial services acquisitions.

Xerox with its monopoly culture, its large bureaucracy, and its forays into new businesses, had difficulty responding to the new competitive pressures in its flagship copier business. Costs and product prices were higher than the competition's, quality and perceived quality had declined, and market share and return on assets had fallen to alarming levels.

Around 1980, Xerox realized that the Japanese had a 40%–50% cost advantage in the copier business and that they were selling machines for almost what it cost Xerox to produce a machine. Despite the emerging competition, Xerox continued to grow, but net income declined as a percentage of revenues. By 1980, Xerox's market share was severely eroded in all product segments of the copier business. Its share dropped from almost 100% in the 1960s to under 40% in 1980.

Turnaround

Beginning in 1980, Xerox undertook a number of initiatives to respond to the increased competition and the company's declining market share. The company was restructured and developed a philosophy emphasizing quality, led by Chairman and CEO David Kearns. He instigated a strong quality movement, in the belief that quality would drive costs down and that getting it right the first time would eliminate costly repairs and replacements and would prevent the unnecessary breakdown that drove customers away. Kearns and top management strove to drive the quest for quality throughout the organization.

Quality at Xerox was defined as "meeting the customer's existing and latent requirements." Xerox believed that becoming more customer and competitor oriented was critical. It began to use competitive "benchmarking" (the continuous process of measuring products, services, and practices against the toughest competitors and those companies renowned as leaders with respect to reliability, cost, and service), to improve quality and achieve cost reductions. By 1983, it developed a corporatewide quality program called Leadership Through Quality (LTQ), which emphasized preventing defects and meeting customers' expectations. Training all employees in quality tools and processes was a major part of the plan, and quality-related goals were set for each year through 1987.

The effort led to some successes. The ratio of support staff to manufacturing worker was reduced from 4.5 in 1980 to 1.5 in 1987, smaller product development teams helped shorten the product development cycle by 30% and reduce the amount of labor required to bring out a new machine by 40%, and the number of parts vendors was reduced from 5,000 in 1980 to 400 by 1987, resulting in higher quality standards, better pricing, and 99.2% of parts arriving defect-free. By some estimates these efforts helped Xerox save as much as $2 billion in the document-processing business.

Xerox underwent another major restructuring in 1988, refocusing its document-processing line on its core copying business. It also focused on new technologies, including color copiers and "smart" multifunction copiers. Xerox Medical Imaging was closed, the electronic-typewriter production capacity was cut back, and the workstation business was closed. Xerox expected to achieve a payback on the 1988 restructuring within three years and to position itself to achieve its goal of 15% pretax ROA by 1990. Xerox's ROA, which peaked at 19% in 1980, was 11.1% in 1988 and 12.6% in 1989.

Business Products and Systems (BP&S)

BP&S developed, manufactured, marketed, and serviced a broad range of document-processing equipment. BP&S products and systems were produced in 15 countries on 5 continents and marketed in 140 countries by a direct sales force of about 15,000 and a growing network of dealers and distributors. It maintained a worldwide service force of about 30,000 technical representatives.

BP&S's three largest product lines—Copier/Duplicators, Printing Systems, and Document Systems—were sold and serviced by the three general sales and service operating companies: United States Marketing Group (USMG), Americas Operations (handling Canada, Latin America, the Middle East and North Africa), and Rank Xerox (handling 80 countries including the European Community).

United States Marketing Group (USMG)

USMG, which handled the marketing of BP&S's main products in the United States, consisted of nine functional areas, including sales, service, business operations, marketing support, services support, finance, information management, personnel, and administration. The first three functions managed the field organization, which consisted of 5 regions and 65 districts.

Starting January 1, 1990, the regions and districts were managed as partnerships of the three functional areas (sales, service, and business operations) with the district partnership reporting to the regional partnership, which in turn reported to headquarters functional managers. The heads of sales, service, and operations at the district (and regional) level operated as equal partners on management decisions and planning processes.

Decision-making authority was decentralized down to the regional and district partnerships. District partnerships were given increased responsibility to resolve customer problems and to take advantage of business opportunities, but were accountable to corporate policies and inspection. Districts had authority to allocate manpower resources among the functional areas within the overall district head count limit. Regions and districts also had flexibility in advertising investments, though they had to choose from a menu of headquarter options that they could customize to local markets. Profit and expense planning (including revenue growth, profit growth, and expense targets) were generated from the district level upward.

In 1990, USMG had four goals:

1. To become an organization with which customers were eager to do business.
2. To create an environment where every employee could take pride in the organization and feel responsible for its success.
3. To grow profits and increase Xerox presence at a rate faster than the markets in which it competed.
4. To use Leadership Through Quality principles in everything it did.

Customers

Xerox categorized its customers into four segments:

1. Commercial Major Accounts (CMA): These were *Fortune 500* firms, and, although accounting for only 5% of Xerox's customers, they accounted for about 32% of its copier revenues.
2. Named Accounts: These were large commercial accounts that were non–*Fortune 500* firms. They accounted for about 18% of Xerox's customers and 28% of its copier revenues.

3. General Markets: These were all other commercial accounts, and accounted for 62% of Xerox's customers and about 15% of its copier revenues.
4. Government/Education: These customers accounted for 15% of Xerox's customers and 25% of its copier revenues.

The first two groups were segmented further into large and small accounts. The average large Named Account provided the same revenues as the average small Commercial Major Account, and there were a larger number of large Named Accounts than small CMAs.

For most customers, product reliability was the top priority. As one Xerox executive put it, "Copiers are not exciting. Most customers don't notice copiers until they break down. Like toasters, they are just a convenience; they should be reliable and look reliable as well."

Apart from product reliability, purchase criteria varied by segment. In the low-volume segment, the emphasis was more on price than on service. These customers wanted the best possible quality at the lowest possible price. In the mid- and high-volume segments, service was a critical purchase consideration. (The relative importance of various purchase criteria for equipment and service purchase decisions for the mid- and high-volume segments is given in Exhibit 2.) Xerox and Kodak maintained their own national service organizations. Equipment service for other vendors was handled by dealer service organizations or by third-party service organizations, a significant emerging trend. Large service organizations such as TRW offered service either directly to customers or via exclusive relationships with producers or dealer organizations. Hicks saw an opportunity for Xerox to gain, through its service capabilities, a competitive advantage over its rivals in the U.S. and global markets.

Distribution

Historically, all Xerox products were sold directly by the Xerox sales force. However, the company recently began to distribute low-volume and low-priced mid-volume machines through dealer networks, and the lowest-priced machines through consumer retail channels.

For the copier industry as a whole, dealers were the primary distribution channel. In 1989, according to industry specialist Dataquest, 54% of placements went through the dealer channel, 26% via the direct sales force, 10% via the retail channel, 9% via national or regional distributors, and 1% via alternate channels (mail order, agents, telemarketing, etc.). Dataquest estimated that, in 1994, dealers would account for 42%, the direct sales force for 27%, retail channels for 16%, distributors for 10%, and alternate channels for 5% of copier sales.

Product Line and Pricing

Although a copier appeared to be a dull, boring, and simple product, it contained some very sophisticated technology: chemical, electronic, optical, and mechanical science all wrapped in one box. For engineers, it was a tremendous technical and

EXHIBIT 2   Relative Importance of Major Criteria in Equipment and
Service Purchase Decisions

	Commercial Major Accounts			Named Accounts		
	Small	Large	Overall	Small	Large	Overall
Equipment Purchase Decision						
Reliability	0.30	0.34	0.32	0.41	0.38	0.40
Ease of operation	0.17	0.24	0.21	0.20	0.07	0.13
Completeness of product line	0.21	0.11	0.16	0.10	0.20	0.15
Service quality	0.29	0.30	0.29	0.18	0.27	0.23
Price	0.03	0.01	0.02	0.11	0.08	0.09
Service Purchase Decision						
Technical expertise	0.35	0.45	0.40	0.33	0.45	0.39
Professionalism	0.26	0.10	0.18	0.18	0.10	0.14
Guaranteed response time	0.23	0.34	0.28	0.35	0.29	0.32
Variety of contract offerings	0.09	0.10	0.10	0.05	0.11	0.08
Price	0.07	0.01	0.04	0.09	0.05	0.07

intellectual challenge to combine these different technologies and at the same time ensure that the product was easy to use.

In 1990, Xerox had two lines of copiers—the 10 series and the 50 series. The 10 series of Xerox copiers, introduced in 1982, helped Xerox regain significant market share. It also helped revitalize the company's financial outlook and rejuvenate its morale and fighting spirit. In 1988, Xerox introduced the 50 series of copiers. In 1990, Xerox had 18 copiers, 4 in the low-end (1020, 1025, 5012, 5014), 9 in the mid-range (1040, 1045, 1048, 1055, 5018, 5028, 5042, 5046, 5052), and 5 in the high-end (1065, 1075, 1090, 9900, 5090). It regained market share in the low- and mid-volume segments and preserved its high share of the high-end market. Xerox copiers ranged in list price (base unit) from $2,440 for the 5012 to $154,000 for the 5090.

Most Xerox copiers carried a 30-day warranty, in line with industry practice. Some of the high-volume machines carried a 90-day warranty. The new 50 series low- and mid-volume copiers (5012, 5014, 5018, and 5028) were launched with a three-year warranty. The longer warranty was an aggressive marketing tool to accelerate new product acceptance and to communicate the products' higher reliability to customers, dealers, and the Xerox sales force. These copiers utilized user-replaceable cartridges, which replaced many of the parts that were likely to need frequent servicing.

Customer Service

USMG provided maintenance and installation of Xerox as well as third-party products, including PCs and printers. Revenues from customer service were approximately $2 billion in 1989, making Xerox the country's third-largest service business (behind

IBM and DEC). Customer service employed 18,000 people, with 15,000 in the field and additional staff of about 3,000, including a telephone support staff of 1,000.

Customer service at Xerox had several dimensions: fixing/repairing of units; providing operating systems support, interface and integration; communicating with customers; resolving customer issues after installation; providing technical product support; selling of services; and giving feedback to manufacturing, sales, marketing, and administration.

Customer service was run as a cost center, with cost as a percentage of revenue being a very important consideration. Some managers believed that customer service should operate as a standalone operation and be a profit center.

The quality of customer service was measured on the following criteria: (1) customer satisfaction, based on customer surveys; (2) the expense to revenue ratio; (3) reliability; and (4) service billing errors. The focus on customer satisfaction, originally initiated in customer service, continued to be championed by customer service. Centralized parts support enabled customer service engineers to order parts on-line and improved the availability of parts in local inventory. In 1985, service marketing was established as a separate organization to focus on the growth of service revenues.

As a result of these kinds of efforts, customer service improved Xerox's service delivery capabilities and reduced service costs. Actual average response time improved from about 5.75 hours in 1987 to 4.75 hours in 1989. Customer satisfaction with service equipment repair had improved to 96%. Customers' wait time on the phone when calling the Service Support Centers improved more than 40% (and was 20% better than the industry average), with most customers waiting fewer than 20 seconds.

Customer Satisfaction at Xerox

During the period 1980 to 1986, Xerox had three corporate priorities: return on assets (ROA), market share, and customer satisfaction. There was no particular order to the three priorities, yet most people focused on ROA, which had a goal of 15%. No specific quantitative corporate goals were set for market share and customer satisfaction.

Studies conducted in 1987 concluded that customer satisfaction was not a top priority in the day-to-day management of Xerox's businesses. The senior management team at Xerox was convinced that success in customer satisfaction would lead to successes in the other two priorities. Customer satisfaction, the team believed, would drive an external focus and give the voice of the customer a critical role. It decided that customer satisfaction should become the number one corporate priority, which, in September 1987, it announced in a series of management communications meetings and published materials. As President Allaire put it:

> We can be the industry leader in all aspects of customer satisfaction. That is our goal. It is our strong conviction that if we meet our customer's expectations, we will improve market share, and if we improve market share, we will improve our financial performance and shareholder value.

In November 1987, the senior management team issued to the operating units a set of requirements and guidelines to ensure that customer satisfaction (CS) became their first priority. These requirements and guidelines focused on reorienting the company at every level to CS as the first priority, and were used by the units to prepare their own operating strategies and plans to meet CS goals and business objectives. Operating units were given the authority and options to respond to their customers' requirements with a range of approved products, services or solutions that would maximize CS for their markets. They were to delegate those authorities and options to the appropriate organizational level, allowing it to respond easily to customers' requirements.

In March 1988, President Allaire asked that a common, core system of measures for managing and improving customer satisfaction be established for use by all operating units worldwide. Each operating unit had been using its own method for surveying customers, asking different questions and using different scales. In Brazil, for example, customer satisfaction was measured on a two-point scale, while Canada used a five-point scale. Hence it was difficult to do any cross-comparisons or determine whether a particular dissatisfaction problem was endemic to one office, a region, an operating company, or the entire organization.

Based on the best methods in use, a common set of guidelines was formulated for tracking and measuring customer satisfaction. In August 1988, the senior management team approved the proposed framework of measures and issued a complete set of requirements and guidelines to all operating units for measuring, managing, and improving customer satisfaction. The units could customize their systems so long as they complied with the mandatory requirements and stayed within the guidelines.

Vision and Goals

In 1990, Xerox's vision for customer satisfaction was "100% of Xerox's customers are very satisfied or satisfied with our products and services through the elimination of defects and errors in our work processes and the achievement of world-class benchmark quality and value in our products and other deliveries to the customer."

The corporate goal was that by 1993 Xerox should be recognized as the industry benchmark in customer satisfaction in all business areas. This goal had two components: For the external world, the goal was to exceed competitive benchmarks for customer satisfaction in all major business areas and to exceed competitive benchmark quality and reliability in all services to the customer by 1993. For the internal world, the goal was that, by 1993, Xerox products should meet customer requirements and exceed competitive benchmarks in quality; there should be fourfold improvements in reliability, a tenfold reduction in defects and errors in the work processes and deliverables that impact the customer, a 50% improvement in cost, and time to market should be reduced by 12 months.

Top management believed that, to achieve the vision and goals, it needed market-driven business strategies, product strategies, and investments that were determined by customer requirements and expectations. Top management also believed that it was critical that the vision and goals be communicated systematically through each level in the organization to ensure understanding, capability, and commitment.

Fundamental to success was the assurance of quality by problem diagnosis, identification of root causes, and corrective actions.

Action Steps

Several actions were taken to enhance customer satisfaction. Management leadership was particularly important. Senior managers in the operating units became role models for appropriate behaviors relative to the customer, by personally taking the lead in acting to totally satisfy customer requirements and resolving customer complaints. They promoted and participated in programs that placed them in direct contact with customers.

Another action was ensuring that all employees developed a proactive attitude, role, and work emphasis focused on customer satisfaction. Every customer contact by a Xerox employee was viewed as an opportunity to manage the customer's experience with and perception of Xerox. Employees who had no direct customer contact focused on supporting those who did.

A customer satisfaction code of conduct was developed for all employees. CS was introduced into all training curricula, where employees learned about the Leadership Through Quality tools and processes. CS training was provided to all front-line employees.

At the end of 1988, customer relations groups (CRG) were initiated at headquarters and at the regions and districts. At each district, the CRG consisted of two to six people. Its objective was to have direct customer contact so it could follow up on dissatisfied customers and customer complaints and to resolve issues better and faster. Problems reached the CRG in one of the following ways: customer surveys, internal sales or service problem referrals, customer losses or contract cancellations, and nonconformance costs such as machine replacement, accommodation, and sales refusals or reversals.

The perceived benefits of the customer relations group were in staying close to the customer, having a cross-functional focus on customer issues, and having a customer closed-loop process that identified problems, resolved them, conducted root-cause analyses, and provided recommendations for avoidance or elimination. The group hoped to be predictive rather than purely reactive. It hoped to resolve issues before receiving negative feedback and to identify potentially dissatisfied customers based on frequency of service, changes in billing history, changes in service contracts, deteriorating supply purchases, and so on.

The regions and districts were reorganized in 1990 as partnerships of sales, service, and business operations. Previously, the sales, service, and business operations used to report to the regional and headquarters levels, and there was not much teamwork at the local district level.

Local empowerment was another tool for increasing customer satisfaction. Processes and systems were developed and authorities were modified to enable first-line sales, service, and administration teams in the branches and districts to rapidly and effectively respond to customers and resolve complaints. All employees were made to feel accountable for CS and to act accordingly. Rewards and recognition programs were modified to ensure that they supported the CS objectives. The bonus plan for general managers, for example, included CS criteria.

Other major steps included the establishment of customer support teams for post-sale follow-up, establishment of a Customer Complaints Management System, improvements in technical service, information systems, and telephone systems. "Zero defects" programs were implemented for continuing quality improvement of those internal processes that directly impacted external customers.

Measurement of Customer Satisfaction

Xerox believed that a critical aspect for achieving CS was the development of tools to continuously measure, manage, and improve customer satisfaction. Two major sets of data were developed and utilized: (1) external customer feedback data, which included a series of customer satisfaction surveys as well as a Customer Complaint Management System; and (2) internal quality and quantity measures of Xerox work processes and outputs that delivered products and services (see Exhibit 3).

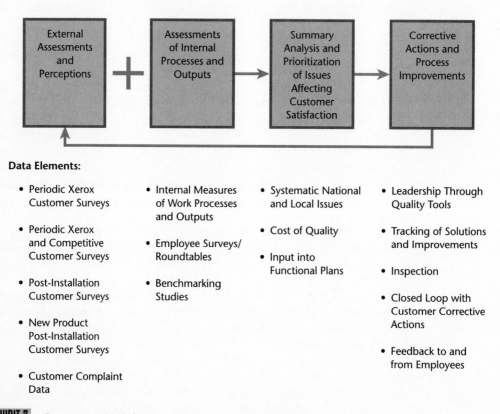

Data Elements:

- Periodic Xerox Customer Surveys

- Periodic Xerox and Competitive Customer Surveys

- Post-Installation Customer Surveys

- New Product Post-Installation Customer Surveys

- Customer Complaint Data

- Internal Measures of Work Processes and Outputs

- Employee Surveys/ Roundtables

- Benchmarking Studies

- Systematic National and Local Issues

- Cost of Quality

- Input into Functional Plans

- Leadership Through Quality Tools

- Tracking of Solutions and Improvements

- Inspection

- Closed Loop with Customer Corrective Actions

- Feedback to and from Employees

EXHIBIT 3   Customer Satisfaction Improvement Model

The External Measurement System

Customer perceptions and market outcomes that resulted from implementing the strategies and action plans were monitored through the external measures of customer satisfaction. The external customer feedback data system consisted of surveys (to solicit from customers their satisfaction with all areas of their interaction with Xerox) and the Customer Complaint Management System, which captured any unsolicited feedback from customers. Four sets of surveys were used: (1) a periodic survey of a random sample of Xerox customers; (2) a post-installation survey of all Xerox customers within 90 days of a new installation; (3) a new-product post-installation survey of a random sample of customers with new products during the launch phase; and (4) a blind survey of Xerox's and competitors' customers to establish benchmark levels of customer satisfaction and to determine Xerox's competitive position.

Periodic Survey   Each month, USMG mailed surveys to 40,000 randomly selected customers; 50% were sent to key operators, 25% to decision makers, and 25% to administrators. About 10,000 surveys were returned to Xerox. The surveys queried customers about satisfaction on a number of levels: overall satisfaction with Xerox, likelihood of acquiring another product from Xerox, likelihood of recommending Xerox to a business associate, and satisfaction with several different aspects of the products, services, and support (see Exhibit 4).

The key measure tracked was the overall satisfaction. Customer satisfaction was measured on a 5-point semantic differential scale (very satisfied—very dissatisfied). Each month, the percentage satisfied (those who marked either very satisfied or somewhat satisfied) was analyzed in terms of a three-month rolling average, the prior month, the current month, actual year to date, and percent of planned target. Results were tracked by district, region, product, product type, and customer segment.

The results of the periodic surveys were used to flag problem areas and measure the effect of corrective actions for individual products, districts, and customer segments. The results were used quite extensively by product managers (to set product, district, and function targets), product development teams, customer relations groups, and various functional areas.

Post-Installation Survey   This survey was administered 7 to 90 days after installation of a machine and enabled the respondent to register any problem, enabled the local field unit to respond rapidly with corrective actions, and allowed Xerox to collect data for work process improvement. Often more than one survey was required: one as soon as possible after the installation, and another within 90 days to cover different interactions and aspects of the transaction.

The operator received the survey, which focused on the product (product performance against expectations, copy quality, ease of use), the sales process (responsiveness of the sales representative, fulfillment of commitments), the order process (availability of product, ease of understanding the options), the delivery process (timing, correctness, attitude of crew), the installation process (time to install, time lag between delivery and installation), and the support activities (user training,

EXHIBIT 4 **Xerox's Customer Satisfaction Questionnaire**

This questionnaire should be completed by the individual who makes decisions about the acquisition of _____ . Please focus on your experiences in the product areas mentioned as you complete the questionnaire.

SECTION 1: GENERAL SATISFACTION

	Very Satisfied	Somewhat Satisfied	Neither Satisfied Nor Dissatisfied	Somewhat Dissatisfied	Very Dissatisfied
1. Based on your recent experience, how satisfied are you with Xerox?	☐	☐	☐	☐	☐

	Definitely	Probably	Might or Might Not	Probably Not	Definitely Not
2. Based on your recent experience, would you acquire another product from Xerox?	☐	☐	☐	☐	☐
3. Based on your recent experience, would you recommend Xerox to a business associate?	☐	☐	☐	☐	☐

	Very Satisfied	Somewhat Satisfied	Neither Satisfied Nor Dissatisfied	Somewhat Dissatisfied	Very Dissatisfied
4. How satisfied are you overall with the qualitty of:					
a) Your Xerox product(s)	☐	☐	☐	☐	☐
b) Sales support you receive	☐	☐	☐	☐	☐
c) Technical service you receive	☐	☐	☐	☐	☐
d) Administrative support you receive	☐	☐	☐	☐	☐
e) Handling of inquiries	☐	☐	☐	☐	☐
f) Supplies support you receive	☐	☐	☐	☐	☐
g) Xerox User training	☐	☐	☐	☐	☐
h) Xerox supplied documentation	☐	☐	☐	☐	☐

Please complete 4i and 4j only if you are the decision maker for systems products (printers, work-stations, personal computers and wordprocessors)

	Very Satisfied	Somewhat Satisfied	Neither Satisfied Nor Dissatisfied	Somewhat Dissatisfied	Very Dissatisfied
i) Your Xerox supplied software	☐	☐	☐	☐	☐
j) Xerox Systems Analyst support	☐	☐	☐	☐	☐
k) Telephone Hotline support	☐	☐	☐	☐	☐

SECTION 2: SALES SUPPORT

	Very Satisfied	Somewhat Satisfied	Neither Satisfied Nor Dissatisfied	Somewhat Dissatisfied	Very Dissatisfied
5. How satisfied are you overall with Xerox Sales Representatives with regard to:					
a) Timeliness of response to your inquiries	☐	☐	☐	☐	☐
b) Frequency of contact to review your needs	☐	☐	☐	☐	☐

(Continued on next page)

EXHIBIT 4 **Continued**

Source: "Xerox Corporation: The Customer Satisfaction Program" (1991), Harvard Business School Case #9-591-055, Boston, MA, 19–20.

	Very Satisfied	Somewhat Satisfied	Neither Satisfied Nor Dissatisfied	Somewhat Dissatisfied	Very Dissatisfied
c) Frequency of contact to provide information about new Xerox products and services	☐	☐	☐	☐	☐
d) Product knowledge	☐	☐	☐	☐	☐
e) Application knowledge	☐	☐	☐	☐	☐
f) Understanding of your business needs	☐	☐	☐	☐	☐
g) Accuracy in explaining terms/ conditions	☐	☐	☐	☐	☐
h) Ability to resolve problems	☐	☐	☐	☐	☐
i) Professionalism	☐	☐	☐	☐	☐

SECTION 3: CUSTOMER SUPPORT

6. What is the purpose of your most recent call to Xerox?

   ☐ Inquiry   ☐ Problem
   ☐ Haven't called, can't answer (skip to Question 10)

7. How long ago did you make this call?

   ☐ Less than 3 months   ☐ 3–6 months
   ☐ 6–12 months   ☐ Greater than 12 months

8. What Xerox function did you contact?

   ☐ Sales   ☐ Service   ☐ Supplies   ☐ Systems Analyst
   ☐ Billing   ☐ Collection   ☐ Customer Relations Group
   ☐ Telephone Hotline Support

	Very Satisfied	Somewhat Satisfied	Neither Satisfied Nor Dissatisfied	Somewhat Dissatisfied	Very Dissatisfied
9. How satisfied are you with the support you received?					
a) Ability to get to the right person(s) quickly	☐	☐	☐	☐	☐
b) Attitude of Xerox personnel who assisted you	☐	☐	☐	☐	☐
c) Ability to provide a solution	☐	☐	☐	☐	☐
d) Time required to provide a solution	☐	☐	☐	☐	☐
e) Effectiveness of the solution	☐	☐	☐	☐	☐
f) Overall satisfaction with support received	☐	☐	☐	☐	☐

10. What specific things can we do to increase your satisfaction with Xerox, our products and our services? Thank you for your feedback!

Your name _____
Position _____
Tel # _____
Date _____

manuals and documentation, ease of contacting Xerox). Any dissatisfaction detected was followed up for quick resolution.

New-Products Post-Installation Survey   This survey was sent to a random sample of customers just after the launch of a new product to help identify any problems that customers might face with the new product. It served as an early warning system for new-product performance.

Competitive Benchmarking Customer Satisfaction Survey   This was a critical tool for comparing Xerox to its key competitors in terms of customer satisfaction and perceptions of the products and services. Other purposes of this survey were to identify which suppliers were the benchmarks in satisfying the customer, and what were customers' requirements and preferences in the quality of products and services. This annual survey focused on the various vendors and brands and used the same core questions as the periodic survey. However, in this survey, the identity of the sponsor was not disclosed.

Internal Measurement Process

The common, core system of measures also required matching external customer assessments of Xerox products and services to the appropriate internal quality measures and standards for the work processes and outputs that produced those deliverables. Xerox management could routinely monitor and inspect internal performance as a leading indicator of CS and as leverage in acting to improve output quality and CS. The process included setting and monitoring quality measures of the internal work processes and deliverables that impact the customer and parallel the customer satisfaction measures. The objective was to provide leading indicators of Xerox performance and improvement opportunities.

Xerox processes that impacted each area of customer interaction were determined, and systems were put in place to measure and monitor these internal processes. For every diagnostic question asked in the periodic and post-installation surveys, there was one or more internal standards and measures that indicated Xerox performance in the applicable work processes or deliverables. Examples of internal measures included service response time, number of billing errors, and number of training hours per sales rep. Benchmark standards were set for all processes (i.e., response time should be less than four hours, or billing errors should be less than 2%, or all sales reps should have four hours of training with a new product).

Data Analyses, Review, and Follow-up

Information on customer satisfaction was received from various sources such as the surveys, the customer complaint management system, the district partners, and the field reports. The data were analyzed to identify segment-specific satisfiers (factors that increased customer satisfaction) and dissatisfiers (factors that when not available in the right amount led to customer dissatisfaction).

Customer satisfaction was reviewed frequently and at various levels in the organization. A Customer Satisfaction Improvement meeting attended by the president of USMG, the president of Development and Manufacturing, the senior vice president of World Wide Marketing, and their direct reports was held once a quarter for one day. This meeting covered CS results, strategic enablers, CS corrective actions, new-product status and future-product customer requirements. Cross-functional teams were assigned to follow up and to initiate Quality Improvement Teams (QITs).

A Customer Satisfaction Improvement Network meeting of representatives from all major operating units worldwide met once a quarter for one to two days. On the agenda were customer satisfaction issues that included survey processes, targeting methodology, benchmark studies, CS results and targets, business results and targets, and best practices. On a regular basis, data were distributed to regions and districts for use by all functional areas so that corrective measures could be taken and results tracked.

At USMG, the senior management team met once every two months for two hours to review customer satisfaction. This group focused on the "top 10" dissatisfiers, the progress made on achieving the CS targets, and the actions to be taken to improve customer satisfaction.

In addition, the USMG Customer Satisfaction team met for two hours twice a month to follow up on the actions initiated at the Customer Satisfaction Improvement meeting and the USMG senior staff meeting. This was a cross-functional team and consisted of members from service, marketing, administration, the headquarters customer relations group, development and manufacturing, and worldwide marketing.

The next step in the customer satisfaction process was to manage a corrective action process that responded to customer dissatisfaction indicators, off-standard internal measures, and performance improvement opportunities. All concerns, including those from customers who indicated through the survey that they were somewhat or very dissatisfied, were acted upon very quickly. About 10,000 complaints per month (150 per district) were followed up. About 35% came from the surveys while the balance were from letters or telephone calls. Personal contact was made with the customer and the problem resolved within 48 hours with a closed-loop follow-up system. The districts' customer relations teams did the callbacks. Planned head-count reductions were likely to reduce the size of the customer relations team by one rep per district, unless a district decided to reallocate personnel from another function.

Root causes of problems were categorized and tracked. The most significant problems involved equipment performance and service, where surveys had revealed that customer expectations were higher than Xerox performance. Corrective measures included setting higher reliability requirements (less than one call per month) on new products, providing dissatisfied customers with better machines and improving response time for service.

Actions were taken to improve customer satisfaction in weak market segments such as General Markets, which constantly had the worst CS performance and was furthest from the 1990 target at 84.2% in the first quarter. This segment was targeted at 87.3%, which was needed to reach the overall target of 1990 by year-end and represented 11,000 machines that needed to move from "dissatisfied" to "satisfied." Likely causes of the problems encountered by General Markets were (a) lack of account ownership, (b) frequent account rep changes, (c) time and material prices perceived as excessive, and (d) low priority in the service-call queue.

Specific actions were also taken for products with below-target CS ratings. For example, retrofit programs were in place to improve the performance of some problem 50 series copiers. Mid-volume copiers as a group were below customer satisfaction performance targets, mainly because these machines were generally treated with less care by customers. Mid-volume machines were the orphans of the copier world, generally placed in common areas for use by a large group of people, as opposed to a low-volume or high-volume machine that had one or a few operators who took good care of the machine.

Results

Xerox set year-by-year, overall customer satisfaction targets: 90% in 1990, 94% in 1991, 97% in 1992, and 100% in 1993. These targets were broken down by customer segment and product line. The percentage of satisfied customers increased significantly in all customer segments (see Exhibit 5).

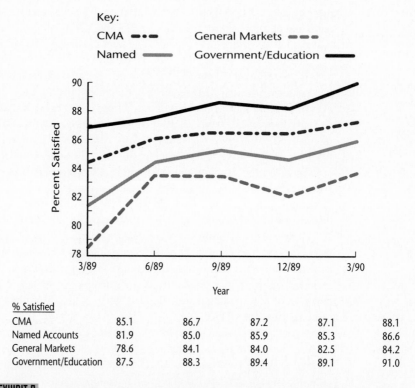

% Satisfied					
CMA	85.1	86.7	87.2	87.1	88.1
Named Accounts	81.9	85.0	85.9	85.3	86.6
General Markets	78.6	84.1	84.0	82.5	84.2
Government/Education	87.5	88.3	89.4	89.1	91.0

EXHIBIT 5   **Percentage Satisfied by Customer Segment (three-month rolling average, reported quarterly)**

Overall customer satisfaction targets were also set for each partnership. These were typically based on the overall improvement required and the previous performance of the partnership relative to internal and competitive benchmarks. Partnerships with the largest variance were expected to improve the most.

The management leadership actions and the focus on changing employee attitudes began to pay off. Prior to these actions, customer satisfaction was the responsibility of the service organization, while sales and business operations did not have much of a customer focus. Customers had complained about lack of follow-up and post-sale support by sales reps who seemed to disappear as soon as the order was signed. Sales reps had focused on new business and had an attitude of "sales at any cost." Many customers were frustrated with inaccurate billing and the difficulty of doing business with Xerox. When a customer problem had involved cross-functional areas, as many did, it seemed as though the sales, service, and administration people did not talk to one another, making it difficult and frustrating to find a solution.

With the district offices as partnerships, their empowerment to resolve customer issues without getting approvals at multiple levels, and the use of customer satisfaction measurements for performance appraisal changed the day-to-day customer interactions. All partners and employees felt responsible for customer satisfaction. Here are the comments of the three partners of one East Coast district:

DISTRICT SERVICE MANAGER: "Three years ago I never went on a sales call; now I go on about three per month. We were not always focused on listening to the customer. We focused on fixing a machine rather than fixing a broken customer who happened to have Xerox equipment."

DISTRICT BUSINESS MANAGER: "Every customer contact—'the 1000 moments of truth'—is now considered an opportunity to improve customer satisfaction with and perception of Xerox."

DISTRICT SALES MANAGER: "We are more customer focused than ever before. Five years ago, there was not that much excitement about customer satisfaction. Today customer satisfaction is everything."

Customer Guarantee

In November 1987, top management of Xerox had considered offering a satisfaction guarantee because it expected that a guarantee would lead to greater customer satisfaction and would also drive the organization to higher levels of performance. It wanted to come up with a guarantee that would be difficult for Xerox's competitors, especially those in the mid- and low-volume segments who distributed through dealers, to emulate. However, it thought that such a guarantee should be offered only after ensuring that the Leadership Through Quality tools and processes as well as the focus on "The Customer" were implemented, and that Xerox was able to consistently perform and deliver on the guarantee. By February 1990, it believed that Xerox had achieved those targets and that the organization was ready to guarantee satisfaction.

Most senior managers believed that a money-back guarantee was the way to go. Based on brainstorming and exploratory research, however, they decided to examine four types of guarantees: (1) A service guarantee (e.g., "If your machine is not operating 98% of the time, you will receive 10% off your next invoice"); (2) A money-back guarantee (e.g., "If you are not satisfied with the product or vendor, you can return your machine, no questions asked"); (3) A product performance guarantee (e.g., "If your machine does not perform at its original specifications or better for at least three years, we will replace your unit at no charge"); and (4) A product-fit guarantee (e.g., "If the product does not meet your needs, you can trade it in for full credit toward any other product").

During May-June 1990, Xerox conducted market research to gather inputs from various customer segments to develop a unique guarantee. The research was done in two phases: focus groups and a telephone survey. First, focus groups were conducted in three cities to test reactions to the four broad categories of guarantees. Several key messages came from the groups:

- The credibility of a guarantee was tied to the reputation of the vendor.
- The length of the guarantee was critical; less than a year was viewed as a normal warranty at best, and at worst, a desperate sales ploy. If a guarantee was for unlimited time, respondents believed that the customer paid a premium.
- Any guarantee could be significantly strengthened by making the customer the sole arbiter.
- For the service guarantee, response time (how quickly a firm responded to a call) was viewed as more appropriate than machine up-time.
- The money-back guarantee was viewed by some as low vendor commitment, i.e., being too easy for the vendor to walk away from.
- The product performance guarantee should be at the customer's request, with no questions asked, for the life of the contract.
- The product-fit guarantee was considered by many to be inappropriate. Many focus group members indicated that customers did not want to switch equipment, but only wanted the equipment to work well and be right for their needs.

Based on the focus groups research, Xerox decided (1) to drop the product-fit guarantee from further consideration, (2) to substitute response time for up-time in the service guarantee, and (3) to change the product performance guarantee to "If your machine does not perform up to your satisfaction for at least three years, we will replace it at no charge at your request." Thus the three guarantees tested in the second phase of the study were:

1. A response-time guarantee, which involved a commitment to send a service person to the customer site within a specified time after the service call was received.
2. A performance guarantee, under which Xerox would commit to a certain customer-determined level of service or product satisfaction. Xerox would replace the machine with another of equal or greater capability at the sole discretion of the customer.

3. A money-back guarantee under which the customer would receive a refund if dissatisfied.

In the second phase of the research, 560 customers (Xerox and non-Xerox), selected from all five customer segments, were surveyed by telephone. The focus group results were used to develop a questionnaire for the telephone survey. The major findings from the survey are presented in Exhibit 6.

Some competitors already offered a guarantee. Kodak had just begun a new campaign touting their "Bend Over Backwards" customer guarantee. Advertised in *Time, Business Week,* and other highly visible publications, Kodak's guarantee of product replacement was at Kodak's discretion and covered a three-year period. Canon also offered a performance guarantee, while Pitney Bowes guaranteed response time, performance, and a parts and supplies price protection. Lanier offered a 98% up-time guarantee.

Whichever guarantee alternative was chosen, Xerox planned an extensive marketing and advertising campaign, its biggest in ten years, around the new guarantee. The guarantee would apply to all Xerox products for a period of three years or for the term of Xerox financing, whichever was longer, and the machines had to be serviced by Xerox (and not by third parties) throughout the guarantee period. Though Xerox executives believed that it would be difficult to link sales specifically to the guarantee, they expected that the guarantee would increase sales by 5%–10%.

Current Situation

Supporters of the money-back guarantee thought it was the only option strong enough to achieve the desired effects—to mobilize the organization and differentiate Xerox's offering from competitors. As one Xerox manager said, "Kodak already offers a performance guarantee, and any competitor could match the rather amorphous 'performance guarantee.' Significant results require a dramatic offering."

Other managers thought that a money-back guarantee carried negative connotations and was a "low commitment" alternative. They thought that a performance guarantee was a better option because it required a higher commitment from Xerox, which customers really wanted. They thought the offering could be differentiated on the basis of who determined whether performance met the customer's requirements. Under existing industry practice, the vendor determined whether the product met the performance criteria. Letting the customer make this decision would be a significantly different, value-added offering to the customer.

Supporters of the response-time guarantee pointed out that competitors had already made response time a critical attribute and that Xerox had to compete on that. Other managers believed that a response time guarantee would not provide enough incentive for all functional areas of the company. Some thought that Xerox did not have the process capacity to guarantee response time and that the option would be too complicated because it would require different response times and pricing based on geographic location (i.e., rural versus large city), among other factors.

Hicks and the other top executives had to decide what type of guarantee Xerox ought to offer.

EXHIBIT 6   **Feedback from the Telephone Survey of Customers, 1990**

• General	Agree	Disagree
Guarantees are a meaningful way to protect the customer	90%	10%
All guarantees are pretty much the same	30%	70%
A company that offers a better guarantee makes a superior product	35%	65%
A better guarantee on a quality product does not increase cost	45%	55%

• **Consideration**

About 63% of those who heard about a guarantee took some action, such as calling for more information, asking for a demo or trial, considering a new vendor, or switching vendors; 37% did nothing on hearing about a guarantee.

Almost half of those who took some action on hearing about a guarantee switched vendors (63% took action, 29% switched vendors).

Named Accounts were most likely to respond to guarantees in the consideration process, exceeding the average by 5%–10%. General Markets were the least responsive.

• **Decision Factors**

In terms of the decision process, the percentage of respondents who thought that guarantees were equal to or more important than the following major criteria were as follows: price (46%), features (42%), vendor reputation (50%), and experience with the vendor (46%).

General Markets and Government/Education were most sensitive to price and features. Among them, 35% view guarantees as equally or more important than price.

Guarantees were equal to or more important than prior experience or vendor reputation for all segments except General Markets, where prior experience was more important.

• **Preferences**

Customers allocated 10 points over the three guarantee offerings as follows:

	Service Response	Product Performance	Money Back
Customer Segments:			
CMA	3.7	3.6	2.7
Named Accounts	3.4	3.6	3.0
General Markets	3.6	3.2	3.2
Government/Education	3.3	3.5	3.2
TOTAL	3.4	3.6	3.0
Product Markets:			
High-Volume	3.7	3.3	3.0
Low- and Mid-Volume	3.3	3.7	3.0

EXHIBIT 6 **Continued**

- **Believability**

    The percentage of respondents who said that such a guarantee was believable:

	Service Response	Product Performance	Money Back
Customer Segments:			
CMA	73%	78%	58%
Named Accounts	62%	73%	61%
General Markets	63%	70%	61%
Government/Education	59%	75%	68%
Total	**63%**	**74%**	**62%**

- The top "Do Not Believe" reasons were as indicated by the following percentage of respondents:

Too open-ended	28%	12%	
Never seen it happen	14%		13%
Unrealistic/Ineffective	15%		24%
Company will try to disregard the guarantee		11%	14%
Will try to repair, not replace		17%	
Company sets rules or specs		13%	

- **Expectations**

    Who would you expect to offer a guarantee? (Numbers represent the percentage of respondents who said they would expect that company to offer a guarantee.)

		Canon	Kodak	Xerox	Other Manufacturers
High-Volume	Xerox Users	9	35	76	10
	Xerox Non-Users	9	30	47	15
	Total	9	33	63	12
Low- and Mid-Volume	Xerox Users	16	5	59	23
	Xerox Non-Users	19	6	32	17
	Total	18	6	38	18
All Respondents		**15**	**12**	**42**	**16**

(Continued on next page)

EXHIBIT 6   **Continued**

- **Current Practices**

  Guarantees typically covered the following items, as indicated by the following percentage of respondents:

	Parts & Labor	Response Time	Uptime	Copy Quality
CMA	83%	42%	36%	22%
Named Accounts	78	38	34	21
General Markets	82	36	31	16
Government/Education	83	47	46	19
Total	**80**	**40**	**38**	**20**

  Response time guarantees typically guaranteed response times of 4 hours (46%), 2 hours (21%), same day (20%), or next day (13%).

- **Response Time Needs**

  What response time will really satisfy you? (Numbers represent the percentage of respondents who indicated that particular amount of time.)

	1 Hour	2 Hours	3 Hours	4 Hours	Same Day	Next Day	Total
Customer Segments							
CMA	7%	22%	9%	32%	22%	8%	100%
Named Accounts	10	17	11	25	28	9	100
General Markets	2	11	6	12	52	17	100
Government/Education	9	12	7	20	34	18	100
Total	**8**	**16**	**9**	**24**	**31**	**12**	**100**
Product Categories							
High-Volume	9	27	13	29	17	5	100
Low- and Mid-Volume	8	11	7	22	37	15	100
Total	**8**	**16**	**9**	**24**	**31**	**12**	**100**

Name Index

Subject Index

512